COMPLICITY AND ITS LIMITS IN THE LAW OF INTERNATIONAL RESPONSIBILITY

This book examines the responsibility of States and international organisations for complicity (aid or assistance) in an internationally wrongful act. Despite the recognition of responsibility for complicity as a rule of customary international law by the International Court of Justice, this book argues that the effectiveness and utility of this form of responsibility is fraught with systemic and operational limits. These limits include a lack of clarity in its constituent elements, its co-existence with primary rules prohibiting complicity and the obligations of due diligence, its implementation and the underlying causal tests, its uncertain relationship to other forms of shared and indirect responsibility, and its potential as a form of attribution of conduct. This book submits that the content and elements of this form of responsibility need adjustments to respond more effectively to the phenomenon of complicity in international affairs.

Volume 59 in the series Studies in International Law

Studies in International Law

Recent titles in this series

Democratic Statehood in International Law: The Emergence of New States in Post-Cold War Practice
Jure Vidmar

International Law and the Construction of the Liberal Peace
Russell Buchan

The OIC, the UN, and Counter-Terrorism Law-Making: Conflicting or Cooperative Legal Orders?
Katja Samuel

Statelessness: The Enigma of the International Community
William E Conklin

The Reception of Asylum Seekers under International Law: Between Sovereignty and Equality
Lieneke Slingenberg

International Law and Child Soldiers
Gus Waschefort

The Contractual Nature of the Optional Clause
Gunnar Törber

Non-State Actors in International Law
Edited by Math Noortmann, August Reinisch and Cedric Ryngaert

The Rule of Law at the National and International Levels: Contestations and Deference
Edited by Machiko Kanetake and André Nollkaemper

Human Rights Obligations of Non-State Armed Groups
Daragh Murray

Security and International Law
Edited by Mary E Footer, Julia Schmidt and Nigel D White

For the complete list of titles in this series, see 'Studies in International Law' link at www.hartpub.co.uk/books/series.asp

Complicity and its Limits in the Law of International Responsibility

Vladyslav Lanovoy

•HART•
OXFORD • LONDON • NEW YORK • NEW DELHI • SYDNEY

HART PUBLISHING
Bloomsbury Publishing Plc
Kemp House, Chawley Park, Cumnor Hill, Oxford, OX2 9PH, UK

HART PUBLISHING, the Hart/Stag logo, BLOOMSBURY and the Diana logo are trademarks of Bloomsbury Publishing Plc
First published in Great Britain 2016

First published in hardback, 2016
Paperback edition, 2019

A catalogue record for this book is available from the British Library.

Library of Congress Cataloging-in-Publication Data

Names: Lanovoy, Vladyslav, author.

Title: Complicity and its limits in the law of international responsibility / Vladyslav Lanovoy.

Description: Oxford ; Portland, Oregon : Hart Publishing, 2016. | Series: Studies in international law ; volume 59 | Includes bibliographical references and index.

Identifiers: LCCN 2016019864 (print) | LCCN 2016020005 (ebook) | ISBN 9781782259404 (hardback : alk. paper) | ISBN 9781782259381 (Epub)

Subjects: LCSH: Government liability (International law) | International criminal law. | Accomplices.

Classification: LCC KZ4080 .L36 2016 (print) | LCC KZ4080 (ebook) | DDC 342.08/8—dc23

LC record available at https://lccn.loc.gov/2016019864

ISBN: HB: 978-1-78225-940-4
PB: 978-1-50992-677-0
ePDF: 978-1-78225-937-4
ePub: 978-1-78225-938-1

Series: Studies in International Law, volume 59

Typeset by Compuscript Ltd, Shannon

To find out more about our authors and books visit www.hartpublishing.co.uk. Here you will find extracts, author information, details of forthcoming events and the option to sign up for our newsletters.

To Heather

Моїм батькам, сестрі Оленці, бабусі Тамілі і дідові Василю

Em memória da Professora Paula Escarameia

Foreword

Why is it that, in recent times, several studies have been published on the issue of complicity in international law? Does it mean that the Articles of the International Law Commission on the Responsibility of States for Internationally Wrongful Acts (ARSIWA) and the Articles on the Responsibility of International Organizations (ARIO) raise more difficulties than they bring solutions to this subject matter? But these Articles do not even speak of complicity! They use a very different expression, that of 'aid or assistance in the commission of an internationally wrongful act'. Is that the same? One may have doubts.

Complicity in the wrongdoing is a separate trigger of responsibility from the principal wrongful act it facilitates. Accordingly, the complicit actor is responsible for the commission of a specific wrongful act that is directly and solely attributed to him, not to the principal wrongdoer. However, if the latter had not committed any breach of international law, then there would not exist any complicit actor. A paradox of complicity is then that it is both *dependent* on the commission of a wrongful act by the principal State (or international organisation) and *autonomous* in that it is a separate wrongdoing attributable to a complicit State (or international organisation). The two responsible subjects of international law are then the authors of two separate violations of two different obligations, distinct one from the other but nevertheless correlated.

As a consequence, is it absolutely necessary to focus on this correlation by claiming the existence of a specific international responsibility for complicity? Wouldn't it be at least more efficient if not even more logical to say that, based on a certain factual situation, two States are to be considered in parallel as internationally responsible, without even considering the actual links existing between their respective behaviour? Such a clear partition between the two would be more in line with the traditional approach of the international responsibility of a State, considered until relatively recent times as a *bilateral* relationship between the State violating an obligation and another State injured by this breach. This relationship characterises the very *unity* of the law of State responsibility on which Paul Reuter, in particular, insisted so much in his general course of international law at the Hague Academy in 1961.

Would the recent care devoted by scholars to the analysis of complicity have something to do with the rising importance of obligations of States towards one another but also in relation with the *international community*, whether it is limited to the States parties to the same treaty or even extended to *the international community as a whole*? The answer to this question is not necessarily the easiest one; but one is forced to recognise that such an approach is in any event far from the one adopted by the ILC in the rules set out in Articles 16 ARSIWA and 14 ARIO.

Now, why is it that, when dealing with interstate responsibility, or, more broadly, the responsibility of different subjects of international law, one should bring into the debate the term 'complicity'? Isn't it a concept which, to say the least, is far from being a neutral one? Complicity belongs to the vocabulary, techniques and theory of *criminal* law. Yes, *international* criminal law does exist. But, as recalled by the International Court of Justice in the *Bosnia Genocide* case in 2007, one must keep completely distinct the international responsibility of States on the one hand and that of internationally criminal individuals on the other, whatever the relationship between the two in the commission of some specific wrongful acts.

Furthermore, once again, one cannot say that reference to complicity in positive international law is simply due to the modern development of international criminal law as this concept was already used well before such a development. There are evident systemic reasons for this. Complicity is the outcome of an intention. Individuals have intentions. States, at least as such, have none. They only act through the means of individual organs; and this is why, rightly or not, Dionisio Anzilotti gave his 'objective' definition of a wrongful act, only depicted as the contradiction between the rule of law and the actual conduct of a State in a given situation. Whatever the criticism which may be exercised against it, there is no room for any psychological subjectivity of a notion like 'complicity' in this definition, one which is still shared by a large number of scholars inspired by the classical voluntary positivism of which Anzilotti was and remains, particularly in Europe, the very champion. He wanted the legal institution of State responsibility to operate as efficiently as possible; and this is another reason why he wanted to free its design of any reference to intention which, in essence, is difficult to prove, in particular if attributed to the State, an artificially created legal person. Should one be led to the conclusion that, if it can be attributed to a State, this is a very special kind of complicity? Complicity without intention? Does this make any sense? Why, then, use such an ambiguous term?

Yes indeed, why complicate the story and analytical theory of this central issue of the international responsibility of States by introducing the term complicity when the ILC ultimately decided not to use it? Would not a reason for this terminological abstention of the Commission lie in the fact that the notion itself, at least for one part, comes very close indeed to simply neglecting the basic distinction between *primary* and *secondary* rules of law?

If complicity, may it be grounded on intention or not, points to another way of defining the *due diligence* rule and, more generally, the way in which one State (or international organisation) should act in respect of assistance given to another State, aren't we dealing here with a *primary* rule of international law? This would then fall *outside* the scope of the theory of international responsibility, at least as ascertained by Roberto Ago, the first and very brilliant Special Rapporteur to the ILC on this subject matter, responsibility being defined by him as a corpus of *secondary* rules of international law, triggered by the prior violation of a primary obligation, of conduct, result or abstention.

Vladyslav Lanovoy engages with the questions set out above, along with many others. With a truly exceptional intellectual maturity and an elegant demonstration of his technical abilities, he does more than ask whether and in which respect the international responsibility for complicity does exist in general international law. Thanks to a critical analysis, based on the effective mastering of the most pertinent legal literature written in at least five languages, the author demonstrates that responsibility for complicity as set out in the ARSIWA and ARIO offers a rather incomplete response to complicit conduct in international law. By contrast, he proposes a revised model of responsibility for complicity which does not overlook the present state of customary international law, to the contrary, but which is at the same time inspired by considering what the law should set as its goals while keeping with the idea that the law must operate independently from the momentary views of its subjects.

This is an extremely stimulating book that provides a set of comprehensive and mature answers to the contemporary questioning on complicity in international law, pointing to *a true legal order* rather than a heterogeneous collection of so-called 'fragmented' rules of law.

Pierre-Marie Dupuy
Emeritus Professor of Public International Law
University of Paris (Panthéon-Assas)
Graduate Institute of International and Development Studies—Geneva
Associate Member of the Institute of International Law

Acknowledgements

This book is a revised version of my PhD thesis in international law (*summa cum laude avec félicitations du jury*) defended in March 2014 at the Graduate Institute of International and Development Studies in Geneva. This work is the result of an intellectual complicity with my supervisor, mentor and friend, Professor Pierre-Marie Dupuy, to whom I extend all my gratitude. I am also grateful to Professors Andrea Bianchi, Vera Gowlland-Debbas and Luigi Condorelli for their insightful comments which have improved this book.

I would also like to thank the staff of the Peace Palace in The Hague, and the Cambridge Lauterpacht Centre for International Law, where I completed the drafting of my PhD thesis. In particular, I would like to thank Professor James Crawford for having shared with me his views on complicity while at the Lauterpacht Centre. I have also benefited immensely from discussions held in the context of the Shares research project in Amsterdam led by Professor André Nollkaemper, Professor Jean d'Aspremont, Dr Ilias Plakokefalos, Dr Dov Jacobs and Dr Christiane Ahlborn. Many other international law scholars have contributed in one way or another to this project, including Professor Marcelo Kohen, Professor Andrew Clapham, Professor Gráinne de Búrca, Professor Ryan Goodman, Professor Jorge Viñuales, Professor Gabrielle Marceau, Professor Santiago Villalpando, Dr Kate Parlett and Dr Arnold Pronto. The three anonymous reviews commissioned by Hart Publishing were particularly helpful in turning my PhD thesis into a book. I would like to thank Sinead Moloney and Emily Braggins for their dedication to this project. Very special thanks go to my dear friends Dr Mamadou Hébié for his thought-provoking comments on earlier drafts and the Arregui, Santos and Emery families, Aua Balde, Dr Meagan Wong and Dr Miriam Cohen.

I would like to dedicate this book to my wife Heather and my family. I cannot thank them enough for their love, patience and support which have been the greatest source of inspiration and which allowed me to bring this project to completion. This book is in memory of Paula Escarameia—my first Professor of Public International Law, my supervisor and mentor at the International Law Commission, a very dear friend and one of the best persons I have ever met. To sadness of her beloved, friends and all the people who have had the chance to meet her, she left us too prematurely in 2010. She not only lived her life with an ever-lasting smile, courage and passion but she also changed the lives of many people, including my own. My passion for international law is a gift from Paula. She was the first Portuguese citizen to obtain an LLM and SJD at Harvard Law School, the first woman ever to be elected to the UN International Law Commission, one of the most influential legal advisors during the elaboration of the Rome Statute of the ICC, and made an immense contribution to the cause of East Timor, including in her capacity as Legal Advisor to the Permanent Mission of Portugal at the United Nations. I hope that the words in the pages below serve as a recognition and appreciation to Paula for everything she taught me in international law and in life.

Vladyslav Lanovoy
London, January 2016

Contents

List of Abbreviations

AFDI	Annuaire français de droit international
AIDI	Annuaire de l'Institut de droit international
AJIL	American Journal of International Law
ARIO	Articles on Responsibility of International Organizations
ARSIWA	Articles on Responsibility of States for Internationally Wrongful Acts
ASIL	American Society of International Law
AVR	Archiv des Völkerrechts
BVerfG	Bundesverfassungsgericht (German Federal Constitutional Court)
BVerwG	Bundesverwaltungsgericht (German Federal Administrative Court)
CJEU	Court of Justice of the European Union
CLF	Criminal Law Forum
Comp	Comparative
CTR	Claims Tribunal Reports
CTS	Consolidated Treaty Series
CUP	Cambridge University Press
EC	European Communities
ECHR	European Convention on Human Rights
ECOSOC	UN Economic and Social Council
ECtHR	European Court of Human Rights
EJIL	European Journal of International Law
EU	European Union
FRY	Federal Republic of Yugoslavia
HMSO	Her Majesty's Stationery Office
HR	Human Rights
HRC	Human Rights Council
HRLR	Human Rights Law Review
IACtHR	Inter-American Court of Human Rights
ICC	International Criminal Court
ICCPR	International Covenant on Civil and Political Rights

ICJ	International Court of Justice
ICLQ	International Comparative Law Quarterly
ICRC	International Committee of the Red Cross
ICSID	International Centre for the Settlement of Investment Disputes
ICTR	International Criminal Tribunal for Rwanda
ICTY	International Criminal Tribunal for the Former Yugoslavia
IHL	International Humanitarian Law
ILDC	Oxford Reports on International Law in Domestic Courts
ILM	International Law Materials
ILR	International Law Reports
ILSA	International Law Students Association
IMT	International Military Tribunal
Intl	International
IOLR	International Organizations Law Review
IRRC	International Review of the Red Cross
ITLOS	International Tribunal on the Law of the Sea
J	Journal
JCSL	Journal of Conflict and Security Law
JICJ	Journal of International Criminal Justice
JIEL	Journal of International Economic Law
L	Law
LJIL	Leiden Journal of International Law
LPICT	Law and Practice of International Courts and Tribunals
LR	Law Revue
LRTWC	Law Reports of Trials of War Criminals
MAT	Mixed Arbitral Tribunal
NYU	New York University
OAS	Organization of American States
OAU	Organization of African Unity
OJLS	Oxford Journal of Legal Studies
OUP	Oxford University Press
PCA	Permanent Court of Arbitration
Pol	Politics/Policy
PUF	Presses Universitaires de France
RBDI	Revue belge de droit international

RCADI	Recueil des cours de l'académie de droit international
RDI	Rivista di diritto internazionale
RDIDC	Revue de droit international et de droit comparé
RGDIP	Revue générale de droit international public
RHDI	Revue hellénique de droit international
RIAA	Report of International Arbitral Awards
SCSL	Special Court for Sierra Leone
SDNY	Southern District of New York
SFDI	Société française pour le droit international
SZIER	Schweizerische Zeitschrift für internationales und europäisches Recht
Transnatl	Transnational
TWC	Trial of War Criminals
UNCLOS	United Nations Convention on the Law of the Sea
UNGA	United Nations General Assembly
UNSC	United Nations Security Council
UNTS	United Nations Treaty Series
UNYB	United Nations Juridical Yearbook
USTIA	United States Treaties and other International Agreements
VCLT	Vienna Convention on the Law of Treaties
WTO	World Trade Organization
YB	Yearbook
YBIL	Yearbook of International Law
YBILC	Yearbook of the International Law Commission
ZaöRV	Zeitschrift für ausländisches öffentliches Recht und Völkerrecht

Table of Treaties

Treaties

Table of Cases

Permanent Court of International Justice and International Court of Justice

International Tribunal for the Law of the Sea

Human Rights Courts

World Trade Organization

Court of Justice of the European Union

International Criminal Courts and Tribunals

Arbitral Awards

Domestic Courts

Table of Other Authorities

UN International Law Commission

UN Security Council

UN General Assembly

Other UN Bodies

Diplomatic Conferences

Other Authorities

Domestic Legislation

1

Introduction

When Pilate saw that he was getting nowhere,
but that instead an uproar was starting,
he took water and washed his hands in front of the crowd:
'I am innocent of this man's blood', he said.
'It is your responsibility'. (Matthew 27:24)

I. RESEARCH QUESTION

A VIOLATION OF an international obligation by one actor is often a result of complicity of another. Complicity is a product of the multifaceted ways in which States, international organisations and other actors interact in modern international affairs.[1] States have assisted others in extraordinary rendition, secret detention and torture in the context of the so-called war on terror. Likewise, there have been cases of military aid for the unlawful use of force or aggression, lethal, technical and financial assistance towards the commission of violations of international human rights and humanitarian law, intelligence sharing and placing of military bases for drone attacks in third States, or financing of non-State actors that commit terrorist activities in a third State. There have also been less common allegations of complicity of international organisations or their Member States in violations of international obligations in the context of joint military and peace-keeping operations. It is certain that many more instances have escaped public scrutiny, or will be revealed years after the event.

As Pilate in front of the crowd, an accomplice actor will seek safe haven from responsibility. This comes as no surprise in international law, a decentralised legal order with weak enforcement mechanisms and perennial institutional flaws. States and international organisations are responsible for actions or omissions attributable to them and which constitute a

[1] P Allott, *The Health of Nations: Society and Law beyond the State* (Cambridge, CUP, 2002) preface x ('The globalising of human society is also a globalising of social evil').

violation of their own obligations.[2] This principle of independent responsibility is paramount throughout the International Law Commission's (ILC) Articles on Responsibility of States for Internationally Wrongful Acts (ARSIWA) and the Articles on Responsibility of International Organizations (ARIO).[3] However, this principle leaves little space for the consideration of how multiple actors may participate in an internationally wrongful act and what their share of responsibility for such participation should be.[4] Complicity is one of the most common means of participating in an internationally wrongful act.[5]

This book examines the existing legal framework of international responsibility for complicity (aid or assistance) as it applies to States and international organisations.[6] What are the limits of complicity as a basis of responsibility in general international law? Does the existing legal framework effectively respond to instances of complicity in the internationally wrongful acts? Is it useful to have a general framework on responsibility for complicity when most practical examples of complicity to date appear to be covered by specific primary rules? These are some of the key

[2] ILC, 'Draft Articles on Responsibility of States for Internationally Wrongful Acts, with Commentaries' (2001) 2 (pt 2) *YBILC* 31, Art 2; ILC, 'Draft Articles on the Responsibility of International Organizations, with Commentaries' (2011) 2 (pt 2) *YBILC* 2, Art 3; see also UNGA, 'Res 56/83' (12 December 2001) UN Doc A/RES/56/83, para 3 (taking note of the ARSIWA); UNGA, 'Res 59/35' (2 December 2004) UN Doc A/RES/59/35, para 1 (commending the ARSIWA 'without prejudice to the question of their adoption or other appropriate action'); UNGA, 'Res 66/100' (9 December 2011) UN Doc A/RES/66/100, para 3 (taking note of the ARIO).

[3] The principle derives from an old Latin maxim 'nemo punitur pro alieno delicto' ('No one is to be punished for the crime or wrong of another'). For an early recognition of this principle in international law which has since been affirmed on multiple occasions see, eg *Paula Mendel and others (United States) v Germany* (1926) 7 RIAA 372; *Phosphates in Morocco (Italy v France)* (Preliminary Objections) [1938] PCIJ Ser A/B No 74, 10, 28; see also J Crawford, *The International Law Commission's Articles on State Responsibility: Introduction, Text and Commentaries* (Cambridge, CUP, 2002) 1–60.

[4] On the existing limitations of the framework of international law for a genuine shared responsibility, including between the complicit and principal wrongdoers, see, eg JE Noyes and BD Smith, 'State Responsibility and the Principle of Joint and Several Liability' (1988) 13 *Yale J Intl L* 225; A Nollkaemper and D Jacobs, 'Shared Responsibility in International Law: A Conceptual Framework' (2013) 34 *Michigan J Intl L* 359; C Dominicé, 'Attribution of Conduct to Multiple States and the Implication of a State in the Act of Another State' in J Crawford et al (eds), *The Law of International Responsibility* (Oxford, OUP, 2010); V Lanovoy, 'Complicity in an Internationally Wrongful Act' in A Nollkaemper and I Plakokefalos (eds), *Principles of Shared Responsibility in International Law: An Appraisal of the State of the Art* (Cambridge, CUP, 2014); on the theory and practice of international responsibility see generally J Crawford, *State Responsibility: The General Part* (Cambridge, CUP, 2013).

[5] ILC, 'ARSIWA' (n 2) 65, para 8 ('the situations covered in Chapter IV [including responsibility for complicity] have a special character. They are exceptions to the principle of independent responsibility and they only cover certain cases').

[6] ILC, 'Report of the International Law Commission on the Work of Its 25th Session (7 May–13 July 1973)' (1973) UN Doc A/9010/Rev 1, reproduced in (1973) 2 *YBILC* 161, 175, para 10 (the term international responsibility covers 'every kind of new relations which may arise, in international law, from the internationally wrongful act').

questions posed in this book which will no doubt continue to generate lively debate in the years to come.

II. THE DEFINITION OF COMPLICITY IN INTERNATIONAL LAW

Complicity is commonly defined as 'being an accomplice; partnership in an evil action ... state of being complex or involved', whereas an accomplice is 'an associate in guilt, a partner in crime'.[7] Black's Law Dictionary defines complicity as '[a]ssociation or participation in a criminal act; the act or state of being accomplice'.[8] However, in international law, the definition of complicity is more complex. According to Jean Salmon, complicity has a tripartite meaning in international law: (i) as a form of international responsibility; (ii) its past use as a mode of attribution of private conduct to the State that has failed to exercise the required degree of vigilance; and (iii) as a form of liability in international criminal law.[9] A fourth dimension of complicity as an emerging standard of corporate liability could be added to this multi-layered definition in international law.[10]

This book focuses on the first dimension of complicity, that is as a form of international responsibility under general international law. Despite their distinct normative functions and foundations, the remaining dimensions of complicity, in particular that of international criminal law, still inform the analysis. This allows a more holistic understanding of the evolution of the concept of responsibility for complicity in general international law, particularly as its elements and criteria of application need

[7] *The Oxford English Dictionary*, vol 2 (Oxford, Clarendon Press, 1983) 729.

[8] *Black's Law Dictionary* (4th edn, St Paul, West Publishing, 2011) 140.

[9] J Salmon, *Dictionnaire de droit international public* (Bruxelles, Bruylant, 2001) 218–29.

[10] See, eg *In re South African Apartheid* (Judgment) [2009] 617 F Supp 2d 228 (SDNY); *Presbyterian Church of Sudan v Talisman Energy Inc* (Judgment) [2005] 374 F Supp 2d 331 (SDNY); *Doe v Unocal* (Judgment) [2002] 395 F 3d 932 (9th Cir 2002); see also International Commission of Jurists, 'Corporate Complicity & Legal Accountability' (Geneva, International Commission of Jurists, 2008); A Clapham, *Human Rights Obligations of Non-State Actors* (Oxford, OUP, 2006) 252–63; C Wells and J Elias, 'Catching the Conscience of the Kings: Corporate Player on the International Stage' in P Alston (ed), *Non-State Actors and Human Rights* (Oxford, OUP, 2005); A Clapham and S Jerbi, 'Categories of Corporate Complicity in Human Rights Abuses' (2000) 24 *Hastings Intl & Comp LR* 339; JP Bohoslavsky and V Opgenhaffen, 'Past and Present of Corporate Complicity: Financing the Argentinean Dictatorship' (2010) 23 *Harvard Human Rights J* 157; JP Bohoslavsky and M Rulli, 'Corporate Complicity and Finance as a "Killing Agent": The Relevance of the Chilean Case' (2010) 8 *JICJ* 829; A Adeyeye, 'Corporate Responsibility in International Law: Which Way to Go' (2007) 11 *Singapore YBIL* 141; A Clapham, 'Extending International Criminal Law beyond the Individual to Corporations and Armed Opposition Groups' (2008) 6 *JICJ* 899; E Mongelard, 'Corporate Civil Liability for Violations of International Humanitarian Law' (2006) 88 *IRRC* 665; H van der Wilt, 'Corporate Criminal Responsibility for International Crimes: Exploring the Possibilities' (2013) 12 *Chinese J Intl L* 43; S Michalowski, 'No Complicity Liability for Funding Gross Human Rights Violations?' (2012) 30 *Berkeley J Intl L* 451.

to be refined in practice. An analysis of the operation of responsibility for complicity in general international law may draw upon the experience of the international criminal tribunals, which have dealt with similar concepts in the context of individual criminal liability. However, this book avoids making any direct analogies. In fact, the use of the term 'complicity' in general international law might be questioned at the outset because of its common criminal connotation.[11] This was seen as a 'source of ambiguity or misinterpretation' by the ILC, which elected to use the term of 'aid or assistance' in the relevant provisions of the ARSIWA and ARIO in its place.[12] However, the reference to 'complicity' in the relations between subjects of international law and in doctrine abounds, and the terms of 'aid or assistance' and 'complicity' are for the most part used interchangeably.[13] One may legitimately doubt, however, whether they are synonymous, particularly when comparing the initial rule in 1978 as proposed by the ILC's Special Rapporteur Roberto Ago and that devised under the leadership of Special Rapporteur James Crawford, which became current Article 16 ARSIWA.[14]

In sum, complicity is a form of participation in the wrongful act of another State or international organisation. Responsibility for complicity in general international law can thus be defined as responsibility of a State or international organisation for its action or omission, knowingly facilitating the commission of an internationally wrongful act by another actor.

III. RESPONSIBILITY FOR COMPLICITY IN AN INTERNATIONALLY WRONGFUL ACT

Complicity in the wrongful act is a separate trigger of responsibility (*fait générateur*) from the principal wrongful act it facilitates. Accordingly, the complicit actor, whether it is a State or international organisation, is

[11] ILC, 'Summary Record of the 1517th Meeting' (13 July 1978), reproduced in (1978) 1 *YBILC* 228, 229, para 4 (Reuter); ILC, 'Summary Record of the 1518th Meeting' (17 July 1978), reproduced in (1978) 1 *YBILC* 232, 233, para 3 (Ushakov); ibid 234, para 11 (Sahović).

[12] ILC, 'Summary Record of the 1524th Meeting' (24 July 1978), reproduced in (1978) 1 *YBILC* 269, para 4 (Schwebel).

[13] ILC, 'ARSIWA' (n 2) 67, para 11 (Art 16 Commentary); see, eg B Graefrath, 'Complicity in the Law of International Responsibility' (1996) 2 *RBDI* 370, 372 ('the term complicity so far has been used in international relations in the political field. It has a pejorative connotation and denounces an act as illegal because it is part of another illegal act or in support of a crime. It always designates a form of participation and derives the moral condemnation from the illegality of the principal act').

[14] See ch 3, s III; for a critical analysis of the drafts of the rule that preceded Art 16 ARSIWA see, eg E Klein, 'Beihilfe zum Völkerrechtsdelikt' in I von Münch (ed), *Staatsrecht, Völkerrecht, Europarecht: Festschrift für Hans-Jürgen Schlochauer zum 75. Geburtstag am 28. März 1981* (Berlin, Walter de Gruyter, 1981); J Quigley, 'Complicity in International Law: A New Direction in the Law of State Responsibility' (1987) 57 *British YBIL* 77; Graefrath (n 13).

responsible not for the act of the principal wrongdoer, but for its own contribution facilitating that same act. However, responsibility for the complicit conduct only accrues once the principal wrongful act is committed. This artificial legal construction of complicity as a separate *fait générateur* of responsibility underlies the relevant provisions of the ARSIWA and ARIO which are reproduced below:

Article 16 ARSIWA

Aid or assistance in the commission of an internationally wrongful act

A State which aids or assists another State in the commission of an internationally wrongful act by the latter is internationally responsible for doing so if:

(a) that State does so with knowledge of the circumstances of the internationally wrongful act; and
(b) the act would be internationally wrongful if committed by that State.

***

Article 41 ARSIWA

Particular consequences of a serious breach of an obligation under this chapter

1. States shall cooperate to bring to an end through lawful means any serious breach within the meaning of article 40.
2. No State shall recognize as lawful a situation created by a serious breach within the meaning of article 40, nor render aid or assistance in maintaining that situation.
3. This article is without prejudice to the other consequences referred to in this part and to such further consequences that a breach to which this chapter applies may entail under international law.

***

Article 14 ARIO

Aid or assistance in the commission of an internationally wrongful act

An international organization which aids or assists a State or another international organization in the commission of an internationally wrongful act by the State or the latter organization is internationally responsible for doing so if:

(a) the former organization does so with knowledge of the circumstances of the internationally wrongful act; and
(b) the act would be internationally wrongful if committed by that organization.

***

Article 42 ARIO

Particular consequences of a serious breach of an obligation under this Chapter

1. States and international organizations shall cooperate to bring to an end through lawful means any serious breach within the meaning of article 41.

2. No State or international organization shall recognize as lawful a situation created by a serious breach within the meaning of article 41, nor render aid or assistance in maintaining that situation.
3. This article is without prejudice to the other consequences referred to in this Part and to such further consequences that a breach to which this Chapter applies may entail under international law.

***

Article 58 ARIO

Aid or assistance by a State in the commission of an internationally wrongful act by an international organization

1. A State which aids or assists an international organization in the commission of an internationally wrongful act by the latter is internationally responsible for doing so if:
   (a) the State does so with knowledge of the circumstances of the internationally wrongful act; and
   (b) the act would be internationally wrongful if committed by that State.
2. An act by a State member of an international organization done in accordance with the rules of the organization does not as such engage the international responsibility of that State under the terms of this article.

These provisions of ARSIWA and ARIO, which combine elements of codification proper and progressive development of international law, have made an important contribution to the regulation of complicity in the wrongdoing. However, their practical added value remains limited for a host of reasons.

First, several treaties and customary law norms prohibit complicity in specific wrongful acts, including genocide, torture, aggression and the use of certain arms.[15] Thus, complicity in such acts generates direct responsibility under those treaties and customary law norms (and may not require satisfaction of the more stringent material, cognitive and opposability requirements that arise under the ARSIWA and ARIO provisions above). However, some of the treaty obligations expressly prohibiting complicity may not be binding upon international organisations, which in and of itself demonstrates the need for a general norm on responsibility for complicity in the ARIO to fill in the gap.[16] In the words of the International

[15] See, eg Convention on the Prevention and Punishment of the Crime of Genocide (adopted 9 December 1948; entered into force 12 January 1951) 78 UNTS 277, Art III(e); UNGA, 'Res 3314 (XXIX) (Declaration on Aggression)' (14 December 1974) UN Doc A/RES/3314, Art 3(f); Convention on the Prohibition of the Use, Stockpiling, Production and Transfer of Anti-Personnel Mines and on their Destruction (adopted 18 September 1997; entered into force 1 March 1999) 2056 UNTS 241, Art 1(1)(c).

[16] For the review of arguments made by some international organisations as to the non-applicability of human rights treaties to them see, eg P Alston, 'The "Not-a-Cat" Syndrome: Can the International Human Rights Regime Accommodate Non-State Actors?' in P Alston (ed), *Non-State Actors and Human Rights* (Oxford, OUP, 2005) 9.

Court of Justice (ICJ), '[i]nternational organizations are … bound by any obligations incumbent upon them under general rules of international law, under their constitutions or under international agreements to which they are parties'.[17] These obligations and their scope may differ from the ones engaged by States.

Second, despite the ILC's efforts, the legal framework for the responsibility of multiple actors in relation to the same internationally wrongful act, or several internationally wrongful acts causing a single injury, is not well-developed in practice. This is evident in the context of the international dispute settlement mechanisms available, which require consent to jurisdiction and the application of the principle of the indispensable third party.[18] Significant structural adjustments are therefore required for the international dispute settlement mechanisms to be able to effectively implement responsibility for complicity in the commission of an internationally wrongful act.

Third, the relevant ARSIWA and ARIO provisions themselves are not free from criticism. Their content is ambiguous and the contradictions between their text and the ILC's Commentary on them are striking. Further, an analysis of practice and *opinio juris* reveals that these contradictions are not insignificant textual niceties—they affect both the existence and scope of responsibility for complicity.

Fourth, as most instances of international responsibility are settled bilaterally and privately between the injured party and the principal wrongdoer, the injured State or international organisation is not always able or willing to invoke responsibility of accomplice actors due to legal and political considerations. A review of the practice of complicity shows that it is usually the stronger actors in international affairs that provide aid or assistance for the commission of an internationally wrongful act by another. This of course presents a difficult balancing exercise for the injured entity as to the way and forum in which to protest or bring a claim.

Fifth, there is a significant problem of evidence. To establish responsibility for complicity in its current ARSIWA/ARIO configuration is a daunting task, particularly where the burden would lie exclusively on the injured entity to bring evidence of the knowledge, and even more so *intention* of the aiding or assisting State or international organisation, or to

[17] *Interpretation of the Agreement of 25 March 1951 between the WHO and Egypt* (Advisory Opinion) [1980] ICJ Rep 73, 90, para 37.

[18] See *Monetary Gold Removed from Rome in 1943 (Italy v France, United Kingdom and United States)* (Preliminary Question) [1954] ICJ Rep 19; *East Timor (Portugal v Australia)* (Judgment) [1995] ICJ Rep 90 (in essence, the principle entails that the Court will not adjudicate on a case where it would necessarily have to pronounce on the rights or responsibility of a non-consenting and absent third State).

show that the latter's assistance *significantly* contributed to the commission of the principal wrongful act.

More generally, the limited impact to date of responsibility for complicity is reminiscent of the still prevailing *Zeitgeist of Lotus*, a view of international law where no restrictions can be presumed on the unlimited freedom of action of sovereigns.[19] Attributing a greater role to responsibility for complicity could substantially limit that freedom of action for States and international organisations. Conversely, it could reinforce the respect of an international obligation and fulfil the legality function of international responsibility.[20]

This book questions the effectiveness and utility of responsibility for complicity as codified in the ARSIWA and ARIO and argues for a slightly different normative model. Many elements of this model are matters of interpretation or adjustment in the application of the rules as codified by the ILC. Some, however, such as the questions of intention and opposability, are more fundamental and go to the very object and purpose of responsibility for complicity in international law. It may be premature to consider the model of complicity advanced in this book as *de lege lata*. However, the existing practice and *opinio juris* analysed in this book do show that the ILC's edifice on responsibility for complicity is not free from criticism. It is submitted that the ARSIWA and ARIO provisions fall short of meeting the object and purpose of regulating legal consequences of complicity in international law. An oversight by the ILC? A deliberate choice of States and international organisations? An immature legal system? All of these explanations, separately or in combination, may have prompted the existing framework in the ARSIWA and ARIO and its limits in positive international law.

[19] *SS 'Lotus' (France v Turkey)* (Judgment) [1927] PCIJ Ser A No 10, 18; *Legality of the Threat or Use of Nuclear Weapons* (Advisory Opinion) [1996] ICJ Rep 226, Declaration of Judge Bedjaoui 268, 270–71, para 13; *Accordance with International Law of the Unilateral Declaration of Independence in Respect of Kosovo* (Advisory Opinion) [2010] ICJ Rep 403, Declaration of Judge Simma 478 ff, paras 2 ff (the Lotus principle reflects no more than an 'old, tired view of international law'); see generally PM Dupuy, 'L'unité de l'ordre juridique international' (2002) 297 *RCADI* 9.

[20] D Anzilotti, *Cours de droit international*, vol 1 (G Gidel tr, Paris, Sirey, 1929) 523 ('l'action de l'État lésé, tendant à une réparation, se concrétise parfois, en tout ou en partie dans le rétablissement de l'ordre juridique comme tel et parce que tel'; author's translation: 'the action of the injured State seeking to obtain reparation sometimes takes the form, in whole or in part, of the re-establishment of the legal order as such'); PM Dupuy, 'Responsabilité et légalité' in SFDI (ed), *La responsabilité dans le système international: Colloque du Mans* (Paris, Pedone, 1991) 278 ('c'est bien plutôt sur l'idée de restauration qu'il conviendrait d'insister. Il s'agira, en effet, de restaurer la situation matérielle de la victime mais aussi de rétablir la situation juridique existant avant la violation du droit'; author's translation: 'it is rather the idea of restoration that should be emphasised. The idea is not only to restore the material situation of the victim but also the legal situation before the breach').

The ICJ identified responsibility for complicity as it has been set out in Article 16 ARSIWA as a rule of customary international law.[21] However, this book calls for analytical caution and a distinction to be drawn between the underlying principle of responsibility for complicity (which is, in the author's view, the limit of what has been recognised by the ICJ) and the constituent elements of responsibility for complicity.[22] While the principle finds overwhelming approval among subjects of international law, the constituent elements of responsibility do not find the same level of support in the existing practice and *opinio juris*.

IV. THE TREATMENT OF RESPONSIBILITY FOR COMPLICITY IN DOCTRINE

In the last decade, three monographs have been published on the subject of complicity in international law, two in the course of preparation of this book. This shows not only the growing interest in the subject, but also its complexity and importance in modern international affairs. Andreas Felder's monograph focuses on the analysis of Articles 16 and 41 of the ARSIWA, arguing that some of its conditions need to be clarified, including the scope of its cognitive requirement which should cover constructive knowledge.[23] Helmut Aust's monograph provides an impressive survey of State practice in respect of complicity, which the present monograph builds upon. Through the theoretical lenses of the rule of law and the doctrine of abuse of rights, Aust concludes that the rule of responsibility for complicity as set out in Article 16 ARSIWA is part of customary international law, at the same time acknowledging the existence of a 'diverse network of rules on complicity' which may have a different scope of application.[24] Most recently, Miles Jackson focuses his monograph on complicity in international criminal law and the law of State responsibility,

[21] *Application of the Convention on the Prevention and Punishment of the Crime of Genocide (Bosnia and Herzegovina v Serbia and Montenegro)* (Merits) [2007] ICJ Rep 43, 217, para 420.

[22] ibid; for a recent analysis of the Court's methodology in identifying customary international law rules see S Talmon, 'Determining Customary International Law: The ICJ's Methodology between Induction, Deduction and Assertion' (2015) 26 *EJIL* 417; see also S Villalpando, 'On the International Court of Justice and the Determination of Rules of Law' (2013) 26 *LJIL* 243, 247–48 (suggesting that we may be 'victims of a normative Ponzi scheme' because of the way the Court and the Commission take each other's work as absolute proof of customary international law); A Alvarez-Jiménez, 'Methods for the Identification of Customary International Law in the International Court of Justice's Jurisprudence: 2000–2009' (2011) 60 *ICLQ* 681; for methodological premises of identifying rules of positive international law see R Ago, 'Droit positif et droit international' (1957) 3 *AFDI* 14.

[23] A Felder, *Die Beihilfe im Recht der völkerrechtlichen Staatenverantwortlichkeit* (Zürich, Schulthess, 2007).

[24] HP Aust, *Complicity and the Law of State Responsibility* (Cambridge, CUP, 2011).

making a normative claim of complicity as a purely derivative form of responsibility. Jackson also criticises the use of complicity as a mode of attribution of conduct in international law.[25]

This book aims to reposition the academic debate from the *normative source* of the rule(s) on responsibility for complicity to their *utility* and *effectiveness* in practice. The author's analysis extends beyond the realm of inter-State relations grappling with how this form of responsibility applies in the context of international organisations. Moreover, the fact that complicity under the law of international responsibility has a distinctive character does not mean that the application of complicity in other fields, such as international criminal law, can be ignored.[26] Likewise, collaboration with non-State actors and the alarming threat now facing international peace and security, as the recent attacks by the Islamic State of Iraq and the Levant (ISIL) demonstrate, demand an investigation of whether complicity could fill the gaps in the existing rules of attribution of conduct under the law of international responsibility.[27]

V. THE MODEL(S) OF RESPONSIBILITY FOR COMPLICITY

Complicity in the commission of an internationally wrongful act is typically described as a form of ancillary, derivative or indirect responsibility.[28] While there may be nuanced differences between these adjectives, they all base the responsibility for complicity upon the actual commission of the principal wrongful act. At a technical level, it is easy to understand why complicity is derivative, as the responsibility for the accomplice arises *after* the commission of the wrongful act by the principal. However, the qualification of responsibility for complicity as ancillary, derivative or indirect may be regarded as undermining the sanctity of an international obligation, and the legal system as a whole.

First, the qualification of responsibility for complicity as derivative diminishes the reprimand associated with it. However, as a matter of principle, there is nothing less reprehensible of complicity than of the principal wrongdoing it occasions. Second, this qualification fosters the idea of responsibility as a purely remedial mechanism, dependent on the commission of the principal wrongful act, and allowing for the responsibility

[25] M Jackson, *Complicity in International Law* (Oxford, OUP, 2015).

[26] See ibid; cf A Bianchi, 'State Responsibility and Criminal Liability of Individuals' in A Cassese (ed), *The Oxford Companion to International Criminal Justice* (Oxford, OUP, 2009).

[27] *Bosnia Genocide (Merits)* (n 21) 217, para 420; ARSIWA (n 2) 65, para 7 ('the idea of the implication of one State in the conduct of another is analogous to problems of attribution').

[28] See, eg Crawford, *State Responsibility: The General Part* (n 4); Jackson (n 25); V Lowe, 'Responsibility for the Conduct of Other States' (2002) 101 *Japanese J Intl L & Diplomacy* 1.

of the accomplice to be a mere afterthought. Third, while complicity is indeed derivative at the level of the origins of responsibility (ie triggering or *fait générateur*), it would be misleading to qualify the content of responsibility for complicity (ie the legal consequences) as derivative. This may result in an undue burden of reparation on weaker principal actors and the provision of a safe haven for stronger complicit actors.

Complicity in the internationally wrongful act should rather be conceived of as a form of shared responsibility, involving a factual relationship of at least two conducts and three actors.[29] The advantage of framing complicity as a form of shared responsibility is to avoid the diminished reprimand attached to complicit conduct vis-à-vis the principal wrongful act. Moreover, the theoretical construction of complicity as a form of shared responsibility permits a more balanced approach to the allocation of responsibility between the accomplice and the principal. It also enhances the prospects for the injured State or international organisation to seek reparation from both the principal and the accomplice.

More generally, responsibility for complicity is a conceptually rare and complex object of analysis for a host of reasons. First, responsibility for complicity contains elements of primary and secondary norms, appearing as a structural or *meta-rule* in the legal order.[30] Second, complicity puts into question the objective character of responsibility through its cognitive requirement. Third, it raises complex issues regarding the nature of obligations in international law, and the legal interests of the international community in their observance. The phenomenon of complicity in a wrongful act makes it 'more essential than ever that the rules developed to ensure the ordered progress of relations between its members should be constantly and scrupulously respected'.[31]

The right to cooperate with other States, international organisations or non-State actors by providing aid or assistance must be limited by a

[29] Nollkaemper and Jacobs (n 4) 396; see also Lanovoy (n 4).

[30] On the classification of primary/secondary norms in international law see HLA Hart, *The Concept of Law* (2nd edn, Oxford, OUP, 1994); R Ago, 'Second Report on State Responsibility' (1970) UN Doc A/CN.4/233, reproduced in (1970) 2 *YBILC* 177, 178–79, para 7–11; 191, para 41; N Bobbio, 'Nouvelles réflexions sur les normes primaires et secondaires' in N Bobbio (ed), *Études de théorie du droit* (Paris, LGDJ, 1988); J Combacau and D Alland, 'Primary and Secondary Rules in the Law of State Responsibility: Categorizing International Obligations' (1985) 16 *Netherlands YBIL* 81; E David, 'Primary and Secondary Rules' in J Crawford et al (eds), *The Law of International Responsibility* (Oxford, OUP, 2010); G Gaja, 'Primary and Secondary Rules in the International Law on State Responsibility' (2014) 97 *RDI* 981; U Linderfalk, 'State Responsibility and the Primary-Secondary Rules Terminology—The Role of Language for an Understanding of the International Legal System' (2009) 78 *Nordic J Intl L* 53; A Marschik, 'Too Much Order? The Impact of Special Secondary Norms on the Unity and Efficacy of the International Legal System' (1998) 9 *EJIL* 212.

[31] *Diplomatic and Consular Staff in Tehran (United States v Iran)* (Judgment) [1980] ICJ Rep 3, 42–43, para 92.

clear and accessible legal framework to determine possible 'abuse' of such a right.[32] Assuming that international law is designed for the benefit of peoples and not merely to justify the action of the most powerful actors,[33] the duty not to knowingly facilitate the wrongful act is inherent to the respect of every international obligation, whether it is bilateral, multilateral or peremptory. No actor should be permitted to knowingly support another in breaching the latter's obligations. To allow otherwise, as the current structure of the ARSIWA and ARIO rules suggests, would be tantamount to promoting a freelance system of 'contracts to break contracts' in international law.[34] In this author's view, there should be no place for such a freelance system in international law.

In assessing the utility and effectiveness of responsibility for complicity in international law, this book addresses several key issues. These can be divided into systemic issues, relating to the role of responsibility for complicity in the legal order, and operational issues, underlying the origins and implementation of responsibility for complicity in practice (in other words, its technical features).

Three systemic issues underlying the role of responsibility for complicity in international law are discussed in this book. First, as the general rule on responsibility for complicity bears resemblance to a primary norm, this poses a fundamental question of whether complicity even belongs to the secondary rules of responsibility in the first place. Second, the 'thin red line' between complicity and the obligations of due diligence raises legitimate questions as to the utility of responsibility for complicity in practice. Can complicity arise from actions and omissions? Does responsibility for complicity have an independent existence parallel to the responsibility that accrues for failure to comply with a specific due diligence obligation? Third, can the framework rule(s) on responsibility for complicity apply to situations of aid or assistance given by a State or international organisation to a non-State actor and, in this sense, complement the existing bases of attribution of conduct?

The book further presents four operational issues that hinder the effectiveness of responsibility for complicity in positive international law. First, the nature, form and degree of aid or assistance required to trigger international responsibility under ARSIWA and ARIO (ie the so-called

[32] *Competence of Assembly regarding Admission to the United Nations* (Advisory Opinion) [1950] ICJ Rep 4, Dissenting Opinion of Judge Alvarez 12, 14 ('[t]he general interest, the interests of international society, must constitute the limits of the rights of states and make it possible to determine whether there has been an abuse of these rights').

[33] MR García-Mora, *International Responsibility for Hostile Acts of Private Persons against Foreign States* (The Hague, Martinus Nijhoff, 1962) 7.

[34] H Lauterpacht, 'Contracts to Break Contracts' in E Lauterpacht (ed), *International Law Being the Collected Papers of Hersch Lauterpacht—The Law of Peace*, vol 4 (Cambridge, CUP, 1978) 340–75.

'material' or 'substantive' element) remain evasive. This raises the question of the utility of any contributory threshold (ie whether the accomplice conduct should 'significantly' or 'materially' facilitate the commission of the principal wrongful act), other than a simple factual link between the accomplice conduct and the principal wrongful act. Second, the knowledge and/or intention that the accomplice entity must possess vis-à-vis the circumstances of the principal wrongful act (ie the so-called 'cognitive' or 'subjective' element) raise doubts as to the actual application of this form of responsibility in practice. As States and international organisations can act only through their agents and representatives,[35] there is a question as to whether the assessment of the 'cognitive' element, particularly if the requirement of intention is to be retained, is similar to that undertaken in the context of individual criminal responsibility. Third, the requirement that the aiding or assisting State or international organisation has to be bound by the same obligation as the one breached by the aided or assisted State or international organisation (ie the opposability requirement or 'bilateralisation' of complicity so to speak) deprives the rule of much of its practical value. Fourth, what are the causal standards of allocation of legal consequences between the principal and the accomplice? Can an injured party seek reparation either from the principal or the accomplice, or both?

A critical analysis of these *systemic* and *operational* issues contributes to the book's main thesis that the responsibility for aid or assistance as set out in the ARSIWA and ARIO offers a partial but incomplete response to the phenomenon of complicity in international affairs. Evidence for this proposition can primarily be found in the *opinio juris* of States and international organisations and the findings, however scarce, of international and domestic courts and formal inquiries into extraordinary renditions and associated human rights violations. It is submitted that the general rule on the responsibility for complicity under customary international law may have a slightly more expansive scope of application and more flexible conditions than those set forth in the relevant provisions of the ARSIWA and ARIO.[36] If the ARSIWA and/or ARIO were to be considered

[35] *Certain Questions Relating to Settlers of German Origin in the Territory Ceded by Germany to Poland* (Advisory Opinion) [1923] PCIJ Ser B No 6, 22.

[36] cf *Bosnia Genocide (Merits)* (n 21) 216–17, paras 419–20; see also *Military and Paramilitary Activities in and against Nicaragua (Nicaragua v United States)* (Merits) [1986] ICJ Rep 14, 98, para 186 ('The Court does not consider that, for a rule to be established as customary, the corresponding practice must be in absolutely rigorous conformity with the rule'); *Military and Paramilitary Activities in and against Nicaragua (Nicaragua v United States)* (Jurisdiction and Admissibility) [1984] ICJ Rep 392, Dissenting Opinion of Judge Schwebel 558, 608, para 74 (asserting that the former draft Art 27, ie the predecessor of Art 16 ARSIWA, was already part of customary international law at that time; crucially, however, that provision had a much broader scope of application than Art 16 ARSIWA); see ch 3, s III.

in the context of a diplomatic conference, the provisions on responsibility for aid or assistance would be good candidates for revision.[37]

This book proposes a revised model of responsibility for complicity, which is partially grounded in the existing *opinio juris* and practice and supplemented by the considerations of justice, rule of law and solidarity in the international legal order. The revised model would bring about at least two systemic benefits: (i) it would allow a greater respect for legality where no actor shall contribute to a wrongdoing by another; and (ii) it would provide an avenue for the injured party to obtain reparation not only from the principal wrongdoer but also from those actors operating behind the scenes. Consider a scenario where the injured party does not maintain diplomatic relations with the principal wrongdoer nor has any other avenues to obtain reparation from the principal wrongdoer, including any jurisdictional link to bring proceedings in court or to arbitration. If complicity were to be among the effective causes of the injury, should the injured State not be able to claim reparation directly from the complicit State?

There are substantive and procedural hurdles that complicate how complicit entities are considered in the law of international responsibility and in contemporary dispute settlement more generally. If complicity in the wrongdoing of another were to be construed as giving rise to a genuine independent responsibility from the moment the principal wrongful act materialises, this could circumvent at least some of those hurdles, such as the indispensable third-party principle. Even if the injured party could bring a claim directly against the complicit actor, this would still leave it in a difficult position in showing the extent to which the complicit conduct had facilitated the commission of the principal wrongdoing and the consequent injury. Outside the dispute settlement mechanisms, *ex gratia* payments, satisfaction, or similar arrangements could ensure that the complicit State or international organisation shares the burden of reparation with the principal wrongdoer.[38]

Finally, a note of caution is welcome. The concept studied in this book is at the juncture between *ethics* and *power*.[39] If the power refuses to translate the ethics embodied in the prohibition of complicity into an effective norm,

[37] For comments of States, including certain resistance to potential convention-route see UNGA, 'Noting Key Role in International Law, Sixth Committee Delegates Disagrees over "Fate" of Drafts on State Responsibility, Diplomatic Protection' (21 October 2013) UN Doc GA/L/3463; see also J Crawford and S Olleson, 'The Continuing Debate on a UN Convention on State Responsibility' (2008) 54 *ICLQ* 959; LT Pacht, 'The Case for a Convention on State Responsibility' (2014) 83 *Nordic J Intl L* 439.

[38] *Certain Phosphate Lands in Nauru (Nauru v Australia)* (Preliminary Objections) [1992] ICJ Rep 240, 262, para 56.

[39] RJ Dupuy, 'Images de Georges Scelle' (1990) 1 *EJIL* 235, 237 (à la conjonction de l'éthique et du pouvoir').

a revolution with the objective of restoring balance between material ordainment and social necessity might be warranted.[40] 'Law exists, it is said, to serve a social need'.[41] It is 'a product of political and social forces … it is dependent on behaviour and … it is an instrument to meet changing needs and values'.[42] Its *normativity* lies in the fact that the rules 'must be accepted as a means of independent control that effectively limits the conduct of the entities subject to law'.[43] Its *concreteness* goes through incremental responsiveness to changing behaviours of entities subject to the law, their will and interests. However, law is not and should not coalesce with a social need; needs are not an objective criterion for they cannot be separated from what States hold as needs in each moment.[44] The law must operate independently from the momentary views of its subjects.[45] Whether the model of responsibility for complicity advocated for in this book adequately meets the above concerns of *normativity* and *concreteness* is a matter to be tested by the social practice of actors operating in international law. For now, responsibility for complicity in its current ILC configuration resembles more a concept of variable content in law.[46] It is the very reason why complicity is so appealing and, at the same time, a complex and challenging object of analysis.

VI. METHODOLOGY

This book aims to provide a critical and systematic analysis of the role of responsibility for complicity in general international law. It does not provide an exhaustive catalogue of instances where complicity has been invoked in the relations between States and international organisations. First, there would be relatively little value in doing so as it would largely overlap with Helmut Aust's monograph. Rather than listing a catalogue of practice, this book takes stock of instances of practice and *opinio juris* which are most helpful to understanding the limits of responsibility for complicity and to rendering its elements and criteria of application more effective (chapters four, five and six). Second, the review of practice (treaties,

[40] ibid ('l'adéquation entre l'ordonnancement matériel et la nécessité sociale'; author's translation: 'the matching of the material order and the social need'); see also P Allott, 'The Concept of International Law' (1999) 10 *EJIL* 31.

[41] *South West Africa (Liberia v South Africa/ Ethiopia v South Africa)* (Second Phase) [1966] ICJ Rep 6, 34, para 49.

[42] O Schachter, 'International Law in Theory and Practice: General Course in Public International Law' (1982) 178 *RCADI* 9, 24.

[43] ibid 25–26.

[44] M Koskenniemi, *From Apology to Utopia* (Cambridge, CUP, 2005) 31.

[45] ibid.

[46] C Perelman and R Vander Elst, *Les notions à contenu variable en droit* (Bruxelles, Bruylant, 1984).

diplomatic correspondence, UN resolutions, international and domestic judgments, commissions of inquiry, etc) undertaken in the preparation of this monograph has shown that there are considerable constraints in generalising the effect of individual incidents where complicity has been invoked without any detailed factual or legal account. These limitations can be grouped in four categories.

First, there are many references to complicity in distinct sources, ranging from official statements and protests by States, the practice of the UN and other regional organisations, and reports by media and non-governmental organisations (NGOs). However, these statements often use the term 'complicity' in a non-technical way (with a purely political or foreign policy connotation and without any reference to a legal framework or consequences). In his monograph, Helmut Aust set out a broad review of practice but quite often he had to concede that many statements did not have any real or apparent legal value.[47]

Second, States tend to simply deny allegations and protests denouncing complicity. It is questionable whether these instances can be considered to support the existence of the general rule on responsibility for complicity. In any event, they shed little light on the actual elements of responsibility for complicity, which is the primary focus of this book.

Third, it is difficult to account for the duplicitous character of complicity, exhibiting elements of both a primary and a secondary norm. In the course of its ARSIWA codification, the ILC collected State practice derivative from specific primary regimes.[48] This practice consisted of protests against the supply of financial and military aid to a belligerent, the permission of the use of a State's territory by another State to carry out an armed attack against a third State, the circumvention of sanctions imposed by the UN Security Council (UNSC), and calls by the UN General Assembly (UNGA) to refrain from supplying arms and other assistance to countries with questionable human rights records.[49] As Nolte and Aust rightly point out this practice raises the question of whether the primary rules referred to are simply exceptions or whether they support the existence of a general rule on responsibility for complicity.[50] Corten takes the argument a step further claiming that there is no need for a general rule on responsibility

[47] Aust (n 24) 107–91.

[48] See R Ago, 'Seventh Report on State Responsibility' (1978) UN Doc A/CN.4/307 and Add 1-2 and Corr 1-2, reproduced in (1978) 2 (pt 1) *YBILC* 31; J Crawford, 'Second Report on State Responsibility' (1999) UN Doc A/CN.4/498 and Add 1-4, reproduced in (1999) 2 (pt 1) *YBILC* 3, 45–57, paras 159–214.

[49] ARSIWA (n 2) 66–67, paras 6–9 (Art 16 Commentary); for surveys of practice see Quigley (n 14); ML Padeletti, *Pluralità di Stati nel fatto illecito internazionale* (Milano, Giuffrè, 1990); Felder (n 23) 179–239; Aust (n 24) 107–91; Jackson (n 25) 125–75.

[50] G Nolte and HP Aust, 'Equivocal Helpers—Complicit States, Mixed Messages and International Law' (2009) 58 *ICLQ* 1, 5.

for complicity when virtually every example of complicity falls under the realm of the existing primary rule (ie aggression, genocide, apartheid, terrorism financing, arms control conventions, etc).[51]

The full extent of interactions between all areas of international law that contain express prohibitions of complicity and the general rules provided in the ARSIWA and ARIO is beyond the scope of this book. A few examples of such areas, namely in the context of the use of force and various arms control treaties that prohibit expressly complicity, show the cross-fertilisation between the general rule on responsibility for complicity and these primary regimes. This, however, does not dissipate the question raised by Corten about the need and function of the rules on responsibility for complicity.[52] In this author's view, so long as the ARSIWA and ARIO provisions are interpreted as requiring intent and opposability of the principal obligation breached, the effectiveness of responsibility for complicity will indeed remain extremely limited. It would leave us in a paradoxical scenario where the so-called secondary norm on responsibility for complicity would require much higher standards than the treaty obligations to which States have adhered. At the same time, this may be simply a reflection of the subjects' will to prohibit complicity in certain breaches of international law, while abiding by a more limited responsibility framework in respect of any other instances of complicit conduct. Moreover, even though complicity is prohibited in different areas of international law, there is little guidance as to what exactly it entails and how responsibility for complicity can be established. It would then be the mission of the general rule of responsibility for complicity to inform a primary rule—ie an unusual situation in international law abiding by a traditional divide between primary and secondary rules.

Fourth, when States protest against alleged complicity in the wrongful act or take action to prevent such complicity, they rarely specify the exact legal basis. Even if there are numerous instances of complicity in the practice of international law, these should not automatically be regarded as undermining the rule on responsibility for complicity nor can they necessarily help to clarify its scope.[53] Similarly, protests invoking complicity as a basis of responsibility or actions taken to prevent possible complicity often arise in respect of factual circumstances that ultimately do not result in the commission of an internationally wrongful act. Even if States

[51] O Corten, 'La "complicité" dans le droit de la responsabilité internationale: un concept inutile?' (2011) 58 *AFDI* 57.

[52] See ibid; see also O Corten and P Klein, 'The Limits of Complicity as a Ground for Responsibility: Lessons Learned from the Corfu Channel Case' in K Bannelier, T Christakis and S Heathcote (eds), *The ICJ and the Evolution of International Law: The Enduring Impact of the Corfu Channel Case* (London, Routledge, 2012).

[53] See *Military and Paramilitary Activities (Merits)* (n 36) 108–09, para 207.

and international organisations may err in their legal or factual assessment, their assertions of the risk of complicity as a justification for acting or avoiding to act tend to translate *opinio juris* into practice.

VII. THE ROLE OF RESPONSIBILITY FOR COMPLICITY IN THE INTERNATIONAL LEGAL ORDER

Finally, a word on the normative foundations of this book is in order. The role of responsibility for complicity depends to a large extent on the conception of the international legal order one adopts.[54] The international legal order today is a complex set of norms, actors, institutions and law-making processes.[55] Generations of lawyers have advanced opposite claims as to the unity or fragmentation of the international legal order.[56] Some have even questioned the qualification of international law as a legal order to begin with.[57] This is not the place to engage with these debates in any

[54] For a detailed account of the differences of the legal order (rules, functions, institutions and societal basis) from a legal system (rules) see Dupuy (n 19) 59–76; P Reuter, 'Principes de droit international public' (1961) 103 *RCADI* 425, 460; B Cheng, 'Custom: The Future of General State Practice in a Divided World' in RSJ MacDonald and DM Johnston (eds), *The Structure and Process of International Law: Essays in Legal Philosophy, Doctrine and Theory* (The Hague, Martinus Nijhoff, 1983) 516 (defining international legal order as 'the structure which results from the existence and operation of the international legal system').

[55] See R Higgins, *Problems and Process: International Law and How We Use It* (Oxford, Clarendon Press, 1994) 1 ('International law is not rules. It is a normative system. All organized groups and structures require a system of normative conduct'); J Combacau, 'Le droit international: bric-à-brac ou système?' (1986) 31 *Archives de philosophie de droit* 85; C Rousseau, 'Principes de droit international public' (1958) 93 *RCADI* 369, 389 (arguing that law is also an instrument of social organisation: 'le droit n'est pas seulement un système de règles ou un ensemble de normes. C'est aussi un élément essentiel de l'organisation sociale. Si l'on considère le droit international en tant qu'ordre normatif, la réponse n'est pas douteuse. Le droit international remplit les deux conditions nécessaires et suffisantes pour être considéré comme un système normatif autonome'; author's translation: 'the law is not only a system of rules or a set of norms. It is also an essential element of social organisation. If one considers international law as a normative order, the answer is without doubt. International law satisfies the two conditions which are necessary and sufficient for it to be considered an autonomous normative system').

[56] See ILC, 'Fragmentation of International Law: Difficulties Arising from the Diversification and Expansion of International Law' (13 April 2006) UN Doc A/CN.4/L.682; G Abi-Saab, 'Fragmentation or Unification: Some Concluding Remarks' (1999) 31 *NYU J Intl L & Pol* 919; J Pauwelyn, 'Bridging Fragmentation and Unity: International Law as a Universe of Inter-Connected Islands' (2003) 25 *Michigan J Intl L* 903.

[57] See Hart (n 30) 213–37; see also M Craven, 'Unity, Diversity and the Fragmentation of International Law' (2003) 14 *Finnish YBIL* 3, 7 (arguing that international law could 'be understood in a number of alternative ways none of which necessarily implies anything particularly systemic: as a category description of the professional outlook of those [who] engage with it; as a domain of discourse between significant agents; as an empirical array of practices; or perhaps merely as the vocabulary employed by a community of scholars and practitioners'); P Bourdieu, *The Logic of Practice* (Cambridge, Polity Press, 1990) 53 (introducing the concept of habitus, as the conditioning assumptions which predispose particular outlooks in a society).

detail. However, it is undeniable that today there is some unifying if not unitary structure of international law, which is far from primitive.[58] Even the greatest apologists of the specialisation trend of international law and the avatars of consent, tend to find comfort in the general international law and its ability to provide a fall back regime, an assurance or appearance of material completeness.[59] Similarly, the classical problems associated with enforcement do not necessarily question the material completeness of the international legal order.

Against this background of perceived maturity and completeness, there is a paradox in an increasingly interconnected world. On the one hand, most actors refrain from directly violating international law primarily because of economic, diplomatic or political repercussions, and only secondarily owing to considerations of law and justice.[60] On the other hand, the number and variety of global issues (ranging from climate change to migration and terrorism) allows actors to evade scrutiny and responsibility for their complicit actions and omissions. As such, more powerful actors procure others to undermine the international legal order thereby channelling more effectively their foreign policy interests.

In this context, the law of responsibility plays a residuary yet crucial role, by ensuring the availability of a remedy to the victim, re-establishing the legal situation prior to the breach, and ultimately deterring future

[58] See, eg Dupuy (n 19); M Virally, *Le droit international en devenir: Essais écrits au fil des ans* (Paris, PUF, 1990) 91–101; MJ Aznar Gómez, 'En torno a la unidad sistémica del derecho internacional' (2007) 59 *Revista Española de Derecho Internacional* 563; N Valticos, 'Pluralité des ordres juridiques internationaux et unité du droit international' in J Makarczyk (ed), *Theory of International Law at the Threshold of the 21st Century: Essays in Honour of Krzysztof Skubiszewski* (The Hague, Kluwer, 1996); I Brownlie, 'Problems Concerning the Unity of International Law', *Le droit international à l'heure de sa codification: études en l'honneur de Roberto Ago*, vol 1 (Milano, Giuffrè, 1987); Craven (n 57); L Barnhoon and K Wellens (eds), *Diversity in Secondary Rules and the Unity of International Law* (The Hague, Martinus Nijhoff, 1995).

[59] See, eg *Amoco Int Finance Corp v Iran* (Award) (14 July 1987) 15 Iran-US CTR 189, 222, para 112 ('the rules of customary international law may be useful to fill in possible lacunae of the law of the Treaty, to ascertain the meaning of undefined terms in its text or, more generally, to aid interpretation and implementation of its provisions'); ILC (n 56) para 137 ('If instead of enhancing the effectiveness of the relevant obligations the regime serves to dilute existing standards … then the need of a residual application, or a "fall-back" onto the general law of State responsibility may seem called for'); ibid para 172 ('None of the treaty-regimes in existence today is self-contained in the sense that the application of general international law would be generally excluded'); B Simma and D Pulkowski, 'Of Planets and the Universe: Self-Contained Regimes in International Law' (2006) 17 *EJIL* 483.

[60] See, eg K Zemanek, 'The Unilateral Enforcement of Obligations' (1987) 32 *ZaöRV* 37, 43; K Zemanek, 'Does the Prospect of Incurring Responsibility Improve the Observance of International Law?' in M Ragazzi (ed), *International Responsibility Today: Essays in Memory of Oscar Schachter* (Leiden, Martinus Nijhoff, 2005) 128; see also J Brunnée and SJ Toope, 'Persuasion and Enforcement: Explaining Compliance with International Law' (2002) 13 *Finnish YBIL* 273; VJ Proulx, *Transnational Terrorism and State Accountability* (Oxford, Hart Publishing, 2012) 14–15.

occurrences of complicity in violations of international law.[61] Hence, the normative agenda of this study is to develop the understanding of responsibility for complicity and its limits in positive international law, and to consider the adjustments necessary to make it an effective and useful tool with a real function in the international legal order. The effectiveness and utility of the rules on responsibility for complicity lie in them being: (i) *predictable* for all the parties involved in either providing or receiving aid or assistance; (ii) *unambiguous* for the party invoking responsibility for complicity and a party defending against a claim of complicity; (iii) *fair* in the sense of not overburdening the extent of responsibility or reparation due from principal and complicit actors; and (iv) *just* for the victim of the violation facilitated by complicity to see that justice is being done.

VIII. STRUCTURE

Chapter two examines complicity through the historical lens of its consolidation as a legal concept in international law and its original bias between individual and collective responsibility. Chapter three reviews the regimes of complicity as a mode of criminal liability of individuals and its codification by the ILC as a form of responsibility of States and international organisations. Chapter four surveys the rules on responsibility for complicity in the codification of the ARSIWA and ARIO, distinguishing complicity from other forms of shared or indirect responsibility, including the responsibility of States in connection with the wrongful act of an international organisation, direction and coercion, circumvention of international obligations, and joint and several responsibility. Chapter five tests each constituent element of responsibility for complicity by reference to examples from practice and *opinio juris*, considering the limits set out in the ARSIWA and ARIO and the need for potential adjustments.

[61] PM Dupuy, 'Le fait générateur de la responsabilité internationale des États' (1984) 188 *RCADI* 9, 21 (arguing that the law shows its degree of effectiveness and integration through its system of responsibility: 'La responsabilité constitue l'épicentre d'un système juridique. La nature des droits, la structure des obligations, la définition des sanctions de leur violation, tout y converge et s'entremêle en des rapports logiques et des relations d'étroite interdépendance. Un droit se dit, avoue ses fondements, trahit ses lacunes, démontre son efficacité et son degré d'intégration à travers son système de responsabilité'; author's translation: 'Responsibility is the epicentre of a legal system. The nature of rights, the structure of obligations, the definition of sanctions for their violation, everything converges and intermingles in the logical connections and closely interdependent relations. A right is recognised, admits its foundations, betrays its shortcomings, demonstrates its effectiveness and degree of integration through its system of responsibility').

Chapter six deals with the content and implementation of responsibility for complicity, including questions of causation and reparation. Chapter seven examines the possibility of construing complicity beyond its original inter-subjects dimension. Finally, chapter eight provides some concluding remarks as to the present function of responsibility for complicity and its prospects for the future.

2

The Origins of Complicity in International Law

I. INTRODUCTION

INTERNATIONAL LAW—BEING originally designed for the external relations of States and based on principles of reciprocity and consent—does not mirror the structure and dynamics of any domestic legal system.[1] This could explain the late integration into international law of responsibility for complicity in the wrongdoing. This late integration may also be explained by the lack of proper forums and mechanisms of invoking and enforcing international responsibility of States before the nineteenth and twentieth centuries.[2]

Responsibility for complicity as we find it codified today in the International Law Commission's (ILC) Articles on Responsibility of States for Internationally Wrongful Acts (ARSIWA) and the Articles on Responsibility of International Organizations (ARIO) was unknown before the second half of the twentieth century. However, the roots of complicity as a legal concept can be traced to the laws of neutrality (section II) and the writings of the founding fathers of international law in the seventeenth and eighteenth centuries, who developed it in the theories about just and unjust wars and as an attribution model to capture the failure of the State to prevent or to punish a harmful conduct by an individual (section III). An analysis of these early uses of complicity sets out the historical

[1] P Malanczuk, *Akehurst's Modern Introduction to International Law* (7th edn, London, Routledge, 1997) 7.

[2] J Crawford, T Grant and F Messineo, 'Towards an International Law of Responsibility: Early Doctrine' in L Boisson de Chazournes and MG Kohen (eds), *International Law and the Quest for its Implementation, Liber Amicorum Vera Gowlland-Debbas* (Leiden, Martinus Nijhoff, 2010) 401 ('the first use of the word "responsibility" in French dates from around 1783—attributed to French Finance Minister Necker. Hamilton and Madison used it later in the same decade in the Federalist Papers, referring for example to the "due responsibility in the government to the people" and its relation to the frequency of elections'); J Henriot, 'Note sur la date et le sens de l'apparition du mot "responsabilité"' (1977) 22 *Archives de philosophie de droit* 59, 60–61.

background which helps understand the current limits of responsibility for complicity, the differences between complicity and due diligence, and the potential utility of complicity as a basis of attribution of conduct.

II. THE ANTECEDENTS OF COMPLICITY IN THE OPERATION OF NEUTRALITY

In contrast to the majority of domestic legal systems, international law was relatively slow to recognise that a third party's contribution to the breach of an international obligation should be subject to legal consequences. To begin with, for a long time, there was no category of responsibility in international law as such. The orthodox understanding of the laws of peace and war revolved around the conception of a perfectly symmetric relationship between sovereign subjective rights and obligations.

Throughout the twentieth century, this relationship served as a foundation for the law of international responsibility. According to Roberto Ago, the architect of the modern conception of international responsibility and the former Special Rapporteur of the ILC, it was 'perfectly legitimate in international law to regard the idea of the breach of an obligation as the exact equivalent of the idea of impairment of the subjective rights of others'.[3] However, the legal relationships arising from complicity in the commission of an internationally wrongful act do not quite fit within Ago's general paradigm of international responsibility. A scenario of complicity involves two separate conducts and three actors, and escapes a simplistic symmetry between the rights and obligations. Instead, complicity is a by-product of the multilateralisation of the relations of responsibility, hesitantly stretching beyond the orthodox bilateralist structure of international law.[4]

Despite the recognition of complicity as a form of responsibility in international law only in the second half of the twentieth century, the concept was not entirely unknown in the earlier stages of development of international law, albeit with important differences from its scope and role today. The first signs of an attempt to regulate the behaviour of third parties can be found in the concept of neutrality and the associated doctrine of

[3] R Ago, 'Second Report on State Responsibility' (1970) UN Doc A/CN.4/233, reproduced in (1970) 2 *YBILC* 177, 192, para 46; see also D Anzilotti, *Teoria generale della responsabilità dello stato nel diritto internazionale* (Firenze, F Lumachi Libraio-Editore, 1902) 83, 91 and 121; R Ago, 'Le délit international' (1939) 68 *RCADI* 417, 441; for the application of this view of responsibility in practice see *Phosphates in Morocco (Italy v France)* (Preliminary Objections) [1938] PCIJ Ser A/B No 74, 10, 28.

[4] cf HP Aust, *Complicity and the Law of State Responsibility* (Cambridge, CUP, 2011) 12–30 (arguing that neutrality shows that complicity is not inconceivable in a purely bilateral framework of international law).

just war.[5] Neutrality allowed a third party to abstain from hostilities and preserve its territorial integrity. As Aust rightly suggests '[b]y regulating how third parties had to position themselves in an ongoing conflict, [the concept of neutrality] defined whether or not assistance to one side of the conflict was permitted'.[6]

However, the analogy between neutrality and complicity lies only in the underlying logic and not in the principle or the legal consequences generated. A violation of neutrality neither amounted to an internationally wrongful act nor did it trigger responsibility, but it did allow the belligerent party to lawfully attack an otherwise neutral State. Thus, the overlap between responsibility for complicity and neutrality lies in the fact that both *cas de figure* expect certain behaviour from a third party vis-à-vis a separate legal relationship (the conduct of hostilities in the case of neutrality and the commission of an internationally wrongful act in the case of complicity).

In the author's view, while it is useful to see some links between the institutions of neutrality and responsibility for complicity, the direct analogies are of limited relevance. It is doubtful whether responsibility for complicity could quite simply exist in a bilateral framework of international law without all the structural adjustments of the international legal order that have taken place since the end of the World War II.[7] In fact, many of the deficiencies in the application of responsibility for complicity are due to the decision of the ILC on the second reading of the ARSIWA to shape complicity within a perfect symmetry of rights and obligations, thereby diminishing its potential role in international law.[8]

A. Rights and Duties of Neutrals

The primary power of a classic sovereign in international law was to have recognition of its right to engage in war in pursuance of its domestic or foreign interests and policies.[9] Military assistance, cooperation and alliances were essential to a State's success in waging war. The corollary of the right

[5] ibid 15–23 (arguing that in terms of historical antecedents to a rule on complicity, 'the law of neutrality comes as close as it gets').

[6] ibid 15.

[7] cf Aust (n 4); see also B Simma, 'From Bilateralism to Community Interest in International Law' (1994) 250 *RCADI* 217, 317.

[8] See, eg P Weil, 'Towards Relative Normativity in International Law' (1983) 77 *AJIL* 413, 422 ('[s]uch terms as "legal conscience of states", "awakening of conscience", "universal conscience", "common good of mankind" recur like a leitmotiv on practically every page of the International Law Commission's work on the theories of jus cogens and international crimes').

[9] For a detailed treatment of neutrality see, eg U Pieper, *Neutralität von Staaten* (Frankfurt am Main, Lang, 1997).

to engage in war was a prerogative of neutrality, a status halfway between war and peace. In the words of Politis, 'from sovereignty … flowed as a logical and necessary consequence the absolute and unconditional right of war; which in its turn had for a no less logical and necessary consequence the equally absolute and unconditional right of neutrality'.[10]

The idea of neutrality is as ancient as the practice of war itself.[11] Nonetheless, as a legal concept, it was unknown to ancient civilisations as well as during the Middle Ages.[12] It first appeared in the diplomatic correspondence of the fifteenth and sixteenth centuries, coming into current use during the Thirty Years' War.[13] Although there is no express reference to neutrality, it is in the writings of Francisco de Vitoria that the germ of the concept lies. Vitoria conceived of an international community based on the ideas of interdependence and solidarity.[14] The main tenet of his theory was that an unjust war affected the international community as a whole, which in turn allowed the sovereign to resort to force on behalf of that community.[15] Neutrality emerged as an inverse corollary of that right to act in community interests.

In the seventeenth century, Hugo Grotius presented his theories on just war and the limits on neutrality, which still carry some weight today. He suggested that while States have a right to abstain, they must do nothing to aid the action of the belligerent whose cause is unjust or to weaken the forces of the one that is fighting for a just cause.[16] He held the view that it was 'the duty of those who keep out of a war to do nothing whereby he who supports a wicked cause may be rendered more powerful, or whereby the movements of him who wages a just war may be hampered'.[17]

Thus, according to Grotius, neutrality did not simply entail non-involvement in a war, but set forth a combination of rights and duties connected to those of the belligerents. However, it was not until the end of the eighteenth century that a more systematic theory of neutrality emerged.[18] During the early stages of the recognition of neutrality in international law, the main duty of the neutral was not to abstain. Instead, the neutral State was entitled to make certain concessions to the belligerents.

[10] N Politis, *Neutrality and Peace* (Washington DC, Carnegie, 1935) 6.

[11] ibid 11.

[12] ibid 4.

[13] ibid 5.

[14] F de Vitoria, *De Indis et de Jure Belli Relectiones [On the Indians and on the Law of War]* (JP Bate tr, Washington DC, Carnegie, 1917) (arguing that third States should not remain passive to the presence of crimes or when injustice is done to one of the members of the community of States).

[15] ibid.

[16] H Grotius, *De Jure Belli Ac Pacis [The Rights of War and Peace]* (FW Kelsey tr, Oxford, Clarendon Press, 1925) bk 2, ch 21.

[17] Grotius (n 16) bk 3, ch 17, § 3.

[18] Politis (n 10) 15.

During the seventeenth and eighteenth centuries, neutrality was regarded as 'particular' or 'imperfect' since it implied abstention from any direct aid except for promises of assistance granted before the outbreak of hostilities. For instance, in 1631 France signed a treaty with Sweden, by which it engaged to assist with funding for the maintenance of the army and to authorise the King of Sweden to enrol soldiers and seek weaponry necessary for the war.[19] Emperor Ferdinand did not see such an act as a breach of France's neutrality, let alone as a sufficient reason for waging war against it.[20] Similarly, during the war of the Austrian Succession, the Dutch, although at peace with France, furnished troops and subsidies to be used against France. Since that aid was given pursuant to an existing treaty, France did not protest when the Dutch forces menaced its Alsatian border.[21] Indeed, before the nineteenth century 'neutrals considered themselves free to grant a certain amount of assistance to one or the other of the belligerents'.[22] According to Politis:

> Neutrals could tolerate, or even authorize several hostile acts, such as a levy of troops upon their territory, the equipping of privateers in their ports, the capture within, or admittance into, their waters of maritime prizes, and indeed, the furnishing of subsidies, arms and munitions of war to the belligerents.[23]

In 1758, Vattel made a particularly important contribution to the understanding of assistance in the context of neutrality and beyond it.[24] In his *Le droit des gens*, he defined the following degrees of involvement of a third State in an unjust war: (i) complete impartiality; (ii) the provision of assistance to one of the belligerents; and (iii) full collaboration with one of the belligerents.[25] The modern law of international responsibility borrowed this theoretical framework to devise and develop categories of involvement of a third State in the internationally wrongful act.

By the end of the eighteenth century, the duty of abstention had been clarified. The international legal system had moved away from a treaty-based neutrality to the regime of so-called institutional neutrality. This meant that, at the moment a war broke out, the non-participating States found themselves automatically having the status of neutrality.[26] Neutral

[19] H Baudenet d'Annoux, *Le développement de la neutralité: De Grotius à Vattel* (Orléans, Imprimerie Auguste Gout et Cie, 1910) 5.

[20] ibid.

[21] Politis (n 10) 17.

[22] ibid 16.

[23] ibid; see also Baudenet d'Annoux (n 19) 6.

[24] On Vattel's contribution to the development of the concept of neutrality see S Oeter, 'Neutrality and Alliances' in V Chetail and P Haggenmacher (eds), *Vattel's International Law in a XXIst Century Perspective* (Leiden, Martinus Nijhoff, 2011).

[25] E de Vattel, *Le droit des gens ou principes de la loi naturelle [The Law of Nations or Principles of Natural Law]* (CG Fenwick tr, Washington DC, Carnegie, 1916) bk 3, ch 6, § 97.

[26] Aust (n 4) 20; WG Grewe, *Epochen der Völkerrechtsgeschichte* (Baden-Baden, Nomos, 1984) 629.

States had to refrain from giving direct aid to one or the other belligerent and from allowing that their citizens give any such aid.[27]

In a state of war, the rights and duties of neutral States were inseparable. Neutrals' rights included the inviolability of their territory and their freedom of commerce. These rights corresponded to the obligations incumbent on belligerents, namely those of abstention and impartiality. A neutral State could not participate in the hostilities, nor could it exercise pressure on the belligerents.[28] Nor could it tolerate acts committed by the belligerents that could signify the neutral's involvement in the war.[29] In fact, the primary duty of the neutrals was simply to oppose any utilisation of their territory by one of the belligerents. Later, this principle found expression in the 1907 Hague Conventions V and XIII.[30] Moreover, the neutral State had to maintain absolute impartiality. This meant that it could not provide the belligerents, directly or indirectly, with any supplies such as arms or ammunition, or in any other way augment their military advantage. In this respect, Article 6 of the 1907 Hague Convention XIII stipulates that '[t]he supply, in any manner, directly or indirectly, by a neutral Power to a belligerent Power, of war-ships, ammunition, or war material of any kind whatever, is forbidden'.[31]

It follows that the idea of complicity, albeit not expressly pronounced, was inherent to the evolution and codification of neutrality in the eighteenth and nineteenth centuries. An interesting parallel can be drawn between complicity's elementary content under the regime of neutrality, and complicity as it is conceived of today. Case law of the nineteenth century is instructive in this regard as it contains applications of the prohibition incumbent on States and its citizens not to provide aid or assistance to foreign belligerents.

The proposition that emerges from this body of law is that a private contract to render aid to a belligerent State in violation of the laws of neutrality was illegal and thus unenforceable. For example, in *Kennett v Chambers*, certain American citizens had contracted with a citizen of Texas to lend money in the war of Texas against Mexico, in return for an

[27] SC Neff, *The Rights and Duties of Neutrals: A General History* (Manchester, Manchester University Press, 2000) 103–08.

[28] L Oppenheim, *International Law—A Treatise: War and Neutrality*, vol 2 (2nd edn, London, Longmans, 1912) 378.

[29] KHL Hammarskjöld, *La neutralité en général*, vol 3 (The Hague, Martinus Nijhoff, 1924) 79.

[30] Hague Convention (V) concerning the Rights and Duties of Neutral Powers and Persons in Case of War on Land (adopted 18 October 1907; entered into force 26 January 1910) 205 CTS 299, Art 5; Hague Convention (XIII) concerning the Rights and Duties of Neutral Powers in Naval War (adopted 18 October 1907; entered into force 26 January 1910) 205 CTS 395, Art 25.

[31] 1907 Hague Convention (XIII) (n 30) Art 6.

agreement to convey certain lands in Texas.[32] Chief Justice Taney held that the American citizens in question violated neutrality of the United States by advancing such money and that the contract itself was illegal and void *ab initio*, hence, not enforceable before the United States courts.[33] Similarly, in *de Wutz v Hendricks*, the English Court of Common Pleas decided that it was contrary to international law for persons residing in England to enter into contracts to raise money for the purpose of supporting subjects of a foreign State in arms against a government that was not at war with England and that no right of action attached to any such contract.[34] The United States-Mexican Claims Commission dealt with similar cases of United States' citizens providing military aid to Mexico in its struggle for independence against Spain.[35] Such claims were usually dismissed on the grounds that, by virtue of their provision of aid to Mexico, the United States' citizen had forfeited his right to the protection of his government.[36]

Two points follow from the foregoing. First, the case law seems to support the proposition that the concept of neutrality contained an early reflection of the prohibition of aid or assistance. Second, it suggests that any contract aimed at rendering an unlawful aid or assistance to the belligerent was void *ab initio* and could not be enforced. We should be careful not to read too much into this old case law as overall States had limited responsibility for trade conducted by private actors in breach of the neutrality regime.[37] However, the above case law points out some interesting analogies in the modern understanding of complicity's legal consequences in the law of treaties and the law of international responsibility, particularly its cognitive and opposability requirements as set out in the ARSIWA and ARIO rules on complicity. For example, does international law prohibit State A from concluding a treaty for the provision of aid or assistance to State B that facilitates the commission of an internationally wrongful act? Is this treaty automatically null and void? If State A is not bound by the obligation breached by State B, but has knowledge thereof, does State A incur responsibility? Can State A go on to conclude such a treaty if it imposes certain conditionalities as to the use of its aid or assistance? Can

[32] *Kennett v Chambers* (1852) 14 Howard 38; cited in EM Borchard, *The Diplomatic Protection of Citizens Abroad or the Law of International Claims* (New York, Banks Law Publishing, 1927) 783.

[33] Borchard (n 32) 783.

[34] *De Wütz v Hendricks* (1824) 9 Moore Rep Cases 586; see also *Cucullu (United States) v Mexico* (1868) 4 Moore Intl Arbitrations 3477, 3479.

[35] Borchard (n 32) 784.

[36] See, eg *Sturm (United States) v Mexico* (1868) 3 Moore Intl Arbitrations 2756; *Brannan (United States) v Mexico* (1868) 3 Moore Intl Arbitrations 2757; *Greene (United States) v Mexico* (1868) 3 Moore Intl Arbitrations 2756.

[37] 1907 Hague Convention (XIII) (n 30) Art 7; see also W Friedmann, 'The Growth of State Control over the Individual, and Its Effect upon the Rules of International State Responsibility' (1938) 19 *British YBIL* 118.

the existence of such conditionalities serve as a circumstance precluding wrongfulness? Does the failure to observe those conditionalities warrant termination or suspension of the treaty? These are some thorny questions to which international law is yet to find conclusive answers. However, they do set some background for this author's critique as developed in chapters four and five of this book.

B. The Prohibition of Aid or Assistance to Belligerents

In many respects, neutrality may be regarded as more instrumental to the crystallisation of the doctrine of due diligence, yet it may have influenced the development of responsibility for complicity too.[38] The abstention from rendering aid or assistance towards one of the belligerents accompanied the legal consolidation of the concept of neutrality.

A pertinent early example of a convoluted coexistence between complicity and due diligence can be found in the *Alabama* arbitration, where the United States claimed that Great Britain violated its neutrality by allowing the *Alabama* ship to be constructed, knowing that it would enter into service with the Confederacy.[39] It is arguable that the underlying dispute did not merely concern due diligence but a deliberate breach of the standards of neutrality applicable during the American Civil War.[40] The parties to the arbitration contended different degrees of due diligence expected on the part of the neutral State, Great Britain. For its part, Great Britain contended that a neutral State can only be held responsible for a reasonable degree of due diligence, which was not clearly established in State practice, and could only be deduced from the nature and content of the obligation together with considerations of justice and equity. However, the tribunal considered that a neutral State has a heightened duty whenever its impartiality vis-à-vis the belligerent party is affected.[41] In that sense, neutral States were to employ due diligence proportionate to the level of danger or risk to which they could be exposed as a result of their failure to comply with the duties of neutrality.[42] Accordingly, the tribunal held that Great Britain could not justify its action on the basis of insufficient legal means in its possession to perform adequate due diligence.[43]

[38] A Ouedraogo, 'La diligence en droit international: Contribution à l'étude d'une notion au contour imprécis' (PhD Thesis, Geneva, Graduate Institute, 2010) 13–29.

[39] *Alabama Claims (United States v Great Britain)* (1872) 29 RIAA 125; see also T Bingham, 'The Alabama Claims Arbitration' (2008) 54 *ICLQ* 1.

[40] ILC, 'Summary Record of the 2641st Meeting' (18 July 2000), reproduced in (2000) 1 *YBILC* 226, 231, para 55 (Brownlie).

[41] *Alabama (Award)* (n 39).

[42] ibid 129.

[43] ibid.

In many respects, the Covenant of the League of Nations and subsequently the UN Charter could be regarded as the requiem of neutrality. Article 16(1) of the Covenant of the League of Nations was already interpreted at the time as abolishing the regime of neutrality:

> Should any Member of the League resort to war in disregard of its covenants under Articles 12, 13 or 15, it shall ipso facto be deemed to have committed an act of war against all other Members of the League, which hereby undertake immediately to subject it to the severance of all trade or financial relations, the prohibition of all intercourse between their nationals and the nationals of the covenant-breaking State, and the prevention of all financial, commercial or personal intercourse between the nationals of the covenant-breaking State and the nationals of any other State, whether a Member of the League or not.[44]

The adoption of the UN Charter arguably superseded neutrality by imposing the framework of collective security. Article 2(5) in particular compels members of the UN to give assistance to the UN in any action taken under the Charter and at the same time to refrain from giving assistance to any State against which the UN is taking preventive or enforcement action. Moreover, Articles 41, 42 and 43 of the Charter accord to the United Nations Security Council (UNSC) the competence to decide upon the enforcement measures and impose an obligation on the members to apply such measures. It follows that no member of the UN may refuse to comply with the binding UNSC resolutions adopted under Chapter VII and opt to remain neutral if the UNSC decides to take military action against a State.

Nevertheless, some exceptions remain in the UN Charter. For instance, according to Article 48(1) of the Charter, even in those cases where the UNSC has decided to take an enforcement action, it may call upon only some States to carry out its decisions. A State may be excused from carrying out a particular obligation imposed by the UNSC due to special economic considerations.[45] For example, Zambia was exempted from carrying out Resolution 232 (1966), which imposed selective mandatory economic sanctions against the illegal white minority regime in Southern Rhodesia.[46] Similarly, in the case of the Iraq–Kuwait conflict, India, Pakistan and the Philippines were allowed to provide humanitarian assistance to their nationals.[47] Of course, even if a State is so exempted from

[44] The Covenant of the League of Nations (adopted 28 June 1919; entered into force 10 January 1920) 13 *AJIL* Supp 128, Art 16; see also R Redslob, *Théorie de la Société des Nations* (Paris, Rousseau, 1927) 96.

[45] Charter of the United Nations (adopted 26 June 1945; entered into force 24 October 1945) 1 UNTS 16, Art 50.

[46] UNSC, 'Res 232' (16 December 1966) UN Doc S/RES/232 (Southern Rhodesia).

[47] UNSC, 'Res 666' (13 September 1990) UN Doc S/RES/666 (Iraq-Kuwait); UNSC, 'Res 669' (24 September 1990) UN Doc S/RES/669 (Iraq-Kuwait).

carrying out a UNSC resolution, its obligation not to assist the belligerent subject to enforcement action remains.[48]

As Brownlie put it '[m]ilitary, economic, and other forms of aid to an aggressor will naturally constitute breaches of the law of neutrality'.[49] In this sense, the primary norm of neutrality co-exists with the general rule on responsibility for complicity. This is confirmed by the recent case of *Attorney of the Federal Armed Forces v Anonymous (a Major of the Armed Forces)*, where the German Federal Administrative Court referred to both responsibility for aid or assistance under Article 16 ARSIWA and the laws of neutrality.[50] By reference to the 1907 Hague Convention V, the German Federal Administrative Court declared that a State not participating in an armed conflict has the status of a neutral, which begins with the outbreak of the armed conflict and entails mutual rights and duties between the neutral States and the parties to the conflict. The territory of a neutral State is inviolable, and belligerents are prohibited from moving 'troops or convoys or either munitions of war or supplies across the territory of a neutral Power'.[51] The German Federal Administrative Court found that Germany violated the above norms with regard to the war led against Iraq. It did so by providing the United States and the United Kingdom with 'overflight rights', allowing the use of German 'installations' and ensuring the 'protection of these installations'.[52] Moreover, the government of the Federal Republic of Germany agreed to deployment of German soldiers in Airborne Warning and Control System (AWACS) aircrafts 'to monitor Turkish airspace'.[53] Ultimately, the German Federal Administrative Court condemned German participation in the war in Iraq and reached the following conclusion: 'aiding or assisting in a wrongful act in international law *is itself* a wrongful act in international law'.[54]

Thus, the twenty-first century has already fulfilled Hersch Lauterpacht's prediction that:

> the more integrated international society will become, the more incompatible will become the rule of law thus established with the continued indifference

[48] Neff (n 27) 193; Aust (n 4) 30.

[49] I Brownlie, *International Law and the Use of Force by States* (Oxford, Clarendon Press, 1963) 369.

[50] *Attorney of the Federal Armed Forces v Major of the Federal Armed Forces* (Judgment) [2005] BVerwG, 2 WD 12.04, ILDC 483 (DE 2005) (German Federal Administrative Court); see also N Schultz, 'Was the War on Iraq Illegal? The German Federal Administrative Court's Judgment of 21st June 2005' (2006) 7 *German LJ* 25.

[51] 1907 Hague Convention (V) (n 30) Arts 1 and 2.

[52] *Attorney of the Federal Armed Forces v Major of the Federal Armed Forces* (n 50) para 4.1.4.1.2.

[53] ibid.

[54] ibid (emphasis added).

> (called neutrality, qualified or absolute) of States to its violation by unlawful recourse to war … In this, as in many other matters, progress in international law and relations is conditioned in their approximation to standards prevailing among individuals.[55]

The somehow elementary logic against complicity in the early regime of neutrality is today superseded by a much stronger multilateral and communitarian orientation of the prohibition of complicity to the commission of an internationally wrongful act and the ensuing consequences of such conduct. Aust has suggested that neutrality shows that 'international law has a tradition of extending the reach of a given legal relationship beyond the parties immediately concerned' and that such a proposition 'challenges the alleged incompatibility between responsibility for complicity and international law's traditional bilateral structure'.[56] This holds true only to a limited extent. First, as we have seen neutrality oscillated between an obligation proper and a right (*faculté*) of the State, particularly at its early stage of development. Second, the violation of neutrality did not give rise to the relationships of responsibility in its modern understanding. In other words, the analogy to neutrality is limited to the positioning of a subject in a triangular structure of rights and obligations, but not so much to the legal consequences that it generated. Thus, it is this author's view that the incremental changes that operated in the structure of the international legal order in the twentieth century were instrumental to the recognition that one entity could bear responsibility for its complicity in the wrongful act of another.[57]

III. COMPLICITY IN THE WRITINGS OF FOUNDING FATHERS OF INTERNATIONAL LAW

In addition to the limited analogies drawn above between complicity and neutrality, the concept of complicity finds further theoretical foundation in the writings of Vattel and Grotius. In many respects, the prohibition of complicity in the wrongdoing preceded the modern understanding of the law of international responsibility. Grotius and Vattel conceptualised complicity as a form of due diligence, and lying on a sliding scale between individual liability and international responsibility, from a negative obligation to a form of attribution of conduct.

[55] H Lauterpacht, 'Neutrality and Collective Security' in E Lauterpacht (ed), *International Law Being the Collected Papers of Hersch Lauterpacht—Disputes, War and Neutrality*, vol 5 (Cambridge, CUP, 1977) 627–28.

[56] Aust (n 4) 22–23.

[57] cf ibid 25.

A. The Emergence of Responsibility as an Independent Legal Category

The law of international responsibility did not always lie at the core of the theory and practice of international law as it does today. In accordance with the classical doctrine of international law, scholars were primarily concerned with certain area of international law, such as the law of the sea, the laws of war, diplomatic relations and the treatment of foreigners.[58] Francisco de Vitoria, Francisco Suárez and others did not deal with international responsibility as an independent legal category. Pierino Belli and Alberico Gentili for their part dealt with the issue of responsibility in a rather rudimentary way,[59] with a particular focus on wrongs committed against ambassadors.[60]

Not even Hugo Grotius identified international responsibility as a separate legal category. However, many of his ideas served as inspiration for international responsibility in general and the responsibility for complicity in particular. For example, Grotius embraced and re-interpreted the Roman law doctrine of liability as dependent on fault (*culpa*), which he described as being 'in conformity with the natural order; [and thereby] equally valid in international law'.[61] In this regard, he perceived the maxim of *qui in culpa non est, natura ad nihil tenetur* (reasonable foreseeability or unconscious negligence) as being applicable to both acts of State through its agents and to acts of individuals. Ultimately, Grotius' major contribution to the law of responsibility has been his conception of a relationship between a wrongful act and the ensuing legal consequences. In this respect, Grotius observed that the wrongdoing (*maleficium*) was an independent source of obligations in the law of nations.[62] This rationale served as an edifice for the theory that an internationally wrongful act creates new international legal relations distinct from those existing before the wrongful act occurred.[63]

The treatment of international responsibility as a legal concept emerged in the early twentieth century with Triepel and Anzilotti, whose writings

[58] Crawford, Grant and Messineo (n 2) 377.

[59] P Belli of Alba, *De Re Militari et Bello Tractatus [A Treatise on Military Matters and Warfare]* (HC Nutting tr, Oxford, Clarendon Press, 1936) pt 10, ch 2, 296–98; A Gentili, *De Legationibus Libri Tres [Three Books on Embassies]* (GJ Laing tr, Oxford, Clarendon Press, 1924) bk 3, ch 6, 72–76.

[60] Gentili (n 59) bk 3, ch 6, 72–76.

[61] MG Cohn, 'La théorie de la responsabilité internationale' (1939) 68 *RCADI* 209, 242.

[62] Grotius (n 16) bk 2, ch 17.

[63] Ago, 'Second Report' (n 3) 180–81, paras 14–15; see also D Anzilotti, *Opere di Dionisio Anzilotti: Corso di diritto internazionale*, vol 1 (4th edn, Padova, CEDAM, 1955) 384; W Wengler, *Völkerrecht* (Berlin, Springer, 1964) 499; G Tunkin, *Droit international public: Problèmes théoriques* (Paris, Pedone, 1965) 220.

were followed by Schoen and Strupp.[64] In *Völkerrecht und Landesrecht*, Triepel criticised Grotius' theory of fault and addressed imputation to the State of the conduct of private actors and federal subdivisions.[65] Anzilotti developed Triepel's critique to its logical conclusion, showing that international responsibility is based on an objective conception of an internationally wrongful act.

Anzilotti concluded that the existence of responsibility required both the existence of a violation of international law and its attribution to the State.[66] He noted that the attribution is distinct from pure factual causation—an act is legally attributed to a subject not because it has been committed or intended by the latter, but because the rule attributes it to the State.[67] For Anzilotti, it was not fault but a mere fact of international obligation being violated that engaged responsibility.[68] Both Strupp and Schoen further developed this theory of objective responsibility, albeit Strupp did consider that fault had a role to play in all cases of omission by State organs.[69]

In further enhancing the theory of objective responsibility, Eagleton found that the principle of State equality required subjection to law and

[64] See D Anzilotti, 'La responsabilité internationale des États à raison des dommages soufferts par des étrangers' (1906) 13 *RGDIP* 5 (considering to be the turning point in the modern conception of responsibility); see also G Nolte, 'From Dionisio Anzilotti to Roberto Ago: The Classical International Law of State Responsibility and the Traditional Primacy of a Bilateral Conception of Inter-State Relations' (2002) 13 *EJIL* 1083.

[65] H Triepel, *Völkerrecht und Landesrecht* (Leipzig, CL Hirschfeld, 1958) 324–71.

[66] Anzilotti (n 64) 285–86 ('La notion de la responsabilité internationale implique l'idée d'un rapport unissant à un État la violation du droit international. En d'autres termes, il faut qu'un acte illicite puisse être rapporté à un État, qu'on puisse le considérer comme son acte à lui, le lui imputer'; author's translation: 'The concept of international responsibility implies the idea of a link between the violation of international law and the State. In other words, it must be possible to link an internationally wrongful act to a State, to consider the act as that of the State, to impute it to the State'.); see also Ago, 'Le délit international' (n 3) 450–98.

[67] Anzilotti (n 63) 228; cf Anzilotti (n 64) 291 (suggesting that the concept of attribution relies on causal considerations: 'l'imputabilité, au point de vue du droit international, n'est pas autre chose que la conséquence du rapport de causalité qui existe entre un fait contraire au droit des gens et l'activité de l'Etat dont ce fait émane'; author's translation: 'imputation, from the point of view of international law, is nothing else than the consequence of causal connection that exists between a fact contrary to the laws of nations and the activity of the State from which this fact originates'); see also Ago, 'Second Report' (n 3) 194, para 52 (defending a distinction between factual or natural causation and causation in law).

[68] Anzilotti (n 3) 172; cf H Lauterpacht, *Private Law Sources and Analogies in International Law* (London, Longmans, 1927) 138–41 (expressing reservations about objective responsibility, suggesting that the question of fault is inherent to determining whether a State has failed to prevent or punish a particular wrongful conduct on its territory).

[69] P Schoen, *Die völkerrechtliche Haftung der Staaten aus unerlaubten Handlungen*, vol 10 (Breslau, Kern, 1917) 57–58 (defending the theory of objective responsibility in respect of both actions and omissions of State organs); K Strupp, *Das völkerrechtliche Delikt* (Stuttgart, Kohlhammer, 1920) 54–60; for the continued application of fault as a benchmark to determine responsibility for the failure of due diligence see, eg *Honduras v Salvador and Guatemala* (Final Conclusions and Award) (1909) 3 *AJIL* 729 (Central American Court of Justice).

the respect for the rights of other States (ie State equality was no longer a simple corollary of an absolute State sovereignty):

> This exclusive territorial control, which is a legal possession of the State, logically results in the acceptance by that State of responsibility for illegal acts occurring within the range of its control. If one nation allows to another a monopoly of jurisdiction within the boundaries of the latter, and thereby excludes itself from the possibility of protecting its own rights therein, this can only be upon the assumption that the latter State makes itself responsible for all internationally illegal acts committed within its control against the former State ... The exclusive territorial jurisdiction of the State, which is concomitant of its independence, is the chief source of its responsibility.[70]

Thus, with Triepel, Anzilotti and Eagleton, the foundations of international responsibility as we regard it today emerged. However, as set out above, complicity may be traced back even further to Grotius and Vattel. This earlier genesis of complicity may be one of the underlying reasons that it does not fit neatly within the modern conception of international responsibility, by retaining the reminiscence of fault in its cognitive requirement, whether in the form of knowledge, intention or both.

B. Complicity—Attribution of Responsibility or Attribution of Conduct

The conception of responsibility, as developed by the founding fathers of international law, hinders the drawing of a clear distinction between individual and State responsibility.[71] Similarly, it does not settle the boundaries between complicity and due diligence.

In 1580, Alberico Gentili wrote that the State 'which knows because it has been warned, and which ought to prevent the misdeeds of its citizens, and through its jurisdiction can prevent them, will be at fault and guilty of a crime if it does not do so'.[72] Similarly, according to Grotius, '[a] community, or its rulers, may be held responsible for the crime of a subject if they know of it and do not prevent it when they could or should prevent it'.[73]

In this context, Grotius developed complicity as an overarching framework for holding a State responsible for the acts perpetrated by its own

[70] C Eagleton, *The Responsibility of States in International Law* (New York, New York University Press, 1928) 7.

[71] Crawford, Grant and Messineo (n 2) 382; see also Y Onuma, 'Just Causes of War' in Y Onuma (ed), *A Normative Approach to War: Peace, War and Justice in Hugo Grotius* (Oxford, OUP, 1993) 88–90.

[72] A Gentili, *De Iure Belli Libri Tres [Three Books on the Law of War]* (JC Rolfe tr, Oxford, Clarendon Press, 1933) bk 1, ch 19, 100.

[73] Grotius (n 16) bk 2, ch 21, § 2.

citizens.[74] Following a distinction between the law of nature and civil laws, Grotius refers to:

> [W]hat is due by the law of nature is consequence of a wrong. By a wrong we here mean every fault, whether of commission or of omission, which is in conflict with what men ought to do, either from their common interest or by reason of a special quality. From such a fault, if damage has been caused, by the law of nature an obligation arises, namely, that the damage should be made good.[75]

Thus, for Grotius, complicity could be interpreted as unlawful in and of itself because it is in conflict with 'what men ought to do', either from their common interest or by reason of a special quality. Grotius also contended that a State could be responsible for the acts of its citizens by operation of *patientia* or *receptus*.[76] Under the principle of *patientia*, the State knows of the crime and fails to prevent it,—and on that basis is to be held responsible.[77] Under the principle of *receptus*, crimes of refugees from justice are attributed to the sovereign.[78] In these ways, the State becomes an accomplice in their citizen's crimes.[79] According to Grotius

> to participate in a crime a person must not only have knowledge of it but also have the opportunity to prevent it. This is what the laws mean when they say that knowledge, when its punishment is ordained, is taken in the sense of toleration, so that he may be held responsible who was able to prevent a crime but did not do so; and that the knowledge to be considered here is that associated with the will, that is, knowledge is to be taken in connection with intent.[80]

It was this final statement that paved the way to an over-simplified solution for separating complicity from due diligence. In respect of complicity, Grotius seemed to rely on knowledge in connection with the element of intent. In contrast, the responsibility for failure to perform due diligence derived from a looser link with the State's involvement (toleration). For Grotius, complicity would arise only in the exceptional cases where the State knew of the intended act beforehand, or in some way intended it to occur. Anzilotti explains that as a result of a State's knowledge of the wrongdoing committed by the individual against a third State and its

[74] ibid bk 2, ch 17, § 2.

[75] ibid § 1.

[76] ibid bk 2, ch 21, § 2; see also T Becker, *Terrorism and the State: Rethinking the Rules of State Responsibility* (Oxford, Hart Publishing, 2006) 14.

[77] Grotius (n 16) bk 2, ch 21, §§ 3–4.

[78] ibid; see also JA Hessbruegge, 'The Historical Development of the Doctrines of Attribution and Due Diligence in International Law' (2004) 36 *NYU J Intl L & Pol* 265, 283.

[79] E Jiménez de Aréchaga and A Tanzi, 'International State Responsibility' in M Bedjaoui (ed), *International Law: Achievements and Prospects* (Paris, UNESCO, 1991) 359; Anzilotti (n 3) 15.

[80] Grotius (n 16) bk 2, ch 21, § 2.

failure to prevent or to punish such individual, the State becomes in a certain way 'complicit in the delict', resulting in State responsibility.[81]

For Grotius, the responsibility of a State derives from its failure to perform its duty to take all reasonable and adequate measures for the prevention of the crime and the pursuit, arrest and bringing to justice of the offender. Thus, in such a scenario, the State is internationally responsible not for the acts of any private individual, but for its own omission, ie the lack of due diligence of its organs.

The emblematic example of such form of responsibility is the obligation incumbent on the State to afford protection to foreign States, their representatives and their nationals against attacks by individuals.[82] The State is only responsible when it has failed to take measures, as in the circumstances that should normally have been taken to prevent, redress or inflict punishment for the acts causing the damage. A State cannot act in such a way that the rights of other States are injured.[83] In this regard, the concept of territorial sovereignty incorporates an obligation on a State to protect within its territory the rights of other States:

> Territorial sovereignty ... involves the exclusive right to display the activities of the State. This right has as corollary a duty: the obligation to protect within the territory the rights of other States, in particular their right to integrity and inviolability in peace and in war, together with the rights which each State may claim for its nationals in foreign territory.[84]

[81] Anzilotti (n 3) 15 ('divengono in certo modo complici del delitto, nasce una specie di solidarietà fra essi ed il reo derivante dalla tacita approvazione del fatto: di qui, no dal fatto solo dell'individuo, prende origine la responsabilità dello stato'; author's translation: 'become in some way complicit in the delict, a kind of solidarity emerges between the accomplice and the principal arising from the approval of the fact; this, and not the individual's action, that triggers State responsibility').

[82] *Diplomatic and Consular Staff in Tehran (United States v Iran)* (Judgment) [1980] ICJ Rep 3 31–33, paras 63–70 (the responsibility of Iran was twofold. In a first phase Iran was held responsible for an omission, ie lack of prevention and of protection (concerning the attack on the United States embassy), while in a second phase it was held directly responsible for the activities carried out by the militants in the occupation of the Embassy and the retention of hostages).

[83] *Territorial Jurisdiction of the International Commission of the River Oder (United Kingdom v Poland)* (Judgment) [1929] PCIJ Ser A No 23, 5, 27 (this obligation was first articulated in connection with international waterways as follows: '[t]his community of interest in a navigable river becomes the basis of a common legal right, the essential features of which are perfect equality of all riparian States in the use of the whole course of the river and the extension of any preferential privilege of any one riparian State in relation to others').

[84] *Island of Palmas (United States v Netherlands)* (1928) 2 RIAA 829 839; *SS 'Lotus' (France v Turkey)* (Judgment) [1927] PCIJ Ser A No 10, Dissenting Opinion of Judge Moore, 88 ('[i]t is well settled that a State is bound to use due diligence to prevent the commission within its dominions of criminal acts against another nation or its people').

A duty incumbent on each State not to permit its subjects to commit offences against other nations was further developed by Vattel, as follows:

> [N]o sovereign should permit those under his rule to violate the precepts of natural law, which forbids such acts … [and] nations should mutually respect one another and avoid any offense, injury or wrong; in a word, anything which might be hurtful to others.[85]

To permit citizens to injure a foreign State would violate the fundamental right of independence, thereby impairing the harmonious relations that nations must maintain at all times.[86] However, like Grotius, Vattel rejected the idea of absolute responsibility for the acts of their citizens, advocating that:

> [I]t is impossible for the best governed State or for the most watchful and strict sovereign to regulate at will all the acts of their subjects and to hold them on every occasion to the most exact obedience; it would be unjust to impute to the nation, or to the sovereign, all the faults of their citizens.[87]

Vattel continues as follows:

> If a sovereign who has the power to see that his subjects act in a just manner permits them to injure a foreign nation, either the State itself or its citizens, he does no less a wrong to that nation than if he injured it himself … A sovereign who refuses to repair the evil done by one of his subjects, or to punish the criminal or, finally, to deliver him up, *makes himself in a way an accessory to the deed, and becomes responsible for it*.[88] (emphasis added)

Vattel considered that a State's failure to repair the wrong committed by an individual or to punish such an individual could result in complicity of the State and thus engage its responsibility. He further argued that a State could be held liable

> if the nation or its ruler, approve and ratify the acts of its citizen, [for] it takes upon itself the act, and may then be regarded by the injured party as the real author of the affront of which the citizen was perhaps only the instrument.[89]

The above principles as proposed by Vattel have found clear reflection in the modern law of international responsibility.

The subjective theory of responsibility as advocated by Grotius was criticised by Pufendorf.[90] In his *Elementa*, Pufendorf asserted that 'guilt'

[85] de Vattel (n 25) bk 2, ch 6, § 72.

[86] MR García-Mora, *International Responsibility for Hostile Acts of Private Persons against Foreign States* (The Hague, Martinus Nijhoff, 1962) 19.

[87] de Vattel (n 25) bk 2, ch 6, § 73.

[88] ibid § 72.

[89] ibid § 74.

[90] S von Pufendorf, *De Jure Naturae et Gentium [On the Law of Nature and Nations]* (WA Oldfather tr, Oxford, Clarendon Press, 1934) bk 8, ch 6, § 12.

was non-transferable, unless there was some form of participation in the misdeed:

> In transgressions guilt does not pass to other persons included in the society, unless they have themselves agreed to it by an efficacious consent, by *rendering aid, or by some other means* ... So a prince or a magistrate, if he has not neglected to announce a moral prohibition, contracts no guilt from the fact that a transgression has been committed by an old subject or a new-comer, or by one who, after committing a crime in one state, flees to another ... Nor, indeed, do subjects contract guilt from the misdeed of princes, unless they themselves have directly contributed to it.[91] (emphasis added)

According to Pufendorf, there was already at that time a legal presumption that 'the State knows about the [wrongful] act, and it is presumed a State can prevent the crime'.[92] This presumption paved the way to the objective conception of responsibility in international law.

As a general point, however, it is clear that the writings of the founding fathers of international law failed to clarify complicity's precise scope and character, namely whether it is a self-standing negative obligation or a mode of attribution of conduct. Nor did they acknowledge complicity as a form of responsibility of one subject of international law in connection with the wrongful act of another (ie the conception that the ILC adhered to in the ARSIWA and ARIO).

However, these early writings prompted the development of complicity as a form of attribution of private conduct to a State (the so-called notion of 'implied complicity'). Arbitral tribunals in the late nineteenth and early twentieth century attributed responsibility to the State for private conduct as a result of a State's implied complicity or acquiescence.[93] For example, in the *Cotesworth and Powell* case, a Mixed Commission established by Colombia and Great Britain held in respect of damages resulting from private acts which were granted immunity by Colombia that:

> One nation is not responsible for the acts of its individual citizens, except when it approves or ratifies them. It then becomes a public concern, and the injured party may consider the nation itself the real author of the injury. And

[91] S von Pufendorf, *Elementorum Jurisprudentiae Universalis Libri Duo [Two Books of the Elements of Universal Jurisprudence]* (WA Oldfather tr, Oxford, Clarendon Press, 1931) bk 1, definitions XII, § 28.

[92] von Pufendorf (n 90).

[93] *Cotesworth and Powell (Great Britain v Colombia)* (1875) 2 Moore Intl Arbitrations 2050, 2082; *The Montijo (United States v Colombia)* (1875) Moore Intl Arbitrations 1421, 1438; *Poglioli (Italy v Venezuela)* (1903) 10 RIAA 669, 689; *Narcisa de Hammer (United States) v Venezuela* (1885) Moore Intl Arbitrations 2969; cf *Laura MB Janes and others (United States) v Mexico* (1925) 4 RIAA 82, 89–90.

> this approval, it is apprehended, need not be in express terms, but may fairly be inferred from a refusal to provide means of reparation when such means are possible; or from its pardon of the offender when such pardon necessarily deprives the injured party of all redress.[94]

The international law doctrine at that time construed implied complicity as a failure of the State to prevent military excursions, trans-border activities and other wrongdoings by private individuals.[95] For instance, Borchard observed that the State was liable 'where it fails to show due diligence in preventing or suppressing the riot, or where the circumstances indicate an insufficiency of protective measures or a complicity of government officers or agents in the disorder'.[96] Borchard also concluded that the responsibility of the State could be engaged where its involvement was relatively limited, for example, where the 'mob was aided by soldiers or gendarmes, or where the police took part in the assault'.[97] Kelsen, for example, underscored that indirect liability, which results from the acts of private persons imputable to the State, arises in situations where the State has clearly been negligent either in preventing the commission of the act or in punishing the responsible private actors.[98] Thus, the theory of 'implied complicity' emerged as a bridge between the model of absolute non-liability for private conduct and strict liability of the State.[99]

In his re-conceptualisation of the law of international responsibility in the second half of the twentieth century, Ago conceived of complicity as an inter-State form of attribution of responsibility rather than of conduct. He rejected the notion of 'implied complicity' (in the sense of pure failure to prevent or punish) as a basis for attribution of private conduct to the State. He considered it to be technically incorrect as the State was not complicit in the wrongful act of the individual but rather incurred responsibility for its own omission in failing to prevent or to punish that wrongdoing.[100] However, at the same time, his conception of a de facto organ of the State was much broader than the one that ended up being consolidated by the

[94] *Cotesworth and Powell (Great Britain v Colombia)* (n 93).

[95] See, eg JL Brierly, *The Basis of Obligation in International Law* (H Lauterpacht and CHM Waldock eds, Oxford, Clarendon Press, 1958) 152–60; JL Brierly, 'The Theory of Implied State Complicity in International Claims' (1928) 9 *British YBIL* 42; A Decencière-Ferrandière, 'La responsabilité internationale des États' (Thèse Doctorat, Paris, Université de Paris, 1925) 61–62; O Hoijer, *La responsabilité internationale des États en matière d'actes législatifs* (Paris, Les Éditions Internationales, 1930) 159–90.

[96] Borchard (n 32) 224.

[97] ibid; see, eg *Don Pacifico (Great Britain v Greece)* (1906) 6 Moore Digest Intl L 852; *USS Baltimore v Chile* (1906) 6 Moore Digest Intl L 854.

[98] H Kelsen, 'Théorie du droit international public' (1953) 84 *RCADI* 5, 90.

[99] García-Mora (n 86) 20.

[100] R Ago, 'Fourth Report on State Responsibility' (1972) UN Doc A/CN.4/264 and Add 1, reproduced in (1972) 2 *YBILC* 71, 119–20, para 135.

Court following its judgment in the *Military and Paramilitary Activities*.[101] In his Fourth Report, Ago acknowledged that cases where the State

> *encourages and even promotes the organization of such groups, that it provides them with financial assistance, training and weapons, and co-ordinates their activities with those of its own forces for the purpose of conducting operations, and so on, the groups in question cease to be individuals from the standpoint of international law*. They become entities which act in concert with, and at the instigation of, the State, and perform missions authorized by or even entrusted to them by that State. Such groups then fall into the category of those organs which are linked, in fact if not formally, with the State machinery, and frequently called 'de facto organs'.[102] (emphasis added)

In other words, the original intention of Ago was merely to restrict the relationships between the State and non-State actors, distinguishing a *pure failure to prevent* the event over which the State had no control or knowledge, from the situation where the State took some *deliberate steps* to encourage or promote the functioning of, and ultimately wrongful conduct by a non-State actor. It follows that Ago's rejection of the notion of 'implied complicity' was solely due to the need of conceptual distinction between pure omission (where the State had no knowledge or control over a private conduct) and those situations where a State had a particular involvement in the wrongdoing by a non-State actor. Only the latter situations, in Ago's view, could result in the State incurring responsibility *for* the conduct of private actors which would then simply be an extended instrumentality of the State.

In sum, Ago's original idea of control that a State needs to exert over a non-State actor for the purposes of attribution, includes complicity. That notion, even if excluding a pure omission to prevent or punish, is certainly broader than the 'effective control' as the applicable test today in order to attribute private actor's conduct to the State. As we shall see in chapter seven, links between the historical foundations of the concept of complicity and its recent developments are evident, as complicity emerges as a new ground of attribution of conduct in international law.

IV. INTERIM CONCLUSIONS

This chapter sought to understand the roots of the concept of complicity in international law. The analysis conducted above showed that in the context of inter-State relations, there is little to no evidence of a legal framework for responsibility for complicity before the twentieth century.

[101] *Military and Paramilitary Activities in and against Nicaragua (Nicaragua v United States)* (Merits) [1986] ICJ Rep 14, 64, para 115.

[102] Ago (n 100) 120, para 136.

One possible exception is found in the practice of neutrality, as an instance where the law acknowledged a set of rights and obligations, with some resemblance to responsibility for complicity. To preserve their status as neutrals States had to refrain from rendering aid or assistance to the belligerents. Intellectual constructions like that of Vattel discussing different degrees of involvement of a third State in an unjust war arguably generated an incipient indicator for a much later distinction between assistance and co-perpetration in the law of responsibility.

Another antecedent of complicity can be found in the general duties of sovereigns not to be implicated in any direct or indirect way in the wrongful acts of their citizens. In general, however, the founding scholars of classical international law did not distinguish between the obligation to prevent and complicity proper. Rather, they construed the obligation of (non)-assistance as a tool in the pursuance of (un)just war. A reading of Grotius reveals an early attempt to draw a distinction between the situations where a State merely fails to prevent a given act on its territory and where the State has direct knowledge of the wrongful act committed by one of its subordinates and deliberately supports or tolerates it.

In the early twentieth century, complicity was thought of as a form of attribution of private conduct to the State; only later did it mutate into an ancillary form of international responsibility of one subject of international law in connection with a wrongful act committed by another subject. Today, surprisingly, there are signs of complicity re-emerging as a ground of attribution of private conduct. These signs, although embryonic and disparate, are analysed in chapter seven of this book.

The emergence of responsibility for complicity, as codified in the ARSIWA and ARIO, may be traced to the period following the conclusion of World War II. Roberto Ago explained during his lectures at The Hague Academy in 1939 that complicity did not at that time exist in international law. According to Ago:

> Any form of complicity, participation or instigation of a delict appears to be inconceivable in international law. The law of nations in its current structure cannot provide for these forms of the common consideration of a plurality of actors with respect to one single delict. These forms appear to be the feature of the elaboration and nature of the domestic criminal law.[103]

[103] Ago (n 3) 523 (translation by the author of the original in French: 'Ce qui paraît … inconcevable en droit international, c'est toute forme de complicité, de participation, ou de provocation au délit. Le droit des gens, dans sa structure actuelle, ne saurait prévoir ces formes de considération commune de plusieurs sujets par rapport à un seul délit, qui apparaissent comme l'œuvre caractéristique de l'élaboration et de la nature du droit pénal étatique'); see also E Klein, 'Beihilfe zum Völkerrechtsdelikt' in I von Münch (ed), *Staatsrecht, Völkerrecht, Europarecht: Festschrift für Hans-Jürgen Schlochauer zum 75. Geburtstag am 28 März 1981* (Berlin, Walter de Gruyter, 1981) 434.

Yet, in 1978, 30 years after this statement was made, now as an experienced scholar and ad hoc judge, Ago presented an entirely opposite reasoning to convince his peers at the ILC. Certainly, international law had mutated into a very different reality in the post-World War II period. The UN Charter proposed collective security to the world, despite it being doomed to remain dormant for some time in light of the interests of the United States and the former Union of Soviet Socialist Republics (USSR). These superpowers consistently used other States and non-State armed groups under their respective zones of influence as proxies for the commission of wrongful acts. Regulating complicity was very much about an ideological choice and contingencies of the time. In fact, it cannot be excluded that Ago found some inspiration in the Soviet doctrine on the law of responsibility, which promoted the notion of responsibility for complicity, with a particular focus on aggression and the use of force.[104]

In such an environment between contingency of co-existence and immaturity of co-operation,[105] Ago conceptualised the foundations of international law of responsibility, gradually moving away from a purely bilateralist structure towards an incipient idea of public order. Responsibility for complicity was part of this public order conception, even though Ago was well aware that it was largely a matter of progressive development of international law.[106] When the time came to consider responsibility of complicit States, it would seem that the formalism of codification was taken over by the call for progressive development.[107] Ago prompted the Commission 'to show intellectual courage in dealing with [complicity]'[108] and supported the comments of his fellow Commission member, Stephen Schwebel, that the rules on complicity reflected the progressive development of international law more than its

[104] See, eg N Ushakov, *Основания международной ответственности государств [Bases of International Responsibility of States]* (Moscow, International Relations, 1983) 145–54.

[105] See W Friedmann, *The Changing Structure of International Law* (London, Stevens & Sons, 1964).

[106] R Ago, 'La codification du droit international et les problèmes de sa réalisation', *Recueil d'études de droit international en hommage à Paul Guggenheim* (Genève, Université de Genève, 1968) 94 ('codifier le droit a toujours signifié le modifier en partie et parfois même profondément'; author's translation: 'to codify the law has always meant to modify it partially and sometimes even significantly').

[107] RJ Dupuy, 'La codification du droit international a-t-elle encore un intérêt à l'aube du troisième millénaire?', *Droit international à l'heure de sa codification: Études en l'honneur de Roberto Ago*, vol 1 (Milano, Giuffrè, 1987) 267 ('[la Commission] est très sensible à poser la primauté de l'éthique sur la technique').

[108] ILC, 'Summary Record of the 1519th Meeting' (18 July 1978), reproduced in (1978) 1 *YBILC* 237, 240, para 21 (Ago).

codification. Ago believed that, 'if there was one case in which the Commission should carry out progressive development, it was surely the case covered by [complicity]'.[109]

It must also be borne in mind that significant structural changes in international law generated conditions favourable for finally attributing relevance to the implication of third parties in a violation of international law. The emergence of international criminal law, the establishment of the Nuremberg and Tokyo military tribunals and the adoption of the Genocide Convention, most certainly exerted influence on the early stages of the ARSIWA codification of responsibility for complicity. Similarly, '[t]he moral and social concerns that inform State responsibility—to express disapproval, to direct behaviour and to distribute social burdens—closely resemble standard justification behind domestic torts but also criminal law'.[110] It is therefore unsurprising that the initial stages of development of responsibility for complicity were influenced by similar concepts as they operate in domestic legal systems.[111] Special Rapporteur Ago attempted to convince his peers at the ILC that he was not incorporating the criminal content of responsibility for complicity in relation to the conduct of States.[112] Yet, the wording of the originally proposed provision and its contextual appearance alongside the concept of delicts and crimes implies the opposite. In fact, it would not be an exaggeration to argue that in general international law, 'complicity's most objectionable characteristics are inherited from domestic exemplars'.[113]

[109] ibid.

[110] Lauterpacht (n 68) viii; for the influence of domestic law concepts on the development of international law and the limited scope for analogies see A Cavaglieri, 'Règles générales du droit de la paix' (1929) 26 *RCADI* 311; *International Status of South-West Africa* (Advisory Opinion) [1950] ICJ Rep 128, Separate Opinion of Judge McNair 146, 148 ('International law has recruited and continues to recruit many of its rules and institutions from private systems of law').

[111] For the analysis of complicity in domestic legal systems see, eg MD Dubber, 'Criminalizing Complicity: A Comparative Analysis' (2007) 5 *JICJ* 977; M Pihou, 'An Argument in Favour of a More Normative Distinction between Principals and Accomplices in International Criminal Law' (2008) 21 *Hague YBIL* 41; M Aksenova, 'Complicity in International Criminal Law: A Case for Clarification' (Mississippi College of Law, New Perspectives in Comparative Law—Inaugural YCC Conference, 2012); S Hasan, 'The Role of Complicity in International Responsibility, with Special Attention to State Responsibility' (PhD Thesis, Geneva, Graduate Institute, 2012) 9–35.

[112] cf, eg UNGA, 'Sixth Committee, Summary Record of the 42nd Meeting' (9 November 1978) UN Doc A/C.6/33/SR.42, 17, para 58 (Federal Republic of Germany).

[113] JG Stewart, 'The End of "Modes of Liability" for International Crimes' (2012) 25 *LJIL* 165, 169.

In the author's view, it is advisable to take brief account of complicity's codification in the Nuremberg Charter, the Genocide Convention, and its adoption in the statutes of the ad hoc international criminal law tribunals and the International Criminal Court (ICC) before focusing our attention on the ARSIWA and ARIO. This will help with explaining the complex questions that the Court faced in the *Bosnia Genocide* case[114] and exploring potential interactions with or influences on the law of international responsibility for complicity.

[114] See especially *Application of the Convention on the Prevention and Punishment of the Crime of Genocide (Bosnia and Herzegovina v Serbia and Montenegro)* (Merits) [2007] ICJ Rep 43, 110–19, paras 161–79.

3

The Regimes of Complicity in International Law

I. INTRODUCTION

THIS CHAPTER LOOKS into the two normative regimes of complicity in modern international law. Complicity is one of the few concepts which applies across qualitatively distinct legal regimes such as international criminal law and the law of international responsibility. Yet a comparative analysis of the application of complicity in these different regimes is often overlooked on the assumption that the law of international responsibility has a nature and purpose that is wholly distinct from the criminal liability of individuals.

Without proposing to question this paradigm generally, in the author's view there is no valid objection to the idea that the interpretation of certain concepts in general international law may be informed by developments in specific branches of international law.[1] There is, in particular, a considerable overlap in the way that certain elements of responsibility for complicity are identified and applied. For instance, the question of whether complicity requires knowledge or intention for the purposes of finding responsibility of States or international organisations implicates *ultima ratio* an analysis of whether their officials or agents (meaning individuals) possessed such knowledge or intention when rendering aid or assistance. Certainly, the standard of proof and other procedural aspects will differ depending on whether State or individual responsibility is involved but an overlap cannot and should not be ignored.

Section II surveys the development of the concept of complicity from the Nuremberg Charter, through its codification in the Genocide Convention and integration in the Statutes of the ad hoc tribunals and the Rome Statute of the International Criminal Court (ICC).

Section III is a critical historical account of the efforts to codify complicity in general international law applicable to States and international organisations. This account reflects a tension between the concept's original

[1] See generally N Valticos, 'Pluralité des ordres juridiques internationaux et unité du droit international' in J Makarczyk (ed), *Theory of International Law at the Threshold of the 21st Century: Essays in Honour of Krzysztof Skubiszewski* (The Hague, Kluwer, 1996).

inspiration in criminal law and the need to adapt its operation and scope to States and international organisations. It also shows a certain tension between the two substantially different conceptions of complicity held by Special Rapporteurs Roberto Ago and James Crawford. This review helps to develop an understanding of the background and the source of justifications behind the current limits to responsibility for complicity in positive international law.

II. COMPLICITY IN INTERNATIONAL CRIMINAL LAW

The law on responsibility for complicity may be usefully informed by the parallel developments and interpretation of the concept in international criminal law.[2] Of course, the differences between these two regimes should not be understated, but there are also areas of overlap, at a conceptual and practical level, which warrant consideration.[3] Both regimes 'can be regarded as forms of social organization aimed at the creation of disciplined, formally free subjects who are able to grasp the relation between liberty, order and responsibility'.[4] Moreover, both regimes 'link past, present and future in a particular way', relating particular wrongs to a given consequence with the view to restoring legality and the *status quo ante*.[5] Thus, while the two regimes of complicity have different functions and objects, their operational elements share similar foundations.

It is beyond the scope of this chapter to provide an exhaustive analysis of complicity as a form of liability in international criminal law.[6] Rather, the intention is to appraise whether nuanced parallels can be drawn from the interpretation of constituent elements of complicity in international criminal law for an improved understanding of similar elements in the law of international responsibility.

[2] *Application of the Convention on the Prevention and Punishment of the Crime of Genocide (Bosnia and Herzegovina v Serbia and Montenegro)* (Merits) [2007] ICJ Rep 43, 116, para 173 (recognising the duality of responsibility of States and individuals as 'a constant feature of international law'); for the without prejudice clauses as to State/individual responsibility, respectively see Rome Statute of the International Criminal Court (adopted 17 July 1998; entered into force 1 July 2002) 2187 UNTS 90, Art 25(4); ILC, 'Draft Articles on Responsibility of States for Internationally Wrongful Acts, with Commentaries' (2001) 2 (pt 2) *YBILC* 31, Art 58.

[3] See especially BI Bonafé, *The Relationship between State and Individual Responsibility for International Crimes* (Leiden, Martinus Nijhoff, 2009); A Nollkaemper, 'Concurrence between Individual Responsibility and State Responsibility in International Law' (2003) 52 *ICLQ* 615; M Spinedi, 'State Responsibility v Individual Responsibility for International Crimes: Tertium Non Datur?' (2002) 13 *EJIL* 895.

[4] WG Werner, 'Responding to the Undesired: State Responsibility, Risk Management and Precaution' (2007) 36 *Netherlands YBIL* 57, 65.

[5] ibid 66–67.

[6] For studies in this area see, eg M Jackson, *Complicity in International Law* (Oxford, OUP, 2015) 59–121; MD Dubber, 'Criminalizing Complicity: A Comparative Analysis' (2007) 5 *JICJ* 977; A Clapham, 'Issues of Complexity, Complicity and Complementarity: From the

A. Complicity in the Nuremberg Charter

Traditionally, the consequences deriving from an unlawful act of an individual in international law were left to the discretion of the respective State of jurisdiction.[7] Individuals were regarded as the objects of international law, not its subjects, and responsibility under international law was limited to inter-State affairs.[8] However, in the twentieth century, the perpetuation of impunity in respect of the most serious internationally wrongful acts became untenable.[9]

Article 228 of the Treaty of Versailles in 1919 was one of the first attempts to impose punishment on individuals for the commission of a category of international crimes, namely war crimes, which traditionally entailed only State responsibility.[10] However, it was not until after the atrocities committed by the Nazis in Europe and by the Japanese in many parts of South East Asia that a new principle of individual criminal responsibility was founded.

The result of the 'Nuremberg revolution' was the disentanglement of individual and State responsibility. As famously described by the International Military Tribunal (IMT) at Nuremberg:

> Crimes against international law are committed by men, not by abstract entities, and only by punishing individuals who commit such crimes can the provisions of international law be enforced.[11]

Nuremberg Trials to the Dawn of the New International Criminal Court' in P Sands (ed), *From Nuremberg to The Hague: The Future of International Criminal Justice* (Cambridge, CUP, 2003); E Kok, 'The Principle of Complicity under International Law—Its Application to States and Individuals in Cases Involving Genocide, Crimes against Humanity and War Crimes' in L van den Herik and C Stahn (eds), *The Diversification and Fragmentation of International Criminal Law* (Leiden, Martinus Nijhoff, 2012).

[7] For an excellent analysis of the evolving role of individual in the international legal order see K Parlett, *The Individual in the International Legal System* (Cambridge, CUP, 2011).

[8] *Jurisdiction of the Courts of Danzig* (Advisory Opinion) [1928] PCIJ Ser B No 15, 17–18.

[9] PM Dupuy, 'International Criminal Responsibility of the Individual and International Responsibility of the State' in A Cassese, P Gaeta and JRWD Jones (eds), *The Rome Statute of the International Criminal Court: A Commentary* (Oxford, OUP, 2002) 1085 (suggesting that 'the promoters of the various international criminal courts undoubtedly intended, by punishing individuals, also to punish the actions of the State to which the acts may be attributed'); see also AA Cançado Trindade, 'Complementarity between State Responsibility and Individual Responsibility for Grave Violations of Human Rights: The Crime of State Revisited' in M Ragazzi (ed), *International Responsibility Today: Essays in Memory of Oscar Schachter* (Leiden, Martinus Nijhoff, 2005) 265; BI Bonafé, 'Responsabilità dello Stato per fatti illeciti particolarmente gravi e responsabilità penale dell'individuo: due approcci a confronto' in M Spinedi, A Gianelli and ML Alaimo (eds), *La codificazione della responsabilità internazionale degli stati alla prova dei fatti: Problemi e spunti di riflessione* (Milano, Giuffrè, 2006); Bonafé (n 3).

[10] Treaty of Versailles (adopted 28 June 1919; entered into force 10 January 1920) 2 USTIA 43, 137, Art 228; see also Bonafé (n 3) 35.

[11] *Trial of the Major War Criminals* (Judgment) (1947) IMT 171, 223; see also WA Schabas, 'State Policy as an Element of International Crimes' (2008) 98 *J Crim L & Criminology* 953.

On the basis of this then-revolutionary principle, Article 8 of the Charter of the Nuremberg Tribunal provided that:

> The fact that the defendant acted pursuant to order of his Government or of a superior shall not free him from responsibility, but may be considered in mitigation of punishment if the Tribunal determines that justice so requires.[12]

Complicity was specifically recognised in the Charters of the Nuremberg and Tokyo Tribunals:

> Leaders, organizers, instigators and accomplices participating in the formulation or execution of a common plan or conspiracy to commit any of the foregoing crimes are responsible for all acts performed by any persons in execution of such plan.[13]

However, notions such as aiding or abetting were often employed without being clearly distinguished from co-perpetration. In addition, due to the particularly complex factual circumstances of World War II, many of these cases could easily fit within the theoretically constructed modes of liability.[14] The passage below illustrates the point:

> The person who persuades another to commit murder, the person who furnishes the lethal weapon for the purpose of its commission, and the person who pulls the trigger are all principals or accessories to the crime.[15]

Many of those convicted at Nuremberg were held liable as accomplices rather than as principals.[16] At these early stages of development of international criminal law, complicity in a crime was not only seen as a mode for attracting liability but also a self-standing and separable crime from the principal one. The 'Nuremberg Principles' that were formulated by the International Law Commission (ILC) stated that 'complicity in the commission of a crime against peace, a war crime, or a crime against humanity as set forth in Principle VI is a crime under international law'.[17]

[12] Charter of the International Military Tribunal at Nuremberg (adopted 8 August 1945) 82 UNTS 279, Art 8.

[13] ibid, Art 6; Charter of the International Military Tribunal for the Far East (adopted 19 January 1946) 4 USTIA 20, Art 5.

[14] *Trial of Franz Schönfeld and Nine others* (Judgment) (1949) 11 LRTWC 64; *Trial of Bruno Tesch and others (The Zyklon B Case)* (Judgment) (1947) 1 LRTWC 93; see also *United States v Otto Ohlendorf (The Einsatzgruppen Case)* (Judgment) (1949) 4 TWC 411.

[15] *United States v Alstötter (Justice Case)* (Judgment) (1948) 3 TWC 1.

[16] *Prosecutor v Tadić* (Judgment) IT-94-1-T (7 May 1997) para 674 (noting that the post-Second World War judgments generally failed to discuss in detail the criteria upon which guilt was determined); see also ILC, 'Principles of International Law Recognised in the Charter of the International Military Tribunal and in the Judgement of the Tribunal' (1950) 2 *YBILC* 374.

[17] ILC (n 16) Principle VII.

The trial of the major Nazi war criminals at Nuremberg also demonstrated a close relationship to the domain of complicity as a form of State responsibility. This is particularly the case for the crime of membership, according to which members of groups or organisations could be convicted simply on the ground of the prior establishment by the IMT of the group's criminality.[18] This application of complicity was extensively used as a basis for liability, as can be seen, for example, in the *United States v Alstötter* (also known as *Justice* case). There, the prosecution framed the accused's provision of legal advice to the Nazi government, which resulted in violations of international law, as a form of complicity in the subject acts.[19]

Similarly, Article II(2) of the Control Council Law No 10, which was used for the domestic prosecution of war criminals in post-war Germany, established the criminal liability of an individual who was (i) an accessory to the crime, (ii) took a consenting part therein, (iii) was connected with plans or enterprises involving its commission, or (iv) was a member of any organisation or group connected with the commission of any such crime.[20] The Tokyo Charter used similar categories. The drafters of the Nuremberg and Tokyo Charters were

> prompted more by concern for efficiency than by concern for legal exactitude or rationality. The use of varied terms and expressions that are often synonymous and that overlap can be explained by the desire to let no act go unpunished.[21]

The way in which the post-World War II IMTs applied accomplice liability was imprecise in its legal content and scope, but it still served as the first real linkage between the individual and State responsibility.[22] The genesis of this linkage has given rise to some rather significant difficulties in the reconciliation of the constituent elements of related offences applicable to

[18] Bonafé (n 3) 37.

[19] *United States v Alstötter (Justice Case)* (n 15); see also JD Ohlin, 'The Torture Lawyers' (2010) 51 *Harvard Intl LJ* 193, 249–50; JE Alvarez, 'Torturing the Law' (2005) 37 *Case Western Reserve J Intl L* 175.

[20] Control Council Law No 10, Punishment of Persons Guilty of War Crimes, Crimes Against Peace and Against Humanity (20 December 1945), reproduced in (1946) 3 Official Gazette Control Council for Germany 50, Art 2(2); see also *United States v Flick* (Judgment) (1952) 6 TWC 1187; *Trial of Bruno Tesch and others (The Zyklon B Case)* (n 14).

[21] D Thiam, 'Fourth Report on the Draft Code of Offences against the Peace and Security of Mankind' (1986) UN Doc A/CN.4/398, reproduced in (1986) 2 (pt 1) *YBILC* 53, 64–65, para 104.

[22] For a continuing influence of the MIT judgments in the context of corporate complicity today see, eg *Corrie v Caterpillar* (Judgment) [2005] Inc 403 F Supp 2d 1019 (WD Wash 2005); see also G Baars, 'Corrie et Al v Caterpillar: Litigating Corporate Complicity in Israeli Violations of International Law in the US Courts' (2004) 11 *YB Islamic & Middle Eastern L* 97.

individual and State. Genocide is used as an example in the next section in order to demonstrate the intricacies of the concurrent operation of responsibility and the concept of complicity therein in respect of individuals and States.

B. Codification of Complicity in the Genocide Convention

During the preparation of the Genocide Convention, the question arose as to whether, in addition to the responsibility for failure to prevent or punish acts of genocide, a provision should be drafted for the responsibility of States for the commission of and complicity in genocide.[23] The United Nations General Assembly (UNGA) Sixth Legal Committee spent 51 meetings discussing the draft Convention on Genocide, including the provisions on complicity and the nature of responsibility that States have under the Convention.[24]

One particularly interesting part of the discussion related to Article IX with the United Kingdom, France and Haiti supporting a civil form of State responsibility for genocide rather than a criminal one.[25] As a result of this discussion, the precise wording of Article IX of the Genocide Convention does not qualify the nature of responsibility for genocide applied to the State:

> Disputes between the Contracting Parties relating to the interpretation, application or fulfilment of the present Convention, including those relating to the responsibility of a State for genocide or for any of the other acts enumerated in article III, shall be submitted to the International Court of Justice at the request of any of the parties to the dispute.[26]

If this provision was meant to apply exclusively to 'the responsibility of a State for failing to prevent or punish genocide' and not to the responsibility of a State for acts enumerated in Article III of the Genocide Convention, then one would have expected to see discussion of this during the negotiations of the Convention. As there was not, the language of this provision

[23] For the travaux préparatoires relied on in this section see H Abtahi and P Webb, *The Genocide Convention: The Travaux Préparatoires* (Leiden, Martinus Nijhoff, 2008).

[24] UNGA, 'Sixth Committee, Summary of Records of Meetings' (21 September 1948) UN Doc A/C.6/SR.61—(1 December 1948) UN Doc A/C.6/312.

[25] UNGA, 'Sixth Committee, Summary of Records of the 103rd Meeting' (12 November 1948) UN Doc A/C.6/SR.103.

[26] Convention on the Prevention and Punishment of the Crime of Genocide (adopted 9 December 1948; entered into force 12 January 1951) 78 UNTS 277, Art IX.

allowed the ICJ to infer that States themselves can be held responsible under international law for genocide and the other acts enumerated under Article III of the Genocide Convention, including complicity.[27]

Article III(e) of the Genocide Convention on complicity in genocide gave rise to a number of specific issues as discussed by the Ad Hoc Committee on Genocide, a body which was set up by the Economic and Social Council to prepare a second draft convention on genocide.[28] One such issue, which was discussed by the Ad Hoc Committee on Genocide entrusted to prepare a second draft convention, was whether complicity of the State in the acts of individuals is an essential element of the crime of genocide.[29] The United States delegation considered that genocide could not be an international crime unless the State participated in its perpetration.[30] The Lebanese delegate contended that State complicity might be an element of genocide, but it was not its necessary condition.[31]

According to the chairman of the Ad Hoc Committee, then speaking as the United States representative, complicity of the State would have to be presumed if, for example, it did not intervene to restore order.[32] In turn, France supported the retention of complicity of the State as an element in the definition of genocide, but advocated a wide interpretation of the term so as to encompass even the mere act of granting immunity to the group that committed a genocide.[33] For its part, the former Union of Soviet Socialist Republics (USSR) considered that the participation of the government was a necessary but sometimes indirect element.[34] China on the other hand resisted the drafting proposal according to which the crime of genocide would necessarily involve State complicity.[35]

In a discussion held on 12 April 1948, the French representative stated that:

> genocide could be committed by an individual or by a group of individuals not connected with the State or without the intervention of the State. It could also be committed at the instance and with the complicity of the State. In that case the State itself could be considered guilty of the crime.[36]

[27] *Application for Revision of the Judgment of 11 July 1996 in the Case Concerning Application of the Convention on the Prevention and Punishment of the Crime of Genocide (Bosnia and Herzegovina v Yugoslavia)* (Judgment) [2003] ICJ Rep 7, 616–17, paras 32–33; *Bosnia Genocide (Merits)* (n 2) 105 ff, para 150 ff.

[28] ECOSOC, 'Res 117(VI)' (3 March 1948) UN Doc E/734.

[29] ECOSOC, 'Ad Hoc Committee on Genocide, Summary Record of the 3rd Meeting' (15 April 1948) UN Doc E/AC.25/SR.4; ECOSOC, 'Ad Hoc Committee on Genocide, Summary Record of the 7th Meeting' (20 April 1948) UN Doc E/AC.25/SR.7.

[30] ECOSOC, 'Ad Hoc Committee on Genocide, Summary Record of the 3rd Meeting' (n 29).

[31] ibid (Lebanon).

[32] ibid (United States).

[33] ibid.

[34] ibid (USSR).

[35] ibid (China).

[36] ibid (France).

The representative for France further noted that genocide was a particularly heinous crime when committed with State complicity or made possible as a result of a State's default.[37] France proposed to draw the following distinction 'if the guilty party were an individual, the crime would be a national one, punishable by national law. If the guilty party were a State, the crime committed would come under international law'.[38] Ultimately, the French proposal was rejected for the following reasons: (i) the persecution of Jews by the Nazis before they were in power showed that genocide could be committed without the involvement of the government in power; (ii) the requirement of governmental involvement was deemed contradictory to the obligation of territorial States to prosecute the offenders as it was unlikely that a government would prosecute acts of genocide in which it was involved; and (iii) the proposal was deemed inconsistent with the UNGA Resolution 96(I),[39] which provided that persons committing genocide shall be punished 'whether they are private individuals, public officials or Statesmen'.[40]

In light of the foregoing, the discussion of whether State complicity is an essential element of the crime of genocide concluded with an agreement that private individuals could commit genocide without the participation of or tolerance by the State. However, the process by which the drafters of the Convention arrived at this result demonstrates that this was an important issue.

Notwithstanding debate concerning the definition of the crime of genocide itself and whether State complicity is an inherent element, the successive drafts of the Convention included complicity in genocide among the punishable acts.[41] Today, Article III of the Genocide Convention describes four forms of participation in the crime: conspiracy, direct and public incitement, attempt and complicity. These crimes or forms of liability arguably do not bear the same stigma as the one attached to the crime of genocide itself. Indeed, many legal systems attach lesser consequences to complicit actors than the principal wrongdoers. Yet, as rightly pointed out

[37] ibid.

[38] ibid.

[39] UNGA, 'Res 96(I): The Crime of Genocide' (11 December 1946) UN Doc A/RES/96(I).

[40] M Boot, *Nullum Crimen Sine Lege and the Subject Matter Jurisdiction of the International Criminal Court: Genocide, Crimes against Humanity, War Crimes* (Antwerpen, Intersentia, 2002) 437.

[41] ECOSOC, 'Prevention and Punishment of Genocide, Comments by Government on the Draft Convention Prepared by the Secretariat, Communications from Non-Governmental Organizations' (30 January 1948) UN Doc E/623; ECOSOC, 'Genocide France: Draft Convention on Genocide' 5 February 1948) UN Doc E/623/Add 1 (draft Art 1 contained the following language '[i]ts authors or their accomplices shall be responsible before International Justice'); ECOSOC, 'Ad Hoc Committee on Genocide, Basic Principles of a Convention on Genocide (Submitted by the Delegation of the Union of Soviet Socialist Republics on 5 April 1958)' (7 April 1948) UN Doc E/AC.25/7; ECOSOC, 'Ad Hoc Committee on Genocide, Draft Articles for the Inclusion in the Convention on Genocide Proposed by the Delegation of China on 16 April 1948' (16 April 1948) UN Doc E/AC.25/9.

by William Schabas, complicity in genocide should not be viewed as being less serious than the commission of genocide itself:[42]

> The accomplice may well be the leader who gives the order to commit genocide, while the 'principal' offender is the lowly subordinate who carries out the instructions. In this scenario, the guilt of the accomplice is really superior to that of the principal offender.[43]

Former draft Article IV(e), the predecessor to Article III(e) of the Genocide Convention, originally referred to complicity not only in respect of the crime of genocide but also 'complicity in conspiracy of genocide, instigation and attempt of genocide'.[44] During the drafting process, two amendments were tabled in relation to that sub-paragraph, one by Belgium, reading 'complicity in crimes of genocide',[45] and the other one by the United Kingdom, reading 'deliberate complicity in crimes of genocide'.[46]

Mr Pescatore, representative of Luxembourg, made a number of observations on the proposed amendment by Belgium. First, he noted that there was a substantial difference between the Ad Hoc Committee's draft and the Belgian amendment. In the former text, complicity applied to all the enumerated acts, ie genocide itself as well as the inchoate crimes of conspiracy, incitement and attempt.[47] Conversely, in the Belgian text, complicity applied only to genocide. Second, he argued that to address complicity in conspiracy was meaningless, that while it was theoretically possible to have complicity in incitement, the result would be unclear and vague, and that it was undesirable to provide for complicity for attempts, especially in light of evidentiary difficulties.[48]

Mr Pescatore pointed out that, in the legal system to which Luxembourg law adhered, complicity meant the rendering of accessory or secondary aid, or simply of facilities, to the perpetrator of an offence.[49] He further clarified that:

> Accomplices were punished only if the crime was actually committed. A person who rendered essential, principal or indispensable aid was termed as a

[42] WA Schabas, *Genocide in International Law: The Crime of Crimes* (2nd edn, Cambridge, CUP, 2009) 307.

[43] ibid.

[44] ECOSOC, 'Ad Hoc Committee on Genocide, Summary Record of the 16th Meeting' (29 April 1948) UN Doc E/AC.25/SR.16; ECOSOC, 'Ad Hoc Committee on Genocide, Summary Record of the 17th Meeting' (30 April 1948) UN Doc E/AC.25/SR.17 (the provision read as follows: 'complicity in any of the acts enumerated in this Article').

[45] ECOSOC, 'Belgium: Amendment to the Draft Convention on Genocide' (5 October 1948) UN Doc A/C.6/217.

[46] ECOSOC, 'United Kingdom of Great Britain and Northern Ireland: Amendments to the Draft Convention on Genocide' (16 October 1948) UN Doc A/C.6/236 and UN Doc A/C.6/236/Corr 1.

[47] UNGA, 'Sixth Committee, Summary Record of the 87th Meeting' (29 October 1948) UN Doc A/C.6/SR.87 (Luxembourg).

[48] ibid.

[49] ibid.

> co-perpetrator and was placed on the same footing in regard to punishment as the perpetrator.[50]

The United Kingdom also challenged the Ad Hoc Committee's former draft Article IV and Mr Fitzmaurice tabled an amended proposal.[51] The object of the latter was to show that complicity applied only to material acts of genocide. On that point, the United Kingdom's amendment was identical to the Belgian one and the reasons overlapped with those set out by the Luxembourg representative. The second aim of the United Kingdom's amendment was to restrict liability to those cases where complicity was deliberate. The reasoning behind such proposal was that as the provision then stood, it was possible to be implicated in a crime in all innocence, and therefore the United Kingdom believed it was essential that complicity be 'deliberate' to constitute a crime.[52]

France supported the Belgian amendment, contending that complicity applied only to the crime of genocide itself. In the view of the French delegation, the United Kingdom's proposal—also supported by Luxembourg and Iran—of introducing the classification 'deliberate' did not add anything to the idea of criminal intent, which according to French criminal law was a necessary factor for a finding of complicity.[53] In response, the United Kingdom suggested that the repetition of 'deliberate' in the Convention would be desirable, considering that some systems do not imply intent as an inherent element of complicity.[54] Indeed, years after, when the United Kingdom incorporated the Genocide Convention into domestic law, it did not include complicity. Parliamentary Secretary Elystan Morgan explained the legislation to Parliament as follows:

> Complicity in genocide has not been included in Clause 2(1) [because] we take the view that the sub-heading in Article III is subsumed in the act of genocide itself in exactly the same way as, under our domestic criminal law, aiding and abetting is a situation in which a person so charged could be charged as a principal [perpetrator] in relation to the offence itself.[55]

Other States like Egypt, the former USSR and the former Yugoslavia were opposed to the limitation of complicity to the act of genocide itself and the exclusion of complicity in the inchoate crimes.[56] The delegation from the former Yugoslavia offered an example of a situation in which an accomplice of a person who had not succeeded in killing his victim, but had

[50] ibid.
[51] ibid (United Kingdom).
[52] ibid.
[53] ibid (France).
[54] ibid (United Kingdom).
[55] 'Official Report, Fifth Series' (3–14 February 1969), reproduced in (1968–69) 777 *Parliamentary Debates Commons* 480–509; cited in Schabas (n 42) 347.
[56] UNGA (n 47).

merely wounded him, would go unpunished, even though he had been well aware of the crime which the principal intended to commit; in that case the accomplice could plead that genocide had not been committed, but merely attempted.[57] The practice of criminal law at that time was considered to have shown that in the majority of cases complicity was very difficult to prove. It was still more so in the case of an attempted crime. It seemed, therefore, that from the legislator's point of view, and in order not to augment the difficulties that would be encountered by those who would have to apply the Convention, it would be wiser to stay within the limits laid down by domestic legislations.[58] Ultimately, the inclusion of the term 'deliberate' was dropped, and the amended wording 'complicity in any act of genocide' was adopted by 25 votes to 14, with three abstentions,[59] which then led to the formulation 'complicity in genocide' as it presently stands in Article III(e) of the Genocide Convention.

The Trial Chamber of the International Criminal Tribunal for Rwanda (ICTR) embraced the proposition that criminal liability for complicity in genocide could only arise where genocide has been committed:

> It appears from the *travaux préparatoires* of the Genocide Convention that only complicity in the completed offence of genocide was intended for punishment and not complicity in an attempt to commit genocide, complicity in incitement to commit genocide nor complicity in conspiracy to commit genocide, all of which were, in the eyes of some States, too vague to be punishable under the Convention.[60]

As demonstrated in this section, the *travaux préparatoires* of the Genocide Convention considered in some depth the modalities of the State responsibility for complicity in genocide. Although a more detailed definition of the term was not included, the compromissory clause of Article IX of the Genocide Convention provides the necessary flexibility to incorporate State responsibility and for its subsequent developments. As for the main elements and criteria that led to the codification of the provision on complicity in genocide, these were inspired from domestic criminal laws, in particular the Anglo-Saxon doctrine of aiding and abetting. After the considerable discussion within the Ad Hoc Committee described above, the scope of complicity was limited only to the consummated crime of genocide and subject to showing of necessary mens rea.

The understanding of the nature of obligations set out in the Genocide Convention, including that of complicity, from a perspective of the law of

[57] ibid (Yugoslavia).
[58] ibid.
[59] ECOSOC, 'Ad Hoc Committee on Genocide, Summary Record of the 13th Meeting' (29 April 1948) UN Doc E/AC.25/SR.13.
[60] *Prosecutor v Akayesu* (Judgment) ICTR-96-4-T (2 September 1998) para 527.

international responsibility, took some time to be consolidated. First, in its 1951 Advisory Opinion, the Court hinted at the special and wide-ranging character of the obligations under the Genocide Convention:

> [I]n a convention of this type one cannot speak of individual advantages or disadvantages to States, or of the maintenance of a perfect contractual balance between rights and duties. The high ideals which inspired the Convention provide, by virtue of the common will of the parties, the foundation and measure of all its provisions.[61]

Second, in the *Bosnia Genocide* case, the Court affirmed States can be held responsible for complicity in genocide:

> The concepts used in paragraphs (b) to (e) of Article III, and particularly that of 'complicity', refer to well known categories of criminal law and, as such, appear particularly well adapted to the exercise of penal sanctions against individuals…it would not be in keeping with the object and purpose of the Convention to deny that the international responsibility of a State—even though quite different in nature from criminal responsibility—can be engaged through one of the acts, other than genocide itself, enumerated in Article III.[62]

The Court's position on the duality of responsibility for genocide (ie that Articles I and III imposed obligations on both individuals and States) was a positive step.[63] Yet the subsequent reasoning of the Court shows that it either used à la carte or ignored elements of complicity in genocide as they have been interpreted in the vast jurisprudence on international criminal law. The Court's interpretation of the cognitive requirement of complicity is telling in that regard.[64] The Court's reasoning is not without criticism and chapter five of this book will examine more closely the statements of the Court and the perceived relationship between Article III(e) of the Genocide Convention and the Articles on Responsibility of States for Internationally Wrongful Acts (ARSIWA)/Articles on Responsibility of International Organizations (ARIO) provisions on complicity. For the time being, it is sufficient to state that the Court's conception of responsibility for complicity in respect of States neither follows strictly Article 16 ARSIWA nor adheres to the general understanding of accomplice liability in international criminal law.

[61] *Reservations to the Convention on Genocide* (Advisory Opinion) [1951] ICJ Rep 15, 23.

[62] *Bosnia Genocide (Merits)* (n 2) 114, para 167; see also *Application of the Convention on the Prevention and Punishment of the Crime of Genocide (Bosnia and Herzegovina v Serbia and Montenegro)* (Preliminary Objections) [1996] ICJ Rep 595, 616, para 32.

[63] *Bosnia Genocide (Merits)* (n 2) 117, para 174; cf ibid Joint Declaration of Judges Shi and Koroma 279; ibid Separate Opinion of Judge Owada 285 (considering that Art I excluded from its scope the issue of direct responsibility of a State for the commission of genocide).

[64] ibid 218, para 421 (holding that at the very least complicity in genocide presupposes awareness of the specific intent of the principal perpetrators, but leaving open the reply as to whether the accomplice must share the intent).

C. Aiding and Abetting in the Practice of the Ad Hoc Tribunals and the ICC

The relationship of individual and State responsibility vis-à-vis the concept of complicity or aid or assistance is not yet settled in positive international law. Certainly, the Court's recognition of the duality of responsibility could be regarded as separating two different normative frameworks. At the same time the Court's analogy-based reasoning in respect of complicity, ie between Article III(e) of the Genocide Convention and Article 16 ARSIWA, leaves open questions as to whether the standards applicable to complicity in these two layers of norms are so fundamentally different. At a more pragmatic level, in the author's view, an analysis of the application of complicity in international criminal law may assist the understanding of the less established areas of international responsibility for complicity.[65]

Complicity in international criminal law is to a large extent an amalgamation of experiences of domestic legal systems.[66] At risk of oversimplifying, domestic criminal and tort laws generally follow either a unitary perpetration model or a differentiated participation model of complicity.[67] Under the framework of the unitary perpetration model, every person who contributed to the commission of the crime is considered guilty as if he were a principal offender.[68] Within this model, every participant carries independent responsibility. Differentiation, if any, regarding the extent of individual contribution to the crime could ultimately be envisaged at the stage of sentencing or its mitigation. Conversely, the differentiated participation model distinguishes the material perpetrator and the secondary participants.[69] This model presupposes that the responsibility of secondary participants is subsidiary or accessorial to the principal offence.

In international criminal law, the inherently collective nature of international crimes and the nature of the sanction renders it particularly

[65] See, eg A Bos, 'Crimes of State: In Need of Legal Rules?' in G Kreijen (ed), *State, Sovereignty, and International Governance* (Oxford, OUP, 2002) 221–37; Nollkaemper (n 3); A Cassese, 'On the Use of Criminal Law Notions in Determining State Responsibility for Genocide' (2007) 5 *JICJ* 875.

[66] For a comparative review see, eg M Aksenova, 'Complicity in International Criminal Law: A Case for Clarification' (Mississippi College of Law, New Perspectives in Comparative Law—Inaugural YCC Conference, 2012); Dubber (n 6).

[67] M Pihou, 'An Argument in Favour of a More Normative Distinction between Principals and Accomplices in International Criminal Law' (2008) 21 *Hague YBIL* 41.

[68] See, eg Italian Criminal Code (Royal Decree No 1398) (enacted 1 July 1931; as amended 1 April 2015) s 110; Austrian Criminal Code (StGB, BGBI 60/1974) (enacted 23 January 1974; as amended 4 November 2013) s 12.

[69] See, eg Russian Criminal Code (No 63-FZ) (enacted 13 June 1996; as amended 1 March 2012) ch 7; German Criminal Code (StGB) (BGBI I S 3799) (enacted 10 October 2013; as amended 10 December 2015) s 27.

important to ascertain the specific role played by the accused and, as a consequence, to differentiate among the various participants.[70] Similar reasoning inspired the codification of State responsibility for complicity, ultimately resulting in complicity as a derivative responsibility in Article 16 ARSIWA and its sister provisions.[71]

The ad hoc tribunals and the *travaux préparatoires* of the Statute of the International Criminal Court (ICC) have adhered to the view that 'international Courts must draw upon the general concepts and legal institutions common to all the major legal systems of the world'.[72] Most, if not all, criminal law systems punish accomplices, ie those who aid, abet, counsel and procure or otherwise participate in criminal offences.[73]

In international criminal law, there are several forms of secondary participation which commonly fall under the concept of complicity in most domestic legal systems. The following forms of secondary participation are now well-established in international criminal law: (i) planning; (ii) instigation—prompting another to commit an offence, which requires proof of a causal connection with the commission of the crime itself; (iii) ordering the commission of an offence, which implies the authority on the part of the accused to make the order; and (iv) aiding (ie giving assistance) and abetting (otherwise being sympathetic to the commission of the offence).[74] However, it is the latter notion of aiding and abetting that most closely resembles the scope of complicity (aid or assistance) in the context of international responsibility.[75]

Aiding and abetting is a well-established form of criminal liability[76] and a general principle of international criminal law.[77] It is a form of secondary participation, which must be distinguished from perpetration.

[70] F Zorzi Giustiniani, 'The Responsibility of Accomplices in the Case-Law of the Ad Hoc Tribunals' (2009) 20 *CLF* 417, 419; see E van Sliedregt, *Individual Criminal Responsibility in International Law* (Oxford, OUP, 2010) 70.

[71] See Jackson (n 6) 18–22; A Eser, 'Individual Criminal Responsibility (Article 25)' in A Cassese, P Gaeta and JRWD Jones (eds), *The Rome Statute of the International Criminal Court: A Commentary*, vol 1 (Oxford, OUP, 2002) 781–83.

[72] *Prosecutor v Furundžija* (Judgment) IT-95-17/1-T (10 December 1998) para 178.

[73] *Trial of Franz Schönfeld and Nine others* (n 14) 69–70; *United Kingdom v Golkel and others* (Judgment) (1948) 5 LRTWC 45, 53.

[74] Statute of the International Criminal Tribunal for Rwanda adopted by UNSC Res 955 (8 November 1994) 33 ILM 1598, Art 6(1); Statute of the International Tribunal for the Prosecution of Persons Responsible for Serious Violations of International Humanitarian Law Committed in the Territory of the Former Yugoslavia since 1991 adopted by UNSC Res 827 (25 May 1993) 32 ILM 1159, Art 7(1); Statute of the Special Court for Sierra Leone (adopted 16 January 2002; entered into force 12 April 2002) 2178 UNTS 138, Art 6(1).

[75] cf Jackson (n 6) 66–69 (suggesting that instigation is also an 'archetypal doctrine of complicity in international criminal law').

[76] *Prosecutor v Musema* (Judgment) ICTR-96-13-T (27 January 2000) para 169; *Prosecutor v Bagilishema* (Judgment) ICTR-95-1A-T (7 June 2001) para 67.

[77] *Prosecutor v Brđanin* (Judgment) IT-99-36-T (1 September 2004) para 724; *Prosecutor v Krstić* (Judgment) IT-98-33-T (2 August 2001) para 640.

While the principal perpetrator has been defined as the one who fulfils 'a key co-coordinating role' and whose 'participation is of an extremely significant nature and at the leadership level',[78] the accomplice is whoever associates himself with the crime committed by another.[79] It follows that complicity necessarily implies the commission of the principal offence.[80] To this end, the International Criminal Tribunal for Rwanda (ICTR) has explained that:

> As far as the Chamber is aware, all criminal systems provide that an accomplice may also be tried, even where the principal perpetrator of the crime has not been identified, or where, for any other reasons, guilt could not be proven.[81]

Both the International Criminal Tribunal for the Former Yugoslavia (ICTY) and ICTR Statutes contain a general liability form which declares individually responsible every person 'who planned, instigated, ordered, committed or otherwise aided and abetted in the planning, preparation or execution of a crime'.[82] The Statutes are 'another example of regulations which, partly due to the wording of earlier conventions such as that on genocide, lack a clear notion of perpetration and participation'.[83] Accordingly, the formulation of this general clause does not clarify whether all participants in a crime are equally liable or whether there is a difference based on the role played in the commission of the offence.[84] Moreover, while incorporating complicity, these provisions do not give 'any indication about its actual content, let alone about its objective and subjective elements'.[85] However, the Tribunals have developed an extensive jurisprudence on aiding and abetting liability. This jurisprudence has been fairly consistent, except for occasional back and forth of the relationship of aiding and abetting vis-à-vis complicity in genocide which by now appears to be settled,[86] and an *accident de parcours* in the *Perišić* case explained in

[78] *Prosecutor v Krstić* (n 77) paras 624–44; *Prosecutor v Stakić* (Judgment) IT-97-24-T (31 July 2003) para 533.

[79] *Prosecutor v Stakić* (n 78) para 533; see also *Prosecutor v Brđanin* (n 77) para 727.

[80] *Prosecutor v Brđanin* (n 77) para 728.

[81] *Prosecutor v Akayesu* (n 60) para 530.

[82] See ICTY Statute (n 74) Art 7(1); ICTR Statute (n 74) Art 6(1).

[83] Eser (n 71) 786.

[84] Zorzi Giustiniani (n 70) 418.

[85] ibid.

[86] See *Prosecutor v Akayesu* (n 60) paras 545–58 (presenting complicity as a substantive crime requiring a different actus reus and mens rea from aiding and abetting); cf *Prosecutor v Semanza* (Judgment) ICTR-97-20-T (15 May 2003) para 394; *Prosecutor v Stakić* (n 78) para 531; but see also *Prosecutor v Krstić* (Judgment) IT-98-33-A (19 April 2004) para 139 (suggesting that complicity in genocide 'may encompass broader conduct than that of aiding and abetting'); in doctrine see E van Sliedregt, 'Complicity to Commit Genocide' in P Gaeta (ed), *The UN Genocide Convention: A Commentary* (Oxford, OUP, 2009); G Dawson and R Boynton, 'Reconciling Complicity in Genocide and Aiding and Abetting Genocide in the Jurisprudence of the United Nations Ad Hoc Tribunals' (2008) 21 *Harvard Human Rights J* 241; C Eboe-Osuji, '"Complicity in Genocide" versus "Aiding and Abetting Genocide": Construing the Difference in the ICTR and ICTY Statutes' (2005) 3 *JICJ* 56.

the following section.[87] The following sections survey the scope and elements of the aiding and abetting liability under international criminal law.

i. Material Element (Actus Reus)

In the *Tadić* case, the ICTY Appeals Chamber introduced a distinction between different participants in the crime that has been further developed in subsequent decisions of the ICTY and ICTR.[88] First, it distinguished between principal and accessory. Second, it distinguished between accomplices and those who take part in a joint criminal enterprise. The Appeals Chamber provided the following clarifications:

i. The aider and abettor is always an accessory to a crime perpetrated by another person, the principal.
ii. In the case of aiding and abetting no proof is required of the existence of a common concerted plan, let alone of the pre-existence of such a plan. No plan or agreement is required: indeed, the principal may not even know about the accomplice's contribution.
iii. The aider and abettor carries out acts specifically directed to assist, encourage or lend moral support to the perpetration of a certain specific crime (murder, extermination, rape, torture, wanton destruction of civilian property, etc), and this support has a substantial effect upon the perpetration of the crime. By contrast, in the case of acting in pursuance of a common purpose or design, it is sufficient for the participant to perform acts that in some way are directed to the furthering of the common plan or purpose.
iv. In the case of aiding and abetting, the requisite mental element is knowledge that the acts performed by the aider and abettor assist the commission of a specific crime by the principal. By contrast, in the case of common purpose or design more is required (i.e., either intent to perpetrate the crime or intent to pursue the common criminal design plus foresight that those crimes outside the criminal common purpose were likely to be committed), as stated above.[89]

The subsequent ICTY case law distinguished between a joint criminal enterprise as a form of co-perpetration, rendering the co-perpetrator liable for the commission of the crime, and aiding and abetting as a form of complicity which could result in a lesser degree of liability.[90] The Appeals

[87] cf *Prosecutor v Perišić* (Judgment) IT-04-81-A (28 February 2013).

[88] *Prosecutor v Tadić* (Judgment) IT-94-1-A (15 July 1999) para 229.

[89] ibid.

[90] *Prosecutor v Vasiljević* (Judgment) IT-98-32-A (25 February 2004) para 102; see also *Prosecutor v Sesay* (Judgment) SCSL-04-15-A (26 October 2009) para 401; *Prosecutor v Krajišnik* (Judgment) IT-00-39-A (17 March 2009) para 675; see also E van Sliedregt, 'Joint Criminal Enterprise as a Pathway to Convicting Individuals for Genocide' (2007) 5 *JICJ* 184, 195 (explaining that while joint criminal enterprise connotes 'a close involvement in the commission of a crime', aiding and abetting 'constitutes mere facilitation'); for different approaches to sentencing of accomplices in international criminal law see Jackson (n 6) 88–91.

Chamber of the Special Court for Sierra Leone (SCSL) in *Taylor* confirmed that the formulation 'assist, encourage or lend moral support to the perpetration' is part and parcel of customary international law.[91] Conduct triggering aiding and abetting liability includes the provision of lethal, technical support, encouragement beyond mere presence at the crime scene, and sharing of information on the location of potential victims.[92]

Aiding and abetting have been considered as two distinct legal concepts in international criminal law, the former meaning 'giving assistance to someone' and the latter meaning 'facilitating the commission of an act by being sympathetic thereto'.[93] However, the Trial Chamber in *Tadić* seemed to consider 'aiding' and 'abetting' as part of a single notion, encompassing 'all acts of assistance by words or acts that lend encouragement or support, as long as the requisite intent is present'.[94] It appears that in the practice of the tribunals, 'the Prosecution has never been requested to specify in any of its indictments whether the accused had been charged in relation to one sort of assistance rather than the other'.[95] However, in a few cases, the accused was convicted only of abetting, which could suggest a disjunctive nature of the count of aiding or abetting.[96]

Importantly, the ad hoc tribunals' jurisprudence consistently reflects the position that actus reus of aiding and abetting need not occur during the act of the principal, but can take place before and after the fact.[97] However, if the assistance is given after the fact, a prior agreement between the principal and the accomplice 'at the time of the planning, preparation or execution of the crime' is required.[98]

The ad hoc tribunals have further upheld that the participation in a crime (and the ensuing liability) may be found in an omission.[99] Such a possibility was first raised by the ICTR Trial Chamber in the *Akayesu* case, which stated that 'aiding and abetting may consist of failing to act or refraining

[91] *Prosecutor v Taylor* (Judgment) SCSL-03-01-A (26 September 2013) para 362.

[92] *Prosecutor v Ntakirutimana* (Judgment) ICTR-96-10-A and ICTR-96-17-A (13 December 2004) paras 530–32; *Prosecutor v Blaškić* (Judgment) IT-95-14-A (29 July 2004) para 46.

[93] *Prosecutor v Akayesu* (n 60) para 484; *Prosecutor v Kayishema and Ruzindana* (Judgment) ICTR-95-1-T (21 May 1999) para 196; *Prosecutor v Ntakirutimana* (Judgment) ICTR-96-10-T and ICTR-96-17-T (21 February 2003) para 787.

[94] *Prosecutor v Tadić* (n 16) para 689.

[95] G Mettraux, *International Crimes and the Ad Hoc Tribunals* (Oxford, OUP, 2005) 284; *Prosecutor v Semanza* (n 86) para 384.

[96] *Prosecutor v Akayesu* (n 60) para 707; *Prosecutor v Musema* (n 76) para 908; *Prosecutor v Muhimana* (Judgment) ICTR-95-1B-T (28 April 2005) para 553.

[97] *Prosecutor v Delalić and others* (Judgment) IT-96-21-A (20 February 2001) para 352; *Prosecutor v Blaškić* (n 92) para 48; *Prosecutor v Ntagerura and others* (Judgment) ICTR-99-46-A (7 July 2006) para 372.

[98] *Prosecutor v Blagojević and Jokić* (Judgment) IT-02-60-T (17 January 2005) para 731; *Prosecutor v Blagojević and Jokić* (Judgment) IT-02-60-A (9 May 2007) para 180.

[99] *Prosecutor v Orić* (Judgment) IT-03-68-A (3 July 2008) para 523; *Prosecutor v Simić* (Judgment) IT-95-9-A (28 November 2006) paras 85–86; *Prosecutor v Seromba* (Judgment) ICTR-2001-66-A (12 March 2008) para 56.

from action'.[100] In 2009, the ICTY Appeals Chamber found *Mrkšić* liable for aiding and abetting exclusively on the basis of his omissions.[101] In the *Furundžija* case, the ICTY Trial Chamber held that 'presence, when combined with authority, can constitute assistance in the form of moral support'.[102] The German Supreme Court in the British Occupied Zone had previously referred to this doctrine as that of 'approving spectator'.[103]

The ad hoc tribunals have not provided further guidance as to the exhaustive list of circumstances which might give rise to liability for aiding and abetting on the basis of an omission.[104] Nevertheless, a review of case law reveals that in some circumstances a failure to act may amount to a 'tacit approval or encouragement' of the crime concerned and consequently trigger aiding and abetting liability.[105] In other cases, a failure to act may amount to an 'omission proper' resulting from the failure to perform one's legal duty to protect against the occurrence of harm.[106] The key requirement is the existence of a *duty to act*, which may have various sources. For instance, a duty to act may be founded in: (i) the laws and customs of war;[107] (ii) the defendant's position of authority;[108] (iii) domestic law;[109] or (iv) State's obligations under general international law.[110] Although there is no provision for omissions liability in the ICC Rome Statute,[111] it remains to be seen whether the ICC will use the case

[100] *Prosecutor v Akayesu* (n 60) para 548.

[101] *Prosecutor v Mrkšić* (Judgment) IT-95-13/1-A (5 May 2009) paras 71–73.

[102] *Prosecutor v Furundžija* (n 72) para 209; see also *Prosecutor v Kunarać, Kovać and Vuković* (Judgment) IT-96-23 and 96-23/1 (22 February 2001) para 393; *Prosecutor v Kayishema and Ruzindana* (n 93) para 202; *Prosecutor v Mpambara* (Judgment) ICTR-01-65-T (11 September 2006) para 22.

[103] See, eg *Urteil vom 10 August 1948 gegen K und A StS 18/48 ('Synagogue case')* (Judgment) 1 Entscheidungen (German Supreme Court Strafsenat) 53–56 (the accused was found guilty of the devastation of a synagogue on the basis of his presence at the crime-scene, combined with his status of authority); see also *Prosecutor v Furundžija* (n 72) para 205.

[104] *Prosecutor v Blaškić* (n 92) para 47; *Prosecutor v Brđanin* (Judgment) IT-99-36-A (3 April 2007) para 274; *Prosecutor v Ntagerura and others* (n 97) para 370; *Prosecutor v Rutaganira* (Judgment) ICTR-95-IC-T (14 May 2005) para 64.

[105] *Prosecutor v Brđanin* (n 104) para 273; see in particular Jackson (n 6) 98–120.

[106] *Prosecutor v Brđanin* (n 104) para 274; cf G Boas, 'Omission Liability at the International Criminal Tribunals—A Case for Reform' in S Darcy and J Powderly (eds), *Judicial Creativity at the International Criminal Tribunals* (Oxford, OUP, 2010) 219–23 (arguing that there is no support in customary international law for aiding and abetting liability arising out of omissions); see also K Ambos, *Der allgemeine Teil des Völkerstrafrechts—Ansätze einer Dogmatisierung* (Berlin, Duncker & Humblot, 2002) 667; M Duttweiler, 'Liability for Omission in International Criminal Law' (2006) 6 *ICLR* 1, 46.

[107] See, eg *Prosecutor v Vasiljević* (Judgment) IT-98-32-T (29 November 2002) para 62.

[108] *Prosecutor v Orić* (Judgment) IT-03-68-T (30 June 2006) para 304.

[109] *Prosecutor v Ntagerura and others* (Judgment) ICTR-99-46-T (25 February 2004) para 660.

[110] *Prosecutor v Rutaganira* (n 104) paras 78–82.

[111] cf 'Report of the Preparatory Committee for the Establishment of an International Criminal Court—Draft Statute for the International Criminal Court' (14 April 1998) UN Doc A/Conf.183/233 (former draft Art 28(1) on omissions liability was ultimately not included in the final version of the Rome Statute).

law on aiding and abetting liability by omission as developed by the ad hoc tribunals.[112]

In the recent years, important jurisprudential developments have taken place in relation to the addition of a requirement of 'specific direction' as part of aiding and abetting liability.[113] In *Perišić*, the ICTY Appeals Chamber overturned his earlier conviction, holding that aiding and abetting liability is subject to the requirement that the assistance rendered was 'specifically directed' at the criminal conduct.[114] The Appeals Chamber took account of temporal and geographic distance between the accused and the Army of the Republika Srpska (VRS) perpetrators of the crimes, and the general independence of VRS from the Yugoslav Army (VJ) of which Perišić was a chief of general staff at the relevant time.[115] Even though the Chamber acknowledged the provision of considerable and comprehensive aid to the VRS, it did not find that Perišić had specifically directed any such aid at relevant crimes:

> Assistance from one army to another army's war efforts is insufficient, in itself, to trigger individual criminal liability for individual aid providers absent proof that the relevant assistance was specifically directed towards criminal activities.[116]

Moreover, in their joint separate opinion in *Perišić* Judges Meron and Agius suggested that the requirement of specific direction could also play a role in the assessment of the mens rea.[117] The *Perišić* judgment, followed by the acquittals of Stanišić and Simatović, was met with criticism and even indignation, including among the ICTY judges.[118] It did not take long for

[112] See, eg *Prosecutor v Lubanga* (Decision on the Confirmation of Charges) ICC-01/04-01/06 (29 January 2007) paras 351–54; see also Duttweiler (n 106) 60; Jackson (n 6) 106–07.

[113] See, eg S Darcy, 'Assistance, Direction and Control: Untangling International Judicial Opinion on Individual and State Responsibility for War Crimes by Non-State Actors' (2014) 96 *IRRC* 243; NHB Jørgensen, 'State Responsibility for Aiding or Assisting International Crimes in the Context of the Arms Trade Treaty' (2014) 108 *AJIL* 722; M Aksenova, 'The Specific Direction Requirement for Aiding and Abetting: A Call for Revisiting Comparative Criminal Law' (2015) 4 *Cambridge J Intl & Comp L* 88.

[114] *Prosecutor v Perišić* (n 87) para 73; cf *Prosecutor v Mrkšić* (n 101) para 159; *Prosecutor v Lukić and Lukić* (Judgment) IT-98-32/1-A (4 December 2012) paras 424 ff; *Prosecutor v Blagojević and Jokić* (n 98) paras 188–89.

[115] *Prosecutor v Perišić* (n 87) para 49.

[116] ibid para 72; see also *Prosecutor v Perišić* (Judgment) IT-04-81-T (6 September 2011) Dissenting Opinion of Judge Moloto on Counts 1 to 4 and 9 to 12, paras 3–34.

[117] *Prosecutor v Perišić* (n 87) Joint Separate Opinion of Judges Meron and Agius 1, 3.

[118] *Prosecutor v Stanišić* (Judgment) IT-03-69-T (30 May 2013) Dissenting Opinion of Judge Picard 852, 866–67, para 2406; M Milanović, 'The Limits of Aiding and Abetting Liability: The ICTY Appeals Chamber Acquits Momcilo Perisic' www.ejiltalk.org/the-limits-of-aiding-and-abetting-liability-the-icty-appeals-chamber-acquits-momcilo-perisic/; JG Stewart, 'The ICTY Loses Its Way on Complicity—Part 1' www.opiniojuris.org/2013/04/03/guest-post-the-icty-loses-its-way-on-complicity-part-1/; JG Stewart, 'The ICTY Loses Its Way on Complicity—Part 2' www.opiniojuris.org/2013/04/03/guest-post-the-icty-loses-its-way-on-complicity-part-2/; see also, eg 'A Tribunal's Legal Stumble' *New York Times* (9 July 2013).

the SCSL Appeals Chamber in *Taylor* and the ICTY Appeals Chamber itself in *Šainović* to unequivocally reject the requirement of 'specific direction', after having provided a comprehensive analysis of customary international law.[119] It would seem that the requirement of specific direction was heavily fact-specific in *Perišić* and is not a factor in assessing either the actus reus or mens rea of the aiding and abetting liability under customary international law.[120]

Possibly, some analysis of remoteness or proximity may on certain facts be relevant to assessing whether the aid or assistance had a substantial effect on the commission of the crime, but it is not *a sine qua non* requirement.[121] The ICTY has on occasion adopted an approach from the ILC's Draft Code of Crimes according to which the contribution must have had a 'direct and substantial effect' on the commission of the offence.[122] The ILC did not clarify the distinction between 'direct' and 'substantial', stating that 'the form of participation of an accomplice must entail assistance which facilitates the commission of a crime in some significant way'.[123] Thus, the reference to 'direct' in the Draft Code of Crimes is 'misleading as it may imply that assistance needs to be tangible or to have a causal effect on the crime'.[124] In any event, most ICTY and ICTR authorities converge that the actus reus of aiding and abetting requires material assistance, encouragement or moral support which need to have a substantial impact on the commission of the principal offence—but not indispensable.[125]

ii. Mental Element (Mens Rea)

The Statutes of the ad hoc tribunals lack a general provision on the mental element, which has led each tribunal to formulate a particular mens rea for each crime and form of participation. In most instances, the interpretation of the mens rea required for complicity has been in conformity with the

[119] *Prosecutor v Taylor* (n 91) para 540; *Prosecutor v Šainović and others* (Judgment) IT-05-87-A (23 January 2014) para 1651; see also LN Sadat, 'Can the ICTY Šainović and Perišić Cases Be Reconciled?' (2014) 108 *AJIL* 475, 481–82.

[120] See Jackson (n 6) 80–85; Aksenova (n 113).

[121] Jørgensen (n 113) 743.

[122] ILC, 'Draft Code of Crimes Against the Peace and Security of Mankind' (1996) 2 (pt 2) *YBILC* 17; *Prosecutor v Tadić* (n 16) para 691; *Prosecutor v Delalić and others* (Judgment) IT-96-21-T (16 November 1998) para 326.

[123] ILC, 'Draft Code of Crimes Against the Peace and Security of Mankind' (n 122) 21, para 11.

[124] ibid; *Prosecutor v Furundžija* (n 72) para 232.

[125] *Prosecutor v Tadić* (n 88) para 229; see also *Prosecutor v Delalić and others* (n 97) para 352; *Prosecutor v Blaškić* (n 92) paras 45–46; *Prosecutor v Brđanin* (n 104) para 151; *Prosecutor v Musema* (n 76) para 126; *Prosecutor v Gacumbitsi* (Judgment) ICTR-01-64 (7 July 2006) para 140.

ILC Draft Code of Crimes, which in its Article 2(3)(d) affirms the criminal responsibility of an individual who '*knowingly* aids, abets or otherwise assists … in the commission of … a crime'.[126]

Generally, 'the requisite mental element is knowledge that the acts performed by the aider and abettor assist the commission of the specific crime of the principal'.[127] In some decisions, however, the liability has been limited to those situations in which the accomplice had intended to provide assistance, or at a minimum, accepted that such assistance would be possible or foreseeable consequence of his conduct.[128] As the ICTY put it in *Furundžija*:

> [A]ction which decisively encourages the perpetrator is sufficient to amount to assistance: the knowledge that he will receive assistance during or after the event encourages the perpetrator in the commission of the crime. From this perspective, willingness to provide assistance, when made known to the perpetrator, would also suffice, if the offer of help in fact encouraged or facilitated the commission of the crime by the main perpetrator.[129]

Thus, the requisite knowledge is met with the awareness that one's actions will aid in the perpetration of a crime. In the *Kunarać* case, for example, the ICTY Trial Chamber declared that the accomplice must 'take the conscious decision to act in the knowledge that he hereby supports the commission of the crime'.[130] In other words, international criminal law has construed the mental element as not requiring a sharing of the principal's intent.[131]

There remains some disagreement in respect of the level of knowledge required and how that level of knowledge should be assessed. For example, in *Blagojević*, the ICTY Appeals Chamber found that the accused's awareness of facts related to the forcible transfer operation was insufficient

[126] ILC (n 122); *Prosecutor v Furundžija* (n 72) paras 237–41; *Prosecutor v Tadić* (n 88) para 229.

[127] *Prosecutor v Tadić* (n 88) para 229; see also *Prosecutor v Kunarać, Kovać and Vuković* (n 102) para 392; *Prosecutor v Krnojelać* (Judgment) IT-97-25-T (15 March 2002) para 90; *Prosecutor v Aleksovski* (Judgment) IT-95-14/1-A (25 March 2000) paras 162–63; *Prosecutor v Krnojelać* (Judgment) IT-97-25-A (17 September 2003) para 33; *Prosecutor v Kordič and Čerkez* (Judgment) IT-95-14/2-T (26 February 2001) para 399; *Prosecutor v Simić* (n 99) para 86; *Prosecutor v Fofana and Kondewa* (Judgment) SCSL 04-14-T (2 August 2007) para 145; *Prosecutor v Ntakirutimana* (n 92) para 501.

[128] *Prosecutor v Blaškić* (Judgment) IT-95-14-T (3 March 2000) para 286; *Prosecutor v Bagilishema* (n 76) para 32.

[129] *Prosecutor v Furundžija* (n 72) para 230.

[130] *Prosecutor v Kunarać, Kovać and Vuković* (n 102) para 392.

[131] ibid; see also *Prosecutor v Delalić and others* (n 122) para 328; *Prosecutor v Mrkšić* (Judgment) IT-95-13-T (27 September 2007) para 556; *Prosecutor v Boškoski and Tarčulovski* (Judgment) IT-04-82-T (10 July 2008) para 403; *Prosecutor v Strugar* (Judgment) IT-01-42-T (31 January 2005) para 333; *Prosecutor v Ntagerura and others* (n 97) para 370; *Prosecutor v Seromba* (n 99) para 56; cf *Prosecutor v Orić* (n 108) para 288 ('the aider and abettor must have "double intent", namely both with regard to the furthering effect of his own contribution and the intentional completion of the crime by the principal perpetrator').

to prove complicity in genocide in the absence of knowledge of mass killings at Srebrenica.[132] Conversely, in the *Furundžija* case, the ICTY Trial Chamber asserted that:

> [I]t is not necessary that the aider and abettor should know the precise crime that was intended and which in the event was committed. *If he is aware that one of a number of crimes will probably be committed, and one of those crimes is in fact committed, he has intended to facilitate the commission of that crime, and is guilty as an aider and abettor.*[133] (emphasis added)

The ICTY Appeal Chambers in the *Blaškić* and *Simić* cases revisited these contradictory interpretations of the degree of the knowledge that is required.[134] In the latter case, it was held that:

> The requisite *mens rea* for aiding and abetting is knowledge that the acts performed by the aider and abettor assist in the commission of the specific crime of the principal perpetrator. The aider and abettor must be *aware of the essential elements of the crime which was ultimately committed by the principal*. In relation to the crime of persecutions, an offence with a specific intent, *he must thus be aware not only of the crime whose perpetration he is facilitating but also of the discriminatory intent of the perpetrators of that crime.* He *need not share the intent but must be aware of the discriminatory context in which the crime is to be committed and know that his support or encouragement has a substantial effect on its perpetration.*[135] (emphasis added)

The above analysis of the ICTY and ICTR jurisprudence on the question of mens rea of aiding and abetting can be summarised as follows. An accomplice needs to know that his aid or assistance will contribute to the commission of the principal offence. However, he need not know to what extent his aid or assistance will contribute to that offence. In principle, he must also be aware of the principal offence and its essential elements (but not all of its elements). If the principal offence requires specific intent, the accomplice must be aware of the fact that the principal has the requisite intent to commit that offence; however, the accomplice need not share the intent of the principal.[136]

iii. Complicity in the ICC Rome Statute

The controversies surrounding the material and mental elements of accomplice liability have not been diminished by the adoption of the Rome

[132] *Prosecutor v Blagojević and Jokić* (n 98) paras 119–24.

[133] *Prosecutor v Furundžija* (n 72) para 246; *Prosecutor v Blaškić* (n 128) para 287; *Prosecutor v Kvočka and others* (Judgment) IT-98-30/1-T (2 November 2001) para 255; *Prosecutor v Naletilić and Martinović* (Judgment) IT-98-34-T (31 March 2003) para 63; *Prosecutor v Brđanin* (n 77) para 272; *Prosecutor v Strugar* (n 131) para 350.

[134] *Prosecutor v Blaškić* (n 92) paras 45 and 50; *Prosecutor v Simić* (n 99) para 86.

[135] *Prosecutor v Simić* (n 99) para 86.

[136] *Prosecutor v Krstić* (n 86) para 140; *Prosecutor v Blagojević and Jokić* (n 98) para 782.

Statute of the ICC.[137] However, the Statute has generally brought some clarity regarding the distinction between principals and accomplices, subjecting the former category to the test of control over the crime.[138] As for complicity proper, Article 25(3)(c) of the Statute provides:

> (3) In accordance with this Statute, a person shall be criminally responsible and liable for punishment for a crime within the jurisdiction of the Court if that person …
>
> (c) For the purpose of facilitating the commission of such a crime, aids, abets or otherwise assists in the commission or its attempted commission, including providing the means for its commission.[139]

Pursuant to this provision, aiding and abetting covers any act that contributes to the commission of a crime.[140] On the one hand, the accomplice need not make a direct or substantial contribution to the commission of the crime. On the other hand, the accomplice's conduct must be 'for the purpose of facilitating the commission of such a crime', which implies a higher threshold of mens rea than knowledge or awareness, as applied by the ICTY and ICTR.[141] The intent and knowledge tests are clearly set out in Article 30 of the ICC Statute, which reads as follows:

> Article 30
>
> Mental element
>
> 1. Unless otherwise provided, a person shall be criminally responsible and liable for punishment for a crime within the jurisdiction of the Court only if the material elements are committed with intent and knowledge.

[137] See, eg G Werle, 'Individual Criminal Responsibility in Article 25 ICC Statute' (2007) 5 *JICJ* 953; V Militello, 'The Personal Nature of Individual Criminal Responsibility and the ICC Statute' (2007) 5 *JICJ* 941.

[138] ICC Rome Statute (n 2) Art 25(3)(a); *Prosecutor v Lubanga* (Judgment) ICC-01/04-01/06 (14 March 2012) paras 977 ('Under Article 25(3)(a), an individual can be convicted of committing a crime: (i) individually; (ii) jointly with another; or (iii) through another person') and 1005 ('the accused does not need to be present at the scene of the crime, so long as he exercised jointly with others, control over the crime'); *Prosecutor v Lubanga* (n 112) paras 326–41; *Prosecutor v Katanga and Chui* (Decision on the Confirmation of Charges) ICC-01/04/01/07 (30 September 2008) paras 480–89.

[139] ICC Rome Statute (n 2) Art 25(3)(c).

[140] Eser (n 71); Werle (n 137).

[141] K Ambos, 'Article 25: Individual Criminal Responsibility' in O Triffterer (ed), *Commentary on the Rome Statute of the International Criminal Court* (2nd edn, Oxford, Hart Publishing, 2008) 760; R Cryer et al, *An Introduction to International Criminal Law and Procedure*, vol 2 (Cambridge, CUP, 2010) 376–77; cf Werle (n 137) 969 (suggesting in respect of Art 25(3)(c) of the Rome Statute of the ICC that 'consonant with the jurisprudence of the ad hoc Tribunals, it is not necessary that the accomplice share particular mental elements possessed by the perpetrator, such as the special intent to destroy required for genocide. It suffices that he or she knows of such intent'); for different views on mens rea as expressed in the Preparatory Committee to the Rome Conference see MC Bassiouni, *The Legislative History of the International Criminal Court*, vol 1 (Ardsley New York, Transnational, 2005) 194.

2. For the purposes of this article, a person has intent where:
   (a) In relation to conduct, that person means to engage in the conduct;
   (b) In relation to a consequence, that person means to cause that consequence or is aware that it will occur in the ordinary course of events.
3. For the purposes of this article, 'knowledge' means awareness that a circumstance exists or a consequence will occur in the ordinary course of events. 'Know' and 'knowingly' shall be construed accordingly.[142]

This creates a rather high threshold for liability to arise. Schabas has argued that Article 30 poses certain problems for Article 25(3)(c).[143] In his view, the purposes underlying abetting (moral encouragement or support) can be inferred from the speech or expression of the abettor.[144] By contrast, the additional proof of mens rea may need to be established in cases of aiding.[145]

Accordingly, if for instance an 'arms dealer knew weapons that he sold to a country were destined to be used for the commission of international crimes, liability would not arise if the sole purpose for selling them was making profit'.[146] As Clapham puts it:

> [A]t least for international crimes within the ICC Statute, the Statute defines the boundaries of complicity in a wide way, casting the net well beyond the principal perpetrators. The objective element seems to require little more than assistance, while the subjective element seems to require *a purpose to facilitate the crime* as well as *knowledge that the assistance will assist in the offence*.[147] (emphasis added)

D. Parallels to Complicity in the Law of International Responsibility

In sum, there are four possible parallels that can be drawn from an overview of the operation of aiding and abetting liability under international criminal law for the concept of complicity under general international law.

[142] ICC Rome Statute (n 2) Art 30.

[143] WA Schabas, *The International Criminal Court: A Commentary on the Rome Statute* (Oxford, OUP, 2010) 436; see also S Finnin, 'Mental Elements under Article 30 of the Rome Statute of the International Criminal Court: A Comparative Analysis' (2012) 61 *ICLQ* 325, 336 ff; C Plomp, 'Aiding and Abetting: The Responsibility of Business Leaders under the Rome Statute of the International Criminal Court' (2014) 30 *Utrecht J Intl & Eur L* 4, 13–15.

[144] Schabas (n 143) 436.

[145] ibid.

[146] Cryer et al (n 141) 377.

[147] A Clapham, 'On Complicity' in M Henzelin and R Roth (eds), *Le droit pénal à l'épreuve de l'internationalisation* (Paris, LGDJ, 2002) 255; see also A Clapham, 'Extending International Criminal Law beyond the Individual to Corporations and Armed Opposition Groups' (2008) 6 *JICJ* 899; Plomp (n 143).

First, the constituent elements of complicity in international criminal law strongly resemble those found in the law of international responsibility, as we will see in the following sections and chapters. In the same way as the ILC, the ad hoc tribunals have distinguished the liability for aiding and abetting from co-perpetration. Notably, the material content of aiding and abetting under international criminal law comprises the idea of encouragement or incitement. Incitement most likely comes closer to instigation as developed by the ad hoc tribunals, or alternatively falls within the concept of 'solicitation or inducement' under Article 25(3)(b) of the ICC Rome Statute.[148] Conversely, the ILC did not consider it to be appropriate for the responsibility for complicity of States to cover encouragement or incitement for lack of sufficient practice. This is so notwithstanding numerous instruments that specifically prohibit incitement.[149] However, the rationale of limited practice did not prevent the ILC from including aid or assistance, direction and control, and coercion as forms of international responsibility. In most scenarios, coercion, for instance, could be regarded as a mere continuation of encouragement, instigation or incitement. In the author's view, had the ILC clarified that responsibility of one actor in connection with the act of another accrues irrespective of the form of contribution to that act, this could have served as a strong incentive for States and international organisations to respect their international obligations.[150]

Second, aiding and abetting liability under international criminal law has been limited to situations where the aid or assistance *substantially* facilitates the commission of the offence. The ICC Rome Statute omits the requirement of substantial impact and prescribes that the accused must facilitate the commission of the principal offence.[151] As we shall see in

[148] ICC Rome Statute (n 2) Art 25(3)(b); Werle (n 137) 966–67; for the application of the doctrine of instigation see *Prosecutor v Semanza* (n 86) para 381; *Prosecutor v Kvočka and others* (n 133) para 252; *Prosecutor v Kordić and Čerkez* (Judgment) IT-95-14/2-A (17 December 2000) paras 29–32; see generally Jackson (n 6) 66–69.

[149] ILC, 'Report of the International Law Commission on the Work of Its 30th Session (8 May–28 July 1978)' (1978) UN Doc A/33/10, reproduced in (1978) 2 (pt 2) *YBILC* 1, 100–01 (former draft Art 27 commentary); see also C Dominicé, 'Attribution of Conduct to Multiple States and the Implication of a State in the Act of Another State' in J Crawford et al (eds), *The Law of International Responsibility* (Oxford, OUP, 2010) 285; cf B Graefrath, E Oeser and PA Steiniger, *Völkerrechtliche Verantwortlichkeit der Staaten* (Berlin, Staatsverlag der DDR, 1977) 64; cf Genocide Convention (n 26) Art III(c); Convention on the Suppression and Punishment of the Crime of Apartheid (adopted 30 November 1973; entered into force 18 July 1976) 1015 UNTS 243, Art 4(a); Convention on the Elimination of All Forms of Racial Discrimination (adopted 21 December 1965; entered into force 4 January 1969) 660 UNTS 195, Art 4.

[150] On the conceptual and practical issues with this distinction of scope of responsibility see *Prosecutor v Taylor* (n 91) paras 344 ff; see also A Nollkaemper, 'The Charles Taylor Judgment: Disconnecting the Responsibilities of Presidents and States' www.sharesproject.nl/the-charles-taylor-judgment-disconnecting-the-responsibilities-of-presidents-and-states/.

[151] ICC Rome Statute (n 2) Art 25(3)(c).

the following section, the ILC's codification constrained the scope of responsibility for complicity to situations where the aid or assistance has *significantly contributed* to the commission of an internationally wrongful act, yet this threshold remains uncertain in practice.

Third, the ad hoc tribunals have accepted that the aid or assistance need not be direct or positive. To trigger individual liability aid or assistance can be found in an omission and can be given through indirect means and channels by which the accomplice facilitates the principal offence. As we shall see in the next chapters, this is certainly one of the most obscure areas in the law of international responsibility.[152] Neither the provisions of the ARSIWA and ARIO nor their commentaries foreclose omissions as constituting complicity.[153] However, the ICJ seems to have excluded omissions from the scope of responsibility under Article 16 ARSIWA.[154]

Fourth, the practice of the ad hoc tribunals shows that the aiding and abetting liability generally requires evidence of knowledge of the principal offence (though this can be deduced from the surrounding circumstances). This is all the more interesting given that for most offences, criminal law requires proof of mens rea beyond a reasonable doubt. Logic demands that international responsibility for complicity, which is much closer to a civil conception of responsibility, should require an equivalent or even more lenient cognitive requirement on the part of the aiding or assisting State and a relaxed standard of proof. Surprisingly, it does not. Responsibility for complicity in the wrongful act, as construed by the ILC's Commentary to Article 16 ARSIWA and some scholars, is conditioned by a sort of double intent.[155] Simply put, according to such a restrictive reading of the provision, a complicit State needs *to intend* to facilitate the commission of the principal wrongful act and need to *know of the intent* of the aided or assisted State to commit an internationally wrongful act.

III. CODIFICATION OF COMPLICITY IN THE LAW OF INTERNATIONAL RESPONSIBILITY

In parallel to its consolidation in international criminal law, the ILC codified complicity as a form of responsibility of one State or international organisation in connection with the wrong committed by another State or international organisation. The evolution of complicity in the

152 HP Aust, *Complicity and the Law of State Responsibility* (Cambridge, CUP, 2011) 209.

153 cf J Crawford, *State Responsibility: The General Part* (Cambridge, CUP, 2013) 403–05.

154 *Bosnia Genocide (Merits)* (n 2) 222, para 432.

155 ARSIWA (n 2) 66, para 5 (Art 16 Commentary); Crawford (n 153) 408; Aust (n 152) 238; cf Jackson (n 6) 160–61; V Lowe, 'Responsibility for the Conduct of Other States' (2002) 101 *Japanese J Intl L & Diplomacy* 1, 8.

law of responsibility is an example of the tension between bilateralism and solidarity, between objective character of responsibility and reminiscence of fault, between the presumption of good faith in the conduct of subjects and the need to ensure the observance of international obligations. But before venturing into these tensions that have shaped the conception of responsibility for complicity in general international law, a few preliminary remarks on the law of international responsibility itself are apposite.

It is a truism by now that Herbert Hart's distinction between primary and secondary rules lies at the heart of the modern conception of the law of responsibility.[156] In essence, while the primary rules define the content of the legal obligations, the secondary rules deal with the consequences of the breach of primary rules and set out the criteria for responsibility to accrue.

Already during the ILC's predecessors' efforts in codifying responsibility such as the 1929 Harvard Law School project on the 'Responsibility of the State for Injuries in its Territory to the Person or Property of Foreigners',[157] the distinction of 'primary and secondary' rules started gaining momentum.[158] However, the initial attempts at codification of the law of responsibility, including that undertaken by the ILC under the leadership of the Special Rapporteur García-Amador, often mixed these two categories of rules by trying to elaborate the substantive norms of treatment of aliens.[159]

It was only in 1963 that Roberto Ago as a newly appointed Special Rapporteur on State responsibility suggested that the ILC should take a more rigorous approach to the codification of the law of responsibility in order to avoid conflating distinct categories of rules of international law.[160]

[156] HLA Hart, *The Concept of Law* (2nd edn, Oxford, OUP, 1994) 79–99.

[157] '1929 Draft on International Responsibility of the State for Injuries Caused in Its Territory to the Persons or Property of Aliens, Prepared by Harvard Law School', reproduced in (1956) 2 *YBILC* 229.

[158] ILC, 'Report of the International Law Commission on the Work of Its 15th Session (6 May–12 July 1963) with Annexes' (1963) UN Doc A/5509, reproduced in (1963) 2 *YBILC* 187, 231 (Briggs) (noting that the 1929 Harvard Law School project 'employed the term "responsibility" in more than one sense, for the most part it correctly treated State responsibility as a secondary obligation, having its source in the non-observance of a primary obligation under international law').

[159] See, eg '1929 Draft on International Responsibility of the State for Injuries Caused in Its Territory to the Persons or Property of Aliens, Prepared by Harvard Law School' (n 157); '1961 Draft Convention on the International Responsibility of States for Injuries to Aliens, Prepared by Harvard Law School', reproduced in (1969) 2 *YBILC* 142; FV Garcia-Amador, 'First Report on State Responsibility' (20 January 1956) UN Doc A/CN.4/96, reproduced in (1956) 2 *YBILC* 173; for other codification projects of responsibility undertaken in the 20th century see R Ago, 'First Report on State Responsibility' (1969) UN Doc A/CN.4/217 and Add 1, reproduced in (1969) 2 *YBILC* 126, 141–55.

[160] ILC (n 158) 227; see also E David, 'Primary and Secondary Rules' in J Crawford et al (eds), *The Law of International Responsibility* (Oxford, OUP, 2010) 28; N Bobbio, 'Nouvelles réflexions sur les normes primaires et secondaires' in N Bobbio (ed), *Études de théorie du droit*

According to Ago, the Commission's masterplan consisted in codifying 'the whole of responsibility, and nothing but responsibility'.[161] Responsibility would only contain secondary rules, an epilogue of the breach so to speak. Ago formulated the distinction between 'primary' and 'secondary' rules as follows:

> The Commission agreed on the need to concentrate its study on the determination of the principles which govern the responsibility of States for internationally wrongful acts, maintaining a strict distinction between this task and the task of defining the rules that place obligations on States, the violation of which may generate responsibility. Consideration of the various kinds of obligations placed on States in international law and, in particular, a grading of such obligations according to their importance to the international community, may have to be treated as a necessary element in assessing the gravity of an internationally wrongful act and as a criterion for determining the consequences it should have. But this must not obscure *the essential fact that it is one thing to define a rule and the content of the obligation it imposes, and another to determine whether that obligation has been violated and what should be the consequence of the violation. Only the second aspect of the matter comes within the sphere of responsibility proper* …[162] (emphasis added)

Critiques of this two-street view thrive in the literature on the law of international responsibility.[163] The main tenets of the critique can be summarised as follows:

> It has been said, for example, that the *'secondary' rules are mere abstractions, of no practical use*; that the assumption of generally applicable secondary rules overlooks the possibility that particular substantive rules, or substantive rules within a particular field of international law, may generate their own specific secondary rules, and that the draft articles themselves fail to apply the distinction consistently, thereby demonstrating its artificiality.[164] (emphasis added)

According to the Commission, any re-consideration of this distinction was prejudicial to the completion of the codification project as a whole.[165]

(Paris, LGDJ, 1988) 109 (suggesting that the secondary rules impose no obligation as such: 'contrairement aux normes primaires, elles ne créent aucune obligation').

161 ILC (n 158) 252.

162 ILC, 'Report of the International Law Commission on the Work of Its 22nd Session (4 May–10 July 1970)' (1970) UN Doc A/8010/Rev 1, reproduced in (1970) 2 *YBILC* 271, 306, para 66.

163 See especially P Allott, 'State Responsibility and the Unmaking of International Law' (1988) 29 *Harvard Intl LJ* 1; see also J Combacau and D Alland, 'Primary and Secondary Rules in the Law of State Responsibility: Categorizing International Obligations' (1985) 16 *Netherlands YBIL* 81; A Marschik, 'Too Much Order? The Impact of Special Secondary Norms on the Unity and Efficacy of the International Legal System' (1998) 9 *EJIL* 212.

164 Crawford (n 153) 64–65; J Crawford, 'The ILC's Articles on Responsibility of States for Internationally Wrongful Acts: A Retrospect' (2002) 96 *AJIL* 874, 878 ('[ARSIWA] are not a repository for all possible secondary rules'); see also J Crawford, 'First Report on State Responsibility' (1998) UN Doc A/CN.4/490 and Add 1-7, reproduced in (1998) 2 (pt 1) *YBILC* 1, 6, para 14.

165 Crawford, 'First Report' (n 164) 6, para 15.

Although the distinction between primary and secondary norms is artificial, the central assumption was that the ARSIWA and subsequently ARIO would provide for the lowest common denominators, which then may be supplemented by demands of a primary norm. In the process, it was inevitable that the Commission's project of 'rules about rules' implied a certain cross-reference to the existing primary rules. However, as long as the Commission did not attempt to deal with the content of those primary rules, it remained faithful to its pre-established mandate.

As will transpire throughout this study, complicity has posed particular challenges in keeping up to this artificial distinction. As proposed by Roberto Ago in 1978, the terms of the original draft of the rule on responsibility for complicity were conceptually much closer to imposing a primary norm. The wording of these earlier drafts of the provision, as adopted in the 1996 ARSIWA Draft on first reading, imposed a particular standard of conduct on States, failing which they would incur responsibility. The responsibility of the aiding or assisting State arose regardless of whether it was bound by the principal obligation breached. However, on ARSIWA's second reading, the provision was effectively limited to meet the concerns of dogmatic primary/secondary norm distinction.[166] Special Rapporteur James Crawford revised the supposed deficiencies (in this author's view quite the opposite) of the earlier drafts of the rule in what later became Article 16 ARSIWA.[167] As we shall see in chapters four and five, the elimination of the alleged deficiencies of the earlier draft did not solve all of the ambiguities in the constituent elements of responsibility for complicity. However, it did effectively limit the practical effect and utility of responsibility for complicity in international law.

A. Complicity's Big Bang (Ago)

It would not be an exaggeration to say that Special Rapporteur Roberto Ago masterminded the modern conception of the law of responsibility, and complicity's place within it. Under his leadership, the ILC embarked upon the examination of responsibility for complicity as part of a broader phenomenon of participation of a State in the wrongful act of another

[166] For a critique of the distinction between primary and secondary rules see, eg Combacau and Alland (n 163); Marschik (n 163).

[167] cf, eg CJ Tams, 'All's Well When It Ends Well: Comments on the ILC's Articles on State Responsibility' (2002) 62 *ZaöRV* 759, 793–94 (arguing that the second reading brought in important and necessary corrections to the scope of responsibility for complicity—suggesting that under the 1996 draft responsibility for aid and assistance 'was broader than responsibility for the principal act').

State. According to Ago, international law was increasingly being challenged by cases where:

> [T]he existence of an internationally wrongful act unquestionably committed by a State, attributable to it as such and without the slightest doubt involving its international responsibility, is accompanied by the existence of participation by another State, or by another subject of international law, in the commission by the first State of its own act.[168]

Several distinctions were drawn between possible forms of participation of one State in the wrongful act of another and cognate concepts that trigger direct responsibility in international law or result in multiple attribution.

First, the ILC excluded the situation of State organs that had been placed at the disposal of another State.[169] The actions or omissions of a foreign organ performing a function in the exercise of the receiving State—when acting under its authority, direction or control—are acts of that State and not of the State to which the organ originally belonged.[170]

Second, the ILC drew a distinction between situations in which a State fails to prevent the occurrence of the breach on its territory and those situations in which it places its territory at the disposal of another State with the intention to subvert a neighbouring State.[171] It was only in the latter case that it was appropriate to speak of complicity. Ago believed that:

> [A] case of 'participation' in the internationally wrongful act of another *cannot be found in the fact or rather the sole fact* that a State failed to take the preventive or repressive measures required of it with respect to actions committed in its territory by an organ of another State to the detriment of the third State.[172] (emphasis added)

Third, the ILC concluded that there can be no question of the participation of a State in the internationally wrongful act of another State where a single wrongful act can be attributed in parallel to several States, or where identical internationally wrongful acts are committed in concert by two or more States, each acting through its own organs.[173]

Applying the above conceptual delimitations, the ILC identified three cases in which the 'participation' by a State in an internationally wrongful act committed by another State could arise.[174] First, the ILC referred to cases in which State A advises or incites State B to commit a breach of

[168] R Ago, 'Seventh Report on State Responsibility' (1978) UN Doc A/CN.4/307 and Add 1-2 and Corr 1-2, reproduced in (1978) 2 (pt 1) *YBILC* 31, 52, para 52.

[169] See ibid 53, para 56; now ARSIWA (n 2) Art 6.

[170] Ago, 'Seventh Report' (n 168) 53, para 56.

[171] ibid 35–36, para 15.

[172] ibid 53, para 57.

[173] ibid 53–54, paras 56–59.

[174] ibid 54, para 61.

its international obligation.[175] Second, it referred to cases in which State A exerts pressure on State B to commit the breach.[176] Third, the Commission identified situations in which State A aids or assists State B in the commission of an internationally wrongful act by the latter.[177]

It was the latter category of situations that the ILC considered to be the only real case of 'complicity'.[178] In such situations, the State in question does not merely incite or encourage another State, whether by oral or written communications, to commit an internationally wrongful act. Nor does it coerce another State to commit an internationally wrongful act. Instead, the State deliberately provides tangible means to another State, which facilitate the commission of an internationally wrongful act by the latter.

As a result, Ago proposed the following draft rule on responsibility for complicity in his 1978 report to the ILC:

> Article 25
>
> Complicity of a State in the Internationally Wrongful Act of another State
>
> The fact that a State renders assistance to another State to commit an international offence against a third State constitutes an internationally wrongful act of the State, which thus becomes an accessory to the commission of the offence and incurs international responsibility thereby, even if the conduct in question would not otherwise be internationally wrongful.[179]

Following discussions within the ILC and the UNGA Sixth Committee, Ago proposed a new iteration of the rule—the former draft Article 27, which the Commission adopted with no changes on first reading of the ARSIWA in 1996:

> Article 27
>
> Aid or Assistance by a State to another State for the Commission of an Internationally Wrongful Act
>
> Aid or assistance by a State to another State, if it is established that it is rendered for the commission of an internationally wrongful act carried out by the latter, itself constitutes an internationally wrongful act, even if, taken alone, such aid or assistance would not constitute the breach of an international obligation.[180]

[175] ibid 54–56, paras 62–65; see also *Military and Paramilitary Activities in and against Nicaragua (Nicaragua v United States)* (Merits) [1986] ICJ Rep 14, 129, para 255; ibid Dissenting Opinion of Judge Schwebel 259, 388–89, para 259 ('Customary international law does not know the delict of "encouragement"').

[176] Ago, 'Seventh Report' (n 168) 55–56, para 64.

[177] ibid 54, para 61.

[178] ibid 57, para 70.

[179] ibid 60, para 77.

[180] ILC (n 149) 99.

Notably, the terms 'complicity' and 'accessory' in the original draft Article 25 were discarded in favour of the term 'aid or assistance' because the provision was not intended to prohibit certain acts that are commonly considered to constitute complicity in domestic law, namely moral aid and incitement.[181] The Commission emphasised that the notion of complicity in State responsibility was far from having the same meaning as the one attributed to it under domestic legal systems.[182] For instance, at the UNGA Sixth Committee, Nigeria 'endorsed the Commission's decision to discard the concepts of "complicity" and "accessory" as pertaining to the field of municipal law'.[183]

The substance of the originally proposed rule remained in draft Article 27, albeit considerably weakened. In Ago's view, the core element of the rule on complicity was the link between the conduct adopted by a State—which in isolation may not in certain cases be internationally wrongful—and the act committed by another State, the wrongfulness of which has been established.[184] Complicity of a State in the commission of an internationally wrongful act by another amounted to an internationally wrongful act in itself.[185]

Ago's conception of responsibility for complicity prompted ruminations from within the ILC, States and in doctrine. A common criticism was that to conceive of complicity as an autonomous wrongful act for the purposes of responsibility equated to generating a primary norm prohibiting complicity in any breach of international law. For example, Quentin-Baxter, a former member of the Commission, opined that:

> The Article as it stood, more than any Article the Commission had adopted, seemed to leap the barrier between secondary and primary rules. Nowhere else in the draft had the Commission said that a particular kind of action constituted an internationally wrongful act of a State. Superficially at least, that statement looked like the identification of a primary rule.[186]

In response, Ago believed and persuaded his peers that 'the Commission should not hesitate to leap that barrier whenever necessary'.[187] At that time, complicity was still part of progressive development of international law. The ILC ultimately concluded that the real purpose and added value of the rule on responsibility for complicity was the recognition that

[181] ibid 100–01, para 5–7 (Former Draft Art 27 Commentary).

[182] ibid 102, para 12 (Former Draft Art 27 Commentary).

[183] UNGA, 'Sixth Committee, Summary Record of the 42nd Meeting' (9 November 1978) UN Doc A/C.6/33/SR.42, 12, para 41 (Nigeria).

[184] Ago, 'Seventh Report' (n 168) 52, para 52.

[185] ibid.

[186] ILC, 'Summary Record of the 1518th Meeting' (17 July 1978), reproduced in (1978) 1 *YBILC* 232, 236, para 32 (Quentin-Baxter).

[187] ILC, 'Summary Record of the 1519th Meeting' (18 July 1978), reproduced in (1978) 1 *YBILC* 237, 240, para 27 (Ago).

'[e]ven if the State could not itself be said to have committed a given internationally wrongful act, it might have committed a separate internationally wrongful act by facilitating the commission of the first'.[188] Two different types of situations were envisaged.

The first situation would be when State A knowingly supplies arms to State B in breach of an embargo regime imposed by a resolution of the United Nations Security Council (UNSC). Such conduct constitutes a direct violation of the relevant UNSC resolution and on that basis alone engages State A's responsibility. The second situation is where State A's supply of arms is not prohibited by a primary norm, or where State B goes on to commit other parallel breaches of international law with the use of State A's arms. In this regard, the ILC was of the view that knowledge or awareness of the specific purpose for which State B intends to use them is vital for ascertaining responsibility for aiding and assisting. This means that State A needs to be aware of the intention of State B to commit a particular wrongful act.[189]

The requirement of intent although not expressly reflected in the original draft Article 25 and former draft Article 27 of the rule, ultimately appeared in the ILC's Commentary, suggesting that aid or assistance must be rendered

> with the specific object of facilitating the commission of the principal internationally wrongful act in question. Accordingly, it is not sufficient for it to be possible for aid or assistance provided without such intention to be used by the recipient State for unlawful purposes, or for the State providing aid or assistance to be aware of the eventual possibility of such use. The aid or assistance must in fact be rendered with a view to its use in committing the principal internationally wrongful act. Nor is it sufficient that this intention be 'presumed'; as the article emphasized, it must be 'established'. Unless these essential requirements are fulfilled, an act which *per se* is lawful cannot become an unlawful act, and a possible wrongful act cannot be invested with additional wrongfulness.[190]

According to Ago:

> The very idea of 'complicity' in the internationally wrongful act of another *necessarily presupposes an intent to collaborate in the commission of an act of this kind,* and hence … *knowledge of the specific purpose* for which the State receiving certain supplies intends to use them. Without this condition, there can be no question of complicity.[191] (emphasis added)

[188] ILC (n 186) 237, para 33 (Quentin-Baxter).

[189] See Ago, 'Seventh Report' (n 168) 58–59, para 73 (referring to several contemporaneous examples of alleged complicity in the wrongful acts).

[190] ILC (n 149) 104, para 18 (Former Draft Art 27 Commentary).

[191] Ago, 'Seventh Report' (n 168) 58, para 72; for contemporaneous reactions to the idea of intent as part of responsibility for complicity see, eg B Graefrath, 'Complicity in the Law of International Responsibility' (1996) 2 *RBDI* 370, 371–72; J Quigley, 'Complicity in International Law: A New Direction in the Law of State Responsibility' (1987) 57 *British YBIL* 77;

In terms of its material content, the ILC examined international practice deriving from primary norms, and stressed that 'aid or assistance must have the effect of making it *materially* easier for the State receiving the aid or assistance in question to commit an internationally wrongful act'.[192] One of the most frequently cited examples of complicity was and still remains today that of a State placing its territory at the disposal of another State to make it possible, or at least easier, for it to commit an offence against a third State.[193] In this context, Article 3(f) of the UNGA Resolution 3314 (XXIX) prohibits aggression, including

> the action of a State in allowing its territory, which it has placed at the disposal of another State, to be used by that other State for perpetrating an act of aggression against a third State.[194]

The Commission also noted that there was a range of possible content and degrees of assistance triggering responsibility. Thus, for example, complicity in an act of aggression could result from the provision of land, sea, air transport, or contributing troops.[195] Another classic example of complicity is when a State supplies another State with weapons to attack a third State, and those weapons are then used to support a regime of apartheid, to maintain a colonial domination by force or to commit genocide.[196] The ILC noted that there might be situations of complicity in the commission of offences that might be considered atypical or less serious such as the closure of an international waterway, abduction of persons on foreign soil, or destruction of property belonging to nationals of a third country.[197]

In sum, in this author's view, Ago's Big Bang consisted of presenting a far-reaching rule on responsibility for complicity, which would reflect the legal interests of third parties in the respect of international obligations, moving beyond the monolithic view of the breach.[198] The notion of

E Klein, 'Beihilfe zum Völkerrechtsdelikt' in I von Münch (ed), *Staatsrecht, Völkerrecht, Europarecht: Festschrift für Hans-Jürgen Schlochauer zum 75. Geburtstag am 28. März 1981* (Berlin, Walter de Gruyter, 1981).

192 ILC, 'Report of the International Law Commission on the Work of Its 30th Sess (n 149) 104, para 17 (former draft Art 27 commentary).

193 Ago, 'Seventh Report' (n 168) 58, para 71; for the example of indirect aggression see ILC, 'Summary Record of the 1312th Meeting' (20 May 1975), reproduced in (1975) 1 *YBILC* 41, 44, para 13 (Ustor); ILC, 'Summary Record of the 1313th Meeting' (21 May 1975), reproduced in (1975) 1 *YBILC* 46, 47, para 4 (Ushakov).

194 UNGA, 'Res 3314 (XXIX) (Declaration on Aggression)' (14 December 1974) UN Doc A/RES/3314, Art 3(f).

195 Ago, 'Seventh Report' (n 168) 58, para 71.

196 ILC (n 149) 102, para 13 (former draft Art 27 commentary).

197 ibid 102, para 13.

198 ILC, 'Report of the International Law Commission on the Work of Its 51st Session (3 May–23 July 1999)' (1999) UN Doc A/54/10, reproduced in (1999) 2 (pt 2) *YBILC* 1, 69, para 251; M Spinedi, 'From One Codification to Another: Bilateralism and Multilateralism in the

complicity, in the terms proposed by Ago, indeed heralded 'the extension of legal responsibility into areas where States have previously carried moral responsibility'.[199] Responsibility for complicity was thus more an instance of *codification sauvage* than *codification sage*.[200]

B. Complicity's Revolution (Crawford)

Special Rapporteur James Crawford made a valuable contribution or rather revolution in the codification of the ARSIWA. His method was marked by Anglo-Saxon pragmatism.[201] In fact, many of the key changes to the text of the ARSIWA can be attributed to Crawford in his capacity as ILC Special Rapporteur on State responsibility. The most notorious ones for the purposes of our discussion are: (i) the deletion of former draft Article 23 dealing with the obligation to prevent; (ii) the introduction of Article 47 on joint and several responsibility; (iii) the removal of the term 'crime' (former draft Article 19) and its transformation into a 'serious breach of a peremptory norm' (Articles 40 and 41); and (iv) the substantial revisiting of the rule on responsibility for complicity.

Special Rapporteur Crawford revisited the rule as it has been designed by Ago, trying to reposition complicity within a classic bilateral straitjacket of the relations of responsibility. Why bilateralisation? The newly crafted Article 16 ARSIWA through its paragraph (b) limits the responsibility to situations where the principal wrongful act would also be wrongful had it been committed by the aiding or assisting State itself. In practice, this means that the complicit State must be bound by the same obligation as the one breached by the principal wrongdoing State receiving former's assistance. Out of more than 40 States that provided comments throughout the codification process, to the best of the author's knowledge, Sweden was the only State directly requesting for such

Genesis of the Codification of the Law of Treaties and the Law of State Responsibility' (2002) 13 *EJIL* 1099, 1109 ff; cf Klein (n 191) 429.

[199] V Lowe, *International Law* (Oxford, OUP, 2007) 121.

[200] See RJ Dupuy, 'Coutume sage et coutume sauvage' in S Bastid (ed), *Mélanges offerts à Charles Rousseau* (Paris, Pedone, 1974); A Mahiou, 'Les objectifs de la codification: Rapport général' in SFDI (ed), *La codification du droit international: Colloque d'Aix-en-Provence* (Paris, Pedone, 1999) 60 (fearing a possible atrophy of codification: 'le mouvement de mondialisation est d'abord porteur d'une stratégie de dérégulation de la vie internationale de nature à susciter une diminution ou une dilution des règles et une atrophie de la codification'; author's translation: 'the globalisation movement brings first of all a strategy of deregulation of international affairs capable of generating a reduction or dilution of the rules and atrophy of codification').

[201] A Pellet, 'The ILC's Articles on State Responsibility for Internationally Wrongful Acts and Related Texts' in J Crawford et al (eds), *The Law of International Responsibility* (Oxford, OUP, 2010) 83.

a limitation to be incorporated.[202] As we shall see in chapter five, the introduction of the opposability limitation was not only unnecessary but also overly restrictive, thereby hindering the utility of responsibility for complicity.

Other elements of responsibility for complicity as revised by Special Rapporteur James Crawford in Article 16 ARSIWA aimed at further limiting its scope of application. Crawford considered that former draft Article 27 gave rise to a primary norm, albeit by reference to the wrongful act by another State.[203] Concerned about the implications of such a broad rule in practice, the Special Rapporteur stressed that the responsibility envisaged under Chapter IV of the ARSIWA is in all senses derivative.[204]

The Special Rapporteur noted in particular that by analogising to domestic laws that prescribe that it is a civil wrong to knowingly assist another person in violating the latter's contractual obligations, one could advocate for a broader formulation of responsibility for aid or assistance in public international law.[205] Crawford pointed out 'that in national legal systems, rules dealing ... with ... complicity and inducing breach of contract may be classified as falling within the "general part" of the law of civil or criminal obligations'.[206] He found that although some national legal systems make it a civil wrong for one person to assist someone else in order to breach their contractual obligation, they usually did so with many qualifications:

> First of all, the principle is not recognized in some legal systems (eg those based on Islamic law), and only to a very limited extent by others (eg German law). In those systems where it is recognized in principle (eg French law, the common law), it is subject to important qualifications. In particular, the contract concerned must be lawful, the interference with it must be intentional and there must be no independent justification for the interference.[207]

[202] ILC, 'Comments of Governments on Part 1 of the Draft Articles on State Responsibility for Internationally Wrongful Acts' (1981) UN Doc A/CN.4/342 and Add 1-4, reproduced in (1981) 2 (pt 1) *YBILC* 71, 77 (Sweden) ('Assuming, for example, that State A, by treaty with State B has undertaken not to increase the size of its navy beyond a certain level, would it be unlawful for a third State to sell warships to State A, if that level is thereby exceeded?'); but see also UNGA, 'Sixth Committee, Summary Record of the 31st Meeting' (26 October 1978) UN Doc A/C.6/33/SR.31, 5, para 11 (Netherlands); ILC, 'Comments and Observations Received from Governments' (2001) UN Doc A/CN.4/515 and Add 1-3, reproduced in (2001) 2 (pt 1) *YBILC* 33, 52 (United States) (welcoming the insertion of the opposability requirement).

[203] J Crawford, 'Second Report on State Responsibility' (1999) UN Doc A/CN.4/498 and Add 1-4, reproduced in (1999) 2 (pt 1) *YBILC* 3, 47, para 166.

[204] *Spanish Zone of Morocco Claims (United Kingdom v Spain)* (1924) 2 RIAA 615, 648 (Max Huber referring to 'responsabilité derivée').

[205] Crawford (n 203) 50–51, para 184; and 97 (where the Special Rapporteur provided an overview of the comparative law on liability for inducing breach of contract as a civil wrong).

[206] ibid 47, para 167.

[207] ibid 51, para 184.

Special Rapporteur Crawford took from that comparative overview that limits on responsibility for complicity in the wrongful act of another were necessary. Otherwise, it would mean that bilateral treaties could be enforced on any third party. In other words, States that are not parties to a particular bilateral treaty would effectively be placed under an obligation not to assist the parties to the treaty in breaching the terms of that treaty. In Crawford's view, even if one were to assume the applicability of domestic analogies to the extended view of responsibility for complicity:

> Treaties reflect the particular policies of the States entering into them, and international law has a strict doctrine of privity in relation to treaties. Moreover, treaties have proliferated, and many obligations to provide finance, materials or technology are incorporated in treaties. National legal systems have more rigorous controls on the legality of contracts than international law currently has for treaties, and there are ways under national law by which third parties can challenge the legality of contracts adversely affecting them which do not yet exist for treaties.[208]

To support his reasoning, Crawford gave the example of the regime for invalidating treaties not in conformity with *jus cogens* which, pursuant to Articles 65 and 66 of the VCLT, is only available to the parties to the treaty in question and not to the affected third parties.[209] Special Rapporteur referred to the *East Timor* case, where Portugal did not purport to challenge the validity of the 1989 Treaty.[210] As we shall see in chapter five, the question of potential invalidity of treaties is without prejudice to the responsibility for complicity that could arise from the conclusion of a treaty, which would be in breach of a pre-existing obligation.

The following passage demonstrates some of the doubts that Special Rapporteur Crawford legitimately raised with regard to complicity's place under the law of international responsibility, which prompted him to limit its scope as much as possible:

> In certain circumstances, it may be justified to attribute the wrongfulness of State A's conduct to State B, which is implicated in that conduct because of assistance given … Depending upon the scope of the responsibility defined by Chapter IV, it is thus possible to defend article 27 … as falling within the scope of a draft concerned with the secondary rules of State responsibility. Care is needed to ensure that the articles do not go beyond the scope of 'implication', turning into substantive and possibly controversial primary rules. Whether they do so, however, depends upon their content rather than their classification.[211]

208 ibid para 185.
209 ibid para 185, fn 359.
210 ibid; *East Timor (Portugal v Australia)* (Judgment) [1995] ICJ Rep 90.
211 Crawford (n 203) 47, para 167.

Given the breadth of the former draft Article 27, a case could have been made for the deletion of the rule on responsibility for aid or assistance.[212] However, Crawford ultimately considered that a better solution was to keep the rule and limit its scope to aid or assistance given with the knowledge of the circumstances of and significantly facilitating the commission of a wrongful act by which the aiding or assisting State is bound.[213] Special Rapporteur stressed the essentially derivative character of responsibility for complicity and the need to ascertain specific intent of a purported complicit actor as to the commission of the principal wrongful act:

> First, the assisting State is only responsible if the assisted State has actually committed an internationally wrongful act. As the commentary makes clear, the responsibility of the assisting State only arises if and when the assisted State carries out the wrongful act. Secondly, the assisting State is only responsible if it is established that the assistance was 'rendered for the commission of an internationally wrongful act'. *What is required is a specific intent to assist in the commission of the wrongful act by the assisted State.*[214] (emphasis added)

In his Second Report, Special Rapporteur Crawford acknowledged many other important issues for the development of a general rule of complicity, some of which were left to be settled by international practice. For example, must the assisting State not only be aware that the aided or assisted conduct will occur, or must it also know of its internationally wrongful character? What degree of inquiry reasonably needs to be conducted by the aiding or assisting State as to the illegality of the ultimate conduct by the State recipient of aid or assistance? Does ignorance of the law by the State officials who give the aid or assistance excuse that State?

Despite its shortcomings, the decision taken by the ILC to limit the scope of responsibility for complicity and retain it in the final version of the ARSIWA is still a victory, a second best scenario for the promotion of solidarity and legality in the law of international responsibility.[215]

C. Complicity's Restatement (Gaja)

Already in 1963, Abdullah El-Erian, the former Special Rapporteur on Relations between States and Intergovernmental Organizations, stressed

[212] See, eg ILC, 'Comments and Observations Received by Governments' (1998) UN Doc A/CN.4/488 and Add 1-3, reproduced in (1998) 2 (pt 1) *YBILC* 81, 128 (Switzerland) ('this provision, which has no basis in positive law and would embody a purely causal responsibility, has no place in the Commission's draft and should therefore be deleted').

[213] Crawford (n 203) 51, para 188.

[214] ibid 47, para 167.

[215] On the historic progression of the concept of solidarity see M Koskenniemi, *The Gentle Civilizer of Nations* (Cambridge, CUP, 2004) 288–352.

that 'the continuous increase of the scope of activities of international organizations [was] likely to give new dimensions to the problem of responsibility of international organizations'.[216]

As discussed above, when Ago masterminded the new approach to the codification of the ARSIWA, focusing exclusively on the secondary norms, the ILC was well aware of the questions surrounding the responsibility of international organisations. However, at that time, the Commission decided to keep the codification of the responsibility of States separate from any considerations of the responsibility of other subjects of international law.[217]

On second reading completed in 2001, the Commission clarified that the question of State responsibility was 'without prejudice' to the responsibility of international organisations.[218] The ARSIWA Commentary to Article 57 explains that 'those cases where the international organization is the actor and the State is said to be responsible by virtue of its involvement in the conduct of the organization or by virtue of its membership of the organization' were more appropriate to be addressed in the law of responsibility applicable to international organisations.[219] It was noted at that time that cases of shared responsibility between States and international organisations could undermine the functioning of international organisations and their internal rules and procedures.[220]

Shortly before the adoption of the ARSIWA in 2001, the ILC foresaw an analogous project for the codification of responsibility in respect of international organisations.[221] Giorgio Gaja was appointed as the Commission's Special Rapporteur on the subject.[222] Under his leadership, the Commission followed closely, perhaps too closely, the structure and content of the ARSIWA.[223] Although Special Rapporteur Gaja was well aware

[216] A El-Erian, 'First Report on Relations between States and Intergovernmental Organizations' (1963) UN Doc A/CN.4/161 and Add 1, reproduced in (1963) 2 *YBILC* 159, 184, para 172; see also C Eagleton, 'International Organization and the Law of Responsibility' (1950) 76 *RCADI* 319; W Meng, 'Internationale Organisationen im völkerrechtlichen Deliktsrecht' (1985) 45 *ZaöRV* 324.

[217] R Ago, 'Report on State Responsibility' (1963) UN Doc A/CN.4/152, reproduced in (1963) 2 *YBILC* 227, 228, para 6, fn 2.

[218] ARSIWA (n 2) Art 57.

[219] ibid 142, para 4 (Art 57 Commentary).

[220] ibid.

[221] ILC, 'Report of the International Law Commission on the Work of Its 52nd Session (1 May–9 June and 10 July–18 August 2000)' (2000) UN Doc A/55/10, reproduced in (2000) 2 (pt 2) *YBILC* 1, 131–32, paras 729–30.

[222] ILC, 'Report of the International Law Commission on the Work of Its 54th Session (29 April–7 June and 22 July–16 August 2002)' (2002) UN Doc A/57/10, reproduced in (2002) 2 (p 2) *YBILC* 1, 93, paras 461–63.

[223] G Gaja, 'First Report on Responsibility of International Organizations' (2003) UN Doc A/CN.4/532, reproduced in (2003) 2 (pt 1) *YBILC* 105, 109, para 11 ('should the study concerning particular issues relating to international organizations produce results that do not differ from those reached by the Commission in its analysis of State responsibility, the

of the *special* character of international organisations and their functioning, the ARIO contain little evidence of any major departure from the logic of the ARSIWA. Arguably, the level of abstraction of the ARIO built upon the mirror image of ARSIWA does not do justice to the specificities of different international organisations, including 'their organizational structure, the nature and composition of their governing organs, and their regulations, rules and special procedures'.[224] The ARIO have often been criticised for not taking into account this essential difference between States and international organisations, perhaps with the only exception in their treatment of countermeasures.[225]

On the one hand, the ARIO's bandwagoning of the ARSIWA is a welcome step for coherence and unity of the law of international responsibility.[226] On the other hand, the effectiveness of and the adherence to the ARIO provisions by the law-determining agents is questionable, not least because of significant differences in the functioning of international organisations and their internal rules.[227] Today, it is widely accepted that while most of the ARSIWA provisions reflect customary international law, the ARIO provisions are largely an outcome of progressive development of international law.[228] This section makes some preliminary remarks on

model of the draft articles on State responsibility should be followed both in the general outline and in the wording of the new text'); cf ILC, 'Responsibility of International Organizations, Comments and Observations Received from International Organizations' (14 February 2011) UN Doc A/CN.4/637, 8, para 1 (ILO); 10–11, para 2 (Joint submission); ILC, 'Summary Record of the 2800th Meeting' (18 May 2004) UN Doc A/CN.4/SR.2800, reproduced in (2004) 1 *YBILC* 65, 69, para 17 (Matheson); ILC, 'Summary Record of the 2801st Meeting' (19 May 2004) UN Doc A/CN.4/SR.2801, reproduced in (2004) 1 *YBILC* 73, 80, para 64 (Escarameia); see also C Ahlborn, 'The Use of Analogies in Drafting the Articles on the Responsibility of International Organizations—An Appraisal of the "Copy-Paste Approach"' (2012) 9 *IOLR* 53.

224 ILC, 'Responsibility of International Organizations: Comments and Observations Received from International Organizations' (17 February 2011) UN Doc A/CN.4/637/Add 1, 4, para 1 (UN); for an excellent analysis of the internal rules of international organizations see C Ahlborn, 'The Rules of International Organizations and the Law of International Responsibility' (2011) 8 *IOLR* 397.

225 A Pellet, 'International Organizations Are Definitely Not States. Cursory Remarks on the ILC Articles on the Responsibility of International Organizations' in M Ragazzi (ed), *Responsibility of International Organizations: Essays in Memory of Sir Ian Brownlie* (Leiden, Martinus Nijhoff, 2013) 46–48; J d'Aspremont, 'The Articles on the Responsibility of International Organizations: Magnifying the Fissures in the Law of International Responsibility' (2012) 9 *IOLR* 15.

226 ILC, 'Draft Articles on the Responsibility of International Organizations, with Commentaries' (2011) 2 (pt 2) *YBILC* 2, para 4 (the similarity between the ARSIWA and ARIO 'is based on appropriate reasons and not on a general presumption that the same principles apply').

227 ibid Art 64 (which provides for the possibility of displacing the general rules of responsibility vis-à-vis applicable special rules or lex specialis); see also K Boon, 'The Role of Lex Specialis in the Articles on the Responsibility of International Organizations' in M Ragazzi (ed), *Responsibility of International Organizations: Essays in Memory of Sir Ian Brownlie* (Leiden, Martinus Nijhoff, 2013).

228 See several contributions making the same point in Ragazzi (ed) (n 227).

the ARIO and the transposition of responsibility for complicity to international organisations, the merits of which will be discussed in chapters four and five.

Today, the actions of many international organisations have an important effect on individuals, private associations, enterprises, States and public institutions.[229] However, this reality has not been accompanied by the development of an adequate system of accountability. As the dealings of international organisations increasingly affect individuals, this absence of a system of accountability is all the more problematic.[230] International responsibility is only one element of a broader discussion on accountability of international organisations, yet a crucial one.[231]

In its First Report, the ILA Committee on the Accountability of International Organizations indicated that any model rules in this area would 'have to keep the balance between preserving the necessary autonomy in decision-making of international organizations and guaranteeing that the international organizations will not be able to avoid accountability'.[232] This safeguarding of the functional autonomy of international organisations is twofold. First, there is a question of immunities from jurisdiction before domestic courts where victims might bring claims against the organisation.[233] Second, there has only been limited application of rules

[229] cf M Steinbrück Platise and A von Bogdandy, 'ARIO and Human Rights Protection: Leaving the Individual in the Cold' (2012) 9 *IOLR* 67; on the role and impact of international organizations see generally JE Alvarez, *International Organizations as Law-Makers* (Oxford, OUP, 2005); HG Schermers and N Blokker, *International Institutional Law: Unity within Diversity* (5th edn, Leiden, Martinus Nijhoff, 2011); J Klabbers, *An Introduction to International Institutional Law* (Cambridge, CUP, 2002).

[230] CA Feinäugle, 'The UN Security Council Al-Qaida and Taliban Sanctions Committee: Emerging Principles of International Law for the Protection of Individuals?' (2008) 9 *German LJ* 1513; P de Visscher, 'Observations sur le fondement et la mise-en-oeuvre du principe de la responsabilité de l'organisation des Nations Unies' (1963) 40 *RDIDC* 165.

[231] See, eg J Brunnée, 'International Legal Accountability through the Lens of the Law of State Responsibility' (2005) 36 *Netherlands YBIL* 21; M Parish, 'An Essay on the Accountability of International Organizations' (2010) 7 *IOLR* 277; A Tzanakopoulos, 'Strengthening Security Council Accountability for Sanctions: The Role of International Responsibility' (2014) 19 *JCSL* 409; R Wilde, 'Enhancing Accountability at the International Level' (2006) 12 *ILSA J Intl & Comp L* 395; E Suzuki and S Nanwani, 'Responsibility of International Organizations: The Accountability Mechanisms of Multilateral Development Banks' (2005) 27 *Michigan J Intl L* 177.

[232] ILA, 'Committee on Accountability of International Organizations, First Report' Taipei Conference (1998) 586, 602.

[233] C Ryngaert, 'The Immunity of International Organizations Before Domestic Courts: Recent Trends' (2010) 7 *IOLR* 121; A Reinisch, *International Organizations before National Courts* (Cambridge, CUP, 2000); A Reinisch, *Challenging Acts of International Organizations before National Courts* (Oxford, OUP, 2010); see more generally on issues of international responsibility before domestic courts S Wittich, 'Domestic Courts and the Content and Implementation of State Responsibility' (2013) 26 *LJIL* 643; A Nollkaemper, 'Internationally Wrongful Acts in Domestic Courts' (2007) 101 *AJIL* 760; S Olleson, 'Internationally Wrongful Acts in the Domestic Courts: The Contribution of Domestic Courts to the Development of Customary International Law Relating to the Engagement of International Responsibility' (2013) 26 *LJIL* 615.

on the basis of which Member States may be held co-responsible for the non-fulfilment by the organisation of its international commitments and obligations vis-à-vis third parties.[234]

Historically, the subject of responsibility of international organisations was obscured by the uncertainties surrounding their legal personality and the scope of their rights and obligations. In the *Reparation for Injuries* Advisory Opinion, the Court recognised that:

> [F]rom the moment that [international] organizations exercise legal competencies of the same type as those of States, it seemed logical that the same consequences should attach to the actions of both one and the other.[235]

The Court stressed that '[t]he subjects of law in any legal system are not necessarily identical in their nature or in the extent of their rights'.[236] International organisations, unlike States, do not possess a general competence.[237] Instead, they are 'invested by the States which create them with powers, the limits of which are a function of the common interests whose promotion those States entrust to them'.[238]

Despite the recognition that international organisations may engage international responsibility for their actions and omissions,[239] the implementation of this responsibility is hampered in practice by both substantive and procedural hurdles, such as immunity from jurisdiction and the internal rules of different organisations. The jurisdiction of most international courts and tribunals has been structured for inter-State cases, and efforts to bring a framework for dispute settlement in respect of international organisations has been much slower and, thus far, approached in an ad hoc manner.[240]

Traditionally, the question of the responsibility of the Member States of an international organisation was raised in cases of private law debts and actions ensuing from bankruptcy proceedings of an international

[234] K Wellens, *Remedies against International Organizations* (Cambridge, CUP, 2004) 25, 46 and 114.

[235] *Reparation for Injuries Suffered in the Service of the United Nations* (Advisory Opinion) [1949] ICJ Rep 174, 178.

[236] ibid 178.

[237] *Legality of the Use by a State of Nuclear Weapons in Armed Conflict* (Advisory Opinion) [1996] ICJ Rep 66, 78–79, para 25.

[238] ibid.

[239] *Difference relating to Immunity from Legal Process of a Special Rapporteur of the Commission on Human Rights* (Advisory Opinion) [1999] ICJ Rep 62, 89, para 66 ('[the] United Nations may be required to bear responsibility for … any damages incurred as a result of acts performed by the United Nations or by its agents acting in their official capacity'); de Visscher (n 230) 167.

[240] J Crawford, 'The System of International Responsibility' in J Crawford et al (eds), *The Law of International Responsibility* (Oxford, OUP, 2010) 18 (referring to examples of the EU that had specifically to be provided for in order to be a party to contentious proceedings under Part XV of UNCLOS and the WTO dispute settlement mechanism. In effect for these purposes it is equated to a State).

organisation. The *Tin Council* cases are emblematic in this context.[241] However, following the end of the Cold War, international organisations have substantially expanded the scope of their activities in different areas ranging from peace and security, trade and investment and human rights. Likewise, the character of the wrongful acts committed by an international organisation in collaboration with its Members has become more complex. Examples of peacekeeping missions and territorial administration by the UN are illustrative of that complexity.[242] The issues of responsibility are even more challenging where States acting on a multilateral basis are able to persuade an international organisation to adopt or at least acquiesce to their cause or when they establish an organisation through which to pursue a particular cause.[243] Despite these challenges, a legal system where international organisations are not subject to any formal responsibility is no longer tenable.[244]

Tentative solutions to the problem have been developed in recent years. These include the establishment of independent inquiries (eg in respect of the genocide in Rwanda and in Srebrenica),[245] forms of internal auditing mechanisms (eg the World Bank Inspection Panel),[246] or the admission

241 *Re International Tin Council* (Judgment) (1988) 77 ILR 18; *JH Rayner (Mincing Lane) Ltd v Department of Trade and Industry and others and Related Appeals* (Judgment) [1990] 2 AC 418 (HL); see also *Westland Helicopters Ltd v Arab Organization for Industrialization, United Arab Emirates, Kingdom of Saudi Arabia, State of Qatar, Arab Republic of Egypt and Arab British Helicopter Company, ICC Case No 3879/AS* (1984) 23 ILM 1071; for the ensuing litigation see *Westland Helicopters Ltd v Arab Organization for Industrialization* (Judgment) [1995] 2 All ER 387; see also A Reinisch, 'Aid or Assistance and Direction and Control between States and International Organizations in the Commission of Internationally Wrongful Acts' (2010) 7 *IOLR* 63.

242 See, eg S Besson, 'La pluralité d'États responsables: Vers une solidarité internationale?' (2007) 1 *SZIER* 13, 13–14.

243 For difficulties of suing States for the wrongs of international organisations see, eg *Maclaine Watson & Co Ltd v International Tin Council* (Judgment) [1990] 2 AC 418, 482 (Templeman LJ).

244 See, eg RJ Araujo, 'Objective Meaning of Constituent Instruments and Responsibility of International Organizations' in M Ragazzi (ed), *International Responsibility Today: Essays in Memory of Oscar Schachter* (Leiden, Martinus Nijhoff, 2005); I Brownlie, 'The Responsibility of States for Acts of International Organizations' in M Ragazzi (ed), *International Responsibility Today: Essays in Memory of Oscar Schachter* (Leiden, Martinus Nijhoff, 2005); Wilde (n 231); A Stumer, 'Liability of Member States for Acts of International Organization: Reconsidering the Policy Objections' (2007) 48 *Harvard Intl LJ* 553; A Geslin, 'Réflexions sur la répartition de la responsabilité entre l'organisation internationale et ses états membres' (2005) 109 *RGDIP* 539.

245 UNSC, 'Report of the Independent Inquiry into the Actions of the United Nations during the 1994 Genocide in Rwanda' (16 December 1999) UN Doc S/1999/1257; UNGA, 'Report of the Secretary-General pursuant to General Assembly Resolution 53/55: The Fall of Srebrenica' (15 November 1999) UN Doc A/54/549.

246 See, eg AG Gualtieri, 'The Environmental Accountability of the World Bank to Non-State Actors: Insights from the Inspection Panel' (2002) 72 *British YBIL* 213 (for example, the World Bank Panel has reviewed matters like the China Western Poverty Reduction Project concerning an irrigation project financed by the World Bank. In that respect, the World Bank faced allegations that the project could lead to adverse environmental impacts in the region); see also A Orakhelashvili, 'The World Bank Inspection Panel in Context: Institutional Aspects of the Accountability of International Organizations' (2005) 2 *IOLR* 57.

of the possibility of any 'separate or concurrent responsibility of a State or of another international organization which participated in the performance of the wrongful act'.[247] The principle of responsibility of Member States in connection with the wrongful act committed by an international organisation is now set out in Article 58 ARIO, which will be discussed in chapter four.

In his third report, Special Rapporteur Gaja drafted a provision on aid or assistance given by an international organisation to another organisation or State in the commission of an internationally wrongful act.[248] The provision (initially former draft Article 12 which became Article 14 ARIO) was inspired by, or rather mirrored, upon Article 16 ARSIWA. Gaja noted that the equivalent formulation to that in Article 16 ARSIWA would be appropriate, being conditional on the knowledge of the circumstances of the internationally wrongful act and requiring that both the assisted and the assisting entities be bound by the obligation breached.[249] Accordingly:

> Although the articles on responsibility of States do not expressly envisage that States aid or assist … an international organization in the commission of an internationally wrongful act, these cases appear to be analogous to those referred to in [Article 16].[250]

Most States and international organisations questioned the transposition of the constituent elements and criteria of responsibility for complicity into the ARIO. These comments will be analysed in detail in the subsequent chapters, but for the time being it suffices to say that there is very limited practice showing the application of these provisions. In defence of Special Rapporteur Giorgio Gaja, his reluctance to change the content of the rule on responsibility for complicity for organisations was prompted by the need for consistency, allowing room for the law-determining agents to further refine and interpret the relevant provisions in their practice. Indeed, as noted by the Special Rapporteur Gaja:

> One difficulty in defining more precisely aid or assistance in the commission of an internationally wrongful act is that, for the purpose of assessing whether aid or assistance occurs, much depends on the content of the obligation breached and on the circumstances. Thus, it seems preferable not to modify the wording that was used in [Article 16 ARSIWA].[251]

[247] ILA, 'Committee on Accountability of International Organizations, Third Report' New Delhi Conference (2002) 16; see also ch 4 for discussion on Art 58 ARIO.

[248] G Gaja, 'Third Report on Responsibility of International Organizations' (2005) UN Doc A/CN.4/553, reproduced in (2005) 2 (pt 1) *YBILC* 7, 13, para 25.

[249] ibid.

[250] ibid para 26; P Klein, *La responsabilité des organisations internationales dans les ordres juridiques internes et en droit des gens* (Bruxelles, Bruylant, 1998) 468–69.

[251] G Gaja, 'Seventh Report on Responsibility of International Organizations' (2009) UN Doc A/CN.4/610, reproduced in (2009) 2 (pt 1) *YBILC* 73, 87, para 75.

The effectiveness of the rule will be tested in the future by the extent to which the unlimited functional immunity of the UN and other international organisations continues to prevail.[252] Insofar as such an approach reigns in international law, the prospects of responsibility of international organisations generally and responsibility for complicity specifically are limited.[253]

IV. INTERIM CONCLUSIONS

This chapter examined the development of complicity as a form of responsibility in international criminal law and in the law of international responsibility applicable to States and international organisations.[254] As set out above, the author does not claim that these regimes are susceptible to any direct analogies. The respective frameworks of international criminal law and the law of international responsibility may differ but the conception of the function and elements of complicity in both regimes bear resemblance. It is undeniable that these different forms of complicity interact with each other, for example, through the question of knowledge of the wrongdoing.

The evolution of complicity in these two fields also demonstrates an apparent legal paradox. While international criminal law has progressively relaxed the conditions triggering liability for complicity or aiding and abetting (apart maybe from a short-lived incongruity in the *Perišić* case), quite an opposite trend has appeared in the ILC's codification process of responsibility for complicity. This is particularly striking in the context of assessing the cognitive criterion of complicity. Why is it

[252] For recent cases upholding the UN immunity from jurisdiction see, eg *Delama Georges and others v United Nations and others* (Judgment) [2015] No 1:13-cv-7146 (SDNY) (relating to the UN role in the cholera epidemics in Haiti); *Stichting Mothers of Srebrenica and others v Netherlands* (Judgment) [2012] Case No 10/04437 (Dutch Supreme Court) (relating to the Srebrenica massacre and the alleged failure of the UN and the Dutchbat to protect the Srebrenica 'safe area'); *Stichting Mothers of Srebrenica v Netherlands* (Judgment) [2013] ECtHR App No 65542/12 (2013) EHRR SE10 paras 140–70; see also M Singer, 'Jurisdictional Immunity of International Organizations: Human Rights and Functional Necessity Concerns' (1995) 36 *Virginia J Intl L* 53; Reinisch, *International Organizations before National Courts* (n 233) 158.

[253] For general trends on the practice of domestic courts in respect of immunity of international organisations see Ryngaert (n 233); see also K Daugirdas, 'Reputation and the Responsibility of International Organizations' (2014) 25 *EJIL* 991 (arguing that the ARIO will force international organisations 'to both participate in transnational discourse about their legal obligations and take action to cease, correct, or make reparations for violations of international law').

[254] *Bosnia Genocide (Merits)* (n 2) 120, para 182 ('State responsibility can arise under the Convention for genocide and complicity, without an individual being convicted of the crime of an associated one').

appropriate to adopt a more stringent test of intention in the law of international responsibility where international criminal law is satisfied with knowledge?

Considering that the law of international responsibility is conceptually closer to civil responsibility, should not a State or international organisation be held responsible if they knowingly rather than intentionally contributed to the wrongful act by another subject of international law? Ultimately, the willingness to consider the scope of the role for responsibility for complicity depends on the needs of the law-determining agents but, even more, on the view of the legal order that they adhere to.

4

The ILC Rules on Responsibility for Complicity

La vérité est que la matière de la responsabilité tient la place d'un immense laboratoire.[1]

I. INTRODUCTION

THIS CHAPTER'S OBJECTIVE is twofold. First, it examines the outcome of the International Law Commission's (ILC) codification of responsibility for complicity so as to better understand the compromises and choices made by the Commission. Second, the present chapter aims at distinguishing complicity from other forms of shared and indirect responsibility in international law.

Section II of this chapter examines the general regime of responsibility for complicity as codified in Articles 16 Articles on Responsibility of States for Internationally Wrongful Acts (ARSIWA) and 14 Articles on Responsibility of International Organizations (ARIO). The analysis of the text of the provisions and the ILC's Commentary to them sets out a background for a critical review in chapter five of each constituent element in light of the existing practice and *opinio juris*. Section III discusses the regime of aggravated complicity as set out in Articles 41(2) ARSIWA and 42(2) ARIO, imposing a duty of non-assistance to the maintenance of the unlawful situation resulting from a serious breach of a peremptory norm (*jus cogens*). Section IV addresses responsibility for complicity of States in connection with the wrongful act of an international organisation (Article 58 ARIO). Finally, section V distinguishes responsibility for complicity from other forms of indirect and shared responsibility in the ARSIWA and ARIO, including direction and control, coercion, circumvention of international obligations, and joint and several responsibility.

[1] P Reuter, 'Principes de droit international public' (1961) 103 *RCADI* 425, 596 (author's translation: 'The truth is that the question of responsibility is a huge laboratory').

II. GENERAL REGIME OF COMPLICITY (ARTICLES 16 ARSIWA AND 14 ARIO)

A. Preliminary Remarks

As demonstrated in chapter three, the content and purpose of Article 16 ARSIWA underwent substantial changes from 1978 until its adoption in 2001. From the early days in the codification process, it was crystal clear that more than any other article in the draft, complicity 'seemed to leap the barrier between secondary and primary rules'.[2] Apart from former draft Article 19 (on distinction between crimes and delicts), which as such dealt with a degree of a particular wrongful act, the provision on responsibility for complicity was the only Article which prescribed that a particular action or omission constituted an internationally wrongful act.[3]

The discussion of complicity in an internationally wrongful act culminated in the adoption of Article 16 ARSIWA, which reads as follows:

> Article 16
>
> Aid or assistance in the commission of an internationally wrongful act
>
> A State which aids or assists another State in the commission of an internationally wrongful act by the latter is internationally responsible for doing so if:
>
> (a) that State does so with the knowledge of the circumstances of the internationally wrongful act;
> (b) the act would be internationally wrongful if committed by that State.[4]

An equivalent provision, rendering an international organisation responsible for aid or assistance in the commission of a wrongful act by another international organisation or a State, was codified in Article 14 ARIO and adopted in 2011:

> Article 14
>
> Aid or assistance in the commission of an internationally wrongful act

[2] ILC, 'Summary Record of the 1518th Meeting' (17 July 1978), reproduced in (1978) 1 *YBILC* 232, 236, para 32 (Quentin-Baxter); ILC, 'Report of the International Law Commission on the Work of Its 22nd Session (4 May–10 July 1970)' (1970) UN Doc A/8010/Rev 1, reproduced in (1970) 2 *YBILC* 271, 306, para 66 (according to Ago 'it is one thing to define a rule and the content of the obligation it imposes, and another to determine whether that obligation has been violated and what should be the consequence of the violation. Only the second aspect of the matter comes within the sphere of responsibility proper'); ILC, 'Report of the International Law Commission on the Work of Its 15th Session (6 May–12 July 1963) with Annexes' (1963) UN Doc A/5509, reproduced in (1963) 2 *YBILC* 187, 252 (Ago's masterplan was to codify the 'whole of responsibility and nothing but responsibility').

[3] ILC, 'Summary Record of the 1518th Meeting' (n 2) 236, para 32 (Quentin-Baxter).

[4] ILC, 'Draft Articles on Responsibility of States for Internationally Wrongful Acts, with Commentaries' (2001) 2 (pt 2) *YBILC* 31 (ARSIWA), Art 16.

> An international organization which aids or assists a State or another international organization in the commission of an internationally wrongful act by the State or the latter organization is internationally responsible for doing so if:
>
> (a) that organization does so with knowledge of the circumstance of the internationally wrongful act; and
>
> (b) the act would be internationally wrongful if committed by that organization.[5]

Notwithstanding the differences in the character and functioning of States and international organisations, the Commission decided to maintain the same structure and content of responsibility for complicity, albeit this is not free from criticism.[6] Be that as it may, the provisions of Article 16 ARSIWA and 14 ARIO can be regarded as the *chapeau* of the other configurations of responsibility for complicity which will be discussed in this chapter.

According to the ILC's Commentary, responsibility for complicity is limited in three ways.[7] The first limitation, which is stated explicitly in the provisions, is that the aiding or assisting State must have knowledge of the circumstances of the wrongful act committed by the assisted State. The second and related limitation concerns the requirement that the aid or assistance be given with a view to facilitating the commission of the wrongful act and the aid or assistance provided must actually facilitate the commission of that act. The third limitation, which also appears in the text of the provisions, is that the principal act must be wrongful had it been committed by the complicit State (the so-called opposability requirement).

B. Constituent Elements

i. The Threshold of Complicity

Although it is theoretically conceivable that 'aid or assistance' comprises every action or omission that facilitates the commission of an internationally wrongful act by another State, the ILC and several scholars have

[5] ILC, 'Draft Articles on the Responsibility of International Organizations, with Commentaries' (2011) 2 (pt 2) *YBILC* 2 (ARIO), Art 14.

[6] G Gaja, 'Third Report on Responsibility of International Organizations' (2005) UN Doc A/CN.4/553, reproduced in (2005) 2 (pt 1) *YBILC* 7, 13, para 28; cf ch 5 for comments from States and international organisations on the copy-pasting of the content of responsibility for complicity in respect of international organizations; see also C Ahlborn, 'The Use of Analogies in Drafting the Articles on the Responsibility of International Organizations—An Appraisal of the "Copy-Paste Approach"' (2012) 9 *IOLR* 53; JE Alvarez, 'Revisiting the ILC's Draft Rules on International Organization Responsibility' (2011) 105 *ASIL Proceedings* 344; several contributions in M Ragazzi (ed), *Responsibility of International Organizations: Essays in Memory of Sir Ian Brownlie* (Leiden, Martinus Nijhoff, 2013).

[7] ARSIWA (n 4) 66, paras 3–6 (Art 16 Commentary).

stressed that it is necessary to exclude aid or assistance that is too remote.[8] In other words, there must be a link (nexus) between the aid or assistance provided and the principal wrongful act committed. During the debates at the ILC, Paul Reuter questioned whether material assistance that is too remote in character could be considered as complicity at all.[9] Another member suggested that in order to trigger responsibility:

> *Participation must be active and direct.* It *must not be too direct,* however, for the participant then [becomes] a co-author of the offence, and that [goes] beyond complicity. If, on the other hand, participation [is] too indirect, there might be no real complicity. For instance, it would be difficult to speak of complicity in an armed aggression if the aid and assistance to a State consisted in supplying food to ensure the survival of the population for humanitarian reasons.[10] (emphasis added)

However, the ILC made it clear that there are no requirements as to the nature and form of the aid or assistance itself. In the absence of any normative element limiting the character of aid or assistance, Ago contended that even in cases where a State concludes a treaty with another State assuring that it will remain neutral in case of the latter's act of aggression against a third State, responsibility for complicity could arise.[11] There is no logical objection to accepting that under certain circumstances a mere promise may constitute aid or assistance in the sense of Article 16 ARSIWA.[12]

In its commentary to the earlier draft of the provision, the ILC stated as follows:

> It is obvious, too, that aid or assistance in an act of aggression may also take other forms, such as the provision of land, sea or air transport, or even the placing at the disposal of the State that is preparing to commit aggression of military or other organs for use for that purpose. Furthermore, it is by no means only in the event of an act of aggression by a State that the possibility of assistance by another State may arise.[13]

[8] ibid 66, para 5 (Art 16 Commentary); C Chinkin, *Third Parties in International Law* (Oxford, Clarendon Press, 1993) 297; V Lowe, 'Responsibility for the Conduct of Other States' (2002) 101 *Japanese J Intl L & Diplomacy* 1, 10; A Felder, *Die Beihilfe im Recht der völkerrechtlichen Staatenverantwortlichkeit* (Zürich, Schulthess, 2007) 236–37.

[9] ILC, 'Summary Record of the 1517th Meeting' (13 July 1978), reproduced in (1978) 1 *YBILC* 228, 229, para 5 (Reuter) (questioning 'whether assistance that is materially too remote could be regarded as complicity').

[10] ILC, 'Summary Record of the 1519th Meeting' (18 July 1978), reproduced in (1978) 1 *YBILC* 237, 239, para 11 (Ushakov); see also ILC (n 9) 229–30, para 1–6 (Reuter); ILC, 'Summary Record of the 1518th Meeting' (n 2) 233, para 8 (Riphagen).

[11] ILC (n 10) 240, para 26 (Ago) ('For example, if a State concluded an agreement with another State undertaking to maintain benign neutrality if the latter committed an act of aggression, that was not mere incitement but aid and assistance, and it would then be proper to speak of complicity').

[12] See ML Padeletti, *Pluralità di Stati nel fatto illecito internazionale* (Milano, Giuffrè, 1990) 76.

[13] ILC, 'Report of the International Law Commission on the Work of Its 30th Session (8 May–28 July 1978)' (1978) UN Doc A/33/10, reproduced in (1978) 2 (pt 2) *YBILC* 1, 102, para 13 (Former Draft Art 27 Commentary).

As noted above, the ILC, by design, did not define what constitutes aid or assistance and did not clarify whether there are cases in which such responsibility could arise on the basis of an omission. The International Court of Justice (ICJ) for its part seems to have ruled out the possibility of complicity by omission in the *Bosnia Genocide* case,[14] although its pronouncements on this issue are not convincing.[15] For example, an assisting State may grant explicit authorisation for flights over its territory but may also simply not object to the use of its airspace. As long as the assisting State behaves in this way with the required knowledge of the circumstances of the principal wrongful act, why would one exclude its potential responsibility for complicity?

The same can be said with regard to proxy-detention facilities purportedly used in the fight against terrorism.[16] By providing intelligence, airspace, personnel and territory, without an explicit or documented decision, many States, though complicit in the torture and ill-treatment of suspects of terrorism, would not be held to account under the ICJ's interpretation. This is because technically there would be no positive act of assistance but rather knowing tolerance of and acquiescence to a third State's unlawful actions.[17] When such omissions take place with knowledge of the circumstances of the wrongdoing, it is conceptually tenable to accept that they should be found to be complicit in the wrongdoing. Where there is no knowledge of the wrongdoing but rather a substantiated risk of that wrongdoing, the more generic framework of due diligence obligations steps in.[18]

[14] *Application of the Convention on the Prevention and Punishment of the Crime of Genocide (Bosnia and Herzegovina v Serbia and Montenegro)* (Merits) [2007] ICJ Rep 43, 222, para 432.

[15] See, eg V Lanovoy, 'Complicity in an Internationally Wrongful Act' in A Nollkaemper and I Plakokefalos (eds), *Principles of Shared Responsibility in International Law: An Appraisal of the State of the Art* (Cambridge, CUP, 2014) 146–47; M Jackson, *Complicity in International Law* (Oxford, OUP, 2015) 156–57.

[16] See, eg *El-Masri v The Former Yugoslav Republic of Macedonia* (Judgment) (GC) [2012] ECtHR App No 39630/09 (2013) 57 EHRR 25; *Al Nashiri v Poland* (Judgment) [2014] ECtHR App No 28761/11 (2015) 60 EHRR 16; *Husayn (Abu Zubaydah) v Poland* (Judgment) [2014] ECtHR App No 7511/13 (2015) 60 EHRR 16; *R (on the Application of Binyam Mohamed) v Secretary of State for Foreign and Commonwealth Affairs* (Judgment) [2008] EWHC 2048; on the practices of rendition and secret detention see also United States Senate Select Committee on Intelligence, 'Committee Study of the Central Intelligence Agency's Detention and Interrogation Program' (2014); N Shah, 'Knocking on the Torturer's Door: Confronting International Complicity in the US Rendition Program' (2007) 38 *Columbia Human Rights LR* 581; F Messineo, '"Extraordinary Renditions" and State Obligations to Criminalize and Prosecute Torture in the Light of the Abu Omar Case in Italy' (2009) 7 *JICJ* 1023; S Borelli, 'Casting Light on the Legal Black Hole: International Law and Detentions Abroad in the "War on Terror"' (2005) 87 *IRRC* 39; P Sands, 'The International Rule of Law: Extraordinary Rendition, Complicity and Its Consequences', *Droit du pouvoir—pouvoir du droit: Mélanges en l'honneur de Jean Salmon* (Bruxelles, Bruylant, 2007).

[17] *Bosnia Genocide (Merits)* (n 14) 222, para 432.

[18] See ch 5, s II.C and see also Lanovoy (n 15) 146–47.

Arguments for the exclusion of omissions from the rubric of complicity include a voluntarist conviction that States should be entitled to presume that other States will act lawfully,[19] and that responsibility for omissions would require constant scrutiny by States and overburden their daily activities.[20] However, these arguments are not persuasive. First and foremost, to bring omissions within the scope of responsibility by aid or assistance would improve the coherence of the ARSIWA and ARIO, which already define internationally wrongful acts as consisting of actions or omissions.[21] Similarly, admitting that complicity can arise from an omission when a State or international organisation has actual knowledge of the wrongful act could facilitate the assessment of causation, which is much more difficult to pin down in the context of due diligence obligations.

Likewise, there is no requirement that the aid or assistance should have been 'essential to the performance of the internationally wrongful act; it is sufficient if it contributed significantly to that act'.[22] Does it mean, for example, more than *de minimis*? Or does it mean making the commission of the act more likely than not because of aid or assistance? The Commission did not provide any examples as to what this 'contributed significantly' standard actually means. Bruno Simma rightly cautioned the ILC at the time of the ARSIWA second reading that

> the substantial or essential element was virtually absent. …[it] was a real problem, namely, how to be more precise and specific about the interrelationship between the aid provided to the State and the wrongful act which it committed.[23]

To resolve this problem, there were three options: (i) to restrict the notion of complicity to the most serious breaches of international law, including violations of *erga omnes* obligations, and then to be less restrictive on the link between aid or assistance and the principal wrongful act; (ii) to confine oneself to forms of aid or assistance which were essential and then require a causal link between the aid or assistance and the wrongful act; or (iii) to emphasise the positive and active nature of the link (ie the existence of a specific link between the aid or assistance and the wrongful act).[24] The Commission did not take up any of these options, resulting in many unanswered questions about the link between the complicit action or omission and the principal wrongful act, as Simma predicted.

[19] Lowe (n 8) 10.

[20] G Nolte and HP Aust, 'Equivocal Helpers—Complicit States, Mixed Messages and International Law' (2009) 58 *ICLQ* 1, 2.

[21] ARSIWA (n 4) Art 2.

[22] ibid 66, para 5 (Art 16 ARSIWA Commentary); see also J Crawford, 'Second Report on State Responsibility' (1999) UN Doc A/CN.4/498 and Add 1-4, reproduced in (1999) 2 (pt 1) *YBILC* 3, 50, para 182 ('To require that the aid should have been an indispensable prerequisite to the wrongdoing would invite speculation as to other contingencies, and might create loopholes to the application of the rule').

[23] ILC, 'Summary Record of the 2578th Meeting' (28 May 1999), reproduced in (1999) 1 *YBILC* 74, 79, para 41 (Simma).

[24] ibid.

Nor did the Commission take the opportunity to provide further guidance on this point when devising Article 14 ARIO, which substantially transposes the same terms of responsibility for complicity to an international organisation aiding or assisting another State or international organisation. The issue of the threshold for complicity has arisen with regard to international and regional organisations operating in the financial sector.[25] It comes as no surprise that 'an international organization could incur responsibility for assisting a State, through financial support or otherwise, in a project that would entail an infringement of human rights of certain affected individuals'.[26]

In its comments on the ARIO, the International Monetary Fund (IMF), for example, rejected 'the blanket application of Article 16 of the draft Articles on State responsibility to international organizations'.[27] Having been 'established, inter alia, to provide financial assistance to its members to assist in addressing their balance of payment problems',[28] the IMF is unable to influence the behaviour of borrowing States—even by loan conditionality.[29] It follows that 'the fungible character of financial resources also means that IMF financial assistance can never be essential, or contribute significantly, to particular wrongful conduct of a member State'.[30]

Other financial organisations have a much closer link between the financial assistance they provide and the potential wrongful conduct resulting from such assistance. The impact of complicity could be seen, for example, in the practice of the International Bank for Reconstruction and Development (IBRD) and its regional counterparts when providing loans for project financing, which could amount to assisting the recipient State in the commission of an internationally wrongful act, whether it is a breach of human rights or environmental laws.[31]

25 For questions of accountability of international and regional financial institutions in matters of human rights violations see, eg DD Bradlow, 'Private Complaints and International Organizations: A Comparative Study of the Independent Inspection Mechanisms in International Institutions' (2005) 36 *Georgetown J Intl L* 403; P Dann, 'Accountability in Development Aid Law: The World Bank, UNDP and Emerging Structures of Transnational Oversight' (2006) 44 *AVR* 381; E Suzuki and S Nanwani, 'Responsibility of International Organizations: The Accountability Mechanisms of Multilateral Development Banks' (2005) 27 *Michigan J Intl L* 177.

26 Gaja (n 6) 13, para 28.

27 ILC, 'Comments and Observations Received from International Organizations' (1 May 2007) UN Doc A/CN.4/582, reproduced in (2007) 2 (pt 1) *YBILC* 17, 22 (IMF).

28 ibid 22 (IMF).

29 See A Reinisch, 'Aid or Assistance and Direction and Control between States and International Organizations in the Commission of Internationally Wrongful Acts' (2010) 7 *IOLR* 63, 68; A Buira, 'An Analysis of IMF Conditionality' *G-24 Discussion Paper Series* (2003); EMG Denters, *Law and Policy of IMF Conditionality* (The Hague, Kluwer, 1996); O Eldar, 'Reform of IMF Conditionality: A Proposal for Self-Imposed Conditionality' (2005) 8 *JIEL* 509.

30 ILC (n 27) 22 (IMF).

31 Reinisch (n 29) 68.

Thus, a distinction may be drawn between those institutions that provide general lending schemes without exerting any influence or control over the actual money and project-oriented lending where the organisation has a stronger degree of control over the flow and use of money.[32] Special Rapporteur Gaja acknowledged that the nature of the lending organisation is an element that can be taken into account when determining its potential responsibility for complicity.[33]

In his third report, Gaja specifically referenced the responsibility of international organisations for providing financial assistance to a State's project that leads to human rights violations, quoting to this effect the former General Counsel of the World Bank, Ibrahim Shihata.[34] According to Shihata, '[a] loan agreement to a country which violates such rights does not in itself violate any human rights rules, or for that matter, condone violations of such rights'.[35] Gaja explained that such a conclusion would only be valid in respect of cases of loans that are not directly linked to a project involving an infringement of human rights.[36] Thus, as long as there is a proven *de minimis* link between the financial assistance and particular circumstances of the wrongful act, the international organisation's responsibility for aid or assistance cannot be excluded in principle.

ii. Knowledge of the Circumstances of the Internationally Wrongful Act

Article 16 ARSIWA envisages that 'a State providing [for example] material or financial assistance or aid to another State does not normally assume the risk that its assistance or aid may be used to carry out an internationally wrongful act'.[37] The ILC's Drafting Committee ultimately decided to retain this requirement explicitly in the text of Article 16, and provided the following explanation:

> [T]he Drafting Committee had considered a suggestion by some Governments to delete it and a proposal by one Government to redraft the subparagraph to include the words 'or should have known'. It had decided that the article should be retained in its entirety and as currently drafted. In particular, it had noted that the knowledge requirement was essential, as a narrow formulation of the chapter was the only approach acceptable to many States. The commentary would clarify the threshold at which aid and assistance became participation in the commission of the act.[38]

[32] ibid 69.

[33] See Gaja (n 6).

[34] ibid 13, para 28, fn 41.

[35] IFI Shihata, 'Human Rights, Development, and International Financial Institutions' (1992) 8 *American University J Intl L & Pol* 27, 35.

[36] Gaja (n 6) 13, para 28.

[37] ARSIWA (n 4) 66, para 4 (Art 16 Commentary).

[38] ILC, 'Summary Record of the 2681st Meeting' (29 May 2001), reproduced in (2001) 1 *YBILC* 90, 95, para 50; see also ILC, 'Summary Record of the 2762nd Meeting' (3 May 2001), reproduced in (2001) 1 *YBILC* 34, 37, para 19 (Simma).

It follows that if an assisting State is not aware of the circumstances of the wrongful act, it cannot be held responsible on this basis. However, the precise extent and standard of knowledge required to find whether a State bears responsibility for its aid or assistance is not settled as a matter of positive law.[39]

Likewise, the terms of Article 16 ARSIWA and the relevant parts of the ILC's Commentary provide little guidance on how knowledge should be proven and what standards of proof apply. There is no unified interpretation under general international law. In some cases, constructive knowledge (ie such that can be expected from the exercise of reasonable care) could satisfy the requirements of responsibility, particularly where assistance is given pursuant to a treaty or an established pattern of cooperation (eg a military alliance). In the majority of cases where no such treaty or pattern exists, a more rigorous standard of actual or direct knowledge is required. The exact degree of knowledge in this context will also depend on the corresponding requirements of the primary obligation.[40] In the absence of a specific requirement in a primary rule, it is this author's view that the standard of 'knowledge of the circumstances of the wrongful act' suffices.

Generally, a State's responsibility should be triggered by the foreseeable consequences of the aid or assistance given under the circumstances. That the unlawful conduct is foreseeable as a consequence of the type or content of assistance in the given circumstances must surely suffice.[41] In other words, knowledge would mean awareness that these circumstances exist or that a particular consequence will occur in the ordinary course of events. Such 'knowledge' can be assessed in light of public statements, diplomatic exchanges and official policies of the relevant organs of the State. Information about a State's record on human rights and humanitarian law may also be available through media reports[42] and the investigations of

[39] See, eg Jackson (n 15) 159–62; HP Aust, *Complicity and the Law of State Responsibility* (Cambridge, CUP, 2011) 236; J Quigley, 'Complicity in International Law: A New Direction in the Law of State Responsibility' (1987) 57 *British YBIL* 77, 108–20; Nolte and Aust (n 20) 14–15.

[40] J Crawford, *The International Law Commission's Articles on State Responsibility: Introduction, Text and Commentaries* (Cambridge, CUP, 2002) 84.

[41] Lowe (n 8) 8.

[42] *Military and Paramilitary Activities in and against Nicaragua (Nicaragua v United States)* (Merits) [1986] ICJ Rep 14, 40, para 62 (even if media reports 'seem to meet high standards of objectivity, the Court regards them not as evidence capable of proving facts, but as material which can nevertheless contribute, in some circumstances, to corroborating the existence of a fact'); ibid 53, para 92 (the Court taking account of the US activities 'as one of public knowledge, and as such, sufficiently established'); ibid, Dissenting Opinion of Judge Schwebel 259, 324; *Application of the Convention on the Prevention and Punishment of the Crime of Genocide (Bosnia and Herzegovina v Serbia and Montenegro)* (Provisional Measures, Order of 13 September 1993) [1993] ICJ Rep 325, Separate Opinion of Judge Shahabuddeen 353, 358 (on admissibility of media material as evidence in the proceedings before the ICJ).

international organisations and non-governmental organisations.[43] As discussed in detail in chapter five, little if no persuasive evidence emerges from practice and *opinio juris* of States and international organisations to support the proposition that an entity giving aid or assistance must not merely know of the circumstances in which it is to be used, but also intend or desire that it should be so used, and know of the intent of the principal wrongdoer.[44]

iii. Complicity with a View to Facilitating the Commission of the Internationally Wrongful Act

According to the ILC's Commentary, the requirement that the aid or assistance must be given with a view to facilitating the commission of the wrongful act 'limits the application of Article 16 to those cases where the aid or assistance given is clearly linked to the subsequent wrongful conduct'.[45] The Commentary explains that:

> A State is not responsible for aid and assistance under article 16 unless the relevant State organ *intended*, by the aid or assistance given, *to facilitate the occurrence of the wrongful act* and the internationally wrongful act is actually committed by the aided or assisted State.[46] (emphasis added)

This would suggest the presence of a requirement of purpose-based intent, absent which the conduct in question would be lawful. However, such a construction would be at odds with the general framework of the ARSIWA and ARIO, because, after protracted discussions, the ILC decided not to include the element of fault as a constituent element of an internationally wrongful act. The Commission stated that, if necessary, the mental element should be defined by the primary obligation on a case-by-case basis.[47] However, 'in the absence of any specific requirement of a mental element in terms of the primary obligation, it is only the act of a State that matters, independently of any intention'.[48]

There is no logical justification to deviate from the objective nature of responsibility in the situations of responsibility for complicity. In most cases, it is extremely difficult, if not impossible, to prove that a State did not only know that its assistance would be used for illegal purposes, but that it had been providing such assistance just for that purpose, ie with the intention to facilitate the commission of that wrongful act.[49]

[43] A Boivin, 'Complicity and Beyond: International Law and the Transfer of Small Arms and Light Weapons' (2005) 87 *IRRC* 467, 470.

[44] cf Aust (n 39) 230–49.

[45] ARSIWA (n 4) 66, para 5 (Art 16 Commentary).

[46] ibid 66, para 5 (Art 16 Commentary).

[47] ibid 36, para 10 (Art 2 Commentary).

[48] ibid.

[49] B Graefrath, 'Complicity in the Law of International Responsibility' (1996) 2 *RBDI* 370, 375.

In this way, it would be problematic to equate knowledge to intent because it would not capture the common scenario where the receiving State commits a violation but the assisting State does not desire the illegal result.[50] The ILC discussed the example of Germany permitting the United States' military bases to be set up in its territory in 1958. These bases were used to send United States' airplanes to Lebanon for a military intervention.[51] Ago was of the opinion that this situation would typically fall within the scope of responsibility for complicity even though it was unlikely that Germany had desired the United States' intervention in Lebanon.[52] Similarly, in 1965 Germany and Turkey allowed United States' balloons to be launched from their territory, prompting the USSR to protest that these States were complicit in the wrongful acts by the United States. In these situations, the responsibility of the two States arose from a knowing omission or toleration of the activities harmful to a third State. In other words, intent could be no more than proof of objective collaboration between two subjects rather than the artificial search for a state of mind or purpose of one subject in respect of the principal wrongful act by another. Ago's general position, however, was that:

> The very 'idea' of complicity in the internationally wrongful act of another necessarily presupposes *an intent to collaborate* in the commission of an act of this kind, and hence, in the cases considered, *knowledge of the specific purpose for which the State receiving supplies intends to use them*. Without this condition, there can be no question of complicity.[53] (emphasis added)

When the Commission discussed the cognitive requirement of complicity, there were opposing views as to whether the intent was necessary or if a more objective standard of knowledge of the circumstances of the wrongful act would suffice. As one of the ILC members suggested at the time: 'too narrow a definition [of the cognitive element] would nullify the scope of the article … No State would admit that it was helping another to commit a wrongful act'.[54] Schwebel did not think this was necessarily the case and recalled, for instance, that 'Hitler's plan of aggression had been published in explicit detail'.[55] Another member of the Commission at the time stressed:

> It did not really seem necessary to emphasize the element of intent … The Commission had never so far taken intent into consideration. *By definition, a State took its decisions knowingly* and there could be no question of responsibility for negligence, as in internal law. It was *enough to establish that aid or assistance had*

[50] Quigley (n 39) 111.
[51] R Ago, 'Seventh Report on State Responsibility' (1978) UN Doc A/CN.4/307 and Add 1-2 and Corr 1-2, reproduced in (1978) 2 (pt 1) *YBILC* 31, 59, para 73.
[52] ibid 59, para 73.
[53] ibid 58, para 72.
[54] ILC, 'Summary Record of the 1518th Meeting' (n 2) 236, para 28 (Njenga).
[55] ibid 237, para 37 (Schwebel).

been provided by one State to another for the former to incur responsibility.[56] (emphasis added)

In preparation for the second reading, Brownlie stated that the inclusion of intent was redundant because complicity presumed the existence of requisite knowledge. According to him '[i]t was also likely to cause misunderstanding, as it might actually set conditions of liability, and set them at rather a high level'.[57]

Some commentators, including James Crawford, have referred to the ICJ's ruling in the *Bosnia Genocide* case as recognising that the general regime on responsibility for complicity requires intent on the part of the aiding or assisting State in relation to the principal wrongful act.[58] Crawford's main response to the critics of the requirement of intent is threefold: (i) the 'character of interstate relations and the great diversity of situations which may arise'; (ii) the fact that intent is not tainted with the requirement of common purpose or cause between the principal and complicit entity; and (iii) the idea that no criticism is valid because in any case Article 16 ARSIWA is 'still a substantial advance of the concept [of complicity] in international law'.[59] Chapter five will examine whether and to what extent Crawford's statements, which are coloured by his conviction that less is more in the law of international responsibility, align with the practice and *opinio juris* of States and international organisations. It will be argued that the requirement of intent is unnecessary and overly restrictive in the general regime of responsibility for complicity.

iv. Opposability of the Obligation Breached

The responsibility under paragraph (b) of Articles 16 ARSIWA and 14 ARIO is further limited by the requirement that the principal act be wrongful for both the principal and the complicit State or international organisation.[60] An aiding or assisting State may not deliberately procure the breach by another State of an obligation by which both States are bound. In other words, 'a State cannot do by another what it cannot do by itself'.[61]

This condition is not free from criticism. Consider the following scenario: State A has a conventional duty toward State B not to build a dam near a given river. State C has sufficient knowledge of the existence of this bilateral obligation between State A and State B. Nonetheless,

[56] ibid 233, para 4 (Ushakov).

[57] ILC, 'Summary Record of the 2577th Meeting' (26 May 1999), reproduced in (1999) 1 *YBILC* 67, 70, para 27 (Brownlie).

[58] J Crawford, *State Responsibility: The General Part* (Cambridge, CUP, 2013) 407–08.

[59] ibid 408; *Bosnia Genocide (Merits)* (n 14) 223, para 432.

[60] G Gaja, 'Seventh Report on Responsibility of International Organizations' (2009) UN Doc A/CN.4/610, reproduced in (2009) 2 (pt 1) *YBILC* 73, 83, para 45.

[61] Crawford (n 22) 51, para 186.

State C supports State A with money and technology for the purposes of construction of the dam by State A. The question arises as to whether State B can sue State C for assisting in the breach of the treaty between States A and B. The response of the ILC is in the negative, stressing that a State is not bound by an obligation of another State vis-à-vis third States. This reasoning is inspired by Articles 34 and 35 of the Vienna Convention on the Law of Treaties (VCLT), also known as the rule of *pacta tertiis nec nocent nec prosunt*:

> Article 34
>
> General rule regarding third States
>
> A treaty does not create either obligations or rights for a third State without its consent.[62]
>
> ***
>
> Article 35
>
> Treaties providing for obligations for third States
>
> An obligation arises for a third State from a provision of a treaty if the parties to the treaty intend the provision to be the means of establishing the obligation and the third State expressly accepts that obligation in writing.[63]

However, as will be discussed in chapter five, outside the realm of the law of treaties, this limitation of the relationships that can give rise to responsibility for complicity is problematic. For example, the ILC did not consider situations in which the absence of the formal obligation is subsumed within multilateral or regional cooperation agreements, containing similar obligations. Taking the scenario outlined above, State C, although not bound by the same obligation as State A vis-à-vis State B, could be held responsible for assisting State A, in the violation of its obligations under a regional instrument, to which all of the three States are parties. The fact that State C is subject to a similar obligation (albeit under a different instrument or under customary international law) would in this scenario actually facilitate proof of the 'knowledge of the circumstances' requirement. Parallel obligations of this kind (with similar content) are relatively common, but would be excluded from the framework of responsibility for complicity because of the opposability requirement.[64]

[62] Vienna Convention on the Law of Treaties (adopted 23 May 1969; entered into force 27 January 1980) 1155 UNTS 331, Art 34; see also E David, 'Art 34 (1969)' in O Corten and P Klein (eds), *The Vienna Conventions on the Law of Treaties: The Commentary* (Oxford, OUP, 2011).

[63] VCLT (n 62) Art 35; see also C Laly-Chevalier, 'Art 35 (1969)' in O Corten and E Klein (eds), *The Vienna Conventions on the Law of Treaties: The Commentary* (Oxford, OUP, 2011).

[64] Aust (n 39) 258–65 (discussing the problem of the overlapping obligations in respect of the same subject matter which stem from different sources).

Similarly, the Commission ignored situations of responsibility that could arise while the treaty is provisionally being applied or while a formal obligation is emerging (*in statu nascendi*). For example, when the State has signed a particular treaty and commenced the procedures for its ratification, at the very minimum, that State is required under Article 18 of the VCLT not to undermine the object and purpose of the treaty.[65] It will certainly do so if it provides aid or assistance to another State (party to the treaty) in order to breach an obligation as essential in character as to undermine the very object and purpose of the treaty. Nor did the Commission take into account the examples of objective regimes, such as the Antarctic Treaty System, and whether a State could by its aid or assistance facilitate the breach of such regimes, even though technically not being a contracting party to them.[66]

Crawford conveyed his message to his fellow members at the ILC that without the requirement of opposability, the provision would be a de facto primary norm imposing an obligation on States not to provide aid or assistance to any internationally wrongful act.[67] Most, but not all of the ILC Members agreed to the addition of this requirement of opposability.[68] One of the members who did not agree explained his objections to the inclusion of opposability as follows:

> That provision considerably reduced, without good reason, the scope of application of [former draft Article 27]. It did not exclude bilateral obligations alone. It also excluded multilateral obligations by which the aiding or assisting State was not bound. The condition was not necessary, since it was most unlikely that a State would knowingly and deliberately help another State to breach its bilateral or multilateral obligations. Neither the commentary to the draft articles adopted on First Reading nor the second report of the Special Rapporteur [Crawford] contained any examples drawn from international practice.[69]

In addition to the absence of relevant practice—as we shall see in chapter five—this 'bilateral straitjacket' of responsibility for complicity in the ARSIWA and ARIO was not the result of a particular pressure from States or international organisations.[70] Elsewhere, James Crawford has acknowledged that 'international law now contains a range of rules which cannot be broken down into mere bundles of bilateral relations between

[65] VCLT (n 62) Art 18; see also L Boisson de Chazournes, AM La Rosa and MM Mbengue, 'Art 18 (1969)' in O Corten and P Klein (eds), *The Vienna Conventions on the Law of Treaties: The Commentary* (Oxford, OUP, 2011).

[66] See Aust (n 39) 255–58.

[67] Crawford (n 22) 50–51, paras 183–86.

[68] See ILC (n 57) 70, para 25 (Simma), para 27 (Brownlie); 71, para 31 (Rosenstock).

[69] ibid 68, para 5 (Economides).

[70] cf ILC, 'Comments of Governments on Part 1 of the Draft Articles on State Responsibility for Internationally Wrongful Acts' (1981) UN Doc A/CN.4/342 and Add 1-4, reproduced in (1981) 2 (pt 1) *YBILC* 71, 77 (Sweden).

States but instead cover a much broader scope'.[71] The ILC (under James Crawford's leadership) failed to recognise that a broader scope of responsibility for complicity could have led to a greater respect for the rule of law and the promotion of the legal interests of international community as a whole in the observance of international obligations.

III. AGGRAVATED REGIME OF COMPLICITY (ARTICLES 41(2) ARSIWA AND 42(2) ARIO)

A. Preliminary Remarks

Articles 16 ARSIWA and 14 ARIO are not the only provisions addressing situations of complicity in a wrongful act. Most notably, Article 41(2) ARSIWA (and its copy for international organisations in Article 42(2) ARIO) expressly prohibit aid or assistance to the maintenance of a situation created by a serious breach of peremptory norms (*jus cogens*):

> Article 41 ARSIWA
>
> Particular consequences of a serious breach of an obligation under this chapter
>
> 1. States shall cooperate to bring to an end through lawful means any serious breach within the meaning of article 40.
> 2. No State shall recognize as lawful a situation created by a serious breach within the meaning of article 40, nor render aid or assistance in maintaining that situation.
> 3. This article is without prejudice to the other consequences referred to in this part and to such further consequences that a breach to which this chapter applies may entail under international law.

They can be said to operate as a *lex specialis* in relation to Article 16 ARSIWA.[72] The operation of these provisions is in some ways quite similar to Articles 16 ARSIWA and 14 ARIO (general regime), but in other ways different. They are similar in the sense that their function is to preserve legality under international law and to ensure the wrongdoing is not assisted. They are different because, contrary to the general regime of responsibility for complicity, they deal exclusively with the prohibition of complicity in relation to the serious breaches of *jus cogens* norms that have already taken place.[73]

[71] J Crawford, 'The System of International Responsibility' in J Crawford et al (eds), *The Law of International Responsibility* (Oxford, OUP, 2010) 24.

[72] Aust (n 39) 336–52.

[73] See generally A Gattini, 'A Return Ticket to "Communitarisme", Please' (2002) 13 *EJIL* 1181.

Articles 41(2) ARSIWA and 42(2) ARIO reflect a shift from bilateralism to solidarity in international law.[74] The regime of serious breaches of peremptory norms, as set out in Articles 40/41 ARSIWA and 41/42 ARIO enhances the idea of relative normativity in international law.[75] After endless academic and ideological debates, the dichotomy of crime/delict in former draft Article 19 was abandoned on second reading of the ARSIWA.[76] Nonetheless, the ILC maintained in part the substance of the idea of a State crime in the Articles 40/41 ARSIWA and 41/42 ARIO.[77] Concretely, it retained the principle that serious breaches of peremptory norms entail additional legal consequences in the law of international responsibility.[78] These are the duties to cooperate to bring the breach to an end, and not to recognise or render aid or assistance to the maintenance of an unlawful situation deriving from a serious breach of peremptory norms.

[74] cf ILC, 'Report of the International Law Commission on the Work of Its 28th Session (3 May–23 July 1976)' (1976) UN Doc A/31/10, reproduced in (1976) 2 (pt 2) *YBILC* 1, 97, para 7 (Former Draft Art 19 Commentary); see also A Pellet, 'Can a State Commit a Crime? Definitely, Yes!' (1999) 10 *EJIL* 425; A Ollivier, 'International Criminal Responsibility of the State' in J Crawford et al (eds), *The Law of International Responsibility* (Oxford, OUP, 2010); G Abi-Saab, 'The Uses of Article 19' (1999) 10 *EJIL* 339; G Abi-Saab, 'Que reste-il du "crime international"', *Droit du pouvoir—pouvoir du droit: Mélanges en l'honneur de Jean Salmon* (Bruxelles, Bruylant, 2007).

[75] See A Pellet, 'The New Draft Articles of the International Law Commission on the Responsibility of States for International Wrongful Acts: A Requiem for States' Crime?' (2001) 32 *Netherlands YBIL* 55; J Barboza, 'State Crimes: A Decaffeinated Coffee' in L Boisson de Chazournes and V Gowlland-Debbas (eds), *The International Legal System in Quest of Equity and Universality: Liber Amicorum Georges Abi-Saab* (The Hague, Martinus Nijhoff, 2001); E Wyler, 'From "State Crime" to Responsibility for Serious Breaches of Obligations under Peremptory Norms of General International Law' (2002) 13 *EJIL* 1147.

[76] J Crawford, 'First Report on State Responsibility' (1998) UN Doc A/CN.4/490 and Add 1-7, reproduced in (1998) 2 (pt 1) *YBILC* 1, 11, para 52 ff; Wyler (n 75); for general discussions on the notion of crime in the former draft Art 19 see, eg JHH Weiler, A Cassese and M Spinedi (eds), *International Crimes of State: A Critical Analysis of the ILC's Draft Article 19 on State Responsibility* (Berlin, Walter de Gruyter, 1989); R Hofmann, 'Zur Unterscheidung Verbrechen und Delikt im Bereich der Staatenverantwortlichkeit' (1985) 45 *ZaöRV* 195.

[77] See generally J Crawford, 'International Crimes of States' in J Crawford et al (eds), *The Law of International Responsibility* (Oxford, OUP, 2010); NHB Jørgensen, *The Responsibility of States for International Crimes* (Oxford, OUP, 2003); cf *Myrna Mack Chang v Guatemala* (Merits, Reparations and Costs) [2003] IACtHR Ser C No 101, Separate Opinion of Judge Cançado Trindade paras 6–8; *Miguel Castro-Castro Prison v Peru* (Merits, Reparations and Costs) [2006] IACtHR Ser C No 160, Concurring Opinion of Judge Cançado Trindade paras 40–57 (criticising the ILC's decision to abandon the notion of crime).

[78] See generally different contributions in PM Dupuy (ed), *Obligations multilatérales, droit impératif et responsabilité internationale des États* (Paris, Pedone, 2003); see also E Cannizzaro, 'On the Special Consequences of a Serious Breach of Obligations Arising out of Peremptory Rules of International Law' in E Cannizzaro (ed), *The Present and Future of Jus Cogens* (Roma, Sapienza, 2015); NHB Jørgensen, 'The Obligation of Non-Assistance to the Responsible State' in J Crawford et al (eds), *The Law of International Responsibility* (Oxford, OUP, 2010); cf CJ Tams, 'Do Serious Breaches Give Rise to Any Specific Obligations of the Responsible State?' (2002) 13 *EJIL* 1161, 1179–80 (concluding that there are no specific legal obligations for the State responsible for a serious breach of peremptory norms).

They are not self-exclusive and rather complement each other in practice. For instance, the duty to cooperate under Article 41(1) ARSIWA is no more than a reverse coin of the duty of non-assistance and could serve a strong preventative function in the future, including in shaping the notion of the responsibility to protect.[79] Aust goes as far as to suggest that the obligation to prevent combined with the obligation to cooperate under Article 41(1) ARSIWA could 'be seen as functional equivalents to the prohibition of complicity in international law'.[80] In this author's view, there are some technical differences in the scope of the duty to cooperate and non-recognition vis-à-vis the obligation of non-assistance, but they are certainly complementary.

There is a close connection between the obligation not to render aid or assistance to and the obligation not to recognise a situation deriving from a serious breach of a peremptory norm.[81] In the words of the ILC, together, they form a 'duty of abstention' in respect of the situation deriving from the serious breach of peremptory norms.[82] In its Commentary to the ARSIWA, the ILC suggests that the obligation of non-assistance could, in some respects, be regarded as an extension of the duty of non-recognition.[83]

The relationship between these duties is uncertain. Some authors have argued that the duty of non-recognition is just one expression of the duty of non-assistance.[84] For example, Joe Verhoeven suggests that an obligation of non-recognition expresses a condemnation of any form of complicity in the violation of international law.[85] Judge Kooijmans took the view

[79] Aust (n 39) 352–65; see different contributions in J Hoffmann and A Nollkaemper (eds), *Responsibility to Protect From Principle to Practice* (Amsterdam, Pallas, 2012); VP Nanda, 'The Future Under International Law of the Responsibility to Protect after Libya and Syria' (2013) 21 *Michigan State Intl LR* 1; NHB Jørgensen, 'The Obligation of Cooperation' in J Crawford et al (eds), *The Law of International Responsibility* (Oxford, OUP, 2010).

[80] Aust (n 39) 364.

[81] S Villalpando, *L'émergence de la communauté internationale dans la responsabilité des États* (Paris, PUF, 2005) 389; on the formulation of the duty of non-recognition as it inspired the ILC's work see *Legal Consequences for States of the Continued Presence of South Africa in Namibia (South West Africa) notwithstanding Security Council Resolution 276 (1970)* (Advisory Opinion) [1971] ICJ Rep 16, 55–56, paras 120–24.

[82] ARSIWA (n 4) 114, para 4 (Art 41 Commentary).

[83] ibid 115, para 12 (Art 41 Commentary).

[84] V Gowlland-Debbas, *Collective Responses to Illegal Acts in International Law: United Nations Action in the Question of Southern Rhodesia* (Dordrecht, Martinus Nijhoff, 1990) 289; cf S Talmon, *Kollektive Nichtanerkennung illegaler Staaten* (Tübingen, Mohr, 2006) 334 (suggesting that the recognition would only constitute psychological encouragement but not assistance).

[85] J Verhoeven, 'La reconnaissance internationale: déclin ou renouveau?' (1993) 39 *AFDI* 7, 36 (the obligation of non-recognition 'n'exprime pas autre chose que la condamnation de toute forme de complicité dans la violation du droit'); see also A Lagerwall, 'The Duty Not to Recognise as Lawful a Situation Created by the Illegal Use of Force: From Kosovo to Abkhazia and South Ossetia' in M Szabó (ed), *State Responsibility and the Law of Treaties* (The Hague, Eleven, 2010).

that, while the obligation of non-assistance is relatively clear in terms of what it entails, the obligation of non-recognition lacks 'real substance' in international law.[86]

Aust has convincingly argued that the two duties complement each other despite their different content.[87] Finding support in a passage of the ILC's Commentary,[88] Aust concludes that while a duty of non-assistance tackles concrete measures of help which impact directly upon the maintenance of the unlawful situations, non-recognition addresses the more general or political forms of support and encouragement.[89] In fact, the duty of non-recognition has arguably a much broader scope of application in international law than as a consequence flowing exclusively from serious breaches of peremptory norms. For instance, the duty of non-recognition also applies in respect of 'territorial acquisition or special advantages obtained by the illicit use of force', which may not necessarily reach the threshold of seriousness as envisaged by the ILC for the regime of Articles 40/41 ARSIWA.[90]

The consequences set out in the ARSIWA and ARIO in respect of breaches of peremptory norms are without prejudice to any other consequences that may arise under general international law.[91] These are, for example, the obligation of cessation, reparation, the guarantees of non-repetition (which are addressed in chapter six), or measures taken by the United Nations Security Council (UNSC).[92] There could of course be consequences in terms of treaty law, including the potential termination or

[86] *Legal Consequences of the Construction of a Wall in the Occupied Palestinian Territory* (Advisory Opinion) [2004] ICJ Rep 136, Separate Opinion of Judge Kooijmans 219, 232, para 44.

[87] Aust (n 39) 326–37.

[88] ARSIWA (n 4) 115, para 12 (Art 41 Commentary).

[89] Aust (n 39) 337.

[90] UNGA, 'Res 2625 (XXV) Declaration on Principles of International Law Concerning Friendly Relations and Co-Operation among States in Accordance with the Charter of the United Nations' (24 October 1970) UN Doc A/RES/25/2625, Principle I ('No territorial acquisition resulting from the threat or use of force shall be recognized as legal'); see also CJ Tams, 'All's Well When It Ends Well: Comments on the ILC's Articles on State Responsibility' (2002) 62 *ZaöRV* 759, 775; S Talmon, 'The Duty Not to "Recognize as Lawful" a Situation Created by the Illegal Use of Force or Other Serious Breaches of a Jus Cogens Obligation: An Obligation without Real Substance?' in C Tomuschat and JM Thouvenin (eds), *The Fundamental Rules of the International Legal Order* (Leiden, Martinus Nijhoff, 2006) 112 (arguing that the obligation of non-recognition amounts to 'more than the prohibition of a formal admission of legality', requiring 'States to refrain from any action implying the recognition of the legality of the situation in question').

[91] ARSIWA (n 4) Art 41(3).

[92] ibid 115–16, paras 13–14 (Art 41 Commentary); for relevant practice of the UNSC see, eg UNSC, 'Res 217' (20 November 1965) UN Doc S/RES/217 (Southern Rhodesia); UNSC, 'Res 1828' (31 July 2008) UN Doc S/RES/1828 (Sudan); UNSC, 'Res 1856' (22 December 2008) UN Doc S/RES/1856 (DRC); UNSC, 'Res 1865' (27 January 2009) UN Doc S/RES/1865 (Ivory Coast); UNSC, 'Res 1756' (15 May 2007) UN Doc S/RES/1756 (DRC); UNSC, 'Res 1572' (15 November 2004) UN Doc S/RES/1572 (Ivory Coast); UNSC, 'Res 1857' (22 December 2008) UN Doc S/RES/1857 (DRC).

suspension.[93] Similarly, a serious breach of peremptory norm could lead to the suspension of the principal and accomplice wrongdoers from their membership of an international organisation.[94] A State responsible for serious breaches of peremptory norms could also be under 'an obligation to change its government, to change its constitution to the extent necessary, and to hold free elections so as to prevent the recurrence' of such acts.[95] In principle, other consequences could be envisaged, as long as these do not amount to punitive damages, reprisals or other manifestly disproportionate measures. As the Appeals Chamber of the International Criminal Tribunal for the former Yugoslavia (ICTY) explained in its *Blaškić subpoena* decision 'under present international law it is clear that States, by definition, cannot be the subject of criminal sanctions akin to those provided for in national criminal systems'.[96] It is thus likely that the ILC's failure to further clarify the content of any such consequences was a deliberate choice to leave the issue to political processes.[97]

B. Constituent Elements of the Obligation of Non-assistance

i. The Existence of a Serious Breach of Peremptory Norm of International Law

Article 40(2) ARSIWA clarifies that to characterise a breach as 'serious', the breach must entail 'a gross or systematic failure by the responsible State to fulfil the obligation'.[98] Further, the ARSIWA Commentary states that there are two criteria that shall be used to distinguish a serious breach from other types of breaches: (i) the character of the obligation that has been breached—it must derive from a peremptory norm of general international law (*jus cogens*), and (ii) the intensity of the breach.[99]

[93] VCLT (n 62), Art 60; B Simma, 'Reflections on Article 60 of the Vienna Convention on the Law of Treaties and Its Background in General International Law' (1970) 20 *Österreichische Zeitschrift für öffentliches Recht* 5.

[94] For examples from practice and discussions on the availability of such remedy and its effectiveness in bringing the wrongdoer to compliance see, eg A Duxbury, *The Participation of States in International Organisations* (Cambridge, CUP, 2011) 214–21; N Singh, *Termination of Membership of International Organizations* (London, Stevens & Sons, 1958) 58; LB Sohn, 'Expulsion or Forced Withdrawal from an International Organization' (1964) 77 *Harvard LR* 1381, 1416; CW Jenks, 'Due Process of Law in International Organizations' (1965) 19 *International Organization* 163, 166.

[95] AJ de Hoogh, *Obligations Erga Omnes and International Crimes* (The Hague, Kluwer, 1996) 195–97.

[96] *Prosecutor v Blaškić* (Subpoena Decision) IT-95-14 (29 October 1997) para 25.

[97] A Nollkaemper, 'State Responsibility for International Crimes: A Review of Principles of Reparation' in A Constantinidis and N Zaikos (eds), *The Diversity of International Law: Essays in Honour of Professor Kalliopi K. Koufa* (Leiden, Martinus Nijhoff, 2009) 511–12 (arguing that 'State responsibility principally remains confined within a bilateral straitjacket and has made little progress towards communitarian responses to situations of system criminality').

[98] ARSIWA (n 4) 113, para 7 (Art 40 Commentary).

[99] ibid 112, para 1 (Art 40 Commentary).

The first criterion concerns the identification of norms that can be qualified as peremptory.[100] Article 53 of the VCLT provides that a peremptory norm of general international law is one which is:

> [A]ccepted and recognized by the international community of States as a whole as a norm from which no derogation is permitted and which can be modified only by a subsequent norm of general international law having the same character.[101]

The notion of *jus cogens* has been affirmed in contexts other than the law of treaties.[102] However, the aggravated legal consequences attaching to breaches of peremptory norms have not been without controversy.[103] It has been argued that there is often insufficient practice and *opinio juris* on the operation of peremptory norms outside of the context of treaty law with the result that international courts and tribunals may inadvertently be diluting *jus cogens* itself.[104] However, it is generally accepted that the following norms are peremptory: the obligation to respect the principle of self-determination, the prohibition of aggression and unlawful use or threat of force, the prohibition against slavery, genocide, torture, racial discrimination and apartheid.[105] Clearly, the 'club' of the peremptory norms is limited as a matter of positive international law.

The second criterion is that the character of the breach of *jus cogens* must be serious.[106] This requirement indicates that a certain order of magnitude of violation is required. However, this does not necessarily mean that lesser violations of these obligations are somehow excusable.[107] The Commission's assumption was that the violations of peremptory norms such as the prohibition of genocide are by definition serious whereas

[100] ibid.

[101] VCLT (n 62) Art 53.

[102] *Prosecutor v Furundžija* (Judgment) IT-95-17/1-T (10 December 1998) para 178; *R v Bow Street Metropolitan Stipendiary Magistrate and others, Ex Parte Pinochet Ugarte (No 3)* (Judgment) [1999] 2 WLR 827; see also *Legality of the Threat or Use of Nuclear Weapons* (Advisory Opinion) [1996] ICJ Rep 226, 257, para 79; cf *Armed Activities on the Territory of the Congo (New Application: 2002) (DRC v Rwanda)* (Jurisdiction and Admissibility) [2006] ICJ Rep 6, 29–31, paras 56–63; ibid, Separate Opinion of Judge ad hoc Dugard 86, 86–91, paras 3–14.

[103] G Gaja, 'Jus Cogens Beyond the Vienna Convention' (1981) 172 *RCADI* 271; B Simma, 'From Bilateralism to Community Interest in International Law' (1994) 250 *RCADI* 217, 288; A Paulus, 'Jus Cogens in a Time of Hegemony and Fragmentation—An Attempt at a Re-Appraisal' (2005) 74 *Nordic J Intl L* 297, 308; A Orakhelashvili, *Peremptory Norms in International Law* (Oxford, OUP, 2006) 205.

[104] A Bianchi, 'Human Rights and the Magic of Jus Cogens' (2008) 19 *EJIL* 491; on the risk of seeing jus cogens everywhere, reference is made to *Juridical Condition and Rights of the Undocumented Migrants* (Advisory Opinion) [2003] IACtHR Ser A No 18 (holding that the principles of non-discrimination, equality before the law, and equal protection before the law can be regarded as peremptory norms).

[105] ARSIWA (n 4) 112–13, paras 4–5 (Art 40 Commentary).

[106] ibid 112, para 2 (Art 40 Commentary).

[107] ibid 113, para 7 (Art 40 Commentary).

the seriousness of other violations such as war crimes depends on the surrounding circumstances.[108] This qualification recalls the distinction between substantial and circumstantial gravity, previously used to differentiate between delicts and crimes.[109] The ILC justified its choice for introducing the threshold of seriousness as follows:

> For example, when reacting against breaches of international law, States have often stressed their systematic, gross or egregious nature. Similarly, international complaint procedures, for example in the field of human rights, attach different consequences to systematic breaches, eg in terms of non-applicability of the rule of exhaustion of local remedies.[110]

This justification sends an unfortunate message that only systematic and gross breaches of peremptory norms trigger the obligations of non-recognition and non-assistance. For example, if a State sporadically commits acts of torture in its detention facilities but those acts of torture do not rise to the level of 'systematic and gross', then other States can continue providing aid or assistance to the State committing torture without incurring responsibility.[111] This normative outcome is disappointing.[112]

Nina Jørgensen uses the hostage-taking of American diplomatic and consular staff in Tehran in 1979 and their subsequent detention until 1981 as an example of the way the seriousness requirement may hamper the application of Article 41(2) ARSIWA.[113] Jørgensen rightly asks if States could have assisted in maintaining the unlawful situation brought about by the hostage taking after the hostages had been released.[114] The problem

[108] UNGA, 'Sixth Committee, Summary Record of the 16th Meeting' (15 November 2001) UN Doc A/C.6/56/SR.16, 10, para 63 (Crawford); see also A Gianelli, 'Le conseguenze delle gravi violazioni di obblighi posti da norme imperative tra norme primarie e norme secondarie' in M Spinedi, A Gianelli and ML Alaimo (eds), *La codificazione della responsabilità internazionale degli stati alla prova dei fatti: Problemi e spunti di riflessione* (Milano, Giuffrè, 2006); Crawford (n 58) 378–94.

[109] See R Ago, 'Fifth Report on State Responsibility' (1976) UN Doc A/CN.4/291 and Add 1-2, reproduced in (1976) 2 (pt 1) *YBILC* 3, 53, para 150; ILC, 'Report of the International Law Commission on the Work of Its 28th Session (3 May–23 July 1976)' (n 74) 121, paras 70–71; G Palmisano, 'Les causes d'aggravation de la responsabilité des États et la distinction entre "crimes" et "délits" internationaux' (1994) 98 *RGDIP* 629; G Palmisano, 'Cronaca di una morte annunciata: la responsabilità dello Stato per crimini internazionali' in M Spinedi, A Gianelli and ML Alaimo (eds), *La codificazione della responsabilità internazionale degli stati alla prova dei fatti: Problemi e spunti di riflessione* (Milano, Giuffrè, 2006); PM Dupuy, 'A General Stocktaking of the Connections between the Multilateral Dimension of Obligations and Codification of the Law of Responsibility' (2002) 13 *EJIL* 1053, 1061; Wyler (n 75) 1157.

[110] ARSIWA (n 4) 113, para 7 (Art 40 Commentary); see, eg *Ireland v United Kingdom* (Judgment) [1978] ECtHR Ser A No 25 (1979–80) 2 EHRR 25, para 159.

[111] cf, eg *A (FC) and others (FC) v Secretary of State for the Home Department, A and others (FC) v Secretary of State for the Home Department (Joined Appeals)* (Judgment) [2005] UKHL 71 para 34.

[112] See, eg Jørgensen (n 77) 114–15; Aust (n 39) 326; BI Bonafé, *The Relationship between State and Individual Responsibility for International Crimes* (Leiden, Martinus Nijhoff, 2009) 75–81.

[113] See Jørgensen (n 78) 692.

[114] ibid.

remains to be solved in practice as to 'where to draw the line between the "ordinary" and "aggravated" breaches' of *jus cogens*, and whether it is necessary to do so at all.[115]

Further, why should the duty of non-assistance only attach to serious breaches of *jus cogens* and not *erga omnes* obligations? The latter already have an important role in the regime of invocation of responsibility (Articles 42/48 ARSIWA and Articles 43/49 ARIO) and implementation (Articles 49–54 ARSIWA and Articles 51–57 ARIO) and it would only be logical to extend the reach of the duty of non-assistance to the maintenance of a situation flowing from breaches of *erga omnes* obligations. According to the ARSIWA Commentary:

> The examples which the [ICJ] has given of obligations towards the international community as a whole all concern obligations which, it is generally accepted, arise under peremptory norms of general international law. Likewise the examples of peremptory norms given by the Commission in its commentary to what became article 53 of the Vienna Convention involve obligations to the international community as a whole.[116]

The ILC appears to suggest that 'obligations *erga omnes* and obligations resulting from peremptory norms [are] two faces of the same coin'.[117] However, the ILC did stress that:

> While peremptory norms of general international law focus on the scope and priority to be given to a certain number of fundamental obligations, the focus of obligations to the international community as a whole is essentially on the legal interest of all States in compliance—ie … in being entitled to invoke the responsibility of any State in breach.[118]

It is questionable whether in substance the notion of *erga omnes* and the notion of *jus cogens* coincide for the purposes of the prohibition of aid or assistance, as enshrined under Articles 41(2) ARSIWA and 42(2) ARIO.[119] If they coincide, the duty of non-assistance would extend in respect of a

[115] ibid.

[116] ARSIWA (n 4) 112, para 7.

[117] LA Sicilianos, 'The Classification of Obligations and the Multilateral Dimension of Relations of International Responsibility' (2002) 13 *EJIL* 1127, 1136; on the relationship between jus cogens and erga omnes obligations see, eg Gaja (n 103) 1136; P Picone, 'La distinzione tra norme internazionali di jus cogens e norme che producono obblighi erga omnes' (2008) 1 *RDI* 5; P Picone, 'Obblighi erga omnes e codificazione della responsabilità degli stati' (2005) 4 *RDI* 893; G Gaja, 'Do States Have a Duty to Ensure Compliance with Obligations Erga Omnes by Other States?' in M Ragazzi (ed), *International Responsibility Today: Essays in Memory of Oscar Schachter* (Leiden, Martinus Nijhoff, 2005); CJ Tams et al, 'Erga Omnes, Jus Cogens and Their Impact on the Law of Responsibility' in M Evans and P Koutrakos (eds), *The International Responsibility of the European Union: European and International Perspectives* (Oxford, Hart Publishing, 2013).

[118] ARSIWA (n 4) 112, para 7.

[119] M Ragazzi, *The Concept of International Obligations Erga Omnes* (Oxford, Clarendon Press, 1997) 189 ff; see also CJ Tams, *Enforcing Obligations Erga Omnes* (Cambridge, CUP, 2005).

much broader range of obligations. In line with the celebrated passage in the *Barcelona Traction* case obligations *erga omnes* result *inter alia* 'from the principles and rules concerning the basic rights of the human person, including protection from slavery and racial discrimination'.[120] The Court's use of the term 'including' suggests that other norms, for example in human rights law, could give rise to obligations *erga omnes*.[121] Thus, at least those norms that are non-derogable 'in time of war or other public emergency threatening the life of the nation' could be qualified as *erga omnes*.[122]

However, the ILC failed to clarify whether States and international organisations are allowed to provide aid or assistance in maintaining an illegal situation deriving from the breach of *erga omnes* obligations and whether these too have to reach a particular level of seriousness.[123] Further, the conceptual differences between the regime of invocation and that applicable to serious breaches of peremptory norms leave many questions unanswered.[124]

In the author's view, the aggravated legal consequences provided by Articles 41(2) ARSIWA and 42(2) ARIO should not be limited *ratione materiae* to 'serious' breaches of peremptory norms in international law.[125] There is no principled obstacle to extending the obligations of non-recognition and non-assistance in respect of violations of *erga omnes* obligations, if not (even more ambitiously) to any illegality which is of continuing character or where its effects persist in time, particularly where the illegality has been determined by a body such as the UNSC or the UNGA (United Nations General Assembly). This said, a State may at its own risk determine whether a situation constitutes an illegality so as not to recognise it and refrain from rendering aid or assistance towards its maintenance.[126]

[120] *Barcelona Traction, Light and Power Company, Limited (Second Phase) (Belgium v Spain)* (Judgment) [1970] ICJ Rep 3, 32, para 34.

[121] Sicilianos (n 117) 1137; IDI, 'Resolution on the Protection of Human Rights and the Principle of Non-Intervention in the Internal Affairs of States' (1989) 63 *AIDI* 338.

[122] European Convention for the Protection of Human Rights and Fundamental Freedoms (adopted 4 November 1950; entered into force 3 September 1953) 213 UNTS 221, Art 15.

[123] See IDI, 'Obligations Erga Omnes in International Law (Resolution)' (2005) 71 *AIDI* 287 (according to Art 5 of the resolution, only 'widely acknowledged grave breaches of an erga omnes obligation' can trigger special consequences under international law').

[124] See PM Dupuy, 'The Deficiencies of the Law of State Responsibility Relating to Breaches of "Obligations Owed to the International Community as a Whole": Suggestions for Avoiding the Obsolescence of Aggravated Responsibility' in A Cassese (ed), *Realizing Utopia: The Future of International Law* (Oxford, OUP, 2012).

[125] See *Legal Consequences of the Construction of a Wall in the Occupied Palestinian Territory* (n 86), Separate Opinion of Judge Higgins 207, 216, para 38 ('That an illegal situation is not to be recognized or assisted by third parties is self-evident').

[126] Talmon (n 90) 113; I Brownlie, *Principles of Public International Law* (6th edn, Oxford, OUP, 2003) 491 (arguing that the duty of non-recognition 'may be observed irrespective of or in the absence of any directives from the United Nations if in the careful judgment of the individual state a situation has arisen the illegality of which is opposable to states in general').

ii. The Operation of the Obligation Not to Render Aid or Assistance

The scope of Articles 41(2) ARSIWA and 42(2) ARIO is limited to situations that occur *after* the commission of the most serious breaches of peremptory norms. In other words the regime comes closer to what is widely known in domestic laws as complicity 'after the fact'.[127] The ILC's Commentary clarifies that the obligation of non-assistance in Article 41(2) ARSIWA 'extends beyond the commission of the serious breach, and it applies whether or not the breach itself is a continuing one'.[128] For instance, States and international organisations must refrain from rendering aid or assistance to a State unlawfully occupying a foreign territory or maintaining in effect legislation which is contrary to peremptory norms of international law.

Most cases of serious breaches of peremptory norms covered by the obligations of non-assistance will be of continuing character and could thus concurrently fall under the scope of general regime on complicity (Articles 16 ARSIWA and 14 ARIO). However, there may also be situations in which the unlawful effects of a *jus cogens* breach continue in time while the breach itself has ceased. In such scenarios, the regime of Articles 41 ARSIWA and 42 ARIO would continue to apply.

In a way, Articles 41(2) ARSIWA and 42(2) ARIO impose a new substantive or primary norm, the violation of which can trigger an independent responsibility. Assuming that no express primary norm prohibits aid or assistance (eg through an obligation under the UNSC resolution), if a State or an international organisation does render aid or assistance that goes to maintaining a situation flowing from a serious breach of *jus cogens*, they breach Article 41 ARSIWA itself. In this situation, the secondary norm may be de facto operating as if it were a primary one.

The obligation codified in Articles 41(2) ARSIWA and 42(2) ARIO applies without necessarily having to establish the same cognitive requirement as under Articles 16 ARSIWA and 14 ARIO (general regime). Under the general regime there is a presumption of a lack of knowledge of the circumstances of the wrongful act and/or lack of intent. In contrast, under Article 41(2) ARSIWA and 42(2) ARIO, the presumption is reversed, ie the putative aiding or assisting actor is imputed with knowledge and/or intention that its aid or assistance will contribute to maintaining the situation resulting from a serious breach of *jus cogens*.[129] Reading into the *Wall* Advisory Opinion, the same rationale could extend to the prohibition of complicity in respect of violations of *erga omnes* obligations.[130]

[127] Gianelli (n 108) 278; Aust (n 39) 338.

[128] ARSIWA (n 4) 115, para 11 (Art 41 Commentary).

[129] ibid 115, para 11 (Art 41 Commentary); Graefrath (n 49) 374 (proposing a presumption of intention in cases of complicity in the commission of most serious breaches of peremptory norms).

[130] *Legal Consequences of the Construction of a Wall in the Occupied Palestinian Territory* (n 86) 199–200, paras 154–59.

In this author's view, it is not coherent to have different standards for the general and aggravated ('after the fact') regimes of complicity, where serious breaches of *jus cogens* or *erga omnes* are being facilitated. The importance of compliance with these rules justifies reversing the *presumption of the absence of knowledge* into a *presumption of knowledge* in the context of general regime on responsibility for complicity too.[131] In other words, a State, which furnishes aid or assistance to the State which is committing serious breaches of international law, is at some point presumed to know of such circumstances and the use that will be given to its aid or assistance.[132] State A cannot simply rely on the presumption of good faith to the effect that State B would not use the aid or assistance for the commission of serious breaches of peremptory norms of international law. The presumption of knowledge in such cases would thus impose a heightened degree of scrutiny on the putative aiding or assisting entity, and support the responsibility's function of upholding legality.

The potential objection to such a heightened degree of scrutiny over the aid or assistance decisions is that it would stray too far in the use of the relative normativity phenomenon in international law.[133] In this author's view, a proposal to presume the requisite knowledge when assistance is given to violations of *jus cogens* and *erga omnes* obligations is not as problematic as other special effects commonly attributed to the hierarchically superior norms in international law (eg in the context of jurisdictional requirements) which have rightly been challenged.[134] Thus, it is our understanding that there is no fundamental objection to the presumption of knowledge in situations of complicity towards the commission of serious breaches of peremptory norms and, arguably, obligations *erga omnes* too.[135]

Moreover, contrary to Articles 16 ARSIWA and 14 ARIO, arguably the aid or assistance under Article 41(2) ARSIWA and 42(2) ARIO need not

[131] On the analysis of presumptions in international law see A Riddell and B Plant, *Evidence before the International Court of Justice* (London, BIICL, 2009) 102–11.

[132] See similarly B Graefrath, E Oeser and PA Steiniger, *Völkerrechtliche Verantwortlichkeit der Staaten* (Berlin, Staatsverlag der DDR, 1977) 374–77; P d'Argent, *Les réparations de guerre en droit international public: La responsabilité internationale des États à l'épreuve de la guerre* (Bruxelles, Bruylant, 2002) 548–54.

[133] cf *Armed Activities (DRC v Rwanda)* (n 102) 32, para 64 ('the fact that a dispute relates to compliance with a norm having [a jus cogens] character … cannot of itself provide a basis for the jurisdiction of the Court'); *East Timor (Portugal v Australia)* (Judgment) [1995] ICJ Rep 90, 102, para 29 ('the erga omnes character of a norm and the rule of consent to jurisdiction are two different things'); see also Aust (n 39) 347–52; Paulus (n 103) 330; Bianchi (n 104) 501.

[134] On the implications of relative normativity see *Armed Activities (DRC v Rwanda)* (n 102) Separate Opinion of Judge ad hoc Dugard 86, para 10; see also K Marek, 'Contribution à l'étude du jus cogens en droit international' in *Mélanges en hommage à Paul Guggenheim* (Genève, HEI, 1968); O Quirico, 'Ius Cogens: A Puzzle' in M Szabó (ed), *State Responsibility and the Law of Treaties* (The Hague, Eleven, 2010); Tams et al (n 117); Gaja (n 103); M Virally, 'Réflexions sur le "jus cogens"' (1966) 12 *AFDI* 5; P Weil, 'Towards Relative Normativity in International Law' (1983) 77 *AJIL* 413.

[135] cf Aust (n 39) 345–52.

significantly contribute to the maintenance of the situation flowing from the serious breach of a peremptory norm.[136] The degree of the required link or contribution can be lower than in the circumstances covered by Articles 16 ARSIWA and 14 ARIO.[137] This is justified by the fact that Articles 41(2) ARSIWA and 42(2) ARIO refer to the maintenance of the situation brought about by the serious breach rather than the circumstances of the wrongful act which is yet to be committed.[138]

In the *Namibia* Advisory Opinion, the Court found that the members of the UN were under an obligation

> to recognize the illegality and invalidity of South Africa's continued presence in Namibia [and] to refrain from lending any support or any form of assistance to South Africa with reference to its occupation of Namibia.[139]

The Court held that

> the termination of the Mandate and declaration of the illegality of South Africa's presence in Namibia [was] opposable to all States in the sense of barring *erga omnes* the legality of a situation which is maintained in violation of international law…[140]

In the *Wall* Advisory Opinion, the Court asserted that—given the character and importance of the rights and obligations involved—other States were under an obligation not to recognise the illegal situation resulting from the construction of the Wall, and not to render aid and assistance to maintain that situation.[141]

However, let us test a different scenario. State A invades State B and is illegally occupying State B's territory with the continued assistance of State C. A regional organisation condemns the occupation and related assistance as unlawful, but the UNSC, ICJ or UNGA make no equivalent pronouncement. Can any State of the international community invoke the responsibility of State C? The temptation is strong to reply in the affirmative following the Court's reasoning in the *Barcelona Traction* case, according to which all States may have legal interest in the observance of

[136] Boivin (n 43) 493.

[137] W Riphagen, 'Third Report on the Content, Forms and Degrees of International Responsibility' (1982) UN Doc A/CN.4/354 and Add 1-2, reproduced in (1982) 2 (pt 1) *YBILC* 22, 23–24, para 6; Aust (n 39) 336.

[138] Similarly see Felder (n 8) 140; Boivin (n 43) 493; cf Aust (n 39) 340–41.

[139] *Namibia (Advisory Opinion)* (n 81) 54, para 119; see also UNSC, 'Res 276' (30 January 1970) UN Doc S/RES/276 (Namibia); UNSC, 'Res 283' (29 July 1970) UN Doc S/RES/283 (Namibia); UNSC, 'Res 301' (20 October 1971) UN Doc S/RES/301 (Namibia).

[140] *Namibia (Advisory Opinion)* (n 81) 56, para 126; see also ARSIWA (n 4) 115, para 11 (Art 41 Commentary).

[141] *Legal Consequences of the Construction of a Wall in the Occupied Palestinian Territory* (n 86) 200, para 160; see also Dissenting Opinion of Judge Kooijmans 219, 231–32, paras 40–45.

obligations *erga omnes*.[142] Under closer scrutiny though the question we are concerned with is a slightly different one. It consists of whether a third State in doubt as to the illegality of particular act, or alternatively in doubt as to the 'seriousness' of the breach, can invoke the responsibility of the State assisting in the maintenance of the situation flowing from a purportedly serious breach of a peremptory norm.[143]

Arguments based on the implications of Article 41(2) ARSIWA have been made in the area of jurisdictional immunities of States and the claims for reparation filed in respect of atrocities committed during World War II.[144] Following the ruling of the Italian Court of Cassation in *Ferrini*, denying immunity to Germany, Andrea Bianchi suggested that 'consideration of the legal consequences stemming, under the law of State responsibility, from a serious violation of a *ius cogens* rule may well lead, by way of interpretation, to the non-recognition of a State's jurisdictional immunity'.[145] The argument was subsequently taken up by Italy in the oral proceedings in the *Jurisdictional Immunities of the State* case.[146] Pierre-Marie Dupuy, acting as counsel for Italy, argued that if the Italian judge had upheld the rule on jurisdictional immunity of Germany, it would have lent support to the commission and maintenance of an internationally wrongful act by Germany.[147]

The response of Germany to this argument in the observations by Robert Kolb was twofold. First, 'if no duty exists (or existed, in 1945) to provide individual compensation for the cases at issue, then that duty cannot have been breached'.[148] The second part of the response is that even if that complicity had occurred, ie if an internationally wrongful act had been committed, 'the consequences could be only those foreseen by

[142] *Barcelona Traction, Light and Power Company, Limited (Second Phase) (Belgium v Spain)* (n 120) 32, paras 33–34; see also P Klein, 'Responsibility for Serious Breaches of Obligations Deriving from Peremptory Norms of International Law and United Nations Law' (2002) 13 *EJIL* 1241; I Scobbie, 'Unchart(er)ed Waters?: Consequences of the Advisory Opinion on the Legal Consequences of the Construction of a Wall in the Occupied Palestinian Territory for the Responsibility of the UN for Palestine' (2005) 16 *EJIL* 941.

[143] See A Lagerwall, 'L'administration du territoire Irakien: Un exemple de reconnaissance et d'aide au maintien d'une occupation résultant d'un acte d'agression' (2006) 39 *RBDI* 249.

[144] *Ferrini v Federal Republic of Germany* (Judgment) (2004) 128 ILR 658 (Italian Court of Cassation) 669; *Case No 137/1997* (Judgment) (1997) 50 RHDI 595 (Greek Court of Levadia).

[145] A Bianchi, 'Ferrini v Federal Republic of Germany. Italian Court of Cassation, March 11, 2004' (2005) 99 *AJIL* 242, 247; see also C Focarelli, 'Denying Foreign State Immunity for Commission of International Crimes: The Ferrini Decision' (2008) 54 *ICLQ* 951.

[146] *Jurisdictional Immunities of the State (Germany v Italy; Greece intervening)* (Judgment) [2012] ICJ Rep 99, 140–42, paras 92–97.

[147] ibid ICJ Pleadings, CR 2011/18 (13 September 2011) 56, paras 16–17 (Dupuy) ('apporter son concours à la réalisation et au maintien d'un fait illicite international accompli par un autre Etat'; author's translation: 'lend its support to the commission and maintenance of a breach of international law by another State').

[148] ibid ICJ Pleadings, CR 2011/20 (15 September 2011) 51, para 16 (Kolb).

relevant secondary norms, those relating to responsibility of States'.[149] Kolb continued that

> the commission of our putative wrongful act could not give rise to the commission of another wrongful act, but only to the elimination of the consequences of the breach in accordance with the current rules of international law. What *jus cogens* does not do, supposed complicity certainly cannot.[150]

It is questionable whether in upholding Germany's immunity Italy would be rendering assistance to the maintenance of the unlawful situation arising from a serious breach of peremptory norm; or rather would it risk becoming complicit in a separate internationally wrongful act (ie denial of justice to the victims)?[151] The ICJ laconically rejected the former proposition and omitted any pronouncement on the latter:

> Assuming for this purpose that the rules of the law of armed conflict which prohibit the murder of civilians in occupied territory, the deportation of civilian inhabitants to slave labour and the deportation of prisoners of war to slave labour are rules of jus cogens, there is no conflict between those rules and the rules on State immunity. The two sets of rules address different matters. *The rules of State immunity are procedural in character and are confined to determining whether or not the courts of one State may exercise jurisdiction in respect of another State. They do not bear upon the question whether or not the conduct in respect of which the proceedings are brought was lawful or unlawful.* That is why the application of the contemporary law of State immunity to proceedings concerning events which occurred in 1943–1945 does not infringe the principle that law should not be applied retrospectively to determine matters of legality and responsibility (as the Court has explained in paragraph 58 above). For the same reason, *recognizing the immunity of a foreign State in accordance with customary international law does not amount to recognizing as lawful a situation created by the breach of a jus cogens rule, or rendering aid and assistance in maintaining that situation, and so cannot contravene the principle in Article 41 of the [ARSIWA].*[152] (emphasis added)

Whether prompted by particular facts of the case or judicial policy considerations, the Court did not take the opportunity to give some content to the legal consequences as contained in Article 41 ARSIWA. The ICJ's cautious language in the *Wall* Advisory Opinion, albeit extending the scope of application of those consequences to *erga omnes* obligations,[153] sheds little light on their content either: 'the United Nations, and especially the

[149] ibid.

[150] ibid.

[151] See, eg *Case No 137/1997* (n 144) (holding that 'the recognition of immunity for an act contrary to peremptory international law would amount to complicity by the national court in the promotion of an act strongly condemned by the international public order').

[152] *Jurisdictional Immunities of the State (Germany v Italy; Greece intervening)* (n 146) 140, para 93.

[153] *Legal Consequences of the Construction of a Wall in the Occupied Palestinian Territory* (n 86) 200, para 159.

General Assembly and the Security Council, should consider what further action is required to bring to an end the illegal situation'.[154] The vagueness of such pronouncements raises doubts as to whether the consequences set out in Article 41 ARSIWA could attract any more substantive content.[155] While States would be able to invoke responsibility of a defaulting State, strictly speaking, they are not under a positive obligation to do so; nor are they expected to take any more substantial actions.[156]

Notwithstanding the possible critiques that may be made of the current formulation and content of Articles 41(2) ARSIWA and 42(2) ARIO, the duty of non-assistance pulls the strings of solidarity in international law.[157] According to Simma, it 'is a remarkable victory of community interest over bilateralist reflexes nowhere more profoundly entrenched than in the field of State responsibility'.[158] The duties of non-assistance, non-recognition and cooperation incumbent on third parties are essential for the 'public order' effects of peremptory norms.[159] Despite the apparent lack of clarity in respect of the content of consequences enshrined in Articles 40/41 ARSIWA and 41/42 ARIO, at least in theory, the duties of cooperation, non-recognition and non-assistance potentially encapsulate 'a whole array of measures, which can be set in motion in order to suppress … non-compliance with peremptory norms'.[160] It is submitted that these measures may also be apposite in respect of situations flowing from serious breaches of obligations *erga omnes*.

[154] ibid 200, para 160.

[155] cf Abi-Saab (n 74) 342–43; see also K Kawasaki, 'The Content and Implementation of the International Responsibility of States: Some Remarks on the Draft Articles on State Responsibility Adopted by the ILC's Drafting Committee in 2000' (2001) 29 *Hitotsubashi JL & Pol* 25 (arguing that a State would have to 'change radically the responsible government structure as appropriate assurances and guarantees of non-repetition because the circumstances so require, if international responsibility arises from an internationally wrongful act that constitutes a serious breach by a State of an obligation owed to the international community as a whole and essential for the protection of its fundamental interests'); B Stern, 'Les dilemmes de la responsabilité internationale aujourd'hui' in *Vers de nouvelles normes en droit de la responsabilité publique: Actes du colloque 11 et 12 mai 2001* (Paris, Sénat, 2001) 277–78.

[156] See *Legal Consequences of the Construction of a Wall in the Occupied Palestinian Territory* (n 86) Separate Opinion of Judge Higgins 207, 216, para 37; ibid Separate Opinion of Judge Kooijmans 219, 231, para 40; see also Tams (n 119) 11; Aust (n 39) 43–45 (who doubts that the Court wanted to present a general concept of obligations for third States flowing from violations of obligations erga omnes); LA Sicilianos, *Les réactions décentralisées à l'illicite: Des contremesures à la légitime défense* (Paris, LGDJ, 1990) 174; J Crawford, 'Third Party Obligations with Respect to Israeli Settlements in the Occupied Palestinian Territories' (2012) www.tuc.org.uk/sites/default/files/tucfiles/LegalOpinionIsraeliSettlements.pdf 16–18, paras 42–45.

[157] Simma (n 103) 317.

[158] ibid.

[159] Orakhelashvili (n 103) 579.

[160] Aust (n 39) 47; see also Tams (n 78); A Pellet, 'Les articles de la CDI sur la responsabilité de l'État pour fait internationalement illicite. Suite—et fin?' (2002) 48 *AFDI* 1, 18; Talmon (n 90); Klein (n 142); A Zimmermann and M Teichmann, 'State Responsibility for International Crimes' in A Nollkaemper and H van der Wilt (eds), *System Criminality in International Law* (Cambridge, CUP, 2009).

IV. COMPLICITY OF STATES IN AN INTERNATIONALLY WRONGFUL ACT OF THE INTERNATIONAL ORGANISATION (ARTICLE 58 ARIO)

The legal construction of ARIO began from an assumption that '[t]he existence for the organization of a distinct legal personality does not exclude the possibility of a certain conduct being attributed both to the organization and to one or more of its members or to all its members'.[161] This assumption partially puts into question the establishment of a genuine agency relationship between an international organisation and its Member States.[162] The nature of the relationships between international organisations and their Member States is a complex and underdeveloped subject of international law, including in respect of the allocation of responsibility.[163]

Thus, Article 58 ARIO represents an important contribution to the progressive development of international law in this area. In part, it remedies a gap contained in Article 16 ARSIWA by extending the responsibility to situations where States aid or assist wrongful acts of international organisations. The formulation of Article 58 ARIO follows verbatim Article 16 ARSIWA:

> Article 58 ARIO
>
> Aid or assistance by a State in the commission of an internationally wrongful act by an international organization
>
> 1. A State which aids or assists an international organization in the commission of an internationally wrongful act by the latter is internationally responsible for doing so if:
>   (a) the State does so with knowledge of the circumstances of the internationally wrongful act; and
>   (b) the act would be internationally wrongful if committed by that State.

[161] ARIO (n 5) 9, para 10 (Art 2 Commentary); for one of the earliest treatments of the problem of Member State responsibility in doctrine see M Perez Conzalez, 'Les organisations internationales et le droit de la responsabilité' (1988) 92 *RGDIP* 63; see especially J d'Aspremont, 'Abuse of the Legal Personality of International Organizations and the Responsibility of Member States' (2007) 4 *IOLR* 91; JM Cortés Martin, 'The Responsibility of Members Due to Wrongful Acts of International Organizations' (2013) 12 *Chinese J Intl L* 679; O Murray, 'Piercing the Corporate Veil: The Responsibility of Member States of an International Organization' (2011) 8 *IOLR* 291; C Ahlborn, 'To Share or Not to Share? The Allocation of Responsibility between International Organizations' SHARES Research Paper No 28 (2013).

[162] *Maclaine Watson v Department of Trade and Industry* (Judgment) (1988) 80 ILR 39, 114; *JH Rayner (Mincing Lane) Ltd v Department of Trade and Industry and Others and Related Appeals* (Judgment) [1990] 2 AC 418 (HL) 1016–017 (Oliver LJ); *JH Rayner (Mincing Lane) Ltd v Department of Trade and Industry and Others and Related Appeals* (Judgment) [1988] 3 WLR 1033 (CA) (Millet J); see also D Sarooshi, *International Organizations and Their Exercise of Sovereign Powers* (Oxford, OUP, 2005) 42–49.

[163] See Ahlborn (n 6); see also V Gowlland-Debbas, 'The Security Council and Issues of Responsibility under International Law' (2011) 353 *RCADI* 185; J d'Aspremont, 'The Articles on the Responsibility of International Organizations: Magnifying the Fissures in the Law of International Responsibility' (2012) 9 *IOLR* 15.

2. An act by a State member of an international organization done in accordance with the rules of the organization does not as such engage the international responsibility of that State under the terms of this article.[164] (emphasis added)

The exception set out in paragraph 2 is problematic at both conceptual and practical levels. Under the construction of Article 58, it is the international organisation that bears the principal responsibility for the wrongful act. The responsibility would then be linked to the aiding or assisting State not for having committed the wrongful act of the international organisation but exclusively for its contribution to that act.[165] Conceptually, however, as in the case of inter-State complicity, the organisation and the State each incur responsibility for two *separate* wrongful acts. In other words, the *fait générateur* of a Member State's responsibility for complicity is only triggered after the principal wrongful conduct is attributable to the international organisation.

Article 58 ARIO seems to create a two-tiered framework. Whereas its paragraph 1 applies to responsibility of any State (ie whether Member or non-Member of the organisation), paragraph 2 applies exclusively to the Member States of the organisation that commits the wrongful act. It is difficult to see why the caveat of paragraph 2 could and should not apply to non-Member States. Assume State A (non-Member) and State B (Member) incur responsibility for complicity in connection with the wrongful act of the international organisation committed against State C (Member). Both States A and B rendered aid or assistance in compliance with the internal rules of an international organisation. In general, the rules of the international organisation do not affect the conduct of State B as a non-Member. Yet it may be questioned whether State B could in theory rely upon the exception provided in paragraph 2 of Article 58 ARIO.

Article 59 ARIO (dealing with direction and control by one State over the internationally wrongful act by an organisation) contains a similar exception. However, by contrast to aid or assistance, where a Member State controls or directs the international organisation to commit an internationally wrongful act, that State incurs responsibility *for* the principal wrongdoing of an international organisation.[166] This also holds true in

[164] ARIO (n 5) Art 58(2).

[165] ibid Art 62 (which provides for limited circumstances in which the Member State could be responsible for an international wrongful act of the international organisation, rather than in connection with that act, ie the case of complicity); see also Cortés Martin (n 161) 705–06; cf A Orakhelashvili, 'The Responsibility of Member-States Due to Wrongful Acts of International Organizations: A Response to Cortes Martin' (2014) 13 *Chinese J Intl L* 621, 625 (concluding that the rule set out in Art 62 ARIO 'should be seen as relevant only in relation to such act and conduct performed by an international organisation which sees no contribution by member-States; it should not be used as a cover for individual or collective state wrongs performed within the organisation's framework').

[166] ARIO (n 5) 92 (Art 59 Commentary); see also ARSIWA (n 4) 68, para 1 (Art 17 Commentary).

respect of the State that coerces an international organisation pursuant to Article 60 ARIO, which contains no exception relating to Member States' compliance with the internal rules of an organisation. The justification for a different treatment of responsibility set out in Articles 59 and 60 ARIO from that in Article 58 ARIO would lie in the *stronger* degree of influence the conduct by the Member State exerts on the commission of an internationally wrongful act in the case of the former. Arguably, in situations of direction/control, and especially coercion, the organisation's autonomy in taking a decision as to the commission of an internationally wrongful act would be impaired.

Thus, with Article 58(2), the Commission effectively elevated the status of internal rules of organisation to a new circumstance precluding wrongfulness for the aiding or assisting State. This follows from the Commission's rationale for including paragraph 2:

> [It] sought to make it clear that the responsibility of a member State for aid or assistance to an international organization in the commission of an internationally wrongful act did not arise in situations where the State was acting as a member in accordance with the rules of the organization. The commentary would explain that that did not affect the State's responsibility for its own actions. In other words, *the provision did not mean that a State member of an organization did not incur responsibility for the breach of its own international obligations arising from its participation in the activities of the organization.* For example, a State voting within an organization in favour of the commission of an act which amounted to genocide continued to be held responsible under international law on its own account. When such a vote was taken in accordance with the rules of the organization, that State would not in addition be considered responsible for aiding or assisting the organization in the commission of the act in question.[167]

In other words, a Member State can directly engage its own responsibility where the impugned conduct constitutes a violation of its own obligation. By virtue of Article 58(2) ARIO, a Member State simply avoids its subsidiary responsibility for aid or assistance in the commission on an internationally wrongful act by an international organisation, if that was performed in accordance with the internal rules.

Having drawn the important distinction between the scope of Article 58 and its neighbours (Articles 59 and 60 ARIO), we shall now discuss possible *cas de figure* which would fall under Article 58 ARIO. A State's complicity in the wrongful act of an international organisation could stem, for example, from the provision of military personnel by the State to an international organisation that attempts to topple a government or from the technical assistance given to an international organisation that sub-

[167] ILC, 'Summary Record of the 3097th Meeting' (3 June 2011) UN Doc A/CN.4/SR.3097, 31 (Report of the Chairman of the ILC Drafting Committee).

sequently commits wrongful acts such as unlawful traffic of cultural objects.[168] Article 58 ARIO could also cover situations of complicit conduct by States in the context of peacekeeping or military operations which result in internationally wrongful acts.[169] Commonly, a State would either allow the use of its territory, airspace, or provide other types of military or logistical assistance to the benefit of military operations led by an international organisation.

In recent years, for instance, the EU has led several operations with the military troops supplied by its Member States in the framework of its Common Foreign and Security Policy (CFSP). Examples of such joint military missions include the operation CONCORDIA in the Former Yugoslav Republic of Macedonia, the anti-piracy operation ATALANTA off the coast of Somalia, the EUFOR RED Congo operations in the Democratic Republic of the Congo (DRC) and the EUFOR Chad/CAR in Chad and the Central African Republic (CAR).[170] For instance, in a case of the German warship *Rheinland Pfalz*, operating in the EUNAVFOR Operation ATALANTA, the Administrative Court of Cologne ruled in 2011 that it was Germany and not the EU that violated Articles 3 European Convention on Human Rights (ECHR) and 7 International Covenant on Civil and Political Rights (ICCPR) by arresting suspected pirates and transferring them to Kenya, pursuant to a bilateral EU–Kenya agreement.[171] However, assuming a particular incident as part of any such EU mission results in an internationally wrongful act, over which a Member State has no effective control, the wrongful act would be attributed exclusively to the EU-centralised command. In such circumstances, the responsibility of a Member State could nonetheless arise under Article 58 ARIO if it had knowingly provided means of facilitating that wrongful act.

[168] ILC, 'Comments and Observations Received from International Organizations' (2006) UN Doc A/CN.4/568 and Add 1, reproduced in (2006) 2 (pt 1) *YBILC* 125, 144 (UNESCO).

[169] On the responsibility of the troops placed at the disposal of an international organizations see, eg B Amrallah, 'The International Responsibility of the United Nations for Activities Carried Out by UN Peace-Keeping Forces' (1976) 32 *Revue égyptienne de droit international* 57, 69; M Hirsch, *The Responsibility of International Organizations Toward Third Parties: Some Basic Principles* (Dordrecht, Martinus Nijhoff, 1995) 175; Sarooshi (n 162) 63–104; B Kondoch, 'The Responsibility of Peacekeepers, Their Sending States, and International Organizations' in TD Gill and D Fleck (eds), *The Handbook of the International Law of Military Operations* (Oxford, OUP, 2010); P Lagrange, 'Responsabilité des États pour actes accomplis en application du chapitre VII de la Charte des Nations Unies' (2008) 1 *RGDIP* 85; CA Bell, 'Reassessing Multiple Attribution: The International Law Commission and the Behrami and Saramati Decision' (2009) 42 *NYU J Intl L & Pol* 501.

[170] See PJ Kuijper and E Paasivirta, 'EU International Responsibility and Its Attribution' in MD Evans and P Koutrakos (eds), *The International Responsibility of the European Union: European and International Perspectives* (Oxford, Hart Publishing, 2013) 51–52; SP Bodini, 'Fighting Maritime Piracy under the European Convention on Human Rights' (2011) 22 *EJIL* 829, 845–46.

[171] *25 K 4280/09* (Judgment) [2011] Köln VerwG (Cologne Administrative Court).

Article 58 ARIO also covers situations where a particular primary rule binding the organisation's Member States prohibits aid or assistance, but no such rule expressly binds the organisation itself. The ILC cited an interesting example where a State would have to refrain from giving aid or assistance under a primary norm to another State and, by implication, to an international organisation:

> Aid or assistance by a State could constitute a breach of an obligation that the State has acquired under a primary norm. For example, a nuclear-weapon State Party to the Treaty on the Non-Proliferation of Nuclear Weapons would have to refrain from assisting a non-nuclear-weapon State in the acquisition of nuclear weapons, and the same would seem to apply to assistance given to an international organization of which some non-nuclear-weapon States are members.[172]

A less common example can be found in the 1999 World Trade Organization (WTO) Panel report on *Turkey—Restrictions on Imports of Textile and Clothing Products*.[173] The case concerned the imposition of import quotas. Turkey argued that the measures at issue had been taken by a separate entity (ie the Turkey-EC). The Panel held that 'even if these measures are taken in the ambit of a customs union, they are implemented, applied and monitored by Turkey, for application in the Turkish territory only. Therefore they are Turkish measures'.[174]

In its analysis, the Panel mentioned that 'in public international law, in the absence of any contrary treaty provision, Turkey could reasonably be held responsible for the measures taken by the Turkey-EC customs union',[175] on the basis of the principle reflected in former draft Article 27 [now Article 16 ARSIWA]. In its report, the Panel reproduced a passage of the ILC's commentary to that provision.[176]

While the case referred to former draft Article 27 ARSIWA, it is conceptually closer to scenarios of Article 58 ARIO. The Panel's decision might be interpreted to stand for the proposition that responsibility for complicity could extend to situations where the State monitors or ensures the implementation of measures, the mandate for which originates from a regional or international organisation. The panel seems to suggest that States may be held responsible in connection with the measures passed by customs unions or regional trade agreements that infringe the WTO law and general international law. However, on a different interpretation of the Panel's conclusions, the Panel seems to be incorrectly referring to responsibility for complicity in this context. On this interpretation, the Panel intended to

[172] ARIO (n 5) 91, para 2 (Art 58 Commentary).

[173] *Turkey—Restrictions on Imports of Textile and Clothing Products* (Panel Report) WT/DS34/R (31 May 1999) paras 9.42–9.44.

[174] ibid para 9.44.

[175] ibid para 9.42.

[176] ibid para 9.43 (where the Panel quotes former draft Art 27 Commentary).

refer to the possibility of concurrent or multiple attribution of the wrongful act that could trigger joint and several responsibility.[177]

More generally, the WTO dispute settlement practice has accepted that Member States implementing the EU measures act 'de facto as organs of the Community, for which the Union would be responsible under WTO law and international law in general'.[178] This can be contrasted with the general approach of the European Court of Human Rights (ECtHR), which held in *Bosphorus* that a State could not simply forego its international obligations by transferring functions to an international organisation as

> absolving Contracting States completely from their Convention responsibility in the areas covered by such a transfer would be incompatible with the purpose and object of the Convention; the guarantees of the Convention could be limited or excluded at will, thereby depriving it of its peremptory character and undermining the practical and effective nature of its safeguards...The State is considered to retain Convention liability in respect of treaty commitments subsequent to the entry into force of the Convention.[179]

The case of the EU and its Member States' responsibility generates numerous controversies, and at the time of writing at least three models of allocation of responsibility between the EU and its Member States can be envisaged.[180] These are: (i) the model of exclusive responsibility of the EU, as demonstrated through the WTO case law; (ii) the model of co-responsibility mechanism as proposed in case the EU were ever to accede to the ECHR in the future, which now seems unlikely;[181] and

[177] ARSIWA (n 4) Art 47.

[178] *EC—Geographic Indications* (Panel Report) WT/DS174/R (15 March 2005) para 7.725; *EC—Selected Customs Matters* (Panel Report) WT/DS315/R (16 June 2006) para 7.553; see also F Hoffmeister, 'Litigating against the European Union and Its Member States—Who Responds under the ILC's Draft Articles on International Responsibility of International Organizations?' (2010) 21 *EJIL* 723.

[179] *Bosphorus Hava Yollari Turizm ve Ticaret Şirketi v Ireland* (Judgment) (GC) [2005] ECtHR App No 45036/98 (2006) 42 EHRR 1 paras 154–55 (even though the Court went on to find that Ireland did not incur responsibility as the EU law contained equivalent framework of human rights protection to that of the ECHR); see also *Waite and Kennedy v Germany* (Judgment) [1999] App No 26083/94 (2000) 30 EHRR 261.

[180] See, eg Kuijper and Paasivirta (n 170); P Eeckhout, 'The EU and Its Member States in the WTO—Issues of Responsibility' in L Bartels and F Ortino (eds), *Regional Trade Agreements and the WTO Legal System* (New York, OUP, 2006); S Talmon, 'Responsibility of International Organizations: Does the European Community Require Special Treatment?' in M Ragazzi (ed), *International Responsibility Today: Essays in Memory of Oscar Schachter* (Leiden, Martinus Nijhoff, 2005); JW van Rossem, 'Interaction between EU Law and International Law in the Light of Intertanko and Kadi: The Dilemma of Norms Binding the Member States but Not the Community'' (2009) 40 *Netherlands YBIL* 183.

[181] 'Draft Revised Agreement on the Accession of the European Union to the Convention for the Protection of Human Rights and Fundamental Freedoms' (10 June 2013) CoE Doc 47+1(2013)008rev2 www.coe.int/t/dghl/standardsetting/hrpolicy/Accession/Meeting_reports/47_1(2013)008rev2_EN.pdf; cf *Opinion 2/13 of the Court (Full Court)* (18 December 2014) CJEU, ECLI:EU:C:2014:2454, para 258 (holding the Draft Accession Agreement to be incompatible with the EU law).

(iii) the model of allocation of responsibility between the EU and Member States, potentially to be implemented in the investment treaty dispute settlement context.[182]

Leaving aside the case of the EU, in general it is a legitimate position that, in light of the organisation's normal functioning, Member States must be assumed to have actual or at least constructive knowledge of an international organisation's actions, so that they cannot claim ignorance of fact or law.[183] As Karel Wellens points out, Member States 'have a right to insist that the international organization remains within the functional limits of its purposes and that it does not adopt decisions that are incompatible with the object and purpose of the constituent treaty'.[184] One is tempted to assert that there is even a duty

> to ensure supervision of the organization, serving two purposes: to protect the member States' own interests in the effective operation of the international organization, and to protect third parties' interests in the case of a failure by the international organization to perform adequately.[185]

Such a duty would be the corollary of the obligation that 'all agents of the United Nations, in whatever official capacity they act, must take care not to exceed the scope of their functions, and should comport themselves [so] as to avoid claims against the United Nations'.[186] Applying a similar rationale, Member States of any international organisation must ensure that no harm is caused through their collective action to non-Members, other international organisations or private actors. They can do so through various means, but particular attention should be paid at the level of decision-making. Sarooshi claims that:

> States should take action within the organization—for example, voting against a decision—to try and ensure that the organization does not commit an internationally wrongful act, and that the failure to do so may engage a secondary responsibility of the State for the act of the organization.[187]

Otherwise, States would be free to use international organisations as means to avoid responsibility, which would impair the systemic integrity

[182] See P Sturma, 'The Responsibility of International Organizations and Their Member States' in M Ragazzi (ed), *Responsibility of International Organizations: Essays in Memory of Sir Ian Brownlie* (Leiden, Martinus Nijhoff, 2013) 319–23; P Sturma, 'Drawing a Line between the Responsibility of an International Organization and Its Member States under International Law' (2011) 2 *Czech YBIL* 3.

[183] Chinkin (n 8) 102.

[184] K Wellens, *Remedies against International Organizations* (Cambridge, CUP, 2004) 29; see also PHF Bekker, *The Legal Position of Intergovernmental Organizations: A Functional Necessity Analysis of Their Legal Status and Immunities* (Dordrecht, Martinus Nijhoff, 1994) 50.

[185] Wellens (n 184) 30.

[186] *Difference relating to Immunity from Legal Process of a Special Rapporteur of the Commission on Human Rights* (Advisory Opinion) [1999] ICJ Rep 62, 89, para 66; cf Chinkin (n 8) 119.

[187] Sarooshi (n 162) 64.

of international law.[188] This brings us to one of the most commonly referenced examples of a Member State's complicity, a vote taken within the international organisation. This example has attracted considerable attention in scholarly debates.[189] Because the vote of Member States potentially allows the international organisation to adopt a particular conduct contrary to its own international obligations, such a vote may constitute aid or assistance. This is also a good example of complicity through omission as a vote, whether it is affirmative, negative or an abstention, is not tangible or physical assistance to the purported wrongdoing. Yet, it does facilitate in the commission of the principal wrongful act. The question of the link between the vote and the principal wrongful act becomes essential in this context. Special Rapporteur Gaja expressed the view that:

> A distinction between States which vote in favour and the other States would not always be warranted. This would reflect also a policy reason, because giving weight to that distinction could negatively affect the decision-making process in many organizations, because the risk of incurring responsibility would hamper the reaching of consensus.[190]

In light of comments received from States and international organizations, Gaja concluded that 'the influence that may amount to aid or assistance could not simply consist in participation in the decision-making process of the organization according to the pertinent rules of the organization'.[191] Hence, unless States' conduct goes clearly beyond the rules of the organisation and its decision-making procedures, responsibility for complicity in the internationally wrongful act of an organisation would not arise.[192]

Nonetheless, factors such as 'the size of the membership and the nature of the involvement [by the Member State]' may affect the consideration of its potential responsibility.[193] Most importantly, establishing responsibility in such cases may be hindered by the difficulties of proving that the vote of the State contributed *significantly* to the wrongful act. In the

[188] I Brownlie, 'The Responsibility of States for Acts of International Organizations' in M Ragazzi (ed), *International Responsibility Today: Essays in Memory of Oscar Schachter* (Leiden, Martinus Nijhoff, 2005) 361; D Sarooshi, 'International Organizations and State Responsibility' in M Ragazzi (ed), *Responsibility of International Organizations: Essays in Memory of Sir Ian Brownlie* (Leiden, Martinus Nijhoff, 2013) 84.

[189] P Klein, *La responsabilité des organisations internationales dans les ordres juridiques internes et en droit des gens* (Bruxelles, Bruylant, 1998) 469–70; see, eg P Palchetti, 'Sulla responsabilità di uno Stato per il voto espresso in seno ad un'organizzazione internazionale' (2012) 2 *RDI* 352.

[190] G Gaja, 'Fourth Report on Responsibility of International Organizations' (2006) UN Doc A/CN.4/564 and Add 1-2, reproduced in (2006) 2 (pt 1) *YBILC* 103, 124, para 93.

[191] Gaja (n 60) 87, para 74.

[192] ARIO (n 5) Art 58(2); see also R Higgins, 'The Legal Consequences for Member States of the Non-Fulfilment by International Organizations of Their Obligations towards Third Parties' (1995) 66 *AIDI* 251, 388–89; cf Klein (n 189) 485.

[193] ARIO (n 5) 91, para 4 (Art 58 Commentary); Palchetti (n 189) 368–73.

Application of the Interim Accord of 13 September 1995 case, the ICJ hinted that such a question could have arisen if Greece's conduct were to be evaluated outside the framework of primary obligation contained in Article 11 of the Interim Accord.[194] Were it not for the Article 11 obligation, the Court would have to examine 'whether the decision taken by NATO at the Bucharest Summit with respect to the Applicant's candidacy was due exclusively, principally, or marginally to the Respondent's objection'.[195]

In the course of elaboration of Article 58 ARIO, States have expressed concern about the possibility of incurring responsibility for aid or assistance in the circumstances of a vote leading to a wrongful act by an organisation. For example, China stated that given that the decisions and actions of an organisation are generally under the control of its Members or depend upon their support, those States voting in favour of a measure should assume international responsibility if it is wrongful.[196]

It could be the case that the degree of responsibility should vary depending on the actual degree of participation in the voting procedures.[197] For example, a State may: (a) direct the adoption of a decision that leads to the commission of an internationally wrongful act; (b) control the proceedings, leading to the adoption of the decision, for instance, when the State's representative chairs the meetings or has a casting vote; (c) exercise a veto in the process leading to a decision that could prevent the commission of the wrongful act; (d) exercise marginal influence or constitute part of the minority in the decision-making process.[198]

In scenarios (a), (b) and (c), it would seem logical to hold the State's contribution to the decision as amounting to aid or assistance in the commission of the wrongful act.[199] In scenario (d), where the State Member has marginal influence on the decision-making process or when it is part of the minority that voted against the commission of the wrongful act, such a State could avoid responsibility. The link in scenario (d) between the participation in the decision-making process and the commission of the wrongful act may not be obvious or simply absent.[200]

[194] *Application of the Interim Accord of 13 September 1995 (Former Yugoslav Republic of Macedonia v Greece)* (Judgment) [2011] ICJ Rep 644, 667, para 70.

[195] ibid.

[196] UNGA, 'Sixth Committee, Summary Record of the 11th Meeting' (24 October 2005) UN Doc A/C.6/60/SR.11, 10, para 53 (China); UNGA, 'Sixth Committee, Summary Record of the 12th Meeting' (25 October 2005) UN Doc A/C.6/60/SR.12, 9, para 51 (Belarus).

[197] JM Cortés Martin, *Las organizaciones internacionales: codificación y desarrollo progresivo de su responsabilidad internacional* (Sevilla, Instituto Andaluz de Administración Pública, 2008) 300.

[198] See ibid.

[199] See ibid; see also Cortés Martin (n 161); Orakhelashvili (n 165).

[200] Cortés Martin (n 197) 300; cf S Yee, 'The Responsibility of States Members of an International Organization for Its Conduct as a Result of Membership or Their Normal Conduct Associated with Membership' in M Ragazzi (ed), *International Responsibility Today: Essays in Memory of Oscar Schachter* (Leiden, Martinus Nijhoff, 2005).

During the proceedings in the *Bosnia Genocide* case, a question arose as to whether a State could violate its obligation to refrain from complicity in genocide by taking part in the decision-making process of an international organisation of which it is a member.[201] In this context, Bosnia and Herzegovina even considered initiating proceedings before the ICJ against the United Kingdom for its alleged violation of Article III(e) of the Genocide Convention arising from its assistance to the maintenance of the arms embargo imposed by the UNSC.[202]

More generally, one could think of cases in which State A, acting as a member of an organisation, did not vote in favour but sponsored or supported the adoption of a measure within the organisation to end the embargo and resume supply of arms to State B. If State A sought such a decision within the organisation, knowing that the supply will be used by State B to commit a wrongful act, it could be thus held to responsibility on the grounds of complicity even though it did not vote. The potential responsibility would of course depend on factual circumstances and the evidence of the influence that the acting State had on the organisation while pursuing the latter's decision.

Cortés Martín has argued that there could be a serious problem in framing a vote or involvement in the decision-making of international organisation as complicity.[203] He states that this would undermine the very concept of separate legal personality that the international organisation is embodied with.[204] The international organisation would not be acting according to its own will but according to that of its members.[205] In temporal terms, the process of voting and taking of a decision takes place before the actual commission of the wrongful act. For responsibility purposes, it is still the organisation that commits the wrongful act and its legal autonomy and capacity to act are not necessarily hindered by the fact that the decision leading to a particular action or omission was taken at the roundtable with its Member States.

The conduct consisting of the voting procedure or decision-making is more akin to one of preparatory character and, taken on its own without the subsequent implementation measure, could rarely be considered to

[201] *Bosnia Genocide (Provisional Measures Order of 13 September 1993)* (n 42), Separate Opinion of Judge ad hoc Elihu Lauterpacht 407, 440–41, para 102 (considering the question of whether the arms embargo could indirectly contribute to a genocide taking place in Bosnia and the relationship between the UNSC Resolution 713 and jus cogens); see also P Palchetti, 'State Responsibility for Complicity in Genocide' in P Gaeta (ed), *The UN Genocide Convention: A Commentary* (Oxford, OUP, 2009) 387.

[202] Palchetti (n 201) 387; see also J Quigley, 'State Responsibility for Ethnic Cleansing' (1998) 32 *University of California Davis LR* 341; cf Klein (n 189) 470 (considering that the case would be much closer to responsibility of the United Kingdom as a principal rather than for its complicity).

[203] Cortés Martin (n 197) 301.

[204] ibid.

[205] ibid.

facilitate a wrongful act.[206] In its judgment in the *Gabčikovo-Nagymaros* case, the Court hinted at such distinction:

> A wrongful act or offence is frequently preceded by preparatory actions which are not to be confused with the act or offence itself. It is as well to distinguish between the actual commission of a wrongful act (whether instantaneous or continuous) and the conduct prior to that act which is of a preparatory character and which 'does not qualify as a wrongful act'.[207]

Unless it is causally foreseeable that the preparatory acts of decision-making and voting would lead to the commission of an internationally wrongful act and the State has actual knowledge of the circumstances of the wrongful act, the State would bear no responsibility for complicity.

While the actual practice is scarce, other situations of potential complicity of Member States in the wrongful acts of an international organisation could be envisaged. For example, aid or assistance could take 'the form of providing funds to the organization for its extrabudgetary technical cooperation activities or hosting its headquarters, offices or meetings' which could be used for the commission of an internationally wrongful act.[208]

Some agreements concluded by international organisations and their Member States, usually called mixed agreements, provide for a joint responsibility of an international organisation and its Member States in case of failure to discharge certain obligations.[209] In these situations, the impact of Article 58(2) ARIO would be limited. However, even if no such arrangement exists a priori there is nothing in positive law that precludes the dual or multiple attribution of conduct to international organisations and its Member States.[210] Commentators disagree on the subject matter.[211]

[206] cf Klein (n 189) 469–70 and 489; see also d'Aspremont (n 161) 114 (arguing that 'when, at the preparatory stage, member states prove to exercise overwhelming control that quells the autonomy of the organization, they must be jointly or concurrently held responsible for the ensuing wrongful acts').

[207] *Gabčikovo-Nagymaros Project (Hungary/Slovakia)* (Judgment) [1997] ICJ Rep 7, 54, para 79; see also ILC, 'Report of the International Law Commission on the Work of Its 45th Session (3 May–23 July 1993)' (1993) UN Doc A/48/10, reproduced in (1993) 2 (pt 2) *YBILC* 1, 57, para 14 (Former Draft Art 41 Commentary).

[208] ILC (n 168) 25 (ILO).

[209] J Heliskoski, *Mixed Agreements as a Technique for Organizing the International Relations of the European Community and Its Member States* (The Hague, Kluwer, 2001); E Steinberger, 'The WTO Treaty as a Mixed Agreement: Problems with the EC's and the EC Member States' Membership of the WTO' (2006) 17 *EJIL* 837.

[210] IDI, 'Resolution on the Legal Consequences for Member States of the Non-Fulfilment by International Organizations of Their Obligations toward Third Parties' (1996) 66 *AIDI* 444, Arts 3, 5 and 8.

[211] See Klein (n 189) 426–521; M Hartwig, *Die Haftung der Mitgliedstaaten für Internationale Organisationen* (Berlin, Springer, 1993); F Messineo, 'Attribution of Conduct' in A Nollkaemper and I Plakokefalos (eds), *Principles of Shared Responsibility in International Law: An Appraisal of the State of the Art* (Cambridge, CUP, 2014); A Geslin, 'Réflexions sur la répartition de la responsabilité entre l'organisation internationale et ses états membres' (2005) 109 *RGDIP* 539; Murray (n 161).

The issue of Member States' responsibility alongside that of the organisation is particularly important in the area of joint military or peacekeeping operations. Although some positive developments have taken place in relation to the responsibility of multinational forces for violations committed in the context of operations authorised by the UN, doubts persist as to the content and scope of the applicable primary norms.[212] This in turn has an impact on the interpretation and application of the relevant secondary rules of responsibility in this context. For example, insofar as the UN exercises operational control of the activities in the course of which wrongful acts have been committed (eg peacekeeping operations), it is indeed the UN that has accepted exclusive responsibility for such acts.[213] It is the position of the UN Legal Counsel that:

> As a subsidiary organ of the United Nations, an act of a peacekeeping force is, in principle, imputable to the Organization, and if committed in violation of an international obligation entails the international responsibility of the Organization and its liability in compensation.[214]

This guiding principle is qualified by the assessment of factual control in every given situation. According to the UN Secretary General:

> The international responsibility of the United Nations for combat-related activities of United Nations is premised on the assumption that the operation in question is under the exclusive command and control of the United Nations …
>
> In joint operations, international responsibility for the conduct of the troops lies where operational command and control is vested according to the arrangements establishing the modalities of cooperation between the State or States providing the troops and the United Nations. *In the absence of formal arrangements between the United Nations and the State or States providing troops, responsibility would be determined in each and every case according to the degree of effective control exercised by either party in the conduct of the operation.*[215] (emphasis added)

[212] LA Sicilianos, 'L'(ir)responsabilité des forces multinationales' in L Boisson de Chazournes and MG Kohen (eds), *International Law and the Quest for its Implementation, Liber Amicorum Vera Gowlland-Debbas* (Leiden, Martinus Nijhoff, 2010); see also R Kolb, G Porretto and S Vité, *L'application du droit international humanitaire et des droits de l'homme aux organisations internationales—Forces de paix et administrations civiles transitoires* (2nd edn, Bruxelles, Bruylant, 2005); F Hampson, '"States" Military Operations Authorized by the United Nations and International Humanitarian Law' in L Condorelli, AM La Rosa and S Scherrer (eds), *The United Nations and International Humanitarian Law* (Paris, Pedone, 1996); for analysis of applicable law in the cases of authorised operations LA Sicilianos, 'Entre multilatéralisme et unilatéralisme: l'autorisation par le Conseil de sécurité de recourir à la force: Une tentative d'évaluation' (2008) 339 *RCADI* 9.

[213] P Klein, 'The Attribution of Acts of International Organizations' in J Crawford et al (eds), *The Law of International Responsibility* (Oxford, OUP, 2010) 299–300.

[214] ILC, 'Report of the International Law Commission on the Work of Its 56th Session (3 May–6 August 2004)' (2004) UN Doc A/59/10, reproduced in (2004) 2 (pt 2) *YBILC* 1, 112 (this quote is from an unpublished letter of 3 February 2004 by the UN Legal Counsel to the Director of the Codification Division).

[215] UNGA, 'Report of the Secretary-General on the Financing of the United Nations Peacekeeping Operations' (20 September 1996) UN Doc A/51/389, 6, paras 17–18.

One of the most emblematic precedents is found in the UN operations in the Congo in the 1960s.[216] As a result of violations committed during those operations, claims were made (and later settled) against the UN by States in respect of injuries suffered by their nationals.[217]

Contrary to situations of wrongful acts committed by the UN peacekeepers, the Security Council frequently gives its authorisation for a particular military action, which is then executed by participating States and in some cases regional organisations. In such military operations, practice has shown that the UN bears no responsibility. For instance, it was the United States and not the UN that had to answer to demands for reparation made by third States due to violations of international obligations committed during the Korean War.[218] The same outcome was transposed *mutatis mutandis* to the violations committed in the course of the 1991 Gulf War, as troops provided by the coalition States operated under a unified command pursuant to the UNSC Resolution 678.[219] Likewise, contributions to cover damage caused by the national troops making up the multinational force that had been deployed under the auspices of NATO in Bosnia and Herzegovina following the Dayton Agreement were made by those participating States and not by NATO itself.[220] In the same vein, it was the United States and not NATO that offered *ex gratia* payment to the Chinese authorities after an incidental bombing of the Chinese embassy in Belgrade in the course of military operations undertaken by NATO States.[221]

The attribution of responsibility may be more problematic in cases of the so-called 'hybrid operations', such as that carried out jointly by the UN and African Union in Darfur (UNAMID).[222] According to Boutin, UNAMID 'presents characteristics comparable ... [and] similar to the command structure of the States' coalitions under multinational integrated command' (ie a structure where the troops are placed under the operation

[216] DW Bowett, *United Nations Forces: A Legal Study of United Nations Practice* (London, Stevens & Sons, 1964) 245.

[217] See ILC, 'The Practice of the United Nations, the Specialized Agencies and the International Atomic Energy Agency Concerning Their Status, Privileges and Immunities: Study Prepared by the Secretariat' (1967) UN Doc A/CN.4/L.118 and Add 1-2, reproduced in (1976) 2 *YBILC* 154, 218–19, paras 54–56.

[218] F Seyersted, 'United Nations Forces. Some Legal Problems' (1961) 37 *British YBIL* 351, 362 ff.

[219] See CF Amerasinghe, 'An Assessment of the ILC's Articles on the Responsibility of International Organizations' in M Ragazzi (ed), *Responsibility of International Organizations: Essays in Memory of Sir Ian Brownlie* (Leiden, Martinus Nijhoff, 2013) 74.

[220] Klein (n 188) 303; M Guillaume, 'La réparation des dommages causés par les contingents français en ex-Yougoslavie et en Albanie' (1997) 43 *AFDI* 151, 152.

[221] See SD Murphy, 'Ex Gratia Payment for Bombing of Chinese Embassy in Belgrade' (2000) 94 *AJIL* 127.

[222] UNSC, 'Res 1769' (31 July 2007) UN Doc S/RES/1769; see also SE Kreps, 'The United Nations-African Union Mission in Darfur: Implications and Prospects for Success' (2007) 4 *African Security Review* 66.

control of a multinational force commander).[223] It remains a legal puzzle on how to distribute potential responsibility and legal consequences deriving from wrongful acts committed in the context of such hybrid operations.

To determine the responsibility of such 'agents of execution', the relevant criterion in the view of attribution lies in the notion of effective control.[224] Control, as such, 'will necessarily comprise a series of competences and attributions, the various elements of which need not necessarily be present in each and every case but which taken as a whole must be sufficiently strong and coherent to justify effective allegiance' of the entity or agent to the organisation.[225] In essence, in the context of military or peacekeeping operations, effective control is equivalent to operational control.[226] However, in complex military operations, there may be different forms and degrees of control alongside the operational control.[227] As Dannenbaum suggests, where several actors are implicated in a given operation, effective control 'is held by the entity that is best positioned to act effectively and within the law to prevent the abuse in question'.[228] Boutin further argues that the conduct of the troops 'should be attributed to the State or/and international organization which exercised a causally proximate element of control over the soldier's conduct'.[229]

The test of effective control set forth in Article 7 ARIO is no magic solution in practice of all joint military operations conducted by States and international organisations. Let us take an example of the intervention

[223] B Boutin, 'The Role of Control in Allocating International Responsibility in Collaborative Military Operations' (PhD Thesis, University of Amsterdam, 2015) 46 (distinguishing such model of a coalition from two others—the multinational command with a dominant State and a national command model).

[224] Sicilianos, 'L'(ir)responsabilité des forces multinationales' (n 212) 97; see also T Dannenbaum, 'Translating the Standard of Effective Control into a System of Effective Accountability: How Liability Should Be Apportioned for Violations of Human Rights by Member State Troop Contingents Serving as United Nations Peacekeepers' (2010) 51 *Harvard Intl LJ* 113, 153–54; Boutin (n 223).

[225] P de Visscher, 'Les conditions d'application des lois de la guerre aux opérations militaires des Nations Unies' (1971) 54 *AIDI* 1, 48.

[226] See, eg ILC, 'Comments and Observations Received from Governments' (13 April 2011) UN Doc A/CN.4/636/Add 1, 11, para 2 (Mexico); KM Larsen, 'Attribution of Conduct in Peace Operations: The "Ultimate Authority and Control" Test' (2008) 19 *EJIL* 509, 523; M Milanović and T Papić, 'As Bad as It Gets: The European Court of Human Rights's Behrami and Saramati Decision and General International Law' (2009) 58 *ICLQ* 267, 289; see also P Klein, 'Responsabilité pour les faits commis dans le cadre d'opérations de paix et étendue du pouvoir de contrôle de la Cour européenne des droits de l'homme: quelques considérations critiques sur l'arrêt Behrami et Saramati' (2007) 53 *AFDI* 43.

[227] Boutin (n 223) 116–21; C Leck, 'International Responsibility in United Nations Peacekeeping Operations: Command and Control Arrangements and the Attribution of Conduct' (2009) 10 *Melbourne J Intl L* 346, 359.

[228] Dannenbaum (n 224) 158.

[229] Boutin (n 223) 120.

in Libya. 'Operation Odyssey Dawn' and 'Operation Unified Protector' aimed to enforce the UNSC Resolution 1973, and individual NATO Member States were initially in command.[230] However, in March 2011 command shifted to NATO forces.[231] The resulting changes in the rules of engagement for contributing States were significant. Some States contributed aircrafts when NATO took control, but they were precluded from participating in air strikes by their individual rules of engagement.[232] For example, the United States chief of staff for Libya mission explained the United States' rules of engagement as follows:

> Where they see a clear situation where civilians are threatened, they have … intervened … When it's unclear that it's civilians that are being attacked, the air crews are instructed to be very cautious …What we look for, to the degree that we can, is to discern intent … There's no simple answer.[233]

In face of the disparate rules of engagement adopted by contributing States, it becomes difficult to discern which party specifically had effective control in a joint military conduct but also which legal standards prevail in each situation. There is good reason to cast doubt on the legal distinction drawn by the ILC between fully and not fully seconded State organs.[234] The former situations are rare in practice, as State's troops placed at the disposal of the organisation frequently retain some organic link to its State and sometimes even continue to exercise certain functions on its behalf, even where it is under an operational control of the organisation.[235] In the case of non-fully seconded State organs, the organisation and its Member

[230] See JM Lehmann, 'All Necessary Means to Protect Civilians: What the Intervention in Libya Says about the Relationship between Jus in Bello and the Jus Ad Bellum' (2012) 17 *JCSL* 117, 139; on the legality of intervention G Ulfstein and HF Christiansen, 'The Legality of the NATO Bombing in Libya' (2013) 62 *ICLQ* 159.

[231] See KP Mueller, *Precision and Purpose: Airpower in the Libyan Civil War* (Santa Monica, RAND Corporation, 2015) 194.

[232] 'Dutch F-16s Join Libyan Raids, but Don't Take Part in Bombing' *Dutch News* (18 May 2011).

[233] 'Rules of Engagement Are Murky in Libya Air War' *Foreign Policy* (21 March 2011).

[234] ARIO (n 5) 19–20, para 1 (Art 7 Commentary); see also ILC, 'Responsibility of International Organizations, Comments and Observations Received from International Organizations' (14 February 2011) UN Doc A/CN.4/637, 23 (ILO) (suggesting that in the law of international civil services, there is also a distinction to be drawn between the officials on 'loan' and 'secondment', and that the international organisation bears no responsibility for the acts committed by an official on 'loan' to the organisation).

[235] See, eg *Mukeshimana-Ngulinzira and others v Belgium and others* (Judgment) [2010] RG No 04/4807/A and 07/15547/A; ILDC 1604 (BE 2010) (Belgium Court of First Instance) (holding that the failure by the UN peacekeeping contingent in Rwanda to prevent the killing of Tutsis in the 1994 genocide in Rwanda could be attributed to Belgium where the Belgian government had decided to withdraw from the peacekeeping operation); A Sari, 'UN Peacekeeping Operations and Article 7 ARIO: The Missing Link' (2012) 9 *IOLR* 77, 79; Dannenbaum (n 224) 148; Leck (n 227); for a detailed analysis of control in the context of operations under the aegis of the UN, NATO and the EU see Boutin (n 223).

State could be jointly and severally responsible for the same wrongful act, but this would raise no question of aid or assistance.[236] According to Gaja:

> Should one assume that conduct could not be simultaneously attributed to a State and an international organization, the positive criteria for attributing conduct to a State would imply corresponding negative criteria with regard to attribution of the same conduct to an international organization. In many cases the question will in practice be whether a certain conduct should be attributed to one or, alternatively, to another subject of international law. However, conduct does not necessarily have to be attributed exclusively to one subject only. Thus, for instance, two States may establish a joint organ, whose conduct will generally have to be attributed to both States. Similarly, one could envisage cases in which conduct should be simultaneously attributed to an international organization and one or more of its members.[237]

Such scenarios could be envisaged in joint border control operations, or in situations of territorial administration under the aegis of international organisation, such as the administration by the UN of Kosovo or East Timor.[238] Probably the best example of a situation where both Member States and international organiation may have been held concurrently responsible is the bombing campaign by NATO in 1999 on the territory of the Federal Republic of Yugoslavia (FRY). Several Member States of NATO appeared before the ICJ in the *Legality of the Use of Force* cases and before the ECtHR in the *Banković* case. In both proceedings, certain of the responding States argued that their conduct was exclusively attributable to NATO.[239] The cases were eventually dismissed on admissibility grounds.

[236] ARIO (n 5) Art 48.

[237] G Gaja, 'Second Report on Responsibility of International Organizations' (2004) UN Doc A/CN.4/541, reproduced in (2004) 2 (pt 1) *YBILC* 1, 4, paras 6–7.

[238] See, eg M Ruffert, 'The Administration of Kosovo and East-Timor by the International Community' (2001) 50 *ICLQ* 613; M Saul, 'The Practice of Shared Responsibility in Relation to Internationally Administered Territories' SHARES Research Paper No 65 (2015); K Schmalenbach, 'Third Party Liability of International Organizations: A Study on Claim Settlement in the Course of Military Operations and International Administrations' (2006) 10 *International Peacekeeping: The Yearbook of International Peace Operations* 33; L Cameron and R Everly, 'Conceptualizing the Administration of Territory by International Actors' (2010) 21 *EJIL* 221; E de Brabandere, 'Immunity of International Organizations in Post-Conflict International Administrations' (2010) 7 *IOLR* 79.

[239] See, eg *Legality of Use of Force (Serbia and Montenegro v Belgium)* (Preliminary Objections) [2004] ICJ Rep 279, ICJ Pleadings, Preliminary Objections of Belgium of 5 July 2000, 155–58 and 171–80; *Legality of Use of Force (Serbia and Montenegro v Canada)* (Preliminary Objections) [2004] ICJ Rep 429, ICJ Pleadings, Preliminary Objections of Canada of 5 July 2000, 46–47, paras 164–65; see also T Stein, 'Kosovo and the International Community. The Attribution of Possible Internationally Wrongful Acts: Responsibility of NATO or of Its Member States?' in C Tomuschat (ed), *Kosovo and the International Community* (The Hague, Kluwer, 2002); A Pellet, 'L'imputabilité d'éventuels actes illicites—Responsabilité de l'OTAN ou des États membres' in C Tomuschat (ed), *Kosovo and the International Community* (The Hague, Kluwer, 2002).

According to Gaja, 'one envisageable solution would be for the relevant conduct to be attributed both to NATO and to one or more of its Member States, for instance because those States contributed to planning the military action or to carrying it out'.[240] This principle of joint attribution to a State and international organisation has been confirmed in *Al Jedda*[241] as well as in the *Nuhanović* and *Mustafić-Mujić* cases.[242] In the latter cases, the Supreme Court of the Netherlands found the Netherlands responsible for the conduct of its peacekeeping troops operating under the UN mandate in Srebrenica.[243] Joint operations of international organisations and their Member States have raised complex questions relating not only to the attribution of conduct for the purposes of responsibility but also to the notion of jurisdiction and the limits of extra-territorial application of the ECHR.[244]

It remains to be seen in practice whether dual or multiple attribution will be more than a qualified exception to the traditional approach of hiding

[240] Gaja (n 237) 4, paras 6–7.

[241] *Al Jedda v United Kingdom* (Judgment) (GC) [2011] ECtHR App No 27021/08 (2011) 53 EHRR 23, para 80.

[242] *Netherlands v Nuhanović* (Judgment) [2013] Case No 12/03324 LZ/TT (Dutch Supreme Court) paras 3.11.2–3.12.3; *Netherlands v Mustafić-Mujić* (Judgment) [2013] Case No 12/03329 (Dutch Supreme Court) paras 3.11.2–3.12.3; see also T Dannenbaum, 'Dutch Supreme Court Affirms That Dutchbat Acted Unlawfully in Srebrenica' www.ejiltalk.org/dutch-supreme-court-affirms-that-dutchbat-acted-unlawfully-in-srebrenica/; B Boutin, 'Responsibility of the Netherlands for the Acts of Dutchbat in Nuhanović and Mustafić: The Continuous Quest for a Tangible Meaning for "Effective Control" in the Context of Peacekeeping' (2012) 25 *LJIL* 521.

[243] *Netherlands v Nuhanović* (n 242) paras 3.11.2–3.12.3; *Netherlands v Mustafić-Mujić* (n 242) paras 3.11.2–3.12.3; see also A Nollkaemper, 'Dual Attribution: Liability of the Netherlands for Conduct of Dutchbat in Srebrenica' (2011) 9 *JICJ* 1143; E Cannizzaro, 'Beyond the Either/Or: Dual Attribution to the European Union and to the Member State for Breach of the ECHR' in MD Evans and P Koutrakos (eds), *The International Responsibility of the European Union: European and International Perspectives* (Oxford, Hart Publishing, 2013); L Condorelli, 'Le statut des forces de l'ONU et le droit international humanitaire' (1995) 78 *RDI* 881, 897.

[244] *Al Jedda v United Kingdom* (n 241) paras 84–86 (re-asserting the conventional test of 'effective control' alongside that of 'ultimate authority and control'); *Al-Skeini v United Kingdom* (Judgment) (GC) [2011] ECtHR App No 55721/07 (2011) 53 EHRR 18, paras 136 and 149; cf *Behrami v France / Saramati v France, Germany and Norway* (Admissibility) (GC) [2007] ECtHR App No 71412/01 and 78166/01 (2007) 45 EHRR SE10, paras 133–43 (coming up with an 'ultimate authority and control' test and thereby attributing actions of the NATO-led forced in Kosovo to the UN); see, eg Bodini (n 170) 843–45, 847–48; M Milanović, *Extraterritorial Application of Human Rights Treaties: Law, Principles, and Policy* (Oxford, OUP, 2011) 41–53 (noting the confusion that reigns in the notions of control for the purposes of ascertaining jurisdiction or establishing responsibility); S Besson, 'The Extraterritoriality of the European Convention on Human Rights: Why Human Rights Depend on Jurisdiction and What Jurisdiction Amounts to' (2012) 25 *LJIL* 857, 870 ff (providing a useful analysis of the typology of control in the assessment of jurisdiction); A Sari, 'Jurisdiction and International Responsibility in Peace Support Operations: The Behrami and Saramati Cases' (2008) 8 *HRLR* 151; F Messineo, 'Things Could Only Get Better: Al-Jedda beyond Behrami' (2012) 50 *Military Law and the Law of War Review* 321, 346 (noting that the ECtHR's ruling in Al-Jedda can be 'read either as an attempt to keep Behrami alive or as a subtle overcoming of that decision').

troops-contributing State's conduct behind the veil of international organisations. Similarly, it shall not be taken for granted that effective control will necessarily be an appropriate standard for a variety of organisations that deal with issues and activities other than those arising in the context of military operations.[245] It is evident after all that international organisations have become much more than 'mere instrumentalities whereby sovereign States can associate and work with each other'.[246]

V. COMPLICITY AND OTHER FORMS OF SHARED OR ANCILLARY RESPONSIBILITY

An analysis of the responsibility for complicity in international law calls for delimitation from its neighbouring concepts. The following operations go to establish these boundaries. On the one hand, complicity must be distinguished from other forms of indirect responsibility, namely coercion, direction and control, and circumvention of obligations through another entity (sub-section V.A). On the other hand, complicity must be distinguished from joint and several responsibility, where two or more States or international organisations jointly commit an internationally wrongful act (sub-section V.B).

A. Other Forms of Indirect Attribution of Responsibility

The ILC originally distinguished complicity from other forms of indirect responsibility, where one State or international organisation is responsible *for* the international wrongful act of another because of a particular legal or factual relationship between the two subjects. The classic case is that of responsibility of a State for the internationally wrongful act of its protectorate.[247] As opposed to complicity, the State exercising direction,

[245] See, eg ILC (n 234) 23 (ILO); UNGA, 'Sixth Committee, Summary Record of the 20th Meeting' (26 October 2011) UN Doc A/C.6/66/SR.20, 9–10, para 53 (France).

[246] RY Jennings, 'Universal International Law in a Multicultural World', *International Law and the Grotian Heritage* (The Hague, TMC Asser, 1985) 49.

[247] *Rights of Nationals of the United States of America in Morocco* (Judgment) [1952] ICJ Rep 176 (France was held responsible for the acts of Morocco); *Mavrommatis Palestine Concessions (Greece v United Kingdom)* (Objection to the Jurisdiction) [1924] PCIJ Ser A No 2, 23 (the United Kingdom was held responsible for administration of Palestine); see also C Eagleton, *The Responsibility of States in International Law* (New York, New York University Press, 1928) 35–40; MG Cohn, 'La théorie de la responsabilité internationale' (1939) 68 *RCADI* 209, 291; F Klein, *Die Mittelbare Haftung im Völkerrecht: Die Haftung eines Völkerrechtssubjektes für das völkerrechtswidrige Verhalten eines anderen Völkerrechtssubjektes* (Frankfurt am Main, Klostermann, 1941) 34–35.

control or coercion bears the responsibility *for* and not *in connection with* the wrongful act committed by the directed, controlled or coerced State.[248]

In the practice and theory of the early twentieth century, the concept of indirect responsibility included cases of responsibility incurred by a State on the commission of wrongful acts by: (i) private individuals; (ii) organs which lacked competence or which had acted *ultra vires*; (iii) territorial governmental entities possessing under the internal legal system a personality separate from that of the State itself.[249] Similarly, between 1932 and 1945 a few cases of 'puppet States' or local administrations of political convenience proliferated, including Manchukuo, Croatia and Slovakia.[250] In all these cases, practice showed that the administering or protector States were not absolved from responsibility for breaches committed by the administered or protected States or ad hoc local administrations.[251]

Under the leadership of Roberto Ago, the ILC circumscribed the concept of indirect responsibility to the 'set of cases in which a State is required to answer for an internationally wrongful act committed by another State or another subject of international law'.[252] In 1979, Ago proposed to codify the responsibility for direction or control and for coercion under former draft Article 28:

> Article 28
>
> Indirect responsibility of a State for an internationally wrongful act of another State
>
> 1. An internationally wrongful act committed by a State in a field of activity in which that State is not in possession of complete freedom of decision, being subject, in law or in fact, to the directions or the control of another State, does not entail the international responsibility of the State committing the wrongful act but entails the indirect international responsibility of the State which is in a position to give directions or exercise control.

[248] R Ago, 'Eighth Report on State Responsibility' (1979) UN Doc A/CN.4/318 and Add 1-4, reproduced in (1979) 2 (pt 1) *YBILC* 4, 25–26, paras 44–47.

[249] ibid.

[250] See I Brownlie, 'State Responsibility: The Problem of Delegation' in K Ginther et al (eds), *Völkerrecht zwischen normativem Anspruch und politischer Realität: Festschrift für Karl Zemanek zum 65. Geburtstag* (Berlin, Duncker & Humblot, 1994) 301; K Marek, *Identity and Continuity of States in Public International Law* (2nd edn, Genève, Droz, 1968) 110 ff; J Crawford, 'The Criteria for Statehood in International Law' (1978) 48 *British YBIL* 93, 130–33.

[251] Brownlie (n 250) 301; see also M Whiteman, *Digest of International Law*, vol 8 (Washington DC, Department of State Publication, 1967) 835 ff; ILC (n 13) 100–01.

[252] Ago (n 248) 5, para 3; see similarly D Anzilotti, *Teoria generale della responsabilità dello stato nel diritto internazionale* (Firenze, F Lumachi Libraio-Editore, 1902); D Anzilotti, 'La responsabilité internationale des États à raison des dommages soufferts par des étrangers' (1906) 13 *RGDIP* 5; see also P Schoen, *Die völkerrechtliche Haftung der Staaten aus unerlaubten Handlungen*, vol 10 (Breslau, Kern, 1917) 42; C de Visscher, *La responsabilité des États: cours professé à l'Académie de droit international de la Haye*, vol 5 (The Hague, Brill, 1924) 93 and 105.

2. An internationally wrongful act committed by a State under coercion exerted to that end by another State does not entail the international responsibility of the State which acted under coercion but entails the indirect international responsibility of the State which exerted it.[253]

This provision intended to deal with situations where a State is responsible for the conduct of another State, but not for the conduct of entities other than States.[254] The commentary to former draft Article 28 listed the following examples: (i) international dependency relationship, especially 'suzerainty' and international protectorate; (ii) relationships between a federal State and member States of a federation which have retained their own international personality; and (iii) relationships between the occupying State and an occupied State in cases of territorial occupation.[255]

Ago's understanding was that indirect responsibility arises because of control exercised by the dominant State over a particular activity of the dependent State.[256] For the establishment of such an indirect responsibility on the part of the dominant State as a result of an internationally wrongful act of the dependent State, a twofold condition must be met. First, organs of the dependent State must have committed the act in question. Second, they must have operated in a field of action in which their freedom of decision was restricted, in one way or another, by the control of the dominant State.[257]

On second reading, the former draft Article 28 ARSIWA was split into two separate provisions, Articles 17 and 18. Article 17 attaches responsibility to the State that directs and controls another State committing the wrongful act. Article 18 sets out the responsibility of a State for coercing another to commit an internationally wrongful act. In the words of the ILC's Commentary, the conduct of the State that actually acts is 'chargeable' to the directing or coercing State which is, one might say, the 'puppet master'; and if the puppet commits a wrongful act the controlling State is responsible because the act is, in effect, the act of the controlling State.[258] Similar provisions were introduced into Articles 15 and 16 ARIO. In addition, owing to the specific nature of the relationship between international organisations and States, the responsibility for circumvention of international obligations was reflected in Articles 17 and 61 ARIO.

[253] Ago (n 248) 26–27, para 47.
[254] ibid.
[255] ibid.
[256] For the discussion of the theories of representation and control traditionally associated with cases of indirect responsibility see ibid 5–7; J Fry, 'Coercion, Causation, and the Fictional Elements of Indirect State Responsibility' (2007) 40 *Vanderbilt J Transnatl L* 611, 616–17.
[257] Ago (n 248) 14, para 18.
[258] ILC (n 13) 100–01, paras 7–8 (Former Draft Art 27 Commentary); ARSIWA (n 4) 67–69 (Art 17 Commentary).

i. Direction and Control

Article 17 ARSIWA (with its twin Article 15 ARIO for international organisations) provides as follows:

> Article 17
>
> Direction and control exercised over the commission of an internationally wrongful act
>
> A State which directs and controls another State in the commission of an internationally wrongful act by the latter is internationally responsible for that act if:
>
> (a) That State does so with knowledge of the circumstances of the internationally wrongful act; and
> (b) The act would be internationally wrongful if committed by that State.[259]

When preparing this provision, Ago had in mind the relationship of dependency upon another State and the question of whether an unlawful act of the dependent State could entail the responsibility of the dominant State. As introduced above, the clearest example of such direction and control is found in the relationship between States and their protectorates, which today is almost non-existent in practice.

However, in theory cases of direction and control by one State over the other may still be found in the situations of military occupation. The *locus classicus* on the responsibility of the dominant State for the acts of the dependent State can be found in the *Rights of Nationals of the United States in Morocco*.[260] In that case, France commenced proceedings in respect of a dispute concerning the rights of the United States' nationals in Morocco under the French protectorate. The United States objected that any eventual judgment might not be considered as binding upon Morocco, which was not a party to the proceedings. France replied that it was acting both on its own name and as the protecting power over Morocco, with the result that the Court's judgment would be binding both on France and Morocco.[261] In the *British Claims in the Spanish Zone of Morocco*, the tribunal had already found that 'the responsibility of the protecting State … proceeds … from the fact that the protecting State alone represents the protected territory in its international relations'.[262]

[259] ARSIWA (n 4) Art 17.

[260] *Rights of Nationals of the United States of America in Morocco* (n 247) 176; cf *Robert E Brown (United States) v United Kingdom* (1923) 6 RIAA 120, 130–31 (where the tribunal held that the authority of Great Britain, as suzerain over the South African Republic prior to the Boer War 'fell far short of what would be required to make her responsible for the wrong inflicted upon Brown').

[261] *Rights of Nationals of the United States of America in Morocco* (n 247) 179; see also ICJ Pleadings vol 1, 235 and vol 2, 431–34.

[262] *Spanish Zone of Morocco Claims (United Kingdom v Spain)* (1924) 2 RIAA 615, 649.

According to the ILC:

> [T]he term 'controls' refers to cases of domination over the commission of wrongful conduct and not simply the exercise of oversight, still less mere influence or concern. Similarly, the word 'directs' does not encompass mere incitement or suggestion but rather connotes actual direction of an operative kind.[263]

In fact, both direction and control must be exercised over the wrongful conduct in order for a dominant State to incur responsibility.[264] As a preliminary requirement, a particular threshold needs to exist for one State to be considered dominated by another. For instance, situations of representation would not fulfil such a threshold. Accordingly, the representation of Liechtenstein by Switzerland or Western Samoa by New Zealand cannot in and of themselves be considered a case of domination.[265] Another case that could be referred to is that of Italy representing San Marino. Similar consideration applies to those entities composing a federal State. Such entities are not considered States and are dealt with by Article 4 of the ARSIWA, notwithstanding the fact that in some jurisdictions like Switzerland cantons possess a quasi-functional sovereignty according to which they can enter into bilateral relations with foreign States.

In other words, the scope of application of Article 17 ARSIWA is relatively narrow, presupposing the existence of a dependency relationship and the actual power of the dominant State to direct acts of the dependent State. As an example, in a case of military occupation, 'if the acts of the occupying power directly engage its responsibility, it is its indirect responsibility which is engaged for the acts of the occupied State undertaken pursuant to its direction and control'.[266] It is questionable whether the requirements of direction and control are cumulative or disjunctive. For instance, in the *Legality of the Use of Force* case, France relied on the 1996 Draft ARSIWA.[267] It argued that:

> This principle [is] fully transposable to cases where the power of direction or control is exercised not by another State but, as is the case here, by one (or two—since NATO is responsible for the 'direction' of KFOR and the United Nations for 'control' of it)—international organization(s).[268]

While the two concepts of 'direction' and 'control' seem closely linked in practice, both must be established cumulatively to trigger

[263] ARSIWA (n 4) 69, para 7 (Art 17 Commentary).
[264] ibid.
[265] See C Dominicé, 'Attribution of Conduct to Multiple States and the Implication of a State in the Act of Another State' in J Crawford et al (eds), *The Law of International Responsibility* (Oxford, OUP, 2010) 287.
[266] ibid 288.
[267] *Legality of Use of Force (Serbia and Montenegro v France)* (Preliminary Objections) [2004] ICJ Rep 575, Preliminary Objections of the French Republic (5 July 2000) 33, para 46.
[268] ibid.

responsibility.[269] Although there is very little practice,[270] the establishment of control and direction by the State over the internationally wrongful act committed by another State raises issues, which are similar in nature to those relating to the responsibility for aid or assistance. For example, Article 17 ARSIWA also imposes the requirement of knowledge of the circumstances of the internationally wrongful act as well as the pre-condition of the opposability of the obligation breached. However, contrary to Article 16, the responsibility of one State for the direction or control of another State, once established, may give rise to the exclusive responsibility of the directing or controlling State, provided the dependent State had no autonomy left as to its decision-making regarding the commission of an internationally wrongful act.[271]

This rule is subject to an exception in those cases where the dependent State maintains a certain degree of freedom in the particular area of the obligation breached; it would be responsible for its own conduct, even if instructed to commit the breach by the directing or controlling State.[272] For example, if the dependent State autonomously runs a nuclear site for enriched uranium and illegally provides it to a third party, albeit encouraged otherwise by the dominant State, the dominant State would incur no responsibility. This outcome is due to the fact that, as we have previously recalled, the ILC did not consider incitement or encouragement as sufficient to generate responsibility.[273]

ii. Coercion

Another example of the responsibility of one State or international organisation in connection with the act of another is that of coercion. Article 18 ARSIWA (with its twin Article 16 ARIO in respect of international organisations) provides as follows:

> Article 18
>
> Coercion of another State
>
> A State which coerces another State to commit an act is internationally responsible for that act if:
>
> (a) The act would, but for the coercion, be an internationally wrongful act of the coerced State; and

[269] Crawford (n 22) 51–55, paras 187–208.

[270] For a notable exception see *Robert E Brown (United States) v United Kingdom* (n 260) 130–31; *Héritiers de SAR Mgr le Duc de Guise (France v Italy)* (1951) 13 RIAA 150, 161; Crawford (n 22) 54; Crawford (n 58) 412–18.

[271] Ago (n 248) 26, para 45.

[272] Ago (n 51) 55–56, para 64; see also *Chevreau (France v United Kingdom)* (1931) 2 RIAA 1113; *Robert E Brown (United States) v United Kingdom* (n 260).

[273] *Military and Paramilitary Activities (Merits)* (n 42) 129, para 255; ibid, Dissenting Opinion of Judge Schwebel 378, para 259; Crawford (n 22) 55–56, para 213.

(b) The coercing State does so with knowledge of the circumstances of the act.[274]

According to the ILC's Commentary, coercion is '[n]othing less than conduct which forces the will of the coerced State ... giving it no effective choice but to comply with the wishes of the coercing State'.[275] The wording of Article 18 is slightly different from Articles 16 and 17 ARSIWA. It protects the coerced State such that coercion may even amount to *force majeure*, a circumstance precluding wrongfulness.[276] As James Crawford explains:

> Under ARSIWA Article 16, the primary wrongdoer is the acting state and the assisting state has a supporting role. By contrast, in the case of coercion under ARSIWA Article 18, the coercing state is the *fons et origo* of the conduct, and the coerced state is its instrument.[277]

Importantly, the notion of coercion in Article 18 ARSIWA covers both lawful and unlawful coercion.[278] Although in most cases coercion is unlawful because it results from the use or threat of the use of force, it is also possible that there is no obligation in place prohibiting the coercive act such as lesser forms of economic or social coercion. The rationale of the provision is that if a State coerces another State to breach an obligation owed to a third State, it is the State exercising the coercion that must bear full international responsibility.

Conversely to responsibility for complicity and to responsibility for direction and control, Article 18 does not require the opposability of the obligation on the coercing and the coerced State.[279] Such a conception was driven by the consideration that otherwise 'the injured State could find itself unable to invoke the coerced State's responsibility, which benefits from a circumstance precluding wrongfulness, and also unable to invoke the coercing State's responsibility, since it is not bound by the obligation breached'.[280]

iii. Circumvention of International Obligations

The scenarios of complicity need to be further distinguished from those situations where an international organisation circumvents its obligations under international law, by requiring its Member States to implement decisions and authorisations which are contrary to international law. This is set out in Article 17 of the ARIO:

274 ARSIWA (n 4) Art 18.
275 ibid 69, para 2 (Art 18 Commentary).
276 ibid 69, para 2 (Art 18 Commentary).
277 Crawford (n 58) 396.
278 ARSIWA (n 4) 70, para 3 (Art 18 Commentary).
279 Crawford (n 22) 55, para 209.
280 Dominicé (n 265) 289.

Article 17

Circumvention of international obligations through decisions and authorizations addressed to members

1. An international organization incurs international responsibility if it circumvents one of its international obligations by adopting a decision binding member States or international organizations to commit an act that would be internationally wrongful if committed by the former organization.
2. An international organization incurs international responsibility if it circumvents one of its international obligations by authorizing member States or international organizations to commit an act that would be internationally wrongful if committed by the former organization and the act in question is committed because of that authorization.
3. Paragraphs 1 and 2 apply whether or not the act in question is internationally wrongful for the member States or international organizations to which the decision or authorization is addressed.[281]

This provision reflects the progressive development of international law, and the 'layered nature of international organizations'.[282] The *fait générateur* of this responsibility presupposes that the organisation adopt a binding decision or authorisation to circumvent its international obligation. The ARIO Commentary notes that this implies 'an *intention* on the part of the international organization to take advantage of the separate legal personality of its members in order to avoid compliance with an international obligation'.[283] As in the case of Articles 16 ARSIWA and 14 ARIO, the requirement of intent is rather problematic and unnecessarily restricts the scope of responsibility.[284]

There is also a *temporal* distinction as to the moment the internationally wrongful act arises, depending on whether a binding decision or authorisation is involved. In the case of binding decisions, the responsibility of an international organisation is engaged at the very moment the decision is passed. In the case of authorisations, it is the moment when the Member State acts upon that authorisation that the responsibility of an international organisation arises.

One area where the question of circumvention could arise is in the context of measures taken by the UNSC.[285] The responsibility for implementing

[281] ARIO (n 5) Art 17.

[282] See C Brölmann, *The Institutional Veil in Public International Law: International Organisations and the Law of Treaties* (Oxford, Hart Publishing, 2007).

[283] ARIO (n 5) 41, para 4 (Art 17 Commentary) (emphasis added); see also A Nollkaemper and N Nedeski, 'Responsibility of International Organizations "in Connection with Acts of States"' (2012) 9 *IOLR* 33, 48 ('Intent appears to function as an on-off switch that to a greater or lesser extent can protect the responsible party or the injured party and, certainly in the absence of much practice, reflects of policy choice').

[284] Nollkaemper and Nedeski (n 283) 48.

[285] See also Gowlland-Debbas (n 163) 378; N Blokker, 'Abuse of the Members: Questions Concerning Draft Article 16 of the Draft Articles on Responsibility of International Organizations' (2010) 7 *IOLR* 35.

and enforcing the UNSC measures lies with Member States of the UN.[286] However, depending on the terms of the resolution, the implementing State could either be left with no or some discretion as to the way in which it could implement a specific measure. The discretion left to the State is a crucial factor in determining whether the responsibility lies with an international organisation, Member State, or both. Thus, if the Member State has no discretion as to the means or manner of implementing the international organisation's decision, 'it would seem unreasonable to make it solely responsible for certain conduct'.[287] In these circumstances, the organisation may be regarded as exerting normative control over the conduct of the Member State, ie 'effective control is not exercised factually on the ground, but normatively through the imposition of an international obligation'.[288] The situation thus closely resembles one of agency as envisaged by Article 4 ARIO (ie the Member State acting as an agent of the organisation), which should thus prompt an exclusive attribution of the impugned conduct to the organisation or, in certain cases, concurrent attribution to the organisation and the Member State.

In parallel, there may be cases where Member States incur responsibility if their implementing measure (even if subject to no discretion in the original decision of the UNSC) is in violation of the State's own international obligations, irrespective of whether the same obligation binds the international organisation. Notwithstanding this conceptual distinction, and more broadly the obligations of Member States under Articles 25 and 103 of the UN Charter, domestic and regional courts no longer shy away from reviewing Member State's implementing measures, even where the decision of an international organisation appears to leave little to no margin of appreciation for the implementing State.[289]

A converse situation of a Member State seeking to avoid one of its international obligations through an organisation is covered by Article 61 ARIO. This inverted scenario is particularly relevant in the context of a recent stream of UNSC resolutions authorising States to use 'all necessary

[286] 'Memorandum of the Office of Legal Affairs of the United Nations' (21 April 1995), reproduced in (1995) *UN Juridical YB* 464–65.

[287] UNGA, 'Sixth Committee, Summary Record of the 22nd Meeting' (5 November 2004) UN Doc A/C.6/59/SR.22, 9, para 66 (Denmark on behalf of Nordic countries).

[288] A Tzanakopoulos, 'Strengthening Security Council Accountability for Sanctions: The Role of International Responsibility' (2014) 19 *JCSL* 409, 416; see also A Tzanakopoulos, *Disobeying the Security Council: Countermeasures against Wrongful Sanctions* (Oxford, OUP, 2011) 40–53.

[289] See, eg Joined Cases C-402/04P and C-415/05P, *Yassin Abdullah Kadi, Al Barakaat International Foundation v Council of the EU* (Judgment) (GC) [2008] ECR I-6351; Joined Cases C-584/10P, C-593/10P and C-595/10P, *EU Commission v Yassin Abdullah Kadi* (Judgment) (GC) [2014] All ER (EC) 123; *Nada v Switzerland* (Judgment) (GC) [2012] ECtHR App No 10593/08 (2013) 56 EHRR 18, paras 176–80.

means'.[290] Arguably, the abuse of such wording in the UNSC resolution could allow States to circumvent their obligations, for instance by de facto derogating from human rights norms under the ECHR instead of taking formal steps required to do so.[291] In a way, Article 61 ARIO serves as an additional guarantee of a well-established position that States parties to the ECHR cannot evade their responsibility by transferring competence to act to an international organisation and they are to ensure that the rights under the ECHR are duly respected.[292]

In sum, by contrast to cases of complicity, the conduct covered by Articles 17 and 61 ARIO does not depend on the unlawfulness of the principal wrongful act.[293] Nor is the responsibility for circumvention of international obligations subject to knowledge or opposability requirements as is the case of responsibility for aid or assistance.[294] In this sense, the responsibility triggered under these provisions is much broader than that for complicity, and creates an additional layer of protection against abuse of the separate personality of an international organisation.[295]

B. Joint and Several Responsibility

Finally, the scenarios of complicity differ from cases of joint and several responsibility.[296] Joint and several responsibility arises in international law in situations where two or more subjects commit in concert an internationally wrongful act. Article 47 ARSIWA and its twin Article 48 ARIO only address a plurality of responsible States (international organisations) in relation to the same internationally wrongful act. Article 47 ARSIWA reads as follows:

> Article 47
>
> Plurality of Responsible States
>
> 1. Where several States are responsible for the same internationally wrongful act, the responsibility of each State may be invoked in relation to that act.

[290] See, eg UNSC, 'Res 2249' (20 November 2015) UN Doc S/RES/2249 (ISIL) para 5; UNSC, 'Res 1973' (17 March 2011) UN Doc S/RES/1973 (Libya) paras 4 and 8.

[291] Gowlland-Debbas (n 163) 382.

[292] *Waite and Kennedy v Germany* (n 179) para 67; *Gasparini v Italy and Belgium* (Admissibility) [2009] App No 10750/03, 6; see also *Bosphorus Hava Yollari Turizm ve Ticaret Şirketi v Ireland* (n 179) para 154.

[293] See ARIO (n 5) Art 17(3); 42, para 14 (Art 17 Commentary).

[294] ibid 42–43, para 15 (Art 17 Commentary).

[295] For a detailed analysis of these provisions see, eg N Voulgaris, 'Rethinking Indirect Responsibility' (2014) 11 *IOLR* 5; Blokker (n 285).

[296] ILC (n 13) 99, para 2 (Former Draft Art 27 Commentary); Graefrath, Oeser and Steiniger (n 132) 371–72.

2. Paragraph 1:
   (a) does not permit any injured State to recover, by way of compensation, more than the damage it has suffered;
   (b) is without prejudice to any right of recourse against the other responsible States.[297]

The Commission emphasised that the situation of complicity was different from the form of responsibility that arises for co-perpetrators or co-participants as a result of their commission of a wrongful act, for example through a joint organ.[298] The conduct in such cases is 'concurrently attributable to each of the States having that organ in common'.[299] The Commission also emphasised that complicity differed from situations where two States participate together as principals in committing two separate internationally wrongful acts.[300]

In practice, however, there may be situations where it is difficult to distinguish whether a State is merely assisting the wrongdoer by providing means or facilitating an outcome, or is actually running an operation together with another State which directly results in the wrongful act. Brownlie argued that

> many strong cases of 'aid or assistance' will be primarily classifiable as instances of joint responsibility and it is only in the more marginal cases that a separate category of delict is called for. No doubt the law is under-developed in this context but the distinction, which is to be sought, is sufficiently clear.[301]

In situations where a State gives economic aid to a party carrying out certain breaches of international law, only complicity would be called for, but where a State is nearly a full partner in aggression, contributing troops, equipment (ie a degree of more substantial support), a finding of joint liability would be warranted. Brownlie suggested that

> the supply of weapons, military aircraft, radar equipment, and so forth, would in certain situations amount to 'aid or assistance' in the commission of an act of aggression but would not give rise to joint responsibility. However, the supply of combat units, vehicles, equipment, and personnel, for the specific purpose of assisting an aggressor, would constitute a joint responsibility.[302]

By this statement, Brownlie implied that the distinction between assistance as an ancillary or derivative form of responsibility and assistance

[297] ARSIWA (n 4) Art 47; see also ARIO (n 5) Art 48.

[298] ARSIWA (n 4) 66, para 1 (Art 16 Commentary); ibid 115, para 11 (Art 41 Commentary); ILC (n 13) 99, para 2 (Former Draft Art 27 Commentary).

[299] ILC, 'Summary Record of the 1516th Meeting' (12 July 1978), reproduced in (1978) 1 *YBILC* 222, 224, para 9 (Ago).

[300] ILC (n 13) 99, para 2 (Former Draft Art 27 Commentary).

[301] I Brownlie, *System of the Law of Nations: State Responsibility Part 1* (Oxford, Clarendon Press, 1983) 191.

[302] ibid.

as amounting to joint responsibility could be just a matter of degree to be determined by the content of 'assistance' and the intention of the assisting party. However, these criteria are not conclusive. Contrary to joint responsibility where the second actor commits the wrongful act, in the scenario of complicity, the responsibility follows from a knowing contribution to the wrongful act of another.[303]

As this author has argued elsewhere:

> In theory, the distinction is one of attribution. Whereas in the scenario of joint or several responsibility the act causing injury is concurrently attributable to two or more States, in the situations of complicity no attribution of the principal wrongful act to the complicit entity takes place. In practice, however, it may be more difficult to distinguish complicity from a fully-fledged commission of the wrongful act in situations where multiple actors contribute to the commission of the same wrongful act and in a similar manner.[304]

For instance, in the case of intervention in Iraq, numerous allied States contributed with different military equipment and troops to the Coalition Provisional Authority (CPA) run by the United States and the United Kingdom.[305] Had it been established that the intervention was unlawful, it would have been very difficult to draw a factual distinction between complicity and joint and several responsibility of those States.[306] Similar issues can arise in the context of joint border enforcement and patrol operations, or under the aegis of an international organisation. For example, with the ongoing migrant and refugee crisis, and potential violations of human rights, the distribution of responsibility between multiple actors poses a serious challenge to international law.[307] One way of distinguishing between complicity and joint and several responsibility in this context is by looking at the actual impact of the contribution to and the

[303] Ago (n 51) 58, para 72.

[304] Lanovoy (n 15) 144.

[305] See C Chinkin, 'The Continuing Occupation? Issues of Joint and Several Liability and Effective Control' in P Shiner and A Williams (eds), *The Iraq War and International Law* (Oxford, Hart Publishing, 2008); S Talmon, 'A Plurality of Responsible Actors: International Responsibility for Acts of the Coalition Provisional Authority in Iraq' in P Shiner and A Williams (eds), *The Iraq War and International Law* (Oxford, Hart Publishing, 2008).

[306] See, eg *Treatment in Hungary of Aircraft and Crew of United States (United States v Hungary; United States v USSR)* (Orders of 12 July 1954; Removal from the List) [1954] ICJ Rep 8 (the United States asserted joint and several responsibility of Hungary and the USSR, demanding full reparation from each State as a result of their cooperation in the interception and detention of a US military plane and its crew. The US also argued that Hungary was 'aided and abetted' by the USSR. The cases were dismissed on jurisdictional grounds).

[307] M den Heijer, 'Europe Beyond Its Borders: Refugee and Human Rights Protection in Extraterritorial Immigration Control' in B Ryan and V Mitsilegas (eds), *Extraterritorial Immigration Control: Legal Challenges* (Leiden, Martinus Nijhoff, 2010) 191–92; E Papastavridis, '"Fortress Europe" and FRONTEX: Within or Without International Law?' 79 *Nordic J Intl L* 75, 107; A Nollkaemper and D Jacobs, 'Shared Responsibility in International Law: A Conceptual Framework' (2013) 34 *Michigan J Intl L* 359, 362.

operational involvement in the wrongful act. If in the situation of multiple contributors, each of their contributions is *essential* for the commission of the wrongful act, they may be held jointly or severally liable. If, however, their contributions *merely facilitate* the commission of the wrongful act, then they may be held responsible for complicity.[308]

Furthermore, dual or even multiple attribution of conduct cannot be excluded when two or more entities exercise concurrently effective control over the conduct in question.[309] This is particularly relevant in the context of peacekeeping operations.[310] According to the ILC:

> [A]ttribution of a certain conduct to an international organization does not imply that the same conduct cannot be attributed to a State; nor does attribution of conduct to a State rule out attribution of the same conduct to an international organization.[311]

If two or more actors take a joint action to the detriment of a third party, they become co-authors or co-perpetrators of the internationally wrongful act.[312] Thus, irrespective of the degree and extent, complicity as such falls short of the regime of joint and several responsibility in international law. As acknowledged by Ago:

> There can be no question, for example, of the participation of a State in the internationally wrongful act of another State in cases where identical offences are committed in concert, or sometimes even simultaneously, by two or more States, each acting through its own organs.[313]

However, it may be the case that under the same treaty provision, one State breaches an obligation by its positive action, whereas another State breaches its obligation by its failure to act, and the combination of their respective conduct causes injury. Although their conduct may be joint and cause the same injury, they will technically be responsible for two distinct internationally wrongful acts.[314]

308 Lanovoy (n 15) 144–45.

309 See, eg *Netherlands v Nuhanović* (n 242) para 3.11.2; see also *Responsibilities and Obligations of States Sponsoring Persons and Entities with Respect to Activities in the Area* (Advisory Opinion) [2011] 11 ITLOS Rep 10, 62, para 192 (the Seabed Chamber recognising the possibility of joint and several liability under Art 139(2) of the Convention on the Law of the Sea); *Eurotunnel Arbitration* (Partial Award) (2007) 132 ILR 1 paras 165–69 (the arbitral tribunal considering whether France and the United Kingdom were jointly responsible for failure to prevent the entry of asylum seekers through the Channel Tunnel).

310 Bell (n 169); Dominicé (n 265).

311 ARIO (n 5) 16, para 4.

312 Dominicé (n 265) 282.

313 ILC (n 13) 99, para 2 (Former Draft Art 27 Commentary).

314 See A Nollkaemper, 'Issues of Shared Responsibility before the International Court of Justice' in E Rieter and H de Waele (eds), *Evolving Principles of International Law: Studies in Honour of Karel C Wellens* (Leiden, Martinus Nijhoff, 2012) 199; J Crawford, 'Third Report on State Responsibility' (2000) UN Doc A/CN.4/507 and Add 1-4, reproduced in (2000) 2 (pt 1) *YBILC* 3, 73, para 268.

Let us take another example. Assume State A and State B are allies and proceed in concert to launch an armed attack on a third State, each acting through their own military organs and with a lapse of time between these two attacks. Hence, two separate acts of aggression have been committed by the two States. According to Ago, such concerted action cannot be considered as a form of 'participation' by one of the two States in an act of aggression committed by the other alone.[315] Brownlie considered that 'the practice of States [was] almost completely non-existent, or, seen differently, strongly suggests by its silence the absence of joint and several liability in delict in State relations'.[316] Brownlie suggests that 'practice in the matter of reparation payments for illegal invasion and occupation rests on the assumption that Axis countries were liable on the basis of individual causal contribution to damage and loss, unaffected by the existence of co-belligerency'.[317]

In this context, Special Rapporteur James Crawford noted that Article 47 ARSIWA was part of the progressive development of international law, emphasising that it would be inappropriate 'to assume that internal law concepts and rules in this field can be applied directly to international law'.[318] He noted nevertheless that careful analogies could be drawn.[319] Even if the application of the notion of joint and several responsibility in international law remains underdeveloped,[320] it is at least arguable that it constitutes a general principle of law within the meaning of Article 38(1)(c) of the Statute of the ICJ.[321]

[315] ILC (n 13) 99, para 2 (Former Draft Art 27 Commentary).

[316] Brownlie (n 301) 189.

[317] ibid; cf *Anglo-Chinese Shipping Co Ltd v United States* (Judgment) (1955) 22 ILR 982 (United States Court of Federal Claims).

[318] ARSIWA (n 4) 124, para 3 (Art 47 Commentary); for a comparative survey of domestic laws on solidary or joint responsibility see T Weir, 'Complex Liabilities' in A Tunc (ed), *International Encyclopedia of Comparative Law: Torts*, vol 11 (Tübingen, Martinus Nijhoff, 1983) ss 43–44, 79–81.

[319] ARSIWA(n 4) 124, para 3 (Art 47 Commentary).

[320] For examples of treaty provisions referring to joint and several responsibility see, eg United Nations Convention on the Law of the Sea (adopted 10 December 1982; entered into force 16 November 1994) 1833 UNTS 3, Art 139; Convention on International Liability for Damage Caused by Space Objects (adopted 29 March 1972; entered into force 1 September 1972) 961 UNTS 187, Art IV.

[321] Statute of the International Court of Justice (adopted 26 June 1945; entered into force 24 October 1945) 3 Bevans 1179, Art 38; see *Oil Platforms (Islamic Republic of Iran v United States)* (Merits) [2003] ICJ Rep 161, Separate Opinion of Judge Simma 324, 358, para 74; *Aerial Incident of 27 July 1955 (United States v Bulgaria)* [1960] ICJ Rep 146, ICJ Pleadings, Memorial of the United States of 2 December 1958, 229; Talmon (n 305) 185; P d'Argent, 'Reparation, Cessation, Assurances and Guarantees of Non-Repetition' in A Nollkaemper and I Plakokefalos (eds), *Principles of Shared Responsibility in International Law: An Appraisal of the State of the Art* (Cambridge, CUP, 2014) 244–49; see also European Group on Tort Law, *Principles of European Tort Law: Text and Commentary* (Vienna, Springer, 2005) 144 ('solidary liability is so deeply embedded in the European systems that to abandon it would be a profound shift in the balance of law').

i. Separability of International Responsibility

While responsibility for complicity under Article 16 ARSIWA is widely conceived as derivative implying responsibility only to the extent of aid or assistance provided, Article 47 sets out a general principle that, in cases of plurality of responsible States in respect of the same wrongful act, each State bears full responsibility for the conduct attributable to it.[322] The ARSIWA Commentary provides an example of where two or more States combine in carrying out together an internationally wrongful act in circumstances where they may be regarded as acting jointly in respect of the entire operation.[323] In such a case, the injured party can hold each responsible State to account for the wrongful conduct as a whole.[324] Nollkaemper and Jacobs give further examples of 'pollution of an international watercourse by two or more riparian states and climate change caused by emissions from several states that contravene obligations under the Kyoto Protocol'.[325]

Existing case law and practice oscillates between the approach of divisibility and non-divisibility of legal consequences in cases of joint wrongdoing.[326] On the one hand, the reasoning of some international decisions seems to favour the divisibility approach. For instance, in the *Anglo-Chinese Shipping* case, the tribunal held that the Axis powers during the Second World War were responsible on the basis of their own individual contributions to the damage caused to Japan, regardless of their quality as co-belligerents.[327] In the *Ilaşcu* case, the ECtHR followed a similar approach by ordering Moldova and Russia to repair their respective parts of the harm caused to the applicants.[328] In the *Samoan Claims* arbitration, the tribunal found both the United States and the United Kingdom responsible for injuries to German citizens in Samoa.[329] Although the tribunal did not render the decision on the allocation of legal consequences, the two States subsequently agreed each to pay one-half of the amounts owed to the subjects of other States, and each assumed sole responsibility for injuries caused to their own citizens.[330]

322 ARSIWA (n 4) 124, para 1 (Art 47 Commentary).

323 ibid 124, para 2 (Art 47 Commentary).

324 ibid.

325 Nollkaemper and Jacobs (n 307) 369; Kyoto Protocol to the United Nations Framework Convention on Climate Change (adopted 11 December 1997; entered into force 16 February 2005) 2303 UNTS 162.

326 S Besson, 'La pluralité d'États responsables: Vers une solidarité internationale?' (2007) 1 *SZIER* 13, 28–29.

327 *Anglo-Chinese Shipping Co Ltd v United States* (n 317) 986.

328 *Ilaşcu and others v Moldova and Russia* (Merits and Just Satisfaction) [2004] ECtHR App No 48787/99 (2005) 40 EHRR 46, paras 484–90.

329 *Samoan Claims Arbitration (Germany v United States and United Kingdom)* (1902) 9 RIAA 15.

330 WS Penfield, 'The Settlement of the Samoan Cases' (1913) 7 *AJIL* 767; JE Noyes and BD Smith, 'State Responsibility and the Principle of Joint and Several Liability' (1988) 13 *Yale J Intl L* 225, 242.

On the other hand, there are cases where courts have avoided considerations of possible divisibility of the injury and the effect this could have on the legal consequences for the respondent. Thus, in the *Corfu Channel* case, Yugoslavia had allegedly laid the mines and would have been responsible for the damage caused. The Court, however, held that Albania was responsible to the United Kingdom for the totality of the damage caused on the basis that it knew or should have known of the presence of the mines and of the attempt by the British ships to exercise their right of transit, but failed to warn the ships.[331] The ICJ did not indicate that Albania's responsibility for failing to warn could be attenuated, let alone excused, on the basis of possible responsibility which could be borne by Yugoslavia that laid the mines. In other words, in such a scenario where the obligations breached are of a different character, each participating State is responsible on an individual basis for the entirety of the injury caused. In the *Corfu Channel* case, two separate wrongful acts were in place, one possibly committed by Yugoslavia in laying the mines, and another by Albania in failing to warn the British ships. However, the wrongful acts led to a single injury. Was it justified then that Albania pay compensation for the entirety of the injury caused?

The only element provided in Article 47(2)(a) ARSIWA which may assist us is that the determination of reparation should not exceed the amount of the damage caused.[332] A brief *tour d'horizon* of the case law is warranted to see whether a trend has emerged as to the idea of solidarity in the reparation for injury suffered and whether such a trend could be potentially extended to responsibility for complicity.[333] For example, in the *Nauru* case, the Court noted that its decision to uphold jurisdiction:

> [Did] not settle the question whether reparation would be due from Australia, if found responsible, *for the whole or only for part of the damage Nauru alleges it has suffered*, regard being had to the characteristics of the Mandate and Trusteeship Systems … and, in particular, the special role played by Australia in the administration of the Territory.[334] (emphasis added)

In the *Oil Platforms* case, the Court had to deal with the issue of attribution regarding minelaying by Iran and Iraq.[335] In addition to minelaying, Iran also carried out attacks by helicopters, other aircraft and patrol boats, which largely contributed to the unsafe shipping conditions in the Gulf.[336] The latter actions could be easily attributed to the responsible

[331] *Corfu Channel (United Kingdom v Albania)* (Merits) [1949] ICJ Rep 4, 22–23; ILC (n 4) 125, para 8 (Art 47 Commentary).

[332] ARSIWA (n 4) 125, para 9 (Art 47 Commentary).

[333] *Oil Platforms (Merits)* (n 321) Separate Opinion of Judge Simma 353–61, paras 63–83.

[334] *Certain Phosphate Lands in Nauru (Nauru v Australia)* (Preliminary Objections) [1992] ICJ Rep 240, 258–59, para 48.

[335] *Oil Platforms (Merits)* (n 321).

[336] ibid, Separate Opinion of Judge Simma 353, para 62.

State. This however was not the case with regard to minelaying which could be attributed either to Iran or Iraq. As emphasised by Judge Simma, the central question faced by the Court was 'how can we hold Iran responsible for acts which, even though they did create impediments to the freedom of commerce and navigation, cannot be attributed to Iran with certainty?'.[337]

Judge Simma noted that it was a common knowledge that the Iran–Iraq war had a destabilising effect on the regional economy, including American commerce going through the Gulf. However, the resulting damage caused by impediments to the freedom of commerce and navigation under the 1955 Treaty, was *indivisible* and *could not be apportioned* between Iran and Iraq.[338]

Judge Simma then engaged in a comparative law overview of the principle of joint tortfeasors as it is applied across jurisdictions to see whether both or neither States could be equally responsible for the impediments caused to commerce and navigation. Some of his findings merit being outlined in this context. For example, Judge Simma makes reference to Section 830 of the German Civil Code which reads as follows:

> 1. If several persons through a jointly committed delict have caused damage, each is responsible for the damage. The *same applies if it cannot be discovered which of several participants has caused the damage through his action.*
> 2. Instigators and *accomplices are in the same position as joint actors.* (emphasis added)

Thus, under Section 830 of the German Civil Code an accomplice bears similar responsibility to that of the joint actors such that it imposes responsibility for damage even when it cannot be discovered which of several participants in the wrongdoing caused the damage as such. The same approach seems to be followed by French, Japanese, Quebec and Swiss law.[339] For instance, Section 1480 of the Civil Code of Québec provides:

> Where several persons have jointly participated in a wrongful act which has resulted in injury or have committed separate faults each of which may have caused the injury, and *where it is impossible to determine*, in either case, which of them actually caused the injury, *they are solidarily liable for reparation thereof.*[340] (emphasis added)

[337] ibid para 63.

[338] ibid para 64.

[339] ibid, Separate Opinion of Judge Simma 355–56, paras 69–71; see also RP Alford, 'Apportioning Responsibility Among Joint Tortfeasors for International Law Violations' (2011) 38 *Pepperdine LR* 233.

[340] Civil Code of Québec, CQLR, c C-1991 s 1480.

Article 50 of the Swiss Code of Obligations contains similar language:

1. Where two or more persons have together caused damage, *whether* as instigator, perpetrator or *accomplice, they are jointly and severally liable to the injured party*.
2. The court determines at its discretion whether and to what extent they have right of recourse against each other.
3. Beneficiaries are liable in damages only to the extent that they received a share in the gains or caused loss or damage due to their involvement.[341] (emphasis added)

Likewise, Article 719(1) of the Japanese Civil Code provides that:

> If more than one person has inflicted damages on others by their joint tortious acts, each of them shall be jointly and severally liable to compensate for those damages. The same shall apply if it cannot be ascertained which of the joint tortfeasors inflicted the damages.[342]

Other countries use the model of joint and several responsibility but are more cautious in distinguishing between this regime as it applies to joint action from situations where tortfeasors' acts can be individualised.[343] In New Zealand, for example, joint and several liability is the rule for the joint action, but several liability arises where 'there is a coincidence of separate acts that by their conjoined effect cause damage'.[344] This means that if two tortfeasors act independently of one another, each is liable only for the respective portion of the damage caused.[345] China also generally adheres to the model of joint and several liability for joint action, but each tortfeasor who commits independent acts will 'bear corresponding compensation liabilities respectively in appropriate proportion to the extent of their faults'.[346] Upon analysis of multiple jurisdictions, one commentator concluded that an appropriate standard would be to impose several liability for independent tortfeasors who cause divisible harm whereas the regime of joint and several liability better fits in situations where they cause indivisible harm.[347] In this author's view, this may well be a solution for situations of complicit conduct in international law, where the injury resulting from the principal wrongful act is often indivisible.

341 Federal Act on the Amendment of the Swiss Civil Code (Part Five: The Code of Obligations) (adopted 30 March 1911; entered into force 1 January 1912) Art 50.

342 Japanese Civil Code (Act No 89 of 27 April 1896) Art 719(1).

343 Alford (n 339) 243–45.

344 S Todd, 'New Zealand' in S Stijns (ed), *International Encyclopaedia of Laws: Tort Law*, vol 3 (The Hague, Kluwer, 2008) 425.

345 ibid.

346 H Shan, 'China' in S Stijns (ed), *International Encyclopaedia of Laws: Tort Law*, vol 1 (The Hague, Kluwer, 2005) 163.

347 WVH Rogers, 'Comparative Report on Multiple Tortfeasors' in WVH Rogers and WH van Boom (eds), *Unification of Tort Law: Multiple Tortfeasors* (The Hague, Kluwer, 2004) 308–09; see also useful comparative references in support of this point in Weir (n 318) 79; Noyes and Smith (n 330) 251–58.

These examples go to show that complicity need not necessarily be seen as an ancillary form of responsibility when one comes to apportioning legal consequences (eg the level of reparation owed). If such a regime is operational in the context of domestic civil responsibility, it is difficult to see why this could not be the case in international law. Certainly, it would be a major improvement from the perspective of the injured party to be able to recover damages jointly and severally from both the complicit and the principal wrongdoers. Furthermore, such an approach to complicity is already grounded in the recognition that complicity in the wrongful act of another constitutes a wrongful act in and of itself.

Conversely, if complicity in an internationally wrongful act is read as a sufficient cause of action, particularly in those cases where the injury cannot be apportioned, it may lead to a situation where the injured party can recover for more harm than had actually been caused. In domestic legal systems, there is some precedent to believe that this is not only an inevitable but also a just consequence when the division of liability among tortfeasors and participants in the wrongdoing is impossible.[348] Importantly, while this possibility of exceeding the amount of damage is excluded from Article 47 ARSIWA, the scope of this provision only covers situations where two or more States acted in concert leading to a single internationally wrongful act. The question then would be whether it is fair and equitable for a complicit entity to bear the same or higher burden of reparation as opposed to the principal wrongdoer.

Finally, an interesting related question arose in the *CME v Czech Republic* arbitration which concerned the involvement of individuals as joint tortfeasors in the internationally wrongful act of a host State in relation to a foreign investor.[349] The issue before the tribunal was whether for the purposes of ascertaining causation, the conduct of an individual could be deemed separate from the conduct of government entity, attributable to the State. The tribunal emphasised that:

> [A] State may be held responsible for injury to an alien investor where it is not the sole cause of the injury; the State is not absolved because of the participation of other tortfeasors in the infliction of injury…[350]

In doing so, the tribunal expressly referred to the ILC's Commentary on the issue of concurrent causation. In relevant part, the Commentary provides that in cases where separate factors combine to cause damage and only one of these factors is to be ascribed to the responsible State, 'international practice and the decisions of international tribunals do not support

[348] See, eg *Maddux v Donaldson* (Judgment) [1961] 362 Mich 425 (108 NW 2d 33) (United States Michigan Supreme Court) 433.

[349] *CME Czech Republic BV v Czech Republic* (Partial Award) [2001] UNCITRAL, 9 ICSID Rep 113.

[350] ibid 230, para 580.

the reduction or attenuation of reparation for concurrent causes'.[351] The tribunal considered that '[s]uch a result should follow *a fortiori* in cases where the concurrent cause is not the act of another State (which might be held separately responsible) but of private individuals'.[352] The tribunal further noted that '[t]his approach [was] consistent with the way in which the liability of joint tortfeasors is generally dealt with in international law and State practice'.[353]

This case is instructive for it brings a new dimension to the concept of joint or several responsibility extending it to situations of possible collaboration between States and non-State actors. Crucially, it raises complex questions as to the relationship between shared forms of responsibility and the principle of causation with particular reference to a number of ICJ cases.[354] As it will be discussed in chapter six, the issue of causation, largely neglected by the ILC, is central to the implementation of responsibility. This issue is common to responsibility for complicity and joint and several responsibility.

First, it is not clear whether Article 16 ARSIWA could constitute an independent cause of action and under which circumstances. This begs the question whether Article 16 is merely concerned with a form of responsibility, falls in between a primary and a secondary norm or quite simply is a primary norm.[355] Second, a determination of causal standards is crucial to ascertaining the extent of reparation in proportion to the contribution of the aiding or assisting conduct to the injury. As shall be discussed in chapter six, the Commission's clarifications are not free from objections. On the one hand, the ILC stated that:

> By assisting another State to commit an internationally wrongful act, *a State should not necessarily be held to indemnify the victim for all the consequences of the act, but only for those which,* in accordance with the principles stated in Part Two of the articles, *flow from its conduct.*[356] (emphasis added)

At the same time, the ILC left open the possibility that 'where the assistance is a necessary element in the wrongful act in absence of which it

[351] ARSIWA (n 4) 93, para 12 (Art 31 Commentary).

[352] *CME Czech Republic BV v Czech Republic* (n 349) 231, para 583.

[353] ibid 230, para 581; see also *Czech Republic v CME Czech Republic BV* (Judicial Review) [2003] Case No T-8735-01, (2003) 42 ILM 919 (Svea Court of Appeal) 967 (holding that the invocation of the principle of joint tortfeasors by the tribunal was no excess of mandate that would lead to the setting aside of the award).

[354] *Diplomatic and Consular Staff in Tehran (United States v Iran)* (Judgment) [1980] ICJ Rep 3, 29–32; *Corfu Channel (United Kingdom v Albania)* (n 331) 17–18 and 22–23; *Armed Activities on the Territory of the Congo (DRC v Uganda)* (Judgment) [2005] ICJ Rep 168.

[355] See Graefrath (n 49) 372; W Riphagen, 'Preliminary Report on the Content, Forms and Degrees of International Responsibility' (1980) UN Doc A/CN.4/330 and Corr 1-3, reproduced in (1980) 2 (pt 1) *YBILC* 107, 121, paras 71 ff.

[356] ARSIWA (n 4) 67, para 10 (Art 16 Commentary).

could not have occurred, the injury suffered can be concurrently attributed to the assisting and the acting State'.[357] Thus, there is a conceptual misunderstanding that needs to be clarified as to whether the implementation (*'mise en oeuvre'*) of the regime of responsibility for complicity is concurrent (solidary) or derivative (ancillary).

Arguably, where aid or assistance facilitates a principal wrongful act, the resulting harm of which cannot be individualised, it is safe to assume that complicity is a necessary cause of the principal wrongful act and by implication of the ensuing injury. In turn, this would mean that the injured party would have recourse either against the principal or complicit wrongdoer, and any potential reparation would be on joint and several basis.[358] Indeed, Article 19 ARSIWA seems to confirm that this is a possibility by indicating that the whole chapter dealing with responsibility of a State in connection with the act of another State is without prejudice to international responsibility arising by virtue of other provisions contained in the Articles.[359]

ii. Wrongful Acts Committed by a Common Organ or Jointly Run Operations

A concerted military operation has regrettably become part of modern international relations. States may wish to run a joint peacekeeping operation, under the unified military command. Two or more States may constitute a joint organ for specific law enforcement activities or to undertake certain conduct outside their territory. As an example, States may create a joint organ to administer the occupied territory as was done with the Coalition Provisional Authority (CPA) in Iraq, or for civilian purposes, such as an organ for nuclear research or the establishment of telecommunications. Such joint organ may breach the obligations incumbent on its respective States and would therefore be attributable to each of the States that have created it, for it acts on their behalf. Likewise, one could also envisage a conduct being simultaneously attributed to two or more international organisations when they establish a joint organ and act through that organ.[360]

In cases of a wrongful act committed by a common organ to at least two States, it is attributable simultaneously to each State which runs that organ.[361] In the absence of particular understanding between the States

[357] ibid 67, para 10 (Art 16 Commentary).

[358] UNGA, 'Sixth Committee, Summary Record of the 38th Meeting' (6 November 1978) UN Doc A/C.6/33/SR.38, 11, para 37 (Romania) (stating that that 'in the case of crimes enumerated in [former] Article 19, paragraph 3, it was important to classify the participation and the principal act in the same manner. It would be possible in that connexion to specify in [former] Article 27 that the gravity of the principal act also affected the classification of the act of assistance').

[359] ARSIWA (n 4) Art 19.

[360] ARIO (n 5) 16, para 4.

[361] ARSIWA (n 4) 124, para 2 (Art 47 Commentary).

running a common organ, it is not clear whether any principle or presumption could be drawn from international practice as to the apportioning of responsibility. Could, for example, a presumption be drawn that, unless otherwise provided by the parties, States running a common organ shall bear a solidary or joint responsibility?

Such a consideration was tackled in a peripheral manner in the Partial Award in the *Eurotunnel* case, where the arbitral tribunal found that no such responsibility exists in general international law, unless otherwise provided for in the primary obligation.[362] The case concerned the construction and operation of a fixed link through the La Manche Channel (Fixed Link), pursuant to a treaty between France and the United Kingdom.[363] The dispute had arisen on the basis of the claim that the protection afforded to the Fixed Link from incursions caused by migrants based at a Red Cross refugee camp in the vicinity of the Eurotunnel entrance was inadequate. The claimants argued that the failure to provide adequate protection was attributable to France and the United Kingdom on an individual and joint basis.[364]

The tribunal had to address the question 'whether the provisions of the Treaty of Canterbury as given effect to by the Concession Agreement and the Concession Agreement [entered into thereafter] establish or imply any general principle of solidary responsibility for breaches of obligation'.[365] The Concession Agreement only provided for joint or several obligations of the concessionaries to France and the United Kingdom as principals but not vice versa. The tribunal further examined the nature of the Intergovernmental Commission (IGC) created pursuant to the Canterbury Treaty with a mandate 'to supervise, in the name and on behalf of the two governments, all matters concerning the construction and operation of the Fixed Link'.[366] The tribunal held:

> [T]here is no equivalent so far as the Principals [France and the United Kingdom] are concerned of the joint and several responsibility and mutual guarantees exacted from the Concessionaries. To the extent that the Claimants' case depends on the thesis of joint and several responsibility, ie the *per se* responsibility of one State for the acts of the other, it must fail. But the Fixed Link required close cooperation between the two Governments, cooperation to be effected in particular through joint organs (the IGC and the Safety Committee). The core commitments towards the Concessionaries—in effect, to facilitate

[362] *Eurotunnel Arbitration* (n 309) paras 163–87.

[363] Treaty between the United Kingdom and France concerning the Construction and Operation by Private Concessionaries of a Channel Fixed Link with Exchanges of Notes (adopted 12 February 1986; registered by France 16 March 1988) 1497 UNTS 334, para 4 (preamble).

[364] *Eurotunnel Arbitration* (n 309) paras 163–87.

[365] ibid para 175.

[366] ibid paras 51 and 179.

> the construction and (with specified exceptions) to permit the uninterrupted operation of the Fixed Link—required the continuing cooperation of both Governments, directly or through the IGC. Whether particular breaches of the Concession Agreement result from the fault of one or the other or both States will depend on the particular obligations violated and on all the circumstances.[367]

The tribunal found that the issue before it was not one of the character of responsibility but whether the conditions for international responsibility had been met in the first place:

> Although issues of policing outside the control zone were exclusively a matter for France, the overall responsibility for the security of the Fixed Link was shared and not divided … Both States shared the responsibility, and under Clause 27.7 they had to ensure that the IGC took the necessary steps to facilitate the implementation of the Agreement … and that in doing so it gave 'due consideration to the reasonable commercial objectives of the Concessionaries, including the avoidance of unnecessary costs and delays'. What the IGC as a joint organ failed to do, the Principals in whose name and on whose behalf the IGC acted equally failed to do.[368]

The finding of the tribunal is instructive for the development of further discussion as to the existence of the principle of joint responsibility in general international law.[369] That said, the tribunal's approach was still very much grounded in the classical notion of independent responsibility, rather than examining the conduct of the common organ through the lenses of shared responsibility proper.[370]

But what happens when such a common organ like the IGC receives aid or assistance from a third State? Does this State bear equal share of responsibility for the resulting wrongful act as the States running that organ? It may be that the assistance is insignificant to the point of having no impact on the principal wrongdoing, and the ensuing injury caused. However, it may also be the case that the assistance provided by a third State is so essential in character that the organ is effectively running its operations not due to its original States' directions but rather owing to the assistance received from a third State. This is particularly relevant in those cases where an organ possesses considerable degree of autonomy from the States that had originally established it.

[367] ibid para 187.

[368] ibid.

[369] S Wittich, 'Joint Tortfeasors in Investment Law' in C Binder et al (eds), *International Investment Law for the 21st Century, Essays in Honour of Christoph Schreuer* (Oxford, OUP, 2009) 721.

[370] Nollkaemper and Jacobs (n 307) 385.

VI. INTERIM CONCLUSIONS

This chapter has examined the history of codification of the provisions on responsibility for complicity presented in Articles 16 and 41(2) ARSIWA and Articles 14, 42(2) and 58 ARIO. Since its origins in Ago's report in 1978, the ILC regarded complicity as giving rise to State responsibility, 'whether the principal wrongful act [was to be] committed against a State or a particular group of States, a subject of international law other than a State, or the international community as a whole'.[371] With the conceptual shift from 'complicity' (original draft Article 25) towards 'aid or assistance' (former draft Article 27, as adopted on first reading in 1996), the scope and character of responsibility for complicity as now set out in Article 16 ARSIWA has been significantly limited over the years.

The final text of Article 16 and its sister provisions is subject to conditions, which in this author's view are overly restrictive and make the entire framework ineffective as a basis for holding States and international organisations responsible for their aid or assistance. Discrepancies and confusion between the terms of the relevant provisions and the ILC's Commentaries leave much to be desired for those who seek certainty and stability in a legal norm. In this chapter, we also sought to show that Articles 16 ARSIWA and 14 ARIO operate alongside other forms of shared or indirect responsibility in international law and the drawing of strict lines between these different regimes is not self-evident. This is true in particular of the concept of joint and several responsibility, which may serve as a useful standard for developing the framework of implementation (*'mise en oeuvre'*) of responsibility for complicity, particularly where the injury flowing from the principal wrongful act is not divisible.

[371] ILC (n 13) 105, para 22 (Former Draft Art 27 Commentary).

5

Establishing Responsibility for Complicity

I. INTRODUCTION

THIS CHAPTER EXAMINES the trigger (*fait générateur*) of responsibility for complicity. Most incidents of complicity occur 'in juridical outer space'[1] and out of judicial scrutiny, often due to jurisdictional constraints. There are also many allegations of complicity, which are factually and legally unsubstantiated and shed little light on the content and limits of responsibility for complicity.[2] It is thus important to identify from the outset the sources of relevant practice and *opinio juris*.

The comments by States and international organisations provided during the codification of the Articles on Responsibility of States for Internationally Wrongful Acts (ARSIWA) and Articles on Responsibility of International Organizations (ARIO), coupled with the sparse judicial decisions (both international and domestic), formal inquiries on complicity in the context of renditions and protests made by one State against alleged complicity of another, constitute the key practice and *opinio juris* for understanding the limits of the conduct that gives rise to responsibility for complicity, and its place and role under general international law. This chapter will focus primarily on the comments of States and international organisations that have provided some substantive analysis of the rule on responsibility for complicity.[3] There will be less emphasis on other

[1] D Luban, *Legal Modernism: Law, Meaning and Violence* (Michigan, University of Michigan Press, 1997) 355.

[2] For a detailed survey of practice of complicity see HP Aust, *Complicity and the Law of State Responsibility* (Cambridge, CUP, 2011) 107–91; A Felder, *Die Beihilfe im Recht der völkerrechtlichen Staatenverantwortlichkeit* (Zürich, Schulthess, 2007) 179–239; J Quigley, 'Complicity in International Law: A New Direction in the Law of State Responsibility' (1987) 57 *British YBIL* 77, 83–107.

[3] See, eg UNGA, 'Sixth Committee, Summary Record of the 31st Meeting' (26 October 1978) UN Doc A/C.6/33/SR.31, 5, paras 9–12 (Netherlands); UNGA, 'Sixth Committee, Summary Record of the 35th Meeting' (1 November 1978) UN Doc A/C.6/33/SR.35, 3, para 9 (Yugoslavia); UNGA, 'Sixth Committee, Summary Record of the 37th Meeting' (3 November 1978) UN Doc A/C.6/33/SR.37, 13, para 47 (Japan).

comments where States or international organisations stressed the importance of the rule, without providing any guidance regarding its constituent elements or application.[4] However, even where these comments lack technical precision and substance, they still show the importance that States and international organisations attach to the rule on responsibility for complicity.

During the International Law Commission (ILC)'s codification process, the majority of those States commenting supported the inclusion of the rule on responsibility for complicity in the ARSIWA. These include Bulgaria,[5] Finland,[6] Denmark,[7] Mali,[8] Mexico,[9] the Netherlands,[10] Jamaica,[11] Japan,[12] Sweden,[13] Venezuela,[14] the United Kingdom,[15] and the United States.[16] By contrast, the German Democratic Republic and Switzerland stated that the provision had no solid basis in positive international law.[17] Similar reservations were expressed by the Federal

[4] See, eg UNGA, 'Sixth Committee, Summary Record of the 21st Meeting' (29 October 1999) UN Doc A/C.6/54/SR.21, 8, para 56 (Poland); ILC, 'Comments and Observations Received from Governments' (2001) UN Doc A/CN.4/515 and Add 1-3, reproduced in (2001) 2 (pt 1) *YBILC* 33, 52 (Poland); UNGA, 'Sixth Committee, Summary Record of the 22nd Meeting' (1 November 1999) UN Doc A/C.6/54/SR.22, 9, para 50 (Slovakia); UNGA, 'Sixth Committee, Summary Record of the 15th Meeting' (28 October 2004) UN Doc A/C.6/59/SR.15, 16, paras 104–05 (Guatemala); UNGA, 'Sixth Committee, Summary Record of the 32nd Meeting' (27 October 1978) UN Doc A/C.6/33/SR.32, 7, para 22 (Jamaica).

[5] UNGA, 'Sixth Committee, Summary Record of the 40th Meeting' (7 November 1978) UN Doc A/C.6/33/SR.40, 7, para 28 (Bulgaria).

[6] UNGA, 'Sixth Committee, Summary Record of the 39th Meeting' (7 November 1978) UN Doc A/C.6/33/SR.39, 3, para 4 (Finland).

[7] ILC (n 4) 52 (Denmark).

[8] ILC, 'Observations and Comments of Governments on Chapters I, II and III of Part 1 of the Draft Articles on State Responsibility for Internationally Wrongful Acts' (1980) UN Doc A/CN.4/328 and Add 1-4, reproduced in (1980) 2 (pt 1) *YBILC* 87, 101, para 5 (Mali).

[9] UNGA, 'Sixth Committee, Summary Record of the 20th Meeting' (14 November 2000) UN Doc A/C.6/55/SR.20, 6, para 42 (Mexico).

[10] ILC (n 4) 52 (Netherlands).

[11] UNGA, 'Sixth Committee, Summary Record of the 32nd Meeting' (n 4) 7, para 22 (Jamaica).

[12] UNGA, 'Sixth Committee, Summary Record of the 22nd Meeting' (n 4) 7, para 37 (Japan).

[13] ILC, 'Comments of Governments on Part 1 of the Draft Articles on State Responsibility for Internationally Wrongful Acts' (1981) UN Doc A/CN.4/342 and Add 1-4, reproduced in (1981) 2 (pt 1) *YBILC* 71, 77 (Sweden).

[14] ILC, 'Comments and Observations of Governments on Part 1 of the Draft Articles on State Responsibility for Internationally Wrongful Acts' (1982) UN Doc A/CN.4/351 and Add 1-3, reproduced in (1982) 2 (pt 1) *YBILC* 15, 19 (Venezuela).

[15] ILC, 'Comments and Observations Received by Governments' (1998) UN Doc A/CN.4/488 and Add 1-3, reproduced in (1998) 2 (pt 1) *YBILC* 81, 128–29 (United Kingdom).

[16] ibid 129 (United States).

[17] ibid 128 (Germany and Switzerland); for an early critique of the customary law status of Art 16 ARSIWA see E Klein, 'Beihilfe zum Völkerrechtsdelikt' in I von Münch (ed), *Staatsrecht, Völkerrecht, Europarecht: Festschrift für Hans-Jürgen Schlochauer zum 75. Geburtstag am 28. März 1981* (Berlin, Walter de Gruyter, 1981) 433–38.

Republic of Germany[18] and the Federal Republic of Yugoslavia (FRY) which questioned the customary law status of the rule during the proceedings of the *Bosnia Genocide* case.[19] France for its part had considered that complicity, because it belonged to the realm of primary rules, should not be part of the law of international responsibility.[20] The United States and the Netherlands also had certain objections to the nature of the proposed responsibility for complicity, which in their view constituted a substantive rule, thereby departing from the general framework of the law of responsibility.[21]

Notwithstanding the above comments made at early stages of the codification process, today there is overwhelming support from States and international organisations for the existence of the rule on responsibility for complicity. However, as will be shown below, the support for the inclusion of the rule in the ARSIWA has not has not been matched with an equivalent approval of its constituent elements. The codification process of the ARIO shows that uncertainties regarding the constituent elements of responsibility for complicity persist.

The critique by States and international organisations of the rules on aid or assistance, as being transposed verbatim from the ARSIWA to the ARIO, confirms that the rule as set out in Article 16 ARSIWA was an imperfect compromise of different conceptions of responsibility. This chapter first aims to translate into practice the underlying conceptual tensions as to the scope of responsibility for complicity. Second, where appropriate, this chapter criticises some of the limits that the Commission artificially imposed on the scope of responsibility for complicity, and points out to possible re-interpretations and adjustments.

Section II deals with the material element of complicity and the link required between the complicit and the principal conduct for responsibility to arise. This section also questions the International Court of Justice (ICJ)'s premature attempt to discard the possibility of obtaining complicity through omission, by looking at the interpretation given by States to primary rules prohibiting complicity and the relationship of complicity to obligations of due diligence. Section III examines the cognitive requirement of responsibility for complicity and seeks to reconcile the criteria of knowledge and intention. The author submits that the knowledge of the circumstances of the wrongful act alone (without intent) is a sufficient requirement for responsibility to arise and sheds some light on the means

[18] UNGA, 'Sixth Committee, Summary Record of the 42nd Meeting' (9 November 1978) UN Doc A/C.6/33/SR.42, 17, para 58 (Federal Republic of Germany).

[19] *Application of the Convention on the Prevention and Punishment of the Crime of Genocide (Bosnia and Herzegovina v Serbia and Montenegro)* (Merits) [2007] ICJ Rep 43, ICJ Pleadings, Counter-Memorial of the FRY 336, para 5.6.1.2.

[20] UNGA (n 18) 6, para 17 (France).

[21] See UNGA (n 5) 2, para 4 (United States); UNGA, 'Sixth Committee, Summary Record of the 31st Meeting' (n 3) 5–6, paras 9–12 (Netherlands).

of determining that knowledge. Finally, section IV discusses the opposability requirement and makes a normative claim against it. This claim is based on a generalised lack of practice and *opinio juris* that could support such a strict and unnecessary limitation to the operation of responsibility for complicity. In many respects, this single requirement frustrates the potential of responsibility for complicity for ensuring legality and deterring violations of international law through proxies.

II. MATERIAL ELEMENT

The ARSIWA and ARIO rules are generally silent on the form or character of conduct capable of generating responsibility for complicity in international law.[22] As demonstrated in chapter four, neither the relevant provisions nor the ILC's Commentaries exclude the possibility that complicity could arise out of both active and passive behaviour, as long as it is given with the knowledge of the circumstances of the wrongful act.

Similarly, former Special Rapporteur James Crawford has argued that '[n]o limitation is placed on the precise form of the aid or assistance in question—all that is required is a causative contribution to the illegal act'.[23] If that is indeed the case, then the content or material element of complicity should be irrelevant and no criteria should be elaborated. However, in the same contribution, Crawford submits that omissions 'may be excluded as a form of aid or assistance'.[24] The Court's reading of complicity in the *Bosnia Genocide* case militates in the same direction, suggesting that complicity only arises in cases of positive action.[25] Moreover, it remains unclear what the link (nexus) between the aid or assistance and the principal wrongful act should be in order to trigger responsibility. The text of the provisions contains no wording to that effect, but the ILC's Commentary suggests that aid or assistance need not be 'essential' but must have contributed 'significantly' to the principal wrongful act.[26]

To a great extent, the finding of complicity depends on the surrounding factual circumstances. In the words of the Irish High Court '"participation" [in the wrongful act] is not a black and white issue. It may well be …

[22] ILC, 'Draft Articles on Responsibility of States for Internationally Wrongful Acts, with Commentaries' (2001) 2 (pt 2) *YBILC* 31 (ARSIWA), Art 16; ILC, 'Draft Articles on the Responsibility of International Organizations, with Commentaries' (2011) 2 (pt 2) *YBILC* 2 (ARIO), Art 14.

[23] J Crawford, *State Responsibility: The General Part* (Cambridge, CUP, 2013) 402; see also V Lowe, 'Responsibility for the Conduct of Other States' (2002) 101 *Japanese J Intl L & Diplomacy* 1, 5–6.

[24] Crawford (n 23) 403.

[25] *Bosnia Genocide (Merits)* (n 19) 223, para 432.

[26] ARSIWA (n 22) 66, para 5.

a matter of "substance and degree"'.[27] This section seeks to reach an understanding of the range of complicit conduct that facilitates the commission of an internationally wrongful act and of the link that must exist between the complicit conduct and the principal wrongful act.

This section reviews the comments of States and international organisations and the most common *fattispecie* of complicity in practice in order to identify the conduct that is typically perceived by the law-determining agents as giving rise to responsibility for complicity (sub-section II.A). Further, as a subsidiary tool, this section surveys the interpretations that States have given to some of the treaty norms that prohibit complicity, or to functionally similar rules, that may shed light on the type of conduct that constitutes complicity and its limits (sub-section II.B). Finally, this section looks into the links between the responsibility for complicity and the responsibility flowing from the breach of due diligence obligations in international law (sub-section II.C).

A. The Content of Complicity and its Link to the Principal Wrongful Act

i. Comments of States and International Organisations

Throughout the ILC's codification process, several States submitted that the rule on responsibility for complicity required further clarification regarding its material element and the necessary link (nexus) between the complicit and the principal conduct. The United States, for instance, expressly requested that the Commission clarify 'what constitutes the threshold of actual participation required by the terms "aids or assists"'.[28] The United States also recalled that aid or assistance in the earlier draft Article 27 did not cover instances of incitement or encouragement, and that such aid or assistance must have made it 'materially easier for the State receiving the aid or assistance in question to commit an internationally wrongful act'.[29] Other States shared the view that incitement does not come within the scope of responsibility for complicity under general international law.[30]

[27] *Horgan v An Taoiseach and others* (Judgment) (2003) 132 ILR 407, ILDC 486 (IE 2003) (Irish High Court) para 174.

[28] ILC (n 4) 52, para 2 (United States).

[29] ibid para 3 (United States); ILC, 'Report of the International Law Commission on the Work of Its 30th Session (8 May–28 July 1978)' (1978) UN Doc A/33/10, reproduced in (1978) 2 (pt 2) *YBILC* 1, 104, para 17 (Former Draft Art 27 Commentary).

[30] See, eg UNGA, 'Sixth Committee, Summary Record of the 37th Meeting' (n 3) 13, para 47 (Japan); R Ago, 'Seventh Report on State Responsibility' (1978) UN Doc A/CN.4/307 and Add 1-2 and Corr 1-2, reproduced in (1978) 2 (pt 1) *YBILC* 31, 54–56, paras 62–64; see also *Notes on some of the questions decided by the Board of Commissioners under the Convention with France of the 4th of July 1831* (1836) 5 Moore Intl Arbitrations 4473.

The United Kingdom for its part submitted that the aid or assistance must be clearly and unequivocally connected to the principal wrongful act.[31] This suggests the requirement of a close connection but does not seem to have any bearing on the actual degree of impact that complicity must exert over a wrongful act.

Certain States were concerned that complicity's material element was being cast too broadly and tried to limit the application of the provision to most serious breaches of international law. For instance, the Netherlands suggested at some point limiting the application of the provision to aid or assistance rendered for the commission of particularly serious violations of international law.[32] This issue came up with some frequency in the Commission's discussions. As noted in chapter four, members of the Commission struggled to find the appropriate ways to circumscribe the character and degree of complicity in the wrongful act, which need to fall short of co-perpetration or joint and several responsibility.[33] Riphagen, for instance, assumed that complicity would need to be 'abnormal' to engage responsibility, and suggested that it was prudent to limit the provision to those breaches that undermine 'the interests of the international community in general'.[34] Scholars put forward similar proposals for limiting the application of responsibility *ratione materiae* as most of the practice of complicity at that time (and still very much so today) related to infringement of *erga omnes* or *jus cogens* obligations.[35]

Taking stock of these views, Crawford considered that limiting complicity to such breaches could bring back the 'delicts/crimes' dichotomy into the ARSIWA and was therefore undesirable.[36] At the same time, there was a generalised concern among the members of the ILC to emphasise the material element of assistance, though this never occurred as the text of the relevant provisions and the ILC's Commentaries show.

The concerns about the material element of responsibility for complicity re-appeared in the context of the copy-pasting of the rule to the ARIO. While overall supporting the inclusion of responsibility for complicity in the ARIO, several organisations noted that the rule had an uncertain scope,

[31] ILC (n 4) 52 (United Kingdom).

[32] ILC (n 14) 18 (Netherlands).

[33] ILC, 'Summary Record of the 1519th Meeting' (18 July 1978), reproduced in (1978) 1 *YBILC* 237, 239, para 11 (Ushakov); ILC, 'Summary Record of the 1517th Meeting' (13 July 1978), reproduced in (1978) 1 *YBILC* 228, 229, paras 3–4 (Reuter).

[34] ILC, 'Summary Record of the 1518th Meeting' (17 July 1978), reproduced in (1978) 1 *YBILC* 232, 233, para 8 (Riphagen).

[35] See, eg B Graefrath, 'Complicity in the Law of International Responsibility' (1996) 2 *RBDI* 370, 380; see also ML Padeletti, *Pluralità di Stati nel fatto illecito internazionale* (Milano, Giuffrè, 1990) 74–76 (discussing the need to limit the material element of complicity).

[36] ILC, 'Summary Record of the 2578th Meeting' (28 May 1999), reproduced in (1999) 1 *YBILC* 74, 79, para 44 (Crawford); see also Quigley (n 2) 104–05.

and could adversely affect the regular activities for which the organisations have been set up.[37] For example, the International Labour Organization (ILO) noted that aid or assistance could occur where the Member States provide 'funds to the organization for its extrabudgetary technical cooperation activities or hosting its headquarters, offices or meetings'.[38] These forms of assistance, according to the ILO, could give rise to concurrent responsibility of the State and international organisation. This is confirmed by the practice of States of concluding agreements to exclude responsibility in connection with third-party claims resulting from the organisation's activities:

> For example, donor Governments of ILO sometimes exclude their responsibility for possible damages caused by activities of ILO under the financed projects. ILO, in turn, regularly passes the primary responsibility for third-party claims in connection with those activities on to the Government of the beneficiary country. Similarly, the headquarters agreement between ILO and Switzerland provides that 'Switzerland shall not incur by reason of the activity of the International Labour Organisation on its territory any international responsibility for acts or omissions of the Organisation or of its agents acting or abstaining from acting within the limits of their functions'.[39]

Agreements excluding a donor's responsibility for third-party claims are fairly common.[40] Yet, it is unclear whether these agreements would be affected by the operation of the rule on responsibility for complicity or rather be conceived of as *lex specialis*.

A number of international organisations have also referred to functional justifications and inherent difficulties with the fact that their regular activities could eventually be framed as aid or assistance for the purposes of international responsibility. The EU, for example, made a case for material content of responsibility for complicity to be kept as narrow as possible:

> Since aid or assistance is often used in a financial context, it would seem desirable that this draft article and its interpretation be kept as narrow as possible so as not to turn it into a disincentive for development aid by international organizations.[41]

Indeed, it was the international organisations providing financing that objected the most to extension of the rule in Article 16 ARSIWA to international organisations. The main thrust of these arguments was that

[37] See ILC, 'Comments and Observations Received from International Organizations' (2006) UN Doc A/CN.4/568 and Add 1, reproduced in (2006) 2 (pt 1) *YBILC* 125, 139–45.

[38] ibid 143 (ILO).

[39] ibid.

[40] ibid; see also ibid 144 (UNESCO).

[41] ILC, 'Responsibility of International Organizations, Comments and Observations Received from International Organizations' (14 February 2011) UN Doc A/CN.4/637, 27 (EU).

with an increasing level of activity in the financial sector, organisations cannot assume the risk that assistance will be used to carry out an internationally wrongful act.[42] Comments by the World Bank and the International Monetary Fund (IMF) emphasised the limitations of responsibility for complicity's material element and the scope of its application in the financial sector. The World Bank, for example, stressed that:

> We are not at all convinced that applying to international organizations the provision … on aid and assistance in the commission of an internationally wrongful act 'is not problematic', as the Commission's commentary suggests. Actually, if not strictly confined to its proper scope, *this provision is worrisome and may create a dangerous chilling effect for any international financial institution providing economic assistance to eligible borrowers and recipients*.[43] (emphasis added)

The IMF took, by far, the strongest position on the matter, which merits being quoted in full:

> [I]n line with the commentary to article 16 of the draft articles on State responsibility, that 'aid or assistance' as used in those draft articles entails … *providing a facility or financing that is essential or contributed significantly to the wrongful conduct in question*.
>
> Given the fungible nature of financial assistance, such references in the case of financial assistance can only mean assistance that is earmarked for the wrongful conduct. This should be distinguished from the aid and assistance, as those words are used colloquially, which international organizations regularly provide their members.
>
> For example, IMF was established, inter alia, to provide financial assistance to its members to assist in addressing their balance of payments problems. Consistent with its charter, IMF regularly provides such financial assistance.
>
> That said, a member receiving financial assistance from IMF may still engage in wrongful conduct. Neither IMF itself, nor the provision of financial assistance by IMF, is capable of precluding such conduct or contributing significantly to it. First, IMF cannot preclude such conduct because … a member always has an effective choice not to follow the conditions on which IMF assistance is provided. Secondly, *IMF cannot contribute significantly to such conduct because IMF financing is not targeted to particular conduct; it is provided to support a member's economic programme that addresses its balance of payments problems. The financial resources utilized by the member to engage in particular conduct can be, and typically are, obtained from a variety of sources—domestic taxpayers, domestic and international creditors and international donors. The fungible character of financial resources also means that IMF financial assistance can never be essential, or contribute significantly, to particular wrongful conduct of a member State …*[44] (emphasis added)

[42] ibid 28 (World Bank).
[43] ibid 27 (World Bank).
[44] ILC, 'Comments and Observations Received from International Organizations' (1 May 2007) UN Doc A/CN.4/582, reproduced in (2007) 2 (pt 1) *YBILC* 17, 22 (IMF).

The IMF's position can be broken down into three elements. First, it suggests that, as a matter of principle, the IMF bears no responsibility for the fact that its Member States may deviate from the conditions imposed by the IMF's assistance. Second, the IMF's assistance is generic in character and there are necessarily multiple concurrent causes (ie other financial resources) that a Member State can use for the commission of an internationally wrongful act. In short, the IMF's assistance would be lost in the causal chains. Third and relatedly, the fungible character of the IMF's assistance precludes it from being 'essential' to or 'significantly' contributing to the commission of an internationally wrongful act.

Each of these elements is problematic. With respect to the first element, Member States retain autonomy as to their decision to commit a wrongful act; however, should the organisation know about the circumstances of that wrongful act, it should bear responsibility for its aid or assistance. With regard to the second element, it is generally recognised in international law that the existence of multiple causes is not a sufficient factor to exclude responsibility and appropriate legal consequences, including the obligation of reparation.[45] With regard to the third point, it is evident from practice and from the ILC's analysis that complicity *need not be essential* to the commission of the wrongful act. Laurence Boisson de Chazournes brings up the example of preferential financing relating to partnership agreements, explaining that 'the conditions offered in such contexts are most probably determinant in implementing a project or engaging in a given activity, which would suffice to presume the test of significance is satisfied'.[46]

Thus, on the basis of the problems identified by the IMF, it is difficult to see why the fungible character of financial assistance should per se exclude responsibility. It does however raise a broader issue as to whether it is wise to require a stringent link (nexus) between the aid or assistance and the principal wrongful act. In this author's view, a more sensible solution—in complex cases of multiple sources of funding—is to structure complicity such that the burden of proof for showing that the funding was given with no knowledge of the circumstances of the wrongful act lies with the international organisation and not with the injured party. Once the injured party would be able to show that the aid or assistance facilitated the commission of an internationally wrongful act, the burden of proof would shift to the international organisation to show that it had no knowledge of the circumstances of the principal wrongful act. Thus,

[45] See ch 6; see also ARSIWA (n 22) 93, para 12 (Art 31 Commentary).

[46] L Boisson de Chazournes, 'United in Joy and Sorrow: Some Considerations on Responsibility Issues under Partnerships Among International Financial Institutions' in M Ragazzi (ed), *Responsibility of International Organizations: Essays in Memory of Sir Ian Brownlie* (Leiden, Martinus Nijhoff, 2013) 222.

the lack of knowledge rather than the fungible character of the assistance should serve as a defence to the claim of complicity. The burden of showing the absence of knowledge is easily satisfied so long as the organisation can demonstrate that it had undertaken some form of due diligence review prior to rendering its aid or assistance.

The EU shared yet another example from its practice to justify a 'high threshold' of complicity for the responsibility to accrue:

> [I]n its practice the European Commission has faced claims, according to which the European Community was said to be liable for aiding or assisting third States in the commission of internationally wrongful acts, thereby allegedly triggering the international responsibility of the Community itself. A pertinent example is a case that was brought in a court of a third State against the Community for allegedly having financed illegal activities of a public body, the employees of which allegedly caused the death of members of the applicant's family. In such a situation, it would be important to apply a similarly *high threshold for triggering international liability as is laid down for assistance or aid by States under article 16 of the rules on State responsibility*.[47] (emphasis added)

Concerns about the material content and scope of responsibility were also raised in relation to complicity of Member States in the wrongful acts committed by international organisations.[48] For example, France expressed its doubts whether the ILC clearly drew a distinction between situations where the Member State could be acting in compliance with the internal rules of an international organisation (eg implementing a decision of the organisation) and those situations where State's influence upon the organisation's commission of the wrongful act would amount to aid or assistance and engage its responsibility.[49] China, for its part, considered this distinction to be one of degree to which complicity affects the commission of an internationally wrongful act:

> [T]he term 'State' [in Article 58 ARIO] could refer to a member or non-member of the international organization. While a State member of an international organization should not be held responsible for an act of the organization merely because it had participated in the decision-making process in accordance with the relevant rules of the organization, a State member having major influence over the commission of an internationally wrongful act by an international organization should bear corresponding responsibility…when a member State *played a major or leading role in the commission of an act by an international organization*, the main responsibility for the consequences of that act should be placed on the member State.[50] (emphasis added)

[47] ILC (n 37) 139 (EU).

[48] ARIO (n 22) Art 58; see also ch 4, s IV for discussion.

[49] UNGA, 'Sixth Committee, Summary Record of the 14th Meeting' (30 October 2006) UN Doc A/C.6/61/SR.14, 12, para 60 (France); see also discussion on Art 58 ARIO in ch 4, s IV.

[50] UNGA, 'Sixth Committee, Summary Record of the 14th Meeting' (n 49) 3, para 9 (China).

But what does constitute a major or leading role? Would such a role only be fulfilled when a State proposes the resolution or co-sponsors it? What would be the position of other States that have voted in favour, against or abstained from voting on a particular decision leading to an internationally wrongful act? As discussed in chapter four, Member State responsibility in connection with the wrongful acts of an international organisation opens an additional set of complex questions to which the ILC did not provide a conclusive answer.

In sum, what transpires from the above overview of comments of States and international organisations is that there is no principled opposition to complicity arising from both actions or omissions, insofar as these facilitate the commission of an internationally wrongful act. A common thread to the comments analysed above suggests that there may be different degrees of facilitation of the wrongful acts, and there is need to ensure a clear connection between aid or assistance and the principal wrongful act. We have also seen that some comments, like that of the IMF, may generate a chilling effect on the scope of responsibility for complicity in the near future. By saying that a particular content of assistance such as fungible funding can never be significant would set an absolute bar to responsibility. Other than this radical position, however, the comments of States and international organisations show little guidance as to what the standard of 'significantly' facilitating or contributing to the principal wrongful act actually entails and how can it be proved.

ii. The Fattispecie *of Complicity in Practice*

A review of international practice allows the discernment of certain types of conduct that States and international organisations consider as facilitating the commission of an internationally wrongful act and triggering international responsibility for complicity. The proposed analysis is non-exhaustive, as its sole purpose is to show that the over-determination of either the required material element of the conduct (ie action or omission) or the requisite link to principal wrongful act is problematic and render the rule ineffective.

a. Delivering Military Aid or Assistance to States and Non-State Actors

The most common scenario of complicity arises where State A provides military assistance to State B, or an organised armed opposition group, in the circumstances where the recipient of aid or assistance is one of the parties to an internal armed conflict. For instance, there have been numerous reports of complicity taking place in the ongoing violations of international human rights law and humanitarian law in Syria, which are committed both by the government forces and the Syrian opposition groups (also known as the National Coalition for Syrian Revolutionary and Opposition Forces). These reports have been produced on the basis of verifiable evidence of several States, including Turkey, Qatar and Saudi Arabia providing weapons to the Syrian opposition groups, while Russia and Iran assisting the government forces.[51]

Similarly, with respect to the Libyan Civil War in 2011, the UN Panel found that Qatar had continued providing ammunition to Libyan insurgents in violation of the embargo regime set under the UNSC Resolution 1973.[52] There have been reports suggesting that the United States was also directly involved in these operations of arms delivery, which may have resulted in violations of international human rights and humanitarian law.[53]

In theory, the general regime of responsibility for complicity could play an important role, alongside any embargos and other measures which third parties may devise to prevent, or put an end to the provision of such aid or assistance. However, in practice, there will be challenging issues of evidence for the injured party to be able to show the link between the aid or assistance provided and a particular wrongful act committed. For example, in *Rasheed Haje Tugar v Italy*, the former European Commission on Human Rights considered that Italy's export of mines to Iraq which resulted in an injury to the applicant, did not necessarily trigger the responsibility of Italy.[54] The applicant had alleged that but for Italy's failure to pass legislation preventing an indiscriminate export of mines to Iraq, he would not have suffered the injury. The former European Commission on Human Rights found that there was 'no immediate relationship between the mere supply, even if not properly regulated, of weapons and the possible "indiscriminate" use thereof in a third State'.[55] While the decision appeared to rely heavily on the absence of a causal link between Italy's failure to pass legislation and the injury sustained by the applicant, the rationale is telling for other scenarios of putative complicity arising from the supply of arms to a third party.

In the context of Syria, where third States have provided different types and forms of military assistance to both government and the opposition,

[51] See, eg 'Syria: Who's Backing Who?' *Guardian* (11 October 2012); 'Turkey Accuses Russia of Supplying Syria with Ammunitions' *Guardian* (11 October 2012); 'Arms Shipments Seen From Sudan to Syria Rebels' *New York Times* (12 August 2013); 'Iran Supplying Syrian Military via Iraqi Airspace' *New York Times* (4 September 2012); 'Iran Boosts Military Support in Syria to Bolster Assad' *Reuters* (21 February 2014).

[52] UNSC, 'Final Report of the Panel of Experts Established pursuant to Resolution 1973 (2011) Concerning Libya' (15 February 2013) UN Doc S/2013/99, paras 60 ff; see also UNSC, 'Res 1973' (17 March 2011) UN Doc S/RES/1973 (Libya).

[53] 'U.S.-Approved Arms for Libya Rebels Fell Into Jihadis' Hands' *New York Times* (5 December 2012).

[54] *Rasheed Haje Tugar v Italy* (Admissibility) [1995] ECHR App No 22869/93 Ser 83-A 26.

[55] ibid 29.

this would mean that any injured party will have a considerable difficulty in showing that a particular aid or assistance significantly facilitated the commission of a given wrongful act. It is questionable whether in determining international responsibility, a simple test of showing a *clear factual* or *causal* link on the balance of probabilities between the aid or assistance and the principal wrongdoing should not suffice for the purposes of establishing responsibility. This is particularly true where widespread war crimes or crimes against humanity are taking place, and a multiplicity of actors and causes are involved. In such circumstances, requiring a more stringent test such that aid or assistance 'significantly' facilitate the commission of the principal wrongful act may not only be impractical but may further the climate of impunity. A stronger or weaker link between complicity and the principal wrongful act may be a relevant factor at the level of implementation of responsibility and legal consequences, but arguably is not determinative of the existence of responsibility in the first place.

b. Delivering Aid or Assistance Pursuant to a Treaty or Export Licences

Another common scenario of complicity occurs where State A provides aid or assistance pursuant to an existing treaty with State B, but in the meantime becomes aware that its aid or assistance is no longer being used in accordance with the purposes set out in the treaty.[56] Holding States responsible in these circumstances gives rise to normative problems.[57] First, it is uncertain whether a State has the duty to inquire that its aid or assistance is being diverted from its original purpose as set out in the treaty. States are a priori expected to rely on the good faith commitment of their counterparts.[58] Second, the State continues to be bound to perform its obligation to deliver specific assistance subject to its right to suspend that obligation or the treaty as a whole in the event of a material breach. Such a suspension of assistance may avoid responsibility for complicity in relation to any ulterior wrongful acts. However, the same cannot be said about the State that simply protests against the unlawful use of its aid or assistance while continuing to deliver it under the treaty.[59]

An example of a claim against the United Kingdom demonstrates how aid or assistance provided pursuant to a treaty or under an export

[56] See examples of the US cutting military aid to Indonesia on the occasion of intervention in East Timor and to Turkey after its invasion of Cyprus, cited in Quigley (n 2) 90.

[57] ibid 123 (on the bill before the US Senate proposing to reduce aid from the US to Israel because of the amount it spent on civilian settlements in the West Bank and Gaza strip).

[58] *Lac Lanoux (France v Spain)* (1957) 12 RIAA 281, 313; *Norwegian Shipowners' Claims (Norway v United States)* (1922) 1 RIAA 309, 324; *Tacna-Arica Question (Chile/Peru)* (1925) 2 RIAA 921, 930.

[59] Quigley (n 2) 124; G Nolte and HP Aust, 'Equivocal Helpers—Complicit States, Mixed Messages and International Law' (2009) 58 *ICLQ* 1, 19.

licence could trigger international responsibility for complicity. In 2009, a Ramallah-based organisation Al-Haq brought a claim for judicial review in relation to the United Kingdom's provision of arms to Israel during the January 2009 violations committed in Palestine. Al-Haq claimed that the United Kingdom was complicit in violations of international law committed by Israel, by continuing to sell substantial quantities of military equipment to Israel under Standard Individual Export Licences and the EU–Israel Association Agreement, a preferential trade agreement.[60] The claimants alleged that the aid or assistance provided under the above-mentioned agreements as well as Defence Systems and Equipment international arms fairs, amounted to violations by the United Kingdom of its customary obligations under Articles 16 and 41(2) ARSIWA.[61] Although the claim was dismissed as non-justiciable before a domestic court, it demonstrates an area of cooperation between States where responsibility for complicity may play an increasing role in the future.

c. Authorising or Failing to Object to the Use of Territory

There are numerous examples of complicity of States allowing their territory to be used by other States to conduct raids, temporary incursions into third States, or full-fledged aggression.[62] In most cases, the alleged complicity in the violations of the norms prohibiting the use of force is denied as, for example, did Kenya in 1976 in relation to its alleged complicity in the Israeli raid against Uganda to liberate hijacked hostages.[63] Kenya was said to have allowed the Israeli planes to be refuelled on its territory. The then president of Uganda stated that 'Uganda has been aggressed by Israel with the close collaboration of some states, including Kenya and other neighbouring states' and declared that Uganda had the right 'to retaliate in whatever she can to redress the aggression against her'.[64] Kenya denied its involvement in that incident.[65] In other cases, a State will normally contend that the use of its airspace or territory was lawful or, in the alternative, that it had no requisite knowledge of the circumstances of the wrongful act.[66]

[60] *R (Al-Haq) v Secretary of State for Foreign and Commonwealth Affairs* (Judgment) [2009] EWHC 1910 (Admin) para 7.

[61] ibid Detailed Grounds paras 58 ff.

[62] See, eg Aust (n 2) 109–15; Quigley (n 2) 83–92.

[63] 'African Nations Bid UN Council Meet on Israeli Raid' *New York Times* (6 July 1976) (Amin warned of taking possible counter-measures against Kenya with the assistance of Libyan long-range bombers).

[64] 'Amin Says Uganda Retains the Right to Reply to Raid' *New York Times* (6 July 1976).

[65] 'Other Political and Security Questions: Complaint of Aggression by Israel against Uganda' (1976) UNYB 315, 316.

[66] See examples in Aust (n 2) 110 ff.

The protests against complicity in breaches committed by third States on its territory have arisen in respect of varied forms of aid or assistance, including political or diplomatic collusion, placement of technology or military bases for launching drone attacks, placing a detention centre at the disposal of a third State, and merely failing to control its territory and prevent a principal wrongful act from occurring. Complicity may arise where a State explicitly authorises flights over its territory but also when it does not object to the use of its airspace knowing that those flights may be instrumental to the commission of an internationally wrongful act.[67]

In this context, an example of alleged complicity can be found in a recent judgment of the Administrative Court of Cologne in Germany.[68] The case arose from the use by the United States of data and technology of the Ramstein military base to execute the United States' drone attack in Yemen in 2012. The applicants, the relatives of individuals killed in that drone attack, filed a claim in 2014, alleging that by permitting the United States to use its airbase at Ramstein and facilitate thereby a launch of drone strikes and the resulting violation of the right to life, Germany breached its constitutionally enshrined duty to protect the right to life. The Administrative Court of Cologne dismissed the claim, holding that the German government is not obliged to prevent the United States from using Ramstein airbase for the execution of drone attacks in Yemen.[69] The decision is currently being appealed, but it shows that the use of drones in extra-judicial killings and executions can often be facilitated directly or indirectly by the collaboration of other States through the provision of airbases, technology, data or personnel.[70]

d. Financing and Granting Export Credit Guarantees

Less conventional forms of complicity may include the provision of export credit guarantees for major infrastructure projects[71] or providing funds to an international organisation for certain extrabudgetary activities of

[67] See, eg 'Iran Supplying Syrian Military via Iraqi Airspace' (n 51); 'Enablers of the Syrian Conflict: How Targeting Third Parties Can Slow the Atrocities in Syria' *Human Rights First* (March 2013) http://www.atrocitysupplychain.org/files/HRF-Syria-case-study.pdf; see also Aust (n 2) 228–30.

[68] *3 K 5625/14* (Judgment) [2015] Köln VerwG (Cologne Administrative Court).

[69] ibid paras 87–92 (German Cologne Administrative Court).

[70] See, eg 'GCHQ Documents Raise Fresh Questions over UK Complicity in US Drone Strikes' *Guardian* (24 June 2015).

[71] See, eg World Bank, 'Investigation Report—China: Western Poverty Reduction Project (Credit No 3255-CHA and Loan No 4501-CHA)' (28 April 2000) Panel Investigation Report paras 81, 237, 244, 254, 420–22 (finding Bank's non-compliance with several policies and procedures); see also AG Gualtieri, 'The Environmental Accountability of the World Bank to Non-State Actors: Insights from the Inspection Panel' (2002) 72 *British YBIL* 213, 238–42 (describing the Qinghai Project); Aust (n 2) 148–49 (describing the Ilisu Dam construction project); see also J McChrystie Adams, 'Environmental and Human Rights Objections Stall Turkey's Proposed Ilisu Dam' (2000) 12 *Colorado J Intl Environmental L & Policy* 173; C Binder, 'Völkerrecht und Staudammbauten: das Ilisu-Projekt' (2007) 1 *Juridikum* 10.

technical cooperation,[72] which may lead to violations of international law. The practice of listing conditionalities regarding the expected use of assistance may be a necessary but not always sufficient tool to avoid potential responsibility. The existence of conditionalities must be accompanied with an establishment of procedures for a periodic review of their compliance and effective reporting mechanisms, particularly where funding is being provided in tranches. Similarly, if funds are knowingly being used for purposes other than those agreed, it may be apposite to generate a presumption of knowledge of the circumstances of the wrongful act.[73]

An illustration of possible financial complicity in violations of international law can be found in the case of a project loan for Turkey in the context of constructing the Ilisu Dam.[74] This project concerned the construction of a dam for irrigation and power supply purposes on the River Tigris. There was limited evidence that the project could be conducive to human rights violations, including forced displacement of the local population, and it could also lead to the exclusion of Syria and Iraq, downstream neighbour States, from their equitable share of water resources.[75] The United Kingdom was providing export credit guarantee for the project.[76] The Syrian Minister of Foreign Affairs sent a note to the United Kingdom in which he accused the latter of violating international law by supporting the construction of the Ilisu Dam project.[77] Ultimately, after discussions took place in the House of Commons, the United Kingdom withdrew from the project.[78] Subsequently, Germany, Austria and Switzerland took up the granting of export credit guarantees for the project but subjected them to a set of conditions, including compliance with international law and certain soft law standards. Following numerous controversies, the Swiss and the Austrian export financing agencies, decided to discontinue funding on the grounds that conditions, including respect for human rights law, had not been observed. Even though the source of funding belonged to State agencies, similar *fattispecie* can be envisaged under the auspices of development banks and other international organisations in their daily practices.

Another recent example of hypothetical complicity is the 2015 EU–Turkey agreement to establish the Turkey Refugee Facility, by virtue

[72] ILC (n 37) 142 (ILO).

[73] A Reinisch, 'Aid or Assistance and Direction and Control between States and International Organizations in the Commission of Internationally Wrongful Acts' (2010) 7 *IOLR* 63, 69; G Verdirame, *The UN and Human Rights: Who Guards the Guardians?* (Cambridge, CUP, 2011) 136.

[74] A Epiney, 'Nachbarrechtliche Pflichten im internationalen Wasserrecht und Implikationen von Drittstaaten' (2001) 39 *AVR* 1; Binder (n 71).

[75] See Aust (n 2) 147–49.

[76] 'World Commission on Dams Report Challenges Financing for Ilisu Dam' *Turkish Daily News* (20 March 2001).

[77] 'Arab League Urges UK to Reconsider Financing Turkish Dam' *Albawada News* (17 July 2000).

[78] United Kingdom House of Commons, 'Written Answers' (30 November 2000) Hansard Commons Debates col 748W.

of which the EU has provided EUR 3 billion to Turkey. The official purpose of the Turkey Refugee Facility is 'to coordinate and streamline actions financed in order to deliver efficient and complementary support to Syrians under temporary protection and host communities in Turkey'.[79] It has been reported, however, that the funding is being used to unlawfully detain and return refugees and asylum-seekers to conflict zones.[80] In the event such allegations could be corroborated and it could be shown that the financial resources provided by the EU indeed facilitated the principal wrongful acts by Turkey, the EU would argue that the financing did not significantly contribute to the commission of principal wrongful acts. More fundamentally, the question would revolve around the EU's knowledge of the purported wrongful acts by Turkey, the absence of which would exonerate the EU from any responsibility. However, where the funding is being provided in tranches which is a common procedure in similar projects, it is likely that the aiding or assisting entity would no longer be able to deny knowledge of the circumstances of the wrongful act when authorising the release of the successive tranche of money.

e. Providing Technical Assistance, Intelligence and Personnel

Complicity can also be based on cooperation under less formal arrangements or memoranda of understanding between States or inter-agencies.[81] These may allow for exchange of intelligence, operational collaboration, common training, and exchanges of technical equipment that could be used, for example, for the commission of human rights violations by other States.[82] Similarly, a State may knowingly fail to inform its officials

[79] 'EU-Turkey Cooperation: A €3 Billion Refugee Facility for Turkey' *European Commission Press Releases* (24 November 2015).

[80] 'Turkey: EU Risks Complicity in Violations as Refugees and Asylum-Seekers Locked up and Deported' *Amnesty International* (16 December 2015); Amnesty International, 'Europe's Gatekeeper: Unlawful Detention and Deportation of Refugees from Turkey' (16 December 2015) EUR 44/3022/2015.

[81] See, eg F Messineo, '"Extraordinary Renditions" and State Obligations to Criminalize and Prosecute Torture in the Light of the Abu Omar Case in Italy' (2009) 7 *JICJ* 1023; S Borelli, 'Rendition, Torture and Intelligence Cooperation' in H Born, I Leigh and A Wills (eds), *International Intelligence Cooperation and Accountability* (Abingdon, Routledge, 2011); D Fleck, 'Individual and State Responsibility for Intelligence Gathering' (2007) 28 *Michigan J Intl L* 687.

[82] See, eg *R v Hape* (Judgment) [2007] SCC 26 (Canadian Supreme Court); *Canada (Justice) v Khadr* (Judgment) [2008] SCC 28 (Canadian Supreme Court); *Amnesty International Canada and British Columbia Civil Liberties Association v Canada* (Judgment) [2008] FC 336 (Canadian Federal Court); *Belhaj & Boudchar v The Rt Hon Jack Straw and others* (Judgment) [2014] EWCA Civ 1394; *Belhaj & Boudchar v The Rt Hon Jack Straw and others* (Judgment) [2013] EWHC 4111 (QB); for documented cases of complicity in rendition, torture and arbitrary detention see Open Society Foundation, 'Globalizing Torture: CIA Secret Detention and Extraordinary Rendition' (2013) https://www.opensocietyfoundations.org/sites/default/files/globalizing-torture-20120205.pdf; United States Senate Select Committee on Intelligence, 'Committee Study of the Central Intelligence Agency's Detention and Interrogation Program' (2014) http://fas.org/irp/congress/2014_rpt/ssci-rdi.pdf.

that intelligence they have shared is being used by another State for the commission of human rights violations.[83]

An example of such collaboration can be found in the *Canada (Justice) v Khadr* case, where the Canadian Security and Intelligence (CSIS) officers shared the results of the interrogations of Mr Khadr with the United States authorities at Guantanamo Bay. The Canadian Supreme Court concluded that the 'regime providing for the detention and trial of Mr Khadr at the time of the CSIS interviews constituted a clear violation of fundamental human rights protected by international law'.[84] In holding that the Canadian Charter of Rights and Freedoms applies to Canadian officials assisting the US authorities at Guantanamo Bay, the Canadian Supreme Court stressed that '[b]y making the product of its interview of Mr Khadr available to US authorities, Canada participated in a process that was contrary to Canada's international human rights obligations'.[85]

Other measures taken by States in countering terrorism are instructive as regards instances of complicity by action or omission.[86] For example, according to the UN Study on Secret Detention:

> Practices such as 'hosting' secret detention sites or providing proxy detention have been supplemented by numerous other facets of complicity, including authorizing the landing of airplanes for refueling, short-term deprivation of liberty before handing over the 'suspect', the covering up of kidnappings, and so on. With very few exceptions, too little has been done to investigate allegations of complicity.[87]

Likewise, the European Commission for Democracy through Law, also known as the Venice Commission, held that providing 'transit facilities to another State could amount to providing assistance to the latter in committing a wrongful act, if the former State is aware of the wrongful character of the act concerned' in line with Article 16 ARSIWA.[88]

Investigations conducted by regional organisations such as the Council of Europe, as well as domestic inquiries, have surfaced evidence of a range of conduct amounting to complicity.[89] For instance, the panel of jurists

[83] See Borelli (n 81).

[84] *Canada (Justice) v Khadr* (n 82) para 24.

[85] ibid para 27.

[86] See M Scheinin and M Vermeulen, 'International Law: Human Rights Law and State Responsibility' in H Born, I Leigh and A Wills (eds), *International Intelligence Cooperation and Accountability* (Abingdon, Routledge, 2011).

[87] 'Joint Study on the Practices in Relation to Secret Detention in the Context of Countering Terrorism' (19 February 2010) UN Doc A/HRC/13/42, 5.

[88] European Commission for Democracy through Law (Venice Commission), 'Opinion on the International Legal Obligations of Council of Europe Member States in Respect of Secret Detention Facilities and Inter-State Transport of Prisoners' (17 March 2006) Opinion No 363/2005, CDL-AD (2006) 009, para 45.

[89] See, eg Council of Europe, Parliamentary Assembly, 'Alleged Secret Detentions and Unlawful Inter-State Transfers of Detainees Involving Council of Europe Member States' (12 June 2006) Doc 10957; Council of Europe, Parliamentary Assembly, 'Alleged Secret Detentions and Unlawful Inter-State Transfers of Detainees Involving Council of Europe Member States: Second Report' (11 June 2007) Doc 11302 rev, para 165 ff.

established by the UK Parliament to inquire into allegations of the United Kingdom's complicity in torture concluded that a State would engage responsibility whenever it:

— asks a foreign intelligence service known to use torture to detain and question an individual;
— provides information to a foreign intelligence service known to use torture, enabling that intelligence service to apprehend an individual;
— gives questions to a foreign intelligence service to put to a detainee who has been, is being or is likely to be tortured;
— sends interrogators to question a detainee who is known to have been tortured by those detaining and interrogating him;
— has intelligence personnel present at an interview with a detainee in a place where he is being, or might have been tortured; or
— systematically receives information known or thought likely to have been obtained from detainees subjected to torture.[90]

The panel's conclusion once again underscores the breadth of conduct that could amount to complicity in torture and could trigger international responsibility.

f. Delivering Aid or Assistance in the Context of Multinational Military Intervention

The United States-led intervention in Iraq shows complicity in operation and the complex issues it raises in practice. In particular, the intervention in Iraq shows a *géometrie variable* of complicity, where dozens of States contributed to hostilities with different degrees and forms of assistance. A few examples demonstrate the difficulty and inappropriateness of ascribing particular content or degree to complicity for it to be able to trigger responsibility.

For example, Australia, Czech Republic, Slovakia and Poland could all be considered as having made a direct and significant contribution to the intervention in Iraq. Other States have either criticised the legality of the war or have occasionally furnished aid or assistance to the United States. In Belgium, for example, the Ministers of Foreign Affairs and Defence declared that they would refuse placing the Belgian territory at the disposal of the American aircrafts if the territory were to be used for the purposes of waging an unlawful war.[91] In Canada, a claim was brought

[90] Joint Human Rights Committee, 'Allegations of UK Complicity in Torture' (21 July 2009) Twenty-third Report of Session 2008–09, United Kingdom House of Lords Paper 152/ House of Commons 230.

[91] See O Corten, 'Quels droits et quels devoirs pour les États tiers? Les effets juridiques d'une assistance à un acte d'agression' in K Bannelier, T Christakis and O Corten (eds), *L'intervention en Irak et le droit international* (Paris, Pedone, 2004) 106.

against the country's participation in the Iraq war. In *Turp v Chrétien*, the Canadian Federal Court dismissed the claim against Canada's participation in the Iraq war.[92] The court found an application to be premature as there was no 'official decision' at that time as to Canada's participation in the war in Iraq.[93] The Canadian Federal Court held that the claim would fail in any event as this was one of the matters of 'high policy', which except for claims based on the Canadian Charter of Rights and Freedoms, would not be judicially reviewable.[94]

Olivier Corten suggests that the varying degrees of third States' involvement in the Iraq war could be divided into three categories.[95] A first group of States neither accepted nor denied rendering aid or assistance to the coalition. These States included China, Russia and India that de facto maintained the status of neutrality.[96] The second group of States included Austria and Switzerland that decided to close their airspace and did not allow any transit through their territory.[97] Both Austria and Switzerland declared that they would give no military or logistical assistance in any form to the intervention in Iraq. Finally, a third group of States accepted to provide full support to the United States. A great majority of States falling under this third category, including Spain, Portugal, Denmark, Bulgaria, Hungary, Romania, Ireland, Georgia, Croatia, Turkey, Oman, Qatar, Jordan and Saudi Arabia, refrained from sending troops but furnished logistical and other substantial military assistance.[98] The involvement of Germany was more significant as their territory was constantly being used as a transfer hub of the United States soldiers in Europe and for overflights with the destination to the Persian Gulf. Kuwait, for example, even accepted that the attacks could be launched from its territory.[99]

Talmon notes that while the Coalition Provisional Authority (CPA) was a common organ under a unified command of the United States and the United Kingdom, other States: (i) seconded government officials and military personnel to the CPA; (ii) hired private contractors and made them available to the CPA; and (iii) funded the activities of the CPA.[100] Australia,

[92] See *Turp v Chrétien* [2003] FCT 301 (T-369-03) (Canadian Federal Court).

[93] ibid para 13.

[94] ibid paras 19–21.

[95] Corten (n 91) 118.

[96] ibid.

[97] See, eg 'Déclaration de Pascal Couchepin, Président de La Confédération Helvétique' *Réseau Voltaire* (20 March 2003) www.voltairenet.org/article9363.html.

[98] For relevant references in the newspapers see Corten (n 91) 118.

[99] 'Les États-Unis tentent de briser leur isolement en mettant en avant une coalition de trente pays' *Le Monde* (20 March 2003).

[100] S Talmon, 'A Plurality of Responsible Actors: International Responsibility for Acts of the Coalition Provisional Authority in Iraq' in P Shiner and A Williams (eds), *The Iraq War and International Law* (Oxford, Hart Publishing, 2008).

for instance, 'provided advisers in some key sectors to assist the CPA in the performance of its duties'.[101] Assuming that the intervention in Iraq was illegal or any specific wrongful acts during the occupation of Iraq are established, assistance from States under the third category above could result in responsibility insofar as the requisite knowledge could be shown.

To give just one example, the German Federal Administrative Court resorted to Article 16 ARSIWA when examining the German participation in the 2003 war in Iraq.[102] The case concerned a professional soldier who in April 2003 refused to execute the order of his superior to work on the further development of military software. He considered that his action could foster an involvement of the Federal Armed Forces in the war against Iraq, which he personally believed to be contrary to international law. The Federal Administrative Court held that:

> Neither the NATO Treaty, the NATO Status of Forces Agreement, the NATO Status of Forces Supplementary Agreement nor the Convention on the Presence of Foreign Forces in Germany require the Federal Republic of Germany to support acts by its NATO partners which contravene the Charter of the United Nations and violate international law...[103]

Importantly, the Federal Administrative Court held that:

> An internationally wrongful act can consist of an action, or—if there is an international obligation to act—an omission ... Aiding or assisting an internationally wrongful act is itself an internationally wrongful act.[104]

The Court concluded that:

> As emerges from the foregoing explanations ... serious concerns in international law exist about several acts of assistance of the Federal Republic of Germany in favour of the USA and the UK in connection with the war against Iraq begun on 20 March 2003...
>
> This applies in any case for the granting of overflight rights for military aircraft of the USA and the UK, flying over federal territory on the way to or returning from the war zone in the Gulf region in the framework of the Iraq war. This also applies to the permission for the sending of troops and the transport of weapons and military supplies to the war zone from German soil and for all undertakings which could lead to German state territory serving as starting point or 'hub' for military operations directed against Iraq ... the objective sense and purpose of these measures was to facilitate or even promote the military action of the USA

[101] ibid 217.

[102] *Attorney of the Federal Armed Forces v Major of the Federal Armed Forces* (Judgment) [2005] BVerwG, 2 WD 12.04, ILDC 483 (DE 2005) (German Federal Administrative Court).

[103] ibid para 4.1.4.1.3 (original references omitted); translation taken from UNGA, 'Responsibility of States for Internationally Wrongful Acts: Comments and Information Received from Governments' (9 March 2007) UN Doc A/62/63, 13, para 28.

[104] *Attorney of the Federal Armed Forces v Major of the Federal Armed Forces* (n 102) para 4.1.4.1.2; translation as per UNGA (n 103) 14, para 28.

> and the UK. Because of these objectives grave concerns in international law exist about the conduct of the federal government in this respect, as regards the prohibition of the use of force in international law and the said provisions of the Fifth Hague Convention ...[105]

This case shows the willingness of domestic courts to frame complicity both arising from actions or omissions. It also shows that domestic courts have referred to the general rule on responsibility for complicity in circumstances where other primary obligations could have been sufficient to reach a decision on the merits of the claims.

g. Extraditing Foreign Nationals

Another area of practice where the responsibility for complicity has been invoked and applied relates to cases of extradition of foreign nationals. For example, in a 1982 decision, the Swiss Federal Court was seized of the case in which a Belgian national was lured out of Belgium to Switzerland to be later extradited to the Federal Republic of Germany. Under the Belgian constitution, Belgium could not extradite its own citizens. Accordingly, the Swiss Federal Court denied extradition considering that otherwise it would become complicit in the violation of Belgian sovereignty.[106]

A more recent matter involving similar allegations was brought before the German Constitutional Court, this time concerning citizens of Yemen who were lured to Germany with the view to being subsequently extradited to the United States. The Court held that:

> Pursuant to article 25 of the [German] Basic Law, general rules of international law must be respected by the legislature when enacting national law and by the executive and courts when interpreting and applying such national law ... From this it follows in particular that the administrative authorities and courts of the Federal Republic of Germany are as a matter of principle barred by article 25 of the Basic Law from interpreting and applying national law in a way that violates such general rules of international law. *They are also obliged to refrain from doing anything that lends effectiveness to acts performed in violation of general rules of international law by non-German sovereign entities within the territorial area of application of the Basic Law and are prohibited from playing any decisive role in such acts by non-German sovereign entities...*
>
> Tortious action on the part of the United States would establish its responsibility under international law vis-à-vis Yemen. In such a case, *there would be the risk that by extraditing the complainant, Germany would be acting in support of the*

[105] *Attorney of the Federal Armed Forces v Major of the Federal Armed Forces* (n 102) para 4.1.4.1.4.

[106] See *P1201/81/fs* (Judgment) (1983) 10 Europäische Grundrechte Zeitschrift 435 (Swiss Federal Tribunal); see also *1B_87/2007* (Judgment) (2007) 34 Europäische Grundrechte Zeitschrift 571 (Swiss Federal Tribunal).

> *potentially illegal actions of the United States and would thus make itself responsible vis-à-vis Yemen under international law. That State responsibility can under specific conditions be established by acting in support of third party actions that are contrary to international law is shown by article 16 of the International Law Commission's draft convention on State responsibility, which codifies customary international law in this field.*[107] (emphasis added)

The Court ultimately found that there was no collusion between Germany and the United States. However, its legal considerations above, including by reference to Article 16 ARSIWA, show that in different circumstances the conduct of luring a foreigner into another State with the view to extraditing him to a third State could give rise to responsibility for complicity. It also shows that principles of international responsibility can be relevant for the purposes of preventing an international wrong from taking place.[108]

iii. Preliminary Conclusions

Two preliminary conclusions follow from this review of practice and *opinio juris* of responsibility for complicity. First, there is no overwhelming support for the eviction of complicity by omission as some authors have suggested on the basis of the genocide-specific and policy-oriented reasoning of the Court in the *Bosnia Genocide* case. The range of conduct triggering responsibility for complicity is wide, covering forms of facilitation which technically may not amount to positive action. Second, it could be argued that there is yet no clear standard as to the required link between the complicit conduct and the principal wrongful act. Evidently, in their comments, States and international organisations have insisted on the fact that the link between complicity and the principal wrongful act must be sufficiently close. However, saying that the link must be close is not tantamount to requiring a particular level or degree of impact that the complicit conduct must have on the commission of the principal wrongful act. This leaves us with certainty in the extremes—that trivial or remote assistance to the wrongdoing would not suffice to trigger international responsibility whereas significant or proximate assistance would.

The ILC Commentary's references to a 'specific causal link'[109] and to the fact that complicity must have 'significantly contributed' to the wrongful

[107] *2 BvR 1243/03 and 2 BvR 1506/03* (Judgment) [2003] BverfG 109 (German Constitutional Court) paras 45 and 47; English translation taken from UNGA (n 103) 12–13, para 25.

[108] A Nollkaemper, 'Internationally Wrongful Acts in Domestic Courts' (2007) 101 *AJIL* 760, 780.

[109] ARSIWA (n 22) 65, para 8. Note that causation here is not being used in its technical sense of linking a given conduct to an injury (damages). It is being referred to more broadly as a factual connector of two conducts.

act[110] are not self-explanatory. The ILC stressed that 'the assisting State will only be responsible to the extent that its own conduct has caused or contributed to the internationally wrongful act'.[111] This could be read to suggest a more lenient approach to the factual link between the complicit and principal act as *causing* and *contributing to* are presented as alternatives.

The ILC's reference to *causing* could include the following scenarios where the variable X is the aid or assistance and the variable Y the principal wrongful act:

— X is the only cause of Y;
— X is the necessary cause of Y (the same as saying that Y would not have occurred but for X); or
— X is the only effective or sufficient cause among other potential causes of Y.

By contrast, the standard of *contributing to* would capture any scenario of X actually facilitating Y (*de minimis*; more likely than not; significantly; substantially; essentially—there is a *continuum* of possible legal standards). A combined reading of the standards of *causing* and *contributing* suggests that the qualifying link between the complicit and principal conduct covers a large spectrum of factual behaviour. Pursuant to this definition, any reasonable observer would understand that complicity encompasses different degrees of involvement or collaboration. As we have seen through the examples from practice discussed in this work, these degrees of complicity in the wrongful act could range from sending direct military support, sharing intelligence, providing credit guarantees, or simply not protesting to the use of airspace. However different they are in terms of their character and forms, all of them contribute to the wrongful act without necessarily *causing* it. In other words, the participation that falls within the scope of responsibility for complicity is sufficiently broad to include omissions as these can, in principle, facilitate the commission of the wrongful act. The key question to be asked is whether a given action or omission made it easier for another State or international organisation to commit its wrongful act.

This conclusion finds support in the ILC's Commentaries to ARSIWA when they stress that 'the assistance may have only been an incidental factor in the commission of the primary act'.[112] Pursuant to this interpretation, arguments such as those advanced by the IMF as analysed above cannot stand. In this author's view, the test only requires a simple factual link between two conducts (complicit and principal) and the more than absolutely trivial form of complicity. Indeed, an objective approach

110 ibid 66, para 5 (Art 16 Commentary).
111 ibid para 1 (Art 16 Commentary).
112 ibid 67, para 10 (Art 16 Commentary).

goes through recognising that any aid or assistance factually related to the principal wrongful act, generates without more a presumption of responsibility, which is rebuttable by showing the absence of knowledge of the circumstances of the principal wrongful act. As we shall see next this position goes in line with the interpretation by States of different primary rules which expressly prohibit complicity. This position is also defensible from a systemic perspective of the international legal order. It is logical to assume that the legality of the international system and the integrity of international obligations can only be guaranteed insofar as any kind of aid or assistance that *makes easier* the commission of the wrongful act generates responsibility.

B. The Content of Complicity in Primary Norms

As mentioned above, many substantive or primary norms in international law expressly prohibit different forms of complicity. Examples can be found in Article III(e) of the Genocide Convention, Article 2(5) of the UN Charter, Article 1 common to the Geneva Conventions, Article 1(1)(c) of the Convention on Cluster Munitions, and so forth. It is important to bear in mind that this 'network of rules on complicity'[113] may influence the way in which the general rule on responsibility for complicity is interpreted and applied. We take examples from the field of arms control, the use of force and human rights law to demonstrate a possible overlap with the general regime on responsibility for complicity in terms of its material content.

i. Arms Control Treaties Prohibiting Complicity

a. The Chemical Weapons Convention

Under Article 1(1)(d) of the Chemical Weapons Convention, States Parties are under an obligation not 'to assist, encourage or induce, in any way, anyone to engage in any military preparations to use chemical weapons'.[114] A commentary on the obligation not to provide assistance under the Chemical Weapons Convention clarifies that assistance

> can be given *by material or intellectual support* ... but also *financial resources, technological-scientific know-how or provision of specialised personnel, military instructions, etc* to anybody who is resolved to commit such prohibited activity or by support in the concealment of such activities.[115] (emphasis added)

[113] Aust (n 2) 376–418.

[114] Convention on the Prohibition of the Development, Production, Stockpiling and Use of Chemical Weapons and on Their Destruction (adopted 13 January 1993; entered into force 29 April 1997) 1974 UNTS 45, Art 1(1)(d).

[115] W Krutzsch and R Trapp (eds), *The Chemical Weapons Convention: A Commentary* (Oxford, OUP, 2014) 17.

As for the prohibition of encouragement or inducement, it implies 'contributing to the emergence of resolve of anybody to commit a prohibited activity by instigating, promising assistance, etc'.[116] It is noteworthy that under the Convention the promise of assistance is excluded from the definition of assistance itself, and rather constitutes encouragement or inducement. By contrast, as we have referred to in chapter three, Ago considered that in certain circumstances the mere promise of assistance or abstention towards an act of aggression, for example, could trigger responsibility for complicity under general international law.

b. The Convention on the Prohibition of Anti-personnel Mines

Article 1(1)(c) of the Convention on the Prohibition of the Use, Stockpiling, Production and Transfer of Anti-Personnel Mines and on their Destruction contains a general obligation prohibiting States Parties 'to assist, encourage, or induce, in any way, anyone to engage in any activity prohibited under the Convention'.[117] The types of prohibited activities include the use, development, acquisition, stockpiling, retention, or transfer of anti-personnel mines.

The use of the qualifier 'in any way' suggests that the assistance can be both direct and indirect; it can consist of actions or omissions. During the negotiations of the Convention, a number of States emphasised that the prohibition of assistance would also apply to a non-party State using anti-personnel mines. There were two groups of States' comments in this context. One group of States, including Australia and Zimbabwe, took the view that assistance could only include positive and direct physical involvement in the acts prohibited by the Convention. Another group of States, including the United Kingdom and Brazil, considered the scope of the prohibition of assistance under the Convention to be over-encompassing.

Australia considered that the term 'assist' under Article 1(1)(c) of the Convention meant:

> [T]he *actual and direct physical participation* in any activity prohibited by the Convention but *does not include permissible indirect support such as the provision of security for the personnel* of a State not party to the Convention engaging in such activities.[118] (emphasis added)

[116] ibid.

[117] Convention on the Prohibition of the Use, Stockpiling, Production and Transfer of Anti-Personnel Mines and on their Destruction (adopted 18 September 1997; entered into force 1 March 1999) 2056 UNTS 241, Art 1(1)(c).

[118] Statement of Australia upon Ratification of the Convention cited in S Maslen, *Commentaries on Arms Control Treaties: The Convention on the Prohibition of the Use, Stockpiling, Production, and Transfer of Anti-Personnel Mines and on Their Destruction*, vol 1 (2nd edn, Oxford, OUP, 2005) 95.

Zimbabwe made a similar declaration on the restrictive reading of the term:

> Our troops will therefore not in any way be directly or otherwise be involved in any activity banned by the Convention wherever they are operating. We therefore in our view, believe that the term *assist* should be interpreted, *relating directly to the activity in question and should not be applied liberally or given too wide a definition*… Active participation also means actively participating in the carrying, laying and training in the use, manufacture, distribution, encouraging or inducing someone in the use of [anti-personnel mines]. It is therefore our humble submission that the terms assist and active participating in the context of Article 1 mean *knowingly and intentionally participating directly or rendering assistance* on the use, transfer and/or production of [anti-personnel] mines.[119] (emphasis added)

The above interpretations show a restrictive reading of complicity in the context of the Convention, pointing to a distinction between direct and indirect assistance. In our view, this distinction is not appropriate as it would create serious loopholes in the enforcement of the Convention. Such an interpretation as proposed by Australia and Zimbabwe also seems to run counter to the ordinary meaning of the terms 'to assist, encourage or induce, in any way'.

While the positions expressed above cannot be simply ignored, other States have subscribed to a more lenient and over-encompassing understanding of the obligation prohibiting assistance. This view is also in line with the object and purpose of the Convention. The statements by the United Kingdom and Brazil are telling in this respect. The United Kingdom declared that the:

> Unacceptable activities include: planning with others for the use of anti-personnel mines (APM); training others for the use of APM; agreeing Rules of Engagement permitting the use of APM; agreeing operation plans permitting the use of APM; agreeing operational plans permitting the use of APM in combined operation; requests to non-State Parties to use APM; and providing security or transport for APM. Furthermore, it is not acceptable for UK forces to accept orders that amount to assistance in the use of APM.[120]

The United Kingdom went as far as to state that 'permitting transit [of anti-personnel mines] across UK territory would amount to assistance under the terms of Article 1'.[121] Brazil in turn expressed the view that:

> Article 1 of the Convention *clearly bans joint operations with non-States Parties that may involve the use of anti-personnel mines*. Even if the States Parties involved in

[119] Statement of Zimbabwe on Issues Concerning Article 1 (General Obligations) of the Anti-Personnel Mine Ban Convention to the Standing Committee on the General Status and Operation of the Convention (31 May 2002) reproduced in Maslen (n 118).

[120] United Kingdom Intervention on Article 1, Statement to the Standing Committee on the General Status and Operation of the Convention (16 May 2003) reproduced in Maslen (n 118) 96.

[121] ibid.

> such operations do not participate directly and actively in the laying of anti-personnel mines, the operations should be considered illegal if the use of land-mines by a non-State Party is of direct military benefit to those States Parties. In the absence of such a broad interpretation of the term 'assist', Article 1 would contain a serious and unfortunate loophole. All States Parties should commit strictly to observe the provisions of Article 1, which would include *giving the term 'assist' as broad an interpretation as possible.*[122] (emphasis added)

The analysis of States' comments reveals that there are, in essence, three main categories of assistance that fall under Article 1(1)(c): logistics, security and planning.[123] Logistical support includes 'fuelling or refuelling an aircraft or a lorry containing anti-personnel mines, or providing medical assistance to a soldier engaged in laying anti-personnel mines'.[124] Security support covers protection that is extended to soldiers laying mines, to a ship transporting the mines or the aircraft launching them.[125] Finally, planning covers training or other strategic exercises aimed at the performance of any prohibited activity under the Convention.[126]

In addition, financial links could also constitute assistance pursuant to Article 1(1)(c) of the Convention. For example, Norway's Petroleum Fund withdrew its investment in Singapore Technologies Engineering, a company which produces anti-personnel mines, because it was considered to be a potential violation of Article 1(1)(c).[127] This example evokes the concerns expressed by IMF, as discussed in section II.A above. It shows a sort of precautionary logic that States are encouraged to apply so as to ensure that their aid or assistance is not being diverted for the commission of an internationally wrongful act.

A State which provides assistance to any of the prohibited activities under the Convention, engages international responsibility even if that assistance is given to a non-party State or an armed opposition group. However, assistance would only engage such responsibility if it can be factually linked to the prohibited activity under the Convention. If the link is too remote, for example, helping the hospital that provides medical care to all soldiers who laid anti-personnel mines, this would not constitute the prohibited assistance for the purposes of the Convention.[128] By contrast, if the State fuels vehicles transporting anti-personnel mines, loads trucks

[122] Statement of Brazil on Issues concerning Article 1 (General Obligations) of the Anti-Personnel Mine Ban Convention to the Standing Committee on General Status and Operation of the Convention (1 February 2002) reproduced in ibid.

[123] E-mail received from Lieutenant-Colonel Mike Kelly, Australian Defence Force (3 June 2002) cited in ibid.

[124] ibid 96–97.

[125] ibid 97.

[126] ibid.

[127] Statement of Norway to the Standing Committee on General Status and Operation of the Convention (1 February 2002) cited in ibid 96.

[128] ibid 97.

with anti-personnel mines or provides drivers for those trucks, this is sufficiently direct and falls under Article 1(1)(c).[129] Hence, there seems to be a requirement in the Convention that the aid or assistance be specifically linked to one of the prohibited activities, whether these are committed by another State party, non-party or an armed opposition group, providing the assisting State has the requisite knowledge of the circumstances of the prohibited activities. There is however no requirement that the assistance significantly or otherwise facilitate any prohibited activity, a simple factual or causal link between the two conducts is sufficient to engage responsibility of the State under Article 1(1)(c) of the Convention.

In the context of the Convention, the application of the obligation not to provide assistance raises particular problems in terms of operational planning and collaboration in joint military coalitions that include both States parties and non-parties. Given that planning and provision of strategic training may amount to assistance to one of the prohibited activities, some States have struggled insofar as the instructions they have to give to their armed forces. For instance, Canada's Office of the Judge Advocate General stated that:

> When engaged in pre-conflict or combined operations with foreign forces, Canada will not agree to operational plans which authorize the use by the combined force of anti-personnel mines. While Canadians may participate in operational planning as members of a multinational staff they *may not participate in planning for the use of anti-personnel mines.* This would not prevent a State that is not a signatory or party to the APM Convention from participating in a multinational force or planning for the use of anti-personnel mines by its own forces for strictly national purposes. However, CF [Canadian forces] personnel will not be involved in any such planning.[130] (emphasis added)

For example, in 2001 Canadian soldiers operating in Afghanistan were ordered by their American commander to lay mines around their camp.[131] When they refused to do so, United States soldiers—whose country has not ratified the Convention—laid the mines for them.[132] This and other examples led Byers to argue that 'the United States' refusal to ratify most humanitarian conventions, combined with its position as the principal military and intelligence ally of dozens of countries, is responsible for a number of the recent, difficult issues of complicity in international law'.[133]

[129] ibid.

[130] Canada's Office of the Judge Advocate General, 'The Law of Armed Conflict', s 5.10, reproduced in ibid 98.

[131] M Byers, 'Helmut P Aust: Complicity and the Law of State Responsibility' (2012) 23 *EJIL* 586.

[132] ibid 587.

[133] ibid.

c. The Convention on Cluster Munitions

The increasing awareness of the legal consequences that may attach to complicity in the wrongdoing was clearly at the forefront of the negotiations of the Convention on Cluster Munitions (CCM). Like the Convention on the Prohibition of Anti-Personnel Mines, Article 1(1)(c) of the CCM stipulates that each Contracting Party undertakes not to 'assist, encourage or induce anyone in any activity prohibited to a State Party under this Convention'.[134]

Throughout the negotiations process, States have proposed amendments to Article 1(1)(c) so as to clarify the meaning of 'assistance'. Germany suggested that the scope of application of this provision would

> not preclude the mere participation in the planning or the execution of operations, exercises or other military activities by the Armed Forces or by an individual national of a State Party to this Convention, conducted in combination with Armed Forces of States not Parties to this Convention which engage in activity prohibited under this Convention.[135]

Morocco, Senegal and Mauritania made a further suggestion for amendment:

> [T]he States not party explain to the States Parties participating in the planning or the execution of operations, the military necessity for engaging in such activities and taking into account the humanitarian concerns addressed by the Convention. The States Parties shall refrain from engaging in activities prohibited under this Convention in any joint military operations with States not parties.[136]

Several delegations raised concerns of interoperability and military efficiency which too broad of a scope for Article 1(1)(c) would undermine.[137] In order to restrict the scope of the obligation under Article 1(1)(c) to accommodate these concerns, an interoperability provision was inserted

[134] Convention on Cluster Munitions (adopted 30 May 2008; entered into force 1 August 2010) 2688 UNTS 39, Art 1(1)(c).

[135] 'Proposal by Germany, Supported by Denmark, France, Italy, Slovakia, Spain, the Czech Republic and the United Kingdom for the Amendment of Article 1' (19 May 2008) Diplomatic Conference Doc CCM/13.

[136] 'Proposal by Morocco, Supported by Senegal and Mauritania, for the Amendment of the Proposal by Germany, Supported by Denmark, France, Italy, Slovakia, Spain, the Czech Republic and the United Kingdom for the Amendment of Article 1' (20 May 2008) Diplomatic Conference Doc CCM/69.

[137] See 'Summary Record of the Tenth Session of the Committee of the Whole' (18 June 2008) Diplomatic Conference Doc CCM/CW/SR/10; see also 'Proposal by France for the Amendment of Article 1' (2008) Diplomatic Conference Doc CCM/16; 'Proposal by the United Kingdom for the Amendment of Article 1' (2008) Diplomatic Conference Doc CCM/14.

as Article 21(3) that, arguably, subverts the purpose of Article 1(1)(c) obligation at best, and the object and purpose of the treaty at worst:

> Notwithstanding the provisions of Article 1 of this Convention and in accordance with international law, States Parties, their military personnel or nationals, may engage in military cooperation and operations with States not party to this Convention that might engage in activities prohibited to a State Party.[138]

This exemption was included as a key compromise for the very adoption of the Convention. In order to slightly minimise the impact of this exemption, paragraph 4 of Article 21 of the CCM stresses that a State party may not 'expressly request the use of cluster munitions in cases where the choice of munitions is within its exclusive control'.[139] Nevertheless, a joint reading of paragraphs 3 and 4 of Article 21 suggests that States Parties to the CCM can lawfully use cluster munitions when cooperating with States non-Parties to the CCM.

Aust suggests that Article 21 CCM and the surrounding discussions that took place show that a mere association or alliance of States Parties and non-Parties would not amount to assistance and any such inference would be far-fetched.[140] In support of his argument Aust cites the example of the European Court of Human Rights (ECtHR), which did not hold members of the 'coalition of States' which had attacked Iraq in 2003 responsible for the capturing and detention of Saddam Hussein on the mere basis that they had formed this alliance.[141] In relevant part, the ECtHR held as follows:

> The Court considers these jurisdiction arguments to be based on submissions which are not substantiated. While the applicant referred to certain UN documents, press releases and academic publications, these referred, without more, to coalition partners acting together. The applicant did not address each respondent State's role and responsibilities or the division of labour/power between them and the US. He did not refer to the fact or extent of the military responsibility of each Division for the zones assigned to them. He did not detail the relevant command structures between the US and non-US forces except to refer to the overall Commander of coalition forces who was at all relevant times a US General. Finally, and importantly, *he did not indicate which respondent State (other than the US) had any (and, if so, what) influence or involvement in his impugned arrest, detention and handover*. Despite the formal handover of authority to the Iraqi authorities in June 2004 and elections in January 2005, the applicant simply maintained, without more, that those forces remained de facto in power in Iraq.[142] (emphasis added)

[138] CCM (n 134) Art 21(3).
[139] ibid Art 21(4).
[140] Aust (n 2) 206–07.
[141] *Saddam Hussein v Albania and others* (Admissibility) [2006] ECtHR App No 23276/04, 3–4.
[142] ibid.

However, the ECtHR reasoned strictly on jurisdictional and admissibility grounds and, in this author's view, the impact of this decision on responsibility for complicity is limited. The case does show, however, that courts are inclined to seek to determine each State's independent responsibility in cases of multiple causes contributing to the same wrongful outcome.

To sum up, the CCM regime shows a tendency of States to adopt a piecemeal approach to complicity, elaborating provisions such as Article 21 CCM to circumvent their obligations not to assist non-Parties to the Convention and to continue benefiting from military alliances with non-Parties. As we shall see further in this chapter, the general regime on responsibility for complicity also suffers a disguised logic of interoperability through its opposability requirement of the obligation breached.

The above overview of treaties dealing with arms control shows that, subject to limited exceptions, States subscribe to a broad definition of assistance that is prohibited under the Conventions and do not require more than a clear factual (causative) link between the conduct of assistance and the performance of prohibited activity.

We now proceed to a different area of international law in which questions of responsibility for complicit conduct have played a major role and where numerous obligations of non-assistance coexist and can shape our understanding of the material element of complicity under the general regime of international responsibility.

ii. Rules Prohibiting Complicity in the Use of Force

Approximately 30 conflicts account for close to 60 per cent of all international crises in the twentieth century.[143] The protracted character of some conflicts is frequently due to complicity by third States and external actors. For example, complicity has played an important role in the ongoing conflicts in Africa, including in the Democratic Republic of the Congo (DRC) or Darfur. Complicity in these and other contexts takes the form of arms trade, sending of military forces, dispatching patrols, or putting facilities, technology or logistics at the disposal of another State or an armed opposition group. Enforcing responsibility for complicity from outside by virtue of an effective sanctions regime and a more transparent scrutiny of decisions as to whether to render aid or assistance may well be one of the elements necessary to get to resolve these conflicts.

In the context of the threat or use of force, States and international organisations bear responsibility for their complicity in the violations of *jus ad bellum* and *jus in bello*.[144] Under the regime of *jus ad bellum*, at least

[143] N Stürchler, *The Threat of Force in International Law* (Cambridge, CUP, 2009) 49.

[144] *Legality of the Threat or Use of Nuclear Weapons* (Advisory Opinion) [1996] ICJ Rep 226, 245, para 42.

four layers of primary norms regulate complicity. Under the regime of *jus in bello*, determinations of complicity are regulated through an extensive interpretation of Article 1 common to the Geneva Conventions. We shall deal separately with these two regimes and try to assess whether their experience can inform the material element of complicity under the law of international responsibility and, in particular, whether they support a broad interpretation of its material element.

a. Complicity in the Violations of *Jus ad Bellum*

A host of rules apply to complicity in relation to the threat or use of force in international law. These are Article 3(f) of the Declaration on Aggression, Article 2(5) of the UN Charter, the general obligation of due diligence under customary international law, and the remnant regime of neutrality.

1. *Article 3(f) of the Declaration on Aggression*

Article 3(f) of the Declaration on Aggression of 1974 stipulates that States shall not allow their territory, which they have placed at the disposal of another State, to be used by that State for the perpetration of an act of aggression against a third State.[145] This formulation generates a quasi-strict liability standard. In other words, placing one's territory at the disposal of another State for an act of aggression constitutes in and of itself an act of aggression in international law, which gives rise to the right of the injured State to resort to self-defence, without prejudice to any other legal consequences.[146] As Aust states, '[t]he mere factual establishment that [the State] has granted the permission to make use of its territory for the commission of aggression suffices to trigger its responsibility'.[147]

The provision set out in Article 3(f) of the Declaration on Aggression finds extensive support in international practice, which has been discussed in great detail by other commentators.[148] Examples of protests against the placing of the territory at the disposal of another State for aggression can be found in the factual circumstances of third States placing their territory or airspace at the disposal of: (i) the US in its attacks on Libyan targets in 1986; (ii) the US in its intervention in Iraq; (iii) Belgium and the US in their intervention in the DRC in 1964; (iv) the US in its armed attack against Lebanon in 1958.

[145] UNGA, 'Res 3314 (XXIX) (Declaration on Aggression)' (14 December 1974) UN Doc A/RES/3314, Art 3(f).

[146] On the history of the definition of aggression see, eg J Zourek, 'Enfin une définition de l'agression' (1974) 20 *AFDI* 9.

[147] Aust (n 2) 381.

[148] See, eg Quigley (n 2); M Jackson, *Complicity in International Law* (Oxford, OUP, 2015); Aust (n 2); KN Trapp, *State Responsibility for International Terrorism* (Oxford, OUP, 2011).

It cannot be excluded that the same conduct of placing the territory at the disposal of another State may trigger in parallel responsibility for the contribution to all the lesser forms of use of force as covered by Article 2(4) of the UN Charter. In other words, the direct responsibility for violating Article 3(f) of the Declaration on Aggression does not necessarily exclude that State's responsibility for complicity in a separate violation. For example, if State A does not ensure border control knowingly to allow the military activities of State B against State C, State A could be directly violating its obligation under Article 3(f) of the Declaration on Aggression.[149] At the same time, State A could in parallel be engaging responsibility for complicity by omission in the violation of the use of force by State B or any other specific wrongful act committed by State B in the context of its intervention. The benefit of construing a direct violation of Article 3(f) of the Declaration on Aggression is that there would be no need to establish the criteria of Article 16 ARSIWA. As the violation of Article 3(f) of the Declaration on Aggression gives rise to direct responsibility, there is limited impact of Article 16 ARSIWA.

A separate question arises whether forms of assistance to an act of aggression other than placing of the territory are prohibited by the Declaration on Aggression and under customary international law. If some lesser forms of assistance than placing the territory at the disposal of aggression are not prohibited, Article 16 ARSIWA could then be of some relevance. For instance, during the elaboration of the Declaration on Aggression, there was considerable disagreement among States as to whether the assistance to or tolerance of armed bands could constitute a form of indirect aggression. The proposal by six States during the negotiation of the Declaration was ultimately not retained, but aimed at including in the scope of aggression:

1. The organization or encouragement of the organization of irregular forces or armed bands, including mercenaries, for incursion into the territory of another State.
2. The organization or instigation of or assistance or participation in acts of civil strife or terrorist acts in another State, or acquiescence in organized activities within its territory directed towards the commission of such acts.[150]

[149] For the recognition of Art 3(g) of the Declaration on Aggression as reflecting customary international law see *Military and Paramilitary Activities in and against Nicaragua (Nicaragua v United States)* (Merits) [1986] ICJ Rep 14, 103, para 195; see also *Armed Activities on the Territory of the Congo (DRC v Uganda)* (Judgment) [2005] ICJ Rep 168, Separate Opinion of Judge Kooijmans 306, 322, para 63 (doubting that the resolution as a whole reflects 'in all its terms' customary international law).

[150] UNGA, 'Report of the Special Committee on the Question of Defining Aggression' (1972) UN Doc A/8719, 18; UNGA, 'Report of the Special Committee on the Question of Defining Aggression' (1970) UN Doc A/8019, 58 ff.

The agreed version of Article 3(g) of the Declaration introduced the wording 'substantial involvement'/'le fait de s'engager d'une manière substantielle' in the acts listed under Article 3, including in the sending of armed bands or groups. Such substantial involvement would itself meet the threshold of an act of aggression. The reference to substantial involvement in the provision could suggest the requirement of active conduct.[151] However, can tolerance of or acquiescence in the activities of armed groups constitute an act of aggression? If the answer is in the affirmative, then this may affect the entitlement of an allegedly injured State to act in self-defence against the complicit State.[152]

During the negotiations,[153] proposals to minimise the level of State involvement required for an act of aggression, including 'assistance to', 'knowing acquiescence in', or 'collaboration in' (all of which would amount to active or passive support for, rather than sponsorship of, armed groups) were rejected in favour of the 'sending by or on behalf of' standard.[154] Kimberley Trapp suggests that 'no form of indirect aggression made its way into the UN Definition of Aggression, which applies only to state sponsorship of terrorism, and not to state support for terrorism involving some lesser form of assistance to non-state terrorist actors'.[155]

Hence, in the context of the Declaration on Aggression, the regulation of forms of assistance other than placing the territory at the disposal of another State is limited. By virtue of its narrow interpretation of the concept of 'armed attack', the Court in the *Military and Paramilitary Activities*

[151] PL Zanardi, 'Aggressione armata indiretta ed elemento soggettivo dell'illecito internazionale' in *Le droit international à l'heure de sa codification: études en l'honneur de Roberto Ago*, vol 3 (Milano, Giuffrè, 1987) 161.

[152] See *Military and Paramilitary Activities (Merits)* (n 149) 103–04, para 195 (where the Court did not consider that an armed attack covered assistance to rebels in the form of furnishing arms or other logistical assistance); cf *Legal Consequences of the Construction of a Wall in the Occupied Palestinian Territory* (Advisory Opinion) [2004] ICJ Rep 136, 194, para 139; on the scope of self-defence in international law see, eg O Corten, *The Law Against War: The Prohibition on the Use of Force in Contemporary International Law* (Oxford, Hart Publishing, 2012) 126–97, 401–94; C Gray, *International Law and the Use of Force* (3rd edn, Oxford, OUP, 2008) 114–253; Y Dinstein, *War, Aggression and Self-Defence* (4th edn, Cambridge, CUP, 2005); J Verhoeven, 'Les "étirements" de la légitime défense' (2002) 48 *AFDI* 49; CJ Tams, 'Swimming with the Tide or Seeking to Stem It? Recent ICJ Rulings on the Law on Self-Defence' (2005) 18 *RQDI* 275; SD Murphy, 'Self-Defense and the Israeli Wall Advisory Opinion: An Ipse Dixit from the ICJ?' (2005) 99 *AJIL* 62; O Corten and F Dubuisson, 'Opération "Liberté Immuable": Une extension abusive du concept de légitime défense' (2002) 1 *RGDIP* 51; CJ Tams, 'Light Treatment of a Complex Problem: The Law of Self-Defence in the Wall Case' (2006) 16 *EJIL* 963.

[153] UNGA, 'Report of the Special Committee on the Question of Defining Aggression' (1973) UN Doc A/9019.

[154] Trapp (n 148) 27.

[155] ibid.

case further contributed to the understanding that not all types of assistance generate the equivalent extent of legal consequences:

> The Court sees no reason to deny that, in customary law, the prohibition of armed attacks may apply to the sending by a State of armed bands to the territory of another State, if such an operation, because of its scale and effects, would have been classified as an armed attack rather than as a mere frontier incident had it been carried out by regular armed forces. But the Court does not believe that the concept of 'armed attack' includes not only acts by armed bands where such acts occur on a significant scale but also assistance to rebels in the form of the provision of weapons or logistical or other support.[156]

The question of whether a particular form of aid or assistance to non-State actors amounts to an armed attack for the purposes of *jus ad bellum* is without prejudice to the potential responsibility of aiding or assisting State for internationally wrongful acts committed as a result of that aid or assistance. Until the ICJ's judgment in the *Bosnia Genocide* case, situations of assistance provided by a State to non-State actors were exclusively treated as part of the tripartite attribution framework (de jure organ, de facto organ, and 'instructions, direction or control' test). As will be discussed in chapter seven, the fact that the provision in Article 16 ARSIWA was initially conceived for exclusively inter-State complicity was no obstacle for the ICJ to test its application to the aid and assistance from Serbia to non-State actors of Republika Srpska.[157]

Finally, an interesting aspect of complicity in the context of *jus ad bellum* arises in the situations of intervention by invitation. Whenever a State or international organisation intervenes in a third State on the basis of the latter's express consent, the circumstance precluding wrongfulness under Article 20 ARSIWA/ARIO applies.[158] There may arise questions in practice, however, as to whether such consent covers also provisions of aid or assistance by third States for purposes of intervention.[159] For example, to what extent were contributions of different African States to

[156] *Military and Paramilitary Activities (Merits)* (n 149) 103–04, para 195; cf ibid Dissenting Opinion of Judge Schwebel 259, 268 ff and 331 ff; ibid Dissenting Opinion of Judge Jennings 528, 543.

[157] *Bosnia Genocide (Merits)* (n 19) 217, para 420.

[158] ARSIWA (n 22) Art 20; ARIO (n 22), Art 20; see also T Christakis and K Mollard-Bannelier, 'Volenti non fit injuria? Les effets du consentement à l'intervention militaire' (2004) 50 *AFDI* 102; C Farhang, 'The Notion of Consent in Part One of the Draft Articles on State Responsibility' (2014) 27 *LJIL* 55; HP Aust, 'Circumstances Precluding Wrongfulness' in A Nollkaemper and I Plakokefalos (eds), *Principles of Shared Responsibility in International Law: An Appraisal of the State of the Art* (Cambridge, CUP, 2014); V Lowe, 'Precluding Wrongfulness or Responsibility: A Plea for Excuses' (1999) 10 *EJIL* 405.

[159] See A Abass, 'Consent Precluding State Responsibility: A Critical Analysis' (2004) 53 *ICLQ* 211, 216.

the intervention of France in Mali covered by the consent of the latter?[160] Unless a specific agreement is elaborated prior to intervention,[161] it is very likely that the State when giving its consent to intervention only contemplated intervention by the particular State addressee of the consent.[162] If that is indeed the case, then technically the contributions of third States to such intervention are illegal and, taken alone, may be seen as constituting an act of aggression or lesser forms of use of force, with the ensuing legal consequences. This would leave little room for a separate operation of the responsibility for complicity as set out in Article 16 ARSIWA.

2. *Article 2(5) UN Charter*

Whenever the UN takes preventive or enforcement action against a particular State, Article 2(5) of the UN Charter applies:

> All Members shall give the United Nations every assistance in any action it takes in accordance with the present Charter, and shall refrain from giving assistance to any state against which the United Nations is taking preventive or enforcement action.[163]

The provision 'highlights the bonds of solidarity between the UN and its Member States'.[164] As Aust rightly argues, the provision is concurrently of a larger and narrower scope as compared to Article 16 ARSIWA:

> It is more far-reaching insofar as Article 2(5) of the Charter can arguably impose more wide-ranging obligations on UN Member States to dissociate themselves from a State against which preventive or enforcement action is being taken as compared with Article 16 [ARSIWA].[165]

Article 2(5) of the UN Charter does not impose any precise causal or cognitive standards while Article 16 ARSIWA does. At the same time, its scope of application is narrower than that of Article 16 ARSIWA, as it only applies to cases where the United Nations Security Council (UNSC) has taken the preventive or enforcement action.[166]

[160] See, eg UNSC, 'Res 2085' (20 December 2012) UN Doc S/RES/2085 (Mali); Aust (n 158) 182–83.

[161] See, eg G Gaja, 'Fourth Report on Responsibility of International Organizations' (2006) UN Doc A/CN.4/564 and Add 1-2, reproduced in (2006) 2 (pt 1) *YBILC* 103, 107, para 13 (referring to an example of Indonesia which in 2005 invited the EU, five Member States of ASEAN, Norway and Switzerland to deploy the 'Aceh Monitoring Mission' in order to supervise the peace process in the province of Aceh).

[162] See, eg *Armed Activities (DRC v Uganda)* (n 149) 196 ff, paras 42 ff.

[163] Charter of the United Nations (adopted 26 June 1945; entered into force 24 October 1945) 1 UNTS 16, Art 2(5).

[164] R Kolb, *An Introduction to the Law of United Nations* (Oxford, Hart Publishing, 2010) 138.

[165] Aust (n 2) 32.

[166] ibid 34.

The first limb of the provision in Article 2(5) of the UN Charter imposes a positive duty on Member States to provide assistance to the organisation. A recent example of implementation of this duty can be found in the UN-authorised intervention and the establishment of the no-fly zone in Libya.[167] However, it is the second limb of the provision that is most relevant to our discussion on complicity. The primary goal of this obligation is 'to prevent any hindrance to any action undertaken by the United Nations'.[168] It is doubtful whether the same obligation extends to situations where the UNSC takes no enforcement action, but simply finds or declares the existence of a particular illegal situation.[169] The obligation of non-assistance also extends to provisional measures taken in light of Article 40 of the UN Charter with the view to prevent a breach of international peace and security.[170]

Further, the UNSC has often imposed specific duties of non-assistance not only on States,[171] which are subject of the enforcement actions, but also on non-State actors.[172] One of the earliest examples of such language concerned the Korean crisis in 1950, during which the UNSC called upon Member States to refrain from giving assistance to North Korea.[173] Another example can be found in respect of the situation in the DRC, where the UNSC demanded, inter alia, 'the cessation of all support, in particular weapons and any other military material, to the armed groups and militias, and further demands that all Congolese parties and all States in the region actively prevent the supply of such support'.[174] In most cases, the duty of non-assistance has been accompanied by the imposition of arms embargoes.[175] The resolutions often refer broadly to specific forms of assistance. As an example of such wording, Resolution 1803 on Iran refers to

> financial support for trade with Iran, including the granting of export credits, guarantees or insurance, to their nationals, or entities involved in such trade,

[167] UNSC, 'Res 1973' (n 52) paras 6 ff.

[168] V Gowlland-Debbas, *Collective Responses to Illegal Acts in International Law: United Nations Action in the Question of Southern Rhodesia* (Dordrecht, Martinus Nijhoff, 1990) 380; M Forteau, *Droit de la sécurité collective et droit de la responsabilité internationale* (Paris, Pedone, 2006) 201.

[169] cf Aust (n 2) 382.

[170] HP Aust, 'Article 2(5)' in B Simma et al (eds), *The Charter of the United Nations: A Commentary* (3rd edn, Oxford, OUP, 2012) 244.

[171] See, eg UNSC, 'Res 1132' (8 October 1997) UN Doc S/RES/1132 (Sierra Leone) para 1; UNSC, 'Res 283' (29 July 1970) UN Doc S/RES/283 (Namibia) para 5.

[172] See, eg UNSC, 'Res 1540' (28 April 2004) UN Doc S/RES/1540 para 1.

[173] UNSC, 'Res 82' (25 June 1950) UN Doc S/RES/82 (North Korea).

[174] UNSC, 'Res 1484' (30 May 2003) UN Doc S/RES/1484 (DRC).

[175] For exceptions to the rule see UNSC, 'Res 1054' (26 April 1996) UN Doc S/RES/1054 (Sudan); UNSC, 'Res 1636' (31 October 2005) UN Doc S/RES/1636 (Lebanon); see also JM Farrall, *United Nations Sanctions and the Rule of Law* (Cambridge, CUP, 2007) 110; F Alabrune, 'La pratique des Comités des sanctions du Conseil de sécurité depuis 1990' (1999) 45 *AFDI* 226; M Forteau, 'La levée et la suspension des sanctions internationales' (2005) 51 *AFDI* 57.

> in order to avoid such financial support contributing to the proliferation of sensitive nuclear activities, or to the development of nuclear weapons delivery systems, as referred to in Res 1737 (2006).[176]

The wording used in the Resolution on the Southern Rhodesia is also instructive as to the scope of aid or assistance the UNSC typically prohibits in its resolutions.[177] In its Resolution 253, the UNSC laid down binding obligations of non-assistance with respect to certain commercial, industrial, investment or tourism related activities carried on with the illegal regime in Southern Rhodesia.[178] On that occasion, the UNSC:

> [D]eplore[d] the attitude of States that have not complied with their obligations under Article 25 of the Charter, and censure[d] in particular those States that have persisted in trading with the illegal *régime* in defiance of the resolutions of the Security Council, and which have given active assistance to the *régime*.[179]

It is interesting to note that the UNSC specifically referred to active assistance in the above. This could imply that, as a matter of principle, whenever the UNSC refers to the prohibition of assistance, it has in mind different forms in which these can take place whether through active or passive behaviour. For example, in a set of resolutions following North Korea's withdrawal from the Non-Proliferation Treaty (NPT), the UNSC referred to the prohibition of assistance covering 'all arms and related material, as well as to financial transactions, technical training, advice, services or assistance related to the provision, manufacture, maintenance or use of such arms, except for small arms and light weapons and their related material'.[180] Likewise, in its Resolution 1718, the UNSC decided that '[a]ll Member States shall prevent the direct or indirect supply, sale or transfer of [different types of arms, war materials and technology]'.[181] Similar wording is used in the resolutions on Libya, indicating that all Member States should 'prevent the *direct or indirect* supply, sale or transfer to [Libya] … of arms and related material of all types, including weapons and ammunition, military vehicles and equipment, paramilitary equipment, and spare parts for the aforementioned'.[182] The reference to 'direct or indirect' suggests that the duty of non-assistance extends to omissions facilitating the commission of the wrongful acts.

176 UNSC, 'Res 1803' (3 March 2008) UN Doc S/RES/1803 (Iran), para 9.
177 UNSC, 'Res 253' (29 May 1968) UN Doc S/RES/253 (Southern Rhodesia), para 3.
178 ibid para 4.
179 ibid para 12.
180 UNSC, 'Res 1874' (12 June 2009) UN Doc S/RES/1874 (DPRK) para 10.
181 UNSC, 'Res 1718' (14 October 2006) UN Doc S/RES/1718 (DPRK) para 8.
182 UNSC, 'Res 1970' (26 February 2011) UN Doc S/RES/1970 (Libya) para 9.

The practice of the United Nations General Assembly (UNGA) is also instructive in calling on States not to provide assistance to the commission of internationally wrongful acts. For example, the UNGA has expressly referred to the obligation set forth in Article 2(5) in the context of Southern Rhodesia.[183] Likewise, it has called for non-assistance in the context of the occupation of the Syrian Golan and the Palestinian Territories in the West Bank.[184] In yet another resolution, condemning the action of the United States against Libya, the UNGA requested 'all States to refrain from extending any assistance or facilities for perpetrating acts of aggression against the Libyan Arab Jamahiriya'.[185] In its Resolution 55/174, relating to the internal conflict in Afghanistan prior to the events of 9/11, the UNGA called upon

> all signatories of the Tashkent Declaration on Fundamental Principles for a Peaceful Settlement of the Conflict in Afghanistan and the Afghan parties to implement the principles contained in that Declaration in support of the efforts of the United Nations toward a peaceful resolution of the Afghan conflict, in particular the agreement *not to provide military support to any Afghan party and to prevent the use of their territories for such purposes,* and recalls their appeal to the international community to take identical measures to prevent the delivery of weapons to Afghanistan.[186] (emphasis added)

In sum, while there are similarities in the policy objective of Article 2(5) of the Charter and Article 16 ARSIWA, their scope is clearly different.[187] Whereas Article 2(5) and specific non-assistance duties in the UNSC resolutions address internationally wrongful acts threatening international peace and security, Article 16 ARSIWA deals with all types of internationally wrongful acts.[188] Nevertheless, the UNSC and UNGA practice of imposing specific duties of non-assistance and the broad definition of conduct captured by these duties corroborates our interpretation of the material element of responsibility for complicity under general international law.

[183] UNGA, 'Res 31/154' (20 December 1976) UN Doc A/RES/31/154 (Southern Rhodesia) paras 1–2; UNGA, 'Res 33/38' (13 December 1978) UN Doc A/RES/33/38 (Southern Rhodesia) paras 1–2.

[184] See, eg UNGA, 'Res 63/99' (5 December 2008) UN Doc A/RES/63/99 (Syrian Golan) para 6; UNGA, 'Res ES-7/4' (28 April 1982) UN Doc A/RES/ES-7/4 (Palestine) para 9; UNGA, 'Res 38/180' (19 December 1983) UN Doc A/RES/38/180 (Middle East) paras 9, 13–14; UNGA, 'Res 39/146' (14 December 1984) UN Doc A/RES/39/146 (Middle East) para 11 (pt A); paras 13–14 (pt B); UNGA, 'Res 41/162' (5 December 1986) UN Doc A/RES/41/162 (Middle East) para 11.

[185] UNGA, 'Res 41/38' (20 November 1986) UN Doc A/RES/41/38 (Libya) para 3.

[186] UNGA, 'Res 55/174' (19 December 2000) UN Doc A/RES/55/174 (Afghanistan) para 16 (pt A).

[187] Aust (n 2) 249.

[188] Felder (n 2) 158–61.

3. *Modern Regulation of Neutrality*

Notwithstanding development of the system of collective security, the traditional laws of neutrality have not yet become obsolete.[189] They may still apply to prevent the involvement of third party in a conflict.[190] As Aust stresses, this will only be possible in situations in which the UNSC 'has not made any determination as to the party to a conflict which bears responsibility for its outbreak'.[191] The Court has also recognised the continued role of neutrality in its *Nuclear Weapons* Advisory Opinion.[192]

As discussed in chapter two, under the operation of the laws of neutrality, neutral States are to refrain from lending assistance to either side of the conflict. The validity of their status as a neutral State is dependent upon full compliance with this obligation.[193] Indeed, there seems to be a considerable overlap in the logic of the rules of neutrality and the responsibility derived from complicit conduct.[194] According to Aust, both regimes 'are aimed to limit the consequences of international conflicts to the degree absolutely necessary'.[195]

Under Article 2(5) of the UN Charter, States are allowed to provide support only to a party to a conflict that is authorised to use force.[196] The provision of assistance in the framework of the UN Charter would not necessarily deprive the assisting States of their benefits of neutrality.[197] Notwithstanding the system of collective security in place under the UN Charter, States still occasionally rely on the policy of non-belligerency. For instance, Italy claimed its non-belligerency status even though it provided limited support to the United States intervention in Iraq.[198] Insofar as

[189] See, eg Dinstein (n 152); E Chadwick, *Traditional Neutrality Revisited: Law, Theory and Case Studies* (The Hague, Kluwer, 2002) 181; DF Vagts, 'The Traditional Law of Neutrality in a Changing Environment' (1998) 14 *American University Intl LR* 83, 91; cf H Kelsen, 'Théorie du droit international public' (1953) 84 *RCADI* 5, 60; L Henkin, 'Force, Intervention and Neutrality in Contemporary International Law' (1963) 57 *ASIL Proceedings* 147, 159.

[190] See generally C Chinkin, *Third Parties in International Law* (Oxford, Clarendon Press, 1993) 291–314.

[191] Aust (n 2) 382–83.

[192] *Nuclear Weapons (Advisory Opinion)* (n 144) 261, para 89.

[193] Dinstein (n 152) 25; SC Neff, *War and the Law of Nations: A General History* (Cambridge, CUP, 2005) 197; I Brownlie, *International Law and the Use of Force by States* (Oxford, Clarendon Press, 1963) 404.

[194] Jackson (n 148) 126 ('the law of neutrality entails an instance where obligations arise on a third state in respect of their relationship with other states').

[195] Aust (n 2) 384; Lowe (n 23) 13.

[196] Neff (n 193) 325.

[197] See WH von Heinegg, '"Benevolent" Third States in International Armed Conflicts: The Myth of the Irrelevance of the Law of Neutrality' in MN Schmitt and J Pejic (eds), *International Law and Armed Conflict: Exploring the Faultlines: Essays in Honour of Yoram Dinstein* (Leiden, Martinus Nijhoff, 2007) 544.

[198] See N Ronzitti, 'Italy's Non-Belligerency During the Iraq-War' in M Ragazzi (ed), *International Responsibility Today: Essays in Memory of Oscar Schachter* (Leiden, Martinus Nijhoff, 2005).

this intervention did not benefit from authorisation of the UNSC nor had any solid legal basis in international law, Italy could not, by virtue of this status alone, justify its participation in the attacks.[199]

An example on how the regime of neutrality coexists with the general rule on responsibility for complicity can be found in the *Oil Platforms* case, where Iran argued that it is a 'general principle of law that participation in a violation of the law committed by a different actor itself constitutes a violation'.[200] It was Iran's submission that:

> The activities of the United States [support provided to Iraq] ... were not only violations of the law of neutrality, they also constituted unlawful assistance to an aggression, i.e. a violation of the prohibition of the use of force. This violation engages the international responsibility of the United States. This means that the United States is liable to make compensation for any damage sustained by the victim of that aggression. At the very least ... the existence of this legal duty must be a bar to any claim for compensation raised by the United States in this case.[201]

The way in which Iran advanced its claim shows the concurrence of possible legal bases of responsibility in situations of complicity of one actor in the breach committed by another.[202] A party claiming complicity of another will often cite other parallel rules, which de facto regulate the same or materially similar conduct, in the expectation of having fewer hurdles to establishing responsibility. The strategic choice on the part of the claimant as to the exact basis of responsibility will often be determined by criteria linked to evidence and any constraints of obtaining relief, including the applicable causal standards. This may explain Iran's reliance above on the laws of neutrality and the notion of indirect aggression *qua* breaches of primary norms directly engaging the responsibility of the United States, rather than pursuing the argument based on the general rules on responsibility for aid or assistance.

4. *Obligations of Due Diligence*

Finally, States are under a general obligation to control the use of their own territory in a way that does not result in wrongful acts against third

199 See Aust (n 2) 30.

200 *Oil Platforms (Islamic Republic of Iran v United States)* (Merits) [2003] ICJ Rep 161, Further Response of the United States Counter-claim submitted by the Islamic Republic of Iran of 24 September 2001, para 7.50.

201 ibid para 7.51.

202 For a similar application of the violation of neutrality and responsibility for complicity see *Attorney of the Federal Armed Forces v Major of the Federal Armed Forces* (n 102); see ch 2 for discussion.

States.[203] The obligation of due diligence predates the UN Charter and is widely accepted as a corollary of the sovereignty and equality of States. In the *Island of Palmas* case, Max Huber held that sovereignty over territory presupposes the effective exercise thereof which includes an obligation not to allow for unlawful conduct harming other States to take place on one's own territory.[204] The ICJ recognised that every State has an 'obligation not to allow knowingly its territory to be used for acts contrary to the rights of other States'.[205] This obligation may capture numerous scenarios of eventual complicity, and as we shall see in section II.C the red line between the two concepts is indeed rather thin.

5. *Concluding Remarks*

In conclusion to our brief survey of the four normative regimes that may directly overlap in regulating the possible involvement of third parties in the resort to threat or use of force, we can see that the conduct covered by these specific norms is broad and could inform the scope of the general rule on responsibility for complicity. What also transpired from our analysis is that the norms operating in the context of the prohibition of the use of force are well-equipped to respond, on their own, to instances of complicity. In this author's view, it is fair to assume that complicity in the threat or use of force amounts to the threat of or use of force in and of itself.

The primary norms analysed above directly or indirectly prohibit complicity and their breach gives rise to direct responsibility, whereas the ARSIWA and ARIO rules impose restrictive conditions for the responsibility of the complicit wrongdoer to arise. The utility of the general regime on responsibility for complicity is obviously residual in this context. Aust suggests that this is no more than a 'network of rules' which 'mutually complement and reinforce each other if explored systematically'.[206]

[203] See, eg R Pisillo-Mazzeschi, *La due diligence e responsabilità internazionale degli Stati* (Milano, Giuffrè, 1989); RP Barnidge, *Non-State Actors and Terrorism: Applying the Law of State Responsibility and the Due Diligence Principle* (The Hague, TMC Asser Press, 2008); R Pisillo-Mazzeschi, 'The Due Diligence Rule and the Nature of the International Responsibility of States' (1992) 35 *German YBIL* 9.

[204] *Island of Palmas (United States v Netherlands)* (1928) 2 RIAA 829, 839.

[205] *Corfu Channel (United Kingdom v Albania)* (Merits) [1949] ICJ Rep 4, 22; see also *Spanish Zone of Morocco Claims (United Kingdom v Spain)* (1924) 2 RIAA 615, 649; *Trail Smelter* (1941) 3 RIAA 1911, 1965; see also S Heathcote, 'State Omissions and Due Diligence: Aspects of Fault, Damage and Contribution to Injury in the Law of State Responsibility' in K Bannelier, T Christakis and S Heathcote (eds), *The ICJ and the Evolution of International Law: The Enduring Impact of the Corfu Channel Case* (London, Routledge, 2012); O Corten and P Klein, 'The Limits of Complicity as a Ground for Responsibility: Lessons Learned from the Corfu Channel Case' in K Bannelier, T Christakis and S Heathcote (eds), *The ICJ and the Evolution of International Law: The Enduring Impact of the Corfu Channel Case* (London, Routledge, 2012).

[206] Aust (n 2) 384.

b. Complicity in the Violations of *Jus in Bello*

Under the law governing the conduct of hostilities (*jus in bello*), the principle of responsibility of the belligerent power violating norms and principles of international humanitarian law (IHL) is well established in a host of conventional instruments and under customary international law. This responsibility exists independently from any responsibility that the same State may incur for its unlawful resort to the use of force (*jus ad bellum*) and from any individual criminal liability that accrues.[207]

What is less clear and nuanced is the extent to which the applicable law (*jus in bello*) warrants responsibility for third States which are complicit in the violation of IHL committed by one of the belligerents.[208] No provision under IHL expressly prohibits complicity in the violations of this body of rules. Article 1 common to the 1949 Geneva Conventions is the closest one gets to directly regulating complicity in the context of *jus in bello*. The provision stipulates that '[t]he High Contracting Parties undertake to respect and to ensure respect for the present Convention in all circumstances'.[209]

According to the International Committee of the Red Cross (ICRC) Commentary, common Article 1 to the Geneva Conventions requires

> that in the event of a Power failing to fulfill its obligations, the other Contracting Parties (neutral, allied or enemy) may, and should, endeavour to bring it back to an attitude of respect for the Convention. The proper working of the system of protection provided by the Convention demands in fact that the Contracting Parties should not be content merely to apply its provisions themselves, but should do everything in their power to ensure that the humanitarian principles underlying the Conventions are applied universally.[210]

In the *Military and Paramilitary Activities* case, the ICJ referred to this obligation as deriving from 'general principles of humanitarian law to which the Conventions merely give expression'.[211] The ruling was crucial in recognising the application of this obligation to internal armed conflicts. Within the meaning of Article 1 common to the Geneva Conventions, 'to respect' entails that the State must do everything it can to ensure that the rules in question are respected by its organs as well as by all others under its

[207] See P d'Argent, *Les réparations de guerre en droit international public: La responsabilité internationale des États à l'épreuve de la guerre* (Bruxelles, Bruylant, 2002) 490–93; see also E David, *Principes de droit des conflits armés* (4th edn, Bruxelles, Bruylant, 2008) 553–54.

[208] See, eg WA Schabas, 'Enforcing International Humanitarian Law: Catching the Accomplices' (2001) 83 *IRRC* 439.

[209] See, eg 1949 Geneva Convention (I) for the Amelioration of the Condition of the Wounded and Sick in Armed Forces in the Field (adopted 12 August 1949; entered into force 21 October 1950) 75 UNTS 31, Art 1.

[210] J Pictet, *Commentary: IV Geneva Convention Relative to the Protection of Civilian Persons in Time of War* (Geneva, ICRC, 1958) 16.

[211] *Military and Paramilitary Activities (Merits)* (n 149) 114, para 220; see also ibid Separate Opinion of Judge Ago 181, 183–84, para 6.

jurisdiction. '"To ensure respect" means that States, whether engaged in a conflict or not, must take all possible steps to ensure that the rules are respected by all, and in particular by parties to conflict'.[212] The ICRC's Commentary on Article 1 common to the four Geneva Conventions clarifies that:

> It is not an engagement concluded on the basis of reciprocity ... It is rather a series of unilateral engagements solemnly contracted before the world as represented by the other Contracting Parties. Each State contracts obligations vis-à-vis itself and at the same time vis-à-vis the others.[213]

In the *Wall* Advisory Opinion, the Court noted that the fundamental norms and principles of IHL are of an *erga omnes* character and that all High Contracting Parties, irrespective of whether they are a party to a conflict, have to ensure compliance with IHL by parties to a conflict.[214] The International Criminal Tribunal for the former Yugoslavia (ICTY) has come to a similar conclusion in the *Furundžija* case.[215] This broad interpretation of Article 1 also appears to cover a negative obligation not to encourage and aid States or armed opposition groups committing IHL violations abroad.[216]

Indeed, this correlation between the positive and negative obligation in Article 1 of the Geneva Conventions is recognised in Rule 144 of the ICRC Study on Customary IHL: 'States may not encourage violations of international humanitarian law by parties to an armed conflict. They must exert their influence, to the degree possible to stop violations of international humanitarian law'.[217] This rule finds recognition in the practice of the UN[218] and other international organisations.[219]

212 L Boisson de Chazournes and L Condorelli, 'Common Article 1 of the Geneva Conventions Revisited: Protecting Collective Interests' (2000) 837 *IRRC* 67, 69; see also C Focarelli, 'Common Article 1 of the 1949 Geneva Conventions: A Soap Bubble?' (2010) 21 *EJIL* 125.

213 J Pictet, *Commentary on the First Geneva Convention of August 12, 1949* (Geneva, ICRC, 1952) 25.

214 *Legal Consequences of the Construction of a Wall in the Occupied Palestinian Territory* (n 152) 199–200, paras 157–58; *Nuclear Weapons (Advisory Opinion)* (n 144) 257, para 79.

215 *Prosecutor v Furundžija* (Judgment) IT-95-17/1-T (10 December 1998) para 142; see also *Prosecutor v Kupreškić and others* (Judgment) IT-95-16-T (14 January 2000) para 519.

216 *Legal Consequences of the Construction of a Wall in the Occupied Palestinian Territory* (n 152) 199–200, para 158; L Doswald-Beck and JM Henckaerts, *Customary International Humanitarian Law*, vol 1 (Cambridge, CUP, 2005) 532.

217 Doswald-Beck and Henckaerts (n 216) 509 ff.

218 UNSC, 'Res 681' (20 December 1990) UN Doc S/RES/681 (Middle East); UNGA, 'Res 32/91' (13 December 1977) UN Doc A/RES/32/91 (Middle East); UNGA, 'Res 37/123' (16 December 1982) UN Doc A/RES/37/123 (Middle East); UNGA, 'Res 38/180' (n 184); UNGA, 'Res 43/21' (3 November 1988) UN Doc A/RES/43/21 (Middle East).

219 See, eg Council of Europe, Parliamentary Assembly, 'Res 823 Activities of the International Committee of the Red Cross (ICRC)' (28 June 1984); Council of Europe, Parliamentary Assembly, 'Res 881 Activities of the International Committee of the Red Cross (ICRC)' (1 July 1987); Council of Europe, Committee of Ministers, 'Declaration on the Rape of Women and Children in the Territory of Former Yugoslavia' (18 February 1993); Organization of American States, 'Respect for International Humanitarian Law' (7 June 1996) AG/RES.1408 (XXVI-O/96); for other references see Doswald-Beck and Henckaerts (n 216) 510.

Interestingly, the Commentary to Rule 144 of the ICRC Study on Customary IHL cites Article 16 ARSIWA, which may suggest some proximity in the material content of the obligations.[220] According to the ICRC Study, Article 1 of the Geneva Conventions requires States at a minimum not to render aid or assistance to the violation of the Geneva Conventions.[221] Sassoli holds the view that in order to meet the legal threshold of 'ensuring respect' under Article 1 of the Geneva Conventions, States are expected to do more than simply not render aid or assistance to violations of IHL.[222] However, the scope of the obligation falls short of compelling third States to take unilateral measures to ensure cessation of the violations of *jus in bello*.[223]

Overall, the above authorities support a broad application of Article 1 of the Geneva Conventions both *ratione personae* and *materiae*.[224] With regard to the former, Article 1 of the Geneva Conventions implies both a right and an obligation of any Contracting Party to demand respect for IHL not only from other States but also non-State actors. In terms of its scope *ratione materiae*, the obligation contained in Article 1 of the Geneva Conventions covers respect for all the rules of IHL applicable both in international and non-international armed conflict. Furthermore, the Court has interpreted Article 1 of the Geneva Conventions as prohibiting third States from encouraging violations of IHL,[225] whereas it held that Article 16 ARSIWA only covers positive actions of aid or assistance.[226] Moreover, the obligation under Article 1 of the Geneva Conventions operates as soon as the State becomes aware that another State or armed opposition group receiving its aid or assistance are committing violations of IHL.[227] In comparison, there are still uncertainties in

[220] Doswald-Beck and Henckaerts (n 216) 511.

[221] Felder (n 2) 149; F Azzam, 'The Duty of Third States to Implement and Enforce International Humanitarian Law' (1997) 66 *Nordic J Intl L* 55, 58–59.

[222] M Sassòli, 'State Responsibility for Violations of International Humanitarian Law' (2002) 84 *IRRC* 401, 413.

[223] Aust (n 2) 388; see also David (n 207) 625–33; Boisson de Chazournes and Condorelli (n 212).

[224] See, eg N Levrat, 'Les conséquences de l'engagement pris par les Hautes Parties Contractantes de "faire respecter" les conventions humanitaires' in F Kalshoven and Y Sandoz (eds), *Implementation of International Humanitarian Law* (Dordrecht, Martinus Nijhoff, 1989); K Sachariew, 'State's Entitlement to Take Action to Enforce International Humanitarian Law' (1989) 270 *IRRC* 177; U Palwankar, 'Measures Available to States for Fulfilling Their Obligations to Ensure Respect for International Humanitarian Law' (1994) 298 *IRRC* 9; H Brollowski, 'The Responsibility to Protect and Common Article 1 of the 1949 Geneva Conventions and Obligations of Third States' in J Hoffmann and A Nollkaemper (eds), *Responsibility to Protect: From Principle to Practice* (Amsterdam, Pallas, 2012).

[225] *Military and Paramilitary Activities (Merits)* (n 149) 114, para 220.

[226] *Bosnia Genocide (Merits)* (n 19) 222, para 432.

[227] See Sassòli (n 222) 413; Quigley (n 2) 90; HP Aust, 'Complicity in Violations of International Humanitarian Law' in H Krieger and J Willms (eds), *Inducing Compliance with International Humanitarian Law* (Cambridge, CUP, 2015).

positive international law as to whether Article 16 ARSIWA requires intent in addition to knowledge. Aust suggests that Article 16 ARSIWA could be construed as *lex generalis* while Article 1 of the Geneva Conventions would operate as a *lex specialis* and by implication lower the threshold for responsibility to arise.[228]

In a nutshell, States Parties to the Geneva Conventions shall not provide any form of assistance, encouragement or inducement to violations of any norm contained therein, including extraterritorially.[229] If this is a legally correct and tenable interpretation, then the general rule on the responsibility for complicity pursuant to Article 16 ARSIWA has little role to play in the context of *jus in bello*.[230]

Having said this, James Crawford, for instance, has argued that the scope of Article 1 of the Geneva Conventions is in fact more limited.[231] The crux of the argument is that Article 1 generates only a faculty upon States to insist upon the application of the Geneva Conventions in armed conflict to which they are not a party.[232] This would suggest, contrary to above references, that Article 1 does not provide for an extraterritorial obligation to respect and ensure respect of the Geneva Conventions by third parties. In this case, Article 16 ARSIWA and its sister provisions would complement the object and purpose of Article 1 of the Geneva Conventions. Otherwise, it would seem that most cases of potential complicity in the context of *jus in bello* would be effectively covered by a far-reaching interpretation of Article 1 of the Geneva Conventions.

iii. Primary Rules Prohibiting Complicity in Human Rights Violations

We have already seen in section II.A.ii several scenarios where responsibility for complicity plays a role in respect of factual circumstances which lead to the commission of human rights law violations. In addition, there are several rules under international human rights treaties and customary international law that specifically address the problem of complicity, or situations akin to it.

[228] Aust (n 2) 389; see also M Brehm, 'The Arms Trade and States' Duty to Ensure Respect for Humanitarian and Human Rights Law' (2008) 12 *JCSL* 359, 385–86.

[229] See, eg H Tonkin, 'Common Article I: A Minimum Yardstick for Regulating Private Military and Security Companies' (2009) 22 *LJIL* 779, 782–86.

[230] See Azzam (n 221) 70; B Kessler, 'The Duty to "Ensure Respect" under Common Article 1 of the Geneva Conventions: Its Implications on International and Non-International Armed Conflicts' (2001) 44 *German YBIL* 489, 503; Sassòli (n 222) 413.

[231] J Crawford, 'Third Party Obligations with Respect to Israeli Settlements in the Occupied Palestinian Territories' (2012) 15–18 www.tuc.org.uk/sites/default/files/tucfiles/LegalOpinionIsraeliSettlements.pdf; see also A Imseis, 'Critical Reflections on the International Humanitarian Law Aspects of the ICJ Wall Advisory Opinion' (2005) 99 *AJIL* 102, 115.

[232] See F Kalshoven, 'The Undertaking to Respect and Ensure Respect in All Circumstances: From Tiny Seed to Ripening Fruit' (1999) 2 *YBIHL* 3, 60.

For example, Article III(e) of the Genocide Convention imposes an obligation on both States and individuals to refrain from complicity in genocide. As noted in chapter three, the ICJ has recognised that States can be found in direct breach of the obligation not to be complicit in genocide.[233] The ICJ's judgment however raised several issues as to the content and scope of the obligation under Article III(e). For example, while the scope of conduct captured by that obligation has been interpreted broadly under international criminal law, the ICJ linked its content to Article 16 ARSIWA, holding that only positive actions could constitute complicity. By conflating the traditional distinction between primary and secondary norms on complicity, the Court essentially made of Article 16 ARSIWA a *meta-rule*. In other words, the Court sought guidance in the general regime of responsibility to interpret and apply a primary norm prohibiting complicity in genocide. It is submitted that had the Court interpreted Article III(e) of the Genocide Convention on its own, relying on its *travaux préparatoires*, its application under customary international law and guidance in the case law of ad hoc tribunals, it would have reached a different outcome in relation to Serbia's responsibility, in particular as far as the material and cognitive elements of complicity in genocide are concerned.

Another example of the rule which proscribes conduct akin to complicity is the obligation of *non-refoulement*. In essence, it prohibits States from returning a person to another State where the person may be tortured or ill-treated.[234] This obligation has its source either expressly or impliedly in customary international law and several treaty provisions, including Article 33 of the Convention relating to the Status of Refugees,[235] Articles 3(1) of the Convention Against Torture (CAT),[236] Article 7 of the International Covenant on Civil and Political Rights (ICCPR),[237] Article 3 of the European Convention on Human Rights (ECHR), Article 5 of the African Charter on Human and Peoples' Rights (ACHPR)[238] and Article 5(2) of the American Convention on Human Rights (ACHR).[239] The scope of the

[233] *Bosnia Genocide (Merits)* (n 19) 114, para 167.

[234] E Lauterpacht and D Bethlehem, 'The Scope and Content of the Principle of Non-Refoulement: Opinion' in E Feller, V Türk and F Nicholson (eds), *Refugee Protection in International Law: UNHCR's Global Consultations on International Protection* (Cambridge, CUP, 2003) 89.

[235] Convention relating to the Status of Refugees (adopted 28 July 1951; entered into force 22 April 1954) 189 UNTS 150, Art 33.

[236] Convention against Torture and Other Cruel, Inhuman or Degrading Treatment or Punishment (adopted 10 December 1984; entered into force 26 June 1987) 1465 UNTS 85, Art 3(1).

[237] International Covenant on Civil and Political Rights (adopted 16 December 1966; entered into force 23 March 1976) 999 UNTS 171, Art 7.

[238] African Charter on Human and Peoples' Rights (adopted 27 June 1981; entered into force 21 October 1986) 1520 UNTS 217, Art 5.

[239] American Convention on Human Rights (21 November 1969; entered into force 18 July 1978) 1144 UNTS 123, Art 5(2).

obligation of *non-refoulement* is broader under international human rights law than under the refugee law, but the merits of such distinction and its evolution are beyond the scope of this section. What is clear, however, from the above rules for the purposes of our discussion is that there is a common denominator—a State incurs responsibility if through its action or omission it allows for an individual within its jurisdiction to be transferred to another State where he faces a risk of torture or other cruel, inhuman or degrading treatment. Evidently, the scope of responsibility for a failure to observe an obligation of *non-refoulement* is substantively broader than that of responsibility for aid or assistance as construed in the ARSIWA and ARIO.

The responsibility of a State transferring the individual in the circumstances described above arises at the moment of transfer, and not at some later moment when the individual is actually exposed to torture or ill-treatment. In other words, responsibility for failure to comply with a non-refoulement obligation arises irrespective of the conduct of the State receiving the individual.[240] Moreover, as the abundant jurisprudence of the ECtHR on the matter shows, a violation of Article 3 ECHR is triggered when a State 'knowingly' transfers the individual to another State where there are 'substantial grounds for believing that he would be in danger of being subjected to torture'.[241] In other words, the requisite knowledge threshold in relation to conduct that can trigger a violation of a *non-refoulement* obligation is much more lenient than under the general rule on responsibility for complicity. In theory, at least, the rule of *non-refoulement* can be regarded as a 'functionally similar rule' to that of Article 16 ARSIWA and 'may provide opportunities to hold complicit States responsible'.[242]

C. Complicity and Due Diligence: Overlap or Parallel Functioning?

As we have seen in the preceding sections, the existing practice and *opinio juris* do not seem to exclude omissions or less direct forms of assistance (whether knowing passive collaboration, association, failure to properly oversee planning of activities, specific promises or other non-tangible assistance) from the rubric of responsibility for complicity in international law. However, if complicity as a ground of responsibility is to include

[240] See, eg *Soering v United Kingdom* (Judgment) [1989] ECtHR Ser A No 161 (1989) 11 EHRR 439, para 86; *Mamatkulov and Askarov v Turkey* (Judgment) [2005] ECtHR App Nos 46827/99 and 46951/99, (2005) 41 EHRR 25, para 67; *Cruz Varas and others v Sweden* (Judgment) [1991] ECtHR App No 15576/89 (1992) 14 EHRR 1, para 60; *Saadi v Italy* (Judgment) [2008] App No 37201/06 (2009) 49 EHRR 30, para 126.

[241] *Soering v United Kingdom* (n 240) para 88.

[242] Aust (n 2) 393.

omissions, the question then arises as to its conceptual demarcation from the responsibility deriving from a State's failure to perform due diligence obligations.

While responsibility for complicity is, at least in theory, a relatively more unified concept, this does not seem to be the case of responsibility for failure to comply with due diligence obligations.[243] These obligations are inherently diverse in their scope.[244] For instance, in those cases where the due diligence obligation is codified as an obligation to prevent, a judicial body limits itself to examining State's capacity to prevent the specific conduct causing or risking to cause harm. If, however, the obligation of due diligence is termed more generally as is the case of the majority of human rights treaties, this may impose a more onerous obligation on States, for example, to ensure that a specific legislation or that adequate law enforcement mechanisms are in place.[245]

The judgments in the *Corfu Channel* and the *Bosnia Genocide* cases show that the Court is reluctant to apply complicity as a basis for responsibility generally, and in cases of omissions in particular.[246] In *Corfu Channel*, the United Kingdom relied on complicity as a potential basis of responsibility of Albania who had allegedly assisted a third party (Yugoslavia) in laying the mines.[247] As presented by the United Kingdom, the argument

[243] ARSIWA (n 22) Art 14(3) ('The breach of an international obligation requiring a State to prevent a given event occurs when the event occurs and extends over the entire period during which the event continues and remains not in conformity with that obligation'); J Crawford, 'Second Report on State Responsibility' (1999) UN Doc A/CN.4/498 and Add 1-4, reproduced in (1999) 2 (pt 1) *YBILC* 3, 27–29, paras 84–90 (justifying the deletion of former draft Art 23 because it amounted to establishing a general primary obligation to prevent).

[244] See, eg Torture Convention (n 236) Art 2; International Convention for the Suppression of Terrorist Bombings (adopted 15 December 1997; entered into force 23 May 2001) 2149 UNTS 284, Art 15; Convention on the Prevention and Punishment of Crimes against Internationally Protected Persons, Including Diplomatic Agents (adopted 14 December 1973; entered into force 20 February 1977) 1035 UNTS 167, Art 11; see also M Hakimi, 'State Bystander Responsibility' (2010) 21 *EJIL* 341; Pisillo-Mazzeschi, *La due diligence e responsabilità internazionale degli Stati* (n 203).

[245] See, eg UN Human Rights Committee, 'General Comment 31, Nature of the General Legal Obligation on States Parties to the Covenant' (29 March 2004) UN Doc CCPR/C/21/Rev.1/Add 13, para 7; *Prosecutor v Furundžija* (n 215) para 150; C Hoppe, 'Positive Human Rights Obligations of the Hiring State in Connection with the Provision of Coercive Services by a Private Military and Security Company' [2009] EUI Working Paper AEL 2009/19; C Hoppe, 'Passing the Buck: State Responsibility for Private Military Companies' (2008) 19 *EJIL* 989, 994 ff; H King, 'The Extraterritorial Human Rights Obligations of States' (2009) 9 *HRLR* 521; R Nigro, 'Giurisdizione e obblighi positivi degli Stati parti della Convenzione Europea dei diritti dell'uomo: Il caso Ilaşcu' (2005) 88 *RDI* 413.

[246] In both cases the applicant argued that the respondent was responsible for its complicity in the principal wrongdoing that caused injury *Corfu Channel (United Kingdom v Albania)* (n 205), ICJ Pleadings, Memorial submitted by the United Kingdom on 30 September 1947, 19, 48, para 94; *Bosnia Genocide (Merits)* (n 19).

[247] See *Corfu Channel (United Kingdom v Albania)* (n 205) ICJ Pleadings, Memorial of the United Kingdom of 30 September 1947, 19, 48, para 94; see also ibid, Reply of the United Kingdom of 30 July 1948, 241, 257–58.

of complicity was presented in the alternative to, and conflated at times with, that of Albania's knowledge of the laying of the mines.[248] This may explain the Court's preference to found Albania's responsibility on the latter's failure of its own duty to inform, without implicating any questions of responsibility in connection with the laying of the mines by a third party Yugoslavia.[249] In the *Bosnia Genocide* case, one possible explanation for the Court's preference to find the responsibility for the failure of the obligation to prevent, even though the case was clearly one of an exemplary complicity, is that it wanted to mitigate the consequences for Serbia. The finding of complicity could arguably have led to greater legal consequences than a mere declaration of illegality. An alternative interpretation is that the Court opted for an obligation of due diligence as it gives rise to greater flexibility in terms of evidence.

However, the fact that in the above cases due diligence was preferred as the legal basis for finding responsibility does not mean that there is no scope for parallel operation of responsibility for complicity as Klein and Corten have suggested.[250] We shall see below that there are essentially two tenets that distinguish responsibility for complicity from the responsibility arising out of violations of due diligence obligations. The *Bosnia Genocide* case serves as an excellent illustration of these borderline phenomena.

i. Knowledge-based Distinction

In the *Bosnia Genocide* case, the ICJ held that the obligation to prevent does not require knowledge that genocide is occurring or is about to be perpetrated; it is sufficient for the relevant State to be *aware of the risk* of genocide.[251] In the Court's view:

> [A] State may be found to have violated its obligation to prevent *even though it had no certainty*, at the time when it should have acted, but failed to do so, that genocide was about to be committed or was under way; for it to incur responsibility on this basis it is enough that the State was aware, or should *normally have been aware*, of the serious danger that acts of genocide would be committed.[252] (emphasis added)

The Court deduced from this distinction that complicity would require that the 'support in perpetrating the genocide [be given] with full knowledge of the facts', whereas for a finding of the breach of the

[248] For a detailed discussion see Corten and Klein (n 205) 316–24.

[249] cf *Corfu Channel (United Kingdom v Albania)* (n 205) Separate Opinion of Judge Alvarez 39, 44–45; ibid Dissenting Opinion of Judge Badawi Pasha 58, 61–64; ibid Dissenting Opinion of Judge ad hoc Ečer 115, 116–17.

[250] Corten and Klein (n 205) 324, 332–34; see also O Corten, 'La "complicité" dans le droit de la responsabilité internationale: un concept inutile?' (2011) 58 *AFDI* 57.

[251] *Bosnia Genocide (Merits)* (n 19) 222–23, para 432.

[252] ibid.

duty to prevent it suffices that a State 'was aware, or should normally have been aware, of the serious danger that acts of genocide would be committed'.[253] In other words, constructive knowledge or risk of the breach would suffice for finding responsibility as a result of failure of the obligation to prevent, while in cases of complicity—actual, or in the Court's words 'full knowledge', appears to be the required standard.

It is further regrettable for the development of the law of international responsibility that the Court did not dwell upon the temporal element of the obligation to prevent and to punish. From the analysis of the facts of the case, and namely the finding that there was no clear-cut plan of genocide before 12 July 1995, just after the taking of the town of Srebrenica, it would seem that the Court inferred the responsibility arising for failure to prevent ex post facto.[254] The Court could have assessed at least part of Serbia's subsequent conduct on the distinct ground of its obligation not to render any aid or assistance to the maintenance of the situation resulting from a serious breach of a peremptory norm of general international law pursuant to Article 41(2) ARSIWA. This might have been a more coherent way out of the unnecessary restrictions that the Court placed on the general understanding of responsibility for complicity as requiring 'full knowledge of facts' even though no such test transpires neither from Article 16 ARSIWA nor from the primary norm that the Court had to apply, ie Article III(e) of the Genocide Convention.

The Court's ambivalent approach to knowledge as regards complicity and the obligation to prevent is not flawless:

> Although it has not found that the information available to the Belgrade authorities indicated as a matter of certainty, that genocide was imminent (which is why complicity in genocide was not upheld in paragraph 424), they could hardly have been unaware of the serious risk of it once the VRS forces had decided to occupy the Srebrenica enclave.[255]

Cassese rightly argues that it seems illogical (besides being unsupported by any authority or legal rule or principle) to hold that the foresight of a risk of genocide is relevant to the obligation to prevent whereas it is irrelevant to the crime of (or to State responsibility for) complicity in genocide.[256] By implication, if State A provides assistance to State B, and is aware of or has reasons to be aware of a serious danger that acts of genocide may be

[253] ibid.

[254] ibid 165, para 295 and 218, para 423.

[255] ibid 224, para 436.

[256] See A Cassese, 'On the Use of Criminal Law Notions in Determining State Responsibility for Genocide' (2007) 5 *JICJ* 875, 887 (domestic criminal legal systems support the proposition that an omissive conduct may be counted for as a form of complicity, and that the threshold of liability for omission will as a general rule be higher than that for conduct, and not the other way round); see also J Quigley, *The Genocide Convention: An International Law Analysis* (Aldershot, Ashgate, 2006) 135.

committed by individuals or groups that State A is assisting, State A is not only under an obligation to prevent, but crucially to stop providing such assistance. All in all the Court's analysis of the distinction between complicity and the obligation to prevent, and worse the apparent generalising remarks it made about these concepts in the law of responsibility, are to be approached with caution.

Indeed, even the then President of the Court stressed in her communication to the press, after the judgment was rendered, that the distinction between these two notions is not self-evident.[257] In this author's view, had the Court found that Serbia was complicit in the acts of genocide committed by the VRS forces, it would have possibly been compelled to go beyond making a simple declaration of illegality as an ultimate remedy.[258] Thus, the Court's over-determination of the distinction appears to have been guided by judicial policy of minimising the blame rather than the legal consistency in applying these notions in the regime of international responsibility.

ii. Character and Control-based Distinction

Apart from the different cognitive framework underlying complicity and due diligence, three other conceptual traits distinguish the two regimes of responsibility. In practice, these traits go *in tandem*. First, whilst the obligation not to be complicit is negative in character, the obligation of due diligence is said to be a positive one. Second, responsibility for failing to prevent a given event, although not territorially bound, in practice requires some degree of effective control exercised, whether legally or illegally, by a State over a territory outside its borders.[259] This is not a relevant criterion for determining whether a State has been complicit in an internationally wrongful act of another actor. Third, as noted by the International Tribunal for the Law of the Sea (ITLOS) Seabed Disputes Chamber, the content of the due diligence obligations is much more likely to fluctuate with the passage of time.[260]

[257] See 'Application of the Convention on the Prevention and Punishment of the Crime of Genocide (Bosnia and Herzegovina v Serbia and Montenegro): Statement to the Press by HE Judge Rosalyn Higgins, President of the International Court of Justice' (2007) www.icj-cij.org/court/index.php?pr=1898&pt=3&p1=1&p2=3&p3=1.

[258] See PM Dupuy, 'Crime sans châtiment ou mission accomplie?' (2007) 111 *RGDIP* 243, 246–49.

[259] *Application of the Convention on the Prevention and Punishment of the Crime of Genocide (Bosnia and Herzegovina v Serbia and Montenegro)* (Preliminary Objections) [1996] ICJ Rep 595, 615–16, para 31; *Bosnia Genocide (Merits)* (n 19) 107, paras 153–54; *Armed Activities (DRC v Uganda)* (n 149) 231, para 179; 252, para 246; 253, para 247.

[260] See *Responsibilities and Obligations of States Sponsoring Persons and Entities with Respect to Activities in the Area* (Advisory Opinion) [2011] 11 ITLOS Rep 10, para 117 ('Among the factors that make such a description difficult is the fact that "due diligence" is a variable concept. It may change over time as measures considered sufficiently diligent at a certain moment may become not diligent enough in light, for instance, of new scientific or technological knowledge').

The *Bosnia Genocide* case shows the importance of these subtle distinctions. On the one hand, the ICJ disentangled the obligation to prevent in Article I of the Genocide Convention from any territorial link, substituting the traditional concept of 'jurisdiction' for the new and considerably vague one of 'capacity to effectively influence'.[261] On the other hand, it endeavoured to build the general scope of the obligations of due diligence. The Court's reasoning was twofold.

First, it attempted to demonstrate that the duty to prevent is not an obligation of result[262] and that much depends on the circumstances of the particular case. The Court stressed that the due diligence standard 'calls for an assessment *in concreto*'.[263] In terms of parameters for such an assessment of the conduct of the State, the Court considered the 'capacity to effectively influence the actions of persons likely to commit genocide'.[264] Although this capacity is subject to variations, the Court referred to elements such as 'geographical distance of the State concerned from the scene of the events, and on the strength of political links, as well as links of all other kinds, between the authorities of that State and the main actors in the events'.[265] Moreover, given that 'every State may only act within the limits permitted by international law', the State's capacity varies 'depending on its particular legal position vis-à-vis the situation and persons facing the danger, or the reality, of genocide'.[266] In assessing the structure and scope of the obligation to prevent, as an obligation to endeavour, Dupuy emphasises two main factors: (i) a breach of the obligation should be judged only by the actual conduct of the responsible State and not by the circumstance of having or not having achieved the result; and (ii) the importance of the

[261] *Bosnia Genocide* (Merits) (n 19) 221, para 430.

[262] ibid; see also *Pulp Mills on the River Uruguay (Argentina v Uruguay)* (Judgment) [2010] ICJ Rep 14, 77, para 187.

[263] *Bosnia Genocide* (Merits) (n 19) 221, para 430; for discussions on the required standard of diligence see, eg A Gattini, *Zufall und force majeure in System der Staatenverantwortlichkeit anhand der ILC-Kodifikationsarbeit* (Berlin, Duncker & Humboldt, 1991) 197 ff; Pisillo-Mazzeschi, *La due diligence e responsabilità internazionale degli Stati* (n 203) 69 ff; for a historical account of the evolution of due diligence obligations see JA Hessbruegge, 'The Historical Development of the Doctrines of Attribution and Due Diligence in International Law' (2004) 36 *NYU J Intl L & Pol* 265; A Ouedraogo, 'La diligence en droit international: Contribution à l'étude d'une notion au contour imprécis' (PhD Thesis, Geneva, Graduate Institute, 2010).

[264] *Bosnia Genocide* (Merits) (n 19) Declaration of Judge Skotnikov 366, 379 (criticising the Court of having introduced 'a politically appealing, but legally vague, indeed, hardly measurable at all in legal terms, concept of a duty to prevent with the essential element of control being replaced with a highly subjective notion of influence'); see also S Forlati, 'The Legal Obligation to Prevent Genocide: Bosnia v Serbia and Beyond' (2011) 31 *Polish YBIL* 189; S Forlati, 'Violazione dell'obbligo di prevenire il genocidio e riparazione nell'affare Bosnia-Erzegovina c. Serbia' (2007) 90 *RDI* 425; A Gattini, 'Breach of the Obligation to Prevent and Reparation Thereof in the ICJ's Genocide Judgment' (2007) 18 *EJIL* 695.

[265] *Bosnia Genocide* (Merits) (n 19) 221, para 430.

[266] ibid.

primary obligation breached that allows to determine the *momentum a quo* of the violation of the obligation to prevent such an occurrence.[267]

A second point deriving from the Court's reasoning is that a State can be held responsible for breaching its obligation to prevent only if the wrongful act is actually committed. This approach is not free from ambiguities. For example, genocide by its nature can be a composite act. It is a pattern of the acts which, while taken individually, may not in and of themselves amount to genocide, but they could constitute related wrongful acts such as crimes against humanity. The Court could have clarified that a State may be held responsible for breaching its obligation to prevent from the moment of the first wrongful act in the chain of acts leading to the commission of genocide.

iii. Implications for the Material Scope of Complicity

As it is not the objective of this book to delineate a theory of due diligence,[268] it is sufficient to draw together principles on the distinction vis-à-vis situations of complicity in order to better understand the latter's material content.

First, while the obligations of due diligence are positive in character, complicity is concurrently a negative obligation and a form of responsibility in connection with the act of another. While due diligence is closer to an obligation of conduct or means, the prohibition of complicity resembles an obligation of result.[269]

Second, even if it is plausible in theory to construe complicity on the basis of omissions or non-tangible assistance, there are serious practical difficulties with such an endeavour. International law has no adequate mechanisms or processes for a factual determination of omissions. The injured party would in most circumstances be unable to bring evidence of the complicit actor's omission since most of such evidence would remain within the exclusive control of the complicit and the principal State.

[267] PM Dupuy, 'Reviewing the Difficulties of Codification: On Ago's Classification of Obligations of Means and Obligations of Result in Relation to State Responsibility' (1999) 10 *EJIL* 371, 384.

[268] See, eg Pisillo-Mazzeschi, *La due diligence e responsabilità internazionale degli Stati* (n 203); Pisillo-Mazzeschi, 'The Due Diligence Rule and the Nature of the International Responsibility of States' (n 203); VJ Proulx, *Transnational Terrorism and State Accountability* (Oxford, Hart Publishing, 2012); Barnidge (n 203); Ouedraogo (n 263).

[269] See, eg *Responsibilities and Obligations of States Sponsoring Persons and Entities with Respect to Activities in the Area* (n 260) para 110; *Pulp Mills (Judgment)* (n 262) 79–80, para 197; for a critique of the conceptual distinction between obligations of means and result see, eg Dupuy (n 267); for the analysis of judicial and arbitral case law distinguishing between obligations of conduct/means and obligations of result see, eg Crawford (n 243) 20–27, paras 52–81 (concluding that 'not all obligations can be classified either as obligations of conduct or of result. There can be hybrids…'); see also A Marchesi, *Obblighi di condotta e obblighi di risultato* (Milano, Giuffrè, 2003) 106–35.

Third, although the Court tried to minimise the importance of the territorial link in respect of the obligation to prevent genocide, the obligations of due diligence in general, by their nature and purpose, do not have an extraterritorial effect and require at least some form of control to be exercised by the State over the territory and the conduct that results in an internationally wrongful act.[270] Thus, the location of the particular wrongdoing may affect the extent to which responsibility for the failure of due diligence would arise.[271] Similarly, the degree of control for the purposes of attribution of particular wrongful conduct to the State varies greatly upon the exact formulation of a given international obligation and the factual circumstances.[272] This idea of territorial constraint and the degree of control is absent from the framework for responsibility for complicity, which theoretically at least makes the latter a relatively more unified and less circumstantial form of responsibility as opposed to responsibility flowing from the violation of due diligence obligations.

D. Concluding Remarks

In conclusion of this section, we have seen through the practice and *opinio juris* of States and international organisations that the material content of complicity is broad enough to theoretically include actions and omissions. Interactions between States and other actors result in numerous forms, degrees and patterns of possible complicity that would ordinarily trigger legal consequences.

As transpires from our analysis, the ARSIWA and ARIO provisions set out a framework for complicity that oscillates between performing its function as a form of responsibility, on the one hand, and imposing a general obligation of non-assistance to the commission of an internationally wrongful act, on the other hand. With some exceptions, the interpretations that

[270] L Condorelli, 'L'imputation à l'État d'un fait internationalement illicite: Solutions classiques et nouvelles tendances' (1984) 189 *RCADI* 9, 109–14 (speaking of territory as 'indicateur de direction' in ascertaining the responsibility of a State for the failure to perform due diligence); Crawford (n 231) 16, para 39 ('due diligence standards must be limited to acts or actors within the jurisdiction and control of the State—a State cannot be responsible for acts conducted by entities outside its control and outside of its jurisdiction').

[271] Condorelli (n 270) 107–09 (explaining a close link between the territorial sovereignty and responsibility: 'à cause de la ratio et du contenu de nombreuses normes internationales prescrivant des obligations relatives à la gestion exclusive d'un espace territorial, responsabilité internationale et souveraineté territoriale se conditionnent mutuellement'; author's translation: 'because of the ratio and content of numerous international norms concerning the exclusive management of territory, international responsibility and territorial sovereignty complement each other').

[272] *Bosnia Genocide (Merits)* (n 19) Dissenting Opinion of Judge Al-Khasawneh 241, 256–57, para 39.

States have given to the conventional prohibitions of assistance indicate a substantial overlap in terms of the material element of complicity. These prohibitions of assistance are usually all-encompassing, extending to forms of behaviour that technically may come closer to omissions than actions.

Finally, there is relatively little practice and *opinio juris* that would require the showing of a particularly stringent link between complicity and the principal wrongful act such as, for example, one of significantly contributing to the wrongful act. In the author's view, it follows that the existence of a clear factual or causal link between complicity and the commission of the principal wrongful act is sufficient to trigger responsibility of the complicit entity under international law.

III. COGNITIVE ELEMENT: KNOWLEDGE AND/OR INTENTION?

'No responsibility without fault'—an old *adage* or a new *ghost* reinvented through Article 16 ARSIWA and its sister provisions? As we have seen in chapter three, responsibility for complicity as it has been construed by the ILC fuels the engines of fault under the modern dichotomy of knowledge vis-à-vis intent. Albeit evicted from the constituent elements of an internationally wrongful act, fault re-appears in different areas of the law of responsibility, including in relation to the forms and content of responsibility. 'La faute n'est plus alors qu'un constituant de l'illicite'?[273]

Special Rapporteur Crawford clarified that just because there is no general principle or presumption about the role of fault in relation to any given primary rule 'it is an error to think that it is possible to eliminate the significance of fault from the [law of international responsibility]'.[274]

273 G Cottereau, 'Système juridique et notion de responsabilité' in SFDI (ed), *La responsabilité dans le système international: Colloque du Mans* (Paris, Pedone, 1991) 24 (author's translation: 'The fault is no longer a constituent element of the wrongful act'; see also R Ago, 'Le délit international' (1939) 68 *RCADI* 417, 491–92; R Ago, *Scritti sulla responsabilità internazionale degli Stati I* (Padova, Jovene, 1978) 273–302 (analysing the role of fault in an internationally wrongful act).

274 J Crawford, *The International Law Commission's Articles on State Responsibility: Introduction, Text and Commentaries* (Cambridge, CUP, 2002) 13; for a detailed analysis of the issue of fault in the law of international responsibility see A Gattini, 'La notion de la faute à la lumière du projet de convention de la Commission du droit international sur la responsabilité internationale' (1992) 3 *EJIL* 253; GJ Perrin, 'Le problème de la faute dans la responsabilité internationale de l'État' in W Haller et al (eds), *Im Dienst an der Gemeinschaft: Festschrift für Dietrich Schindler zum 65. Geburtstag* (Basel, Helbing & Lichtenhahn, 1989); A Gattini, 'Smoking/No Smoking: Some Remarks on the Current Place of the Fault in the Draft Articles on State Responsibility' (1999) 10 *EJIL* 397; PM Dupuy, 'Faute de l'État et fait internationalement illicite' (1987) 5 *Revue Droits* 51; A Ouedraogo, 'Évolution du concept de faute dans la théorie de la responsabilité internationale des États' (2008) 21 *RQDI* 129; G Arangio-Ruiz, 'State Fault and the Forms and Degrees of International Responsibility: Questions of Attribution and Relevance' in *Le droit international au service de la paix, de la justice et du développement: Mélanges Michel Virally* (Paris, Pedone, 1991).

Elsewhere, Crawford stated that '[i]f the primary rules require fault (of a particular character) ... then they do; if not, then not'.[275] This bears the question as to whether responsibility can arise in the absence of proof of fault or intention to cause harm, when the primary rule requires such fault or intention.[276] Even where primary rules posit some mental requirement, they rarely contain explicit guidance as to the ways of ascertaining knowledge vis-à-vis intention, the degree of knowledge or intention, nor their impact on the content of responsibility.[277]

The prevailing view today is that international responsibility is objective in character (ie the finding of the conduct contrary to international law is sufficient irrespective of any considerations of fault on the part of the State or international organisation).[278] A relatively small number of authors still suggest that fault is to be taken into account in the examination of the existence and consequences of internationally wrongful acts.[279] Pisillo-Mazzeschi acknowledges that three groups of theories can be distinguished: (i) those favouring a general regime of fault; (ii) those favouring the regime of objective responsibility; and (iii) those reconciling the fault theory with that of objective responsibility.[280] He reaches the conclusion that none of these theories are convincing and argues that questions of fault are only relevant to the domain of the obligations of due diligence.[281] In our view, fault has a broader reach than that. In the law of international responsibility, fault is present in many ways (eg the circumstances precluding wrongfulness, the content of reparation, the contribution to injury, and prominently in the forms of responsibility of one actor in connection with the wrongful act of another). As stated by a former ILC member '[fault] is like when you enter a room, and you can tell that somebody has just smoked a cigarette. You can't see the smoker, but you know he's there'.[282]

[275] J Crawford, 'Revising the Draft Articles on State Responsibility' (1999) 10 *EJIL* 435, 438.

[276] I Brownlie, *System of the Law of Nations: State Responsibility Part 1* (Oxford, Clarendon Press, 1983) 37–47.

[277] J Salmon, 'L'intention en matière de responsabilité internationale' in *Le droit international au service de la paix, de la justice et du développement: Mélanges Michel Virally* (Paris, Pedone, 1991) 413–22 (referring to intention as an 'avatar de la faute').

[278] *Bosnia Genocide (Merits)* (n 19) 202, para 385; *Armed Activities (DRC v Uganda)* (n 149) 242, para 215.

[279] For a comprehensive overview see G Arangio-Ruiz, 'Second Report on State Responsibility' (1989) UN Doc A/CN.4/425 and Add 1, reproduced in (1989) 2 (pt 1) *YBILC* 1, 47–55, paras 164–90.

[280] Pisillo-Mazzeschi, 'The Due Diligence Rule and the Nature of the International Responsibility of States' (n 203).

[281] ibid 46–51.

[282] See Gattini, 'Smoking/No Smoking: Some Remarks on the Current Place of the Fault in the Draft Articles on State Responsibility' (n 274) (the expression is attributed to Satya Pal Jagota, a former member of the ILC); PM Dupuy, 'Le fait générateur de la responsabilité internationale des États' (1984) 188 *RCADI* 9, 20 ff; Perrin (n 274); Ouedraogo (n 274).

Modern reminiscence of fault finds some support in the ICJ's reasoning in the *Corfu Channel* case, in particular the dissenting opinions of the judges.[283] In that case, the Court had to establish knowledge, or more precisely the means of obtaining knowledge, on the part of Albania as to the existence of the mines in its territorial sea. For example, Judge Azevedo in his Dissenting Opinion held that '[t]he notion of *culpa* (faute) is always changing and undergoing a slow process of evolution; moving away from the classical elements of imprudence and negligence, it tends to draw nearer to the system of objective responsibility'.[284] Although he failed to further clarify the content of the notion of fault, Judge Azevedo noted that wherever a link of causation could be established between State's conduct and the injury, the responsibility was presumed and the State incurred the burden of exculpating itself.[285]

By contrast, Brownlie argued that knowledge in the *Corfu Channel* case was the prerequisite of the legal duty of a territorial sovereign to give warning concerning the existence of the mines.[286] In his view, the Court was far from 'deciding on the basis of an acceptance of some general theory of fault or otherwise'.[287] He also strongly supported the prevailing policy arguments against the adoption of the fault approach. Given that governments act necessarily through their agents:

> [T]he effectiveness of international duties would be much reduced if the complainant State had to prove some level of knowledge or intention at a high level of government in respect of the acts or omissions of subordinate officials.[288]

A few years later, Brownlie took an opposite view when defending Serbia before the ICJ in the *Bosnia Genocide* case, arguing that Serbia did not have sufficient knowledge of the intention of the funded Army of the Republika Srpska (VRS) forces that went on to commit genocide in Srebrenica.[289] The proof of absence of knowledge or intention on the part of the aiding or assisting actor thus emerges as a circumstance precluding wrongfulness.[290] The controversy on the role of fault in the law of

283 *Corfu Channel (United Kingdom v Albania)* (n 205).

284 ibid Dissenting Opinion of Judge Azevedo 78, 85.

285 ibid 86.

286 I Brownlie, 'State Responsibility and the International Court of Justice' in M Fitzmaurice and D Sarooshi (eds), *Issues of State Responsibility before International Judicial Institutions* (Oxford, Hart Publishing, 2004) 12.

287 ibid; cf *Corfu Channel (United Kingdom v Albania)* (n 205) Dissenting Opinion of Judge Azevedo 78, 82–86; ibid Dissenting Opinion of Judge Badawi Pasha 58, 65.

288 Brownlie (n 286) 12.

289 *Bosnia Genocide* (Merits) (n 19) ICJ Pleadings CR 2006/16 (13 March 2006) 52, paras 155–58 (Brownlie); ibid CR 2006/40 (3 May 2006) 50–51, paras 60–65 (Brownlie); cf ibid CR 2006/31 (18 April 2006) 34–43, paras 61–81 (Pellet); ibid CR 2006/35 (21 April 2006) 37–49, paras 3–29 (Condorelli).

290 For an insightful discussion as to the nature of the circumstances precluding wrongfulness (ie whether they are exculpatory or excuses) see Lowe (n 158); see also Ago, 'Le délit international' (n 273) 532–33 (arguing that the circumstances precluding wrongfulness are defence to illegality rather than to responsibility—they are not pleas in mitigation).

international responsibility may well be a 'dialogue de sourds'.[291] However, if that is indeed the case, then responsibility for complicity shall be no exception to the rule; it should carry no reference to any particular state of *mental* or *psychological* predisposition, let alone intention on the part of the State or international organisation.

Under a closer scrutiny, however, practice and *opinio juris* show that some form of cognitive requirement is inseparable from an effective rule on responsibility for complicity. If that were not the case, the scope of responsibility would be too broad. Hence, international law needs to reconcile the predominantly objective character of responsibility and the exceptionally subjective contours of complicity. One option would be to subscribe to the approach of Schwarzenberger, according to whom there is no rule that obliges an international tribunal to apply an objective or subjective test of responsibility.[292] Instead, courts and tribunals should, in the exercise of their discretion in light of equity and reason, suggest a solution that takes account of subjective elements for each particular case.[293] Another, and more complex alternative, is to propose a framework of responsibility for complicity that keeps its cognitive element without reinventing the wheel of fault full circle.[294]

This section makes a claim that only knowledge of the circumstances of the wrongful act rather than intent is a requirement of responsibility for complicity. Several objective factors and criteria may be used when determining the knowledge of the State or international organisation vis-à-vis the circumstances of the principal wrongful act. Ultimately, it is argued that if there is any role left for intention in the context of responsibility for complicity this is limited to the implementation of responsibility (eg as a possible aggravating circumstance in determining the level of reparation due by the complicit actor) but not for the determination of responsibility (*fait générateur*).

A. Knowledge: 'Circumstances of the Internationally Wrongful Act'

As we have seen in chapter four, the requirement of 'knowledge of the circumstances' of the principal wrongful act appears in the text of the relevant provisions on responsibility for complicity. This requirement only

[291] M Koskenniemi, 'Doctrines of State Responsibility' in J Crawford et al (eds), *The Law of International Responsibility* (Oxford, OUP, 2010) 49.

[292] G Schwarzenberger, *International Law as Applied by International Courts and Tribunals*, vol 4 (3rd edn, London, Stevens, 1957) 649.

[293] ibid.

[294] See, eg R Luzzatto, 'Responsabilità e colpa in diritto internazionale' (1968) 51 *RDI* 53; see also J Salmon, 'La place de la faute de la victime dans le droit de la responsabilité internationale' in *Le droit international à l'heure de sa codification: études en l'honneur de Roberto Ago*, vol 3 (Milano, Giuffrè, 1987); Perrin (n 274); O Diggelman, 'Fault in the Law of State Responsibility—Pragmatism Ad Infinitum?' (2006) 49 *German YBIL* 293; Arangio-Ruiz (n 274).

emerged on the second reading of the rule in Article 16 ARSIWA and, at first glance, appears to be straightforward. However, and even though we ultimately take the position that it is preferable to the requirement of intent, it does raise a range of theoretical and practical issues.

First, it is apparent that one can derive little certainty from the word 'knowledge' alone. How much can a State or international organisation know about the consequences of its decisions abroad? How much can it know in advance of taking those decisions and according to which or whose benchmarks? Even less certainty exists regarding the meaning of the word 'circumstances'. As demonstrated in chapter four, the ILC's Commentaries are not of much assistance on these questions, mixing the standards of knowledge, intent, and the knowledge of intent.

Likewise, the views of States and international organisations show a lack of consistency in their approach to the cognitive standard of responsibility for complicity. A few examples follow. Argentina, for instance, considered the introduction of a subjective element:

> *[P]rima facie* to be incompatible with the general rules in the preceding chapters [of the ARSIWA]. There is, however, clearly some merit in the idea behind this 'subjective' requirement: to limit a number of potential author States 'participating' in the wrongful act, which otherwise could increase indefinitely.[295]

The Republic of Korea expressed doubts about the cognitive test:

> The meaning of the phrase 'with knowledge of the circumstances of the internationally wrongful act' is rather vague and it does not seem to provide any practical guidance to determine the 'responsibility of a State in respect of the act of another State'.[296]

The Netherlands for its part suggested that 'knowledge of the circumstances' encompassed actual and constructive knowledge—ie the applicable test would read as 'knows or should have known the circumstances of the internationally wrongful act'.[297] By contrast, the United Kingdom and the United States argued for a more restrictive reading of the phrase 'knowledge of the circumstances'.[298]

During the transposition of this provision to the ARIO, several organisations pointed out to the need to clarify the cognitive standard. Further to the position expressed above by the United Kingdom and the United States, the World Bank, for example, explicitly requested the ILC to clarify that knowledge means 'actual' and not presumed.[299]

[295] ILC (n 4) 51 (Argentina); UNGA (n 9) 6, para 42 (Mexico).

[296] ILC (n 4) 52 (South Korea).

[297] ibid 52 (Netherlands); see also ILC, 'Summary Record of the 1312th Meeting' (20 May 1975), reproduced in (1975) 1 *YBILC* 41, 44, para 13 (Ustor).

[298] ILC (n 4) 52 (United Kingdom and United States).

[299] ILC (n 41) 28 (World Bank).

Some States also expressed strong reservations regarding the need of the cognitive standard altogether. Denmark questioned

> the wisdom of introducing the qualification of 'knowledge of the circumstances' … as this requirement did not figure—and rightly so—in [A]rticle 2 stating the essential elements of an internationally wrongful act.[300]

Similarly, Cuba questioned whether it was appropriate to build in the cognitive standards in the area of responsibility for complicity, suggesting that the presumption of the requisite knowledge arises from the objective proof of aid or assistance that has facilitated the commission of an internationally wrongful act. Cuba's written comments to the ARIO provisions are self-explanatory:

> Cuba notes that such responsibility is limited by three theoretical requirements of progressive development … Such requirements make it difficult to attribute responsibility to an international organization for the aid, direction or control that it has provided or exercised in the commission of an internationally wrongful act, *which undoubtedly facilitates the proliferation of acts in breach of international law.*
>
> … Cuba considers that a new provision of progressive development, relating to the attribution of responsibility to a State or international organization for its participation in the internationally wrongful act, should be introduced. This new provision should contain a *presumption establishing that any State or international organization that aids another in the commission of a wrongful act does so with knowledge of the circumstances of the same.*
>
> Cuba proposes *removing the requirement whereby the aid or assistance must have been provided with the intention of facilitating the commission of the violation and the violation must actually have been committed, or, as another variant, reversing the burden of proof through a presumption establishing that any entity that aids another to commit a wrongful act, knowing that to be the objective, does so in order that the wrongful act may be committed.*[301] (emphasis added)

The views of Denmark and Cuba clearly represent the minority, but they are relevant as they help us in the balancing of the dialectics of intent vis-à-vis knowledge. These more radical views are actually easier to reconcile with the knowledge of the circumstances (ie a less stringent standard) than with the requirement of intent.

The test of 'knowledge of the circumstances of the wrongful act' has found some expression in practice.[302] In 2009, the UN Legal Counsel expressed an opinion regarding the collaboration of the UN Mission in the

[300] ILC (n 4) 52 (Denmark, on behalf of Nordic countries).

[301] ILC, 'Comments and Observations Received from Governments' (14 February 2011) UN Doc A/CN.4/636, 16 (Cuba).

[302] Lowe (n 23) 8.

DRC (MONUC) and the Forces armées de la République démocratique du Congo (FARDC) that supports the knowledge of the circumstances test:

> If MONUC *has reason to believe* that FARDC units involved in an operation are violating one or the other of those bodies of law [international humanitarian law, human rights law and refugee law] and if, despite MONUC's intercession with the FARDC and with the Government of the DRC, MONUC has reason to believe that such violations are still being committed, then *MONUC may not lawfully continue to support that operation, but must cease its participation in it completely. … MONUC may not lawfully provide logistic or 'service' support to any FARDC operation if it has reason to believe that the FARDC units involved are violating any of those bodies of law.* …This follows directly from the Organization's obligations under customary international law and from the Charter to uphold, promote and encourage respect for human rights, international humanitarian law and refugee law.[303] (emphasis added)

Following on from these allegations, the UNSC, on advice from the Secretary-General, adopted a 'conditionality policy', which made the UN assistance to Congolese troops conditional on their respect for human rights and international humanitarian law.[304] In its Resolution 1906, the UNSC called upon MONUC

> to intercede with the FARDC command if elements of a FARDC unit receiving MONUC's support are suspected of having committed grave violations of such laws, and if the situation persists … to withdraw support from these FARDC units.[305]

The test of knowledge of the circumstances also appears to be a common ground in the context of partnership agreements, which foresee mechanisms of consultation and monitoring. For instance, Article IV of the Co-financing Agreement between the Nordic Development Fund, the African Development Bank and the African Development Fund provides that:

> The Parties shall promptly inform each other of any condition or development which in its opinion is likely to interfere with the implementation or the successful completion of a project or programme being co-financed hereunder and shall consult with each other regarding the appropriate remedial action to be taken by the parties.[306]

303 ARIO (n 22) 37, para 6 (Art 14 Commentary).

304 UNSC, 'Thirtieth Report of the Secretary-General on the United Nations Organization Mission in the Democratic Republic of the Congo' (4 December 2009) UN Doc S/2009/623, para 13; see also HP Aust, 'The UN Human Rights Due Diligence Policy: An Effective Mechanism against Complicity of Peacekeeping Forces?' (2015) 20 *JCSL* 61, 68–70.

305 UNSC, 'Res 1906' (23 December 2009) UN Doc S/RES/1906 (DRC) para 22.

306 Co-financing Agreement between the Nordic Development Fund, the African Development Bank and the African Development Fund (adopted 17 May 2013) Art IV(3); see also Standard Conditions for Loans Made by the World Bank out of the Climate Investment Funds (adopted 31 July 2010) sections 2.06 and 2.08.

As Laurence Boisson de Chazournes puts it,

> If the parties abide by their duty to exchange information concerning the implementation of the co-financed project, each of them can keep abreast of the injurious developments potentially arising from the project. In such conditions, the partner organizations possess, at least in principle, enough knowledge to argue that maintaining the contractual relationship concerning the injurious project is tantamount to willingly providing aid or assistance to a wrongful act. However, that does not hold when the instrument establishing a partnership only foresees a generic exchange of information between the parties.[307]

Devising similar exchange of information provisions in other treaties, agreements or memoranda for the provision of aid or assistance would serve as a reasonable way of inferring knowledge of the circumstances should such aid or assistance be used for the commission of an internationally wrongful act.

The test of knowledge rather than intent finds further support in the case law of the ECtHR addressing the violations committed by the ECHR Member States when collaborating with the United States in so-called extraordinary renditions. In the *El-Masri* case, the ECtHR seemed to support a more lenient approach to the question of knowledge in cases of complicity.[308] The Court emphasised that

> the Macedonian authorities not only failed to comply with their positive obligation to protect the applicant from being detained in violation of Article 5 of the ECHR, but *they also actively facilitated his subsequent detention in Afghanistan* by handing him over to the CIA, despite the fact that they *were aware or ought to have been aware of the risk of that transfer*.[309] (emphasis added)

The Court pointed out that Macedonia not only failed to prevent the violations of Mr El-Masri's rights, but also *actively* facilitated those violations by the CIA operatives in transferring and subsequently mistreating Mr El-Masri. The Court cited Article 16 ARSIWA, which appears to have constituted at least a partial basis for Macedonia's responsibility.[310] If this reading of the Court's rationale is correct, then it seems to subscribe to a more lenient interpretation of the knowledge standard, ie either actual or constructive.

However, despite the reference to Article 16 ARSIWA as one of the legal bases in the Court's judgment, its interpretation of the cognitive standard may be justifiably construed as being limited to the operation of the specific primary norms under the ECHR, and thus of little benefit to the

[307] Boisson de Chazournes (n 46) 223.

[308] *El-Masri v The Former Yugoslav Republic of Macedonia* (Judgment) (GC) [2012] ECtHR App No 39630/09 (2013) 57 EHRR 25.

[309] ibid para 239.

[310] ibid para 97.

general regime of responsibility for complicity. Certainly, the standard of the required knowledge is more expansive in cases of torture under Article 3 of the ECHR, admitting of actual, constructive or even risk-based responsibility. This is not necessarily the case of the general regime on responsibility for complicity, which requires the actual knowledge of the circumstances of the principal wrongful act. While the *standard* of knowledge may differ from one primary rule to another, it is submitted that the ECtHR case law is nonetheless relevant, not least because it recognises knowledge and not intent as a determinative element of international responsibility for complicity.[311]

The jurisprudence of the UN treaty bodies is further confirmatory of the knowledge standard.[312] The choice of knowledge rather than intent in the context of international responsibility was also reached a few years earlier by the UK panel investigating allegations of the UK's complicity in torture. The Panel found that 'States are … complicit … where they have constructive as well as actual knowledge—that is, they should have known of the use of torture'.[313]

In the context of international responsibility, knowledge is relevant insofar as it relates to the circumstances of the wrongful act. An ordinary interpretation of the term 'circumstances' indicates the pattern surrounding the wrongful act, and not necessarily the specific facts that establish its constituent elements. If, for example, State A gives State B aid or assistance for environmental protection programmes, but allows State B to occasionally divert the aid or assistance for breaches of State B's obligation vis-à-vis State C, the requirement of knowledge of the circumstances would be met. Likewise, such aid or assistance would be regarded as contributing to the commission of an internationally wrongful act even though its initial objective may have been different.[314]

Let us take another example. If State A sends its drones to State B, the latter being continuously reproached by international organisations and other States for using drones in extrajudicial executions, a foreseeable consequence of such action is that State A cannot invoke its absence of knowledge of the circumstances surrounding the internationally wrongful act.[315] In cases where State A supports State B in the commission of

[311] See ibid; *Al Nashiri v Poland* (Judgment) [2014] ECtHR App No 28761/11 (2015) 60 EHRR 16, paras 441–42 and 517–19; *Husayn (Abu Zubaydah) v Poland* (Judgment) [2014] ECtHR App No 7511/13 (2015) 60 EHRR 16, paras 441–42 and 517–19.

[312] See, eg *Agiza v Sweden* (20 May 2005) UN Doc CAT/C/34/D/233/2003 (UN Committee against Torture), para 13.4; *Alzery v Sweden* (10 November 2006) UN Doc CCPR/C/88/D/1416/2005 (UN Human Rights Committee), paras 11.5–11.6.

[313] Joint Human Rights Committee (n 90) 13–14, paras 24–26.

[314] See J Quigley, 'State Responsibility for Ethnic Cleansing' (1998) 32 *University of California Davis LR* 341, 359.

[315] V Lanovoy, 'Complicity in an Internationally Wrongful Act' in A Nollkaemper and I Plakokefalos (eds), *Principles of Shared Responsibility in International Law: An Appraisal of the State of the Art* (Cambridge, CUP, 2014) 153.

an internationally wrongful act, the assessment of the knowledge of the *circumstances* does not entail the full awareness of the content, specific form or modalities of the wrongful act as executed.[316] State A only needs to know the circumstances of the wrongdoing, ie that its drones will be used to commit extrajudicial killings by State B. State A need not know that they will be used to kill a particular individual or the modalities of such execution. It may also be that State A gives drones to State B for a lawful purpose of conducting a topographic survey of a remote region. If then these drones were unexpectedly used for an unlawful activity, State A would of course bear no responsibility.[317]

The 'knowledge of the circumstances' requires a relatively more flexible link as opposed to the standard of intent. Further, while a test of intent to facilitate would necessarily be examined only upon the moment of giving aid or assistance, the knowledge of the circumstances implicates an assessment that can be affected by the existence of prior cooperation between the two States in question and a more general pattern of conduct by the recipient State. This has important implications for the scope of responsibility, and evidence on which it can be established. Indeed, the jurisprudence of international courts and tribunals in assessing knowledge has shown the use of indirect evidence and the drawing of inferences of fact which could not be proved beyond any reasonable doubt, a standard typically employed for the proof of intent.[318]

B. Intention: 'With the View to Facilitating the Commission of the Wrongful Act'

In his excellent monograph on complicity, Aust suggests that 'at the current stage of the development of the law, there is no way around the requirement of intent'.[319] He argues that the '[d]ifficulties in proving the intent in question should thus not lead to the abandonment of intent as a requirement for triggering responsibility under Article 16 [ARSIWA]'.[320]

It is true that a number of States and international organisations have expressed support for the requirement of intent throughout the codification of the provisions on responsibility for complicity.[321] For instance,

[316] *Corfu Channel (United Kingdom v Albania)* (n 205) Dissenting Opinion of Judge Azevedo 78, 85–86.

[317] Lanovoy (n 315) 153.

[318] See, eg *El-Masri v The Former Yugoslav Republic of Macedonia* (n 308) paras 151–53 and 167; *Al Nashiri v Poland* (n 311) paras 395–96; cf *Corfu Channel (United Kingdom v Albania)* (n 205) 18 ('The proof may be drawn from inferences of fact, provided that they leave no room for reasonable doubt'); *Bosnia Genocide (Merits)* (n 19) 129–30, paras 209–10; 218, para 422.

[319] Aust (n 2) 377.

[320] ibid.

[321] See, eg ILC (n 4) 52; Nolte and Aust (n 59) 15.

Canada 'welcomed the inclusion of the element of intent in [the former draft] article 27'.[322] The United Kingdom for its part stressed that the rule on responsibility for complicity would be 'too sweeping' unless

> [t]he granting State must know that the aid or assistance being given was being used or would be used by the receiving State to commit an internationally wrongful act, and the granting State must intend to facilitate that act by giving the aid or assistance.[323]

Some States advocated for a narrow interpretation of the knowledge element of Article 16 in the sense of wrongful intent,[324] conceiving it as a 'guarantee that only the real forms of participation by a State in the internationally wrongful act of another State would constitute a breach of a given international obligation'.[325] Similar views in relation to the necessity of intent transpired from some of the comments in the context of the ARIO codification. For instance, the representative of Greece to the UNGA Sixth Committee suggested that for the provision on aid or assistance to be effective in the context of responsibility of international organisations

> a clarification was needed in the commentary to the effect that relevant intention would be required, as had been specified in the commentary to the corresponding article on State responsibility. Such a clarification was proposed, not only for reasons of consistency with the [ARSIWA], but also to explain that mere involvement of a member State in the day-to-day functioning of an international organization could not amount to 'aid or assistance' giving rise to the responsibility of the State for an act of the organization.[326]

The EU agreed and added that '[g]iven that the threshold for the application of the rule seems low (knowledge), one should add in the commentary some limitative language (intent) in line with the commentaries of the [ARSIWA]'.[327]

However, when State A regularly exports military material to State B and it is obvious that State B is systematically violating human rights with the help of this material, State A should not be allowed to hide behind the position that it did not intend to support the commission of such wrongful acts. This approach is also in conformity with what appears to be a more

[322] UNGA, 'Sixth Committee, Summary Record of the 37th Meeting' (n 3) 15, para 53 (Canada).

[323] ibid 8, para 18 (United Kingdom).

[324] UNGA, 'Sixth Committee, Summary Record of the 22nd Meeting' (n 4) 7, para 37 (Czech Republic).

[325] UNGA (n 18) 2, para 2 (Trinidad and Tobago).

[326] UNGA, 'Sixth Committee, Summary Record of the 15th Meeting' (15 November 2006) UN Doc A/C.6/61/SR.15, 7, para 37 (Greece).

[327] ILC (n 41) 27 (EU).

extensive obligation of due diligence, particularly in the domains of arms export and transfer control.[328]

What if the assisting State imposes a priori restrictions to the use of its aid or assistance? Is this tantamount to exempting prima facie that State from any responsibility for the ultimate use of that aid or assistance? Thailand raised a similar query in its comments at the UNGA Sixth Legal Committee:

> The difficulties inherent in the engagement of State responsibility under that article [former draft Article 27] centred upon the element of intention. The sale of arms and military equipment, for instance, need not be a breach of an international obligation, unless otherwise prohibited by a convention. However, restrictive conditions in the contract of sale of such armaments could not preclude the responsibility of the State exporting the weapons, if there were no apparent means of enforcing such restrictions.[329]

In principle, it is difficult to envisage that international law at its current state of development requires more from an otherwise complicit State than the imposition of conditionalities or restrictions to its aid or assistance. However, the response needs to be nuanced. If the State becomes aware that its aid or assistance is no longer abiding by the conditions it had set before, it would have an immediate duty to interrupt any further supplies.

A number of commentators have argued that the requirement of intent renders the whole provision on responsibility for complicity unworkable.[330] It may be extremely difficult to determine the mind and desire of a State or international organisation. A State 'may attempt to conceal the provision of aid, possibly through the dissemination of conflicting statements by multiple organs'.[331] In most cases, a State would provide aid or assistance without desiring a specific result. The requirement of intent in the context of responsibility for complicity could simply mean that the provision of aid or assistance must be a deliberate conduct, ie a result of some form of deliberation or decision-making on the part of the State or

[328] On the obligations of neutral States to control export of weapons to the belligerents see S Oeter, *Neutralität und Waffenhandel* (Berlin, Springer, 1992); see also TA DiPerna, 'Small Arms and Light Weapons: Complicity With A View Toward Extended State Responsibility' (2008) 20 *Florida J Intl L* 25; NHB Jørgensen, 'State Responsibility for Aiding or Assisting International Crimes in the Context of the Arms Trade Treaty' (2014) 108 *AJIL* 722; Brehm (n 228); A Boivin, 'Complicity and Beyond: International Law and the Transfer of Small Arms and Light Weapons' (2005) 87 *IRRC* 467.

[329] UNGA, 'Sixth Committee, Summary Record of the 38th Meeting' (6 November 1978) UN Doc A/C.6/33/SR.38, 5, para 14 (Thailand).

[330] Quigley (n 2) 111; A Orakhelashvili, 'Division of Reparation between Responsible Entities' in J Crawford et al (eds), *The Law of International Responsibility* (Oxford, OUP, 2010) 650–51.

[331] Crawford (n 23) 408; Quigley (n 2) 111.

international organisation.[332] In line with this argument, it has also been suggested that for the assisting State to incur responsibility, there is no requirement that it intended for the wrongful act to be committed or that it desired that particular outcome.[333]

Other commentators have taken the position that in the absence of such purpose or desire as to the ultimate outcome of the aid or assistance, no responsibility can follow.[334] They tend to find support in the rationale of the Court in the *Bosnia Genocide* case. This reliance is exaggerated. In the view of this author, the Court's finding that Serbia did not violate its obligations under the Genocide Convention on the subsidiary grounds of complicity in genocide pursuant to Article III(e) is unconvincing. Indeed, the question of complicity has generated considerable disagreement among judges.[335] The ICJ compared complicity in genocide to a neighbouring notion of aid or assistance in the law of international responsibility in an apparent attempt to safeguard coherent delimitation between individual criminal responsibility and State responsibility.[336] Hence, the Court addressed Serbia's responsibility on the basis of Article 16 ARSIWA, operating on the assumption that there is no distinction in substance between the latter concept and that of complicity within the purview of Article III(e) of the Genocide Convention. However, in the opinion of this author, this assumption should have warranted a more in-depth elaboration by the Court.[337]

In the proceedings before the Court, Bosnia and Herzegovina invoked Article 16 ARSIWA with the view to diverting the ICJ's attention from the intent requirement, or *dolus specialis*, which characterises the crime of genocide itself. For instance, in international criminal law as shown in chapter three, the awareness or knowledge of the intent of the perpetrator suffices for triggering responsibility for complicity in a specific-intent

[332] P Palchetti, 'State Responsibility for Complicity in Genocide' in P Gaeta (ed), *The UN Genocide Convention: A Commentary* (Oxford, OUP, 2009) 389.

[333] ibid; see also Quigley (n 2) 108–17; Padeletti (n 35) 226–27; H Ascensio, 'La responsabilité selon la Cour internationale de justice dans l'affaire du génocide bosniaque' (2007) 111 *RGDIP* 285, 298 (for a broad reading of the meaning of 'aiding or assisting'); M Milanović, 'State Responsibility for Genocide: A Follow-Up' (2007) 18 *EJIL* 669, 683 (highlighting the distinction between general and specific intent in relation to complicity); cf Graefrath (n 35) 375.

[334] Crawford (n 23) 408; Aust (n 2) 235 ff.

[335] See, eg *Bosnia Genocide (Merits)* (n 19) Declaration of Judge Keith 352; ibid Dissenting Opinion of Judge Al-Khasawneh 241; ibid Dissenting Opinion of Judge ad hoc Mahiou 381, 451 ff, para 124 ff.

[336] ibid 216–17, para 419; see also P Gaeta, 'On What Conditions Can a State Be Held Responsible for Genocide?' (2007) 18 *EJIL* 631; P Gaeta, 'Genocide d'Etat et responsabilité pénale individuelle' (2007) 111 *RGDIP* 273; AC Asuncion, 'Pulling the Stops on Genocide: The State or the Individual?' (2010) 20 *EJIL* 1195.

[337] See Gattini (n 264) 696.

crime.[338] In the *Bosnia Genocide* case, even though conceptually the Court seemed to be using the knowledge criterion, its reasoning came out much closer to the purpose-based approach of complicity in genocide.[339] This is why the Court's interpretation and conclusions on the cognitive criterion in that case cannot and should not be transposable to the general regime of responsibility for complicity in any internationally wrongful act.

While Article 16 ARSIWA requires knowledge of the circumstances of the wrongful act on the part of the assisting State, the Court stated:

> there is no doubt that the conduct of an organ or a person furnishing aid or assistance to a perpetrator of the crime of genocide cannot be treated as complicity in genocide unless *at the least* that organ or person acted knowingly, that is to say, *in particular*, was aware of the specific intent (*dolus specialis*) of the principal perpetrator.[340] (emphasis added)

According to the Court, knowledge of the specific intent constitutes a *sine qua non* condition for State complicity in genocide to arise. Commentators have given this passage a life of its own, suggesting that the general regime of international responsibility should be construed restrictively so as to require at least the showing of the knowledge of the intent.[341] In this author's view, such an interpretation misconstrues the Court's statement placing it outside a very peculiar context of the case.[342] The Court itself in the above passage refers to such peculiarity when using the qualifier 'in particular', which suggests that it was the nature of the genocide that prompted the need to establish a higher threshold of knowledge.[343]

Furthermore, the Court deemed it appropriate to 'establish beyond any doubt' whether the authorities of the FRY supplied—and continued to supply—the VRS leaders who decided upon and carried out those acts of

[338] See, eg *Prosecutor v Jelisić* (Judgment) IT-95-10-A (5 July 2001) para 47 (where it was concluded that intent may be inferred from 'the general context, the perpetration of other culpable acts systematically directed against the same group, the scale of atrocities committed, the systematic targeting of victims on account of their membership of a particular group, or the repetition of destructive and discriminatory acts').

[339] See A Abass, 'Proving State Responsibility for Genocide: The ICJ in Bosnia v Serbia and the International Commission of Inquiry for Darfur' (2007) 31 *Fordham Intl LJ* 871; JC Barker and S Sivakumaran, 'I. Application of the Convention on the Prevention and Punishment of the Crime of Genocide (Bosnia and Herzegovina v Serbia and Montenegro)' (2008) 56 *ICLQ* 695; AB Loewenstein and SA Kostas, 'Divergent Approaches to Determining Responsibility for Genocide: The Darfur Commission of Inquiry and the ICJ's Judgment in the Genocide Case' (2007) 5 *JICJ* 839; D Groome, 'Adjudicating Genocide: Is the International Court of Justice Capable of Judging State Criminal Responsibility?' (2008) 31 *Fordham Intl LJ* 911.

[340] *Bosnia Genocide (Merits)* (n 19) 218, para 421.

[341] Crawford (n 23) 405–08; Aust (n 2) 230 ff.

[342] For a similar view see Jackson (n 148) 160.

[343] Cassese (n 256) 881; A Gattini, 'Evidentiary Issues in the ICJ's Genocide Judgment' (2007) 5 *JICJ* 889, 896–97; see also M Gibney, 'Genocide and State Responsibility' (2007) 7 *HRLR* 760; Barker and Sivakumaran (n 339).

genocide with their aid or assistance.[344] In this respect, the Court emphasised the importance of the fact that the decision by the Bosnian Serb leaders to commit genocide was taken only shortly before it was actually carried out and, even assuming that Serbia knew of mass atrocities about to be committed, it did not possibly know that the perpetrators had the *dolus specialis* of genocide.[345] Essentially, in the view of the Court, the relevant aid or assistance provided by Serbia to the VRS forces of Republika Srpska began long before the tragic events of Srebrenica and continued thereafter. Put otherwise, the ICJ found a lack of necessary knowledge or better shared intent on the part of Serbia, on the basis that the resources, which the perpetrators of the acts of genocide possessed, were the result of a general policy of aid or assistance and not specifically addressed towards facilitating the commission of genocide.[346] At the crucial time, it could not be established that the FRY supplied aid or assistance to the VRS forces of Republika Srpska in full awareness that the same aid would be used to commit genocide.[347]

In the author's opinion, this is an overly restrictive reading of the cognitive element of responsibility for complicity in general international law, which does not find support in practice and *opinio juris*. Even where States have called for the ILC to bring in the requirement of intent, they never suggested that temporal distancing between the specific form of complicity and the commission of the principal wrongful act would be a sufficient factor to break the existing factual/causal link (nexus) between these two conducts. Nor did they envisage the application of a heightened standard of proof in all cases of responsibility for complicity.

Arguably, the choice of the Court in *Bosnia Genocide* to use the highest standard of proof (ie beyond any doubt) led to the finding that Serbia did not have the requisite knowledge. The Court has applied a similar standard in other cases.[348] The choice of applying such a high standard of proof was premeditated by the serious nature of the crime of genocide.[349] However, generally, the appropriateness of such a high standard of proof is questionable in respect of responsibility of States and international organisations.

[344] *Bosnia Genocide (Merits)* (n 19) 218, para 422.

[345] ibid 219, para 424.

[346] ibid 218, para 422.

[347] ibid 219, para 424.

[348] *The Temple of Preah Vihear (Cambodia v Thailand)* (Merits) [1962] ICJ Rep 6, 21 and 58; see also *Oil Platforms (Merits)* (n 200) Separate Opinion of Judge Higgins 225, 234, para 33 (noting that 'beyond a general agreement that the graver the charge the more confidence must there be in the evidence relied on, there is thus little to help parties appearing before the Court').

[349] cf M Frulli, 'Un passo avanti e due indietro: responsabilità individuale e responsabilità statale nella sentenza della Corte internazionale di giustizia nel caso Bosnia-Erzegovina c. Serbia' (2007) 3 *Diritti umani e diritto internazionale* 579, 588–91; Gattini, 'Evidentiary Issues in the ICJ's Genocide Judgment' (n 343) 898.

For example, other international dispute settlement mechanisms have addressed differently the issue of State responsibility for serious breaches of international law.[350] In the *Velásquez Rodríguez* case, for instance, the Inter-American Court of Human Rights (IACtHR) ascertained that in the presence of grave breaches of human rights attributable to armed units or police forces of the State, the standard of proof beyond a reasonable doubt can be relaxed.[351] There is merit to the argument that the evidentiary standards need to be less rigid than those followed by the international criminal tribunals for the purposes of establishing criminal liability.[352] This is particularly so when the respondent State does not cooperate in the disclosure of evidence. In the *Corfu Channel* case, the ICJ itself admitted that the

> fact of [an] exclusive territorial control exercised by a State within its frontiers *has a bearing upon the methods of proof available to establish the knowledge of that State as to such events.* By reason of this exclusive control, the other State, *the victim of a breach of international law, is unable to furnish direct proof of facts giving rise to responsibility.* Such a State should be allowed a *more liberal recourse to inferences of fact and circumstantial evidence.* This indirect evidence is admitted in all systems of law, and its use is recognized by international decisions. It must be regarded as of special weight when it is based on a series of facts linked together and leading logically to a single conclusion.[353] (emphasis added)

As Judge Azevedo stressed in his dissenting opinion:

> It would be going too far for an international court to insist on direct and visual evidence and to refuse to admit, after reflection, a reasonable amount of human presumptions with a view to reaching that state of moral, human certainty with which, despite the risks of occasional errors, a court of justice must be content.[354]

In light of the foregoing, it is all the more surprising that in terms of responsibility for complicity the ICJ demands a virtual certainty of genocide, whereas in terms of the obligation to prevent the Court suggests that some general knowledge or risk that genocide is likely to occur would be sufficient for the duty to arise. In other words, in the light of the Court's reasoning, the State that is actively involved in arming and equipping a regime responsible for the acts of genocide must be absolutely sure that genocide is about to occur. Conversely, the State entitled to prevent genocide would be held responsible even if it was not absolutely sure

[350] See, eg Loewenstein and Kostas (n 339); Abass (n 339).

[351] See *Velásquez Rodríguez v Honduras* (Judgment) [1988] IACtHR Ser C No 4, paras 127 ff.

[352] See *Bosnia Genocide (Merits)* (n 19) 132–34, paras 216–24; 134–37, paras 225–30 (for a different value attributed to the elements of proof from that in the ICTY); on the degree of proof see *Corfu Channel (United Kingdom v Albania)* (n 205) 18; *Military and Paramilitary Activities (Merits)* (n 149) 24–25, paras 29–30; 39–40, paras 59–60.

[353] *Corfu Channel (United Kingdom v Albania)* (n 205) 18.

[354] ibid Dissenting Opinion of Judge Azevedo 78, 90–91.

that genocide is about to ensue. This would lead to a paradoxical result in which the systemic need of proscribing complicity in the commission of genocide would be of a lesser importance than the need to prevent genocide.

In addition, the Court in the *Bosnia Genocide* case was unwilling to relax the standard of proof in relation to the 'redacted' sections of documents of the Supreme Defence Council of Serbia.[355] Nor did the Court draw any adverse inferences in relation to Serbia's refusal to disclose the contents of the unedited documents, even though Article 49 of the Statute of the Court provides for this possibility, and even though these could have shed light on whether Serbia had the requisite knowledge at the time genocide was about to be committed. According to Judge Al-Khasawneh, this would have shifted the *onus probandi* or allowed a more liberal recourse to inferences, which could have eventually led to a different conclusion on Serbia's responsibility.[356]

C. Normative Solution(s)

Let us now try to put in perspective the conflicting normative trends discussed in the preceding two sub-sections. In order to do so, we believe that two questions must be answered: (i) why do we need a subjective element at all?; and (ii) is there such thing as a more appropriate cognitive standard for States and international organisations or could we somehow reconcile knowledge and intention under one single test?

Regarding the first question, it is surprising that during the codification of the provisions on responsibility for complicity some States proposed deleting the subjective requirement altogether. This, of course, was a minority view and it was not retained in the final version of the ARSIWA and ARIO. But it does prompt us to ask why we really need a cognitive limitation for responsibility for complicity?

The basic explanation lies in the general obligation of good faith. States and international organisations, just like individuals in domestic legal systems, 'must be able to assume that those with whom they deal in the general intercourse of society will act in good faith'.[357] As complicity creates a tripartite connection (involving complicit, principal and injured entity), it is necessary to circumscribe the legal consequences only to those

[355] See *Bosnia Genocide (Merits)* (n 19) Dissenting Opinion of Judge Al-Khasawneh 241, 254–55, para 35.

[356] See ibid.

[357] R Pound, *An Introduction to the Philosophy of Law* (New Haven, Yale University Press, 1922) 188; for a clear recognition of this principle in international law see *Lac Lanoux (France v Spain)* (n 58) 281; see also *Tacna-Arica Question (Chile/Peru)* (n 58) 930.

situations where aid or assistance is given with the actual knowledge of the circumstances surrounding the breach. Certainly, some flexibility is needed in evaluating whether circumstances are such as to require from the State to halt its assistance. In general only the actual knowledge will trigger responsibility. However, depending on the overall pattern and degree of cooperation between States as well as the primary rule breached, the mere existence of constructive knowledge could suffice in certain circumstances. This follows indirectly from a general approach to evidence of knowledge in international law, as set out in the *Corfu Channel* case, for example:

> international practice shows, that a State on whose territory or in whose waters an act contrary to international law has occurred, *may be called upon to give an explanation. It is also true that that State cannot evade such a request by limiting itself to a reply that it is ignorant of the circumstances of the act and of its authors*. The State may, up to a certain point, be *bound to supply particulars of the use made by it of the means of information and inquiry at its disposal*.[358] (emphasis added)

In similar terms, a complicit State could be required to collaborate in showing that its decision as to rendering aid or assistance was well informed and took account of the surrounding circumstances. A simple claim of ignorance is not an automatic excuse against the potential misuse of aid or assistance given by the State. In this context, the absence of knowledge is conceptually closer to being regarded as a circumstance precluding wrongfulness of complicit conduct. No knowledge—no responsibility for complicity.

It is difficult to strike a balance between knowledge and intent through a simple mathematical equation between the numbers of (i) States and international organisations expressing preference for intent, (ii) those clearly emphasising the knowledge of the circumstances as a sufficient standard, and yet (iii) those few voices arguing for a broader approach to complicity either based on constructive knowledge or deleting any cognitive requirement altogether. Practice has not yet confirmed which of these routes is best suited for the operation of responsibility for complicity.

The requirement of knowledge of the circumstances, supplemented by proper causal analysis, responds to normative and policy concerns of complicity being cast as too broad a basis of responsibility.[359] The

[358] *Corfu Channel (United Kingdom v Albania)* (n 205) 18; see also *Lac Lanoux (France v Spain)* (n 58) 281; on the significance of the principle of good faith in international law see R Kolb, *La bonne foi en droit international public: Contribution à l'étude des principes généraux de droit* (Paris, PUF, 2000); GS Goodwin-Gill, 'State Responsibility and the "Good Faith" Obligation in International Law' in M Fitzmaurice and D Sarooshi (eds), *Issues of State Responsibility before International Judicial Institutions* (Oxford, Hart Publishing, 2004); B Cheng, *General Principles of Law as Applied by International Courts and Tribunals* (Cambridge, CUP, 2006) 105–60.

[359] See Crawford (n 23) 408; Aust (n 2) 237 ff.

establishment of the knowledge of the circumstances of the wrongful act is a more objective framework, more easily ascertainable, and avoids any inherently criminal constructions borrowed from domestic laws. More importantly, it allows for the responsibility for complicity to be an effective norm and facilitate access to justice for victims.[360] Such a conclusion is further buttressed from the ILC's retention of the 'knowledge of the circumstances' test in the ARIO without any amendment and despite occasional invitations to do so by some of its members, State delegates and international organisations.

Despite the fact that the elements of intent and knowledge are closely imbricated in the ILC's reports and commentaries,[361] the overall framework of ARSIWA and ARIO is conceptually closer to an objectivised standard of the knowledge of the circumstances requirement rather than that of intention. Irrespective of where the proper equilibrium is struck, this dichotomy emerges as a counter-force to the two-pronged conception of the internationally wrongful act (ie breach and attribution). A sort of 'fin de la faute [mais] la recherche aléatoire des intentions coupables'.[362]

This state of ambiguity and uncertainty as to the precise subjective standard comforts States and international organisations, troubles judges and legal practitioners, and frustrates the expectations of the injured party to get redress for the injury suffered. It only confirms that 'it is an error to think that it is possible to eliminate the significance of fault from the [law of international responsibility]'.[363]

In this author's view, there are four normative solutions that can be considered for a prospective modelling of responsibility for complicity. The first solution is to delineate the test purely based on the 'knowledge of the circumstances' standard. This reading is faithful to the 'ordinary meaning' of the current text of the ARSIWA and ARIO provisions and finds considerable support in practice and *opinio juris*. However, it would leave unrepresented the strong views of a handful of States and international organisations that insisted on emphasising the requirement of intent.

The second solution would be to reconcile the cognitive standard of complicity with the opposability requirement. It would consist in generating a rebuttable presumption of knowledge or intention in those cases where both the complicit and the principal entity are bound by the same international obligation. If the entities are not bound by the same

[360] See Orakhelashvili (n 330) 650.

[361] See, eg Ago (n 30), 58, para 72; d'Argent (n 207) 550–51; Quigley (n 2) 111 ('[the complicit State] gains politically from providing the aid, even though the gain has nothing to do with the wrongful act committed by the donee State').

[362] PM Dupuy, 'Quarante ans de codification du droit de la responsabilité internationale des États: un bilan' (2003) 2 *RGDIP* 305, 314 (author's translation: 'end of the fault [but] a random search of culpable intentions').

[363] Crawford (n 274) 13.

international obligation, then the responsibility for complicity would only arise if the assisting entity knew of the circumstances of the wrongful act or, alternatively, intended to facilitate the commission of the wrongful act. By generating such a rebuttable presumption, one would make use of the requirement of opposability and at the same time respond to both apologists of knowledge and intention. However, as we have briefly introduced in chapters three and four and will discuss in more detail below, the requirement of opposability is in itself highly problematic and unsupported in practice and *opinio juris*.

The third proposal is to accept the knowledge of the circumstances as a generally applicable test yet recognise that the intention, in addition to knowledge, could play a role at the level of the content of responsibility. In other words, the showing of the intention on behalf of the complicit State could be an aggravating factor at the level of the content of responsibility and could affect the actual share of reparation that complicit State would owe to the injured party.[364] There is some old case law that supports the award of compensation, even for remote consequences, in cases where intent could be shown.[365] This would mean that intention would only play a role at the level of the actual apportioning of the injury between the principal and complicit wrongdoers and not as a necessary condition to establish responsibility of the complicit wrongdoer.

Finally, the fourth proposal would be to adhere to intention as a relevant criterion of responsibility for complicity, but to admit that such intention could be inferred from the pattern of cooperation between the principal and the complicit State. The ILC's Commentary on the first reading of the provision on responsibility for complicity suggested that certain or near-certain knowledge as to the outcome could fulfil the requirement of intent.[366]

All of these proposals can be defended and criticised. In the author's view, however, the first proposal is the closest to the reality of international law and the need to ensure an effective norm on responsibility for complicity. It is true that even if one accepts that the 'knowledge of the circumstances of the wrongful act' is the sole and only standard for responsibility for complicity to arise, this does not dissipate all possible objections. First, applied full circle, this standard could mean that the State

[364] See, eg JE Noyes and BD Smith, 'State Responsibility and the Principle of Joint and Several Liability' (1988) 13 *Yale J Intl L* 225, 261.

[365] See, eg *Venable (United States v Mexico)* (1927) 4 RIAA 224 (holding the existence of 'outrage and wilful neglect of duty' as an aggravating circumstance); *Dix (United States v Venezuela)* (1903) 9 RIAA 121 (holding that international law 'rejected compensation for remote consequences, in the absence of evidence of deliberate intention to injure'); cf *Cresceri (Italy v Peru)* (1901) 15 RIAA 452 (holding the absence of intent as an attenuating circumstance).

[366] ILC (n 29) 99–105 (Former Draft Art 27 Commentary); Lowe (n 23) 8–9; Crawford (n 23) 408.

is almost pre-emptively engaging its responsibility as, on a literal reading of the standard, it would not need to be shown that the State knew about the actual nature and content of the wrongful act of another but only the surrounding circumstances. This objection is not convincing as, in any event, the responsibility for potential complicity is triggered only upon the moment that the principal wrongful act is committed. Second, it is not clear how the standard of knowledge of the circumstances is to be assessed and what is the exact level or degree of knowledge required.

Graefrath argued that the rule on responsibility for complicity would have been much more effective had it been limited to serious violations of international law because this would have circumvented difficulties related to the establishment of the knowledge criterion.[367] The knowledge of the assisting State could be presumed on the basis of the character of the norm violated by the assisted State and, in most cases, recognition of the existence of an internationally wrongful act by the UN or any other international or regional body.[368] As we have seen in chapter four, this presumption is warranted at least in relation to the duty of non-assistance under Articles 41(2) ARSIWA and 42(2) ARIO.

The ICJ case law, particularly that dealing with acquiescence, allows extrapolating the following set of criteria to establish the knowledge of the circumstances of the wrongful act: (i) the notoriety of facts where 'the circumstances were such as called for some reaction, within a reasonable time';[369] (ii) the special interest of the aiding or assisting State in the region;[370] and (iii) the geographical proximity.[371] Other relevant indicators would include the existence of legal proceedings involving the State recipient of aid or assistance or other independent inquiries into the allegations of complicity.[372] The nature of the aid or assistance and of the breach itself, whether instantaneous or continuous in character, may further influence the examination of whether the State or international organisation knew of the circumstances of the wrongful act. If for the first act in the chain of a continuous breach, one cannot presume that the State knew that it was contributing to the commission of the wrongful act, this assumption is

[367] Graefrath (n 35) 380; cf *Bosnia Genocide (Merits)* (n 19) 222, para 432.

[368] See, eg UNSC, 'Res 301' (20 October 1971) UN Doc S/RES/301 (Namibia); UNSC, 'Res 418' (4 November 1977) UN Doc S/RES/418 (South Africa); UNSC, 'Res 569' (26 July 1985) UN Doc S/RES/569 (South Africa); UNSC, 'Res 218' (23 November 1965) UN Doc S/RES/218 (Portuguese colonial territories); *Legal Consequences for States of the Continued Presence of South Africa in Namibia (South West Africa) notwithstanding Security Council Resolution 276 (1970)* (Advisory Opinion) [1971] ICJ Rep 16, 54–55, paras 119–20; *Legal Consequences of the Construction of a Wall in the Occupied Palestinian Territory* (n 152) 196 and 200, paras 146 and 159.

[369] *The Temple of Preah Vihear (Cambodia v Thailand)* (n 348) 23.

[370] *Fisheries (United Kingdom v Norway)* (Judgment) [1951] ICJ Rep 116, 139.

[371] *Bosnia Genocide (Merits)* (n 19) 221, para 430; *Armed Activities (DRC v Uganda)* (n 149) 230–31, paras 174–80.

[372] *El-Masri v The Former Yugoslav Republic of Macedonia* (n 308) para 157; Boivin (n 328) 470.

reversed from the moment the violation extends in time and the State fails to suspend its aid or assistance. Furthermore, in situations where violations of *jus cogens* or *erga omnes* norms are implicated, or where the illegality of a particular conduct by the recipient State has been declared prior to the decision by the aiding or assisting State to contribute, the rebuttable presumption of knowledge would be justified.[373]

Moreover, the establishment of the knowledge of the circumstances in judicial proceedings would possibly require an inversion of the burden of proof.[374] Once the injured State shows that the complicit conduct has indeed facilitated the commission of the principal wrongful act, a rebuttable presumption (*juris tantum*) that the complicit conduct was being given with the knowledge of the circumstances arises, and the burden shifts to the otherwise complicit State to rebut such presumption.[375] At first glance, this could seem as a rather radical suggestion in general international law, which for centuries has embraced the maxim of *onus probandi incumbit actori*. In the *Diallo* case, the Court hinted at the limited circumstances in which the burden of proof would not lie primarily with the party invoking a particular fact.[376] Similarly, there is some support in the existing arbitral practice that there are exceptional circumstances in which the burden of proof could be reversed.

For example, in the *Zafiro* case, the arbitral tribunal placed the onus of proof on the respondent State to demonstrate what proportion of the damage was not attributable to its conduct.[377] The principles of evidence are largely matters of logic and common sense.[378] In this author's view, it is logical that once complicity's material element is established, the aiding or assisting State would have to establish that it was not aware of or that it took all reasonably available measures to ensure that its aid or assistance would not facilitate the commission of an internationally wrongful act. Alternatively, the burden should lie on the principal State to show that part of the injury flowing from its wrongful act was caused by complicity of another. The approach also appears to be accepted in domestic courts. For example, in the *Bridge of Varvarin* case, the German Constitutional Court in a case brought against Germany for its participation in the NATO-led operation in Kosovo, noted that an effective judicial review could justify

[373] Graefrath (n 35) 377; Lowe (n 23) 14.

[374] ILC (n 301) 16 (Cuba).

[375] See, eg C Gutiérrez Espada, *El hecho ilícito internacional* (Madrid, Dykinson, 2005) 219; on presumptions in international law see P Sandonato de Leon, *Les présomptions judiciaires en droit international public* (Paris, Pedone, 2015); A Riddell and B Plant, *Evidence before the International Court of Justice* (London, BIICL, 2009) 101–11.

[376] *Ahmadou Sadio Diallo (Republic of Guinea v DRC)* (Merits) [2010] ICJ Rep 639, 660–61, paras 54–55.

[377] *D Earnshaw and others (United Kingdom v United States) ('Zafiro Case')* (1925) 6 RIAA 160, 164–65.

[378] *Corfu Channel (United Kingdom v Albania)* (n 205) Dissenting Opinion of Judge Badawi Pasha 58, 59–60.

placing the burden of proof on the State to explain its military conduct and to disclose facts that had been kept secret.[379] Moreover, where the aiding or assisting State fails to disclose material evidence of its involvement in the principal wrongful act, courts may draw adverse inferences as regards its knowledge of the circumstances of that wrongful act.[380] As we shall see in chapter six, these considerations are crucial at the level of determination of the content of responsibility and allocation of legal consequences.

The practice and *opinio juris* of the law-determining agents will show whether knowledge is a sufficient standard for the responsibility to arise. In our view, the test of knowledge of the circumstances of the wrongful act is adequate and should be further enhanced without bringing in intention as an additional condition for responsibility to arise. However, as the discussion of the cognitive element of complicity shows that the objectivity in this context is difficult to sustain.[381]

IV. OPPOSABILITY ELEMENT

In addition to the convoluted cognitive requirement as discussed above, the ARSIWA and ARIO rules limit the responsibility for complicity to cases where 'the act would be internationally wrongful if committed by that State [or international organisation]'.[382] As referred to in chapters three and four, this was a major revolution that Special Rapporteur Crawford introduced on the second reading of the ARSIWA. Articles 16(b) ARSIWA and 14(b) ARIO entail that in order to incur responsibility the complicit State or international organisation has to be bound by the same international obligation as the principal wrongdoer (the so-called 'opposability requirement'). Crawford suggested that failure to introduce this requirement 'would have enabled an aiding and assisting State to be held independently liable for the breach of a bilateral treaty to which it was not itself a party'.[383] It is submitted in this section that the opposability requirement has unnecessarily reduced the scope of the application of responsibility for complicity and by implication its function in the international legal order.

[379] *2 BvR 2660/06, 2 BvR 487/07 ('Bridge of Varvarin')* (Judgment) [2013] BverfG 1–70 (German Constitutional Court) para 64; for an analysis of the decision see KF Gärditz, 'Bridge of Varvarin' (2014) 108 *AJIL* 86.

[380] See, eg *Al Nashiri v Poland* (n 311) paras 395–96; *Husayn (Abu Zubaydah) v Poland* (n 311) paras 395–96; *Agiza v Sweden* (n 312) para 12.34.

[381] G Abi-Saab, 'Cours général de droit international public' (1987) 207 *RCADI* 9, 29 ('même quand nous nous efforçons subjectivement d'être objectifs, nous restons objectivement un peu subjectifs').

[382] ARSIWA (n 22) Art 16(b); ARIO (n 22) Art 14(b).

[383] Crawford (n 23) 409; see also C Dominicé, 'Attribution of Conduct to Multiple States and the Implication of a State in the Act of Another State' in J Crawford et al (eds), *The Law of International Responsibility* (Oxford, OUP, 2010) 286; Crawford (n 243) 50–51, paras 181–86.

A. Importing the *Pacta Tertiis* Rule: Is it Appropriate in the Law of International Responsibility?

Crawford's contribution, if examined under the lens of the law of treaties, is fully justified because, in principle, the existence of particular bilateral obligation does not impose any duties on third parties.[384] As it was already referred to in chapter four, the conception of this requirement follows closely the provisions of Articles 34 and 35 of the Vienna Convention on the Law of Treaties (VCLT). In simple terms, the *pacta tertiis nec nocent nec prosunt* rule establishes that a treaty cannot, by its own force alone, create obligations for third parties, as it is only effective as between the parties in their relations *inter se*.[385] The principle is well established in public international law. For example, in the *German Interests in Polish Upper Silesia*, the PCIJ recognised the principle that a treaty 'only creates law as between the States which are parties to it; in the case of doubt, no rights can be deduced from it in favour of third States'.[386]

Crawford extrapolated from that principle in treaty law that the rule on responsibility for aid or assistance could not 'be applied to bilateral obligations in an unqualified form'.[387] He gave the following example:

> Take a case where finance or goods are to be provided pursuant to a treaty by State A to State B, and State A realizes that to comply with the treaty will produce a breach of State B's obligation to State C. Under international law both treaties are presumably valid, although this is without prejudice to the international responsibility of State B. In such circumstances, why should State A be the judge of State B's compliance? If State B insists upon performance of its treaty with State A, is State A entitled to refuse? Yet under [former] article 27, it would appear that if State A knowingly provides the assistance, it is responsible to State C.[388]

Crawford further clarified that:

> It might be argued that State A's intention here is not to injure State C, but rather to comply with its State B's obligation. Refined judgments of the 'intention' of States, based on casuistical doctrines such as 'double effect', are not a

[384] Vienna Convention on the Law of Treaties (adopted 23 May 1969; entered into force 27 January 1980) 1155 UNTS 331, Art 34.

[385] G Fitzmaurice, 'Fifth Report on the Law of Treaties' (21 March 1960) UN Doc A/CN.4/130, reproduced in (1960) 2 *YBILC* 69, 72 ff; CHM Waldock, 'Third Report on the Law of Treaties' (1964) UN Doc A/CN.4/167 and Add 1-3, reproduced in (1964) 2 *YBILC* 517 ff; ILC, 'Report of the International Law Commission on the Work of Its 16th Session (11 May–24 July 1964)' (1964) UN Doc A/5809, reproduced in (1964) 2 *YBILC* 173, 180–84; ILC, 'Report of the International Law Commission on the Work of the Second Part of Its 17th Session (3–28 January 1966)' (1966) UN Doc A/6309/Rev 1, reproduced in (1966) 2 *YBILC* 169, 226–30.

[386] *German Interests in Polish Upper Silesia (Germany v Poland)* (Merits) [1926] PCIJ Ser A No 7, 5, 29; A McNair, *The Law of Treaties* (2nd edn, Oxford, Clarendon Press, 1961) 309–21.

[387] Crawford (n 243) 51, para 186.

[388] ibid.

> very secure basis for State responsibility. A broad rule such as that specified in [former] article 27 [current article 16] could only work satisfactorily if it were open to the assisting State to justify its assistance, e.g., on the ground of an equally valid moral or legal duty. But to enact a principle of justification would plainly involve legislating in the field of the primary rules of responsibility.[389]

The question of potentially conflicting treaties was discussed by the ILC during the elaboration of the VCLT. Ultimately, the Commission did not retain the incompatibility of the subsequent treaty with the previous treaty among the grounds of nullity listed in the VCLT.[390] The Special Rapporteurs on the law of treaties expressed different views on the matter. For example, Hersch Lauterpacht believed that a second treaty would affect the rights of States Parties to the first, and this illegality would result in the nullity of the second treaty.[391] Gerald Fitzmaurice considered that the second treaty would be null only where (i) the first treaty prohibited the conclusion of the second treaty incompatible with the provisions of the former or (ii) the second treaty was being concluded in breach of a multilateral treaty of an interdependent or integral character (eg human rights treaties).[392] By contrast, Humphrey Waldock regarded the question of whether a second treaty impinges on the rights of the parties to the first treaty as a matter of *international responsibility* and not as a condition of validity of treaties.[393] In fact, there is no precedent in which a validly concluded treaty was declared to be null and void on the basis

389 ibid.

390 For discussions within the ILC see, eg ILC, 'Summary Record of the 685th Meeting' (22 May 1963), reproduced in (1963) 1 *YBILC* 73, 78–79, paras 53–65; ILC, 'Summary Record of the 703rd Meeting' (19 June 1963), reproduced in (1963) 1 *YBILC* 196, 196–202; ILC, 'Summary Record of the 742nd Meeting' (10 June 1964), reproduced in (1964) 1 *YBILC* 119; ILC, 'Summary Record of the 743rd Meeting' (11 June 1964), reproduced in (1964) 1 *YBILC* 126; ILC, 'Summary Record of the 857th Meeting' (24 May 1966), reproduced in (1966) 1 (pt 2) *YBILC* 94; ILC, 'Summary Record of the 858th Meeting' (25 May 1966), reproduced in (1966) 1 (pt 2) *YBILC* 102; see also P Cahier, 'Les caractéristiques de la nullité en droit international et tout particulièrement dans la Convention de Vienne de 1969 sur le droit des traités' (1972) 76 *RGDIP* 646, 670–71.

391 H Lauterpacht, 'Report on the Law of Treaties' (24 March 1953) UN Doc A/CN.4/63, reproduced in (1953) 2 *YBILC* 90, 156–59; see also H Lauterpacht, 'Consistency with Prior Treaty Obligations' in E Lauterpacht (ed), *International Law Being the Collected Papers of Hersch Lauterpacht—The Law of Peace*, vol 4 (Cambridge, CUP, 1978) 308–09; McNair (n 386) 221–24.

392 G Fitzmaurice, 'Third Report on the Law of Treaties' (18 March 1958) UN Doc A/CN.4/115, reproduced in (1958) 2 *YBILC* 20, 27–28 and 42–46.

393 CHM Waldock, 'Second Report on the Law of Treaties' (1963) UN Doc A/CN.4/156 and Add 1-3, reproduced in (1963) 2 *YBILC* 36, 55–64; see also JHW Verzijl, 'La validité et la nullité des actes juridiques internationaux' (1935) 9 *Revue de droit international* 184, 320; C Rousseau, *Principes généraux du droit international public* (Paris, Pedone, 1944) 813; P Guggenheim, 'La validité et la nullité des actes juridiques internationaux' (1949) 74 *RCADI* 191, 223.

of its incompatibility with a previous treaty entered into by one of the parties.[394]

However, even if both treaties are valid, there is still scope for potential responsibility as a result of entering into the second treaty in order to breach the obligation engaged under the first treaty.[395] Take the following example: State A has a bilateral treaty with State B not to construct a power plant on a river between the two States. State A goes on to conclude another treaty with State C for the provision of funding towards the construction of the power plant on the river between States A and B. State C knows of the obligation binding State A. While both treaties are technically valid, why should not State C engage its responsibility for complicity in the violation of State A's obligation? The ultimate question would be the exact timing of the *fait générateur* of responsibility, ie when do the internationally wrongful acts of State A and State C occur? Is it the moment of the conclusion of the treaty or when State A actually starts building the power plant? Both views are defensible. As explained by Reuter, State C could indeed become an accomplice in the violation by State A of its pre-existing obligations:

> si le fait illicite réside dans la conclusion du traité (le deuxième en date) on pourrait toujours imaginer que la répartition adéquate soit l'élimination de ce traité; il pourrait en être ainsi si le deuxième était conclu de mauvaise foi et que les circonstances soient telles que l'autre partie à ce traité puisse être considérée comme un complice de la violation de l'obligation déjà souscrite par A, ce qui sera rarement le cas.[396]

Nor does Article 30(4) VCLT provide a solution, ignoring that in the presence of two valid but conflicting obligations, a State would be compelled

[394] For examples of disputes dealing with incompatible treaties see, eg *Costa Rica v Nicaragua* (Judgment) (1917) 11 *AJIL* 181 (Central-American Court of Justice); *El Salvador v Nicaragua* (Judgment) (1917) 11 *AJIL* 674 (Central American Court of Justice); *Customs Regime between Germany and Austria* (Advisory Opinion) [1931] PCIJ Ser A/B No 41, 37 ff; cf *The Oscar Chinn (United Kingdom v Belgium)* (Judgment) [1934] PCIJ Ser A/B No 63, Separate Opinion of Judge Van Eysinga 131, 131–36; ibid, Separate Opinion of Judge Schückling 148–49 (opining in favour of absolute nullity); see also *Jurisdiction of the European Commission of the Danube between Galatz and Braila* (Advisory Opinion) [1928] PCIJ Ser B No 14, 23; cf ibid, Observations by Judge Nyholm 71, 73 and Dissenting Opinion by Judge Negulesco 84, 129; see generally J Barberis, 'Le concept de "traité international" et ses limites' (1984) 30 *AFDI* 239, 261–62.

[395] P Guggenheim, *Traité de droit international public: avec mention de la pratique internationale et suisse*, vol 1 (2nd edn, Genève, Georg et Cié, 1967) 269.

[396] P Reuter, *Introduction au droit des traités* (3rd edn, Paris, PUF, 1995) 99 (author's translation: 'If the wrongful act lies in concluding the treaty (the second in time) we could imagine that the proper outcome is the extinction of this treaty; it might be so if the second treaty was signed in bad faith and that the circumstances are such that the other party to the treaty could be considered an accomplice to the breach of the obligation already incurred by [State] A, which is rarely the case').

to breach one of those obligations to be able to perform the other one. As Aust rightly suggests this is a non-solution to the issue of the responsibility of the State.[397]

Accordingly, while opposability of obligation makes sense in treaty law, the matter could appear differently in the context of international responsibility.[398] In this author's view, it is the knowledge of the principal State's obligation rather than a bond of obligation that triggers responsibility for complicity. Vaughan Lowe gives an example of the restrictive effect of the opposability requirement. For instance, if State A, a persistent objector to claims to extended security zones at sea, assists State B, which has acquiesced in such claims, to engage in unlawful military activities within the security zone of State C, State A would incur no responsibility under the current formulation of Article 16 ARSIWA.[399] Lowe rightly questions whether this should be the result of the law of responsibility, since State A is, after all, assisting the violation by State B of an obligation owed by State B to State C.[400] Similar issues may arise prominently in the context of human rights violations assisted by third States.[401]

As one member of the ILC rightly noted at the time of the second reading, the requirement of opposability

> was a typically private-law approach to responsibility. If an entity, while assisting another entity, breached the obligations stemming from a contract concluded with a third party, it was not considered to be liable. *Even in private law, however, such acts were not deemed to be acts of good faith*, something that would be all the more unacceptable in public law. The *specific nature of international law and international responsibility certainly had to be borne in mind*. Many States had pointed that out in the Sixth Committee, stating that the responsibility of States under

[397] Aust (n 2) 254; see also J Pauwelyn, *Conflict of Norms in Public International Law* (Cambridge, CUP, 2003) 427.

[398] cf *Rainbow Warrior Affair (France/New Zealand)* (1990) 20 RIAA 215, 251, para 75 ('in international law there is no distinction between contractual and tortious responsibility, so that any violation of a State of any obligation, of whatever origin gives rise to State responsibility').

[399] Lowe (n 23) 7; for the definition of security zones see N Klein, *Maritime Security and the Law of the Sea* (Oxford, OUP, 2011) 58.

[400] cf *Gabčikovo-Nagymaros Project (Hungary/Slovakia)* (Judgment) [1997] ICJ Rep 7, 38, para 47 ('Nor does the Court need to dwell upon the question of the relationship between the law of treaties and the law of State responsibility…as those two branches of international law obviously have a scope that is distinct. A determination of whether a convention is or is not in force, and whether it has or has not been properly suspended or denounced, is to be made pursuant to the law of treaties. On the other hand, an evaluation of the extent to which the suspension or denunciation of a convention, seen as incompatible with the law of treaties, involves the responsibility of the State which proceeded to it, is to be made under the law of state responsibility').

[401] See, eg M Milanović, *Extraterritorial Application of Human Rights Treaties: Law, Principles, and Policy* (Oxford, OUP, 2011) 124–26 (discussing the restrictive effect of the opposability requirement by reference to the facts of the case of Binyam Mohamed); see *R (on the Application of Binyam Mohamed) v Secretary of State for Foreign and Commonwealth Affairs* (Judgment) [2008] EWHC 2048.

> international law had a *sui generis* quality and was neither civil nor criminal. It was on that basis that *several States, including Israel, had called for the deletion of the provision that the obligation breached must also be binding upon the State that provided assistance.*[402] (emphasis added)

To justify the inclusion of this limitation to responsibility for complicity, Special Rapporteur Crawford conducted a comparative review of domestic legal systems and the way in which they deal with the question of interference in contractual rights. Special Rapporteur considered that the initial option to have responsibility for complicity without any such limitation would have amounted to a recognition that it is wrongful as such to induce others to breach an international obligation. Crawford's comparative analysis

> showed that legal practice in that field was very diverse, but also that chapter IV of the draft articles [including Article 16 ARSIWA] seemed to have been strongly influenced by the principle of liability applicable to interference in contractual rights under French law. According to that principle, anyone who assisted others in committing an act that was wrongful for that person was himself responsible. In practice, however, that principle was often nuanced. German law adopted a restrictive position on that question, whereas English law adopted an intermediate position, whereby anyone who knowingly induced another person to breach a contractual obligation could be held liable for a wrongful act, but there might be grounds justifying his conduct. The analogies had their limitations, but it had been interesting to note that chapter IV transposed a general assumption of responsibility from a national legal system and that that had proved a source of difficulties.[403]

He deduced that the provision as it stood in former draft Article 27 was too broad and would contravene the logic of the law of treaties. So, rather than adjusting other constituent elements to constraint its scope, Special Rapporteur Crawford introduced the requirement of opposability. In this author's view, to accept opposability as the condition of responsibility for complicity is to recognise that there is nothing wrong in aiding and assisting in the violation of an international obligation that one is not per se bound by.[404]

The 'bilateralisation' of complicity in Articles 16 ARSIWA and 14 ARIO is regrettable in two respects. First, it perpetuates a particular vision of normativity without considering whether it is still appropriate in the modern state of international law.[405] According to this vision, reciprocity

[402] ILC, 'Summary Record of the 2672nd Meeting' (3 May 2001), reproduced in (2001) 1 *YBILC* 34, 42, para 52 (Lukashuk); see also I Lukashuk, 'Ответственность одного субъекта международного права в связи с деянием другого' (2003) 1 *Iurist-mezhdunarodnik* 9.

[403] ILC, 'Summary Record of the 2574th Meeting' (19 May 1999), reproduced in (1999) 1 *YBILC* 48, 54, para 53 (Crawford).

[404] See, eg Gutiérrez Espada (n 375) 216–17.

[405] Lanovoy (n 315) 159.

between the obligation and the right prevails over an *ordre relationnel* in which the observance of the law is a corollary of international legal personality. It removes not only breaches of bilateral obligations but also breaches of multilateral obligations from the scope of responsibility for complicity. Second, it forecloses the development or extension of international responsibility to cover wrongful acts by States in combination with non-State actors which are not explicitly and directly bound by the same obligations.[406] Most importantly, such non-State actors do so with the aid or assistance coming from States. It suffices to consider the situation that gave rise to the *Kosovo* Advisory Opinion.[407] Assume for a moment that the 'authors of the declaration of independence' would be aided or assisted by third States. Had the Court deemed such declaration not in conformity with general international law, could one possibly raise the question of whether the aiding or assisting States would incur responsibility for their complicity in an act concluded with the view to undermining the sovereignty of the territorial State?[408]

More fundamentally, the construction of opposability in the rule on responsibility for complicity was more of an intellectual and legal policy choice of the Special Rapporteur rather than a reflection of available practice and *opinio juris*. First, an overwhelming majority of the States' comments approving the rule on responsibility for aid or assistance were made in respect of former draft Article 27. As demonstrated in previous chapters, that former draft Article 27 of the rule on responsibility for aid or assistance was not limited to cases where the accomplice and the principal were bound by the same obligation. This is a crucial indication that the requirement of opposability fails to capture the scope of responsibility for complicity that States were ready to attribute to former draft Article 27, the predecessor of current Article 16 ARSIWA. Second, Sweden was the only State expressly inviting the Commission to bring the provision on responsibility for complicity into conformity with the logic of Articles 34 and 35 of the VCLT.[409] The Netherlands had made a similar argument in 1978 but then retracted it at a later stage.[410] Quite naturally, after its insertion into what was destined to become Article 16 ARSIWA, a few States

406 ibid.

407 *Accordance with International Law of the Unilateral Declaration of Independence in Respect of Kosovo* (Advisory Opinion) [2010] ICJ Rep 403.

408 J Crawford, 'Sovereignty as a Legal Value' in J Crawford and M Koskenniemi (eds), *The Cambridge Companion to International Law* (Cambridge, CUP, 2012) 117–33; cf B Kingsbury, 'Sovereignty and Inequality' (1998) 9 *EJIL* 599.

409 ILC (n 13) 77 (Sweden).

410 UNGA, 'Sixth Committee, Summary Record of the 31st Meeting' (n 3) paras 9–10 (Netherlands).

welcomed the opposability requirement perceiving in it a positive curtailment of the scope of responsibility for complicity.[411]

According to Lukashuk, an ILC member at the time of the second reading, the requirement of opposability ran:

> [C]ounter to the principles of good faith, whose importance as a principle of positive law had been underlined both in the 1969 Vienna Convention and by ICJ. According to article 16, a State which aided or assisted another State in the commission of an internationally wrongful act was not responsible for doing so if the act would not have been internationally wrongful had it committed it itself. *That provision essentially legalized aid or assistance provided with the intention of infringing international law.*[412] (emphasis added)

We could not agree more with this proposition, which was clearly overlooked by the ILC's Drafting Committee. Lukashuk proceeds by stating that:

> The Special Rapporteur had wrongly referred to articles 34 and 35 of the [VCLT] in that connection. True, those articles provided that a treaty was not binding on third States, but that did not mean that a third State had the right to assist another State in the commission of a breach of the Convention. Acts committed in bad faith were contrary to the Convention.[413]

Moreover, considering that the subjects of law in any legal system are not necessarily identical in their nature or in the way in which they exercise their rights and duties, the opposability requirement may not necessarily be transposed wholesale and unmodified to international organisations.[414] Article 14 ARIO, by analogy to Article 16 ARSIWA, appears to assume that the assisting and assisted entities are under the same obligation.[415] This may lead to problems in practice. Although it is increasingly accepted that international organisations may commit human rights violations, uncertainties remain as to the precise scope and legal source of obligations governing the conduct of multiple international organisations.[416]

[411] See, eg UNGA, 'Sixth Committee, Summary Record of the 22nd Meeting' (n 4) 7, para 37 (Czech Republic); ILC (n 4) 28 (United States).

[412] ILC (n 402) 42, para 53 (Lukashuk).

[413] ibid.

[414] See A Pellet, 'The Definition of Responsibility in International Law' in J Crawford et al (eds), *The Law of International Responsibility* (Oxford, OUP, 2010) 7.

[415] ARSIWA (n 22) 66, para 6 (Art 16 Commentary).

[416] See Reinisch (n 73) 73; A Reinisch, 'Developing a Human Rights and Humanitarian Law Accountability of the UN Security Council for the Imposition of Economic Sanctions' (2001) 95 *AJIL* 851; E de Wet, 'Human Rights Limitations to Economic Enforcement Measures under Article 41 of the United Nations Charter and the Iraqi Sanctions Regime' (2001) 14 *LJIL* 277; E de Wet, 'Holding International Institutions Accountable: The Complementary Role of Non-Judicial Oversight Mechanisms and Judicial Review' in A von Bogdandy et al (eds), *The Exercise of Public Authority by International Institutions*, vol 210 (Heidelberg, Springer, 2010); P Klein, *La responsabilité des organisations internationales dans les ordres juridiques internes et en droit des gens* (Bruxelles, Bruylant, 1998).

A number of States and international organisations took issue with the opposability requirement in the context of the elaboration of Article 14 ARIO. For example, the Russian Federation criticised the opposability requirement in Article 14 ARIO for the reason that 'some actions could be taken only by States and not by international organizations'—this would not necessarily make the act lawful if performed by the international organisation.[417] Similarly, the United States, which a few years earlier favoured the opposability requirement in the context of the ARSIWA, expressed serious reservations as to the operation of this requirement when applied to the responsibility of international organisations.[418] In the view of the representative of Guatemala

> there was no country in the world in which an individual who was not a party to a contract with two other individuals could knowingly assist one of them in violating that contract without incurring responsibility for injuries caused to the other party to the contract as a consequence of the violation. However, in order for an international organization to act as set out in [Article 14 ARIO] …, but without the application of [opposability requirement], *the rule that the international organization would be violating would be a fundamental principle of international law*. Naturally, the same could be said, *mutatis mutandis*, for such conduct carried out by a State.[419] (emphasis added)

The Israeli representative for its part asserted that:

> As a general principle, her delegation considered that the rule had potential relevance. At the time article 16 on State responsibility had been considered, Israel had questioned whether it was appropriate to limit a State's responsibility in situations of aid or assistance only to cases in which the act would be internationally wrongful if committed by that State. Similarly, it questioned whether the same limiting condition should be included in [the ARIO] … concerning … an international organization aiding or assisting … a State or another international organization in the commission of an internationally wrongful act'.[420]

Furthermore, Israel pointed out that the requirement of opposability

> appeared to be of equal relevance in the case of State assistance to an international organization. Nevertheless, it might be necessary to ensure that such a principle did not provide States with a pretext to avoid implementing properly adopted and lawful decisions of an international organization.[421]

417 UNGA, 'Sixth Committee, Summary Record of the 12th Meeting' (25 October 2005) UN Doc A/C.6/60/SR.12, 11, para 67 (Russian Federation).

418 ibid 5, para 24 (United States).

419 ibid 17, para 103 (Guatemala).

420 UNGA, 'Sixth Committee, Summary Record of the 16th Meeting' (28 October 2005) UN Doc A/C.6/60/SR.16, 9, para 55 (Israel).

421 ibid.

Cuba suggested the deletion of the requirement of opposability altogether:

> The requirement that the act would be wrongful if committed by the State or international organization providing the aid or assistance should be removed. The progressive development of a *rule establishing that States and international organizations are duty-bound not to facilitate the commission of an act in breach of international law is proposed instead.*[422] (emphasis added)

These comments attest to the thesis of 'bilateralisation' of complicity as an assassin of its utility and progressive development of international law in this area. Such a requirement is entirely misconceived regarding the responsibility of international organisations. If relatively valid counter-arguments could be made for its retention in the law of State responsibility, it is difficult, if not impossible, to see any rationale for requiring that the international organisation knowingly supporting a State in the commission of internationally wrongful act shall only bear responsibility if subject to the same obligation breached by the assisted State.[423] It is practically impossible to find examples where the organisation is bound by the same treaty obligation as the State, with the exception of customary international law obligations. One solution might be to relax the requirement of opposability to the existence of the obligation with a similar content, rather than identical one.

Aust rightly advances the argument:

> Although the aiding and assisting State would not technically be barred from granting such support, it is reasonably clear that through its conduct it will harm a third State [or] an individual protected by the given human rights treaty. Moreover, the State would have to rely on the purely formal argument that, although it is contributing to a violation of a rule to which it is bound, it could avoid responsibility due to the rule in question being laid down in differing sources.[424]

James Crawford rebuts Aust's reading of the opposability requirement. He suggests that the conditioning of responsibility was not meant to require the existence of the identity in terms of the source of a particular international obligation.[425] Yet, as discussed above, the comments by States and international organisations demonstrate that this is exactly the meaning that they attached to the terms of paragraph (b) in Article 16 ARSIWA and its sister provisions in the ARIO.

In this author's view, the opposability requirement is purely formalistic and fails to perceive the international responsibility as a real epicentre of the international legal order. Indeed, Article 16(b) ARSIWA has a direct

[422] ILC (n 301) 16 (Cuba).
[423] Crawford (n 23) 409–10.
[424] Aust (n 2) 264–65.
[425] Crawford (n 23) 410.

effect of allowing the otherwise complicit State or international organisation to escape responsibility by arguing that it is bound by a different rule from the one breached by the assisted State.[426]

B. Opposability Element: A Requiem of Responsibility for Complicity?

Obligation is above all 'a necessary instrument of social co-operation, and cannot be denied by individual free will'.[427] In this manner, Eagleton linked the premises of responsibility to the theoretical underpinning of an international obligation in international law. Indeed, with the idea of membership in any society or community comes the idea of shared responsibility for the preservation of that structure. Today, membership in the international community presupposes not only the acceptance of the existent rules but also standards, fundamental principles and values which shape the compliance with an international obligation.

It is difficult to see how the requirement of opposability fits into this idea that every international obligation must be performed without undue interferences by third parties. In Crawford's view, the basis of responsibility for complicity without the opposability requirement would stretch too far.[428] However, his only inspiration was taken from the realm of the law of treaties. With due respect, in this author's view the question of compliance with a treaty obligation and its scope under the treaty law could and should differ from the establishment and consequences of responsibility. Lauterpacht's remarks elsewhere are of assistance to our argument:

> It is consonant with State sovereignty to refuse to recognize any source of liability other than that grounded in consent given by treaty or in a rule of law evidenced as binding by custom. But that limitation of liability to defined categories may not be consistent with justice and with the requirements of law in a progressive society. *Conduct which has hitherto been in accordance with the purpose of the law may cease to be so owing to developments which the law has not yet had time to take into account; behaviour which the law is as a rule content to regard as not in contradiction with social needs ceases to be so when the advantage accruing to one party from the exercise of an otherwise legal right results in disproportionately grave injury to others; action which is described as lawful may cease to be so if pursued in an unsocial manner or in a manner contrary to the purpose for which it has been allowed.* In all

[426] ibid.

[427] C Eagleton, *The Responsibility of States in International Law* (New York, New York University Press, 1928) 5.

[428] Crawford (n 23) 409–10.

> these cases such conduct, while *prima facie* lawful, amounts to an abuse of a right conferred by the law.[429] (emphasis added)

Without the condition of opposability, the responsibility of a complicit actor is already sufficiently limited by the requirement of knowledge, which ensures that it does not unduly hamper cooperation between subjects of international law. In a nutshell, the requirement of opposability contained in Article 16(b) ARSIWA and Article 14(b) ARIO shows the conflicting approaches to understanding the enforcement of international obligations. On the one hand, lawyers take it for granted that the law of treaties could dictate its logic upon the development of the law of responsibility. On the other hand, it is said that the law of treaties and the law of responsibility fulfil two different functions in international law. In the *Gabčíkovo-Nagymaros* case, the Court emphasised that:

> A determination of whether a convention is or is not in force, and whether it has or has not been properly suspended or denounced, is to be made pursuant to the law of treaties. On the other hand, an evaluation of the extent to which the suspension or denunciation of a convention, seen as incompatible with the law of treaties, involves the responsibility of the State which proceeded to it, is to be made under the law of state responsibility.
>
> Thus the Vienna Convention of 1969 on the Law of Treaties confines itself to defining—in a limitative manner—the conditions in which a treaty may lawfully be denounced or suspended; while the effects of a denunciation or suspension seen as not meeting those conditions are, on the contrary, expressly excluded from the scope of the Convention by operation of Article 73. It is moreover well established that, when a State has committed an internationally wrongful act, its international responsibility is likely to be involved whatever the nature of the obligation it has failed to respect …[430]

The discussion on opposability shares some similarities with the question of interoperability of obligations under some treaty regimes. As we have seen earlier in this chapter, during the negotiations of the CCM, the issue of interoperability arose due to the concerns about joint military operations and eventual collaboration with States non-parties to the CCM. Several States expressed reservations as to the unlimited prohibition to assist States non-parties in the performance of activities which are prohibited under the CCM. Having strategic interests in alliances and cooperation with these non-parties, some States negotiating the Convention were concerned that this could lead to criminal liability of their officials and

[429] H Lauterpacht, 'General Rules of the Law of Peace' in E Lauterpacht (ed), *International Law Being the Collected Papers of Hersch Lauterpacht—The General Works*, vol 1 (Cambridge, CUP, 1970) 384.

[430] *Gabčikovo-Nagymaros Project (Hungary/Slovakia)* (n 400) 38–39, paras 47–48.

potentially State responsibility. This led to the adoption of a controversial provision contained in Article 21(3) of the CCM, which largely undermines the effectiveness of the obligation not to assist:

> Notwithstanding the provisions of Article 1 of this Convention and in accordance with international law, States Parties, their military personnel or nationals, *may engage* in military cooperation and operations with States not party to this Convention that might engage in activities prohibited to a State Party.[431] (emphasis added)

Let us imagine the following scenario. State A is a party to the CCM and therefore is under an obligation not to use cluster munitions and to reduce its stockpiles. State B is not a party to the Convention. If State A (party to the Convention) transfers its stockpiles, knowing that State B (non-party to the Convention) uses cluster munitions in its military activities against State C (party to the Convention), would State A bear responsibility? From a treaty law perspective, Article 21(3) of the CCM excludes such responsibility of State A. But what is and should be the response under the law of international responsibility? Is not here an evident case of abuse of right by State A, which uses State B as a proxy to inflict harm on State C?

An alternative example is equally problematic. Assume State B (non-party to the Convention) provides cluster munitions to State A (party to the Convention) for the latter's joint operation with other States (both parties and non-parties). Assume B knows of the existence of an obligation incumbent on A and the circumstances of the wrongful act. Why should international law admit that B does no wrong by assisting another State in the latter's violations of its obligation? The assumption is rather problematic. At the end of the day, State B takes an informed decision to aid and assist State A in the breach of the latter's obligations.

The adoption of this language in Article 21(3) of the CCM shows how States are exploring law-making techniques to circumvent their obligations. Regrettably, the same logic is reproduced through the opposability requirement in the context of international responsibility for complicity. The wrongfulness of the conduct of the aiding or assisting State derives primarily from its knowledge. The requirement of knowledge covers both the circumstances of the principal's conduct and whether that conduct constitutes a violation of the principal State or international organisation. From the moment the complicit State or international organisation has knowledge of the fact that its aid or assistance will facilitate a breach of an international obligation by the recipient entity, responsibility for complicity should arise. There is no question here of extending the obligation that the recipient State has vis-à-vis the putative injured party. In other words, if the complicit State has actual knowledge of the wrongfulness of

[431] CCM (n 134) Art 21(3).

the principal's conduct this makes its aid or assistance wrongful per se. The finding of wrongfulness of the conduct in the context of responsibility for complicity does not follow the same paradigm as the breach in the treaty relations. The idea of opposability of the obligation breached rather than that of constructive wrongfulness gives too restrictive of a view on the legal interests protected by the law of international responsibility.

As James Crawford himself accepts elsewhere, the provision in Article 16(b) ARSIWA was never intended to require identity of norms or sources.[432] However, this is not what transpires from the provision as set out in Article 16 and its sister provisions, nor the way in which the provision has been interpreted by States and international organisations. It is thus important to clarify whether responsibility for complicity can and should arise in situations where the assisting and assisted States are not bound by the same obligation. It is interesting to note that in a different context James Crawford was in favour of drawing a sharp distinction between the logics of the law of treaties and international responsibility.[433]

On the flipside to our argument on opposability, one could suggest that 'there is no general legal obligation for States to keep themselves informed of legislative and constitutional developments in other States which are or may become important for the international relations of these States'.[434] In the same vein, there does not seem to be any obligation on the State to keep itself informed of the international commitments of its partner States. Indeed, bilateral treaties continue to thrive, and it would be a practical challenge to impute responsibility in respect of third parties assisting in the breach of such obligation.[435] However, if on facts it could be proven that State A knows of the obligation of State B vis-à-vis State C and knows of the circumstances of the wrongful act, it should incur international responsibility. From the perspective of cogent legal and normative policy at least, State A knowingly contributes to an action that is harmful to a third State. If the law is to keep a blind eye on this conduct, then there is certainly an important lacuna. In this author's view, the demonstration of knowledge of the circumstances coupled with a clear factual link (nexus) between complicity and the principal wrongful act are sufficient for the purposes of responsibility for complicity. Let us take two further conceptual issues that demonstrate the inadequacy of the opposability requirement in practice.

[432] Crawford (n 23) 410.

[433] J Crawford, 'Third Report on State Responsibility' (2000) UN Doc A/CN.4/507 and Add 1-4, reproduced in (2000) 2 (pt 1) *YBILC* 3, 87, para 325.

[434] *Land and Maritime Boundary between Cameroon and Nigeria (Cameroon v Nigeria: Equatorial Guinea intervening)* (Judgment) [2002] ICJ Rep 303, 430, para 266.

[435] See JHH Weiler, 'The Geology of International Law—Governance, Democracy and Legitimacy' (2004) 64 *ZaöRV* 547, 6–7 (who notes that the change occuring in the international legal system is one of the 'stratification' rather than a genuine shift from bilateralism to multilateralism).

i. The Character of the Obligation Breached

Let us assume the following scenario. State A is not a party to the Convention on the Elimination of All Forms of Discrimination against Women (CEDAW). State B is a party to the Convention. State A assists State B with funding to abduct and traffic women in the region located in State C. Due to the requirement of opposability, State C will only be able to bring proceedings against State B for violations of the CEDAW, namely Article 6 of that Convention and not against State A.

Take another example of a bilateral treaty binding State A not to exploit natural resources in the area within the territory of State B. Assume State C knowingly supports State A with drilling material which is exclusively needed to exploit the type of natural resources available in the area. In other words, State C procures State A's breach of its obligation. Under the limitation set forth in Article 16(b) ARSIWA, State C carries no responsibility as it is not bound by the obligation of State A.

Any, even if minimal, conception of legality would militate against such a state of the law. The fact that a particular State does not have a given obligation cannot excuse that State from aiding or assisting others in violation of their respective obligations. Clearly, in this kind of scenario the knowledge of the aiding or assisting State is crucial. In our first example above, it should suffice that the aiding or assisting State knows of the general policy or plan of discrimination as practised by the assisted State. In the second example, the State's actual knowledge as to the use that is expected for its drilling materials should be sufficient to determine its responsibility for the contribution to the violation of the bilateral obligation by State A.

The opposability requirement would thus seem to curtail most of the situations of breaches of bilateral or multilateral obligations. Nonetheless, the requirement has no impact when obligations under customary international law are at stake. However, even here, State A may be a persistent objector to the existence of a particular obligation, the commission of which it has aided or assisted. Would this mean technically that the wrongful act would not be opposable within the meaning of Article 16(b) ARSIWA?

Of course, the requirement of opposability is met by default when the internationally wrongful act implicates a serious breach of international law, whether it is a *jus cogens* or *erga omnes* obligation. However, limiting the possibility of responsibility for complicity to cases where the obligation breached is *erga omnes* or *jus cogens* unnecessarily restricts the role that the responsibility for complicity could play in practice. Moreover, even in cases of assistance to the commission of an *erga omnes* or *jus cogens* violation, State A would still face a serious hurdle in bringing the claim. As the Court stated in the *Armed Activities on the Territory of the Congo (DRC v*

Rwanda) case, the nature of the obligation breached does not affect the fact that the court of law based on the assumption of consent, needs to be satisfied that it has jurisdiction.[436] In that case, the Court held that Rwanda's reservation to Article IX of the Genocide Convention could not be deemed invalid by the sole fact that a dispute relates to compliance with a norm having *jus cogens* character.[437] It cannot of itself provide a basis for the jurisdiction of the Court to entertain that dispute.[438] In sum, although the criterion of opposability may be rendered irrelevant depending on the nature of the obligation breached, in this author's view this limitation to responsibility for complicity is still not justified in practice and *opinio juris*, and renders the relevant provision extremely difficult to operationalise.

ii. The Moment in Time for Assessing the Opposability Requirement

In addition to the character of the obligation breached, it is not clear whether the opposability requirement is to be verified at the moment when the aid or assistance is provided or at the moment the principal wrongful act takes place. There is often a considerable period of time in between the two events.[439]

Articles 13 ARSIWA and 11 ARIO posit a well-established rule that conduct of the State or international organisation only constitutes a breach if that conduct is not in conformity with the obligation binding upon that State or international organisation '*at the time the act occurs*'.[440] These provisions thus build the general principle of intertemporal law into the domain of international responsibility, ie that 'a juridical fact must be appreciated in the light of the law contemporary with it, and not of the law in force at the time when a dispute in regard to it arises or falls to be settled'.[441]

While Article 16 ARSIWA is silent in this regard, the ILC's Commentary to Article 58 ARIO posits that 'no distinction is made with

[436] *Armed Activities on the Territory of the Congo (New Application: 2002) (DRC v Rwanda)* (Jurisdiction and Admissibility) [2006] ICJ Rep 6, 29–31, para 55–63.

[437] ibid 31, para 64; similarly in respect of erga omnes obligations see *East Timor (Portugal v Australia)* (Judgment) [1995] ICJ Rep 90, 102, para 29.

[438] *Armed Activities (DRC v Rwanda)* (n 436) 31, para 64.

[439] On issues of time in the law of international responsibility see P Weckel, 'Les instantanés du droit international' in SFDI (ed), *Le droit international et le temps* (Paris, Pedone, 2001); J Wolfram, 'The Time Factor in the Law of State Responsibility' in M Spinedi and B Simma (eds), *United Nations Codification of State Responsibility* (New York, Oceana, 1987); E Wyler, 'Quelques réflexions sur la réalisation dans le temps du fait internationalement illicite' (1991) 95 *RGDIP* 881; MJ Ayissi, 'La réalisation dans le temps de l'illicite international et ses conséquences dans le droit de la responsabilité internationale' (PhD Thesis, Geneva, Graduate Institute, 2011).

[440] ARSIWA (n 22) 57 (Art 13 Commentary) (emphasis added).

[441] *Island of Palmas (United States v Netherlands)* (n 204) 845.

regard to the temporal relation between the conduct of the State and the internationally wrongful act of the international organization'.[442] This can be read as implying that there can be a time lapse between the complicit and the principal conduct, which reinforces our critique of the opposability requirement and the lack of clarity as to when it must be established.

Consider a scenario in which a State started the ratification process of a treaty, which contains a particular obligation, and it gives aid to another State to violate this obligation. However, the aided State only commits the wrongful act one year after. By that time the aiding State has already ratified the treaty and an obligation binds it. Should the aiding State be held responsible or should it be exempted taking into account the moment it had provided aid? In addition to the principle of intertemporal law, as incorporated into Articles 13 ARSIWA and 11 ARIO, Article 28 of the VCLT further clarifies that:

> Unless a different intention appears from the treaty or is otherwise established, its provisions do not bind a party in relation to any act or fact which took place or any situation which ceased to exist before the date of the entry into force of the treaty with respect to that party.[443]

Accordingly, it is the moment when the obligation is in force and is breached that determines whether responsibility for complicity unfolds. Hence, hypothetically, a State could render aid or assistance to another State well in advance of the commission of an internationally wrongful act. The aiding or assisting State will, however, only incur responsibility if at the moment of the commission of the principal wrongful act it is bound by the obligation breached.

Some reflection on this problem can be found by analogy in case law. For instance, in *Mondev International Limited v United States*, the arbitral tribunal, referring to Article 13 ARSIWA and Article 28 VCLT, emphasised that

> events or conduct prior to the entry into force of an obligation for the respondent State may be relevant in determining whether the State has subsequently committed a breach of the obligation. However, it must still be possible to point to conduct of the State after that date which is itself a breach....The mere fact that earlier conduct has gone unremedied or unredressed when a treaty enters into force does not justify a tribunal applying the treaty retrospectively to that conduct. Any other approach would subvert both the intertemporal principle in the law of treaties and the basic distinction between breach and reparation which underlies the law of State responsibility.[444]

[442] ARIO (n 22) 91, para 3 (Art 58 Commentary).

[443] VCLT (n 384) Art 28.

[444] *Mondev International Ltd v United States* (Award) [2002] ICSID Case No ARB(AF)/99/2, para 70.

The ECtHR in the *Blečić v Croatia* case also reaffirmed the principle contained in Articles 13 ARSIWA:

> [W]hile it is true that from the ratification date onwards all of the State's acts and omissions must conform to the [1950 ECHR] ... the Convention imposes no specific obligation on the Contracting States to provide redress for wrongs or damage caused prior to that date ... Any other approach would undermine both the principle of non-retroactivity in the law of treaties and the fundamental distinction between violation and reparation that underlines the law of State responsibility.[445]

The distinction thus needs to be drawn as to whether situations of aid or assistance to a breach of a given obligation may under certain circumstances constitute an act of a continuing character or are always an instantaneous act with continuing effects.[446] This distinction is particularly relevant in those cases where aid or assistance is given with the knowledge of a general State policy expected to bring about a particular outcome. If the assisted State uses the aid in implementation of such a policy which in turn results in a series of wrongful acts dispersed in time and place, including at the point when the assisting State itself becomes party to the treaty containing the obligation breached, an argument could be made that the provision of such aid amounts to a continuing internationally wrongful act.[447] The point is of practical importance, particularly considering a variety of continuing wrongful acts in international law, including the non-adoption of certain legislative measures prescribed by international obligation,[448] an unlawful occupation or blockade,[449] occupation of embassies or taking of hostages of diplomatic and consular representatives.[450]

Further, in those situations where the State is bound by an obligation and knowingly renders assistance to another State to breach that obligation,

[445] *Blečić v Croatia* (Judgment) [2006] ECtHR App No 59532/00 (2005) 41 EHRR 13, para 48.

[446] *Mondev International Ltd v United States* (n 444) para 58; *Phosphates in Morocco (Italy v France)* (Preliminary Objections) [1938] PCIJ Ser A/B No 74, 10, 23; *Namibia (Advisory Opinion)* (n 368) 54, para 118; *Diplomatic and Consular Staff in Tehran (United States v Iran)* (Judgment) [1980] ICJ Rep 3, 35–36, paras 76–77; *Ilaşcu and others v Moldova and Russia* (Merits and Just Satisfaction) [2004] ECtHR App No 48787/99 (2005) 40 EHRR 46, para 321 ff.

[447] See generally J Pauwelyn, 'The Concept of a Continuing Violation of an International Obligation: Selected Problems' (1996) 66 *British YBIL* 415; G Distefano, 'Fait continu, fait composé et fait complexe dans le droit de la responsabilité' (2006) 52 *AFDI* 1; Ayissi (n 439); J Salmon, 'Le fait étatique complexe—une notion contestable' (1982) 28 *AFDI* 709.

[448] See *Phosphates in Morocco (Italy v France)* (n 446) Separate Opinion of Judge Cheng Tien-Hsi 36, 36–37; see also O Hoijer, *La responsabilité internationale des États en matière d'actes législatifs* (Paris, Les Éditions Internationales, 1930) 9–35; E Vitta, *La responsabilità internazionale dello Stato per atti legislativi* (Milano, Giuffrè, 1953).

[449] *Legal Consequences of the Construction of a Wall in the Occupied Palestinian Territory* (n 152) 199–200, paras 155–59.

[450] *Diplomatic and Consular Staff in Tehran (United States v Iran)* (n 446) 41, para 90; 43–44, para 94.

but the principal wrongful act takes place when State A has already withdrawn from the treaty containing that obligation, State A could also bear responsibility. This construction would be controversial as it could eventually be tainted with retrospectivity *in mitius* in international law. Yet, some support for this proposition can be found in the work of the Institut de droit international (IDI) and the existing case law.[451] In the *Nauru* case, for instance, Australia argued that the case was inadmissible on the ground that the termination of the trusteeship by the UN, before the date of the proceedings, precluded Nauru from making claims of breaches of that Agreement.[452] The Court rejected this objection implying it would apply the Trusteeship Agreement in its decision on the merits even though at the time of the proceedings it was no longer in force.

The core question that emerges is what is 'the extent of the Government's obligation to satisfy itself that no internationally illegal acts are occurring [implicating its aid or assistance]?'.[453] At the crucial moment when a State is asked to provide aid or assistance, what should be the scope of its inquiry into the use and channelling of that aid or assistance by the recipient State? If the State knows that its counterpart is bound by the specific obligation and that the aid or assistance provided will facilitate the breach of that obligation (immediately or at some later point), the aiding or assisting State should not avoid international responsibility. This is where the existing ILC provisions fail to ensure the integrity of international obligations and the legality function of the law of international responsibility, allowing its private/contractual logic to prevail over the public/systemic one.

V. INTERIM CONCLUSIONS

This chapter has cast doubt on the constituent requirements of responsibility for complicity as it currently stands in the ARSIWA and ARIO provisions. As Rosenne rightly posited, 'the ILC independent though it is, does not work in an "ivory tower" but is kept close to the political currents which will in the end have to adopt its proposals'.[454] These proposals may not always be the most representative ones. As we have seen, States and international organisations hold different views on almost every

[451] IDI, 'Resolution on the Intertemporal Problem in Public International Law' (1975) 56 *AIDI* 537 para 1; see also *Island of Palmas (United States v Netherlands)* (n 204) 845.

[452] *Certain Phosphate Lands in Nauru (Nauru v Australia)* (Preliminary Objections) [1992] ICJ Rep 240, 250–53; *Island of Palmas (United States v Netherlands)* (n 204) 845.

[453] P Sands, 'The International Rule of Law: Extraordinary Rendition, Complicity and Its Consequences' in *Droit du pouvoir—pouvoir du droit: Mélanges en l'honneur de Jean Salmon* (Bruxelles, Bruylant, 2007) 419.

[454] S Rosenne (ed), *The International Law Commission's Draft Articles on State Responsibility: Part I, Articles 1-35* (Dordrecht, Martinus Nijhoff, 1991) 19.

condition of responsibility for complicity apart from the underlying rule or principle itself.

First, it transpires from the analysis of practice and *opinio juris* of States and international organisations that the concept of responsibility for complicity is now well entrenched in the relevant standards of behaviour that the law-determining agents expect from each other. However, there remain some difficult questions about the role of this form of responsibility in the context of international organisations as the comments made by financial institutions demonstrate. However, all international organisations commenting on the ARIO recognised the importance of responsibility for complicity as a matter of progressive development of international law. Implicitly, what this also shows is that the recognition of responsibility in Article 16 ARSIWA as a rule of customary international law has not yet closed the doors for further development and refinement of its content and operation in practice.

Second, our analysis of the material element of complicity has shown that States and international organisations have generally expressed preference for an exacting link between the complicit and the principal conduct. The author, however, claimed that a clear factual or causal link between the aid or assistance and the principal wrongful act is sufficient for the responsibility for complicity to arise. Further, no State or international organisation has specifically argued that Article 16 ARSIWA and its sister provisions could not apply to situations of aid or assistance arising out of omissions. This led us to examine the main traits that go on to distinguish responsibility for complicity from the responsibility flowing from the violation of the due diligence obligations. This author proposed that a distinction be drawn on varying knowledge and control-based criteria.

Third, while the existing practice is still relatively scant, it is fair to say that references to responsibility for complicity are increasingly common in the interactions between States and international organisations. In order to better understand the extent and type of conduct covered by the general rule of responsibility for complicity, this chapter examined some of the specific treaty regimes containing prohibitions on complicity that are generally broader in scope than the corresponding ARSIWA and ARIO rules. The analysis of these regimes shows an interesting dynamic in the relations between primary rules on complicity and what one could call a general *meta-rule* (a hybrid of a primary and secondary rule) of responsibility for complicity: where the injured State argues that a direct violation of a treaty obligation prohibiting complicity has occurred, and nonetheless cites Article 16 ARSIWA as well. This is despite the fact that where a treaty contains a specific prohibition of complicity, it is much easier to find responsibility, thus enhancing the chances of success in obtaining reparation.

In principle, where complicity is directly regulated under a primary norm, the injured State would be able to claim a suitable remedy for the totality of the injury from the complicit State. Because of its inherent qualifications, Article 16 ARSIWA will thus be of little strategic value for an injured party. However, when no primary rule expressly regulates complicity, Article 16 ARSIWA and its sister provisions are extremely important. These situations are rare in practice and to date Article 16 ARSIWA has only been cited as a principle of support rather than an exclusive basis for the legal argument.

This limited or residual function of the general rule on the responsibility for complicity is not necessarily a bad thing. From a practical perspective, the fact that States agree to specific prohibitions of complicity in the treaties they conclude shows that they may give different value to the prohibition of complicity depending on the nature of rights and interests that are to be safeguarded. On the one hand, this is a legitimate aspect of treaty-making and normative selectivity. On the other hand, from a systemic perspective, the fragmentation of the norms regulating complicit conduct may dilute the role it could play in upholding legality and the rule of law.[455] The effect of such a dilution would be particularly felt with respect to international organisations that are not bound by the arsenal of treaty obligations prohibiting complicity, with the exception of those norms that concurrently form part of customary international law.

Further, this chapter examined the cognitive and opposability requirements of the responsibility for complicity in the ARSIWA and ARIO. An argument was made that an exclusive test of the 'knowledge of the circumstances' is preferred to that of intent. The author argued that such an approach is more consistent with the objective nature of international responsibility, and shed light on possible ways to demonstrate knowledge of the circumstances of the wrongful act. However, there is still a large degree of ambiguity in respect of this dichotomy knowledge vis-à-vis intent. Accordingly, our main objective was to try to identify normative options that the law-determining agents could follow in adjusting the cognitive requirement and operationalising it. Finally, this author has argued against the opposability requirement which has undermined the current utility of the rule on responsibility for complicity. The author has shown that the introduction of this limitation into the general rule on responsibility for complicity finds no basis in the existing practice and *opinio juris*. Based on the imitation of the logic of the law of treaties, the requirement is not justified both from a conceptual and practical point of view. If international law is to be regarded as a genuine legal order then the limitation of opposability should have no place in the rules on responsibility for complicity.

[455] See PM Dupuy, 'Back to the Future of a Multilateral Dimension of the Law of State Responsibility for Breaches of "Obligations Owed to the International Community as a Whole"' (2012) 23 *EJIL* 1059; PM Dupuy, 'Dionisio Anzilotti and the Law of International Responsibility of States' (1992) 3 *EJIL* 139, 146.

6

Legal Consequences and Implementation of Responsibility for Complicity

I. INTRODUCTION

THE PREVIOUS CHAPTERS have addressed the *fait générateur* and constituent elements of responsibility for complicity. We have seen that there are a number of open questions in relation to the application and effectiveness of these elements for the purposes of establishing international responsibility. This chapter moves to the analysis of a subsequent phase in the lifecycle of responsibility, namely its content and implementation.

In general, there are three legal consequences of a finding of international responsibility: i) cessation; ii) assurances and guarantees of non-repetition; and iii) reparation (restitution, compensation and satisfaction). Section II examines the way in which these legal consequences apply to complicit actors. This is followed by a review of the available forms of reparation and the extent to which the existing causal standards provide an adequate solution to scenarios involving a complicit State or international organisation.

The question of causation is crucial in the context of any claim of reparation before courts and tribunals, including in respect of complicity. There are two dimensions of causal analysis in the context of responsibility for complicity which must be carefully distinguished.[1]

First, as demonstrated in chapter five, complicit conduct must *facilitate* the commission of the principal wrongful act. However, the threshold or degree of facilitating is not set out in the text of the Articles on Responsibility of States for Internationally Wrongful Acts (ARSIWA) and Articles on Responsibility of International Organizations (ARIO) provisions. The International Law Commission (ILC)'s Commentary notes briefly that the

[1] See, eg J d'Aspremont, 'The Articles on the Responsibility of International Organizations: Magnifying the Fissures in the Law of International Responsibility' (2012) 9 *IOLR* 15, 21.

complicit conduct must have 'significantly' contributed to the principal wrongful act. This requirement also finds some support in the *opinio juris* and practice. However, this author has argued that a lower threshold of a *clear factual link* on the balance of probabilities would meet the concerns of States and international organisations about the content of the qualifying aid or assistance and its connection to the principal wrongdoing.

Secondly, after it is established that the State or international organisation incurs responsibility for complicity, a causal analysis must take place in order to determine the reparation due. This causal analysis examines whether the complicit conduct is sufficiently proximate to the injury flowing from the commission of the principal wrongful act and/or whether it was foreseeable.

The causal link between the complicit conduct and the injury must be present for the injured party to claim reparation from the complicit State or international organisation. In the traditional understanding of the *content* of responsibility, this link is not necessarily present by virtue of the fact that the complicit conduct has facilitated the commission of the internationally wrongful act.[2] Although this causal analysis complicates any award of monetary compensation, it is argued here that the policy objectives (ie public order and legality function) of the ARSIWA and ARIO dictate that at least a more flexible causal approach to satisfaction be taken. Indeed, it is imperative that greater emphasis be placed on foreseeability in the causation analysis. Failing this, two other constructions of complicity could take hold. The first is to develop further the conceptual fiction of complicity in a wrongful act as a *separable wrongful act*, causing a *separable injury*, which would be likely to result in the eventual elimination of the causal analysis at all. The second would be to apportion responsibility for complicity in accordance with the existing standards of joint and several responsibility.

Section III examines the implementation of responsibility for complicity. There are essentially three major issues to be addressed in this area. The first issue is whether *any* State or international organisation can invoke the responsibility of others for complicity in breaches of *erga omnes* obligations. The second issue is that the reactions by States to breaches of international obligations by others appear to be premised, at least partially, on attempts of avoiding their own complicity in such breaches. The third issue is that implementation of responsibility for complicity, as an inherently multidimensional phenomenon, is difficult in the current

[2] HP Aust, *Complicity and the Law of State Responsibility* (Cambridge, CUP, 2011) 274–75 (arguing that '[i]t is apparent that in the case of complicity, at least two States have "caused" the injury to be remedied. Put more precisely, through its aid or assistance, the complicity State has contributed to the injury caused by the main actor. Although two separate wrongful acts exist, the injury is one and the same').

framework for dispute settlement, which is inherently bilateral. Significant structural adjustments would be required for courts and tribunals to adjudge the responsibility of complicit actors, without first adjudging on the responsibility of the principal wrongdoer.

II. LEGAL CONSEQUENCES AND CONTENT OF RESPONSIBILITY FOR COMPLICITY

In practice, an establishment of responsibility is a necessary but not sufficient condition for the implementation of the legal consequences flowing from an internationally wrongful act in respect of one or several responsible actors. The obligation of cessation arises only where the internationally wrongful act is of a continuing character;[3] assurances and guarantees of non-repetition must only be given 'if circumstances so require';[4] and the 'obligation to make full reparation' arises under general international law only when an internationally wrongful act has caused an injury.[5] These consequences are of course without prejudice to the continued duty of performance of the obligation breached.[6]

In the particular context of complicity, it is questionable whether, formally speaking, legal consequences can attach to the complicit actors '*telle quelle*'.[7] Without the conceptual fiction of 'complicity in the wrongful act = separable wrongful act', it cannot be assumed that legal consequences will attach to complicit actors. As Aust rightly posits, the complicit State enters 'indirectly into the legal relationship between the main actor and the injured State'.[8] In other words, it is the connection between the complicit conduct and the principal wrongful act that can transform otherwise lawful conduct into wrongful conduct.

[3] ILC, 'Draft Articles on Responsibility of States for Internationally Wrongful Acts, with Commentaries' (2001) 2 (pt 2) *YBILC* 31 (ARSIWA) Art 30(a); ILC, 'Draft Articles on the Responsibility of International Organizations, with Commentaries' (2011) 2 (pt 2) *YBILC* 2 (ARIO) Art 30(a).

[4] ARSIWA (n 3) Art 30(b); ARIO (n 3) Art 30(b).

[5] ARSIWA (n 3) Art 31; ARIO (n 3) Art 31; see P d'Argent, 'Reparation, Cessation, Assurances and Guarantees of Non-Repetition' in A Nollkaemper and I Plakokefalos (eds), *Principles of Shared Responsibility in International Law: An Appraisal of the State of the Art* (Cambridge, CUP, 2014) 209; on the notion of injury in the law of international responsibility see J Barboza, 'Legal Injury: The Tip of the Iceberg in the Law of State Responsibility?' in M Ragazzi (ed), *International Responsibility Today: Essays in Memory of Oscar Schachter* (Leiden, Martinus Nijhoff, 2005); B Stern, 'Et si on utilisait la notion de préjudice juridique? Retour sur une notion délaissée à l'occasion de la fin des travaux de la C.D.I. sur la responsabilité des États' (2001) 47 *AFDI* 3; B Stern, 'A Plea for "Reconstruction" of International Responsibility Based on the Notion of Legal Injury' in M Ragazzi (ed), *International Responsibility Today: Essays in Memory of Oscar Schachter* (Leiden, Martinus Nijhoff, 2005).

[6] ARSIWA (n 3) Art 29; ARIO (n 3) Art 29.

[7] A Felder, *Die Beihilfe im Recht der völkerrechtlichen Staatenverantwortlichkeit* (Zürich, Schulthess, 2007) 271–74.

[8] Aust (n 2) 273.

This chapter will address the following questions. What legal consequences are triggered by complicity? What considerations inform the allocation of legal consequences to the complicit actor? What remedy, if any, is available and appropriate for complicity under general international law? Can or should such remedy go beyond satisfaction in the form of a declaration of illegality?[9] Does the nature and extent of the injury affect the allocation of legal consequences between the principal and complicit wrongdoer vis-à-vis an injured State? These are all complex and relatively unexplored matters in international law, particularly as far as the impact of complicity is concerned. The remarks made in this chapter represent only a small portion of the analysis of legal consequences that could be conducted in cases of attribution of responsibility (ie cases of complicity, direction and control, and coercion) as well as in situations of joint and several responsibility.[10]

A. Cessation (Articles 30(a) ARSIWA/ARIO)

In most cases, complicity in the wrongful act continues over a period of time, as does the principal wrongful act itself. For example, State A could be providing State B with the financial means to unlawfully run the administration of the occupied territory of State C. Similarly, it could be supplying arms on a regular basis for the commission of human rights violations or sharing intelligence which is used to torture detainees. In all these cases, both States A and B are under an obligation of cessation pursuant to Article 30(a) ARSIWA (to cease the principal wrongful act and complicity in that wrongful act). The same framework is provided by Article 30(a) ARIO for international organisations.

The obligation of cessation does not fit neatly within the strict dichotomy of primary and secondary obligations in international law.[11] As its

[9] *Application of the Convention on the Prevention and Punishment of the Crime of Genocide (Bosnia and Herzegovina v Serbia and Montenegro)* (Merits) [2007] ICJ Rep 43, 236, para 469.

[10] See generally A Nollkaemper and D Jacobs, 'Shared Responsibility in International Law: A Conceptual Framework' (2013) 34 *Michigan J Intl L* 359; J Fry, 'Coercion, Causation, and the Fictional Elements of Indirect State Responsibility' (2007) 40 *Vanderbilt J Transnatl L* 611; A Orakhelashvili, 'Division of Reparation between Responsible Entities' in J Crawford et al (eds), *The Law of International Responsibility* (Oxford, OUP, 2010); Y Chen, 'Attribution, Causation and Responsibility of International Organizations' in D Sarooshi (ed), *Remedies and Responsibility for the Actions of International Organizations* (Leiden, Martinus Nijhoff, 2014).

[11] G Arangio-Ruiz, 'Preliminary Report on State Responsibility' (1988) UN Doc A/CN.4/416 and Add 1, reproduced in (1988) 2 (pt 1) *YBILC* 6, 11; For comments of States on the nature of the obligation of cessation see UNGA, 'Sixth Committee, Summary Record of the 31st Meeting' (2 November 1989) UN Doc A/C.6/44/SR.31, 2, para 2 (Iran) and 8, para 23 (Morocco); UNGA, 'Sixth Committee, Summary Record of the 27th Meeting' (4 November 1999) UN Doc A/C.6/54/SR.27, 3, para 9 (Costa Rica); UNGA, 'Sixth Committee, Summary Record of the 32nd Meeting' (3 November 1989) UN Doc A/C.6/44/SR.32, 5, para 24 (German Democratic Republic).

object is the wrongful act in progress, cessation does not annul or repair the consequences of the breach of an international obligation. Cessation merely aims to put an end to the breach and, by implication, prevent any further injury.[12] Deman rightly contends that the obligation of cessation appears as a *préalable* to the triggering of responsibility and as an *intermédiaire* between primary and secondary norms.[13] The ILC recognised that

> cessation may be ascribed either to the continued normal operation of the 'primary' rule of which the wrongful conduct constitutes a violation or to the operation of the 'secondary' rule coming into play as an effect of the occurrence of the wrongful act ... The Commission is of the view that the *very distinction between primary and secondary rules is a relative one and that cessation is situated, so to speak, in between the two categories of rules*.[14] (emphasis added)

In the *Rainbow Warrior* arbitration, the arbitral tribunal considered New Zealand's request for the cessation of the wrongful act by France. The tribunal relied on the ILC's endorsement of the principle that 'cessation has inherent properties of its own which distinguish it from reparation'.[15] The tribunal held that the delivery of an order of cessation generally requires 'two essential conditions intimately linked, namely that the wrongful act has a continuing character and that the violated rule is still in force at the time in which the order is issued'.[16]

Cessation is best construed as a general principle that attaches to any ongoing breach of an international obligation.[17] Special Rapporteur Riphagen observed that in numerous cases 'stopping the breach was involved, rather than reparation or *restitutio in integrum stricto sensu*'.[18]

[12] See, eg *Diplomatic and Consular Staff in Tehran (United States v Iran)* (Judgment) [1980] ICJ Rep 3, 20 and 44; *Diplomatic and Consular Staff in Tehran (United States v Iran)* (Provisional Measures) [1979] ICJ Rep 7, 17 and 20, paras 29 and 42; *Nuclear Tests (New Zealand v France)* (Provisional Measures) [1973] ICJ Rep 135, 139 and 142, paras 21 and 36; *Nuclear Tests (Australia v France)* (Provisional Measures) [1973] ICJ Rep 99, 103–04, paras 17 and 20; *Military and Paramilitary Activities in and against Nicaragua (Nicaragua v United States)* (Provisional Measures) [1984] ICJ Rep 169, 173, para 8.

[13] C Deman, 'La cessation de l'acte illicite' (1990) 2 *RBDI* 477, 495; O Corten, 'The Obligation of Cessation' in J Crawford et al (eds), *The Law of International Responsibility* (Oxford, OUP, 2010).

[14] ILC, 'Report of the International Law Commission on the Work of Its 45th Session (3 May–23 July 1993)' (1993) UN Doc A/48/10, reproduced in (1993) 2 (pt 2) *YBILC* 1, 55, para 4.

[15] *Rainbow Warrior Affair (France/New Zealand)* (1990) 20 RIAA 215, 270, para 113.

[16] ibid para 114; see also J Charpentier, 'L'affaire du Rainbow Warrior: La sentence arbitrale du 30 avril 1990 (Nouvelle-Zélande c/ France) (1)' (1990) 36 *AFDI* 395, 404.

[17] For examples of practice of the UNSC imposing an obligation on States to cease a wrongful act see, eg UNSC, 'Res 545' (20 December 1983) UN Doc S/RES/545 (South Africa); UNSC, 'Res 326' (2 February 1973) UN Doc S/RES/326 (South Africa); UNSC, 'Res 661' (6 August 1990) UN Doc S/RES/661 (Iraq-Kuwait); UNSC, 'Res 471' (5 June 1980) UN Doc S/RES/471 (Israel); UNSC, 'Res 1973' (17 March 2011) UN Doc S/RES/1973 (Libya); UNSC, 'Res 2085' (20 December 2012) UN Doc S/RES/2085 (Mali); UNSC, 'Res 2118' (27 September 2013) UN Doc S/RES/2118 (Syria).

[18] W Riphagen, 'Second Report on the Content, Forms and Degrees of International Responsibility' (1981) UN Doc A/CN.4/344, reproduced in (1981) 2 (pt 1) *YBILC* 79, 88, para 76.

For his part, Special Rapporteur Arangio-Ruiz stressed that cessation should be applied to all unlawful acts extending in time, regardless of whether the conduct of a State is an action or an omission.[19] By implication, the obligation of cessation should also apply to aid or assistance facilitating the commission or maintenance of such breach.

However, where the aid or assistance has already been rendered and the breach of international law has already ceased, there are two additional general obligations that may be invoked by the injured party: assurances and guarantees of non-repetition and reparation.

B. Assurances and Guarantees of Non-repetition (Articles 30(b) ARSIWA/ARIO)

Another set of important legal consequences of a wrongful act lies in the obligation to provide assurances and guarantees of non-repetition, a sort of 'bombe à retardement'.[20] These consequences may have an important deterring role, preventing complicit conduct from occurring in the future.[21] There is much ongoing debate as to the real substance of these legal consequences. In principle, they are of a 'rather exceptional character'.[22] The ILC's Commentary to Article 30(b) ARSIWA suggests that these so-called prospective remedies depend on the nature of the obligation breached and the seriousness of that breach.[23] This could be interpreted, in practice, as restricting the obligation to provide the assurances and guarantees of non-repetition to cases of serious breaches of international law, including *jus cogens* and *erga omnes*.[24]

The author does not agree with this interpretation. The prospective nature of these remedies justifies their application to all situations of complicity in an internationally wrongful act regardless of the nature of the

[19] ILC, 'Report of the International Law Commission on the Work of Its 40th Session (9 May–29 July 1988)' (1988) UN Doc A/43/10, reproduced in (1988) 2 (pt 2) *YBILC* 1, 105, para 537.

[20] A Pellet, 'Remarques sur une révolution inachevée, le projet d'articles de la Commission du Droit international sur la responsabilité des États' (1996) 42 *AFDI* 7, 16 (English translation: 'time bomb').

[21] See, eg L Dubin, 'Les garanties de non-repetition a l'aune des affaires LaGrand et Avena: La révolution n'aura plus lieu' (2005) 4 *RGDIP* 859, 870–75; see also CJ Tams, 'Recognizing Guarantees and Assurances of Non-Repetition: La Grand and the Law of State Responsibility' (2002) 27 *Yale J Intl L* 441.

[22] ARSIWA (n 3) 91, para 13.

[23] ibid.

[24] See B Graefrath, 'Responsibility and Damages Caused: Relationship between Responsibility and Damages' (1984) 185 *RCADI* 9, 72; cf CJ Tams, 'Do Serious Breaches Give Rise to Any Specific Obligations of the Responsible State?' (2002) 13 *EJIL* 1161, 1164–66.

obligation and the severity of the breach.[25] This flows from the threat that unsanctioned complicity poses to the international legal order as a whole, irrespective of the seriousness of the principal wrongful act. In addition, in practical terms, it may be difficult to obtain reparation *stricto sensu* from the complicit actor, as explained in the sections below. An obligation to provide assurances and guarantees of non-repetition of such a complicit conduct would at least provide a partial remedy to the injured party regardless of the issues of causation and divisibility of the injury, which would be required to obtain any reparation from the complicit actor.

These assurances and guarantees of non-repetition could take the form of a note verbale, public statement or the distribution of official policy documents or manuals to the officials of the State who provided the aid or assistance that facilitated the commission of the wrongful act in question.[26] On a few occasions, the International Court of Justice (ICJ) has taken into account requests for guarantees of non-repetition or has implied that the respondent State has already provided such guarantees in one way or another.[27]

While an order requesting the party to provide assurances and guarantees of non-repetition could be applied to situations of complicity, recent decisions of the ICJ suggest that the Court is reluctant to make such orders, even in respect of the principal wrongdoers. In two relatively recent cases, the Court has taken a firm view that good faith in the future conduct of States must be presumed, which would warrant against any such additional legal consequences:

> [W]hile the Court may order, as it has done in the past, a State responsible for internationally wrongful conduct to provide the injured State with assurances and guarantees of non-repetition, it will only do so if the circumstances so warrant, which it is for the Court to assess.
>
> As a general rule, *there is no reason to suppose that a State whose act or conduct has been declared wrongful by the Court will repeat that act or conduct in the future, since its good faith must be presumed* … There is thus no reason, except in special circumstances … to order [assurances and guarantees of non-repetition].[28] (emphasis added)

[25] See Tams (n 24) 1166 (concluding that the duty to provide such guarantees does not constitute a specific consequence of serious breaches in the sense of Art 40 ARSIWA).

[26] See, eg CA Kiss, *Répertoire de la pratique française en matière de droit international public*, vol 3 (Paris, Centre national de la recherche scientifique, 1962–72) 549–50 (in Affaire des Boxers, China had to provide for several measures with the aim of preventing similar incidents taking place in the future).

[27] See *LaGrand (Germany v United States)* (Judgment) [2001] ICJ Rep 466, 513, paras 123–25; *Avena and Other Mexican Nationals (Mexico v United States)* (Judgment) [2004] ICJ Rep 12, 69, para 150; *Armed Activities on the Territory of the Congo (DRC v Uganda)* (Judgment) [2005] ICJ Rep 168, 256, para 257.

[28] *Navigational and Related Rights (Costa Rica v Nicaragua)* (Judgment) [2009] ICJ Rep 213, 267, para 150; see also *Pulp Mills on the River Uruguay (Argentina v Uruguay)* (Judgment) [2010] ICJ Rep 14, 105, para 278; *Land and Maritime Boundary between Cameroon and Nigeria (Cameroon v Nigeria: Equatorial Guinea intervening)* (Judgment) [2002] ICJ Rep 303, 453, para 321.

The example of the *Bosnia Genocide* judgment seems to go in line with this good faith presumption. Even after having found that Serbia failed to prevent and punish genocide, the Court was reluctant to order any such legal consequences other than a declaration:

> There remains however the question whether it is appropriate to direct that the Respondent provide guarantees and assurances of non-repetition in relation to the established breaches of the obligations to prevent and punish genocide. The Court … considers that these indications do not constitute sufficient grounds for requiring guarantees of non-repetition. The Applicant also referred in this connection to the question of non-compliance with provisional measures, but this matter has already been examined above …. In the circumstances, *the Court considers that the declaration referred to in paragraph 465 above is sufficient as regards the Respondent's continuing duty of punishment, and therefore does not consider that this is a case in which a direction for guarantees of non-repetition would be appropriate*.[29] (emphasis added)

Other courts and tribunals have taken an approach which is less deferential to sovereign States, emphasising the need for assurances and guarantees of non-repetition, particularly in the field of human rights law. For instance, the Inter-American Court of Human Rights (IACtHR) has ordered changes to national legislation and domestic policy as a form of assurance and guarantee of non-repetition. In *Moivana Community v Suriname*, the IACtHR ordered the performance of 'public acts or works that seek, *inter alia*, to commemorate and dignify victims, as well as to avoid the repetition of human rights violations'.[30] In *Castillo-Petruzzi v Peru*, the IACtHR held that 'domestic laws that place civilians under the jurisdiction of the military are a violation of the principles of the American Convention' thus ordering Peru 'to adopt the appropriate measures to amend those laws'.[31] Other forms of guarantees of non-repetition may be appropriate, such as strengthening the independence of the judiciary and promoting the training of law enforcement officials and military and security forces, etc.[32]

It is the author's view that assurances and guarantees of non-repetition constitute an important preventative measure against complicity.

[29] *Bosnia Genocide* (Merits) (n 9) 235–36, para 466; see also *Nuclear Tests (Australia v France)* (Judgment) [1974] ICJ Rep 253, 272, para 60; *Nuclear Tests (New Zealand v France)* (Judgment) [1974] ICJ Rep 547, 477, para 63; *Military and Paramilitary Activities in and against Nicaragua (Nicaragua v United States)* (Jurisdiction and Admissibility) [1984] ICJ Rep 392, 437, para 101.

[30] *Moivana Village (Moivana Community v Suriname)* (Preliminary Objections, Merits, Reparations and Costs) [2005] IACtHR Ser C No 124, para 191.

[31] *Castillo-Petruzzi v Peru* (Merits, Reparations and Costs) [1999] IACtHR Ser C No 52, para 222; see also *'The Last Temptation of Christ' (Olmedo-Bustos and others) v Chile* (Merits, Reparations and Costs) [2001] IACtHR Ser C No 73, paras 97–98.

[32] UNGA, 'Res 60/147, Annex: Basic Principles and Guidelines on the Right to a Remedy and Reparation for Victims of Gross Violations of International Human Rights Law and Serious Violations of International Humanitarian Law' (16 December 2005) UN Doc A/RES/60/147.

However, while the assurances and guarantees of non-repetition may deter future complicity, they will still only partially satisfy the injured State or international organisation. States injured by such conduct naturally expect to be able to avail themselves of the right to claim and obtain reparation. As we shall see below, there are though serious substantive and procedural hurdles to obtaining reparation for complicity.

C. Reparation (Articles 31 ARSIWA/ARIO)

While *injury* and *damage* are not the constituent elements of international responsibility, they are essential for determining its content and implementation.[33] As Ago stressed:

> *The extent of the material damage caused may be a decisive factor in determining the amount of the reparation to be made.* But it cannot be of any assistance in establishing whether a subjective right of another State has been impaired and so whether an internationally wrongful act has occurred. It therefore seems inappropriate to take this element of damage into consideration in defining the conditions for the existence of an internationally wrongful act.[34] (emphasis added)

The existing forms of reparation are (a) restitution (Articles 35 ARSIWA and 35 ARIO); (b) compensation (Articles 36 ARSIWA and 36 ARIO); and (c) satisfaction (Articles 37 ARSIWA and 37 ARIO). In practice, these forms of reparation can be combined or intervene at different moments in time, depending on the content, duration and gravity of the breach.[35] The determination of the form and extent of reparation follows the establishment of a clear and unbroken causal link between the wrongful act and the injury suffered.[36]

[33] ARSIWA (n 3), Art 2; ILC, 'Report of the International Law Commission on the Work of Its 25th Session (7 May–13 July 1973)' (1973) UN Doc A/9010/Rev 1, reproduced in (1973) 2 *YBILC* 161, 183, para 12.

[34] R Ago, 'Second Report on State Responsibility' (1970) UN Doc A/CN.4/233, reproduced in (1970) 2 *YBILC* 177, 195, para 54.

[35] For the analysis of State practice see, eg M Iovane, *La riparazione nella teoria e nella prassi dell'illecito internazionale* (Milano, Giuffrè, 1990) 61 ff; C Gray, *Judicial Remedies in International Law* (Oxford, Clarendon Press, 1987); on the forms and function of reparation see I Brownlie, *System of the Law of Nations: State Responsibility Part 1* (Oxford, Clarendon Press, 1983) 199–227; B Stern, 'The Obligation to Make Reparation' in J Crawford et al (eds), *The Law of International Responsibility* (Oxford, OUP, 2010); Y Kerbat, 'Interaction between the Forms of Reparation' in J Crawford et al (eds), *The Law of International Responsibility* (Oxford, OUP, 2010); J Crawford, *State Responsibility: The General Part* (Cambridge, CUP, 2013) 506–38.

[36] B Stern, *Le préjudice dans la théorie de la responsabilité internationale* (Paris, Pedone, 1973) 180 ('il ne suffit pas qu'existe un dommage susceptible d'indemnisation pour que naisse un droit à réparation, il faut encore que l'acte qui est à l'origine de l'obligation de réparer et le préjudice soient unis par un lien suffisamment étroit pour justifier cette réparation'; author's translation: 'for the right to reparation to arise it is not sufficient that a reparable injury exists; it is also necessary that the act which was the source of the obligation to repair the injury and the injury itself are sufficiently close to justify reparation').

The seminal passage in the *Chorzów Factory* case is a basic starting point for any study of reparation in international law: '[i]t is a principle of international law that the breach of an engagement involves an obligation to make reparation in an adequate form'.[37] The Court emphasised that

> reparation must, so far as possible, *wipe-out all the consequences of the illegal act and re-establish the situation which would, in all probability, have existed if that act had not been committed*. Restitution in kind, or, if this is not possible, payment of a sum corresponding to the value which a restitution in kind would bear; the award, if need be, of damages for loss sustained would not be covered by restitution in kind or payment in place of it—such are the principles which should serve to determine the amount of compensation due for an act contrary to international law.[38] (emphasis added)

In other words, reparation arises from a new legal relationship between the wrongdoer and the injured entity that originates from the breach, 'une prétention ou créance d'un côté, de l'autre l'obligation correspondante'.[39] The modern regime applicable to the content and allocation of responsibility, as reflected in the Permanent Court of International Justice (PCIJ)'s judgment above, is premised on a bilateral relationship between the breach of a subjective right and the duty to make good the injury. This *tête-à-tête* construction is still dominant but as more complex breaches involving multiple actors arise, a different conception of the obligation to repair may be developing in international law. When complicity facilitates the commission of the wrongful act, which of the consequences of the breach give rise to reparation, and which are attributable to the complicit actor? Do these consequences need to be proximally related to the ultimate injury? If so, is not the injury technically caused by the principal wrongful act and not the complicity in that wrongful act?

Many factors influence the form and the extent of reparation. These factors include the character of injury, its natural or artificial divisibility, the establishment of causal links, and the circumstances surrounding

[37] *The Factory of Chorzów (Germany v Poland)* (Merits) [1928] PCIJ Rep Ser A No 17, 29; see also D Anzilotti, 'La responsabilité internationale des États à raison des dommages soufferts par des étrangers' (1906) 13 *RGDIP* 5; C Eagleton, *The Responsibility of States in International Law* (New York, New York University Press, 1928) 21; K Strupp, *Das völkerrechtliche Delikt* (Stuttgart, Kohlhammer, 1920) 6.

[38] *The Factory of Chorzów* (Merits) (n 37) 47.

[39] J Belhumeur and L Condorelli (eds), *Christian Dominicé: L'ordre juridique international entre tradition et innovation—Recueil d'études* (Paris, PUF, 1997) 277 (author's translation: 'a claim or debt on the one hand, and the corresponding obligation on the other'); for studies on reparation significant to complicity scenarios see, eg L Reitzer, *La réparation comme conséquence de l'acte illicite en droit international* (Paris, Sirey, 1938); Gray (n 35); Stern (n 35); D Shelton, 'Righting Wrongs: Reparations in the Articles on State Responsibility' (2002) 96 *AJIL* 833; P d'Argent, 'Reparation and Compliance' in K Bannelier, T Christakis and S Heathcote (eds), *The ICJ and the Evolution of International Law: The Enduring Impact of the Corfu Channel Case* (London, Routledge, 2012); Orakhelashvili (n 10); d'Argent (n 5).

the breach.[40] In particular, depending on how causation is construed, the injured party may have a higher or lower probability of obtaining reparation from the complicit actor. For example, the Eritrea–Ethiopia Claims Commission adhered to a relatively broad and flexible standard of causation.[41] On the other hand, the UN Compensation Commission applied a more stringent standard of causation in awarding compensation for damages resulting from the invasion of Kuwait by Iraq in 1990.[42] Adherence to relaxed foreseeability criteria in the applicable causal test in cases of complicity could mitigate but is not likely to resolve problems with the traditional understanding of the content and consequences of responsibility.[43]

i. Causal Analysis—Linking Injury to the Wrongful Conduct

In most cases involving a simple or instantaneous breach, the question of cause and effect does not give rise to major issues. Take a situation where a State expropriates the property of a foreign national in violation of an investment treaty standard. In such a case, the State's act of taking the property amounts to a breach of the treaty norm (*origins* of responsibility) and constitutes the cause of the injury suffered by the investor (*content* of responsibility). In these circumstances, the investor will have no difficulty proving that the State's taking of the property is the proximate cause of the injury sustained by the investor, whether in the form of material or moral damages.

However, as breaches are often found to be the result of different factors and varying degrees of involvement by one or multiple entities, the causal chain towards injury becomes substantially more difficult to establish. Assume that State A knowingly provides technology to State B in order to

[40] For examples of extra-legal considerations affecting the extent of reparation see, eg *Final Award: Eritrea's Damages Claims* (2009) 26 RIAA 505, 522–24 and 630; *Final Award: Ethiopia's Damages Claims* (2009) 26 RIAA 631, 650–51 and 770; see also *Responsibility of Germany for Damage Caused in the Portuguese Colonies in the South of Africa (Portugal v Germany)* (1928) 2 RIAA 1011.

[41] See, eg *Decision No 7 Regarding Jus ad Bellum Liability* (2007) 26 RIAA 10 (the Eritrea–Ethiopia Claims Commission applying a broad standard of causation).

[42] UNSC, 'Res 687' (3 April 1991) UN Doc S/RES/687 (Iraq-Kuwait), para 16 (referring to directness of the loss and damages as a requirement for compensation). Note, however, how the UNCC has relaxed this standard in particular regarding Claims F in relation to the environmental damages suffered as a result of the Iraqi invasion of Kuwait; for the analysis of the UN Compensation Commission's practice see A Kolliopoulos, *La Commission d'indemnisation des Nations Unies et le droit de la responsabilité internationale* (Paris, LGDJ, 2001) 369 ff.

[43] cf *Lighthouse Arbitration (France v Greece)* (1956) 23 RIAA 155, 352–53 (rejecting a claim for damage which was 'neither a foreseeable nor a normal consequence of the evacuation'); *Samoan Claims Arbitration (Germany v United States and United Kingdom)* (1902) 9 RIAA 15; see also AW Rovine and G Hanessian, 'Toward a Foreseeability Approach to Causation Questions at the United Nations Compensation Commission' in RB Lillich (ed), *The United Nations Compensation Commission: Thirteenth Sokol Colloquium* (Irvington New York, Transnational, 1995).

construct a dam that would be in breach of a treaty of cooperation in the management of the river resources between States B and C. In such cases, it is the construction of the dam that constitutes the proximate cause of the injury suffered by State C. But what about the transfer of technology by State A that facilitated the construction of that dam? Is it a cause of the injury suffered by State C? If so, is it sufficient to warrant reparation on the part of State A that had knowingly provided that technology?

It is thus easy to identify the challenges posed by complicity for the legal consequences deriving from a wrongful act. Complicit conduct *intervenes* in a legal relationship between the principal wrongful act and the injury. It leads to an asymmetrical paradigm of causation. In this paradigm, the first act is a condition or contributing factor of the second act that actually causes injury.

International law has not yet developed a framework for causation in cases of multiple wrongful acts leading to the same injury or multiple contributors to the same wrongful act, which results in a single injury. Until recently, there has been relatively little research in this area.[44] However, as the schemes for multilateral cooperation grow in numbers and complexity, this matter is likely to attract more attention in the near future.

a. The ILC's Approach to Causation in General

It is said that international 'responsibility is both very simple and yet sophisticated'.[45] This is particularly true of causation in the law of international responsibility. In this section, we discuss the guidelines that the ILC has given in its work as to how to establish causation for the purpose of reparation and what sort of criteria should apply. We will then see whether these guidelines are sufficient to deal with the problem of complicity.

The starting point is that 'international law, like domestic law, draws a basic distinction between the remoteness of damage and the proximity which is associated with the natural and causal consequences of an act'.[46] Compensation is usually apposite for injury which is not

[44] For notable exceptions see I Plakokefalos, 'Causation in the Law of State Responsibility and the Problem of Overdetermination: In Search of Clarity' (2015) 26 *EJIL* 471; C Ahlborn, 'Remedies against International Organizations—A Relational Account of International Responsibility' in D Sarooshi (ed), *Remedies and Responsibility for the Actions of International Organizations* (Leiden, Martinus Nijhoff, 2014); M Strauss, 'Causation as an Element of State Responsibility' (1984) 16 *Law & Policy in International Business* 893; T Becker, *Terrorism and the State: Rethinking the Rules of State Responsibility* (Oxford, Hart Publishing, 2006) 285–364; Stern (n 36); L Castellanos-Jankiewicz, 'Causation and International State Responsibility' ACIL Research Paper SHARES Series (2012–05); Fry (n 10).

[45] Brownlie (n 35) 1.

[46] *Dispute concerning responsibility for the deaths of Letelier and Moffitt (United States v Chile)* (1992) 25 RIAA 1, 15; for an excellent review of causation see *Barcelona Traction, Light and Power Company, Limited (Second Phase) (Belgium v Spain)* (Judgment) [1970] ICJ Rep 3, ICJ Pleadings CR 1969/22 (20 May 1960) 526–37 (Weil); see also B Cheng, *General Principles of Law as Applied by International Courts and Tribunals* (Cambridge, CUP, 2006) 241–53.

remote from the relevant cause(s).[47] Article 31 ARSIWA encapsulates the basic rule:

> The responsible State is under an obligation to make full reparation for the injury caused by the internationally wrongful act, [where] [i]njury includes any damage, whether material or moral, *caused by* the internationally wrongful act.[48] (emphasis added)

The construction of the injury here circumscribes responsibility for material or moral damages to that *caused by* the internationally wrongful act *itself*. The ILC explained that the allocation of injury or loss to a wrongful act is both a factual and legal process—the determination of the *in-fact* (factual) causation is 'a necessary but not a sufficient condition of reparation'.[49] The ILC observed that various legal standards for causation can be found in case law, including 'remoteness', 'directness', 'foreseeability', and 'proximity',[50] but considered that the manner in which the causal link is classified will vary with different primary norms.[51]

Causation thus plays a central role in any dispute settlement proceedings when it comes to determining the content of responsibility. It is then all the more surprising that the ILC left this concept in the shadows when codifying the ARSIWA and ARIO:[52]

> [T]he most that can be said is that the ILC is particularly silent on causation. The only assertion is that the injury can only be repaired if it is 'caused by the internationally wrongful act'. Nothing more. It is therefore left to States and judges to give some content to the causal link which is necessary for international responsibility to arise.
>
> The ILC justified the fact that the issue of causal link has not been dealt with by saying that '[t]he need for causal link was usually stated in primary rules'. Nevertheless, it is clear that this is not the case and that, even if in certain cases the primary rule gives rise to some causal link problems, it cannot be the same causation as the one which arises when the primary rule is breached. It is regrettable that the ILC did not clarify the difficult issues relating to the causal link.[53]

[47] *Dispute concerning responsibility for the deaths of Letelier and Moffitt (United States v Chile)* (n 46) ('international law does not rely so much in the distinction of being damages 'direct' or 'indirect' as in that they shall be 'proximate' and not 'remote'').

[48] ARSIWA (n 3) Art 31.

[49] ibid 92–93, para 10 (Art 31).

[50] See, eg *Antippa (the Spyros) v Germany, Case No 285* (1926) 7 German-Greek Mixed Arbitral Tribunal 23; *War Risk Insurance Premium Claims—Administrative Decision No II* (1923) 7 RIAA 23, 29–30 ('[i]t matters not how many links there may be in the chain of causation connecting with the loss sustained, provided there is no break in the chain and the loss can be clearly, unmistakably and definitely traced link by link, to Germany's act').

[51] ILC, 'Summary Record of the 2662nd Meeting' (17 August 2000), reproduced in (2000) 1 *YBILC* 386, 388, para 17.

[52] DD Caron, 'The Basis of Responsibility: Attribution and Other Substantive Rules' in RB Lillich and DB Magraw (eds), *The Iran-United States Claims Tribunal: Its Contribution to the Law of State Responsibility* (Irvington New York, Transnational, 1998) 153.

[53] Stern (n 35) 569–70; see generally Stern (n 36).

In defence of the ILC's silence, James Crawford has argued that the requirement of causation in the ARSIWA could not be elaborated in more detail in that context and that it was impossible to 'devise more specific criteria that are applicable across the wide range of primary obligations'.[54] Crawford confirms the ILC Drafting Committee's conclusion on the matter:[55]

> The Drafting Committee had considered a number of suggestions for qualifying that causal link, but, in the end, it had taken the view that, since the requirements of a causal link were not necessarily the same in relation to every breach of an international obligation, it would not be prudent or even accurate to use a qualifier.[56]

Certainly, the Drafting Committee was right in pointing out that some primary obligations contain elements that indicate the exact extent to which an action or omission must have caused injury (eg *de minimis*, more than *de minimis*, substantially, significantly, not too remote, etc). The primary rules may even qualify the injury itself when, for example, referring to such *formulae* as 'serious' or 'irreparable'.[57] However, in most cases, the primary rules are silent on causal standards. Where the primary rules are silent, the causal analysis under general law of responsibility applies.

With the above caveat in respect of primary rules,[58] the development of a unified set of causal guidelines would have greatly assisted the understanding of shared forms of responsibility.[59] The ILC's failure to do so has left responsibility for complicity in *limbo*. In the best case scenario when the responsibility of complicit entity has been established, neither ARSIWA nor ARIO contain any clear guidance as to how to apportion the share of reparation owed by the complicit entity and by reference to which legal benchmarks.

The Commission implied that the link must be sufficient in the sense of not being too remote from the injury.[60] Generally, the requirement of

[54] Crawford (n 35) 493.

[55] ibid.

[56] ILC (n 51) 388; J Crawford, 'Third Report on State Responsibility' (2000) UN Doc A/CN.4/507 and Add 1-4, reproduced in (2000) 2 (pt 1) *YBILC* 3, 18–19, paras 27 ff; ARSIWA (n 3) 92–93, para 10.

[57] Convention on the Law of the Non-Navigational Uses of International Watercourses (adopted 21 May 1997; not yet in force) (1997) 36 ILM 700, Art 7 (referring to 'significant harm'); UNCED, 'Agenda 21: Programme of Action for Sustainable Development ('Rio Declaration')' (14 June 1992) UN Doc A/Conf.151/26, Art 17 (referring to 'significant adverse impact'); United Nations Convention on the Law of the Sea (adopted 10 December 1982; entered into force 16 November 1994) 1833 UNTS 3, Art 206 (referring to 'substantial pollution or significant harmful changes'); see also ILC, 'Summary Record of the 2664th Meeting' (8 June 2000), reproduced in (2000) 1 *YBILC* 171, 174, para 19 (Brownlie); I Brownlie, *Principles of Public International Law* (6th edn, Oxford, OUP, 2003) 446–47.

[58] ILC (n 57) 177, para 54 (Crawford).

[59] G Arangio-Ruiz, 'Second Report on State Responsibility' (1989) UN Doc A/CN.4/425 and Add 1, reproduced in (1989) 2 (pt 1) *YBILC* 1, 15, para 46; for reflections on the absence of a single test of causation in international law see A Gattini, 'Breach of the Obligation to Prevent and Reparation Thereof in the ICJ's Genocide Judgment' (2007) 18 *EJIL* 695, 708; Becker (n 44) 285–330; Plakokefalos (n 44).

[60] ARSIWA (n 3) 92–93, para 10 (Art 31 Commentary).

sufficient cause means that the injury must flow from the wrongful act in a natural sequence, whereas proximate cause would require directness or an uninterrupted chain between the conduct and the injury. The Commission stressed that

> unless some part of the injury can be shown to be *severable in causal terms from that attributed to the responsible State*, the latter is held responsible for all the consequences, not being too remote, of its wrongful conduct.[61] (emphasis added)

To sum up, the Commission's general approach to causation follows the rationale of Hart and Honoré, who sought the answers to the following questions, in sequence: (i) would Y not have occurred but for X? Is there any principle which precludes the treatment of Y as the consequence of X for legal purposes?[62] In the following section, we shall test the appropriateness of this causal analysis in the scenarios of complicity.

b. Applying Causal Tests to Complicity

During the codification of Article 16 ARSIWA, only a few members took issue with the possibility of reparation attaching to responsibility for complicity. On the first reading of the former draft Article 27 ARSIWA, Riphagen noted that it was not clear how the responsibility of the complicit entity was different from the responsibility of the main actor.[63] Similarly, Yamada invited the Commission to consider the question of 'how to determine the distribution of responsibility between the assisting State, and the assisted State'.[64]

As a result, the final guidelines from the Commission on the issue of apportionment in cases of complicity are limited and inconsistent. The ILC presumed that reparation would attach to the principal wrongdoer whose act generates the injury. It is only when a portion of that injury can be traced back to prior conduct lying outside of the main causal chain that possible reparation from a complicit actor would be warranted. As Special Rapporteur Arangio-Ruiz noted, there could be situations in practice where the injury is not exclusively caused by one uniform wrongful act:

> Consideration must be given to cases in which the injuries are not caused exclusively by an unlawful act but have been produced also by concomitant

[61] ibid, 93, para 13 (Art 31 Commentary).

[62] HLA Hart and T Honoré, *Causation in the Law* (2nd edn, Oxford, Clarendon Press, 1985) 110.

[63] W Riphagen, 'Preliminary Report on the Content, Forms and Degrees of International Responsibility' (1980) UN Doc A/CN.4/330 and Corr 1-3, reproduced in (1980) 2 (pt 1) *YBILC* 107, 111, para 14.

[64] ILC, 'Summary Record of the 2576th Meeting' (25 May 1999), reproduced in (1999) 1 *YBILC* 60, 66, para 46 (Yamada).

> causes among which the unlawful act plays a decisive but not exclusive role. *In such cases, to hold the author State liable for full compensation would be neither equitable nor in conformity with a proper application of the causal link criterion.* The solution should be the payment of partial damages, *in proportion to the amount of injury presumably to be attributed to the wrongful act and its effects,* the amount to be awarded on the basis of the *criteria of normality and predictability*.[65] (emphasis added)

Arangio Ruiz noted that these concurrent causes would include actions by third parties.[66] The Commission realised that there could be situations in which a complicit conduct might contribute to the principal wrongful act, but would have little or no effect on the actual injury.[67] Two passages from the ILC Commentary show the evident confusion as to how to trace injury deriving from the principal wrongful act to a prior complicit conduct:

> In cases where the *internationally wrongful act would clearly have occurred in any event*, the responsibility of the assisting State *will not extend to compensating for the act itself*.[68] (emphasis added) [*1]

> By assisting another State to commit an internationally wrongful act, *a State should not necessarily be held to indemnify the victim for all the consequences of the act*, but only for those which, in accordance with the principles stated in Part Two of the [ARSIWA], flow from its own conduct.[69] [*2] (emphasis added)

Technically, and without trying to read too much into these statements, what the Commission appears to be saying is that the reparation due from the complicit State requires a *two-sided* causal analysis. First, a showing that *but for* complicity the principal wrongful act *would clearly not have occurred* [*1] is required. This undermines the idea that the complicit conduct need not be essential, arguably not even significant, with regard to facilitating the principal wrongful act at the stage of determining responsibility. Second, the exact extent of contribution to the injury must be individualised, but leaves open the possibility that the complicit State indemnify the totality of the injury [*2]. Once reconciled in one single formula, the result would be surprising: when complicity is the necessary

65 Arangio-Ruiz (n 59) 14, para 44.

66 ibid.

67 ARSIWA (n 3) 67, para 10 (Art 16 Commentary).

68 ibid 66, para 1 (Art 16 Commentary); see also ILC, 'Summary Record of the 2703rd Meeting' (6 August 2001), reproduced in (2001) 1 *YBILC* 247, 251, para 43 (Crawford) (explaining that 'in a situation when there was no causal relationship between the assistance and the act, the assisting State did not assume responsibility for the act, although it could still be responsible for its own assistance. In some situations, the assistance was so central to the conduct that the State was deemed to have produced the conduct, but in other cases that was not so. The point was controversial, however, and there was no question of inserting anything in [A]rticle 16').

69 ARSIWA (n 3) 67, para 10 (Art 16 Commentary).

cause of the principal wrongful act [*1], the complicit State can be required to compensate for the *act itself* [*1] and to indemnify the victim for all the consequences of that act [*2]. This would effectively transform complicity into joint and several responsibility for the purposes of injury allocation and reparation.[70] Complicity would no longer be, if it ever was, an 'intermediate' situation.[71]

In the alternative to submitting scenarios of complicity to the regime of joint and several responsibility, the existing legal fiction of 'complicity in a wrongful act = separable wrongful act' could be advanced to its logical conclusion, namely 'complicity in a wrongful act = separable wrongful act causing separable injury'. With such a construction, the injured party would be in a position to seek the full amount of reparation from the complicit State without going first to the principal wrongdoer. This construction would entail the following sequence of reasoning: 1) complicity in the wrongdoing *on its own* distresses the international legal order and represents a legal injury in its broadest meaning (ie an injury arising from the mere fact that the breach of an international obligation has occurred); and 2) the injured State can accordingly seek full reparation for the injury flowing from complicity in the wrongful act.[72]

However, the notion of legal injury is conspicuously absent from the ARSIWA and ARIO provisions and commentaries.[73] Crawford suggests that such notion is rightly not included in the conception of the injury in

[70] See ch 4 discussing this approach in the context of comparative tort law principles of joint tortfeasors. It would seem that joint and several responsibility would apply to tortfeasors knowingly participating in the wrong by others which causes damage to the victim: see WVH Rogers, 'Comparative Report on Multiple Tortfeasors' in WVH Rogers and WH van Boom (eds), *Unification of Tort Law: Multiple Tortfeasors* (The Hague, Kluwer, 2004) 308–09; for the transposition of this model to complicity see B Graefrath, 'Complicity in the Law of International Responsibility' (1996) 2 *RBDI* 370, 379; cf V Lowe, 'Responsibility for the Conduct of Other States' (2002) 101 *Japanese J Intl L & Diplomacy* 1, 11; Aust (n 2) 281–83 (arguing that it would be inappropriate to mix the regime of complicity with that of joint and several responsibility but ultimately concedes that a strict separation may not be beneficial particularly from the perspective of the injured party); see also C Chinkin, 'The Continuing Occupation? Issues of Joint and Several Liability and Effective Control' in P Shiner and A Williams (eds), *The Iraq War and International Law* (Oxford, Hart Publishing, 2008) 178 (arguing against solidary responsibility for situations of aid or assistance).

[71] ILC, 'Summary Record of the 1518th Meeting' (17 July 1978), reproduced in (1978) 1 *YBILC* 232, 233, para 7 (Riphagen).

[72] Stern, 'A Plea for "Reconstruction" of International Responsibility Based on the Notion of Legal Injury' (n 5) 93; Stern, 'Et si on utilisait la notion de préjudice juridique?' (n 5); for a distinction between legal and moral injury see Stern (n 36) 31–35; A Tanzi, 'Is Damage a Distinct Condition for the Existence of an Internationally Wrongful Act?' in M Spinedi and B Simma (eds), United Nations Codification of State Responsibility (New York, Oceana, 1987) 8–11; Arangio-Ruiz (n 59) 6, para 14.

[73] ILC, 'Summary Record of the 2705th Meeting' (7 August 2001), reproduced in (2001) 1 *YBILC* 263, 265, para 10 (Simma) ('a lack of consensus on [the issue of legal injury] seemed to have been 'papered over' at some stage'); for case law supportive of the notion of legal injury see, eg *SS 'Wimbledon' (United Kingdom and others v Germany)* (Judgment) [1923] PCIJ Ser A No 1, 15, 20; *Rainbow Warrior Affair (France/New Zealand)* (n 15) 267, para 110.

the law of international responsibility.[74] He brings up two key reasons for that exclusion: i) the forms of reparation only address material and moral damages and ii) if legal injury by virtue of mere breach were accepted, this would have rendered the whole duality of the invocation regime unworkable.[75]

Considering that often the complicit State is a more powerful actor in international relations, either of the above alternatives would substantially enhance the victim's chances of obtaining redress. Moreover, this would be linked with the overall conception of international responsibility as an objective phenomenon and its function as a guardian of legality. These alternative constructions of complicity at the level of content of responsibility could also represent a solution to those situations where the injury is non-divisible,[76] for example where States are complicit in the wrongful act committed by an international organisation, or where several contributions facilitate indistinguishably the injury caused to a third party. Further, this legal construction could circumvent problems relating to the potential lack of a jurisdictional link between the injured and the principal wrongdoing State or issues of indispensable third-party principle.[77] Either option would allow mechanisms of international dispute settlement to pronounce directly on the responsibility of the complicit State. The absence from the proceedings of the principal wrongdoing State would not necessarily constitute the object of the case in hand as two distinct wrongful acts and two distinct injuries would be implicated.

However, at the current stage of development of international law, it is difficult to see how any of the above alternative constructions to causation in respect of injury caused by complicity (ie joint and several responsibility regime for complicity or a presumed independent injury approach) could become operational. Notably, both constructions could lead to seemingly unfair and inequitable situations where a complicit State might carry a higher burden of reparation than the principal wrongdoer. Similarly, even if such a construction could work, it would be difficult to prove the

[74] Crawford (n 35) 487.

[75] ibid 487–88; for relevant comments of States see ILC, 'Comments and Observations Received from Governments' (2001) UN Doc A/CN.4/515 and Add 1-3, reproduced in (2001) 2 (pt 1) *YBILC* 33, 58–59; see also Barboza (n 5) 9.

[76] For examples of cases where tribunals have been able to partition the injury see *Alliance (United States v Venezuela)* (1903) 9 RIAA 140, 143 (the tribunal distinguishing damages for physical harm to vessel caused by storm, and damages for vessel's detention attributable to the defaulting State); *D Earnshaw and others (United Kingdom v United States) ('Zafiro Case')* (1925) 6 RIAA 160, 164–65 (distinguishing the injury caused by the vessel's crew from damage caused by unidentified wrongdoers); *Martini (Italy v Venezuela)* (1930) 10 RIAA 644, 666–68 (distinguishing an injury caused by the State from that caused by the acts of revolutionaries); *Petrocelli (Italy v Venezuela)* (1903) 10 RIAA 591, 592.

[77] *Monetary Gold Removed from Rome in 1943 (Italy v France, United Kingdom and United States)* (Preliminary Question) [1954] ICJ Rep 19, 32.

responsibility of the complicit actor without the evidence being shared with, provided and contested by the principal wrongdoer. At the end of the day, even though complicity is construed as a separable wrongful act for the purposes of incurring responsibility, in terms of the content of responsibility it bears a *lien biologique* of wrongfulness with the principal wrongful act and the resulting injury.

c. Multiple Chains of Causation and Attenuation of Responsibility

This *lien biologique* is even more difficult to establish where different chains of causation, separately or cumulatively, contribute to the coming into being of the same injury. For instance, in the case of the 2003 Iraq war, described in chapter five, it may be shown that specific injury deriving from the wrongful acts allegedly committed by the Common Provisional Authority (CPA) would not have occurred or would have been less likely to occur in the circumstances *but for* multiple and parallel contributions from other States.[78] To use an example, the sending of a battalion of soldiers by State A to assist the military forces of State B in committing a wrongful act against State C might not be a *sufficient* nor *necessary* cause of the resulting injury without the concurrent use of helicopters and weapons provided by other States to State B.

Likewise, in the context of the UN Compensation Commission proceedings dealing with the specific claims of environmental damages suffered as a result of invasion of Kuwait, Iraq argued that it was 'impossible to limit the causes of environmental pollution in a particular region to one cause and hold one state liable for that and oblige it to compensate the damages, especially when many factors and States contributed to the pollution'.[79]

In *Trail Smelter*, the tribunal awarded damages notwithstanding the existence of multiple causes of the injury, finding that the air pollution originating at the smelter in Trail, Canada was nevertheless a sufficient cause.[80] A number of recent investment treaty arbitrations show that multiple causes may bar the award of damages, but they will not necessarily affect the finding of responsibility. For instance, in *Biwater Gauff v Tanzania*, the tribunal found Tanzania to have violated the protections of the Bilateral Investment Treaty between the United Kingdom and Tanzania, but considered that it owed no compensation to the claimant who had

[78] For a detailed analysis see S Talmon, 'A Plurality of Responsible Actors: International Responsibility for Acts of the Coalition Provisional Authority in Iraq' in P Shiner and A Williams (eds), *The Iraq War and International Law* (Oxford, Hart Publishing, 2008).

[79] *Report and Recommendations made by the Panel of the Commissioners concerning the Third Instalment of 'F4' Claims* [2003] UN Compensation Commission Governing Council, reproduced in (2004) 43 ILM 704, 711–12, para 37.

[80] *Trail Smelter* (1941) 3 RIAA 1911, 1930 ff.

failed to establish causation as other causes had led first to the loss in value of its investment.[81] In *Lauder v Czech Republic*, the tribunal was able to find a breach of the provision but considered that the breach was 'too remote to qualify as a relevant cause for the harm caused'.[82] Similar reasoning can be found in the arbitral awards in *Petrobart v Kyrgyz Republic*[83] and *Rompetrol v Romania*.[84]

By analogy, the above cases confirm the idea that while the complicit conduct may as such be sufficiently linked to the principal wrongful act and therefore trigger responsibility, it is not automatic that it will be causally linked to the injury suffered. Mackie has argued against the causal over-determination in situations of additional or alternative causes (ie situations where the causes are sufficient either cumulatively or separately but are neither necessary nor sufficient on their own). Mackie illustrates the point through a hypothetical of two indeterminate machines each of which, after the insertion of a coin of a given value, produces a bar of chocolate.[85] In other words, State A gives arms, State B gives arms, and State C (with arms of A and B) commits a wrongful act against State D. *Quid juris*?

Even if complicity is construed as a sufficient cause, it is doubtful that it can be reparable. Indeed, in most cases, complicity would be a sufficient cause in the sense that its contribution facilitates the effect of the wrongful act (ie the triggering cause of the injury). However, it will not automatically become a necessary cause of the injury. In our example above this would mean that arms from State A and arms from State B are each a sufficient but not a necessary cause of the wrongful act by State C, even less of the injury that that act causes to State D. Similarly, does it matter in which order the arms of State A and State B were used by State C when committing its wrongful act?

In *CME v Czech Republic*, the tribunal explored different aspects of causation that are relevant to the problem of complicity.[86] As detailed in chapter four, although the tribunal was dealing with the possible joint

[81] *Biwater Gauff (Tanzania) Ltd v United Republic of Tanzania* (Award) [2008] ICSID Case No ARB/05/22, para 798; see also ibid, Concurring and Dissenting Opinion of Gary Born, para 19.

[82] *Lauder v Czech Republic* (Final Award) [2001] UNCITRAL, reproduced in 9 ICSID Rep 66, para 235.

[83] *Petrobart Limited v Kyrgyz Republic* (Award) [2005] SCC Case No 126/2003, reproduced in (2005) IIC 184, 73.

[84] *Rompetrol Group NV v Romania* (Award) [2013] ICSID Case No ARB/06/3, para 190.

[85] JL Mackie, *The Cement of the Universe: A Study of Causation* (Oxford, Clarendon Press, 1980) 41; see also A Reinisch, 'Aid or Assistance and Direction and Control between States and International Organizations in the Commission of Internationally Wrongful Acts' (2010) 7 *IOLR* 63, 71.

[86] *CME Czech Republic BV v Czech Republic* (Partial Award) [2001] UNCITRAL, 9 ICSID Rep 113.

responsibility of an individual and the State, parts of its discussion are relevant to the problem of complicity too. In particular, the tribunal applied in practice the ILC's rationale that 'a State may be held responsible for injury to an alien investor where it is not the sole cause of the injury; the State is not absolved because of the participation of other tortfeasors in the infliction of the injury'.[87] Accordingly, the fact that an extraneous third party intervenes into a given causal chain does not automatically break that chain.

Even more complex is the scenario of several causal factors contributing effectively to the relevant outcome, where the extent of specific contribution is not technically capable of determination. These are, for example, the cases of carbon emissions contributing to climate change or various forms of maritime pollution damaging the marine biodiversity. In such cases of cumulative or contributory causes, it is only reasonable and logical to depart from the classical 'but for', *sine qua non* or similar causal tests.[88]

From the analysis conducted so far, it is quite evident that for the injured party proving 'causation is often a bugbear that can turn into a nightmare'.[89] For the principal or complicit entity, on the other hand, 'causation can be a salvation'.[90] In other words, the application of a traditional proximity standard in the situations of complex, composite or cumulative chains of causation leads to the conclusion that the obligation of reparation would rarely apply to complicit actors. Causation analysis is particularly relevant to compensation as a form of reparation but it also informs to a lesser extent the determination of other forms of reparation, such as restitution and satisfaction.

ii. *Forms of Reparation*

a. Restitution (Articles 35 ARSIWA/ARIO)

Restitution implies the idea of 'reestablishment as far as possible of the situation which existed prior to the commission of the internationally wrongful act, to the extent that any changes that have occurred in that situation may be traced to that act'.[91] This definition builds upon the principle that can be found in the *Chorzów Factory* case, quoted at the

[87] ibid para 580.

[88] See, eg R Verheyen, *Climate Change Damage and International Law* (Leiden, Martinus Nijhoff, 2005) 253; PN Okowa, *State Responsibility for Transboundary Air Pollution in International Law* (Oxford, OUP, 2000) 185.

[89] G Vos, 'Linking Chains of Causation: An Examination of New Approaches to Causation in Equity and the Common Law' (2001) 60 *Cambridge LJ* 337, 338.

[90] ibid.

[91] ARSIWA (n 3) 96, para 1 (Art 35).

beginning of this section. In the relevant part of that principle, the Court spoke about the re-establishment of a 'situation which would, in all probability, have existed' but for the commission of the wrongful act.[92]

It is difficult to conceive of scenarios in which restitution as such could be an adequate remedy against the complicit State or international organisation. Usually, the injured party would request restitution of particular objects, goods or persons from the principal wrongdoer.[93] For example, the principal wrongdoer may have transferred some of the unlawfully confiscated property to an accomplice. In such situations, the injured party would have a potential claim for restitution against the complicit entity directly.

Aust rightly suggests that in most traditional examples of situations giving rise to demands for restitution, it is the principal and not the complicit actor who has the necessary control over persons, goods or objects in order to re-establish a situation that would have existed but for its wrongful act.[94] As Dominicé puts it:

> Si l'on fait abstraction des cas où la restitution n'est autre que le retour à l'obligation initiale, il faut bien convenir qu'elle apparaît peu fréquemment comme forme de réparation proprement dite.[95]

In other words, the statement by the ILC that 'there are often situations where restitution is not available'[96] applies to most cases of complicity. Accordingly, in line with the ILC's guidance, 'other forms of reparation [could] take priority'.[97]

b. Compensation (Articles 36 ARSIWA/ARIO)

Compensation is probably the most commonly applied form of reparation. In most cases, it will apply to situations where the injury is material and quantifiable. However, there may also be cases where the injury is immaterial or moral and would nevertheless be subject to compensation. Traditionally, these are the cases where nationals suffer a moral wrong and the State would exercise diplomatic protection on their behalf. With the development of international law, the question of whether moral injury is appropriate for compensation has been supplemented by the development of the doctrine of satisfaction, which is specifically tailored for moral injury.

[92] *The Factory of Chorzów* (Merits) (n 37) 47.

[93] See, eg *The Temple of Preah Vihear (Cambodia v Thailand)* (Merits) [1962] ICJ Rep 6, 36.

[94] Aust (n 2) 277.

[95] See Belhumeur and Condorelli (n 39) 278 (author's translation: 'If we exclude cases where restitution is nothing else than the return to the original obligation, it must be admitted that it is infrequent as a form of reparation proper').

[96] ARSIWA (n 3) 97, para 5 (Art 35).

[97] ibid 97, para 4 (Art 35).

The existing case law points to full and adequate compensation that may come as close as possible to re-placing the injured party in a situation *ex ante*. To give just a few classic examples, in the *Norwegian Shipowners' Claims* case it was held that 'just compensation implies a complete restitution of the *status quo ante*'.[98] The rationale is best expressed in the *Lusitania* case: 'la réparation doit être proportionnée au préjudice, de façon que la partie lésée retrouve son intégrité'.[99]

In short, the 'role of compensation is to fill in any gaps so as to ensure full reparation for damage suffered'.[100] Of course, there are many technicalities and debates in the literature about the scope of compensation, but these are not particularly important for the present study.[101] What is of interest for our purposes is that the situations of complicity do not quite fit into the traditional standards of assessing compensation. As Brownlie rightly noted '[t]he duty to pay compensation is a normal consequence of responsibility, but is not conterminous with it'.[102] Complicity shows that this indeed is the case.

It follows that, unless it can be established that the complicit conduct has caused material damage, compensation would not be given.[103] The Court's holding in the *Bosnia Genocide* case dissipates any doubts in respect of compensation for eventual complicity:

> Since it now has to rule on the claim for reparation, it must ascertain whether, and to what extent, the injury asserted by the Applicant is the consequence of wrongful conduct by the Respondent with the consequence that the Respondent should be required to make reparation for it, in accordance with the principle of customary international law stated above. In this context, the question just mentioned, whether the genocide at Srebrenica would have taken place even if the Respondent had attempted to prevent it by employing all means in its possession, becomes directly relevant, for the definition of the extent of the obligation of reparation borne by the Respondent as a result of its wrongful conduct. The question is whether there is a sufficiently direct and certain causal nexus between the wrongful act, the Respondent's breach of the obligation to prevent genocide, and the injury suffered by the Applicant, consisting of all damage of any type, material or moral, caused by the acts of genocide. Such a nexus could be considered established only if the Court were able to conclude from the case as a whole and with a sufficient degree of certainty that the genocide

[98] *Norwegian Shipowners' Claims (Norway v United States)* (1922) 1 RIAA 309, 338.

[99] *Lusitania* (1923) 7 RIAA 32, 39 (author's translation: 'reparation must be proportionate to the damage, so that the injured party recovers its integrity').

[100] ARSIWA (n 3) 99, para 3 (Art 36 Commentary).

[101] See generally J Barker, 'The Different Forms of Reparation: Compensation' in J Crawford et al (eds), *The Law of International Responsibility* (Oxford, OUP, 2010); for major developments in this area see particularly the practice of investment law tribunals, eg S Ripinsky and K Williams, *Damages in International Investment Law* (London, BIICL, 2008); I Marboe, *Calculation of Compensation and Damages in International Investment Law* (Oxford, OUP, 2009).

[102] Brownlie (n 57) 421.

[103] On the role of damage in the context of implementation of responsibility see, eg Tanzi (n 72); Graefrath (n 24).

> at Srebrenica would in fact have been averted if the Respondent had acted in compliance with its legal obligations. However, the Court clearly cannot do so. As noted above, the *Respondent did have significant means of influencing the Bosnian Serb military and political authorities* which it could, and therefore should, have employed in an attempt to prevent the atrocities, but it has not been shown that, in the specific context of these events, those *means would have sufficed to achieve the result which the Respondent should have sought*. Since the Court cannot therefore regard as proven a causal nexus between the Respondent's violation of its obligation of prevention and the damage resulting from the genocide at Srebrenica, *financial compensation is not the appropriate form of reparation for the breach of the obligation to prevent genocide*.[104] (emphasis added)

If the Court has adopted such a stringent reading of the causal nexus in relation to a failure of the obligation to prevent, it is safe to assume that a similar reading would apply to complicity. Naturally, there could be a slight variation with a possible application of this rationale to complicity, which most frequently arises out of acts and not omissions. Because causation based on omissions is a particularly difficult exercise, Aust suggests that the Court could take a more lenient approach when in presence of an active conduct.[105]

However, even in the cases of omissions, it is arguable that courts may take a more lenient approach to evidence required to show causation. This could be, for instance, by de facto shifting the burden of proof from the injured party claiming omission to the purported complicit or principal wrongdoer. So if a principal wrongdoer State fails to intervene in the chain of causation leading to the injury, which is possible thanks to the assistance from several complicit actors, the principal wrongdoer is best placed to furnish evidence of the exact proportions of aid or assistance used from each of the complicit actors.[106] In any event, the Court's passage certainly casts doubt on the practical value of the extensive interpretation it has given to Article I of the Genocide Convention.[107]

On the one hand, even if complicity were to be treated as a concurrent or intervening cause of the injury, it is likely that the principal State will bear the full share of responsibility vis-à-vis the injured party.[108] As the

[104] *Bosnia Genocide* (Merits) (n 9) 233–34, para 462.

[105] Aust (n 2) 283–84.

[106] *Corfu Channel (United Kingdom v Albania)* (Merits) [1949] ICJ Rep 4, 18 (even though the State's exclusive control over the territory does not shift the burden of proof, '[t]he State may, up to a certain point, be bound to supply particulars of the use made by it of the means of information and inquiry at its disposal').

[107] M Milanović, 'State Responsibility for Genocide: A Follow-Up' (2007) 18 *EJIL* 669, 691; PM Dupuy, 'Crime sans châtiment ou mission accomplie?' (2007) 111 *RGDIP* 243, 255–56.

[108] See, eg *Aerial Incident of 27 July 1955 (United States v Bulgaria)* [1960] ICJ Rep 146 ICJ Pleadings, Memorial of the United States of 2 December 1958, 167, 229 ('An aggrieved plaintiff may sue any or all joint tortfeasors, jointly or severally, although he may collect from them, or any one or more of them, only the full amount of his damage'); see also T Weir, 'Complex Liabilities' in A Tunc (ed), *International Encyclopedia of Comparative Law: Torts*, vol 11 (Tübingen, Martinus Nijhoff, 1983) 43.

ILC points out, even where the injury was caused by a combination of factors, only one of which ascribed to the responsible State, 'international practice and the decisions of international tribunals do not support the reduction or attenuation of reparation for concurrent causes'.[109] On the other hand, this may lead to double recovery for an injured party from both the principal and the complicit wrongdoer for more than its actual injury. This brings us back to the initial problem for unless causation is disposed of as a requirement or adjusted, it will be impossible to operationalise the content of responsibility for complicity.

c. Satisfaction (Articles 37 ARSIWA/ARIO)

In international law, satisfaction has always had a slightly different connotation from the reparation *stricto sensu*. As Dominicé put it, '[i]l s'agit d'une sorte de sanction morale'.[110] Satisfaction aims to remedy all types of non-pecuniary damages suffered. With limited exceptions, moral damages cannot be expressed in pecuniary terms. Traditionally, satisfaction may take different forms, including simple or solemn excuses, honours to the flag, punishment of responsible officials, extradition, and other similar conduct.[111]

As confirmed in the *Rainbow Warrior* arbitration:

> Unlawful action against non-material interests, such as acts affecting the honor, dignity or prestige of a State, entitle the victim State to receive adequate reparation, even if those acts have not resulted in a pecuniary or material loss for the claimant State.[112]

Accordingly, the Tribunal held that the breach by France had

> provoked indignation and public outrage in New Zealand and caused a new, additional non-material damage … of a moral, political and legal nature, resulting from the affront to the dignity and prestige not only of New Zealand as such, but of its highest judicial and executive authorities as well.[113]

Satisfaction emerges as a remedy *par excellence* for moral damages caused either to the honour of the State or its nationals.[114]

[109] ARSIWA (n 3) 93, para 12 (Art 31 Commentary); see, eg *Corfu Channel (United Kingdom v Albania)* (n 106); see also Aust (n 2) 281–84; JE Noyes and BD Smith, 'State Responsibility and the Principle of Joint and Several Liability' (1988) 13 *Yale J Intl L* 225, 246.

[110] Belhumeur and Condorelli (n 39) 279 (author's translation: 'it is a kind of moral sanction').

[111] PA Bissonnette, *La satisfaction comme mode de réparation en droit international* (Genève, HEI, 1952) 24; see also Reitzer (n 39).

[112] *Rainbow Warrior Affair (France/New Zealand)* (n 15) 266–67, paras 107–09.

[113] ibid 267, para 110.

[114] Arangio-Ruiz (n 59) 40, para 136; see also Bissonnette (n 111); EJ de Aréchaga, 'International Responsibility' in M Sørensen (ed), *Manual of Public International Law* (London, MacMillan, 1968) 572.

Conceptually, '[l]a réparation du dommage moral a sans doute un caractère un peu troublé, la victime recevant une satisfaction de remplacement: il y a pourtant réparation et non punition'.[115] The ILC made an effort to emphasise the point that satisfaction does not entail punishment from its 1996 draft through the adoption of the Articles in 2001. Satisfaction emerges as one of the most flexible forms of reparation and, arguably, best fit for the inter-State relations.[116]

It may be argued that, in most cases, complicity will only lead to moral, indirect or consequential damages. These are generally, but not always, rejected in international law as being insufficient for compensation to be awarded.[117] Hence, in general, absent a material damage that can be individualised as a result of complicit conduct, the finding by the Court of a wrongful act and of responsibility constitutes appropriate satisfaction.[118] In the author's view, considering the difficulties that complicity raises for causation, this is indeed the most suitable form of reparation.

A separate issue is whether from a policy and equity perspective this remedy wipes out all the consequences of breach linked to complicity. For example, it is doubtful whether in cases of most serious breaches of international law, whether *jus cogens* or *erga omnes*, satisfaction in the form of declaration of unlawfulness and finding of responsibility is sufficient in respect of complicity in such a wrongdoing. The Court's unwillingness in the *Bosnia Genocide* case to come up with remedies beyond a declaration is telling.[119] At the same time, a declaration of unlawfulness of particular

[115] G Ripert, 'Les règles du droit civil applicables aux rapports internationaux' (1933) 44 *RCADI* 565, 622 (author's translation: '[t]he reparation of moral injury has undoubtedly a slightly problematic character as the victim receives a satisfaction: nonetheless it is reparation and not punishment').

[116] Belhumeur and Condorelli (n 39) 349; for early doctrinal views on the content of satisfaction see Bissonnette (n 111) 25–32; see also C Barthe-Gay, 'Réflexions sur la satisfaction en droit international' (2003) 49 *AFDI* 105; E Wyler and A Papaux, 'The Different Forms of Reparation: Satisfaction' in J Crawford et al (eds), *The Law of International Responsibility* (Oxford, OUP, 2010).

[117] See, eg *Woodward-Clyde Consultants v Iran and others* (Award) (2 September 1983) 3 Iran-US CTR 239, 249–50, para 17; *McCollough and Co Inc v The Ministry of Post, Telegraph and Telephone and others* (Award) (22 April 1986) 11 Iran-US CTR 3, 18, para 52; cf *Ulterwyk Corp and others v Iran and others* (Award) (6 July 1988) 19 Iran-US CTR 107, 140, para 117; *Watkins-Johnson Co and others v Iran and others* (Award) (28 July 1989) 22 Iran-US CTR 218, 250–51, paras 114–17; *General Electric Co v Iran and others* (Award) (15 March 1991) 26 Iran-US CTR 148, 168–69, paras 67–69 (holding that consequential or incidental damages can be compensated as long as they are reasonably incurred expenses).

[118] ARSIWA (n 3) 107, para 6 (Art 37); *Corfu Channel (United Kingdom v Albania)* (n 106) 35; *Rainbow Warrior Affair (France/New Zealand)* (n 15) 272–73, paras 121–23; *Arrest Warrant of 11 April 2000 (DRC v Belgium)* (Judgment) [2002] ICJ Rep 3, 31, para 75; *Certain Questions of Mutual Assistance in Criminal Matters (Djibouti v France)* (Judgment) [2008] ICJ Rep 177, 245, para 204; *Pulp Mills* (Judgment) (n 28) 102, para 269; *Bosnia Genocide (Merits)* (n 9) 234 and 236, paras 463 and 469; for an earlier authority see, eg *The 'Manouba' (France v Italy)* (1913) 11 RIAA 471, 475.

[119] Gattini (n 59) 711; see generally N Scandamis, *Le jugement déclaratoire entre États* (Paris, Pedone, 1976).

complicit conduct by a Court avoids the potential abuses associated in the past with satisfaction, which often fell short of humiliation of another State or could be regarded as of a quasi-punitive nature.[120]

Other courts, in particular in the area of human rights law, take a more proactive approach to the remedies that are akin to satisfaction (ie rehabilitation, symbolic recognition of victims, the right to the truth, etc) and, arguably, such remedies could become available to injured parties in respect of complicit actors. As complicity is of increasing concern in international human rights law, it is appropriate that courts depart from a strict vision of satisfaction to ensure that victims get full redress from both principal and complicit actors. As we have seen in chapter five, when dealing with the knowledge element, courts and tribunals may resort to certain evidentiary presumptions and foreseeability criteria in ascertaining whether there is sufficient link between complicity and the injury for which satisfaction is claimed.[121]

The reality is that 'when [courts] have to condemn a State, international courts prefer to do it at the lowest possible moral cost for the State in question'.[122] In the relations between States and international organisations, a declaration of illegality by international court or tribunal or by a regional or international body such as the United Nations Security Council (UNSC) usually provides adequate satisfaction. This is particularly so in situations where compensation is sought in respect of relatively trivial head of damages, such as infringement of certain rights of the flag State without a measurable loss.[123]

However, where the pattern of complicity is endemic between two particular States more is required from international law to secure compliance with an international obligation. In such circumstances, other forms of satisfaction may be appropriate, such as the obligation to prosecute the complicit State's officials domestically, or, depending on the wrongful acts in question, internationally (eg arresting and surrendering the individuals for prosecution before the International Criminal Court).

Another potential form of satisfaction would be to require that the impugned party regularly report to the UNSC or other bodies on its progress in reviewing domestic structures or policies that allowed the

[120] See Dupuy (n 107).

[121] See, eg Rovine and Hanessian (n 43); CF Amerasinghe, 'Presumptions and Inferences in Evidence in International Litigation' (2004) 3 *LPICT* 395.

[122] F Rigaux, 'International Responsibility and the Principle of Causality' in M Ragazzi (ed), *International Responsibility Today: Essays in Memory of Oscar Schachter* (Leiden, Martinus Nijhoff, 2005) 81–82; R Ago, 'Le délit international' (1939) 68 *RCADI* 417, 503 (arguing that in the case of omissions the causality can be assessed only in a purely normative terms).

[123] See, eg *M/V Saiga (No 2) (Saint Vincent and the Grenadines v Guinea)* (Judgment) [1999] ITLOS Rep (1999) 120 ILR 143, 200 (the tribunal granted compensation in respect of damages to the vessel and its crew, but not in respect of infringement of other rights of the flag State).

provision of the aid or assistance to the internationally wrongful act (eg in cases of extraordinary renditions). A formal diplomatic apology may also fulfil the purpose of satisfaction in certain circumstances.

III. IMPLEMENTATION OF RESPONSIBILITY FOR COMPLICITY

A. Invocation of Responsibility for Complicity

While a finding of responsibility for complicity generates legal consequences the injured State or international organisation must have a right or legal interest that has been affected in order to invoke responsibility of the complicit entity. In other words, while responsibility exists *in abstracto* from the moment the principal wrongful act that benefited from complicity occurs, giving effect to the legal consequences is a separate exercise to which we shall now turn.

Two questions in relation to the invocation of responsibility for complicity will be addressed here. Who can invoke responsibility for complicity, only injured States or international organisations or also other than injured States or international organisations? Assuming States and international organisations other than injured ones can invoke responsibility, is such invocation limited to giving effect to specific legal consequences such as cessation and/or reparation?

The answers to these questions depend on the interpretation of injury and the legal rights and interests that the international community has in regulating complicity.[124]

Already at the beginning of the twentieth century Anzilotti considered that it was difficult to seek to determine which violations of international law can be reprimanded by one, several or all States—States which take measures to prevent or repress a violation of the right of another exercise neither a legal right nor a duty, but simply a lawful activity.[125] As discussed

[124] SFDI, *La responsabilité dans le système international: Colloque du Mans* (Paris, Pedone, 1991) 91.

[125] D Anzilotti, *Teoria generale della responsabilità dello stato nel diritto internazionale* (Firenze, F Lumachi Libraio-Editore, 1902) 93 ('Gli stati che agiscono per impedire o reprimere una violazione del diritto altrui non esercitano dunque nè un diritto nè un dovere giuridico, ma semplicemente un'attività lecita. Di qui deriva una conseguenza molto importante dal punto di vista teorico e pratico, vale a dire che è inutile cercare dei criteri, d'altronde molto difficili a stabilire, per determinare quali violazioni del diritto internazionale possono venir represse da tutti gli stati e quali no'; author's translation: 'The States which act to prevent or repress a breach of the rights of others neither exercise a right nor perform an obligation, but simply undertake a lawful activity. Thus, an important consequence from both theoretical and practical view is that it is useless to devise the criteria, which in any case would be difficult to establish, to determine which breaches of international law can be repressed by all States and those which cannot').

in greater detail below, subsequent developments in international law have progressively imposed restrictions on the States' right to resort to unilateral enforcement measures and have generated a dual regime for the invocation of responsibility.

Accordingly, Articles 42 and 48 ARSIWA draw a distinction between 'injured States' and 'other' States that are entitled to invoke responsibility. The same distinction is transposed to international organisations through Articles 43 and 49 ARIO. According to the ILC Commentary to ARSIWA, an injured State is the State whose individual right has been denied or impaired by the internationally wrongful act or which has otherwise been particularly affected by that act:[126]

> Article 42 ARSIWA
>
> Invocation of responsibility by an injured State
>
> A State is entitled as an injured State to invoke the responsibility of another State if the obligation breached is owed to:
>
> (a) that State individually; or
> (b) a group of States including that State, or the international community as a whole, and the breach of the obligation:
>   (i) specially affects that State; or
>   (ii) is of such a character as radically to change the position of all the other States to which the obligation is owed with respect to the further performance of the obligation.[127]

This definition is modelled upon Article 60 of the Vienna Convention on the Law of Treaties (VCLT) and uses a similar two-tier framework for invocation of responsibility. Under Article 42 ARSIWA, an injured State or especially affected State has the right to invoke responsibility of the wrongdoing State. This provision is evidently inspired by a classical dualistic model of inter-State responsibility. Conceptually, it is possible to envisage situations in which any State considers itself injured by complicity of another State depending on the primary obligation breached. Article 42 ARSIWA, which bears some *a contrario* resemblance to Article 16(b) ARSIWA, requires the opposability of the obligation breached. For a State to be able to validly invoke responsibility pursuant to Article 42 ARSIWA in relation to a complicit conduct, all the three States (ie principal wrongdoer, complicit and injured) would have to be bound by the same international obligation. Customary international law obligations aside, this excludes a great number of situations of breaches of bilateral or multilateral treaty obligations the responsibility for which will never be invoked.

[126] ARSIWA (n 3) 116, para 2.
[127] ibid Art 42.

In terms of the mechanics, invoking complicity of one actor in the wrongful act of another is relatively easier in respect of breaches of certain types of obligations as set out under Article 48 ARSIWA. The provision reads:

> Article 48
>
> Invocation of responsibility by a State other than an injured State
>
> 1. Any State other than an injured State is entitled to invoke the responsibility of another State in accordance with paragraph 2 if:
>   (a) the obligation breached is owed to a group of States including that State, and is established for the protection of a collective interest of the group; or
>   (b) the obligation breached is owed to the international community as a whole.
> 2. Any State entitled to invoke responsibility under paragraph 1 may claim from the responsible State:
>   (a) cessation of the internationally wrongful act, and assurances and guarantees of non-repetition in accordance with article 30; and
>   (b) performance of the obligation of reparation in accordance with the preceding articles, in the interest of the injured State or of the beneficiaries of the obligation breached.
> 3. The requirements for the invocation of responsibility by an injured State under articles 43, 44 and 45 apply to an invocation of responsibility by a State entitled to do so under paragraph 1.[128]

The basis for the invocation is thus the common or general interests of the international community, as expressed either through obligations *erga omnes partes* or *erga omnes*. As discussed in chapter four, these obligations usually include (but are not limited to) norms relating to the protection of human rights, the environment, the prohibition of genocide, use of force and aggression, the prohibition of slavery and the right to self-determination. Doctrine also generally agrees that there is no definite answer as to the relationship between *jus cogens* and *erga omnes* obligations.[129] The ILC Commentary suggests that the former 'focus on the scope and priority to be given to a certain number of fundamental obligations' while the latter emphasise 'the legal interest that all the States have in compliance'.[130]

[128] ibid Art 48.

[129] See, eg G Gaja, 'Jus Cogens Beyond the Vienna Convention' (1981) 172 *RCADI* 271; G Gaja, 'Do States Have a Duty to Ensure Compliance with Obligations Erga Omnes by Other States?' in M Ragazzi (ed), *International Responsibility Today: Essays in Memory of Oscar Schachter* (Leiden, Martinus Nijhoff, 2005); CJ Tams et al, 'Erga Omnes, Jus Cogens and Their Impact on the Law of Responsibility', *The International Responsibility of the European Union: European and International Perspectives* (Oxford, Hart Publishing, 2013); P Picone, 'La distinzione tra norme internazionali di jus cogens e norme che producono obblighi erga omnes' (2008) 1 *RDI* 5.

[130] ARSIWA (n 3) 112, para 7 (Art 39 Commentary).

Some commentators rather present the problem as constituting concentric circles, where *jus cogens* norms form part of the larger spectrum of *erga omnes* obligations.[131]

International law has not yet formed a sound theory by which the following problem may be resolved: who has *locus standi* to bring judicial proceedings based on 'general interests' (*intérêt pour agir)* as opposed to 'subjective right' (*droit pour agir*)? It is questionable whether under the current state of development of international law there are 'general interests' which entitle all States to require due performance of an obligation by the target State to restore legality *statu quo ante*.[132]

The ICJ seemed to reject upfront any such *actio popularis*. In the *South West Africa* cases, the Court declined *locus standi* with regard to the alleged collective interests of States not directly injured. In doing so, the Court stated that 'a right of this kind could be known to certain municipal systems of law... [but] as it stands at present it is not known to international law'.[133] Judge Jessup in his Dissenting Opinion suggested instead that 'international law has accepted and established situations in which States are given a right of action without any showing of individual prejudice or individual substantive interest as distinguished from the general interest'.[134]

The Court seemed to cautiously embrace Judge Jessup's rationale in the *Barcelona Traction* case in its *obiter dictum*, to which we usually attribute more meaning than is warranted:

> [A]n essential distinction should be drawn between the obligations of a State towards the international community as a whole and those arising vis-à-vis another State ... by their nature the former are the concern of all States. In view of the importance of the rights involved, all States can be held to have a legal interest in their protection; they are obligations *erga omnes*.[135]

[131] See Gaja, 'Jus Cogens Beyond the Vienna Convention' (n 129); LA Sicilianos, 'The Classification of Obligations and the Multilateral Dimension of Relations of International Responsibility' (2002) 13 *EJIL* 1127.

[132] See, eg *Arrest Warrant of 11 April 2000 (DRC v Belgium)* (n 118) ICJ Pleadings (15 October 2001) CR 2001/05, 14 and 16 (Rigaux) ('the Congo seeks reparation for the offence—iniuria—committed against it, but at the same time the Congo is defending an objective principle of international law, namely respect for the immunities guaranteed by international law. In so doing, the Congo is arguing on behalf of the entire international community, for it is certain that the violation of those immunities would truly lead to chaos in interstate relations').

[133] See *South West Africa (Liberia v South Africa/ Ethiopia v South Africa)* (Preliminary Objections) [1962] ICJ Rep 319; *South West Africa (Liberia v South Africa/ Ethiopia v South Africa)* (Second Phase) [1966] ICJ Rep 6.

[134] *South West Africa (Liberia v South Africa/ Ethiopia v South Africa)* (n 133), Dissenting Opinion of Judge Jessup 325, 388.

[135] *Barcelona Traction, Light and Power Company, Limited (Second Phase) (Belgium v Spain)* (n 46), 32, para 33.

Without entering into the merits of the Court's rationale and its contextual understanding which is often overlooked,[136] international law has come to accept that States do have an interest in other States' compliance with the *erga omnes* obligations. The way to achieve that compliance can differ depending on the norm in question, but the basic principle seems well entrenched in modern international law. It thus appears reasonable that States and international organisations should be entitled to invoke responsibility of other States or international organisations whenever the latter contribute to the infringement of *erga omnes* obligations.

Even if *locus standi* is given to States other than the directly injured State, that standing does not necessarily mean that they have the power to claim reparation for the injury caused to the primary victim. Article 48(2)(b) ARSIWA builds in the possibility for such recourse. In the *Military and Paramilitary Activities* case, the Court held that States which were not victims of an armed attack could only exercise collective self-defence upon a prior request by the direct victim.[137] Similarly, in the *East Timor* case, Judge Vereshchetin expressed the view that if Portugal wanted to protect the right to self-determination of the Timor people, it had to establish that it had acted in accordance with the interests of that people.[138] By analogy, it would seem that some form of approval would be required from the injured State for another State to act on its behalf in a claim for reparation.

As Tams suggested, the claims of reparations in the interests of the injured State or the beneficiaries of the obligation breached may be further complicated by the identity of the beneficiary, which may be a State, a non-State organised group or an individual.[139] A recent German Constitutional Court case confirms that claims of compensation by individuals against a State for complicity in violations committed as part of operations led by an international organisation are bound to fail.[140] Similarly, 'there may also be situations where the wrongful act in question affects a common good which cannot be personified (such as biological diversity or the safety of the marine environment)'.[141] Complicity in any such violations *erga omnes* or *erga omnes partes* would then in principle entitle a third party (not a primary victim) to invoke the responsibility of the principal and

[136] See, eg R Higgins, 'Aspects of the Case Concerning the Barcelona Traction, Light and Power Company, Ltd' (1970) 11 *Virginia J Intl L* 327; CJ Tams, *Enforcing Obligations Erga Omnes* (Cambridge, CUP, 2005)lpage.

[137] *Military and Paramilitary Activities in and against Nicaragua (Nicaragua v United States)* (Merits) [1986] ICJ Rep 14, 105, para 199.

[138] *East Timor (Portugal v Australia)* (Judgment) [1995] ICJ Rep 90 Separate Opinion of Judge Vereshchetin 135, 135-38.

[139] CJ Tams, 'All's Well When It Ends Well: Comments on the ILC's Articles on State Responsibility' (2002) 62 *ZaöRV* 759, 782.

[140] *2 BvR 2660/06, 2 BvR 487/07 ('Bridge of Varvarin')* (Judgment) [2013] BverfG 1-70 (German Constitutional Court).

[141] Tams (n 139) 782; see ARSIWA (n 3) 126–27, paras 7 and 12 (Art 48 Commentary); Crawford (n 56) 34, para 106(b).

the accomplice wrongdoer.[142] The question remains open as to whether complicity in such violations entitles third States or international organisations to do more, such as taking countermeasures to demand reparation on behalf of the injured party or to induce compliance.[143]

B. Countermeasures Against Complicit States or International Organisations

According to Arthur Watts:

> It is evident that it is in this general area of enforcement of international law, particularly where questions of peace and security are in issue, that the international rule of law is at its weakest. Paradoxically, it is this weakness which, when coupled with the growing concern of States that international law should be properly applied and enforced, can *lead to action which while intended to strengthen the international rule of law in practice may weaken it even further*.[144] (emphasis added)

If none of the traditional forms of reparation and legal consequences or ways of diplomatic pressure suffice to bring the complicit actor into compliance, the question arises whether international law can do more about it? Does it admit *ultima ratio* a sort of *vendetta* justice solution against complicity in the wrongful act?[145]

[142] ILC (n 75) 79 (China) (questioning the breadth of the regime in Art 48 ARSIWA and possible application of Art 54); 80 (France) (noting that '[t]he State which has only a legal interest can only demand the cessation of the breach committed by another State. It cannot seek reparation for the damage caused by the internationally wrongful act which has not directly affected it'); see generally DN Hutchinson, 'Solidarity and Breaches of Multilateral Treaties' (1988) 59 *British YBIL* 151.

[143] For a critique of the current regime in the ARSIWA and the inability of third parties to properly react to serious breaches of international and to induce compliance see, eg A Cassese, *International Law* (2nd edn, Oxford, OUP, 2005) 269–71; DD Caron, 'The ILC Articles on State Responsibility: The Paradoxical Relationship Between Form and Authority' (2002) 96 *AJIL* 857; see also M Dawidowicz, 'Third-Party Countermeasures: Observations on a Controversial Concept' in C Chinkin and F Baetens (eds), *Sovereignty, Statehood and State Responsibility: Essays in Honour of James Crawford* (Cambridge, CUP, 2015); M Dawidowicz, 'Public Law Enforcement without Public Law Safeguards? An Analysis of State Practice on Third-Party Countermeasures and Their Relationship to the UN Security Council' (2007) 77 *British YBIL* 333.

[144] A Watts, 'The International Rule of Law' (1993) 36 *German YBIL* 15, 44.

[145] Reitzer (n 39) 49–50 ('Le problème de la réparation en droit international rappelle, à beaucoup de points de vue, celui de la composition dans le droit primitif des clans et des tribus … La tribu lésée par quelque forfait est-elle libre de se livrer immédiatement à la vengeance (vendetta) ou doit-elle d'abord recourir à un autre moyen? … le clan offensé avait une option entre la vengeance et un arrangement à l'amiable'; author's translation: 'The problem of reparation in international law recalls in many respects that of the composition of clans and tribes in the primitive law … The tribe injured by a conduct, is it free to revenge immediately (vendetta) or should it first resort to other means? … the injured clan had a choice of revenge and amicable settlement'); see also K Zemanek, 'The Unilateral Enforcement of Obligations' (1987) 32 *ZaöRV* 37; A Nissel, 'The ILC Articles on State Responsibility: Between Self-Help and Solidarity' (2006) 38 *NYU J Intl L & Pol* 355.

For example, as discussed in chapter five, many forms of complicity are derived from non-compliance with duties under treaties that provide for assistance or mutual cooperation. The question arises as to whether States can unilaterally sever those legal obligations in situations where the aid is being diverted for wrongful acts. While the suspension of such treaties may be an available route under the limited circumstances that the law of treaties provides for, it can also constitute a countermeasure within the realm of the law of international responsibility.[146] However, in the context of multilateral or so-called 'integral treaties' to which Article 60(2)(d) of the VCLT applies, 'a state injured by the breach of such a treaty cannot suspend the performance of its obligations towards the defaulting state without at the same time infringing the rights of other parties'.[147] In case of breaches of such obligations, all States parties are entitled to respond.[148]

Aust discusses a few examples of States' conduct that could be regarded as either an adoption of countermeasures in the collective interest or as a consequence of the prohibition of complicity.[149] For example, in 1982, the Netherlands suspended a treaty on development cooperation with Suriname because of human rights violations following a *coup d'état*.[150] That treaty stipulated the delivery of economic assistance and subsidies for the maintenance of the Surinamese military. Other examples explored by Aust include the United States' suspension of aid to the regime of Idi Amin in Uganda in 1978[151] or the United States' suspension of its military

[146] On countermeasures see generally *Air Service Agreement of 27 March 1946 (United States/ France)* (1978) 18 RIAA 417; *Responsibility of Germany for Damage Caused in the Portuguese Colonies in the South of Africa (Portugal v Germany)* (n 40) 1011; PM Dupuy, 'Observations sur la pratique récente des sanctions de l'illicite' (1983) 87 *RGDIP* 505; C Leben, 'Les Contre-Mesures Inter-étatiques et Les Réactions à L'illicite Dans La Société Internationale' (1982) 28 *AFDI* 9; E Zoller, 'Quelques Réflexions Sur Les Contre-Mesures En Droit International', *Mélanges Claude-Albert Colliard* (Paris, Pedone, 1984); LA Sicilianos, *Les réactions décentralisées à l'illicite: Des contre-mesures à la légitime défense* (Paris, LGDJ, 1990); D Simon and LA Sicilianos, 'La "contre-violence" unilatérale: Pratiques étatiques et Droit international' (1986) 32 *AFDI* 53; CJ Tams, 'Countermeasures against Multiple Responsible Actors' in A Nollkaemper and I Plakokefalos (eds), *Principles of Shared Responsibility in International Law: An Appraisal of the State of the Art* (Cambridge, CUP, 2014).

[147] LA Sicilianos, 'The Relationship between Reprisals and Denunciation or Suspension of a Treaty' (1993) 4 *EJIL* 341, 347–48.

[148] Crawford (n 56) 31, para 91.

[149] Aust (n 2) 365–73; see generally D Alland, 'Countermeasures of General Interest' (2002) 13 *EJIL* 1221.

[150] 'Note Verbale of 16 December 1982 (Netherlands)' (1983) Tractatenblad No 6; reprinted in HH Lindemann, 'Die Auswirkungen der Menschenrechtsverletzungen in Surinam auf die Vertragsbeziehungen zwischen den Niederlanden und Surinam' (1984) 44 *ZaöRV* 64, 81.

[151] United States Uganda Embargo Act (10 October 1978) 22 USC 287, § 5(b) ('the United States should take steps to dissociate itself from any foreign government which engages in the international crime of genocide'); SJ Fredman, 'US Trade Sanctions against Uganda: Legality under International Law' (1979) 11 *Law and Policy International Business* 1149; Dawidowicz, 'Public Law Enforcement Without Public Law Safeguards?' (n 143) 356–60.

aid to Indonesia following the latter's invasion of the East Timor.[152] Similar actions were taken in order to suspend military assistance to Argentina, Ethiopia, Chile and Uruguay.[153]

These examples may also be regarded as part of international practice on complicity.[154] Indeed, it is only logical to assume that in reacting to instances where a State interrupts or suspends the aid or assistance that it has undertaken to provide under a given treaty, it has dual purpose. The State aims to ensure compliance with the treaty, and only in case of a material breach of that treaty can it resort to consequences available under the law of treaties, namely suspension and termination.[155] At the same time, its reaction may constitute a countermeasure to ensure compliance of the other State in an attempt to avoid its own international responsibility for complicity in that violation.

While Aust suggests that the above examples fall within the category of countermeasures in the collective interest (Article 54 ARSIWA), it may well be the case that they are countermeasures proper, ie taken by the injured State under the regime of Articles 49 to 53 ARSIWA, depending on how one construes the injury in each of those factual scenarios. For instance, if it could be argued that State A is injured in its own subjective right by the breach of State B, in the form of the latter's diversion in the use of aid provided by State A in order to commit a wrongful act to State C, then there is a good foundation for framing State A's reaction as a countermeasure *proper* against State B (ie Articles 49–53). This could circumvent operational uncertainties underlying the regime of Article 54 ARSIWA.[156]

[152] 'Statement of GH Aldrich, Deputy Legal Adviser, US Department of State, before the Subcommittee on International Organizations, Committee of International Relations, US House of Representatives' (19 July 1977), reproduced in (5 September 1977) *Department of State Bulletin* 324–26 (stating that the intervention raised a question of 'uses of US-furnished equipment under applicable US law and agreements between the United States and Indonesia').

[153] Leben (n 146) 23.

[154] Aust (n 2) 365.

[155] Vienna Convention on the Law of Treaties (adopted 23 May 1969; entered into force 27 January 1980) 1155 UNTS 331, Art 60; see also *Legal Consequences for States of the Continued Presence of South Africa in Namibia (South West Africa) notwithstanding Security Council Resolution 276 (1970)* (Advisory Opinion) [1971] ICJ Rep 16, 47 ('the general principle of law that a right of a termination on account of breach must be presumed to exist in respect of all treaties, except as regards provisions relating to the protection of the human person contained in treaties of humanitarian character' referring to Art 60(5) VCLT); B Simma, 'Reflections on Article 60 of the Vienna Convention on the Law of Treaties and Its Background in General International Law' (1970) 20 *Österreichische Zeitschrift für öffentliches Recht* 5.

[156] For States' concerns in relation to potentially wide-ranging consequences of Art 54 ARSIWA see ILC (n 75) 90 ff; for the practice of measures taken in the collective interest see, eg Dawidowicz, 'Public Law Enforcement Without Public Law Safeguards?' (n 143); Tams (n 136) 207 ff; M Koskenniemi, 'Solidarity Measures: State Responsibility as a New International Order?' (2002) 72 *British YBIL* 337; Crawford (n 56) paras 391–94; for States' criticism of an earlier draft of this provision which specifically allowed for third-party countermeasures in response to serious breaches of obligations erga omnes see J Crawford, 'Fourth Report on State Responsibility' (2001) UN Doc A/CN.4/517 and Add 1, reproduced in (2001) 2 (pt 1) *YBILC* 1, 17–18, paras 70–74.

The flipside of this argument is that the primary subject sustaining injury in its narrow meaning is State C. This could bring about a practical imbroglio where both States A and C argue that they have been injured by different aspects of State B's conduct. This is reminiscent of the initial attempt by the ILC to distinguish between directly and indirectly injured States.[157]

Regardless of whether these reactions in practice are framed as countermeasures proper or as measures taken by States in the collective interest, they are all subject to important limitations. These measures constitute a breach of international obligations and their wrongfulness is precluded to the extent they are a response to a prior breach by another entity.[158] Quite naturally, they cannot implicate breaches of the prohibition against the threat or use of force, other peremptory norms and fundamental human rights and humanitarian law obligations. Classic examples of lawful countermeasures include: (i) the withdrawal of trade concessions; (ii) the suspension of the landing rights of offending State aircrafts; (iii) imposition of visa requirements or additional immigration controls against the offending State's nationals; (iv) withdrawal of diplomatic representatives or expulsion of the offending State's diplomats; (v) blocking credits or aid; and (vi) the freezing of offending State financial assets.

Importantly, countermeasures should be temporary in nature and 'must not be aimed at revenge'.[159] As these measures are 'of later (if not final) resort aimed at securing compliance',[160] they must meet several substantive and procedural requirements, including that of proportionality and prior notice.[161] Countermeasures must be 'commensurate with the injury suffered, taking into account the gravity of the internationally wrongful act and the rights in question'.[162] Technically, however, countermeasures are not merely a response to a violation of primary norm per se but also to the violation of the obligations arising from the original breach (eg failure of the defaulting State to cease the breach or to provide for compensation).

[157] ILC, 'Draft Articles on State Responsibility with Commentaries Thereto Adopted by the International Law Commission on First Reading' reproduced in (1996) 2 (pt 2) *YBILC* 58 (Art 19); PM Dupuy, 'A General Stocktaking of the Connections between the Multilateral Dimension of Obligations and Codification of the Law of Responsibility' (2002) 13 *EJIL* 1053, 1069 (noting that this distinction brought by Riphagen could be criticized for 'confusing the nature of the interest attacked and the intensity of the attack'); see also W Riphagen, 'Third Report on the Content, Forms and Degrees of International Responsibility' (1982) UN Doc A/CN.4/354 and Add 1-2, reproduced in (1982) 2 (pt 1) *YBILC* 22, 45, para 140 (holding a strong view against countermeasures in the collective interest 'a single State cannot take upon itself the role of "policeman" of the international community').

[158] ARSIWA (n 3) Art 22; ARIO (n 3) Art 22.

[159] E Katselli, 'Countermeasures by Non-Injured States in the Law on State Responsibility' [2005] *ESIL Proceedings* 1, 2.

[160] J Crawford, 'Overview of Part Three of the Articles on State Responsibility' in J Crawford et al (eds), *The Law of International Responsibility* (Oxford, OUP, 2010) 932.

[161] ARSIWA (n 3) Art 52(1).

[162] ibid Art 51.

This explains in part why the scope of countermeasures under the law of responsibility is broader than under Article 60 of the VCLT.[163]

Much controversy surrounds the availability and application of countermeasures in international law and it is not within the scope of this study to cover this debate in detail.[164] Briefly, however, one view is that the recognition of countermeasures within the ARSIWA and ARIO reflects an imperfection of the international community, an idea of private justice of the most powerful ones, a sort of regression of international law.[165] Another view is that it is preferable to control the use of countermeasures within rather than outside of the sphere of the law.[166]

As Couttereau eloquently summarised the view of the doctrine on the subject:

> Une réaction optimiste voit dans les réactions décentralisées à l'illicite un moyen de pousser l'Etat récalcitrant à rentrer dans la légalité. Cette vision s'inspire donc surtout d'une analyse des circonstances excluant l'illicéité, sous l'angle politique; ces moyens de pression à défaut de mieux permettent aux Etats de disposer de procédés que ne sortent pas du droit pour obliger ceux qui l'ont quitté à y revenir. L'autre vision est plus pessimiste et les voit comme une justification à la déstabilisation des rapports juridiques en renforçant l'émiettement des réactions licites, les éloignant encore plus du modèle du droit qui suppose un tiers arbitre indépendant.[167]

According to Alland, countermeasures, whether taken by injured States or by third States in the collective interest against a complicit entity, represent

[163] See, eg Simma (n 155) 14 and 23; see also more generally on termination and suspension of treaties R Pisillo-Mazzeschi, 'Termination and Suspension of Treaties for Breach in the International Law Commission Works on State Responsibility' in M Spinedi and B Simma (eds), *United Nations Codification of State Responsibility* (New York, Oceana, 1987); see also C Binder, 'Does the Difference Make a Difference? A Comparison between the Mechanisms of the Law of Treaties and of State Responsibility as Means to Derogate from Treaty Obligations in Cases of Subsequent Changes of Circumstances' in M Szabó (ed), *State Responsibility and the Law of Treaties* (The Hague, Eleven, 2010) 23 (arguing that the procedures for treaty non-performance under the law of responsibility 'are much less onerous that those established by the VCLT for a lawful treaty termination').

[164] See generally B Simma and CJ Tams, 'Reacting Against Treaty Breaches' in DB Hollis (ed), *The Oxford Guide to Treaties* (Oxford, OUP, 2012); J Charney, 'Third State Remedies in International Law' (1989) 10 *Michigan J Intl L* 57.

[165] See, eg Y Daudet, 'Travaux de la Commission du droit international' (1994) 40 *AFDI* 575, 591–92.

[166] Pellet (n 20) 21.

[167] G Cottereau, 'Système juridique et notion de responsabilité' in SFDI (ed), *La responsabilité dans le système international: Colloque du Mans* (Paris, Pedone, 1991) 88 (author's translation: 'An optimist reaction sees in the decentralised responses a means to push the recalcitrant State to return to legality. This vision is inspired above all by an analysis of the circumstances precluding wrongfulness, from a political angle; in the absence of a better mechanism, these means of pressure allow States to resort to lawful methods to bring the transgressing to legality. Another view is a more pessimist one and regards the countermeasures as a justification to destabilise legal relationships by reinforcing the scope of lawful reactions, distancing them even further from the model of law that presupposes a third party adjudicator').

a clash of incompatible logic.[168] On the one hand there is a logic of a 'private justice entrenched in the defence of subjective rights' and on the other hand that of 'public order attached to the defence of objective law'.[169] Certainly, many questions remain to be answered, in particular in relation to possible third-party (in the collective interests) countermeasures. Boisson de Chazournes illustrates well the danger of abuse of countermeasures with the following examples in relation to the environment protection:

> Diverting a watercourse as a countermeasure might not only damage another riparian state that allegedly is responsible for a wrongful act, it may also damage other states in a region, not to mention the international community as a whole. Restrictions on trade exchanges with one country might lead to deforestation, to the detriment not only of the state responsible but also possibly other states.[170]

Finally, it is interesting to note that the scenarios discussed in this section may lead to a normative conflict in practice. It is evident that considerations of avoiding complicity may be an additional legitimising factor for suspending or terminating a given treaty relationship (owing to the counterpart's diversion of the use of aid or assistance).[171] However, the question may become more complicated when the assistance through the performance of a given treaty-based obligation contributes to a breach of an international obligation by the counterparty. In such cases, a State is entitled, if not obliged, to suspend, or terminate that treaty. There is some resemblance between this scenario and *exceptio non adimpleti contractus; inadimplenti non est adimplendum*, commonly known as the exception of non-performance.[172] In other words, a treaty-based obligation to provide

[168] D Alland, *Justice privée et ordre juridique international* (Paris, Pedone, 1994) 371.

[169] ibid (celle de la justice privée, qui s'enracine dans la défense de droits subjectifs, celle de la défense de l'ordre public, qui s'attache à la défense du droit objectif, celle des relations juridiques interétatiques, où s'éparpille le pouvoir d'auto-appréciation; author's translation: 'that of private justice, entrenched in the defence of subjective rights, that of the defence of public order attached to the defence of objective law, that of inter-State legal relations, where the power of self-assessment prevails').

[170] L Boisson de Chazournes, 'The State of State Responsibility' (2002) 96 *ASIL Proceedings* 169, 171.

[171] Aust (n 2) 371.

[172] *Diversion of Water from the Meuse (Netherlands v Belgium)* (Judgment) [1937] PCIJ Ser A/B No 70, 4, Separate Opinion of Judge Anzilotti 45, 50 (suggesting that the principle is 'so just, so equitable, so universally recognized, that it must be applied in international relations also'); ibid Individual Opinion of Judge Hudson 73, 77; cf *Application of the Interim Accord of 13 September 1995 (Former Yugoslav Republic of Macedonia v Greece)* (Judgment) [2011] ICJ Rep 644, Separate Opinion of Judge Simma 695, 706, para 26 ('the … exception is to be declared dead'); see also J Crawford and S Olleson, 'The Exception of Non-Performance: Links between the Law of Treaties and the Law of State Responsibility' (2000) 21 *Australian YBIL* 55; F Fontanelli, 'The Invocation of the Exception of Non-Performance, A Case-Study on the Role and Application of General Principles of International Law of Contractual Origin' (2012) 1 *Cambridge J Intl & Comp L* 119; S Forlati, 'Reactions to Non-Performance of Treaties in International Law' (2012) 25 *LJIL* 759.

aid or assistance may lead to situations where the violations committed with that aid or assistance will directly affect the continuing validity of that treaty as a whole.

There is an even stronger argument for the existence of a *duty* to suspend or terminate the performance of that treaty where the aid or assistance would facilitate a breach of a *jus cogens* obligation, or where performance of the treaty could amount to ex post facto assistance to maintaining a situation arising from the serious breach of *jus cogens* norm.[173] Pursuant to Article 41(2) ARSIWA, the otherwise lawful treaty-based assistance would be in violation of the obligation not to assist in the maintenance of the unlawful situation deriving from such breach. As referred to in chapter three, whether the same logic, both pre- and post-breach could extend to situations of complicity in the violations of *erga omnes* obligations is not yet settled in international law.[174] As a matter of principle, States have a legal interest in compliance but it is doubtful whether it could be said that they also have a legal duty to ensure such compliance.[175]

Be that as it may, this discussion demonstrates the importance that responsibility for complicity could have in ensuring legality and the integrity of the international legal order as a whole. It is also yet another example of how complicity bridges the 'territorial sea' between the law of treaties and the law of responsibility.[176] The connections between these two fields are subtle and merit further study, particularly insofar as the concept of breach is concerned.[177] This discussion has also shown that the regime(s) of responsibility for complicity in the ARSIWA and ARIO may

[173] ARSIWA (n 3) Art 41(2); ILC, 'ARIO' (n 3) Art 42(2).

[174] G Gaja, 'States Having an Interest in Compliance with the Obligation Breached' in J Crawford et al (eds), *The Law of International Responsibility* (Oxford, OUP, 2010); Gaja, 'Do States Have a Duty to Ensure Compliance with Obligations Erga Omnes by Other States?' (n 129); S Villalpando, *L'émergence de la communauté internationale dans la responsabilité des États* (Paris, PUF, 2005) 371–410; A Orakhelashvili, *Peremptory Norms in International Law* (Oxford, OUP, 2006) 272.

[175] *R (Al Rawi and Others) v Secretary of State for Foreign and Commonwealth Affairs and Secretary of State for the Home Department* (Judgment) [2006] EWHC 972 QB (Admin) para 70 (Latham LJ); cf *A (FC) and others (FC) v Secretary of State for the Home Department, A and others (FC) v Secretary of State for the Home Department (Joined Appeals)* (Judgment) [2005] UKHL 71, para 34 (Bingham LJ).

[176] See generally S Rosenne, 'Breach of Treaty in the Codification of the Law of State Responsibility' in S Rosenne (ed), *Essays on International Law and Practice* (Leiden, Martinus Nijhoff, 2007); Binder (n 163); PM Dupuy, 'Droit des traités, codification et responsabilité internationale' (1997) 43 *AFDI* 7; P Weckel, 'Convergence du droit des traités et du droit de la responsabilité internationale' (1998) 102 *RGDIP* 647.

[177] ILC, 'Report of the International Law Commission on the Work of Its 50th Session: Topical Summary of the Discussion Held in the Sixth Committee' (16 February 1999) UN Doc A/CN.4/496, 20, para 127 (States supported the notion of lex specialis but considered it important 'to respect the parallelism between the law of treaties and the law of international responsibility, while making clear the complementarity of the draft articles with the Vienna Convention'); see generally S Rosenne, *Breach of Treaty* (Cambridge, CUP, 1985).

be more far-reaching than a simple reflection of the negative character of an obligation to abstain from rendering aid or assistance. The author has also submitted that in certain circumstances a positive duty to sever the operation of treaty-based obligations providing for a certain military, economic, or financial assistance may be warranted.

C. Responsibility for Complicity in Consent-based Dispute Settlement

Our analysis of the implementation of responsibility would not be complete without tackling the question of how the problem of complicity is addressed in a predominantly bilateral and consensualist system of international dispute settlement. It is true that due to, inter alia, political and diplomatic interests, evidentiary issues, and the structural deficiencies of the current framework for dispute settlement in international law, States will rarely consider bringing a case against the complicit wrongdoer before international courts and tribunals. Such cases are unlikely to succeed before the ICJ by virtue of its reliance on the indispensable third-party principle. The situation seems more flexible in the case of other dispute settlement mechanisms such as the ECtHR, as the recent cases of *El-Masri*, *Al-Nashiri* and *Abu Zubaydah* have demonstrated.[178]

The ICJ's docket in recent years has been filled with claims of international responsibility that implicate third entities, whether States other than the respondent State, international organisations or non-state actors.[179] These situations raise complex substantive and procedural issues.[180] The Court has repeatedly circumvented any discussion of the content of and challenges presented by shared forms of responsibility, including

[178] See ch 5; on the dispute settlement mechanisms other than the ICJ see Aust (n 2) 311–18; for application of the rule in the WTO and ITLOS dispute settlement contexts see respectively L Bartels, 'Procedural Aspects of Shared Responsibility in the WTO Dispute Settlement System' (2013) 4 *JIDS* 343, 356–57; I Plakokefalos, 'Shared Responsibility Aspects of the Dispute Settlement Procedures in the Law of the Sea Convention' (2013) 4 *JIDS* 385, 394.

[179] See, eg *Application of the International Convention on the Elimination of All Forms of Racial Discrimination (Georgia v Russian Federation)* (Preliminary Objections) [2011] ICJ Rep 70, 77–80, paras 16–17; *Application of the Interim Accord of 13 September 1995 (Former Yugoslav Republic of Macedonia v Greece)* (n 172), 659 ff, paras 39–44; *Jurisdictional Immunities of the State (Germany v Italy; Greece intervening)* (Judgment) [2012] ICJ Rep 99, 149 ff, paras 121–33; *Questions Relating to the Obligation to Prosecute or Extradite (Belgium v Senegal)* (Judgment) [2012] ICJ Rep 422, 460, paras 111–13.

[180] See A Nollkaemper, 'Issues of Shared Responsibility before the International Court of Justice' in E Rieter and H de Waele (eds), *Evolving Principles of International Law: Studies in Honour of Karel C Wellens* (Leiden, Martinus Nijhoff, 2012); M Paparinskis, 'Procedural Aspects of Shared Responsibility in the International Court of Justice' (2013) 4 *JIDS* 295; F Baetens, 'Procedural Issues Relating to Shared Responsibility in Arbitral Proceedings' (2013) 4 *JIDS* 319.

complicity, and how they might influence the legal relationship between the applicant and respondent. This is partly because in these cases, the Court has been able to adjudge the responsibility of the respondent within the confines of primary norms.[181]

For example, in the *Corfu Channel* case, the primary obligation regarding notification of other States about minefields in one's territory was formulated in terms that permitted the Court to find Albania responsible for its breach, without finding any State responsible for laying of the mines.[182] Yet, the presence of a third party Yugoslavia was well known to the Court even though it was not a party to the proceedings.[183] The fact that the Court even considered the allegation about a third party's implication 'involved examining claims that a State not before the Court had committed an internationally wrongful act'.[184] In this respect, Judge Schwebel in his dissenting opinion in the *Certain Phosphate Lands in Nauru* case stressed that the Court in the *Corfu Channel* case could have found Albania responsible on the basis that it had conspired with an unknown third State.[185] This would have meant finding Albania complicit in the wrongful act of a third State without actually having the opportunity to pronounce on the responsibility of that third State for its wrongful act. In Judge Schwebel's words:

> [W]here it appears from the facts alleged or shown that there was some unknown joint tortfeasor, the Court will not dismiss the claim against the named tortfeasor *proprio motu*. There would have been no good ground for it so doing, since *a holding against Albania could not have entailed the effective liability of an unnamed and unknown joint tortfeasor for the very reason that it was unnamed and unknown*.[186] (emphasis added)

While Judge Schwebel did not need to fully develop this argument, it may follow that a finding of responsibility for complicity in the wrongful act of another does not necessarily require the Court to pronounce on the responsibility of the principal wrongdoer—it may suffice that the evidence before the Court links complicit conduct to the circumstances of that wrongful act.[187] One could also reach this result from 'a rather

181 Paparinskis (n 180) 298.

182 *Corfu Channel (United Kingdom v Albania)* (n 106) 16–23.

183 ibid 16–17 (it seems that Yugoslavia communicated with the Court and even submitted documents which the Court considered).

184 H Thirlway, 'The Law and Procedure of the International Court of Justice 1960–1989: Part Nine' (1998) 69 *British YBIL* 1, 35.

185 *Certain Phosphate Lands in Nauru (Nauru v Australia)* (Preliminary Objections) [1992] ICJ Rep 240, Dissenting Opinion of Judge Schwebel 329, 330.

186 ibid.

187 cf Thirlway (n 184) 35 (citing the content former draft Art 27 and stressing that '[i]t is difficult to see how a finding of connivance could be made without identifying the co-conspirator').

sophisticated legal construction' of complicity as a separable wrongful act as such.[188] In any event, the Court ultimately reached a similar outcome through different means, while stressing that 'the authors of the minelaying remain unknown'.[189]

In the *Military and Paramilitary Activities* case, the rules on the prohibition of the use of force were formulated in such terms that the Court could decide upon the United States' responsibility for unlawful use of force without addressing the responsibility of States through the territory of which it had acted.[190] However, in most cases, even if the Court were to show willingness to examine matters of potential complicity of third States, such claims would likely fail on procedural grounds, including the indispensable third party principle. According to Rosenne:

> The existence of this limitation on the Court's jurisdiction following from the absence from the litigation of essential parties, as a principle of general international law and as a feature of the law of international judicial procedure, is not open to question.[191]

The interpretation of the Court's decisions that deal with third parties' responsibility may lead us to two opposite conclusions. On the one hand, there is the *Monetary Gold* case, where the Court held that it could not decide the main dispute between Italy and the United Kingdom without pronouncing on a necessary preliminary question relating to the responsibility of a third State, Albania.[192] The Court found that if it were to hold otherwise, Albania's 'legal interests would not only be affected by the decision, but would form the very-subject matter of the decision'.[193]

The Court followed a similar rationale in the *East Timor* case, denying jurisdiction on the basis that any decision on the question raised by the parties would pre-judge the responsibility of Indonesia, which was not party to the proceedings.[194] The Court nevertheless stated that 'it is not

[188] Graefrath (n 70) 371.

[189] *Corfu Channel (United Kingdom v Albania)* (n 106) 17.

[190] *Military and Paramilitary Activities* (Jurisdiction and Admissibility) (n 29) 430, paras 86–87; *Military and Paramilitary Activities* (Provisional Measures) (n 12) 34 and 36–37, paras 48 and 51–54.

[191] S Rosenne, *The Law and Practice of the International Court, 1920–2004* (4th edn, Leiden, Martinus Nijhoff, 2005) 546.

[192] *Monetary Gold Removed from Rome in 1943 (Italy v France, United Kingdom and United States)* (n 77) 32.

[193] ibid; see also *East Timor (Portugal v Australia)* (n 138) 105, para 34; *Continental Shelf (Libyan Arab Jamahiriya v Malta)* (Application to Intervene) [1984] ICJ Rep 3, 25, para 40; *Land, Island and Maritime Frontier Dispute (El Salvador/Honduras: Nicaragua intervening)* (Application to Intervene) [1990] ICJ Rep 92, 134-35, para 99.

[194] *East Timor (Portugal v Australia)* (n 138) 104–05, para 34; see also RS Clark, 'Obligations of Third States in the Face of Illegality—Ruminations Inspired by the Weeramantry Dissent in the Case Concerning East Timor' in A Anghie and G Sturgess (eds), *Legal Visions of the 21st Century: Essays in Honour of Judge Christopher Weeramantry* (The Hague, Kluwer, 1998); B Delcourt, 'Un seul État vous manque…L'application de la jurisprudence de l'Or monétaire à l'affaire du Timor oriental' (1996) 1 *RBDI* 191, 206–12.

necessarily prevented from adjudicating when the judgment it is asked to give might affect the legal interests of a State which is not party to the case'.[195] If such reasoning is upheld, then any case of complicity coming before the Court would be necessarily barred on jurisdictional grounds unless the injured State, the assisted State committing the wrongful act, and the assisting State are all parties to the proceedings.

On the other hand, in the *Military and Paramilitary Activities*[196] or *Certain Phosphate Lands in Nauru*,[197] the Court dismissed the argument that the indispensable third party principle would prevent the Court from exercising its jurisdiction. In the *Certain Phosphate Lands in Nauru* case, Nauru brought a claim against Australia for having violated its obligations as one of the three administering powers under the Trusteeship Agreement. During the proceedings before the Court, Australia contested that it could be sued alone and argued that the alleged responsibility of the three States making up the Administrative Authority (Australia, New Zealand and the United Kingdom) was 'solidary' rather than joint and several. According to Australia, they had to be sued collectively—a claim could not be entertained against only one of them.[198] The Court ultimately held that the issue was not one of admissibility but rather related to the merits of the dispute:

> The Court does not consider that any reason has been shown why a claim brought against only one of the three States should be declared inadmissible in *limine litis* merely because that claim raises questions of the administration of the Territory, which was shared with two other States. It cannot be denied that Australia had obligations under the Trusteeship Agreement, in its capacity as one of the three States forming the Administering Authority, and there is nothing in the character of that Agreement which debars the Court from considering a claim of a breach of those obligations by Australia.[199]

It follows that the principle of the indispensable third party should be no obstacle to the admissibility of complicity before the Court in those cases where: (i) the complicit State's conduct constitutes a breach of a primary rule which does not require examination of the responsibility of the principal wrongdoer; (ii) the responsibility of the principal wrongdoer has already been established; and (iii) the injury flowing from the principal wrongful act is divisible. However, in those cases where the harm is technically indivisible or cannot be apportioned between the aiding or assisting State and the principal wrongdoing State, the principle of the

[195] *East Timor (Portugal v Australia)* (n 138) 104, para 34.
[196] *Military and Paramilitary Activities* (Jurisdiction and Admissibility) (n 29) 392, paras 86–88.
[197] *Certain Phosphate Lands in Nauru (Nauru v Australia)* (n 185) 258, para 48.
[198] ibid.
[199] ibid.

indispensable third party is likely to be invoked and to bar the exercise of the Court's jurisdiction in respect of complicit States.[200]

IV. INTERIM CONCLUSIONS

Three actors. Two breaches. One injury or two injuries? Responsibility for complicity raises a number of complex technical issues, including at the level of legal consequences and their allocation. The ILC has, for all purposes and intents, given little guidance on some of the crucial aspects that could operationalise responsibility for complicity in international law. This can be regarded as both a challenge and an opportunity for the evolving international legal order. As discussed above, there are three areas in which the law posited by the ILC has not yet found sufficient reflection in the practice of States and international organisations as well as in the case law of international and domestic tribunals determining international responsibility for complicity.

First, the Commission has not delineated a standard of causation, which could be applied to link the complicit conduct to the injury that follows from the commission of the principal wrongful act. We have discussed different ways in which complicit wrongful act might be examined in the relationship between the principal wrongdoing and the injury. While much uncertainty reigns in this area, a proper causation model may well be 'the law's quintessential solution to responsibility problems' in general[201] and cases of multiple wrongdoers in particular. The ICJ has never had the opportunity to examine these situations and to set out guidelines on how to determine and allocate reparation between two or more entities contributing to the same injury.[202] In the *Nauru* case, the Court suggested that this issue could have been dealt together with the merits. However, that case was settled and the Court did not have the opportunity to provide any guidance on the matter. After having conducted a detailed review of the Court's case law, Paparinskis concludes that the '[e]xisting cases may be read to tentatively suggest that issues of reparations may be either resolved within the limits of traditional rules and principles or by making certain limited readjustments'.[203] We have shown that this is

[200] ARSIWA (n 3) 67, para 11 (Art 16 Commentary).

[201] Becker (n 44) 286.

[202] See, eg S Besson, 'La pluralité d'États responsables: Vers une solidarité internationale?' (2007) 1 *SZIER* 13, 23.

[203] Paparinskis (n 180) 298.

hardly the case of genuine situations of complicity if reliance on the traditional analysis of causation is to be applied. In the alternative, this author has argued that there is a need to either submit situations of complicity to the de facto regime of joint and several responsibility or to develop the fictitious legal construction 'complicity in a wrongful act = separable wrongful act causing separable injury'.

In section III of this chapter, we examined whether States or international organisations other than those injured by the aided or assisted act may invoke the responsibility of the complicit entity, particularly when the aid or assistance contributes to breaches of *jus cogens* or *erga omnes* obligations. We also examined the eventuality of countermeasures being taken by the injured but also other than injured States or international organisations in respect of complicit actor. The third and final aspect of our analysis related to the ICJ's case law on the doctrine of indispensable third party in the context of dispute settlement, which makes the adjudication of claims of complicity difficult but not impossible.

7

Complicity as a Basis of Attribution of Conduct

Our words make our worlds.[1]

I. INTRODUCTION

The phenomenon of a wrongful act committed through the 'use of private proxies' is not new in international law.[2] For example, '[m]ercenaries were used by former colonial powers to destabilize established governments; states in the Cold War relied on private groups as a more or less covert means to pursue foreign policy goals hoping they would escape both domestic and international scrutiny'.[3] The phenomenon is ever more alarming nowadays, with organised militant groups like the Islamic State of Iraq and the Levant (ISIL) seizing control over the territory in Iraq and Syria, Somali pirates capturing ships in the Indian Ocean, rebel groups committing violations of international law in Ukraine, or Syrian Revolutionary and Opposition Forces committing war crimes and other breaches of international law in the armed conflict against the Syrian government.

Non-State actors carry out harmful activities, ranging from sporadic cross-border armed attacks to war crimes and crimes against humanity. States often enable such activities by providing aid or assistance to non-State actors.[4] The responsibility for such assistance to non-State actors has

[1] P Allott, *Eunomia—New Order for a New World* (Oxford, OUP, 1990) 6.

[2] C Lehnardt, 'Private Military Companies and State Responsibility' in S Chesterman and C Lehnardt (eds), *From Mercenaries to Market, The Rise and Regulation of Private Military Companies* (Oxford, OUP, 2007) 143.

[3] ibid.

[4] This chapter focuses exclusively on the responsibility of States for their aid or assistance to the wrongful conduct of non-State actors, albeit similar considerations could apply in the future to international organisations. There is a vast literature on the attribution of private conduct to the State, see, eg A Epiney, *Die völkerrechtliche Verantwortlichkeit von Staaten für rechtswidriges Verhalten im Zusammenhang mit Aktionen Privater* (Baden-Baden, Nomos, 1992); O de Frouville, 'Attribution of Conduct to the State: Private Individuals' in J Crawford et al (eds), *The Law of International Responsibility* (Oxford, OUP, 2010); R Wolfrum, 'State Responsibility for Private Actors: An Old Problem or Renewed Relevance' in

traditionally been limited by the agency paradigm, and the (in)famous test of effective control for the purposes of attribution of conduct.[5] As for complicity (aid or assistance) in Article 16 of the Articles on Responsibility of States for Internationally Wrongful Acts (ARSIWA), we have seen in the previous chapters that the International Law Commission (ILC) conceptualised it in a purely inter-subject framework, as a form of attribution of responsibility rather than of conduct. However, the developments in international law taking place after the adoption of the ARSIWA in 2001 seem to build momentum for extending complicity's scope to cover situations of knowing collaboration in the wrongful acts committed by non-State actors. This begs the question as to whether responsibility for complicity could and should be conceived of as a new basis of attribution of conduct in international law.[6]

This analysis is timely, given the growing role of non-State actors and the challenges they pose to the international legal order in general, and the existing rules of attribution in particular, which are not well suited to the task. At the outset it raises an important legal policy question: should the attribution framework be adjusted to address forms of cooperation between States and non-State actors that fall short of effective control? Or should States rather devise specific primary rules to proscribe any such forms of unlawful collaboration between States and non-State actors in particular areas of international law? Scholars have often approached these options as mutually exclusive in response to the so-called accountability gap of non-State actors.[7] In this author's view, the prohibitions

M Ragazzi (ed), *International Responsibility Today: Essays in Memory of Oscar Schachter* (Leiden, Martinus Nijhoff, 2005).

[5] See, eg VJ Proulx, *Transnational Terrorism and State Accountability* (Oxford, Hart Publishing, 2012); T Becker, *Terrorism and the State: Rethinking the Rules of State Responsibility* (Oxford, Hart Publishing, 2006) 43–79; D Amoroso, 'Moving towards Complicity as a Criterion of Attribution of Private Conducts: Imputation to States of Corporate Abuses in the US Case Law' (2011) 24 *LJIL* 989; E Savarese, 'Issues of Attribution to States of Private Acts: Between the Concept of De Facto Organs and Complicity' (2005) 15 *RDI* 111; AJ de Hoogh, 'Articles 4 and 8 of the 2001 ILC Articles on State Responsibility, the Tadić Case and Attribution of Acts of Bosnian Serb Authorities to the Federal Republic of Yugoslavia' (2002) 72 *British YBIL* 255; GA Christenson, 'Attributing Acts of Omission to the State' (1991) 12 *Michigan J Intl L* 312.

[6] cf M Jackson, *Complicity in International Law* (Oxford, OUP, 2015) 177 ff (arguing that '[c]omplicity cannot be properly accounted for by relaxing the rules of attribution in international law').

[7] See, eg D Jinks, 'State Responsibility for the Acts of Private Armed Groups' (2003) 4 *Chicago J Intl L* 83, 84 (arguing that the 'most effective strategy to restrain and deter state support for, or toleration of, terrorism is to define more clearly the primary obligations of states and the consequences of non-compliance with those obligations'); KN Trapp, *State Responsibility for International Terrorism* (Oxford, OUP, 2011) 61 (insisting on the self-sufficiency of the primary rules on terrorism and the existing bases of attribution of private conduct to the State, and concluding that 'there is absolutely no reason at all to label complicity a basis of attribution for the purposes of state responsibility'); on the analysis of the so-called 'accountability gap' see L Zegveld, *Accountability of Armed Opposition Groups in International Law* (Cambridge, CUP, 2002).

of complicity in treaties and customary law, and complicity as a basis of attribution in the law of responsibility, may reinforce each other in response to the growing accountability gap surrounding the non-State actors' conduct.

In international law, there are three normative layers that capture different degrees of involvement of a State in the wrongdoing committed by non-State actors. Firstly, States may be responsible for failing to prevent and/or punish the unlawful activities of non-State actors (ie under the due diligence obligations). However, as discussed in chapter five, these obligations often lack content, in particular they do not always indicate the degree of diligence to which States are expected to act. Moreover, these are obligations of means and not result, leaving considerable margin of appreciation for the State. Secondly, there are primary obligations that prohibit the provision of aid or assistance to non-State actors. This is a common feature of counter-terrorism instruments as well as instruments dealing with the threat or use of force.[8] The United Nations Security Council (UNSC) has also occasionally imposed obligations on States prohibiting aid or assistance to non-State actors.[9] Thirdly, the conduct of a non-State actor can be attributed to the State under the existing rules of attribution of conduct as set out in Articles 4 to 11 ARSIWA.

However, where the aid or assistance provided to a non-State actor is not covered by a specific primary rule and does not meet the required threshold of agency and effective control under the rules on attribution, the question arises whether the resulting wrongful act could nonetheless be attributable to the State under a broader complicity rule. This proposition is of course *de lege ferenda* and conceptually controversial in light of the ILC's attribution framework and the rule on responsibility for complicity in the ARSIWA. However, there are some early indications of the law-determining agents referring to the rule on responsibility for complicity in situations of aid or assistance from a State to non-State actor. At the outset, one could make a cogent argument that any lower standards of attribution other than those set out in the ARSIWA are a matter of special regimes (*lex specialis*).[10] However, it is not excluded that

[8] See, eg UNGA, 'Res 2625 (XXV) Declaration on Principles of International Law Concerning Friendly Relations and Co-Operation among States in Accordance with the Charter of the United Nations' (24 October 1970) UN Doc A/RES/25/2625, Principle 1, para 10; see also *Military and Paramilitary Activities in and against Nicaragua (Nicaragua v United States)* (Merits) [1986] ICJ Rep 14, 119, para 228.

[9] See, eg UNSC, 'Res 1304' (16 June 2000) UN Doc S/RES/1304 (DRC) para 10; UNSC, 'Res 1373' (28 September 2001) UN Doc S/RES/1373 para 2; UNSC, 'Res 2170' (15 August 2014) UN Doc S/RES/2170 para 10; UNSC, 'Res 864' (15 September 1993) UN Doc S/RES/864 (Angola) para 19 (pt B).

[10] ILC, 'Draft Articles on Responsibility of States for Internationally Wrongful Acts, with Commentaries' (2001) 2 (pt 2) *YBILC* 31 (ARSIWA) Art 55; for an example of such a special regime see United Nations Convention on the Law of the Sea (adopted 10 December 1982;

developments in different areas of international law may influence the conception of responsibility and the limits of attribution in general international law. Hence, in this author's opinion there is merit in exploring whether complicity is emerging as a standard of attribution in the law of international responsibility. Would it operate in the same or similar terms to those of Article 16 ARSIWA, ie only when the conduct of the non-State actor would first be attributed to another State, for example, a territorial State that failed to prevent their conduct, and only thereafter to a putative accomplice State? Or would it be an altogether new standard of attribution?

There are two immediate conceptual problems with framing Article 16 ARSIWA as a mode of attribution of conduct through the lens of classical international law. First, a non-State actor's conduct as such may not even constitute an internationally wrongful act.[11] This is because non-State actors are not directly bound by most international obligations and their conduct would not be wrongful and thus nothing for the State to be complicit in.[12] However, this holds true only insofar as we regard complicity as a purely derivative form of responsibility. The more one accepts an alternative conception of complicity in the law of international responsibility as advocated in this book, ie as a hybrid of direct and derivative responsibility and materially closer to a primary rule, the less objectionable becomes the idea of complicity as a standard of attribution of conduct.

Non-State actors do not operate in a vacuum. They hold ties to a particular territory and quite often exercise effective control over such territory. As a result of those ties and by virtue of their capacity rather than subjectivity they are to comply with rights and obligations of their territorial State.[13] To admit that they cannot commit wrongful acts where their

entered into force 16 November 1994) 1833 UNTS 3, Art 139; J Crawford, *State Responsibility: The General Part* (Cambridge, CUP, 2013) 114–15 (noting that there may also arise mechanisms of attribution which are 'inherent in the primary rule to which the secondary rules of state responsibility apply', referring to the ICTY's *Tadić* case); see also L Condorelli and C Kress, 'The Rules of Attribution: General Considerations' in J Crawford et al (eds), *The Law of International Responsibility* (Oxford, OUP, 2010) 227.

[11] See Jackson (n 6) 176; cf for several theories explaining the extension of obligations under general international law to armed opposition groups see A Clapham, *Human Rights Obligations of Non-State Actors* (Oxford, OUP, 2006); Zegveld (n 7); S Sivakumaran, 'Binding Armed Opposition Groups' (2008) 55 *ICLQ* 369.

[12] de Frouville (n 4) 276; for a notable exception of an obligation directly binding armed opposition groups see 1949 Geneva Convention (IV) Relative to the Protection of Civilian Persons in Time of War (adopted 12 August 1949; entered into force 21 October 1950) 75 UNTS 287, Art 3; see also A Clapham, 'Human Rights Obligations of Non-State Actors in Conflict Situations' (2006) 88 *IRRC* 491.

[13] See DP O'Connell, *International Law* (2nd edn, London, Stevens & Sons, 1970) 81–82.

conduct is either tolerated by the territorial State or directly facilitated by a third State is problematic, as it would further an accountability gap. The question whether a non-State actor is directly bound by *all* of the obligations incumbent on the territorial State is controversial, but the notion of subjectivity or legal personality should not serve as an automatic bar to responsibility.[14] As Klabbers puts it, 'personality, like "subjectivity", is but a descriptive notion: useful to describe a state of affairs, but normatively empty, as neither rights nor obligations flow automatically from a grant of personality'.[15] At the very least, there are convincing theories for extending *certain* rights and obligations to non-State actors involved in an armed conflict or those exercising de facto governmental functions of the State.[16] Ultimately, the only real question for our purposes is whether the assisted conduct of the non-State actor is attributable to a State, and if so, does it amount to a breach of an international obligation binding on that State.

Section II briefly examines the existing rules of attribution in international law, in order to identify the extent to which they cover participation of States in the conduct by non-State actors. Section III makes a claim that the standard of complicity is a necessary addition to the existing rules of attribution of conduct.

II. EXISTING GROUNDS OF ATTRIBUTION OF CONDUCT

Almost a century ago, the tribunal in *Dickson Car Wheel Company* recognised that for a State to 'incur responsibility it is necessary that an unlawful international act be imputed to it, that is, that there exist a violation of a duty imposed by an international juridical standard'.[17] Case law and practice have refined this normative process of linking an act to the State under its multiple iterations, using the notions of *imputability*

[14] See *Reparation for Injuries Suffered in the Service of the United Nations* (Advisory Opinion) [1949] ICJ Rep 174, 178 (the 'subjects of law in any legal system are not necessarily identical in their nature or in the extent of their rights, and their nature depends upon the needs of the community'); see also A Clapham, 'The Subject of Subjects and the Attribution of Attribution' in L Boisson de Chazournes and MG Kohen (eds), *International Law and the Quest for its Implementation, Liber Amicorum Vera Gowlland-Debbas* (Leiden, Martinus Nijhoff, 2010) 45; R Higgins, *Problems and Process: International Law and How We Use It* (Oxford, Clarendon Press, 1994) 49 ('We have erected an intellectual prison of our own choosing and then declared it to be an unalterable constraint').

[15] J Klabbers, *An Introduction to International Institutional Law* (Cambridge, CUP, 2002) 57.

[16] See, eg Clapham (n 11) 278–85; Zegveld (n 7) 17.

[17] *Dickson Car Wheel Company (United States) v Mexico* (1931) 4 RIAA 669, 678; for a historical account of the concept of attribution see, eg GA Christenson, 'The Doctrine of Attribution in State Responsibility' in RB Lillich (ed), *International Law of State Responsibility for Injuries to Aliens* (Charlottesville, University Press of Virginia, 1983).

or *attribution* interchangeably.[18] Today, attribution as a normative process occupies a prominent place in the law of international responsibility as a necessary element of an internationally wrongful act.[19] The various bases of attribution of conduct as set out in the ARSIWA are indisputably reflective of customary international law.[20] Yet, these bases are neither exhaustive nor static. As the impact of actors other than States expands, the attribution criteria will have to adjust to the evolving needs of justice and rule of law. The current limitations in the attribution framework are no more than a reflection of a particular conception of sovereignty in international law.[21]

It is a truism that States 'can act only by and through their agents and representatives'.[22] Nonetheless, the existing framework of international responsibility has been repeatedly criticised for neglecting the emerging role of an individual, both as a potential *catalyst* and *victim* of an internationally wrongful act.[23] The fiction of a State as a metajuridical or abstract entity pervades the whole body of international responsibility, continuing to generate a hiatus between public and private spheres which are no longer as easily distinguishable as in the 1970s when the foundations of the ARSIWA were laid down.[24] It is then easy to understand why the very logic of attribution is geared towards the notion and degree of *control* that a State exerts over a private actor. The rules on the attribution of private conduct have received detailed treatment in case

[18] For the use of the term imputability see, eg *Diplomatic and Consular Staff in Tehran (United States v Iran)* (Judgment) [1980] ICJ Rep 3, 29; *Military and Paramilitary Activities (Merits)* (n 8), 51; however, the ILC ultimately preferred the term attribution to avoid any suggestion that the normative process of linking a conduct to the State was a mere fiction, see R Ago, 'Third Report on State Responsibility' (1971) UN Doc A/CN.4/246 and Add 1-3, reproduced in (1971) 2 (pt 1) *YBILC* 199, 214; J Crawford, 'First Report on State Responsibility' (1998) UN Doc A/CN.4/490 and Add 1-7, reproduced in (1998) 2 (pt 1) *YBILC* 1, 33; see also *Armed Activities on the Territory of the Congo (DRC v Uganda)* (Judgment) [2005] ICJ Rep 168, 223–42.

[19] ARSIWA (n 10) Art 2.

[20] See, eg UNGA, 'Responsibility of States for Internationally Wrongful Acts: Compilation of Decisions of International Courts, Tribunals and Other Bodies' (2007) UN Doc A/62/62; UNGA, 'Responsibility of States for Internationally Wrongful Acts: Compilation of Decisions of International Courts, Tribunals and Other Bodies' (17 April 2007) UN Doc A/62/62/Add 1; S Olleson, *The Impact of the ILC's Articles on Responsibility of States for Internationally Wrongful Acts* (London, BIICL, 2007).

[21] R Ago, 'Second Report on State Responsibility' (1970) UN Doc A/CN.4/233, reproduced in (1970) 2 *YBILC* 177, 189–90, para 38.

[22] *Certain Questions Relating to Settlers of German Origin in the Territory Ceded by Germany to Poland* (Advisory Opinion) [1923] PCIJ Ser B No 6, 22.

[23] See, eg P Allott, 'State Responsibility and the Unmaking of International Law' (1988) 29 *Harvard Intl LJ* 1, 13–14; R Pisillo-Mazzeschi, 'The Marginal Role of the Individual in the ILC's Articles on State Responsibility' (2004) 14 *Italian YBIL* 39; R Pisillo-Mazzeschi, 'Il ruolo marginale dell'individuo nel progetto della commissione del diritto internazionale sulla responsabilità degli stati' in M Spinedi, A Gianelli and ML Alaimo (eds), *La codificazione della responsabilità internazionale degli stati alla prova dei fatti: Problemi e spunti di riflessione* (Milano, Giuffrè, 2006).

[24] See C Chinkin, 'A Critique of the Public/Private Dimension' (1999) 10 *EJIL* 387.

law and doctrine, and this chapter cannot do justice to all or even a good part of the relevant aspects of the debate.[25] The sole intention is to test the argument of complicity as a new standard of attribution of conduct in international law.

In a nutshell, the modern framework of attribution of conduct to the State revolves around the concept of agency. Broadly speaking, there are three sets of attribution rules in customary international law which are closely connected. First, there are several rules that place emphasis on the organic or quasi-institutional links to the State.[26] Articles 4 to 7 ARSIWA provide for different ways in which the acts of an organ or entity exercising governmental authority may be attributed to the State.[27] Second, there is Article 8 ARSIWA, which looks into specific links of a non-State actor to the State. The rationale is that private actors possess an overwhelming autonomy underlying their decision-making and conduct. As a general rule it would thus be unfair or inequitable to place an undue burden of responsibility on the State in respect of their conduct. It is only in the exceptional circumstances where such autonomy is subjugated to that of a State that the private actor's conduct becomes attributable to that State.[28] Third and finally, there are three exceptional bases of attribution, as set out in Articles 9 to 11 of the ARSIWA, which flow from particular changes in the State apparatus or a certain positioning of the State vis-à-vis the private conduct. A brief survey is in order to discern the main parameters and limitations of the existing rules of attribution, examining whether and to what extent they capture the typical scenarios of complicity of a State in the conduct of non-State actor.

Article 4 ARSIWA codifies a customary international law rule that the conduct of any State organ shall be considered an act of that State

[25] de Hoogh (n 5); M Hébié, 'L'attribution aux États des actes des sociétés militaires et de leurs employés à la lumière de l'article 4 du projet d'articles sur la responsabilité des États de 2001' in H Ruiz Fabri, R Wolfrum and J Gogolin (eds), *Select Proceedings of the European Society of International Law*, vol 2 (Oxford, Hart Publishing, 2008); C Kress, 'L'organe de facto en droit international public. Réflexions sur l'imputation à l'État de l'acte d'un particulier à la lumière des développements récents' (2001) 105 *RGDIP* 93; P Palchetti, *L'organo di fatto dello Stato nell'illecito internazionale* (Milano, Giuffrè, 2007); G Bartolini, 'Il concetto di "controllo" sulle attività di individui quale presupposto della responsabilità dello Stato' in M Spinedi, A Gianelli and ML Alaimo (eds), *La codificazione della responsabilità internazionale degli stati alla prova dei fatti: Problemi e spunti di riflessione* (Milano, Giuffrè, 2006); VP Tzevelekos, 'Reconstructing the Effective Control Criterion in Extraterritorial Human Rights Breaches: Direct Attribution of Wrongfulness, Due Diligence, and Concurrent Responsibility' (2015) 36 *Michigan J Intl L* 129.

[26] F Messineo, 'Attribution of Conduct' in A Nollkaemper and I Plakokefalos (eds), *Principles of Shared Responsibility in International Law: An Appraisal of the State of the Art* (Cambridge, CUP, 2014) 65.

[27] For a detailed analysis of different bases of attribution of conduct in international law see Crawford, *State Responsibility: The General Part* (n 10) 113–211.

[28] de Frouville (n 4) 261.

under international law.[29] This includes both de jure and de facto organs. As James Crawford helpfully points out, 'a state cannot evade responsibility for the conduct of a body which as a matter of practice is considered to be or acts as an organ merely by denying it status as such under internal law'.[30] It goes without saying that most non-State actors rarely if ever are considered de jure organs.[31] Whether an organ may be regarded as de facto is more challenging and fact-specific—the characterisation of a non-State actor as a de facto organ would only arise if the test of 'complete dependence' is satisfied. This test entails a very high threshold that is unlikely to be met in normal circumstances.[32] Over the years the Court has given some indication regarding the sort of criteria that would need to be ascertained for a group to constitute a de facto organ. These include the determination whether the State: (i) created the non-State entity; (ii) was involved in its conduct beyond the provision of training, logistical or financial assistance; (iii) exercised *complete* control in fact; and (iv) selected, installed or paid the political leaders of the non-State entity.[33]

For example, in the *Bosnia Genocide* case, despite the clear dependence of Republika Srpska on the Federal Republic of Yugoslavia (FRY), the Court considered that Republika Srpska had some degree of autonomy vis-à-vis the FRY, taking as an example the rejection by Republika Srpska to sign a peace plan.[34] In other words, the Court seemed to imply the need of total political alignment of positions between the State and non-State actor for the latter to be regarded as a de facto organ.[35] Obviously, in light of such a restrictive approach taken by the Court, a receipt of financial, military or technical aid or assistance by a non-State actor, even more so a sporadic one, would never put into question the autonomy of the non-State actor nor transform it into a de facto organ of the State.[36]

[29] See, eg *Salvador Commercial Company (El Salvador/United States)* (1902) 15 RIAA 455, 477; *Finnish Shipowners (United Kingdom/Finland)* (1934) 3 RIAA 1479, 1501; *Difference relating to Immunity from Legal Process of a Special Rapporteur of the Commission on Human Rights* (Advisory Opinion) [1999] ICJ Rep 62, 87, para 62; *Francisco Mallén (Mexico v United States)* (1927) 4 RIAA 173, 174.

[30] Crawford, *State Responsibility: The General Part* (n 10) 124–25; ARSIWA (n 10) 42, para 11 (Art 4 Commentary); M Milanović, 'State Responsibility for Genocide' (2006) 17 EJIL 553, 582.

[31] See, eg *Application of the Convention on the Prevention and Punishment of the Crime of Genocide (Bosnia and Herzegovina v Serbia and Montenegro)* (Merits) [2007] ICJ Rep 43, ICJ Pleadings, CR 2006/9 (6 March 2006) 56, para 15 (Condorelli); CR 2006/34 (21 April 2006) 37, para 4 (Condorelli); CR 2006/31 (18 April 2006) 34 ff (Pellet).

[32] ibid, 205, para 392; *Military and Paramilitary Activities (Merits)* (n 8) 61–63, paras 108–12.

[33] *Military and Paramilitary Activities (Merits)* (n 8) 61–63, paras 108–12.

[34] *Bosnia Genocide* (Merits) (n 31) 141, para 394.

[35] See similarly O Corten, 'L'arrêt rendu par la CIJ dans l'affaire du crime de génocide (Bosnie-Herzégovine c. Serbie): vers un assouplissement des conditions permettant d'engager la responsabilité d'un État pour génocide?' (2007) 53 AFDI 249, 266.

[36] For a comprehensive overview see Palchetti (n 25).

Article 5 ARSIWA deals with the conduct of a person or entity which is empowered by the law of that State to exercise elements of governmental authority and is thus considered an act of the State. This basis has been used to attribute conduct of private military contractors or other entities that States empower to exercise immigration control, run prisons or specific financial regulatory functions.[37] There are numerous precedents of private military and security companies' (PMSCs) allegedly unlawful activities financed or supported by other States in Afghanistan, Iraq, Sierra Leone and Angola, among others.[38] Different considerations may impact the determination of whether an entity exercises elements of governmental authority, including the existence of a contractual relationship or other forms of conferral of powers, the circumstances of the entity's establishment, mode of governance, the content of the powers, etc.[39] Article 5 could thus capture some of the situations of aid or assistance where, for instance, a private security company or contractor running the prison uses funds from the State to commit a wrongful act. However, this mode of attribution is generally limited to situations where there is some form of legislative or contractual evidence of the link to the State, a form of quasi-institutional recognition of conferral of powers or delegation of the State's prerogatives to a non-State actor within a prescribed domain of activities. This mode of attribution of conduct would then not cover scenarios of complicity where non-State actors hold no such quasi-institutional ties to the State.

Another mode of attribution of conduct is set out in Article 6 ARSIWA and concerns those situations where one State places its own organs at the disposal of another State. At first glance, the act of State A providing State B with its own organ for the commission of an internationally

[37] See, eg Crawford (n 10) 127–28; C Hoppe, 'Passing the Buck: State Responsibility for Private Military Companies' (2008) 19 *EJIL* 989; C Beaucillon, J Fernandez and H Raspail, 'State Responsibility for Conduct of Private Military and Security Companies Violating Ius Ad Bellum' in F Francioni and N Ronzitti (eds), *War by Contract: Human Rights, Humanitarian Law and Private Contractors* (Oxford, OUP, 2011).

[38] See, eg D Momtaz, 'State Organs and Entities Empowered to Exercise Elements of Governmental Authority' in J Crawford et al (eds), *The Law of International Responsibility* (Oxford, OUP, 2010); A Tarzwell, 'In Search of Accountability: Attributing the Conduct of Private Security Contractors to the United States Under the Doctrine of State Responsibility' (2009) 11 *Oregon Review of Intl Law* 179; L Vierucci, 'Private Military and Security Companies in Non-International Armed Conflicts' [2009] EUI Working Paper AEL 2009/14; Beaucillon, Fernandez and Raspail (n 37); Hoppe (n 37); C Hoppe, 'Positive Human Rights Obligations of the Hiring State in Connection with the Provision of Coercive Services by a Private Military and Security Company' [2009] EUI Working Paper AEL 2009/19; S Ranganathan, 'Between Complicity and Irrelevance —Industry Associations and the Challenge of Regulating Private Security Contractors' (2009) 41 *Georgetown J Intl L* 303.

[39] ARSIWA (n 10) 43, para 6 (Art 5 Commentary); see, eg *Hyatt International Corp v Iran* (Award) (17 September 1985) 9 Iran-US CTR 72, 94; see also Crawford (n 10) 128–29; H Tonkin, *State Control over Private Military and Security Companies in Armed Conflict* (Cambridge, CUP, 2011) 101.

wrongful act could be regarded as a form of complicity. The Commission, however, came to a different conclusion in favour of an exclusive attribution approach—from the moment the organ is placed at the disposal of one State it acts on behalf of the receiving State, engaging its own responsibility.[40] In practice, however, if that same organ maintains a close relationship with its original State, this rule of attribution would have to be adjusted on the facts, and could result in dual or multiple attribution.[41] Interestingly, Article 7 of the Articles on Responsibility of International Organizations (ARIO) eliminates any doubts in relation to the attribution of conduct by organs or agents of a State or international organisation placed at the disposal of another organisation. Conduct by such organs or agents is attributable to the receiving organisation, provided it exercises effective control over it. As we have seen in chapter four, in complex transnational operations, such as that of peacekeeping forces, the determination and degree of control remains highly controversial.

A conduct of State organs or instrumentalities that is ultra vires (ie in excess of authority or in contravention of instructions) is also attributable to a State under the ARSIWA.[42] Further, conduct of private actors may be attributable if States acknowledge or adopt it as their own ex post facto, as happened for example in the *Diplomatic and Consular Staff in Tehran* case.[43] These are situations akin to complicity after the fact, ie where the wrong in the first instance committed by a non-State actor without any State involvement, becomes nonetheless attributable at some later point in time owing to the State's acknowledgement thereof. Finally, two special cases of attribution of conduct are set out in Articles 9 and 10 ARSIWA, dealing with particular categories of non-State actors. Article 9 ARSIWA covers situations of absence of State's official authorities, while Article 10 ARSIWA attributes conduct of an insurrectional movement in situations where it succeeds in establishing a new State or government.[44]

Article 8 ARSIWA is by far the most relevant provision for the purposes of our discussion on complicity. At first glance, it could appear as covering all instances of aid or assistance by a State to non-State actor. The rule

[40] ARSIWA (n 10) 44, para 1 (Art 6 Commentary); Ago (n 18) 269.

[41] See ch 4. See generally Messineo (n 26).

[42] ARSIWA (n 10) Art 7; for an application of ultra vires doctrine see, eg *Union Bridge Company (United States) v Great Britain* (1924) 9 RIAA 138; *Caire (France) v Mexico* (1929) 5 RIAA 516, 530; *Youmans (United States) v Mexico* (1926) 4 RIAA 110, 116, para 14; *Velásquez Rodríguez v Honduras* (Judgment) [1988] IACtHR Ser C No 4, para 170.

[43] ARSIWA (n 10), Art 11; ILC, 'Draft Articles on the Responsibility of International Organizations, with Commentaries' (2011) 2 (pt 2) *YBILC* 2, Art 9; see, eg *Diplomatic and Consular Staff in Tehran (United States v Iran)* (n 18).

[44] ARSIWA (n 10) 50–52 (Art 10 Commentary); see also J d'Aspremont, 'Rebellion and State Responsibility: Wrongdoing by Democratically Elected Insurgents' (2009) 58 *ICLQ* 427.

provides that the conduct of a person or group of persons shall be considered an act of a State under international law if such person or group is acting *on the instructions, direction or control* of that State in carrying out the conduct.[45] As Dupuy suggests:

> This formulation leaves much room for interpretation. In particular, it is not quite clear whether 'acting on the instructions' of a State is considered by the ILC as being exactly on the same level as being 'under the direction or control' of the State. This ambiguity was most probably left purposely in order to maintain some flexibility for different possible interpretations.[46]

In line with the *locus classicus* on the attribution of private conduct to the State in the *Military and Paramilitary Activities* case, the conduct of a non-State actor falling short of the following tests (de jure organ, de facto organ, or acting under the effective control of the State) could not be attributed to the State.[47] Is there room to consider such aid or assistance to the wrongdoing as part of control, directions or instructions under Article 8 ARSIWA? The Court stated that for the responsibility of the United States to arise in respect of the contras' (a rebel group fighting the Nicaraguan government at the time) conduct, which was in breach of international humanitarian law (eg killing of prisoners, indiscriminate killing of civilians, torture, rape and kidnapping),[48] the United States' involvement had to be proven to exist beyond mere financing or equipping—the United States should have 'directed or enforced the perpetration of the acts contrary to human rights and humanitarian law alleged by the applicant State'.[49] In other words, the Court required either 'the issuance of directions to the *contras* by the US concerning specific operations … or … the enforcement by the US of each specific operation of the *contras*, namely forcefully making the rebels carry out specific operations'.[50] The Court held that the:

> United States participation, *even if preponderant or decisive, in the financing, organizing, training, supplying and equipping of the contras, the selection of its military or paramilitary targets, and the planning of the whole of its operation, is still insufficient in itself* … for the purpose of attributing to the United States the acts committed by the contras in the course of their military or paramilitary operations in Nicaragua. For this conduct to give rise to legal responsibility of the United States, it would in principle have to be proved that that State had effective

45 ARSIWA (n 10) Art 8.

46 PM Dupuy, 'State Sponsors of Terrorism: Issues of International Responsibility' in A Bianchi (ed), *Enforcing International Law Norms Against Terrorism* (Oxford, Hart Publishing, 2004) 10.

47 *Military and Paramilitary Activities* (Merits) (n 8) 62–67.

48 ibid 21 and 63–64, paras 20 and 113.

49 ibid para 115.

50 A Cassese, 'The Nicaragua and Tadić Tests Revisited in Light of the ICJ Judgment on Genocide in Bosnia' (2007) 18 *EJIL* 649, 653.

> control of the military or paramilitary operations in the course of which the alleged violations were committed.[51] (emphasis added)

The International Criminal Tribunal for the former Yugoslavia (ICTY) Appeals Chamber in *Tadić* challenged the primacy of the effective control, configuring a more lenient overall control test for the attribution of non-State actors' conduct to the State, where such non-State actors are organised and hierarchically structured groups, such as military or paramilitary units.[52] Such overall control implicated not only equipping, financing, training or providing operational support to the group, but also coordinating or assisting in the general planning of its military or paramilitary activities.[53] Crucially, however, the ICTY Appeals Chamber did not challenge the application of the effective control test in respect of non-organised private groups, in which case specific instructions for the performance of each specific conduct continue to be required.[54]

However, the International Court of Justice (ICJ) re-affirmed the effective control as the applicable standard in respect of all types of non-State actors' conduct both in the *Armed Activities on the Territory of the Congo*[55] and the *Bosnia Genocide*[56] cases. In the latter case, the Court decisively held that:

> [T]he particular characteristics of genocide do not justify the Court in departing from the criterion elaborated in the Judgment in the case concerning *Military and Paramilitary Activities in and against Nicaragua* … The rules for attributing alleged internationally wrongful conduct to a State do not vary with the nature of the wrongful act in question in the absence of a clearly expressed *lex specialis*.[57]

The Court's re-affirmation of the 'effective control' standard was met with some criticism among the judges on the bench. Vice-President Al-Khasawneh was among the most vocal on this point:

> Unfortunately, the Court's rejection of the standard in the *Tadić* case fails to address the crucial issue raised therein—namely that *different types of activities, particularly in the ever evolving nature of armed conflict, may call for subtle variations in the rules of attribution.* In the *Nicaragua* case, the Court noted that the United States and the Contras shared the same objectives—namely the overthrowing of the Nicaraguan Government. These objectives, however, were achievable without the commission of war crimes or crimes against humanity. The Contras could indeed have limited themselves to military targets in the accomplishment of their objectives. As such, in order to attribute crimes against humanity in

[51] *Military and Paramilitary Activities* (Merits) (n 8) 64–65, para 115.
[52] *Prosecutor v Tadić* (Judgment) IT-94-1-A (15 July 1999) para 120.
[53] ibid paras 131 and 137.
[54] ibid paras 118–19, 132–36 and 141.
[55] *Armed Activities (DRC v Uganda)* (n 18) 226, para 160.
[56] *Bosnia Genocide* (Merits) (n 31) 206–14, paras 396–412.
[57] ibid 208–09, para 401.

> furtherance of the common objective, the Court held that the crimes themselves should be the object of control. *When, however, the shared objective is the commission of international crimes, to require both control over the non-State actors and the specific operations in the context of which international crimes were committed is too high a threshold.* The inherent danger in such an approach is that it gives States the opportunity to carry out criminal policies through non-state actors or surrogates without incurring direct responsibility therefore. *The statement in paragraph 406 of the Judgment to the effect that the '"overall control" test is unsuitable, for it stretches too far, almost to breaking point, the connection which must exist between the conduct of a State's organs and its international responsibility' is, with respect, singularly unconvincing because it fails to consider that such a link has to account for situations in which there is a common criminal purpose. It is also far from self-evident that the overall control test is always not proximate enough to trigger State responsibility.*[58] (emphasis added)

Irrespective of whether the test of effective control finds sufficient support in customary international law[59] or a less stringent threshold of overall control could be apposite in certain circumstances, as outlined by the ICTY in *Tadić*, the aid or assistance would only lead to attribution of non-State actor's conduct to the State in cases where the group is at least hierarchically structured with a proper chain of command, such as a military or paramilitary group.[60] In other words, both tests of attribution do not capture all instances of aid or assistance to the wrongful acts committed by a non-State actor.

In sum, although Article 8 ARSIWA employs seemingly broad concepts such as instructions, direction and control, it fails to capture situations where the link between the State and the non-State actor, whether sporadic or systematic, does not involve the interference of the State in the structure of a non-State actor (ie its leadership, chain of command or hierarchy) and control over each operation of the non-State actor. According to Jinks, in particular following the 9/11 attacks, there has been a shift in the very nature of 'state action'.[61] He claimed that the new rule of attribution in the context of the use of force against terrorist organisations—the so-called harbouring—could be viewed in parallel with the development of Article 16 ARSIWA as a basis of responsibility in general international law.[62] Regardless of the merits of complicity as a basis of attribution of conduct in the context of *jus ad bellum*,[63] the question we are concerned

[58] ibid Dissenting Opinion of Judge Al-Khasawneh 241, 256–57, para 39.

[59] Cassese (n 50) 654 (arguing that the Court has cited no relevant practice and opinio juris for its test of effective control).

[60] *Prosecutor v Tadić* (n 52) paras 131–37.

[61] Jinks (n 7) 90.

[62] ibid.

[63] See, eg A Nollkaemper, 'Attribution of Forcible Acts to States: Connections Between the Law on the Use of Force and the Law of State Responsibility' in N Blokker and N Schrijver (eds), *The Security Council and the Use of Force: Theory and Reality, a Need for a Change?* (Leiden, Martinus Nijhoff, 2005).

with is whether the general rule of complicity can be used as a basis of attribution of a non-State actor's conduct to the State for the purposes of international responsibility.

III. COMPLICITY FILLING THE GAPS IN THE CURRENT REGIME OF ATTRIBUTION

Article 16 ARSIWA was envisaged to apply exclusively between States.[64] When delineating the scope of responsibility for complicity in the ARSIWA, Special Rapporteur Ago noted that:

> Cases in which a State incurs international responsibility for the act of a subject of international law other than a State (eg an international organization or an insurrectional movement), although intellectually conceivable, are not covered, because there are no known cases in which this has actually happened and such cases are unlikely to occur in the future.[65]

This statement clearly left some room for future developments. Already during the final stages leading to the adoption of the ARSIWA, Special Rapporteur James Crawford recognised the parallels between the implication of one State in the conduct of another, including complicity as set out in Article 16 ARSIWA, and questions of attribution of conduct.[66] The adoption of the rules on complicity in the ARIO was a further move away from a strict inter-State conception of responsibility for complicity. The logical progress is now to accept that the responsibility for complicity may play a role as a standard of attribution of a non-State actor's conduct to the aiding or assisting State.

Indeed, there are some indications in practice of complicity moving in the direction of serving as a basis of attribution of conduct.[67] What was intellectually conceivable in the 1970s is becoming a reality today. Complicity of States in the wrongdoings by non-State actors cannot and should not be ignored. The key legal development for construing complicity as a rule of attribution of conduct occurred in the *Bosnia Genocide* case. In that case the ICJ ignored the limitation of the inter-State understanding of responsibility for complicity, when it applied Article 16 ARSIWA to a

[64] HP Aust, *Complicity and the Law of State Responsibility* (Cambridge, CUP, 2011) 52.

[65] R Ago, 'Eighth Report on State Responsibility' (1979) UN Doc A/CN.4/318 and Add 1-4, reproduced in (1979) 2 (pt 1) *YBILC* 4, para 3.

[66] J Crawford, 'Second Report on State Responsibility' (1999) UN Doc A/CN.4/498 and Add 1-4, reproduced in (1999) 2 (pt 1) *YBILC* 3, 47, para 167.

[67] See, eg Amoroso (n 5); Savarese (n 5); E Savarese, 'Fatti di privati e responsabilità dello Stato tra organo di fatto e "complicità" alla luce di recenti tendenze della prassi internazionale' in M Spinedi, A Gianelli and ML Alaimo (eds), *La codificazione della responsabilità internazionale degli stati alla prova dei fatti: Problemi e spunti di riflessione* (Milano, Giuffrè, 2006).

situation, involving alleged complicity between a State—Serbia—and a non-State actor—the self-proclaimed Republika Srpska.[68] The importance of this extension cannot be underestimated—the Court examined the possible responsibility for complicity of Serbia in the acts of genocide committed by the VRS forces of Republika Srpska, even though a few paragraphs earlier in the judgment the Court re-affirmed the correctness of the effective control standard for the purposes of attribution.[69] This strongly suggests that the Court was ready to consider complicity as a separate ground of attribution of conduct in general international law.

The growing pattern of complicity between different States and organised groups of non-State actors that hold effective control over parts of a State's territory calls for a re-evaluation of the modern attribution framework. The following cases serve as a useful background: Iran allegedly providing missiles and other weapons to Hezbollah in their attacks against Israel; different States supplying rebels with weaponry during the conflicts in Libya and in Syria, or by now the classic example of Afghanistan which sheltered Al Qaeda members on its territory.[70] These cases are well documented in the existing literature on questions of terrorism and hence there is no need for duplication here.[71]

What is interesting about these and many other similar cases is that they all point in the same direction—under the current framework of attribution, States have considerable freedom left to engage with private actors and to avoid responsibility. The existing attribution threshold is set very high and the primary rules do not always cover all possible types of financing, logistical, military or technical aid or assistance that States render to non-State actors for the commission of internationally wrongful acts.

Let us take a hypothetical case scenario to illustrate the problem. State A provides aid or assistance to a non-State actor operating in State B. Assume that the aid or assistance consists of financial contributions and training, which facilitate the commission of military raids and human rights violations by that non-State actor against State C. The question arises as to whether it is possible to attribute the acts of this non-State actor to State A because of the latter's aid or assistance. None of the existing forms of attribution of conduct are sufficiently robust to capture complicity, which falls foul of effective control or interference with the very structure

[68] *Bosnia Genocide* (Merits) (n 31) para 420; see also A Pellet, 'Some Remarks on the Recent Case Law of the International Court of Justice on Responsibility Issues' in P Kóvacs (ed), *International Law—A Quiet Strength: Miscellanea in Memoriam Géza Herczegh* (Budapest, Pázmány Press, 2011) 126.

[69] *Bosnia Genocide* (Merits) (n 31) 206–11, paras 396–407; *Military and Paramilitary Activities* (Merits) (n 8) 64–65, para 115; *Armed Activities (DRC v Uganda)* (n 18) 226, paras 160–62.

[70] See generally Proulx (n 5); Trapp (n 7); Becker (n 5).

[71] See, eg Becker (n 5); Trapp (n 7); Proulx (n 5); B Saul, *Defining Terrorism in International Law* (Oxford, OUP, 2008).

and operational aspects of activities carried out by non-State actors. Why should such complicity go unnoticed? Whom is the international legal system trying to protect? Why should the interests of the assisting State prevail over the interests of the State that suffers injury as a result of non-State actors' wrongful conduct made possible by that same aid or assistance? Thus, in this author's view, there is an inherent gap in the modern view of attribution from a systemic perspective of responsibility in international law, in the sense that States have a broad leverage to avoid responsibility in connection with their own decision-making and aid or assistance they provide to non-State actors for the commission of activities which result in harm to third States.

Responsibility for complicity, if adequately construed, could eventually remedy this gap. Special Rapporteur Ago's analysis a few decades ago is still very much the starting point of the attribution framework in the law of international responsibility:

> [T]he acts of private individuals are never taken into account in determining the international responsibility of the State unless they are accompanied by certain actions or omissions of organs of the State.[72]

According to Ago, the possible 'participation' or 'complicity' of organs of the State in the action of an individual does not make that individual a member—even an incidental or de facto member—of the State.[73] As we have seen in chapter two, Ago discarded the approach of arbitral tribunals and scholars in the late nineteenth and early twentieth century of conceiving complicity as a form of attribution of conduct whenever a State failed to prevent or punish the harmful activities of a private actor. Ago believed that this was an altogether different scenario from that of action committed by certain individuals at the instigation and on behalf of the State (ie cases of persons who, without really being organs of the State, act on behalf of the State in certain circumstances, so that their actions would then be attributed to the State in the same way as those of organs in the strict sense of the term).[74] Importantly, for the purposes of attribution, the State organ needs in some way to have connived in the act of the private actor. Ago justified his limited conception of attribution of private actors' conduct as follows:

> The strictly negative conclusion reached regarding the attribution to the State of the acts of private natural and legal persons and of the other persons ... does not imply, however, that the State cannot incur international responsibility for such

[72] R Ago, 'Fourth Report on State Responsibility' (1972) UN Doc A/CN.4/264 and Add 1, reproduced in (1972) 2 *YBILC* 71, 96, para 64.

[73] ibid 96, para 64, n 119.

[74] ibid.

> acts on other grounds … A State has often been held internationally responsible on the occasion of acts or omissions whose material perpetrator was a private natural or legal person who, on that occasion, was not acting on the State's behalf.[75]

In this author's opinion, the growing intensity and variety of interactions between States and non-State actors casts doubt on the continuing validity of the limitations artificially inculcated on the attribution framework.[76] Take an example of modern cyber terrorist attacks performed by private actors with the support of one State against a third State, which may result in a variety of international law violations. The showing of complete dependence, effective and even overall control by a State in such cases is simply a *probatio diabolica* as in the modern technology world the identity and geographical location of the cyber attacker is easily concealed.[77] It is not submitted here that such acts should by default be attributable to the State—there is no place in international law for such a strict or absolute conception of responsibility. However, assuming there is evidence of aid or assistance knowingly provided to a cyber-group committing such attacks, why should a State providing such aid or assistance escape its responsibility (even if the group is not fully dependent on it or operating under its instructions, directions or control)?

Authors have taken different views on whether complicity as a basis of attribution of conduct is a viable pursuit particularly in the context of terrorist activities. Christian Tams, among other commentators, has suggested that 'the concept of "aiding and abetting" in terrorist activities captures the essence of new practice… Notably, it broadens the forms of support which trigger a territorial state's responsibility'.[78] By extension, the provision of assistance by third States may effectively raise the issue of whether any such responsibility may be shared or apportioned between the assisting and the territorial State where the harm occurs. While Tams makes a case for complicity as a new basis of attribution of conduct of terrorist groups to the State, Kimberly Trapp contends that the primary

[75] ILC, 'Report of the International Law Commission on the Work of Its 27th Session (5 May–25 July 1975)' (1975) UN Doc A/10010/Rev.1, reproduced in (1975) 2 *YBILC* 47, 71, paras 4–5 ('The acts of private persons or of persons acting in a private capacity then constitute … an external event which serves as a catalyst for the wrongfulness of the State's conduct').

[76] cf, eg Ago (n 72) 96, para 64.

[77] R Garnett and P Clarke, 'Cyberterrorism: A New Challenge for International Law' in A Bianchi (ed), *Enforcing International Law Norms Against Terrorism* (Oxford, Hart Publishing, 2004) 479; see also Y Dinstein, 'Computer Network Attacks and Self Defence' in M Schmitt and B O'Donnell (eds), *Computer Network Attacks and International Law* (Oxford, Hart Publishing, 2004) 111; J Barkham, 'Information Warfare and International Law on the Use of Force' (2001) 34 *NYU J Intl L & Pol* 57, 99.

[78] CJ Tams, 'The Use of Force against Terrorists' (2009) 20 *EJIL* 359, 386.

norms of due diligence are sufficiently robust to capture different forms of State involvement in terrorist activities of non-State actors.[79] According to Trapp:

> If a state is complicit in its territory being used as a base of terrorist operations, then a use of defensive force in response to terrorist attacks by non-state actors from that state's territory is necessary, and the complicity provides the justification for the violation of the host state's territorial integrity.[80]

In aiming to uphold the distinction between primary and secondary rules, Trapp submits that:

> An argument that states should be held directly responsible for positive conduct (the commission of a terrorist act) on the basis of attributability, when all they may be 'guilty' of is an omission renders many of the primary rules of international law in the terrorist context redundant...[81]

This author is not convinced that the distinction between primary and secondary rules is sufficient reason on its own to dispose of complicity as a possible basis of attribution of conduct. As we have shown throughout this book, the normative model of responsibility for complicity is a hybrid between a primary and secondary norm, if not an actual primary norm. Of course, Trapp is right that certain due diligence obligations could provide an answer to a number of assistance-related scenarios particularly when the wrongful act takes place within the territory of the State that assists the non-State actors.[82] However, the situation is legally more complex when the State supplies arms, finances or otherwise supports the non-State actor operating in a different State or transnationally. In these situations, we are conceptually closer to attributing the wrongful acts committed by the non-State actor to the assisting State. The responsibility for these same acts could be concurrently attributed to the State where they take place on the grounds of the latter's failure to exercise due diligence. In other words, in most cases of wrongful acts committed by a non-State actor funded from abroad, the responsibility of the assisting State and the territorial State could be concurrently engaged on different legal grounds.

Moreover, the qualification of a certain conduct as complicity arguably carries more weight both symbolically (in terms of its deterrent effect to

[79] KN Trapp, 'The Use of Force against Terrorists: A Reply to Christian J Tams' (2010) 20 *EJIL* 1049, 1055.

[80] ibid 1051.

[81] Trapp (n 7) 61.

[82] RP Barnidge, 'The Due Diligence Principle under International Law' (2006) 8 *Int CL Rev* 81; R Pisillo-Mazzeschi, 'The Due Diligence Rule and the Nature of the International Responsibility of States' (1992) 35 *German YBIL* 9; S Heathcote, 'State Omissions and Due Diligence: Aspects of Fault, Damage and Contribution to Injury in the Law of State Responsibility' in K Bannelier, T Christakis and S Heathcote (eds), *The ICJ and the Evolution of International Law: The Enduring Impact of the Corfu Channel Case* (London, Routledge, 2012).

future analogous conduct) and practically (as reparation is likely to be more significant in form and content as compared to the breach of a due diligence obligation). By aiding or assisting a wrongful conduct of a non-State actor, the latter becomes attributable to the State. In contrast, by failing to exercise reasonable due diligence within its territory and allowing thereby the wrongful act by a non-State actor to occur, the State is responsible for its omission. The State's omission in the context of a due diligence obligation is not linked specifically to the non-State actor's *conduct* but rather to the effects flowing from that conduct. Accordingly, at least in theory the injury for which the State may be responsible as a result of its complicity may be greater than that incurred as a result of its failure to exercise due diligence over its territory.

This interpretation is also in line with James Crawford's view of the boundaries of State responsibility in relation to private actors' conduct:

> The different rules of attribution…have a cumulative effect, such that a State may be *responsible for the effects of the conduct of private parties*, if it failed to take necessary measures to prevent those effects. For example, a receiving State is not responsible, as such, for the acts of private individuals in seizing an embassy, but it will be responsible if it fails to take all necessary steps to protect the embassy from seizure, or to regain control over it. In this respect, there is often a close link between the basis of attribution and the particular obligation said to have been breached, even though the two elements are analytically different.[83] (emphasis added)

According to the former ILC Member Ushakov

> the possibility of a kind of complicity of a State organ going beyond mere failure to prevent or punish, should not be ruled out. A whole range of intermediate situations could be envisaged, which might involve elements other than mere failure to prevent or punish, including the extreme case in which the act of an individual became an act of the State because it was proved that the individual had, in fact, acted on behalf of the State.[84]

The need for complicity as another form of attribution of conduct can also be seen in the progressive enlargement of the concept of de facto organ and from the reasoning of international bodies in trying to attribute terrorist acts to the States that support the terrorist groups.[85] The responsibility for

[83] J Crawford, *The International Law Commission's Articles on State Responsibility: Introduction, Text and Commentaries* (Cambridge, CUP, 2002) 92; N Wigneswaran, 'Responsive Responsibility: Counter-Terrorism Obligations and Responsibilities of States under International Law' in MJ Glennon and S Sur (eds), *Terrorism and International Law* (Leiden, Martinus Nijhoff, 2007) 282–85; Christenson (n 5) 341–46.

[84] ILC, 'Summary Record of the 1311th Meeting' (20 May 1975), reproduced in (1975) 1 *YBILC* 38, 41, para 24 (Ushakov).

[85] See Savarese (n 5) 112–16; L Condorelli, 'The Imputability to States of Acts of International Terrorism' (1989) 19 *Israel YB Human Rights* 233; Condorelli and Kress (n 10).

complicity in the context of manifold collaborations between a State and a non-State actor, as the Court seemed to apply it in the *Bosnia Genocide* case, could be distinguished from the classic scenario of the effective control test insofar as three elements are established.

The first element relates to the evidence of awareness by the State that its aid or assistance is used for the commission of internationally wrongful acts. Knowledge rather than control of the ultimate conduct is determinative of whether the aided or assisted conduct of the non-State actor can be attributed to the State. In the *Bosnia Genocide* case, the evidence was clear that Yugoslavia and the Bosnian Serb forces were in close collaboration and shared a common aim in Bosnia and Herzegovina, including several acknowledgements of such assistance by Yugoslavia itself. By contrast, in the *Military and Paramilitary Activities* case, the United States had consistently denied the fact of the provision of material assistance and it also denied that any assistance was given for the contras to overthrow the Nicaraguan government.

In other words, responsibility of a State for its complicity in the wrongdoing of a non-State actor requires a certain degree of knowledge of the circumstances of that wrongdoing. Arguably, it is sufficient that some of the State's higher officials support by their acts or statements the idea that their aid or assistance is being used for the commission of unlawful conduct, without necessarily showing that it knows the particular form of the acts. While in the *Bosnia Genocide* case the Court did not find the evidence of such knowledge fully conclusive (beyond reasonable doubt), in other cases the distinction would be valid, particularly where less serious offences are at stake, and where the Court would apply a lower standard of proof to demonstrate knowledge.

Secondly, the complicit State must be aware of the circumstances of the wrongful act *at the time* of providing aid or assistance. This awareness can be inferred from several sources, including media reports, actions of international organisations and the extent of contacts with the non-State group committing the violations. For example, while such information was widely available in the *Bosnia Genocide* case, that element could not be proven in respect of the contras in the *Military and Paramilitary Activities* case.

Thirdly, Article 16 ARSIWA may find increasing application to those situations where an organisation is more than a mere private grouping. For instance, in the *Bosnia Genocide* case, the Bosnian Serb forces were not seeking to become the government of Bosnia and Herzegovina but rather to establish their own State in a part of Bosnia and Herzegovina's territory. They also called themselves a State. Even though at no time it was formally constituted or recognised as such, the Bosnian Serb forces were clearly operating on a different scale of control over the territory where the wrongful acts were committed from that of the contras in the *Military and Paramilitary Activities* case. In this context, the extension of complicity responsibility, at the very minimum, to situations of aid or assistance by a State to a de facto territorial authority seems warranted.

The ICJ, purposefully or not, seemed to engage into progressive development by expanding the scope of application of responsibility for complicity to collaboration between States and non-State actors. The relationship between State and non-State actors, while traditionally assessed on the basis of the de facto (complete dependency) test and Article 8 test of direction, control or instructions, may well be subject to an emerging test for complicity (aid or assistance) in the years to come.[86] There are embryonic signs of the test of complicity in the context of counter-terrorism, and the case law of regional human rights courts.[87] Rather than construing such a complicity-based rule of attribution of conduct as *lex specialis*, there is merit in making the test operational in general international law, not least due to the gaps discussed above in the operation of the existing rules of attribution of conduct.[88]

There have been occasional references in the practice of States to Article 16 ARSIWA in respect of aiding or assisting by a State in the commission of internationally wrongful acts by non-State actors. For instance, in its official position on an arms embargo to Syria, Austria has referred to Article 16 ARSIWA in relation to arms being provided for the Syrian opposition in the commission of war crimes. Austria stated that:

> Should supplied arms be used by armed opposition groups in Syria in the commission of internationally wrongful acts, the States who had supplied these arms and had knowledge of these acts would incur State responsibility for their aid or assistance in the commission of such acts.[89]

The regional human rights courts have also applied complicity as a standard of attribution of conduct. For example, the Inter-American Court of Human Rights (IACtHR) ruled that Colombia was responsible 'for the violations committed by paramilitary groups who have acted with the *support, acquiescence, involvement, and cooperation of State security forces*'.[90]

[86] Pellet (n 68) 126 (arguing that, following the Bosnia Genocide judgment, complicity assimilated with aid or assistance is an addition to the commonly known typology of the hypotheses of attribution).

[87] See Jackson (n 6) 179–200.

[88] In the context of the global fight against terrorism see Jinks (n 7); Savarese (n 5) 123.

[89] 'The Austrian Position on Arms Embargo in Syria—Official Document' *Guardian* (15 May 2013) www.theguardian.com/world/julian-borger-global-security-blog/interactive/2013/may/15/austria-eu-syria-arms-embargo-pdf.

[90] *Rochela Massacre v Colombia* (Merits, Reparations and Costs) [2007] IACtHR Ser C No 163, para 78 (emphasis added); *Ituango Massacres v Colombia* (Preliminary Objections, Merits, Reparations and Costs) [2006] IACtHR Ser C No 148, paras 125 and 133; *Mapiripán Massacre v Colombia* (Merits, Reparations and Costs) [2005] IACtHR Ser C No 134, paras 121–23; see also Amoroso (n 5) 994 ff.

Notably, the IACtHR has even admitted of acquiescence as a sufficient basis for attribution of private actors' conduct to the State.

Similarly, the European Court of Human Rights (ECtHR) has found 'military, economic, financial and political support' from a State to a non-State actor to be sufficient for the purposes of attribution of conduct.[91] The Court found the responsibility not only on the part of Moldova as a territorial State, but also on the part of Russia holding that the Transnistria regime 'remains under the effective authority, or at the very least under the decisive influence, of the Russian Federation and in any event that it survives by virtue of the military, economic, financial and political support given to it by the Russian Federation'.[92] The ECtHR has attributed non-State actors' conduct to Russia as the latter was 'fully aware that [it] was handing [the applicants] over to an illegal and unconstitutional regime'.[93]

Likewise, in *Social and Economic Rights Action Centre (SERAC) and another v Nigeria*, the African Commission held that

> the government of Nigeria *facilitated* the destruction of the Ogoniland. Contrary to its Charter obligations and despite such internationally established principles, the Nigerian government has given the green light to private actors, and the oil companies in particular, to devastatingly affect the well-being of the Ogonis.[94] (emphasis added)

An argument based on complicity was also made before the United States courts in relation to Libya's assistance to the Provisional Irish Republican Army (PIRA) committing international crimes throughout the 1980s and 1990s.[95] The applicants in *McDonald and others v The Socialist People's Libyan Arab Jamahiriya* argued that Libya knowingly provided arms, training and facilities which were 'used to carry out crimes against humanity against the civilian populations in Great Britain and Northern Ireland by the PIRA'.[96]

It may well be that the above cases need to be treated with some caution (in terms of general regime of responsibility) for the following reasons.

[91] *Ilaşcu and others v Moldova and Russia* (Merits and Just Satisfaction) [2004] ECtHR App No 48787/99 (2005) 40 EHRR 46, paras 377–94.

[92] ibid, para 392; see also ibid, paras 379, 381 and 387.

[93] *Ilaşcu and others v Moldova and Russia* (n 91) para 384.

[94] *Social and Economic Rights Action Centre (SERAC) and another v Nigeria* (Decision) [2001] AHRLR 60, 71; see also J Cerone, 'Re-Examining International Responsibility: Inter-State Complicity in the Context of Human Rights Violations' (2007) 14 *ILSA J Intl & Comp L* 525, 530; C Rose, 'The Application of Human Rights Law to Private Sector Complicity in Governmental Corruption' (2011) 24 *LJIL* 715.

[95] *McDonald and others v The Socialist People's Libyan Arab Jamahiriya* (Complaint) [2006] Civil Action Case 1:06-cv-00729-JR (United States District Court for the District of Columbia), paras 313–20.

[96] ibid, para 322; see also A Clapham, 'Extending International Criminal Law beyond the Individual to Corporations and Armed Opposition Groups' (2008) 6 *JICJ* 899, 921–22.

First, the regional courts of human rights often do not set out a clear-cut distinction as to whether they are primarily analysing breaches of positive or negative obligations of the State in respect of the conduct of non-State actors.[97] Second, the soundness of their reasoning may be justifiably reproached for conflating the standards of attribution for the purposes of jurisdiction and for the purposes of responsibility proper.[98] Most recently, in *Jaloud v Netherlands*, the ECtHR stressed that the tests for jurisdiction and responsibility are fundamentally different, notwithstanding the Court's longstanding confusion of those standards.[99] Third, the expansive standard of complicity as developed by regional human rights courts may be conceived of as *lex specialis* to the general rules on attribution of conduct as set out in the ARSIWA. However, it is interesting that whenever regional human rights courts have to deal with issues of responsibility they acknowledge that they are applying the general rules of international responsibility rather than devising any special rules of attribution of conduct.

The logical question to be asked is whether there is any benefit in extending the scope of application of responsibility for complicity. If applied to States vis-à-vis non-State actors, Article 16 ARSIWA could by implication lead to a lowering standard of attribution, somewhere *in-between* the *Nicaragua* and *Tadić* thresholds.[100] It would require that the assisting State merely possess knowledge of the circumstances in which its aid or assistance is being used by the non-State actor for the commission of an internationally wrongful act, rather than the need to exercise any specific type or degree of control over that non-State actor's conduct. Conversely, if the cognitive requirement is interpreted too strictly (ie requiring the showing of intent), the expansion of responsibility for complicity to situations of collaboration between States and non-State actors will have no real impact or benefit to the integrity of the international legal order.

IV. INTERIM CONCLUSIONS

Apart from the notion of subjectivity in international law which is more artificial than real, there is no fundamental objection to developing

[97] Cerone (n 94) 530.

[98] See, eg *Loizidou v Turkey* (Judgment) [1996] ECtHR App No 15318/89 (1997) 23 EHRR 513; *Ilaşcu and others v Moldova and Russia* (n 91).

[99] *Jaloud v Netherlands* (Judgment) [2015] App No 47708/08 (2015) 60 EHRR 29, para 154; see also M Milanović, 'Jurisdiction, Attribution and Responsibility in Jaloud' http://www.ejiltalk.org/jurisdiction-attribution-and-responsibility-in-jaloud/.

[100] *Military and Paramilitary Activities* (Merits) (n 8) 64, para 115 ff; cf *Prosecutor v Tadić* (n 52) paras 120–45; see also C Tomuschat, 'Attribution of International Responsibility: Direction and Control' in MD Evans and P Koutrakos (eds), *The International Responsibility of the European Union: European and International Perspectives* (Oxford, Hart Publishing, 2013); de Hoogh (n 5).

complicity as a mode of attribution of conduct in general international law, in addition to its common conception as a form of attribution of responsibility. After all, the ARSIWA and ARIO shall not act as a barrier to the adaptation of the law of responsibility to the changing circumstances of the international community. While it may be premature to draw any *de lege lata* conclusions in this area, the chapter's purpose was to examine complicity's role in the context of *attribution of conduct* and whether it could progressively supplement the classic agency/control paradigm.

The problem of responsibility of States for their knowing contribution to wrongs committed by non-State actors is an excellent illustration of the tension between the 'dynamic idea of participation and the static concepts of subject, personality, rules and responsibility inherent in any legal system'.[101] The expanding number and diversity of non-State actors, and the varying degrees of control non-State actors exercise over wrongful acts (which often put the values of the international community at stake), warrant a re-examination of the most suitable forms to holding them accountable as well as to ensuring that States do not use them as a tool for avoiding their own responsibility.

The over-reliance in recent years on domestic enforcement mechanisms and international criminal liability explains the lack of emphasis on the general regime of international responsibility. It may well be the case that the most effective way to address violations committed by non-State actors may lie in the accountability mechanisms other than international responsibility.[102] However, it is inevitable that the stricter the rules of attribution, the more emphasis will be placed on privatising the problem of complicity of States in the acts of non-State armed groups.[103] This in turn will perpetuate the lack of State responsibility proper, and possibly ignoring the grassroots of the wrongdoing and leaving room for 'system criminality'.[104]

[101] J d'Aspremont, 'Non-State Actors in International Law: Oscillating between Concepts and Dynamics' in J d'Aspremont (ed), *Participants in the International Legal System: Multiple Perspectives on Non-State Actors in International Law* (London, Routledge, 2013) 1.

[102] J Brunnée, 'International Legal Accountability through the Lens of the Law of State Responsibility' (2005) 36 *Netherlands YBIL* 21, 47–48 and 53–55.

[103] Becker (n 5) 4 (speaking in similar terms of the problem of terrorism).

[104] A Nollkaemper and H van der Wilt (eds), *System Criminality in International Law* (Cambridge, CUP, 2009) 15; see also NHB Jørgensen, *The Responsibility of States for International Crimes* (Oxford, OUP, 2003) 112.

8

Conclusion

What you hold to be true about the world
depends on what you take into account,
and what you take into account
depends on what you think matters.[1]

I. COMPLICITY AND ITS LIMITS IN THE LAW OF INTERNATIONAL RESPONSIBILITY

THE PROHIBITION OF complicity in a wrongful act and the resulting responsibility are an essential part of any legal system, including the international one. As aptly put by Kelsen, '[i]f a State supports another State which is acting in violation of the law, it participates in an illegal action, and its duty to refrain from illegal actions is implied in the concept of international law'.[2] International law has now developed rules for holding responsible States and international organisations which aid or assist in the commission of internationally wrongful acts by another actor. This book aimed to explore the limits of such responsibility, testing its effectiveness and utility in the international legal order.

Our inquiry started in the early signs of the logic of responsibility for complicity in the concept of neutrality and the writings of the founding fathers of international law. We have seen in chapter two that third parties to armed conflicts were required to refrain from rendering any assistance to one of the belligerents in order to retain their status as neutrals. Complicity was introduced in the writings of the founding fathers of international law, and further developed in the early twentieth century as a mode of attribution of private actor's conduct to the State which failed to prevent or punish it.

In the second half of the twentieth century, complicity secured its place as a form of responsibility in two distinct regimes, international criminal

[1] S Marks, *The Riddle of All Constitutions: International Law, Democracy and the Critique of Ideology* (Oxford, OUP, 2000) 121.

[2] H Kelsen, 'The Draft Declaration on Rights and Duties of States—Critical Remarks' (1950) 44 *AJIL* 259, 271.

law and the law of international responsibility. While there is a strict line between these two regimes in terms of their function and purposes, our intention was to look into the evolution of complicity in a holistic manner. The analysis of international criminal law in chapter three was limited to drawing a comparison of the manner in which the elements of complicity, which share similar features in both regimes, are interpreted and applied. However, we found that the elements applicable to complicity within the framework of individual responsibility for international crimes can only inform the regime of complicity in the law of international responsibility to a limited extent. Nevertheless, in the course of this analysis, it was concluded that there is a paradox in how complicity is treated in different regimes of international law. While in international criminal law, the mental element required for complicity has gradually been relaxed, the opposite has been demonstrated by the ILC's codification of responsibility for aid or assistance in the relevant provisions of the Articles on Responsibility of States for Internationally Wrongful Acts (ARSIWA) and the Articles on Responsibility of International Organizations (ARIO). On the one hand, the International Law Commission (ILC) rushed to delete the word 'complicity' from these texts in order to remove (or hide) any apparent linkage to criminal law. At the same time, the ILC retained a requirement of intent, which of course has criminal origins. This is so notwithstanding the fact that international responsibility, however *sui generis* it may be, is generally much closer to a civil theory of responsibility than a criminal one.[3] In this author's view, knowledge of the circumstances of the principal wrongful act, as established on the balance of probabilities, is sufficient, and no intent on the part of the complicit entity is required.

This book has shown that the scope for application of responsibility for complicity was substantially curtailed between the first and the second reading of the ARSIWA by the ILC, in particular with the introduction of the opposability requirement. Chapter four explored the different facets of complicity in the ARSIWA and ARIO, including the obligation of non-assistance to maintenance of a situation resulting from a serious breach of a peremptory norm, its application in the context of international

[3] See, eg J Crawford, 'First Report on State Responsibility' (1998) UN Doc A/CN.4/490 and Add 1-7, reproduced in (1998) 2 (pt 1) *YBILC* 1, 13–14, para 60 (emphasising that responsibility in international law is 'neither civil nor criminal, but purely and simply international'); G Arangio-Ruiz, 'Fifth Report on State Responsibility' (1993) UN Doc A/CN.4/453 and Add 1-3, reproduced in (1993) 2 (pt 1) *YBILC* 1, 54–57, paras 250–63; R Ago, 'Fifth Report on State Responsibility' (1976) UN Doc A/CN.4/291 and Add 1-2, reproduced in (1976) 2 (pt 1) *YBILC* 3, 33, fn 154; see also A Nollkaemper, 'Concurrence between Individual Responsibility and State Responsibility in International Law' (2003) 52 *ICLQ* 615, 616 ('state responsibility neither depends on nor implies the legal responsibility of individuals').

organisations, and the boundaries of complicity vis-à-vis other forms of shared and indirect responsibility in international law.

The effectiveness and utility of the constituent elements of responsibility for complicity was then tested in view of existing practice and *opinio juris*. Five main conclusions transpired from the analysis conducted in chapter five.

First, the regulation of complicit conduct in international law shows that '[m]ore often than not, the legal situation in which the parties find themselves falls within the ambit of several rules of international law at the same time'.[4] There are, indeed, several rules expressly prohibiting complicity in specific wrongful acts across different areas of international law. There is nevertheless a considerable overlap in the material scope of the conduct that amounts to complicity in these different areas, including *jus ad bellum*, human rights and humanitarian laws, and different conventions on arms control.

Second and relatedly, our findings show that there is far less support for the exclusion of omissions from the scope of complicity than some authors have suggested. Certainly, it may be difficult as a matter of law and fact to establish complicity by omission proper but it is equally important not to constrain complicity's scope unnecessarily and prematurely. The silence of the law-determining agents on this issue should not be interpreted as an exclusion of omissions. Nor can the Court's decision in the *Bosnia Genocide* case be given an overly broad interpretation in terms of the general regime of responsibility for complicity, particularly because the Court was dealing with complicity in genocide which entails specific considerations in terms of knowledge/intent. Had the Court indeed followed a rigid line between international criminal law and the law of international responsibility, between a primary and secondary norm, it is arguable that the outcome of its judgment would have been different. Still in relation to the material content of complicity, this study has shown that there is some basis for the application of the test of 'significantly' facilitating or contributing to the commission of the internationally wrongful act in order to incur responsibility. Although this requirement is mentioned only once in a cursory manner in the ILC's Commentary, States and international organisations have expressed the view in favour of a narrowly defined link between the aid or assistance and the principal wrongful act. In the *Bosnia Genocide* case, the Court also seems to suggest that some degree of influence must be borne by the complicit conduct on the principal wrongful act before responsibility can be triggered. Yet the precise legal qualification of a factual link (nexus) that

[4] *Gabčikovo-Nagymaros Project (Hungary/Slovakia)* (Judgment) [1997] ICJ Rep 7 Dissenting Opinion of Judge Herczegh 176, 196.

must exist between the complicit and the principal conduct has not yet been unveiled in practice. This book advocated that a simple and clear factual link insofar as it is not manifestly trivial or remote is sufficient for responsibility to be found.

Third, there is a significant overlap between complicity and due diligence, particularly in respect of omissions. A line may be drawn between these two concepts on the basis of the following elements—the character of conduct, the degree of knowledge of the conduct, and the requirement of control over the conduct and the territory where it takes place.

Fourth, our analysis has shown that while the cognitive element is central to complicity, if it is defined too narrowly, it will hinder the rule on responsibility for complicity and its utility. No unified interpretation of knowledge vis-à-vis intention dilemma has emerged to date. States and international organisations show conflicting preferences in this regard. We have tried to unpack the different parameters and conceptions that the cognitive element seems to have and have made arguments in support of the use of 'knowledge of the circumstances' as a prevailing test. This is without prejudice to the possibility that the content of the primary norms breached could affect how knowledge is determined and following which standard. However, there is no primary norm in international law that would require a sort of double intent, ie a showing that State A must with its aid or assistance *intend to facilitate* the commission of the wrongful act by State B and must do so *with the knowledge of the intention* of State B to commit that specific wrongful act. In fact, certain primary norms only seem to require that State A know of the intention of State B to use aid or assistance for the commission of a given internationally wrongful act. This is emblematically the case of genocide. However, the examples of other primary norms requiring specific intent are extremely limited and the way in which they affect the examination of the cognitive element cannot and should not be hastily transposed to the general regime of responsibility for complicity.

Fifth, this book raised serious doubts not only about the utility of the opposability limitation in Article 16(b) ARSIWA, which was transposed verbatim to Articles 14(b) and 58(1)(b) ARIO, but also about its validity in the law of international responsibility. The construction of this limitation is heavily driven by the *pacta tertiis* rule as it operates in treaty law. The *opinio juris* and practice of States and international organisations do not provide any support for the need of this requirement in the law of international responsibility. The issue was specifically raised by only one State in the process of the ARSIWA codification in the form of a remark about a potential contradiction with the regime of Articles 34 and 35 Vienna Convention on the Law of Treaties (VCLT). The opposability limitation has received, justifiably in our view, the lion's share of criticism in legal doctrine dealing with this subject and, most importantly, in the comments of States and international organisations during the codification of the same text in the ARIO.

Chapter six examined the legal consequences and implementation of responsibility for complicity, making three main arguments aimed at operationalising the enforcement of responsibility for complicity in practice.

First, it was shown that the ILC's failure to provide guidance on the applicable standards for causation where there are multiple wrongdoers causing or contributing to causing the same injury is problematic. It has effectively left responsibility for complicity in limbo. Even where a State is found to be complicit in the wrongful act of another, the injured State will not automatically be able to recover any damages from the complicit State. This deficiency is not addressed by the existing standards for causation as applied by international courts and tribunals. Accordingly, the phenomenon of complicity in a wrongful act requires active refinement of these causal standards. The introduction of foreseeability criteria can only to a certain extent remedy the problem of causation. We have reviewed two alternative solutions such as developing the existing fiction underlying the regime of responsibility for complicity from 'complicity in a wrongful act = separable wrongful act' to 'complicity in a wrongful act = separable wrongful act causing separable injury' or subjecting the apportioning of the injury to the regime of joint and several responsibility. Technical issues of evidence and proof will of course be equally problematic for both options.

Second, we have argued that the issues that arise from the application of a causal analysis requiring that complicit conduct be the proximate cause of the injury for the purposes of eventual compensation can be partially resolved by other forms of reparation and legal consequences. These include satisfaction, cessation and the guarantees and assurances of non-repetition.

Third, we have argued that States and international organisations are legitimately entitled to invoke the responsibility of others who are being complicit in the violations of *erga omnes* obligations. However, it is much more problematic to make this assumption in respect of countermeasures that States and international organisations could take in regard to actors complicit in such violations. Examples from practice show that reacting to complicity in the wrongful act is not only possible but may also be necessary. Where States render aid or assistance under a treaty obligation and know that their aid or assistance is being diverted from the original stipulation in the treaty, it is arguable that States not only have the right but also the duty, which partially derives from Article 41(2) ARSIWA, to suspend any such aid or assistance. This would de facto amount to a suspension of the operation of the treaty; then the question would become whether such conduct falls under the regime of the VCLT (provided that the conditions of Article 60 VCLT are met) or whether the wrongfulness of suspension is precluded by virtue of Article 22 ARSIWA. Finally, we found that the existing system of international dispute settlement is ill-equipped as a matter of both substance and procedure to consider responsibility for complicity. The International Court of Justice (ICJ) is a perfect example of a bilateralist vision of consent to jurisdiction and its adherence to the principle of the indispensable third party. However, on a closer scrutiny, this principle may not be as rigid as it seems and this book argued that there is room for adjustment to developments in the area of shared and indirect forms of responsibility.

Finally, chapter seven examined the emerging use of complicity as a form of attribution of conduct. Limited practice of States in the field of counter-terrorism operations and in respect of the aid or assistance to the rebels in Syria, coupled with the Court's approach in the *Bosnia Genocide* case and the jurisprudence of regional human rights courts seem to support the construction of complicity as a form of attribution of conduct. However, the more restrictive and traditional view of attribution, as set out in the agency paradigm and the notion of effective control, clearly militates against such a construction. In this author's view, the use of complicity as a ground of attribution of conduct would strengthen the role of the law of responsibility and fill in the grey areas of non-responsibility for States that pursue violations of international law through private actors. It is submitted that the material and cognitive requirements would prevent complicity from becoming too broad a rule of attribution of conduct.

II. A REVISED MODEL OF COMPLICITY: FROM CONCEPT TO FUNCTION?

The limits of the legal framework of responsibility for complicity do not attract simple solutions. Responsibility for complicity is at the core of the tension between the 'intrinsically *bilateral* character of international legal accountability and an incipient international *social* responsibility'.[5] In the words of one commentator, '[t]he hidden promise of complicity is the conception of community upon which it draws'.[6]

[5] P Allott, *Eunomia—New Order for a New World* (Oxford, OUP, 1990) 333; more generally on the shift of the international legal order from pure co-existence of sovereigns as 'billiard balls' toward cooperation where subjects try to deal more effectively with some global/common problems see W Friedmann, *The Changing Structure of International Law* (London, Stevens & Sons, 1964); for an expression of States as 'billiard balls' in international affairs as used above see A Wolfers, *Discord and Collaboration: Essays on International Politics* (Baltimore MD, John Hopkins Press, 1962) 19–24.

[6] C Kutz, *Complicity: Ethics and Law for a Collective Age* (Cambridge, CUP, 2000) 259.

While this promise of a genuine international community remains to be fulfilled,[7] responsibility for complicity in the ARSIWA and ARIO resembles an acknowledgement of Durkheim's *conscience collective*.[8] Durkheim suggested that a society nurtures certain shared sentiments and beliefs. Solidarity and cohesion are the traits of this *conscience collective*. When a breach of these common sentiments occurs, a society calls for a collective response against the offender in order to repair and reinforce the injured conscience.[9] Arguably, Article 41(2) ARSIWA strives to achieve this solidarity by imposing a duty of non-assistance in respect of serious breaches of a peremptory norm.[10] As for the general regime on complicity as set out in Article 16 ARSIWA, its bilateral straitjacket leaves much to be desired from the perspective of solidarity of the international legal order. Finally, the verbatim ARIO provisions on complicity in Articles 14, 42(2) and 58 are yet to garner more than just an embryonic support among States and international organisations.

Having examined the limits of responsibility for complicity in positive international law, the time has come to reflect on the key *leitmotif* of this book: is this form of responsibility effective and useful in public international law? This book has shown that the existing regime on responsibility for complicity in the ARSIWA and ARIO is an important step towards the recognition of multiplicity of causes and actors that may be involved in a violation of international law. There is also recognition that complicity in the wrongful act disturbs the existence of a *legal* order and, therefore as a matter of pure principle and logic, must generate legal consequences.

Although treaty provisions in different domains of international law directly regulate complicity in certain wrongful acts, the law-determining agents still refer to general rules on responsibility for complicity. The fact that the law-determining agents increasingly refer to the general regime on responsibility for complicity where they could simply be applying substantive treaty obligations is significant. It is significant because it shows that the law-determining agents wish to (i) emphasise the *responsibility* as such and (ii) elevate the status of otherwise sporadic normative

[7] G Abi-Saab, 'Whither the International Community?' (1998) 9 *EJIL* 248, 249 ('rather than referring to a group as a community in general, it is better, for the sake of precision, to speak of the degree of community').

[8] É Durkheim, *The Division of Labour in Society* (New York, Free Press, 1964) 73.

[9] ibid.

[10] Allott (n 5) 254–57 and 285–88; K Wellens, 'Solidarity as a Constitutional Principle: Its Expanding Role and Inherent Limitations' in RSJ MacDonald and DM Johnston (eds), *Towards World Constitutionalism: Issues in the Legal Ordering of the World Community* (Leiden, Martinus Nijhoff, 2005); G Abi-Saab, 'International Law and the International Community: The Long Road to Universality' in RSJ MacDonald (ed), *Essays in Honour of Wang Tieya* (Dordrecht, Martinus Nijhoff, 1994); RSJ MacDonald, 'The Principle of Solidarity in Public International Law' in C Dominicé, R Patry and C Reymond (eds), *Etudes de droit international en l'honneur de Pierre Lalive* (Basel, Helbing & Lichtenhahn, 1993).

prescriptions to a degree of relative unity, consistency and universality. Moreover, the responsibility for complicity, whether in its current format or in a slightly revised one as has been proposed in this book, may be a more manageable and acceptable solution to the law-determining agents than an overly broad obligation of due diligence without a territorial link and evaluated by reference to elusive tests such as the 'capacity to influence effectively the action of persons likely to commit, or already committing' a wrongful act.[11]

Conversely, the formal or technical advantage for an injured party to rely on a violation of a specific treaty rule that prohibits complicity or a treaty rule on due diligence is twofold: (i) they would be subject to less onerous evidentiary obligations as they would not have to prove all the requirements of Article 16 ARSIWA or its sister provisions and (ii) they would be more likely to be able to take advantage of the presumption of a causal link between the action or omission (amounting to either complicity or failure of due diligence) and the injury suffered. As it has been demonstrated in chapter six, this formal or technical advantage holds insofar as the legal construction 'complicity in a wrongful act = separable wrongful act' is applied as a derivative form of responsibility at the level of implementation of legal consequences. However, if the formula 'complicity in a wrongful act = separable wrongful act' is extended to 'complicity in a wrongful act = separable wrongful act causing separable injury', then the problems related to the determination of responsibility's content would be reduced.

Further, this apparent formal or technical advantage does not outweigh the practical disadvantage of exclusively relying on multiple primary regimes of complicity. First, as we have seen, they are slightly different in content and may lead to situations where in a single case an injured State would have to plead two or three different standards of complicity. Second, reliance on a particular treaty rule prohibiting complicity will not preclude the Court from looking beyond it into the applicable rules on responsibility for complicity, as the case of *Bosnia Genocide* or cases on extraordinary renditions illustrate.[12] It is reasonable for courts to use the general rule on responsibility for complicity, particularly where the specific prohibition of complicity does not provide any further guidance

[11] *Application of the Convention on the Prevention and Punishment of the Crime of Genocide (Bosnia and Herzegovina v Serbia and Montenegro)* (Merits) [2007] ICJ Rep 43, 221, para 430.

[12] ibid, 217, para 420; see, eg *El-Masri v The Former Yugoslav Republic of Macedonia* (Judgment) (GC) [2012] ECtHR App No 39630/09 (2013) 57 EHRR 25, paras 206, 235–40; *Al Nashiri v Poland* (Judgment) [2014] ECtHR App No 28761/11 (2015) 60 EHRR 16, paras 452 and 517; *Husayn (Abu Zubaydah) v Poland* (Judgment) [2014] ECtHR App No 7511/13 (2015) 60 EHRR 16, paras 449 and 512.

on how to ascertain responsibility of a complicit actor or determine the extent of reparation due.

Accordingly, our findings have shown that the existence of treaty and customary rules prohibiting complicity does not preclude a general norm on responsibility for complicity, which is a hybrid of primary and secondary norms. If there is room for constructive criticism of the function and purpose of the general rule on responsibility for complicity as it stands in Article 16 ARSIWA and its sister provisions, this does not lie in the self-exclusivity argument with regard to treaty norms prohibiting complicity or existing due diligence obligations.[13] Instead, what does cast doubt on the function and purpose of the ARSIWA and ARIO rules is the way they are currently formulated and limited by the requirements of intention and opposability. The former is unrealistically difficult to prove while the latter unnecessarily withdraws bilateral and even multilateral legal relationships from the scope of responsibility for complicity.

How to reconcile the apparent unity of the norm with a duality or multiplicity of its source?[14] After all, this is one of the most challenging issues that the responsibility for complicity raises in terms of its normative analysis. There seems to be one common rule on responsibility for complicity and yet a multiplicity of underlying sources. This generates an interesting imbroglio for international lawyers. Can it be that the rule or principle of responsibility for complicity itself is part of positive international law but its content and modalities are yet in gestation? For any rule or principle

[13] cf O Corten, 'La "complicité" dans le droit de la responsabilité internationale: un concept inutile?' (2011) 58 *AFDI* 57, 83–84 (concluding that primary rules effectively cover all possible situations of complicity: 'la pratique pertinente renvoie en réalité à une série de règles primaires qui énoncent les obligations spécifiques, que ce soit dans le domaine de l'interdiction du recours à la force, du droit international humanitaire ou des droits de la personne, notamment. Plus généralement, on a constaté que des principes comme celui de la diligence requise, ou de la bonne foi et du raisonnable, sont susceptibles d'expliquer bon nombre de précédents parfois envisagés sous l'angle de la complicité'; author's translation: 'in reality, the relevant practice refers to a range of primary rules that set out the specific obligations, whether in the field of the prohibition of the use of force, international humanitarian law or human rights, in particular. More generally, we have noted that the principles such as that of due diligence, good faith and reasonableness, may explain a number of precedents which are sometime considered under the rubric of complicity'); O Corten and P Klein, 'The Limits of Complicity as a Ground for Responsibility: Lessons Learned from the Corfu Channel Case' in K Bannelier, T Christakis and S Heathcote (eds), *The ICJ and the Evolution of International Law: The Enduring Impact of the Corfu Channel Case* (London, Routledge, 2012) 331–34 (concluding that 'it appears that the concept of due diligence covers in an adequate manner all the examples mentioned by the ILC on complicity').

[14] G Abi-Saab, 'Les sources du droit international: un essai de déconstruction' in M Rama-Montaldo (ed), *El derecho internacional en un mundo en transformación: Lieber Amicorum en homenaje al profesor Eduardo Jiménez de Aréchaga*, vol 1 (Montevideo, Fundación de Cultura Universitaria, 1984) 46 ('Comment concilier l'unicité de la norme et la dualité ou la multiplicité de la source?'; author's translation: 'How to reconcile the unity of the norm with the duality or multiplicity of its sources?').

to be 'essential' in international law it must be operational and effective, ie susceptible of invocation and application to concrete cases.[15] This book has argued that at present, the systemic and symbolic value of Article 16 ARSIWA and its sister provisions is lacking in effectively responding to occurrences of complicity, much less deterring them.

The regime on complicity shows that certainty and change are the two apparently irreconcilable essentials of the law.[16] The book advanced the claim for a slightly revised model of responsibility for complicity in an internationally wrongful act. The signs of this model being applied, while still somewhat chaotic and inconclusive, appear in practice and *opinio juris*. The relevant features of the revised model are that: (i) both actions and omissions constitute complicity as long as they have facilitated the commission of a wrongful act; (ii) the knowledge of the circumstances of the wrongful act applies as an exclusive test of responsibility for complicity; (iii) the aid or assistance provided with the knowledge of the principal obligation and the circumstances of its breach generates responsibility without the need to show that both the complicit and principal actor are bound by the obligation breached; and (iv) a State (international organisation) is responsible for knowingly facilitating the conduct of non-State actors, which is attributed to the State (international organisation) and constitutes a violation of its international obligation.

An intuitive objection to a revised model of responsibility as advocated in the book is inevitable. Would it not stretch too far into the sovereign rights of States and the functional mandates of international organisations? Would it not have a chilling effect on their ability to cooperate? The apologists of such an objection naturally find comfort in the concepts of opposability and intent. Yet, let us not hide what these concepts really mean.

A plea for the opposability is no more than a continuing rhetoric of restrictive consent-based vision of treaty relations transposed to the law of international responsibility, a regime with a life and function of its own. Looking beyond the legal rhetoric is the only way for the international legal order to progress and ensure its very survival. Complicity in the wrongdoing is too serious a phenomenon to be hidden behind the rhetoric of consent and reciprocity.

A plea for intent is a reminiscence of fault. Fault … so diligently assassinated by Anzilotti. In the law of responsibility that is today regarded as characteristically objective, to require the showing of intent is to require something that States and international organisations do not

[15] C Chaumont, 'L'ambivalence des concepts essentiels du droit international' in J Makarczyk (ed), *Essays in International Law in Honour of Judge Manfred Lachs* (The Hague, Martinus Nijhoff, 1984) 55.

[16] RY Jennings, 'Judicial Legislation in International Law' (1938) 26 *Kentucky LJ* 122, 127.

possess. These artificial 'monstres froids'[17] or 'figments of imagination'[18] have no soul, mind or desire. They put in place policies, make decisions, take or fail to take actions through their officials. Within the two extremes, knowledge or awareness of the circumstances of the wrongful act is a much more objective criterion and a sufficient safeguard against an overly broad scope of responsibility for complicity.

In conclusion, notwithstanding the author's critique of the ARSIWA and ARIO rules on responsibility for complicity, it is evident that the international legal order is better off with them than without. Law develops organically over time and codification does not necessarily eliminate all gaps nor foresees all developments and often even accentuates them.[19] Accordingly, the ultimate verdict on the exact scope and function of responsibility for complicity is yet to come 'dans les tourments de la lente gestation de la communauté internationale'.[20] As it stands, it is a sign, even if an imperfect one, of this community's shift towards a greater degree of solidarity. After all, international law is not a hard science in the same sense as physics, chemistry or astronomy. It is not a value-free environment and its concepts and norms are necessarily embroiled in the shifting interests of States, international organisations and individuals and in their philosophic, political and ideological attitudes.[21] In the view of Paula Escarameia we are witnessing the change of paradigms, an actual transition from the State-oriented model towards a model that has to reflect new actors, realities and foremost the impact of the individual. The humanising of the international community is no longer a choice of subjects but an inherent component of international relations.[22] Like Goethe's 'Weltkind in der Mitten', the responsibility for complicity fuses concerns about voluntarism and cooperation on the one hand and the necessity of ensuring an orderly, transparent and accountable legal order on the other.

[17] PM Dupuy, 'Faute de l'État et fait internationalement illicite' (1987) 5 *Revue Droits* 51.

[18] C Eagleton, *The Responsibility of States in International Law* (New York, New York University Press, 1928) 11.

[19] H Lauterpacht, *The Function of Law in the International Community* (Oxford, OUP, 2012) 66; cf P Allott, 'State Responsibility and the Unmaking of International Law' (1988) 29 *Harvard Intl LJ* 1.

[20] B Stern, 'Les dilemmes de la responsabilité internationale aujourd'hui' in *Vers de nouvelles normes en droit de la responsabilité publique: Actes du colloque 11 et 12 mai 2001* (Paris, Sénat, 2001) 283 (author's translation: 'in the torment of the slow consolidation of the international community').

[21] O Schachter, 'Invisible College of International Lawyers' (1977) 72 *Northwestern University LR* 217, 218; C de Visscher, *Théories et réalités en droit international public* (2nd edn, Paris, Pedone, 1955); see also A Bianchi, 'Ad-Hocism and the Rule of Law' (2002) 13 *EJIL* 263, 266 (arguing that broad analytical categories are instrumental to maintaining the unity of the system and that their content and scope of application must be constantly revised in line with the changing social paradigms and demands of international community).

[22] P Escarameia, *O direito internacional público nos princípios do século XXI* (Lisboa, Almedina, 2003) 195–211.

Bibliography

Abass A, 'Consent Precluding State Responsibility: A Critical Analysis' (2004) 53 *ICLQ* 211

——, 'Proving State Responsibility for Genocide: The ICJ in Bosnia v Serbia and the International Commission of Inquiry for Darfur' (2007) 31 *Fordham Intl LJ* 871

Abi-Saab G, 'Cours général de droit international public' (1987) 207 *RCADI* 9

——, 'Whither the International Community?' (1998) 9 *EJIL* 248

——, 'Fragmentation or Unification: Some Concluding Remarks' (1999) 31 *NYU J Intl L & Pol* 919

——, 'The Uses of Article 19' (1999) 10 *EJIL* 339

——, 'International Law and the International Community: The Long Road to Universality' in RSJ MacDonald (ed), *Essays in Honour of Wang Tieya* (Dordrecht, Martinus Nijhoff, 1994)

——, 'Les sources du droit international: un essai de déconstruction' in M Rama-Montaldo (ed), *El derecho internacional en un mundo en transformación: Lieber Amicorum en homenaje al profesor Eduardo Jiménez de Aréchaga*, vol 1 (Montevideo, Fundación de Cultura Universitaria, 1984)

——, 'Que reste-il du "crime international"', *Droit du pouvoir—pouvoir du droit: Mélanges en l'honneur de Jean Salmon* (Bruxelles, Bruylant, 2007)

Abtahi H and Webb P, *The Genocide Convention: The Travaux Préparatoires* (Leiden, Martinus Nijhoff, 2008)

Adeyeye A, 'Corporate Responsibility in International Law: Which Way to Go' (2007) 11 *Singapore YBIL* 141

Ago R, 'Le délit international' (1939) 68 *RCADI* 417

——, 'Droit positif et droit international' (1957) 3 *AFDI* 14

——, 'La codification du droit international et les problèmes de sa réalisation', *Mélanges en hommage à Paul Guggenheim* (Genève, HEI, 1968)

——, *Scritti sulla responsabilità internazionale degli Stati I* (Padova, Jovene, 1978)

Ahlborn C, 'The Rules of International Organizations and the Law of International Responsibility' (2011) 8 *IOLR* 397

——, 'The Use of Analogies in Drafting the Articles on the Responsibility of International Organizations—An Appraisal of the "Copy-Paste Approach"' (2012) 9 *IOLR* 53

——, 'Remedies against International Organizations—A Relational Account of International Responsibility' in D Sarooshi (ed), *Remedies and Responsibility for the Actions of International Organizations* (Leiden, Martinus Nijhoff, 2014)

——, 'To Share or Not to Share? The Allocation of Responsibility between International Organizations' SHARES Research Paper No 28 (2013)

Aksenova M, 'The Specific Direction Requirement for Aiding and Abetting: A Call for Revisiting Comparative Criminal Law' (2015) 4 *Cambridge J Intl & Comp L* 88

——, 'Complicity in International Criminal Law: A Case for Clarification' (Mississippi College of Law, New Perspectives in Comparative Law—Inaugural YCC Conference, 2012)

Alabrune F, 'La pratique des Comités des sanctions du Conseil de sécurité depuis 1990' (1999) 45 *AFDI* 226

Alford R, 'Apportioning Responsibility Among Joint Tortfeasors for International Law Violations' (2011) 38 *Pepperdine LR* 233

Alland D, 'Countermeasures of General Interest' (2002) 13 *EJIL* 1221

——, *Justice privée et ordre juridique international* (Paris, Pedone, 1994)

Allott P, 'State Responsibility and the Unmaking of International Law' (1988) 29 *Harvard Intl LJ* 1

——, 'The Concept of International Law' (1999) 10 *EJIL* 31

——, *Eunomia—New Order for a New World* (Oxford, OUP, 1990)

——, *The Health of Nations: Society and Law beyond the State* (Cambridge, CUP, 2002)

Alston P, 'The "Not-a-Cat" Syndrome: Can the International Human Rights Regime Accommodate Non-State Actors?' in P Alston (ed), *Non-State Actors and Human Rights* (Oxford, OUP, 2005)

Alvarez J, 'Torturing the Law' (2005) 37 *Case Western Reserve J Intl L* 175

——, 'Revisiting the ILC's Draft Rules on International Organization Responsibility' (2011) 105 *ASIL Proceedings* 344

——, *International Organizations as Law-Makers* (Oxford, OUP, 2005)

Alvarez-Jiménez A, 'Methods for the Identification of Customary International Law in the International Court of Justice's Jurisprudence: 2000–2009' (2011) 60 *ICLQ* 681

Ambos K, 'Article 25: Individual Criminal Responsibility' in O Triffterer (ed), *Commentary on the Rome Statute of the International Criminal Court* (2nd edn, Oxford, Hart Publishing, 2008)

——, *Der allgemeine Teil des Völkerstrafrechts—Ansätze einer Dogmatisierung* (Berlin, Duncker & Humblot, 2002)

Amerasinghe C, 'Presumptions and Inferences in Evidence in International Litigation' (2004) 3 *LPICT* 395

——, 'An Assessment of the ILC's Articles on the Responsibility of International Organizations' in M Ragazzi (ed), *Responsibility of International Organizations: Essays in Memory of Sir Ian Brownlie* (Leiden, Martinus Nijhoff, 2013)

Amoroso D, 'Moving towards Complicity as a Criterion of Attribution of Private Conducts: Imputation to States of Corporate Abuses in the US Case Law' (2011) 24 *LJIL* 989

Amrallah B, 'The International Responsibility of the United Nations for Activities Carried Out by UN Peace-Keeping Forces' (1976) 32 *Revue égyptienne de droit international* 57

Anzilotti D, 'La responsabilité internationale des États à raison des dommages soufferts par des étrangers' (1906) 13 *RGDIP* 5

——, *Cours de droit international*, vol 1 (G Gidel tr, Paris, Sirey, 1929)

——, *Opere di Dionisio Anzilotti: Corso di diritto internazionale*, vol 1 (4th edn, Padova, CEDAM, 1955)

——, *Teoria generale della responsabilità dello stato nel diritto internazionale* (Firenze, F Lumachi Libraio-Editore, 1902)

Arangio-Ruiz G, 'State Fault and the Forms and Degrees of International Responsibility: Questions of Attribution and Relevance', *Le droit international au service de la paix, de la justice et du développement: Mélanges Michel Virally* (Paris, Pedone, 1991)

Araujo R, 'Objective Meaning of Constituent Instruments and Responsibility of International Organizations' in M Ragazzi (ed), *International Responsibility Today: Essays in Memory of Oscar Schachter* (Leiden, Martinus Nijhoff, 2005)

Ascensio H, 'La responsabilité selon la Cour internationale de justice dans l'affaire du génocide bosniaque' (2007) 111 *RGDIP* 285

Asuncion A, 'Pulling the Stops on Genocide: The State or the Individual?' (2010) 20 *EJIL* 1195

Aust H, 'The UN Human Rights Due Diligence Policy: An Effective Mechanism against Complicity of Peacekeeping Forces?' (2015) 20 *JCSL* 61

——, 'Article 2(5)' in B Simma et al (eds), *The Charter of the United Nations: A Commentary* (3rd edn, Oxford, OUP, 2012)

——, 'Circumstances Precluding Wrongfulness' in A Nollkaemper and I Plakokefalos (eds), *Principles of Shared Responsibility in International Law: An Appraisal of the State of the Art* (Cambridge, CUP, 2014)

——, *Complicity and the Law of State Responsibility* (Cambridge, CUP, 2011)

——, 'Complicity in Violations of International Humanitarian Law' in H Krieger and J Willms (eds), *Inducing Compliance with International Humanitarian Law* (Cambridge, CUP, 2015)

Ayissi M, 'La réalisation dans le temps de l'illicite international et ses conséquences dans le droit de la responsabilité internationale' (PhD Thesis, Geneva, Graduate Institute, 2011)

Aznar Gómez M, 'En torno a la unidad sistémica del derecho internacional' (2007) 59 *Revista Española de Derecho Internacional* 563

Azzam F, 'The Duty of Third States to Implement and Enforce International Humanitarian Law' (1997) 66 *Nordic J Intl L* 55

Baars G, 'Corrie et Al. v Caterpillar: Litigating Corporate Complicity in Israeli Violations of International Law in the US Courts' (2004) 11 *YB Islamic & Middle Eastern L* 97

Baetens F, 'Procedural Issues Relating to Shared Responsibility in Arbitral Proceedings' (2013) 4 *JIDS* 319

Barberis J, 'Le concept de "traité international" et ses limites' (1984) 30 *AFDI* 239

Barboza J, 'Legal Injury: The Tip of the Iceberg in the Law of State Responsibility?' in M Ragazzi (ed), *International Responsibility Today: Essays in Memory of Oscar Schachter* (Leiden, Martinus Nijhoff, 2005)

——, 'State Crimes: A Decaffeinated Coffee' in L Boisson de Chazournes and V Gowlland-Debbas (eds), *The International Legal System in Quest of Equity and Universality: Liber Amicorum Georges Abi-Saab* (The Hague, Martinus Nijhoff, 2001)

Barker J, 'The Different Forms of Reparation: Compensation' in J Crawford et al (eds), *The Law of International Responsibility* (Oxford, OUP, 2010)

Barker J and Sivakumaran S, 'I. Application of the Convention on the Prevention and Punishment of the Crime of Genocide (Bosnia and Herzegovina v Serbia and Montenegro)' (2008) 56 *ICLQ* 695

Barkham J, 'Information Warfare and International Law on the Use of Force' (2001) 34 *NYU J Intl L & Pol* 57

Barnhoon L and Wellens K (eds), *Diversity in Secondary Rules and the Unity of International Law* (The Hague, Martinus Nijhoff, 1995)

Barnidge R, 'The Due Diligence Principle under International Law' (2006) 8 *Int CL Rev* 81

——, *Non-State Actors and Terrorism: Applying the Law of State Responsibility and the Due Diligence Principle* (The Hague, TMC Asser Press, 2008)

Bartels L, 'Procedural Aspects of Shared Responsibility in the WTO Dispute Settlement System' (2013) 4 *JIDS* 343

Barthe-Gay C, 'Réflexions sur la satisfaction en droit international' (2003) 49 *AFDI* 105

Bartolini G, 'Il concetto di "controllo" sulle attività di individui quale presupposto della responsabilità dello Stato' in M Spinedi, A Gianelli and ML Alaimo (eds), *La codificazione della responsabilità internazionale degli stati alla prova dei fatti: Problemi e spunti di riflessione* (Milano, Giuffrè, 2006)

Bassiouni M, *The Legislative History of the International Criminal Court*, vol 1 (Ardsley New York, Transnational, 2005)

Baudenet d'Annoux H, *Le développement de la neutralité: De Grotius à Vattel* (Orléans, Imprimerie Auguste Gout et Cie, 1910)

Beaucillon C, Fernandez J and Raspail H, 'State Responsibility for Conduct of Private Military and Security Companies Violating Ius Ad Bellum' in F Francioni and N Ronzitti (eds), *War by Contract: Human Rights, Humanitarian Law and Private Contractors* (Oxford, OUP, 2011)

Becker T, *Terrorism and the State: Rethinking the Rules of State Responsibility* (Oxford, Hart Publishing, 2006)

Bekker P, *The Legal Position of Intergovernmental Organizations: A Functional Necessity Analysis of Their Legal Status and Immunities* (Dordrecht, Martinus Nijhoff, 1994)

Belhumeur J and Condorelli L (eds), *Christian Dominicé: L'ordre juridique international entre tradition et innovation—Recueil d'études* (Paris, PUF, 1997)

Bell C, 'Reassessing Multiple Attribution: The International Law Commission and the Behrami and Saramati Decision' (2009) 42 *NYU J Intl L & Pol* 501

Belli of Alba P, *De Re Militari et Bello Tractatus [A Treatise on Military Matters and Warfare]* (HC Nutting tr, Oxford, Clarendon Press, 1936)

Besson S, 'La pluralité d'États responsables: Vers une solidarité internationale?' (2007) 1 *SZIER* 13

——, 'The Extraterritoriality of the European Convention on Human Rights: Why Human Rights Depend on Jurisdiction and What Jurisdiction Amounts to' (2012) 25 *LJIL* 857

Bianchi A, 'Ad-Hocism and the Rule of Law' (2002) 13 *EJIL* 263

——, 'Ferrini v Federal Republic of Germany. Italian Court of Cassation, March 11, 2004' (2005) 99 *AJIL* 242

——, 'Human Rights and the Magic of Jus Cogens' (2008) 19 *EJIL* 491

——, 'State Responsibility and Criminal Liability of Individuals' in A Cassese (ed), *The Oxford Companion to International Criminal Justice* (Oxford, OUP, 2009)

Binder C, 'Völkerrecht und Staudammbauten: das Ilisu-Projekt' (2007) 1 *Juridikum* 10

——, 'Does the Difference Make a Difference? A Comparison between the Mechanisms of the Law of Treaties and of State Responsibility as Means to Derogate from Treaty Obligations in Cases of Subsequent Changes of Circumstances' in M Szabó (ed), *State Responsibility and the Law of Treaties* (The Hague, Eleven, 2010)

Bingham T, 'The Alabama Claims Arbitration' (2008) 54 *ICLQ* 1

Bissonnette P, *La satisfaction comme mode de réparation en droit international* (Genève, HEI, 1952)

Black's Law Dictionary (4th edn, St Paul, West Publishing, 2011)

Blokker N, 'Abuse of the Members: Questions Concerning Draft Article 16 of the Draft Articles on Responsibility of International Organizations' (2010) 7 *IOLR* 35

Boas G, 'Omission Liability at the International Criminal Tribunals—A Case for Reform' in S Darcy and J Powderly (eds), *Judicial Creativity at the International Criminal Tribunals* (Oxford, OUP, 2010)

Bobbio N, 'Nouvelles réflexions sur les normes primaires et secondaires' in N Bobbio (ed), *Études de théorie du droit* (Paris, LGDJ, 1988)

Bodini S, 'Fighting Maritime Piracy under the European Convention on Human Rights' (2011) 22 *EJIL* 829

Bohoslavsky J and Opgenhaffen V, 'Past and Present of Corporate Complicity: Financing the Argentinean Dictatorship' (2010) 23 *Harvard Human Rights J* 157

Bohoslavsky J and Rulli M, 'Corporate Complicity and Finance as a "Killing Agent": The Relevance of the Chilean Case' (2010) 8 *JICJ* 829

Boisson de Chazournes L, 'The State of State Responsibility' (2002) 96 *ASIL Proceedings* 169

——, 'United in Joy and Sorrow: Some Considerations on Responsibility Issues under Partnerships Among International Financial Institutions' in M Ragazzi (ed), *Responsibility of International Organizations: Essays in Memory of Sir Ian Brownlie* (Leiden, Martinus Nijhoff, 2013)

Boisson de Chazournes L and Condorelli L, 'Common Article 1 of the Geneva Conventions Revisited: Protecting Collective Interests' (2000) 837 *IRRC* 67

Boisson de Chazournes L, La Rosa A-M and Mbengue M, 'Art 18 (1969)' in O Corten and P Klein (eds), *The Vienna Conventions on the Law of Treaties: The Commentary* (Oxford, OUP, 2011)

Boivin A, 'Complicity and Beyond: International Law and the Transfer of Small Arms and Light Weapons' (2005) 87 *IRRC* 467

Bonafé B, 'Responsabilità dello Stato per fatti illeciti particolarmente gravi e responsabilità penale dell'individuo: due approcci a confronto' in M Spinedi, A Gianelli and ML Alaimo (eds), *La codificazione della responsabilità internazionale degli stati alla prova dei fatti: Problemi e spunti di riflessione* (Milano, Giuffrè, 2006)

——, *The Relationship between State and Individual Responsibility for International Crimes* (Leiden, Martinus Nijhoff, 2009)

Boon K, 'The Role of Lex Specialis in the Articles on the Responsibility of International Organizations' in M Ragazzi (ed), *Responsibility of International Organizations: Essays in Memory of Sir Ian Brownlie* (Leiden, Martinus Nijhoff, 2013)

Boot M, *Nullum Crimen Sine Lege and the Subject Matter Jurisdiction of the International Criminal Court: Genocide, Crimes against Humanity, War Crimes* (Antwerpen, Intersentia, 2002)

Borchard E, *The Diplomatic Protection of Citizens Abroad or the Law of International Claims* (New York, Banks Law Publishing, 1927)

Borelli S, 'Casting Light on the Legal Black Hole: International Law and Detentions Abroad in the "War on Terror"' (2005) 87 *IRRC* 39

——, 'Rendition, Torture and Intelligence Cooperation' in H Born, I Leigh and A Wills (eds), *International Intelligence Cooperation and Accountability* (Abingdon, Routledge, 2011)

Bos A, 'Crimes of State: In Need of Legal Rules?' in G Kreijen (ed), *State, Sovereignty, and International Governance* (Oxford, OUP, 2002)

Bourdieu P, *The Logic of Practice* (Cambridge, Polity Press, 1990)

Boutin B, 'Responsibility of the Netherlands for the Acts of Dutchbat in Nuhanović and Mustafić: The Continuous Quest for a Tangible Meaning for "Effective Control" in the Context of Peacekeeping' (2012) 25 *LJIL* 521

——, 'The Role of Control in Allocating International Responsibility in Collaborative Military Operations' (Amsterdam, University of Amsterdam, 2015)

Bowett D, *United Nations Forces: A Legal Study of United Nations Practice* (London, Stevens & Sons, 1964)

Bradlow D, 'Private Complaints and International Organizations: A Comparative Study of the Independent Inspection Mechanisms in International Institutions' (2005) 36 *Georgetown J Intl L* 403

Brehm M, 'The Arms Trade and States' Duty to Ensure Respect for Humanitarian and Human Rights Law' (2008) 12 *JCSL* 359

Brierly J, 'The Theory of Implied State Complicity in International Claims' (1928) 9 *British YBIL* 42

——, *The Basis of Obligation in International Law* (H Lauterpacht and CHM Waldock eds, Oxford, Clarendon Press, 1958)

Brollowski H, 'The Responsibility to Protect and Common Article 1 of the 1949 Geneva Conventions and Obligations of Third States' in J Hoffmann and A Nollkaemper (eds), *Responsibility to Protect: From Principle to Practice* (Amsterdam, Pallas, 2012)

Brölmann C, *The Institutional Veil in Public International Law: International Organisations and the Law of Treaties* (Oxford, Hart Publishing, 2007)

Brownlie I, *International Law and the Use of Force by States* (Oxford, Clarendon Press, 1963)

——, *Principles of Public International Law* (6th edn, Oxford, OUP, 2003)

——, 'Problems Concerning the Unity of International Law', *Le droit international à l'heure de sa codification: études en l'honneur de Roberto Ago*, vol 1 (Milano, Giuffrè, 1987)

——, 'State Responsibility and the International Court of Justice' in M Fitzmaurice and D Sarooshi (eds), *Issues of State Responsibility before International Judicial Institutions* (Oxford, Hart Publishing, 2004)

——, 'State Responsibility: The Problem of Delegation' in K Ginther et al (eds), *Völkerrecht zwischen normativem Anspruch und politischer Realität: Festschrift für Karl Zemanek zum 65. Geburtstag* (Berlin, Duncker & Humblot, 1994)

——, *System of the Law of Nations: State Responsibility Part 1* (Oxford, Clarendon Press, 1983)

——, 'The Responsibility of States for Acts of International Organizations' in M Ragazzi (ed), *International Responsibility Today: Essays in Memory of Oscar Schachter* (Leiden, Martinus Nijhoff, 2005)

Brunnée J, 'International Legal Accountability through the Lens of the Law of State Responsibility' (2005) 36 *Netherlands YBIL* 21

Brunnée J and Toope S, 'Persuasion and Enforcement: Explaining Compliance with International Law' (2002) 13 *Finnish YBIL* 273

Buira A, 'An Analysis of IMF Conditionality', *G-24 Discussion Paper Series* (2003)

Byers M, 'Helmut P Aust: Complicity and the Law of State Responsibility' (2012) 23 *EJIL* 586

Cahier P, 'Les caractéristiques de la nullité en droit international et tout particulièrement dans la Convention de Vienne de 1969 sur le droit des traités' (1972) 76 *RGDIP* 646

Cameron L and Everly R, 'Conceptualizing the Administration of Territory by International Actors' (2010) 21 *EJIL* 221

Cançado Trindade A, 'Complementarity between State Responsibility and Individual Responsibility for Grave Violations of Human Rights: The Crime of State Revisited' in M Ragazzi (ed), *International Responsibility Today: Essays in Memory of Oscar Schachter* (Leiden, Martinus Nijhoff, 2005)

Cannizzaro E, 'Beyond the Either/Or: Dual Attribution to the European Union and to the Member State for Breach of the ECHR' in MD Evans and P Koutrakos (eds), *The International Responsibility of the European Union: European and International Perspectives* (Oxford, Hart Publishing, 2013)

——, 'On the Special Consequences of a Serious Breach of Obligations Arising out of Peremptory Rules of International Law' in E Cannizzaro (ed), *The Present and Future of Jus Cogens* (Roma, Sapienza, 2015)

Caron D, 'The ILC Articles on State Responsibility: The Paradoxical Relationship Between Form and Authority' (2002) 96 *AJIL* 857

——, 'The Basis of Responsibility: Attribution and Other Substantive Rules' in RB Lillich and DB Magraw (eds), *The Iran-United States Claims Tribunal: Its Contribution to the Law of State Responsibility* (Irvington New York, Transnational, 1998)

Cassese A, 'On the Use of Criminal Law Notions in Determining State Responsibility for Genocide' (2007) 5 *JICJ* 875

——, 'The Nicaragua and Tadić Tests Revisited in Light of the ICJ Judgment on Genocide in Bosnia' (2007) 18 *EJIL* 649

——, *International Law* (2nd edn, Oxford, OUP, 2005)

Castellanos-Jankiewicz L, 'Causation and International State Responsibility' ACIL Research Paper SHARES Series (2012-05)

Cavaglieri A, 'Règles générales du droit de la paix' (1929) 26 *RCADI* 311

Cerone J, 'Re-Examining International Responsibility: Inter-State Complicity in the Context of Human Rights Violations' (2007) 14 *ILSA J Intl & Comp L* 525

Chadwick E, *Traditional Neutrality Revisited: Law, Theory and Case Studies* (The Hague, Kluwer, 2002)

Charney J, 'Third State Remedies in International Law' (1989) 10 *Michigan J Intl L* 57

Charpentier J, 'L'affaire du Rainbow Warrior: La sentence arbitrale du 30 avril 1990 (Nouvelle-Zélande C/ France) (1)' (1990) 36 *AFDI* 395

Chaumont C, 'L'ambivalence des concepts essentiels du droit international' in J Makarczyk (ed), *Essays in International Law in Honour of Judge Manfred Lachs* (The Hague, Martinus Nijhoff, 1984)

Cheng B, 'Custom: The Future of General State Practice in a Divided World' in RSJ MacDonald and DM Johnston (eds), *The Structure and Process of International*

Law: Essays in Legal Philosophy, Doctrine and Theory (The Hague, Martinus Nijhoff, 1983)

——, *General Principles of Law as Applied by International Courts and Tribunals* (Cambridge, CUP, 2006)

Chen Y, 'Attribution, Causation and Responsibility of International Organizations' in D Sarooshi (ed), *Remedies and Responsibility for the Actions of International Organizations* (Leiden, Martinus Nijhoff, 2014)

Chinkin C, 'A Critique of the Public/Private Dimension' (1999) 10 *EJIL* 387

——, 'The Continuing Occupation? Issues of Joint and Several Liability and Effective Control' in P Shiner and A Williams (eds), *The Iraq War and International Law* (Oxford, Hart Publishing, 2008)

——, *Third Parties in International Law* (Oxford, Clarendon Press, 1993)

Christakis T and Mollard-Bannelier K, 'Volenti non fit injuria? Les effets du consentement à l'intervention militaire' (2004) 50 *AFDI* 102

Christenson G, 'Attributing Acts of Omission to the State' (1991) 12 *Michigan J Intl L* 312

——, 'The Doctrine of Attribution in State Responsibility' in RB Lillich (ed), *International Law of State Responsibility for Injuries to Aliens* (Charlottesville, University Press of Virginia, 1983)

Clapham A, 'Human Rights Obligations of Non-State Actors in Conflict Situations' (2006) 88 *IRRC* 491

——, 'Extending International Criminal Law beyond the Individual to Corporations and Armed Opposition Groups' (2008) 6 *JICJ* 899

——, *Human Rights Obligations of Non-State Actors* (Oxford, OUP, 2006)

——, 'Issues of Complexity, Complicity and Complementarity: From the Nuremberg Trials to the Dawn of the New International Criminal Court' in P Sands (ed), *From Nuremberg to The Hague: The Future of International Criminal Justice* (Cambridge, CUP, 2003)

——, 'On Complicity' in M Henzelin and R Roth (eds), *Le droit pénal à l'épreuve de l'internationalisation* (Paris, LGDJ, 2002)

——, 'The Subject of Subjects and the Attribution of Attribution' in L Boisson de Chazournes and MG Kohen (eds), *International Law and the Quest for its Implementation, Liber Amicorum Vera Gowlland-Debbas* (Leiden, Martinus Nijhoff, 2010)

Clapham A and Jerbi S, 'Categories of Corporate Complicity in Human Rights Abuses' (2000) 24 *Hastings Intl & Comp LR* 339

Clark R, 'Obligations of Third States in the Face of Illegality—Ruminations Inspired by the Weeramantry Dissent in the Case Concerning East Timor' in A Anghie and G Sturgess (eds), *Legal Visions of the 21st Century: Essays in Honour of Judge Christopher Weeramantry* (The Hague, Kluwer, 1998)

Cohn M, 'La théorie de la responsabilité internationale' (1939) 68 *RCADI* 209

Combacau J, 'Le droit international: bric-à-brac ou système?' (1986) 31 *Archives de philosophie de droit* 85

Combacau J and Alland D, 'Primary and Secondary Rules in the Law of State Responsibility: Categorizing International Obligations' (1985) 16 *Netherlands YBIL* 81

Condorelli L, 'L'imputation à l'État d'un fait internationalement illicite: Solutions classiques et nouvelles tendances' (1984) 189 *RCADI* 9

——, 'The Imputability to States of Acts of International Terrorism' (1989) 19 *Israel YB Human Rights* 233
——, 'Le statut des forces de l'ONU et le droit international humanitaire' (1995) 78 *RDI* 881
Condorelli L and Kress C, 'The Rules of Attribution: General Considerations' in J Crawford et al (eds), *The Law of International Responsibility* (Oxford, OUP, 2010)
Corten O, 'L'arrêt rendu par la CIJ dans l'affaire du crime de génocide (Bosnie-Herzégovine c. Serbie): vers un assouplissement des conditions permettant d'engager la responsabilité d'un État pour génocide?' (2007) 53 *AFDI* 249
——, 'La "complicité" dans le droit de la responsabilité internationale: un concept inutile?' (2011) 58 *AFDI* 57
——, 'Quels droits et quels devoirs pour les États tiers? Les effets juridiques d'une assistance à un acte d'agression' in K Bannelier, T Christakis and O Corten (eds), *L'intervention en Irak et le droit international* (Paris, Pedone, 2004)
——, *The Law Against War: The Prohibition on the Use of Force in Contemporary International Law* (Oxford, Hart Publishing, 2012)
——, 'The Obligation of Cessation' in J Crawford et al (eds), *The Law of International Responsibility* (Oxford, OUP, 2010)
Corten O and Dubuisson F, 'Opération "Liberté Immuable": Une extension abusive du concept de légitime défense' (2002) 1 *RGDIP* 51
Corten O and Klein P, 'The Limits of Complicity as a Ground for Responsibility: Lessons Learned from the Corfu Channel Case' in K Bannelier, T Christakis and S Heathcote (eds), *The ICJ and the Evolution of International Law: The Enduring Impact of the Corfu Channel Case* (London, Routledge, 2012)
Cortés Martin J, 'The Responsibility of Members Due to Wrongful Acts of International Organizations' (2013) 12 *Chinese J Intl L* 679
——, *Las organizaciones internacionales: codificación y desarrollo progresivo de su responsabilidad internacional* (Sevilla, Instituto Andaluz de Administración Pública, 2008)
Cottereau G, 'Système juridique et notion de responsabilité' in SFDI (ed), *La responsabilité dans le système international: Colloque du Mans* (Paris, Pedone, 1991)
Craven M, 'Unity, Diversity and the Fragmentation of International Law' (2003) 14 *Finnish YBIL* 3
Crawford J, 'The Criteria for Statehood in International Law' (1978) 48 *British YBIL* 93
——, 'Revising the Draft Articles on State Responsibility' (1999) 10 *EJIL* 435
——, 'The ILC's Articles on Responsibility of States for Internationally Wrongful Acts: A Retrospect' (2002) 96 *AJIL* 874
——, 'Third Party Obligations with Respect to Israeli Settlements in the Occupied Palestinian Territories' (2012) www.tuc.org.uk/sites/default/files/tucfiles/LegalOpinionIsraeliSettlements.pdf
——, 'International Crimes of States' in J Crawford et al (eds), *The Law of International Responsibility* (Oxford, OUP, 2010)
——, 'Overview of Part Three of the Articles on State Responsibility' in J Crawford et al (eds), *The Law of International Responsibility* (Oxford, OUP, 2010)
——, 'Sovereignty as a Legal Value' in J Crawford and M Koskenniemi (eds), *The Cambridge Companion to International Law* (Cambridge, CUP, 2012)

——, *State Responsibility: The General Part* (Cambridge, CUP, 2013)

——, *The International Law Commission's Articles on State Responsibility: Introduction, Text and Commentaries* (Cambridge, CUP, 2002)

——, 'The System of International Responsibility' in J Crawford et al (eds), *The Law of International Responsibility* (Oxford, OUP, 2010)

Crawford J, Grant T and Messineo F, 'Towards an International Law of Responsibility: Early Doctrine' in L Boisson de Chazournes and MG Kohen (eds), *International Law and the Quest for its Implementation, Liber Amicorum Vera Gowlland-Debbas* (Leiden, Martinus Nijhoff, 2010)

Crawford J and Olleson S, 'The Exception of Non-Performance: Links between the Law of Treaties and the Law of State Responsibility' (2000) 21 *Australian YBIL* 55

——, 'The Continuing Debate on a UN Convention on State Responsibility' (2008) 54 *ICLQ* 959

Cryer R et al, *An Introduction to International Criminal Law and Procedure*, vol 2 (Cambridge, CUP, 2010)

Dannenbaum T, 'Translating the Standard of Effective Control into a System of Effective Accountability: How Liability Should Be Apportioned for Violations of Human Rights by Member State Troop Contingents Serving as United Nations Peacekeepers' (2010) 51 *Harvard Intl LJ* 113

——, 'Dutch Supreme Court Affirms That Dutchbat Acted Unlawfully in Srebrenica' www.ejiltalk.org/dutch-supreme-court-affirms-that-dutchbat-acted-unlawfully-in-srebrenica/

Dann P, 'Accountability in Development Aid Law: The World Bank, UNDP and Emerging Structures of Transnational Oversight' (2006) 44 *AVR* 381

Darcy S, 'Assistance, Direction and Control: Untangling International Judicial Opinion on Individual and State Responsibility for War Crimes by Non-State Actors' (2014) 96 *IRRC* 243

d'Argent P, *Les réparations de guerre en droit international public: La responsabilité internationale des États à l'épreuve de la guerre* (Bruxelles, Bruylant, 2002)

——, 'Reparation and Compliance' in K Bannelier, T Christakis and S Heathcote (eds), *The ICJ and the Evolution of International Law: The Enduring Impact of the Corfu Channel Case* (London, Routledge, 2012)

——, 'Reparation, Cessation, Assurances and Guarantees of Non-Repetition' in A Nollkaemper and I Plakokefalos (eds), *Principles of Shared Responsibility in International Law: An Appraisal of the State of the Art* (Cambridge, CUP, 2014)

d'Aspremont J, 'Abuse of the Legal Personality of International Organizations and the Responsibility of Member States' (2007) 4 *IOLR* 91

——, 'Rebellion and State Responsibility: Wrongdoing by Democratically Elected Insurgents' (2009) 58 *ICLQ* 427

——, 'The Articles on the Responsibility of International Organizations: Magnifying the Fissures in the Law of International Responsibility' (2012) 9 *IOLR* 15

——, 'Non-State Actors in International Law: Oscillating between Concepts and Dynamics' in J d'Aspremont (ed), *Participants in the International Legal System: Multiple Perspectives on Non-State Actors in International Law* (London, Routledge, 2013)

Daudet Y, 'Travaux de La Commission Du Droit International' (1994) 40 *AFDI* 575

Daugirdas K, 'Reputation and the Responsibility of International Organizations' (2014) 25 *EJIL* 991

David E, 'Art 34 (1969)' in O Corten and P Klein (eds), *The Vienna Conventions on the Law of Treaties: The Commentary* (Oxford, OUP, 2011)

——, 'Primary and Secondary Rules' in J Crawford et al (eds), *The Law of International Responsibility* (Oxford, OUP, 2010)

——, *Principes de droit des conflits armés* (4th edn, Bruxelles, Bruylant, 2008)

Dawidowicz M, 'Public Law Enforcement without Public Law Safeguards? An Analysis of State Practice on Third-Party Countermeasures and Their Relationship to the UN Security Council' (2007) 77 *British YBIL* 333

——, 'Third-Party Countermeasures: Observations on a Controversial Concept' in C Chinkin and F Baetens (eds), *Sovereignty, Statehood and State Responsibility: Essays in Honour of James Crawford* (Cambridge, CUP, 2015)

Dawson G and Boynton R, 'Reconciling Complicity in Genocide and Aiding and Abetting Genocide in the Jurisprudence of the United Nations Ad Hoc Tribunals' (2008) 21 *Harvard Human Rights J* 241

de Aréchaga E, 'International Responsibility' in M Sørensen (ed), *Manual of Public International Law* (London, MacMillan, 1968)

de Brabandere E, 'Immunity of International Organizations in Post-Conflict International Administrations' (2010) 7 *IOLR* 79

Decencière-Ferrandière A, 'La responsabilité internationale des États' (Thèse Doctorat, Paris, Université de Paris, 1925)

de Frouville O, 'Attribution of Conduct to the State: Private Individuals' in J Crawford et al (eds), *The Law of International Responsibility* (Oxford, OUP, 2010)

de Hoogh A, 'Articles 4 and 8 of the 2001 ILC Articles on State Responsibility, the Tadić Case and Attribution of Acts of Bosnian Serb Authorities to the Federal Republic of Yugoslavia' (2002) 72 *British YBIL* 255

——, *Obligations Erga Omnes and International Crimes* (The Hague, Kluwer, 1996)

Delcourt B, 'Un seul État vous manque … L'application de la jurisprudence de l'Or monétaire à l'affaire du Timor oriental' (1996) 1 *RBDI* 191

Deman C, 'La cessation de l'acte illicite' (1990) 2 *RBDI* 477

Denters E, *Law and Policy of IMF Conditionality* (The Hague, Kluwer, 1996)

de Vattel E, *Le droit des gens ou principes de la loi naturelle [The Law of Nations or Principles of Natural Law]* (CG Fenwick tr, Washington DC, Carnegie, 1916)

de Visscher C, *La responsabilité des États: cours professé à l'Académie de droit international de la Haye*, vol 5 (The Hague, Brill, 1924)

——, *Théories et réalités en droit international public* (2nd edn, Paris, Pedone, 1955)

de Visscher P, 'Observations sur le fondement et la mise-en-oeuvre du principe de la responsabilité de l'organisation des Nations Unies' (1963) 40 *RDIDC* 165

——, 'Les conditions d'application des lois de la guerre aux opérations militaires des Nations Unies' (1971) 54 *AIDI* 1

de Vitoria F, *De Indis et de Jure Belli Relectiones [On the Indians and on the Law of War]* (JP Bate tr, Washington DC, Carnegie, 1917)

de Wet E, 'Human Rights Limitations to Economic Enforcement Measures under Article 41 of the United Nations Charter and the Iraqi Sanctions Regime' (2001) 14 *LJIL* 277

——, 'Holding International Institutions Accountable: The Complementary Role of Non-Judicial Oversight Mechanisms and Judicial Review' in A von Bogdandy et al (eds), *The Exercise of Public Authority by International Institutions*, vol 210 (Heidelberg, Springer, 2010)

Diggelman O, 'Fault in the Law of State Responsibility—Pragmatism Ad Infinitum?' (2006) 49 *German YBIL* 293

Dinstein Y, 'Computer Network Attacks and Self Defence' in M Schmitt and B O'Donnell (eds), *Computer Network Attacks and International Law* (Oxford, Hart Publishing, 2004)

——, *War, Aggression and Self-Defence* (4th edn, Cambridge, CUP, 2005)

DiPerna T, 'Small Arms and Light Weapons: Complicity With A View Toward Extended State Responsibility' (2008) 20 *Florida J Intl L* 25

Distefano G, 'Fait continu, fait composé et fait complexe dans le droit de la responsabilité' (2006) 52 *AFDI* 1

Dominicé C, 'Attribution of Conduct to Multiple States and the Implication of a State in the Act of Another State' in J Crawford et al (eds), *The Law of International Responsibility* (Oxford, OUP, 2010)

Doswald-Beck L and Henckaerts J-M, *Customary International Humanitarian Law*, vol 1(Cambridge, CUP, 2005)

Dubber M, 'Criminalizing Complicity: A Comparative Analysis' (2007) 5 *JICJ* 977

Dubin L, 'Les garanties de non-répétition à l'aune des affaires LaGrand et Avena: La révolution n'aura plus lieu' (2005) 4 *RGDIP* 859

Dupuy P-M, 'Observations sur la pratique récente des sanctions de l'illicite' (1983) 87 *RGDIP* 505

——, 'Le fait générateur de la responsabilité internationale des États' (1984) 188 *RCADI* 9

——, 'Faute de l'État et fait internationalement illicite' (1987) 5 *Revue Droits* 51

——, 'Dionisio Anzilotti and the Law of International Responsibility of States' (1992) 3 *EJIL* 139

——, 'Droit des traités, codification et responsabilité internationale' (1997) 43 *AFDI* 7

——, 'Reviewing the Difficulties of Codification: On Ago's Classification of Obligations of Means and Obligations of Result in Relation to State Responsibility' (1999) 10 *EJIL* 371

——, 'A General Stocktaking of the Connections between the Multilateral Dimension of Obligations and Codification of the Law of Responsibility' (2002) 13 *EJIL* 1053

——, 'L'unité de l'ordre juridique international' (2002) 297 *RCADI* 9

——, 'Quarante ans de codification du droit de la responsabilité internationale des États: un bilan' (2003) 2 *RGDIP* 305

——, 'Crime sans châtiment ou mission accomplie?' (2007) 111 *RGDIP* 243

——, 'Back to the Future of a Multilateral Dimension of the Law of State Responsibility for Breaches of "Obligations Owed to the International Community as a Whole"' (2012) 23 *EJIL* 1059

——, 'International Criminal Responsibility of the Individual and International Responsibility of the State' in A Cassese, P Gaeta and JRWD Jones (eds), *The Rome Statute of the International Criminal Court: A Commentary* (Oxford, OUP, 2002)

—— (ed), *Obligations multilatérales, droit impératif et responsabilité internationale des États* (Paris, Pedone, 2003)

——, 'Responsabilité et légalité' in SFDI (ed), *La responsabilité dans le système international: Colloque du Mans* (Paris, Pedone, 1991)

——, 'State Sponsors of Terrorism: Issues of International Responsibility' in A Bianchi (ed), *Enforcing International Law Norms Against Terrorism* (Oxford, Hart Publishing, 2004)

——, 'The Deficiencies of the Law of State Responsibility Relating to Breaches of "Obligations Owed to the International Community as a Whole": Suggestions for Avoiding the Obsolescence of Aggravated Responsibility' in A Cassese (ed), *Realizing Utopia: The Future of International Law* (Oxford, OUP, 2012)

Dupuy R-J, 'Images de Georges Scelle' (1990) 1 *EJIL* 235

——, 'Coutume sage et coutume sauvage' in S Bastid (ed), *Mélanges offerts à Charles Rousseau* (Paris, Pedone, 1974)

——, 'La codification du droit international a-t-elle encore un intérêt à l'aube du troisième millénaire?', *Droit international à l'heure de sa codification: Études en l'honneur de Roberto Ago*, vol 1 (Milano, Giuffrè, 1987)

Durkheim É, *The Division of Labour in Society* (New York, Free Press, 1964)

Duttweiler M, 'Liability for Omission in International Criminal Law' (2006) 6 *ICLR* 1

Duxbury A, *The Participation of States in International Organisations* (Cambridge, CUP, 2011)

Eagleton C, 'International Organization and the Law of Responsibility' (1950) 76 *RCADI* 319

——, *The Responsibility of States in International Law* (New York, New York University Press, 1928)

Eboe-Osuji C, '"Complicity in Genocide" versus "Aiding and Abetting Genocide": Construing the Difference in the ICTR and ICTY Statutes' (2005) 3 *JICJ* 56

Eeckhout P, 'The EU and Its Member States in the WTO—Issues of Responsibility' in L Bartels and F Ortino (eds), *Regional Trade Agreements and the WTO Legal System* (New York, OUP, 2006)

Eldar O, 'Reform of IMF Conditionality: A Proposal for Self-Imposed Conditionality' (2005) 8 *JIEL* 509

Epiney A, 'Nachbarrechtliche Pflichten im internationalen Wasserrecht und Implikationen von Drittstaaten' (2001) 39 *AVR* 1

——, *Die völkerrechtliche Verantwortlichkeit von Staaten für rechtswidriges Verhalten im Zusammenhang mit Aktionen Privater* (Baden-Baden, Nomos, 1992)

Escarameia P, *O direito internacional público nos princípios do século XXI* (Lisboa, Almedina, 2003)

Eser A, 'Individual Criminal Responsibility (Article 25)' in A Cassese, P Gaeta and JRWD Jones (eds), *The Rome Statute of the International Criminal Court: A Commentary*, vol 1 (Oxford, OUP, 2002)

European Group on Tort Law, *Principles of European Tort Law: Text and Commentary* (Vienna, Springer, 2005)

Farhang C, 'The Notion of Consent in Part One of the Draft Articles on State Responsibility' (2014) 27 *LJIL* 55

Farrall J, *United Nations Sanctions and the Rule of Law* (Cambridge, CUP, 2007)

Feinäugle C, 'The UN Security Council Al-Qaida and Taliban Sanctions Committee: Emerging Principles of International Law for the Protection of Individuals?' (2008) 9 *German LJ* 1513

Felder A, *Die Beihilfe im Recht der völkerrechtlichen Staatenverantwortlichkeit* (Zürich, Schulthess, 2007)

Finnin S, 'Mental Elements under Article 30 of the Rome Statute of the International Criminal Court: A Comparative Analysis' (2012) 61 *ICLQ* 325

Fleck D, 'Individual and State Responsibility for Intelligence Gathering' (2007) 28 *Michigan J Intl L* 687

Focarelli C, 'Denying Foreign State Immunity for Commission of International Crimes: The Ferrini Decision' (2008) 54 *ICLQ* 951

——, 'Common Article 1 of the 1949 Geneva Conventions: A Soap Bubble?' (2010) 21 *EJIL* 125

Fontanelli F, 'The Invocation of the Exception of Non-Performance, A Case-Study on the Role and Application of General Principles of International Law of Contractual Origin' (2012) 1 *Cambridge J Intl & Comp L* 119

Forlati S, 'Violazione dell'obbligo di prevenire il genocidio e riparazione nell'affare Bosnia-Erzegovina c. Serbia' (2007) 90 *RDI* 425

——, 'The Legal Obligation to Prevent Genocide: Bosnia v Serbia and Beyond' (2011) 31 *Polish YBIL* 189

——, 'Reactions to Non-Performance of Treaties in International Law' (2012) 25 *LJIL* 759

Forteau M, 'La levée et la suspension des sanctions internationales' (2005) 51 *AFDI* 57

——, *Droit de la sécurité collective et droit de la responsabilité internationale* (Paris, Pedone, 2006)

Fredman S, 'US Trade Sanctions against Uganda: Legality under International Law' (1979) 11 *Law and Policy International Business* 1149

Friedmann W, 'The Growth of State Control over the Individual, and Its Effect upon the Rules of International State Responsibility' (1938) 19 *British YBIL* 118

——, *The Changing Structure of International Law* (London, Stevens & Sons, 1964)

Frulli M, 'Un passo avanti e due indietro: responsabilità individuale e responsabilità statale nella sentenza della Corte internazionale di giustizia nel caso Bosnia-Erzegovina c Serbia' (2007) 3 *Diritti umani e diritto internazionale* 579

Fry J, 'Coercion, Causation, and the Fictional Elements of Indirect State Responsibility' (2007) 40 *Vanderbilt J Transnatl L* 611

Gaeta P, 'Genocide d'Etat et responsabilité pénale individuelle' (2007) 111 *RGDIP* 273

——, 'On What Conditions Can a State Be Held Responsible for Genocide?' (2007) 18 *EJIL* 631

Gaja G, 'Jus Cogens Beyond the Vienna Convention' (1981) 172 *RCADI* 271

——, 'Primary and Secondary Rules in the International Law on State Responsibility' (2014) 97 *RDI* 981

——, 'Do States Have a Duty to Ensure Compliance with Obligations Erga Omnes by Other States?' in M Ragazzi (ed), *International Responsibility Today: Essays in Memory of Oscar Schachter* (Leiden, Martinus Nijhoff, 2005)

——, 'States Having an Interest in Compliance with the Obligation Breached' in J Crawford et al (eds), *The Law of International Responsibility* (Oxford, OUP, 2010)

García-Mora M, *International Responsibility for Hostile Acts of Private Persons against Foreign States* (The Hague, Martinus Nijhoff, 1962)

Gärditz K, 'Bridge of Varvarin' (2014) 108 *AJIL* 86

Garnett R and Clarke P, 'Cyberterrorism: A New Challenge for International Law' in A Bianchi (ed), *Enforcing International Law Norms Against Terrorism* (Oxford, Hart Publishing, 2004)

Gattini A, 'La notion de la faute à la lumière du projet de convention de la Commission du droit international sur la responsabilité internationale' (1992) 3 *EJIL* 253

——, 'Smoking/No Smoking: Some Remarks on the Current Place of the Fault in the Draft Articles on State Responsibility' (1999) 10 *EJIL* 397

——, 'A Return Ticket to "Communitarisme", Please' (2002) 13 *EJIL* 1181

——, 'Breach of the Obligation to Prevent and Reparation Thereof in the ICJ's Genocide Judgment' (2007) 18 *EJIL* 695

——, 'Evidentiary Issues in the ICJ's Genocide Judgment' (2007) 5 *JICJ* 889

——, *Zufall und force majeure in System der Staatenverantwortlichkeit anhand der ILC-Kodifikationsarbeit* (Berlin, Duncker & Humboldt, 1991)

Gentili A, *De Iure Belli Libri Tres [Three Books on the Law of War]* (JC Rolfe tr, Oxford, Clarendon Press, 1933)

——, *De Legationibus Libri Tres [Three Books on Embassies]* (GJ Laing tr, Oxford, Clarendon Press, 1924)

Geslin A, 'Réflexions sur la répartition de la responsabilité entre l'organisation internationale et ses états membres' (2005) 109 *RGDIP* 539

Gianelli A, 'Le conseguenze delle gravi violazioni di obblighi posti da norme imperative tra norme primarie e norme secondarie' in M Spinedi, A Gianelli and ML Alaimo (eds), *La codificazione della responsabilità internazionale degli stati alla prova dei fatti: Problemi e spunti di riflessione* (Milano, Giuffrè, 2006)

Gibney M, 'Genocide and State Responsibility' (2007) 7 *HRLR* 760

Goodwin-Gill G, 'State Responsibility and the "Good Faith" Obligation in International Law' in M Fitzmaurice and D Sarooshi (eds), *Issues of State Responsibility before International Judicial Institutions* (Oxford, Hart Publishing, 2004)

Gowlland-Debbas V, 'The Security Council and Issues of Responsibility under International Law' (2011) 353 *RCADI* 185

——, *Collective Responses to Illegal Acts in International Law: United Nations Action in the Question of Southern Rhodesia* (Dordrecht, Martinus Nijhoff, 1990)

Graefrath B, 'Responsibility and Damages Caused: Relationship between Responsibility and Damages' (1984) 185 *RCADI* 9

——, 'Complicity in the Law of International Responsibility' (1996) 2 *RBDI* 370

Graefrath B, Oeser E and Steiniger P, *Völkerrechtliche Verantwortlichkeit der Staaten* (Berlin, Staatsverlag der DDR, 1977)

Gray C, *International Law and the Use of Force* (3rd edn, Oxford, OUP, 2008)

——, *Judicial Remedies in International Law* (Oxford, Clarendon Press, 1987)

Grewe W, *Epochen der Völkerrechtsgeschichte* (Baden-Baden, Nomos, 1984)

Groome D, 'Adjudicating Genocide: Is the International Court of Justice Capable of Judging State Criminal Responsibility?' (2008) 31 *Fordham Intl LJ* 911

Grotius H, *De Jure Belli Ac Pacis [The Rights of War and Peace]* (FW Kelsey tr, Oxford, Clarendon Press, 1925)

Gualtieri A, 'The Environmental Accountability of the World Bank to Non-State Actors: Insights from the Inspection Panel' (2002) 72 *British YBIL* 213

Guggenheim P, 'La validité et la nullité des actes juridiques internationaux' (1949) 74 *RCADI* 191

——, *Traité de droit international public: avec mention de la pratique internationale et suisse*, vol 1 (2nd edn, Genève, Georg et Cié, 1967)

Guillaume M, 'La réparation des dommages causés par les contingents français en ex-Yougoslavie et en Albanie' (1997) 43 *AFDI* 151

Gutiérrez Espada C, *El hecho ilícito internacional* (Madrid, Dykinson, 2005)

Hakimi M, 'State Bystander Responsibility' (2010) 21 *EJIL* 341

Hammarskjöld K, *La neutralité en général*, vol 3 (The Hague, Martinus Nijhoff, 1924)

Hampson F, '"States" Military Operations Authorized by the United Nations and International Humanitarian Law' in L Condorelli, AM La Rosa and S Scherrer (eds), *The United Nations and International Humanitarian Law* (Paris, Pedone, 1996)

Hart H, *The Concept of Law* (2nd edn, Oxford, OUP, 1994)

Hart H and Honoré T, *Causation in the Law* (2nd edn, Oxford, Clarendon Press, 1985)

Hartwig M, *Die Haftung der Mitgliedstaaten für Internationale Organisationen* (Berlin, Springer, 1993)

Hasan S, 'The Role of Complicity in International Responsibility, with Special Attention to State Responsibility' (PhD Thesis, Geneva, Graduate Institute, 2012)

Heathcote S, 'State Omissions and Due Diligence: Aspects of Fault, Damage and Contribution to Injury in the Law of State Responsibility' in K Bannelier, T Christakis and S Heathcote (eds), *The ICJ and the Evolution of International Law: The Enduring Impact of the Corfu Channel Case* (London, Routledge, 2012)

Hébié M, 'L'attribution aux États des actes des sociétés militaires et de leurs employés à la lumière de l'article 4 du projet d'articles sur la responsabilité des États de 2001', *Select Proceedings of the European Society of International Law*, vol 2 (Oxford, Hart Publishing, 2008)

Heijer M den, 'Europe Beyond Its Borders: Refugee and Human Rights Protection in Extraterritorial Immigration Control' in B Ryan and V Mitsilegas (eds), *Extraterritorial Immigration Control*

Heliskoski J, *Mixed Agreements as a Technique for Organizing the International Relations of the European Community and Its Member States* (The Hague, Kluwer, 2001)

Henkin L, 'Force, Intervention and Neutrality in Contemporary International Law' (1963) 57 *ASIL Proceedings* 147

Henriot J, 'Note sur la date et le sens de l'apparition du mot 'responsabilité' (1977) 22 *Archives de philosophie de droit* 59

Hessbruegge J, 'The Historical Development of the Doctrines of Attribution and Due Diligence in International Law' (2004) 36 *NYU J Intl L & Pol* 265

Higgins R, 'Aspects of the Case Concerning the Barcelona Traction, Light and Power Company, Ltd' (1970) 11 *Virginia J Intl L* 327

——, 'The Legal Consequences for Member States of the Non-Fulfilment by International Organizations of Their Obligations towards Third Parties' (1995) 66 *AIDI* 251

——, *Problems and Process: International Law and How We Use It* (Oxford, Clarendon Press, 1994)

Hirsch M, *The Responsibility of International Organizations Toward Third Parties: Some Basic Principles* (Dordrecht, Martinus Nijhoff, 1995)

Hoffmann J and Nollkaemper A (eds), *Responsibility to Protect From Principle to Practice* (Amsterdam, Pallas, 2012)

Hoffmeister F, 'Litigating against the European Union and Its Member States—Who Responds under the ILC's Draft Articles on International Responsibility of International Organizations?' (2010) 21 *EJIL* 723

Hofmann R, 'Zur Unterscheidung Verbrechen und Delikt im Bereich der Staatenverantwortlichkeit' (1985) 45 *ZaöRV* 195

Hoijer O, *La responsabilité internationale des États en matière d'actes législatifs* (Paris, Les Éditions Internationales, 1930)

Hoppe C, 'Passing the Buck: State Responsibility for Private Military Companies' (2008) 19 *EJIL* 989

——, 'Positive Human Rights Obligations of the Hiring State in Connection with the Provision of Coercive Services by a Private Military and Security Company' [2009] EUI Working Paper AEL 2009/19

Hutchinson D, 'Solidarity and Breaches of Multilateral Treaties' (1988) 59 *British YBIL* 151

Imseis A, 'Critical Reflections on the International Humanitarian Law Aspects of the ICJ Wall Advisory Opinion' (2005) 99 *AJIL* 102

International Commission of Jurists, 'Corporate Complicity & Legal Accountability' (2008)

Iovane M, *La riparazione nella teoria e nella prassi dell'illecito internazionale* (Milano, Giuffrè, 1990)

Jackson M, *Complicity in International Law* (Oxford, OUP, 2015)

Jenks C, 'Due Process of Law in International Organizations' (1965) 19 *International Organization* 163

Jennings R, 'Judicial Legislation in International Law' (1938) 26 *Kentucky LJ* 122

——, 'Universal International Law in a Multicultural World', *International Law and the Grotian Heritage* (The Hague, TMC Asser, 1985)

Jiménez de Aréchaga E and Tanzi A, 'International State Responsibility' in M Bedjaoui (ed), *International Law: Achievements and Prospects* (Paris, UNESCO, 1991)

Jinks D, 'State Responsibility for the Acts of Private Armed Groups' (2003) 4 *Chicago J Intl L* 83

Jørgensen N, 'State Responsibility for Aiding or Assisting International Crimes in the Context of the Arms Trade Treaty' (2014) 108 *AJIL* 722

——, 'The Obligation of Cooperation' in J Crawford et al (eds), *The Law of International Responsibility* (Oxford, OUP, 2010)

——, 'The Obligation of Non-Assistance to the Responsible State' in J Crawford et al (eds), *The Law of International Responsibility* (Oxford, OUP, 2010)

——, *The Responsibility of States for International Crimes* (Oxford, OUP, 2003)

Kalshoven F, 'The Undertaking to Respect and Ensure Respect in All Circumstances: From Tiny Seed to Ripening Fruit' (1999) 2 *YBIHL* 3

Katselli E, 'Countermeasures by Non-Injured States in the Law on State Responsibility' [2005] *ESIL Proceedings* 1

Kawasaki K, 'The Content and Implementation of the International Responsibility of States: Some Remarks on the Draft Articles on State Responsibility Adopted by the ILC's Drafting Committee in 2000' (2001) 29 *Hitotsubashi JL & Pol* 25

Kelsen H, 'The Draft Declaration on Rights and Duties of States—Critical Remarks' (1950) 44 *AJIL* 259

——, 'Théorie du droit international public' (1953) 84 *RCADI* 5

Kerbat Y, 'Interaction between the Forms of Reparation' in J Crawford et al (eds), *The Law of International Responsibility* (Oxford, OUP, 2010)

Kessler B, 'The Duty to "Ensure Respect" under Common Article 1 of the Geneva Conventions: Its Implications on International and Non-International Armed Conflicts' (2001) 44 *German YBIL* 489

King H, 'The Extraterritorial Human Rights Obligations of States' (2009) 9 *HRLR* 521

Kingsbury B, 'Sovereignty and Inequality' (1998) 9 *EJIL* 599

Kiss C, *Répertoire de la pratique française en matière de droit international public*, vol 3 (Paris, Centre national de la recherche scientifique, 1962–72)

Klabbers J, *An Introduction to International Institutional Law* (Cambridge, CUP, 2002)

Klein E, 'Beihilfe zum Völkerrechtsdelikt' in I von Münch (ed), *Staatsrecht, Völkerrecht, Europarecht: Festschrift für Hans-Jürgen Schlochauer zum 75. Geburtstag am 28. März 1981* (Berlin, Walter de Gruyter, 1981)

Klein F, *Die Mittelbare Haftung im Völkerrecht: Die Haftung eines Völkerrechtssubjektes für das völkerrechtswidrige Verhalten eines anderen Völkerrechtssubjektes* (Frankfurt am Main, Klostermann, 1941)

Klein N, *Maritime Security and the Law of the Sea* (Oxford, OUP, 2011)

Klein P, 'Responsibility for Serious Breaches of Obligations Deriving from Peremptory Norms of International Law and United Nations Law' (2002) 13 *EJIL* 1241

——, 'Responsabilité pour les faits commis dans le cadre d'opérations de paix et étendue du pouvoir de contrôle de la Cour européenne des droits de l'homme: quelques considérations critiques sur l'arrêt Behrami et Saramati' (2007) 53 *AFDI* 43

——, *La responsabilité des organisations internationales dans les ordres juridiques internes et en droit des gens* (Bruxelles, Bruylant, 1998)

——, 'The Attribution of Acts of International Organizations' in J Crawford et al (eds), *The Law of International Responsibility* (Oxford, OUP, 2010)

Kok E, 'The Principle of Complicity under International Law—Its Application to States and Individuals in Cases Involving Genocide, Crimes against Humanity and War Crimes' in L van den Herik and C Stahn (eds), *The Diversification and Fragmentation of International Criminal Law* (Leiden, Martinus Nijhoff, 2012)

Kolb R, *An Introduction to the Law of United Nations* (Oxford, Hart Publishing, 2010)

——, *La bonne foi en droit international public: Contribution à l'étude des principes généraux de droit* (Paris, PUF, 2000)

Kolb R, Porretto G and Vité S, *L'application du droit international humanitaire et des droits de l'homme aux organisations internationales—Forces de paix et administrations civiles transitoires* (2nd edn, Bruxelles, Bruylant, 2005)

Kolliopoulos A, *La Commission d'indemnisation des Nations Unies et le droit de la responsabilité internationale* (Paris, LGDJ, 2001)

Kondoch B, 'The Responsibility of Peacekeepers, Their Sending States, and International Organizations' in TD Gill and D Fleck (eds), *The Handbook of the International Law of Military Operations* (Oxford, OUP, 2010)

Koskenniemi M, 'Solidarity Measures: State Responsibility as a New International Order?' (2002) 72 *British YBIL* 337

——, 'Doctrines of State Responsibility' in J Crawford et al (eds), *The Law of International Responsibility* (Oxford, OUP, 2010)

——, *From Apology to Utopia* (Cambridge, CUP, 2005)

——, *The Gentle Civilizer of Nations* (Cambridge, CUP, 2004)
Kreps S, 'The United Nations-African Union Mission in Darfur: Implications and Prospects for Success' (2007) 4 *African Security Review* 66
Kress C, 'L'organe de facto en droit international public. Réflexions sur l'imputation à l'État de l'acte d'un particulier à la lumière des développements récents' (2001) 105 *RGDIP* 93
Krutzsch W and Trapp R (eds), *The Chemical Weapons Convention: A Commentary* (Oxford, OUP, 2014)
Kuijper P and Paasivirta E, 'EU International Responsibility and Its Attribution' in MD Evans and P Koutrakos (eds), *The International Responsibility of the European Union: European and International Perspectives* (Oxford, Hart Publishing, 2013)
Kutz C, *Complicity: Ethics and Law for a Collective Age* (Cambridge, CUP, 2000)
Lagerwall A, 'L'administration du territoire Irakien: Un exemple de reconnaissance et d'aide au maintien d'une occupation résultant d'un acte d'agression' (2006) 39 *RBDI* 249
——, 'The Duty Not to Recognise as Lawful a Situation Created by the Illegal Use of Force: From Kosovo to Abkhazia and South Ossetia' in M Szabó (ed), *State Responsibility and the Law of Treaties* (The Hague, Eleven, 2010)
Lagrange P, 'Responsabilité des États pour actes accomplis en application du chapitre VII de la Charte des Nations Unies' (2008) 1 *RGDIP* 85
Laly-Chevalier C, 'Art 35 (1969)' in O Corten and E Klein (eds), *The Vienna Conventions on the Law of Treaties: The Commentary* (Oxford, OUP, 2011)
Lanovoy V, 'Complicity in an Internationally Wrongful Act' in A Nollkaemper and I Plakokefalos (eds), *Principles of Shared Responsibility in International Law: An Appraisal of the State of the Art* (Cambridge, CUP, 2014)
Larsen K, 'Attribution of Conduct in Peace Operations: The "Ultimate Authority and Control" Test' (2008) 19 *EJIL* 509
Lauterpacht E and Bethlehem D, 'The Scope and Content of the Principle of Non-Refoulement: Opinion' in E Feller, V Türk and F Nicholson (eds), *Refugee Protection in International Law: UNHCR's Global Consultations on International Protection* (Cambridge, CUP, 2003)
Lauterpacht H, 'Consistency with Prior Treaty Obligations' in E Lauterpacht (ed), *International Law Being the Collected Papers of Hersch Lauterpacht—The Law of Peace*, vol 4 (Cambridge, CUP, 1978)
——, 'Contracts to Break Contracts' in E Lauterpacht (ed), *International Law Being the Collected Papers of Hersch Lauterpacht—The Law of Peace*, vol 4 (Cambridge, CUP, 1978)
——, 'General Rules of the Law of Peace' in E Lauterpacht (ed), *International Law Being the Collected Papers of Hersch Lauterpacht—The General Works*, vol 1 (Cambridge, CUP, 1970)
——, 'Neutrality and Collective Security' in E Lauterpacht (ed), *International Law Being the Collected Papers of Hersch Lauterpacht—Disputes, War and Neutrality*, vol 5 (Cambridge, CUP, 1977)
——, *Private Law Sources and Analogies in International Law* (London, Longmans, 1927)
——, *The Function of Law in the International Community* (Oxford, OUP, 2012)
Leben C, 'Les Contre-Mesures Inter-étatiques et Les Réactions à L'illicite Dans La Société Internationale' (1982) 28 *AFDI* 9

Leck C, 'International Responsibility in United Nations Peacekeeping Operations: Command and Control Arrangements and the Attribution of Conduct' (2009) 10 *Melbourne J Intl L* 346

Lehmann J, 'All Necessary Means to Protect Civilians: What the Intervention in Libya Says about the Relationship between Jus in Bello and the Jus Ad Bellum' (2012) 17 *JCSL* 117

Lehnardt C, 'Private Military Companies and State Responsibility' in S Chesterman and C Lehnardt (eds), *From Mercenaries to Market, The Rise and Regulation of Private Military Companies* (Oxford, OUP, 2007)

Levrat N, 'Les conséquences de l'engagement pris par les Hautes Parties Contractantes de "faire respecter" les conventions humanitaires' in F Kalshoven and Y Sandoz (eds), *Implementation of International Humanitarian Law* (Dordrecht, Martinus Nijhoff, 1989)

Lindemann H, 'Die Auswirkungen der Menschenrechtsverletzungen in Surinam auf die Vertragsbeziehungen zwischen den Niederlanden und Surinam' (1984) 44 *ZaöRV* 64

Linderfalk U, 'State Responsibility and the Primary-Secondary Rules Terminology—The Role of Language for an Understanding of the International Legal System' (2009) 78 *Nordic J Intl L* 53

Loewenstein A and Kostas S, 'Divergent Approaches to Determining Responsibility for Genocide: The Darfur Commission of Inquiry and the ICJ's Judgment in the Genocide Case' (2007) 5 *JICJ* 839

Lowe V, 'Precluding Wrongfulness or Responsibility: A Plea for Excuses' (1999) 10 *EJIL* 405

——, 'Responsibility for the Conduct of Other States' (2002) 101 *Japanese J Intl L & Diplomacy* 1

——, *International Law* (Oxford, OUP, 2007)

Luban D, *Legal Modernism: Law, Meaning and Violence* (Michigan, University of Michigan Press, 1997)

Lukashuk I, 'Ответственность одного субъекта международного права в связи с деянием другого' (2003) 1 *Iurist-mezhdunarodnik* 9

Luzzatto R, 'Responsabilità e colpa in diritto internazionale' (1968) 51 *RDI* 53

MacDonald R, 'The Principle of Solidarity in Public International Law' in C Dominicé, R Patry and C Reymond (eds), *Etudes de droit international en l'honneur de Pierre Lalive* (Basel, Helbing & Lichtenhahn, 1993)

Mackie J, *The Cement of the Universe: A Study of Causation* (Oxford, Clarendon Press, 1980)

Mahiou A, 'Les objectifs de la codification: Rapport général' in SFDI (ed), *La codification du droit international: Colloque d'Aix-en-Provence* (Paris, Pedone, 1999)

Malanczuk P, *Akehurst's Modern Introduction to International Law* (7th edn, London, Routledge, 1997)

Marboe I, *Calculation of Compensation and Damages in International Investment Law* (Oxford, OUP, 2009)

Marchesi A, *Obblighi di condotta e obblighi di risultato* (Milano, Giuffrè, 2003)

Marek K, 'Contribution à l'étude du jus cogens en droit international', *Mélanges en hommage à Paul Guggenheim* (Genève, HEI, 1968)

——, *Identity and Continuity of States in Public International Law* (2nd edn, Genève, Droz, 1968)

Marks S, *The Riddle of All Constitutions: International Law, Democracy and the Critique of Ideology* (Oxford, OUP, 2000)

Marschik A, 'Too Much Order? The Impact of Special Secondary Norms on the Unity and Efficacy of the International Legal System' (1998) 9 *EJIL* 212

Maslen S, *Commentaries on Arms Control Treaties: The Convention on the Prohibition of the Use, Stockpiling, Production, and Transfer of Anti-Personnel Mines and on Their Destruction*, vol 1 (2nd edn, Oxford, OUP, 2005)

McChrystie Adams J, 'Environmental and Human Rights Objections Stall Turkey's Proposed Ilisu Dam' (2000) 12 *Colorado J Intl Environmental L & Policy* 173

McNair A, *The Law of Treaties* (2nd edn, Oxford, Clarendon Press, 1961)

'Memorandum of the Office of Legal Affairs of the United Nations' (21 April 1995), reproduced in (1995) *UN Juridical YB* 464–65

Meng W, 'Internationale Organisationen im völkerrechtlichen Deliktsrecht' (1985) 45 *ZaöRV* 324

Messineo F, '"Extraordinary Renditions" and State Obligations to Criminalize and Prosecute Torture in the Light of the Abu Omar Case in Italy' (2009) 7 *JICJ* 1023

——, 'Things Could Only Get Better: Al-Jedda beyond Behrami' (2012) 50 *Military Law and the Law of War Review* 321

——, 'Attribution of Conduct' in A Nollkaemper and I Plakokefalos (eds), *Principles of Shared Responsibility in International Law: An Appraisal of the State of the Art* (Cambridge, CUP, 2014)

Mettraux G, *International Crimes and the Ad Hoc Tribunals* (Oxford, OUP, 2005)

Michalowski S, 'No Complicity Liability for Funding Gross Human Rights Violations?' (2012) 30 *Berkeley J Intl L* 451

Milanović M, 'State Responsibility for Genocide' (2006) 17 *EJIL* 553

——, 'State Responsibility for Genocide: A Follow-Up' (2007) 18 *EJIL* 669

——, 'The Limits of Aiding and Abetting Liability: The ICTY Appeals Chamber Acquits Momcilo Perisic' www.ejiltalk.org/the-limits-of-aiding-and-abetting-liability-the-icty-appeals-chamber-acquits-momcilo-perisic/

——, 'Jurisdiction, Attribution and Responsibility in Jaloud' http://www.ejiltalk.org/jurisdiction-attribution-and-responsibility-in-jaloud/

——, *Extraterritorial Application of Human Rights Treaties: Law, Principles, and Policy* (Oxford, OUP, 2011)

Milanović M and Papić T, 'As Bad as It Gets: The European Court of Human Rights's Behrami and Saramati Decision and General International Law' (2009) 58 *ICLQ* 267

Militello V, 'The Personal Nature of Individual Criminal Responsibility and the ICC Statute' (2007) 5 *JICJ* 941

Momtaz D, 'State Organs and Entities Empowered to Exercise Elements of Governmental Authority' in J Crawford et al (eds), *The Law of International Responsibility* (Oxford, OUP, 2010)

Mongelard E, 'Corporate Civil Liability for Violations of International Humanitarian Law' (2006) 88 *IRRC* 665

Mueller K, *Precision and Purpose: Airpower in the Libyan Civil War* (Santa Monica, RAND Corporation, 2015)

Murphy S, 'Ex Gratia Payment for Bombing of Chinese Embassy in Belgrade' (2000) 94 *AJIL* 127

——, 'Self-Defense and the Israeli Wall Advisory Opinion: An Ipse Dixit from the ICJ?' (2005) 99 *AJIL* 62

Murray O, 'Piercing the Corporate Veil: The Responsibility of Member States of an International Organization' (2011) 8 *IOLR* 291

Nanda V, 'The Future Under International Law of the Responsibility to Protect after Libya and Syria' (2013) 21 *Michigan State Intl LR* 1

Neff S, *The Rights and Duties of Neutrals: A General History* (Manchester, Manchester University Press, 2000)

——, *War and the Law of Nations: A General History* (Cambridge, CUP, 2005)

Nigro R, 'Giurisdizione e obblighi positivi degli Stati parti della Convenzione Europea dei diritti dell'uomo: Il caso Ilaşcu' (2005) 88 *RDI* 413

Nissel A, 'The ILC Articles on State Responsibility: Between Self-Help and Solidarity' (2006) 38 *NYU J Intl L & Pol* 355

Nollkaemper A, 'Concurrence between Individual Responsibility and State Responsibility in International Law' (2003) 52 *ICLQ* 615

——, 'Internationally Wrongful Acts in Domestic Courts' (2007) 101 *AJIL* 760

——, 'Dual Attribution: Liability of the Netherlands for Conduct of Dutchbat in Srebrenica' (2011) 9 *JICJ* 1143

——, 'The Charles Taylor Judgment: Disconnecting the Responsibilities of Presidents and States' www.sharesproject.nl/the-charles-taylor-judgment-disconnecting-the-responsibilities-of-presidents-and-states/

——, 'Attribution of Forcible Acts to States: Connections Between the Law on the Use of Force and the Law of State Responsibility' in N Blokker and N Schrijver (eds), *The Security Council and the Use of Force: Theory and Reality, a Need for a Change?* (Leiden, Martinus Nijhoff, 2005)

——, 'Issues of Shared Responsibility before the International Court of Justice' in E Rieter and H de Waele (eds), *Evolving Principles of International Law: Studies in Honour of Karel C Wellens* (Leiden, Martinus Nijhoff, 2012)

——, 'State Responsibility for International Crimes: A Review of Principles of Reparation' in A Constantinidis and N Zaikos (eds), *The Diversity of International Law: Essays in Honour of Professor Kalliopi K Koufa* (Leiden, Martinus Nijhoff, 2009)

Nollkaemper A and Jacobs D, 'Shared Responsibility in International Law: A Conceptual Framework' (2013) 34 *Michigan J Intl L* 359

Nollkaemper A and Nedeski N, 'Responsibility of International Organizations "in Connection with Acts of States"' (2012) 9 *IOLR* 33

Nollkaemper A and van der Wilt H (eds), *System Criminality in International Law* (Cambridge, CUP, 2009)

Nolte G, 'From Dionisio Anzilotti to Roberto Ago: The Classical International Law of State Responsibility and the Traditional Primacy of a Bilateral Conception of Inter-State Relations' (2002) 13 *EJIL* 1083

Nolte G and Aust H, 'Equivocal Helpers—Complicit States, Mixed Messages and International Law' (2009) 58 *ICLQ* 1

Noyes J and Smith B, 'State Responsibility and the Principle of Joint and Several Liability' (1988) 13 *Yale J Intl L* 225

O'Connell D, *International Law* (2nd edn, London, Stevens & Sons, 1970)

Oeter S, *Neutralität und Waffenhandel* (Berlin, Springer, 1992)
——, 'Neutrality and Alliances' in V Chetail and P Haggenmacher (eds), *Vattel's International Law in a XXIst Century Perspective* (Leiden, Martinus Nijhoff, 2011)
Ohlin J, 'The Torture Lawyers' (2010) 51 *Harvard Intl LJ* 193
Okowa P, *State Responsibility for Transboundary Air Pollution in International Law* (Oxford, OUP, 2000)
Olleson S, 'Internationally Wrongful Acts in the Domestic Courts: The Contribution of Domestic Courts to the Development of Customary International Law Relating to the Engagement of International Responsibility' (2013) 26 *LJIL* 615
——, *The Impact of the ILC's Articles on Responsibility of States for Internationally Wrongful Acts* (London, BIICL, 2007)
Ollivier A, 'International Criminal Responsibility of the State' in J Crawford et al (eds), *The Law of International Responsibility* (Oxford, OUP, 2010)
Onuma Y, 'Just Causes of War' in Y Onuma (ed), *A Normative Approach to War: Peace, War and Justice in Hugo Grotius* (Oxford, OUP, 1993)
Open Society Foundation, 'Globalizing Torture: CIA Secret Detention and Extraordinary Rendition' (2013)
Oppenheim L, *International Law—A Treatise: War and Neutrality*, vol 2 (2nd edn, London, Longmans, 1912)
Orakhelashvili A, 'The World Bank Inspection Panel in Context: Institutional Aspects of the Accountability of International Organizations' (2005) 2 *IOLR* 57
——, 'The Responsibility of Member-States Due to Wrongful Acts of International Organizations: A Response to Cortes Martin' (2014) 13 *Chinese J Intl L* 621
——, 'Division of Reparation between Responsible Entities' in J Crawford et al (eds), *The Law of International Responsibility* (Oxford, OUP, 2010)
——, *Peremptory Norms in International Law* (Oxford, OUP, 2006)
Ouedraogo A, 'Évolution du concept de faute dans la théorie de la responsabilité internationale des États' (2008) 21 *RQDI* 129
——, 'La diligence en droit international: Contribution à l'étude d'une notion au contour imprécis' (PhD Thesis, Geneva, Graduate Institute, 2010)
Pacht L, 'The Case for a Convention on State Responsibility' (2014) 83 *Nordic J Intl L* 439
Padeletti M, *Pluralità di Stati nel fatto illecito internazionale* (Milano, Giuffrè, 1990)
Palchetti P, 'Sulla responsabilità di uno Stato per il voto espresso in seno ad un'organizzazione internazionale' (2012) 2 *RDI* 352
——, *L'organo di fatto dello Stato nell'illecito internazionale* (Milano, Giuffrè, 2007)
——, 'State Responsibility for Complicity in Genocide' in P Gaeta (ed), *The UN Genocide Convention: A Commentary* (Oxford, OUP, 2009)
Palmisano G, 'Les causes d'aggravation de la responsabilité des États et la distinction entre "crimes" et "délits" internationaux' (1994) 98 *RGDIP* 629
——, 'Cronaca di una morte annunciata: la responsabilità dello Stato per crimini internazionali' in M Spinedi, A Gianelli and ML Alaimo (eds), *La codificazione della responsabilità internazionale degli stati alla prova dei fatti: Problemi e spunti di riflessione* (Milano, Giuffrè, 2006)
Palwankar U, 'Measures Available to States for Fulfilling Their Obligations to Ensure Respect for International Humanitarian Law' (1994) 298 *IRRC* 9
Paparinskis M, 'Procedural Aspects of Shared Responsibility in the International Court of Justice' (2013) 4 *JIDS* 295

Papastavridis E, '"Fortress Europe" and FRONTEX: Within or Without International Law?' 79 *Nordic J Intl L* 75

Parish M, 'An Essay on the Accountability of International Organizations' (2010) 7 *IOLR* 277

Parlett K, *The Individual in the International Legal System* (Cambridge, CUP, 2011)

Paulus A, 'Jus Cogens in a Time of Hegemony and Fragmentation—An Attempt at a Re-Appraisal' (2005) 74 *Nordic J Intl L* 297

Pauwelyn J, 'The Concept of a Continuing Violation of an International Obligation: Selected Problems' (1996) 66 *British YBIL* 415

——, 'Bridging Fragmentation and Unity: International Law as a Universe of Inter-Connected Islands' (2003) 25 *Michigan J Intl L* 903

——, *Conflict of Norms in Public International Law* (Cambridge, CUP, 2003)

Pellet A, 'Remarques sur une révolution inachevée, le projet d'articles de la Commission du Droit international sur la responsabilité des États' (1996) 42 *AFDI* 7

——, 'Can a State Commit a Crime? Definitely, Yes!' (1999) 10 *EJIL* 425

——, 'The New Draft Articles of the International Law Commission on the Responsibility of States for International Wrongful Acts: A Requiem for States' Crime?' (2001) 32 *Netherlands YBIL* 55

——, 'Les articles de la CDI sur la responsabilité de l'État pour fait internationalement illicite. Suite—et fin?' (2002) 48 *AFDI* 1

——, 'International Organizations Are Definitely Not States. Cursory Remarks on the ILC Articles on the Responsibility of International Organizations' in M Ragazzi (ed), *Responsibility of International Organizations: Essays in Memory of Sir Ian Brownlie* (Leiden, Martinus Nijhoff, 2013)

——, 'L'imputabilité d'éventuels actes illicites—Responsabilité de l'OTAN ou des États membres' in C Tomuschat (ed), *Kosovo and the International Community* (The Hague, Kluwer, 2002)

——, 'Some Remarks on the Recent Case Law of the International Court of Justice on Responsibility Issues' in P Kóvacs (ed), *International Law—A Quiet Strength: Miscellanea in Memoriam Géza Herczegh* (Budapest, Pázmány Press, 2011)

——, 'The Definition of Responsibility in International Law' in J Crawford et al (eds), *The Law of International Responsibility* (Oxford, OUP, 2010)

——, 'The ILC's Articles on State Responsibility for Internationally Wrongful Acts and Related Texts' in J Crawford et al (eds), *The Law of International Responsibility* (Oxford, OUP, 2010)

Penfield W, 'The Settlement of the Samoan Cases' (1913) 7 *AJIL* 767

Perelman C and Vander Elst R, *Les notions à contenu variable en droit* (Bruxelles, Bruylant, 1984)

Perez Conzalez M, 'Les organisations internationales et le droit de la responsabilité' (1988) 92 *RGDIP* 63

Perrin G, 'Le problème de la faute dans la responsabilité internationale de l'État' in W Haller et al (eds), *Im Dienst an der Gemeinschaft: Festschrift für Dietrich Schindler zum 65. Geburtstag* (Basel, Helbing & Lichtenhahn, 1989)

Picone P, 'Obblighi erga omnes e codificazione della responsabilità degli stati' (2005) 4 *RDI* 893

——, 'La distinzione tra norme internazionali di jus cogens e norme che producono obblighi erga omnes' (2008) 1 *RDI* 5

Pictet J, *Commentary: IV Geneva Convention Relative to the Protection of Civilian Persons in Time of War* (Geneva, ICRC, 1958)

——, *Commentary on the First Geneva Convention of August 12, 1949* (Geneva, ICRC, 1952)

Pieper U, *Neutralität von Staaten* (Frankfurt am Main, Lang, 1997)

Pihou M, 'An Argument in Favour of a More Normative Distinction between Principals and Accomplices in International Criminal Law' (2008) 21 *Hague YBIL* 41

Pisillo-Mazzeschi R, 'The Due Diligence Rule and the Nature of the International Responsibility of States' (1992) 35 *German YBIL* 9

——, 'The Marginal Role of the Individual in the ILC's Articles on State Responsibility' (2004) 14 *Italian YBIL* 39

——, 'Il ruolo marginale dell'individuo nel progetto della commissione del diritto internazionale sulla responsabilità degli stati' in M Spinedi, A Gianelli and ML Alaimo (eds), *La codificazione della responsabilità internazionale degli stati alla prova dei fatti: Problemi e spunti di riflessione* (Milano, Giuffrè, 2006)

——, *La due diligence e responsabilità internazionale degli Stati* (Milano, Giuffrè, 1989)

——, 'Termination and Suspension of Treaties for Breach in the International Law Commission Works on State Responsibility' in M Spinedi and B Simma (eds), *United Nations Codification of State Responsibility* (New York, Oceana, 1987)

Plakokefalos I, 'Shared Responsibility Aspects of the Dispute Settlement Procedures in the Law of the Sea Convention' (2013) 4 *JIDS* 385

——, 'Causation in the Law of State Responsibility and the Problem of Overdetermination: In Search of Clarity' (2015) 26 *EJIL* 471

Plomp C, 'Aiding and Abetting: The Responsibility of Business Leaders under the Rome Statute of the International Criminal Court' (2014) 30 *Utrecht J Intl & Eur L* 4

Politis N, *Neutrality and Peace* (Washington DC, Carnegie, 1935)

Pound R, *An Introduction to the Philosophy of Law* (New Haven, Yale University Press, 1922)

Proulx V-J, *Transnational Terrorism and State Accountability* (Oxford, Hart Publishing, 2012)

Quigley J, 'Complicity in International Law: A New Direction in the Law of State Responsibility' (1987) 57 *British YBIL* 77

——, 'State Responsibility for Ethnic Cleansing' (1998) 32 *University of California Davis LR* 341

——, *The Genocide Convention: An International Law Analysis* (Aldershot, Ashgate, 2006)

Quirico O, 'Ius Cogens: A Puzzle' in M Szabó (ed), *State Responsibility and the Law of Treaties* (The Hague, Eleven, 2010)

Ragazzi M (ed), *Responsibility of International Organizations: Essays in Memory of Sir Ian Brownlie* (Leiden, Martinus Nijhoff, 2013)

——, *The Concept of International Obligations Erga Omnes* (Oxford, Clarendon Press, 1997)

Ranganathan S, 'Between Complicity and Irrelevance-Industry Associations and the Challenge of Regulating Private Security Contractors' (2009) 41 *Georgetown J Intl L* 303

Redslob R, *Théorie de la Société des Nations* (Paris, Rousseau, 1927)

Reinisch A, 'Developing a Human Rights and Humanitarian Law Accountability of the UN Security Council for the Imposition of Economic Sanctions' (2001) 95 *AJIL* 851

——, 'Aid or Assistance and Direction and Control between States and International Organizations in the Commission of Internationally Wrongful Acts' (2010) 7 *IOLR* 63

——, *Challenging Acts of International Organizations before National Courts* (Oxford, OUP, 2010)

——, *International Organizations before National Courts* (Cambridge, CUP, 2000)

Reitzer L, *La réparation comme conséquence de l'acte illicite en droit international* (Paris, Sirey, 1938)

Reuter P, 'Principes de droit international public' (1961) 103 *RCADI* 425

——, *Introduction au droit des traités* (3rd edn, Paris, PUF, 1995)

Riddell A and Plant B, *Evidence before the International Court of Justice* (London, BIICL, 2009)

Rigaux F, 'International Responsibility and the Principle of Causality' in M Ragazzi (ed), *International Responsibility Today: Essays in Memory of Oscar Schachter* (Leiden, Martinus Nijhoff, 2005)

Ripert G, 'Les règles du droit civil applicables aux rapports internationaux' (1933) 44 *RCADI* 565

Ripinsky S and Williams K, *Damages in International Investment Law* (London, BIICL, 2008)

Rogers W, 'Comparative Report on Multiple Tortfeasors' in WVH Rogers and WH van Boom (eds), *Unification of Tort Law: Multiple Tortfeasors* (The Hague, Kluwer, 2004)

Ronzitti N, 'Italy's Non-Belligerency During the Iraq-War' in M Ragazzi (ed), *International Responsibility Today: Essays in Memory of Oscar Schachter* (Leiden, Martinus Nijhoff, 2005)

Rose C, 'The Application of Human Rights Law to Private Sector Complicity in Governmental Corruption' (2011) 24 *LJIL* 715

Rosenne S, *Breach of Treaty* (Cambridge, CUP, 1985)

——, 'Breach of Treaty in the Codification of the Law of State Responsibility', *Essays on International Law and Practice* (Leiden, Martinus Nijhoff, 2007)

—— (ed), *The International Law Commission's Draft Articles on State Responsibility: Part I, Articles 1–35* (Dordrecht, Martinus Nijhoff, 1991)

——, *The Law and Practice of the International Court, 1920–2004* (4th edn, Leiden, Martinus Nijhoff, 2005)

Rousseau C, 'Principes de droit international public' (1958) 93 *RCADI* 369

——, *Principes généraux du droit international public* (Paris, Pedone, 1944)

Rovine A and Hanessian G, 'Toward a Foreseeability Approach to Causation Questions at the United Nations Compensation Commission' in RB Lillich (ed), *The United Nations Compensation Commission: Thirteenth Sokol Colloquium* (Irvington New York, Transnational, 1995)

Ruffert M, 'The Administration of Kosovo and East-Timor by the International Community' (2001) 50 *ICLQ* 613

'Rules of Engagement Are Murky in Libya Air War' *Foreign Policy* (21 March 2011)

Ryngaert C, 'The Immunity of International Organizations Before Domestic Courts: Recent Trends' (2010) 7 *IOLR* 121

Sachariew K, 'State's Entitlement to Take Action to Enforce International Humanitarian Law' (1989) 270 *IRRC* 177

Sadat L, 'Can the ICTY Šainović and Perišić Cases Be Reconciled?' (2014) 108 *AJIL* 475

Salmon J, 'Le fait étatique complexe—une notion contestable' (1982) 28 *AFDI* 709

——, 'L'intention en matière de responsabilité internationale', *Le droit international au service de la paix, de la justice et du développement: Mélanges Michel Virally* (Pedone 1991)

——, *Dictionnaire de droit international public* (Bruxelles, Bruylant, 2001)

——, 'La place de la faute de la victime dans le droit de la responsabilité internationale', *Le droit international à l'heure de sa codification: études en l'honneur de Roberto Ago*, vol 3 (Milano, Giuffrè, 1987)

Sandonato de Leon P, *Les présomptions judiciaires en droit international public* (Paris, Pedone, 2015)

Sands P, 'The International Rule of Law: Extraordinary Rendition, Complicity and Its Consequences', *Droit du pouvoir—pouvoir du droit: Mélanges en l'honneur de Jean Salmon* (Bruxelles, Bruylant, 2007)

Sari A, 'Jurisdiction and International Responsibility in Peace Support Operations: The Behrami and Saramati Cases' (2008) 8 *HRLR* 151

——, 'UN Peacekeeping Operations and Article 7 ARIO: The Missing Link' (2012) 9 *IOLR* 77

Sarooshi D, 'International Organizations and State Responsibility' in M Ragazzi (ed), *Responsibility of International Organizations: Essays in Memory of Sir Ian Brownlie* (Leiden, Martinus Nijhoff, 2013)

——, *International Organizations and Their Exercise of Sovereign Powers* (Oxford, OUP, 2005)

Sassòli M, 'State Responsibility for Violations of International Humanitarian Law' (2002) 84 *IRRC* 401

Saul B, *Defining Terrorism in International Law* (Oxford, OUP, 2008)

Saul M, 'The Practice of Shared Responsibility in Relation to Internationally Administered Territories' SHARES Research Paper No 65 (2015)

Savarese E, 'Issues of Attribution to States of Private Acts: Between the Concept of De Facto Organs and Complicity' (2005) 15 *RDI* 111

——, 'Fatti di privati e responsabilità dello Stato tra organo di fatto e "complicità" alla luce di recenti tendenze della prassi internazionale' in M Spinedi, A Gianelli and ML Alaimo (eds), *La codificazione della responsabilità internazionale degli stati alla prova dei fatti: Problemi e spunti di riflessione* (Milano, Giuffrè, 2006)

Scandamis N, *Le jugement déclaratoire entre États* (Paris, Pedone, 1976)

Schabas W, 'Enforcing International Humanitarian Law: Catching the Accomplices' (2001) 83 *IRRC* 439

——, 'State Policy as an Element of International Crimes' (2008) 98 *J Crim L & Criminology* 953

——, *Genocide in International Law: The Crime of Crimes* (2nd edn, Cambridge, CUP, 2009)

——, *The International Criminal Court: A Commentary on the Rome Statute* (Oxford, OUP, 2010)

Schachter O, 'Invisible College of International Lawyers' (1977) 72 *Northwestern University LR* 217

——, 'International Law in Theory and Practice: General Course in Public International Law' (1982) 178 *RCADI* 9

Scheinin M and Vermeulen M, 'International Law: Human Rights Law and State Responsibility' in H Born, I Leigh and A Wills (eds), *International Intelligence Cooperation and Accountability* (Abingdon, Routledge, 2011)

Schermers H and Blokker N, *International Institutional Law: Unity within Diversity* (5th edn, Leiden, Martinus Nijhoff, 2011)

Schmalenbach K, 'Third Party Liability of International Organizations: A Study on Claim Settlement in the Course of Military Operations and International Administrations' (2006) 10 *International Peacekeeping: The Yearbook of International Peace Operations* 33

Schoen P, *Die völkerrechtliche Haftung der Staaten aus unerlaubten Handlungen*, vol 10 (Breslau, Kern, 1917)

Schultz N, 'Was the War on Iraq Illegal? The German Federal Administrative Court's Judgment of 21st June 2005' (2006) 7 *German LJ* 25

Schwarzenberger G, *International Law as Applied by International Courts and Tribunals*, vol 4 (3rd edn, London, Stevens, 1957)

Scobbie I, 'Unchart(er)ed Waters?: Consequences of the Advisory Opinion on the Legal Consequences of the Construction of a Wall in the Occupied Palestinian Territory for the Responsibility of the UN for Palestine' (2005) 16 *EJIL* 941

Seyersted F, 'United Nations Forces. Some Legal Problems' (1961) 37 *British YBIL* 351

SFDI, *La responsabilité dans le système international: Colloque du Mans* (Paris, Pedone, 1991)

Shah N, 'Knocking on the Torturer's Door: Confronting International Complicity in the US Rendition Program' (2007) 38 *Columbia Human Rights LR* 581

Shan H, 'China' in S Stijns (ed), *International Encyclopaedia of Laws: Tort Law*, vol 1 (The Hague, Kluwer, 2005)

Shelton D, 'Righting Wrongs: Reparations in the Articles on State Responsibility' (2002) 96 *AJIL* 833

Shihata I, 'Human Rights, Development, and International Financial Institutions' (1992) 8 *American University J Intl L & Pol* 27

Sicilianos L-A, 'The Relationship between Reprisals and Denunciation or Suspension of a Treaty' (1993) 4 *EJIL* 341

——, 'The Classification of Obligations and the Multilateral Dimension of Relations of International Responsibility' (2002) 13 *EJIL* 1127

——, 'Entre multilatéralisme et unilatéralisme: l'autorisation par le Conseil de sécurité de recourir à la force: Une tentative d'évaluation' (2008) 339 *RCADI* 9

——, *Les réactions décentralisées à l'illicite: Des contre-mesures à la légitime défense* (Paris, LGDJ, 1990)

——, 'L'(ir)responsabilité des forces multinationales' in L Boisson de Chazournes and MG Kohen (eds), *International Law and the Quest for its Implementation, Liber Amicorum Vera Gowlland-Debbas* (Leiden, Martinus Nijhoff, 2010)

Simma B, 'Reflections on Article 60 of the Vienna Convention on the Law of Treaties and Its Background in General International Law' (1970) 20 *Österreichische Zeitschrift für öffentliches Recht* 5

——, 'From Bilateralism to Community Interest in International Law' (1994) 250 *RCADI* 217

Simma B and Pulkowski D, 'Of Planets and the Universe: Self-Contained Regimes in International Law' (2006) 17 *EJIL* 483

Simma B and Tams C, 'Reacting Against Treaty Breaches' in DB Hollis (ed), *The Oxford Guide to Treaties* (Oxford, OUP, 2012)

Simon D and Sicilianos L-A, 'La "contre-violence" unilatérale: Pratiques étatiques et Droit international' (1986) 32 *AFDI* 53

Singer M, 'Jurisdictional Immunity of International Organizations: Human Rights and Functional Necessity Concerns' (1995) 36 *Virginia J Intl L* 53

Singh N, *Termination of Membership of International Organizations* (London, Stevens & Sons, 1958)

Sivakumaran S, 'Binding Armed Opposition Groups' (2008) 55 *ICLQ* 369

Sohn L, 'Expulsion or Forced Withdrawal from an International Organization' (1964) 77 *Harvard LR* 1381

Spinedi M, 'From One Codification to Another: Bilateralism and Multilateralism in the Genesis of the Codification of the Law of Treaties and the Law of State Responsibility' (2002) 13 *EJIL* 1099

——, 'State Responsibility v Individual Responsibility for International Crimes: Tertium Non Datur?' (2002) 13 *EJIL* 895

Steinberger E, 'The WTO Treaty as a Mixed Agreement: Problems with the EC's and the EC Member States' Membership of the WTO' (2006) 17 *EJIL* 837

Steinbrück Platise M and von Bogdandy A, 'ARIO and Human Rights Protection: Leaving the Individual in the Cold' (2012) 9 *IOLR* 67

Stein T, 'Kosovo and the International Community. The Attribution of Possible Internationally Wrongful Acts: Responsibility of NATO or of Its Member States?' in C Tomuschat (ed), *Kosovo and the International Community* (The Hague, Kluwer, 2002)

Stern B, 'Et si on utilisait la notion de préjudice juridique? Retour sur une notion délaissée à l'occasion de la fin des travaux de la C.D.I. sur la responsabilité des États' (2001) 47 *AFDI* 3

——, 'A Plea for "Reconstruction" of International Responsibility Based on the Notion of Legal Injury' in M Ragazzi (ed), *International Responsibility Today: Essays in Memory of Oscar Schachter* (Leiden, Martinus Nijhoff, 2005)

——, *Le préjudice dans la théorie de la responsabilité internationale* (Paris, Pedone, 1973)

——, 'Les dilemmes de la responsabilité internationale aujourd'hui', *Vers de nouvelles normes en droit de la responsabilité publique: Actes du colloque 11 et 12 mai 2001* (Paris, Sénat, 2001)

——, 'The Obligation to Make Reparation' in J Crawford et al (eds), *The Law of International Responsibility* (Oxford, OUP, 2010)

Stewart J, 'The End of "Modes of Liability" for International Crimes' (2012) 25 *LJIL* 165

——, 'The ICTY Loses Its Way on Complicity—Part 1' www.opiniojuris.org/2013/04/03/guest-post-the-icty-loses-its-way-on-complicity-part-1/

——, 'The ICTY Loses Its Way on Complicity—Part 2' www.opiniojuris.org/2013/04/03/guest-post-the-icty-loses-its-way-on-complicity-part-2/

Strauss M, 'Causation as an Element of State Responsibility' (1984) 16 *Law & Policy in International Business* 893

Strupp K, *Das völkerrechtliche Delikt* (Stuttgart, Kohlhammer, 1920)
Stumer A, 'Liability of Member States for Acts of International Organization: Reconsidering the Policy Objections' (2007) 48 *Harvard Intl LJ* 553
Stürchler N, *The Threat of Force in International Law* (Cambridge, CUP, 2009)
Sturma P, 'Drawing a Line between the Responsibility of an International Organization and Its Member States under International Law' (2011) 2 *Czech YBIL* 3
——, 'The Responsibility of International Organizations and Their Member States' in M Ragazzi (ed), *Responsibility of International Organizations: Essays in Memory of Sir Ian Brownlie* (Leiden, Martinus Nijhoff, 2013)
Suzuki E and Nanwani S, 'Responsibility of International Organizations: The Accountability Mechanisms of Multilateral Development Banks' (2005) 27 *Michigan J Intl L* 177
Talmon S, 'Determining Customary International Law: The ICJ's Methodology between Induction, Deduction and Assertion' (2015) 26 *EJIL* 417
——, 'A Plurality of Responsible Actors: International Responsibility for Acts of the Coalition Provisional Authority in Iraq' in P Shiner and A Williams (eds), *The Iraq War and International Law* (Oxford, Hart Publishing, 2008)
——, *Kollektive Nichtanerkennung illegaler Staaten* (Tübingen, Mohr, 2006)
——, 'Responsibility of International Organizations: Does the European Community Require Special Treatment?' in M Ragazzi (ed), *International Responsibility Today: Essays in Memory of Oscar Schachter* (Leiden, Martinus Nijhoff, 2005)
——, 'The Duty Not to "Recognize as Lawful" a Situation Created by the Illegal Use of Force or Other Serious Breaches of a Jus Cogens Obligation: An Obligation without Real Substance?' in C Tomuschat and JM Thouvenin (eds), *The Fundamental Rules of the International Legal Order* (Leiden, Martinus Nijhoff, 2006)
Tams C, 'All's Well When It Ends Well: Comments on the ILC's Articles on State Responsibility' (2002) 62 *ZaöRV* 759
——, 'Do Serious Breaches Give Rise to Any Specific Obligations of the Responsible State?' (2002) 13 *EJIL* 1161
——, 'Recognizing Guarantees and Assurances of Non-Repetition: La Grand and the Law of State Responsibility' (2002) 27 *Yale J Intl L* 441
——, 'Swimming with the Tide or Seeking to Stem It? Recent ICJ Rulings on the Law on Self-Defence' (2005) 18 *RQDI* 275
——, 'Light Treatment of a Complex Problem: The Law of Self-Defence in the Wall Case' (2006) 16 *EJIL* 963
——, 'The Use of Force against Terrorists' (2009) 20 *EJIL* 359
——, 'Countermeasures against Multiple Responsible Actors' in A Nollkaemper and I Plakokefalos (eds), *Principles of Shared Responsibility in International Law: An Appraisal of the State of the Art* (Cambridge, CUP, 2014)
——, *Enforcing Obligations Erga Omnes* (Cambridge, CUP, 2005)
——, 'Erga Omnes, Jus Cogens and Their Impact on the Law of Responsibility', *The International Responsibility of the European Union: European and International Perspectives* (Oxford, Hart Publishing, 2013)
Tanzi A, 'Is Damage a Distinct Condition for the Existence of an Internationally Wrongful Act?' in M Spinedi and B Simma (eds), *United Nations Codification of State Responsibility* (New York, Oceana, 1987)

Tarzwell A, 'In Search of Accountability: Attributing the Conduct of Private Security Contractors to the United States Under the Doctrine of State Responsibility' (2009) 11 *Oregon Review of Intl Law* 179

The Oxford English Dictionary, vol 2 (Oxford, Clarendon Press, 1983)

Thirlway H, 'The Law and Procedure of the International Court of Justice 1960–1989: Part Nine' (1998) 69 *British YBIL* 1

Todd S, 'New Zealand' in S Stijns (ed), *International Encyclopaedia of Laws: Tort Law*, vol 3 (The Hague, Kluwer, 2008)

Tomuschat C, 'Attribution of International Responsibility: Direction and Control' in MD Evans and P Koutrakos (eds), *The International Responsibility of the European Union: European and International Perspectives* (Oxford, Hart Publishing, 2013)

Tonkin H, 'Common Article I: A Minimum Yardstick for Regulating Private Military and Security Companies' (2009) 22 *LJIL* 779

——, *State Control over Private Military and Security Companies in Armed Conflict* (Cambridge, CUP, 2011)

Trapp K, 'The Use of Force against Terrorists: A Reply to Christian J Tams' (2010) 20 *EJIL* 1049

——, *State Responsibility for International Terrorism* (Oxford, OUP, 2011)

Triepel H, *Völkerrecht und Landesrecht* (Leipzig, CL Hirschfeld, 1958)

Tunkin G, *Droit international public: Problèmes théoriques* (Paris, Pedone, 1965)

Tzanakopoulos A, *Disobeying the Security Council: Countermeasures against Wrongful Sanctions* (Oxford, OUP, 2011)

——, 'Strengthening Security Council Accountability for Sanctions: The Role of International Responsibility' (2014) 19 *JCSL* 409

Tzevelekos V, 'Reconstructing the Effective Control Criterion in Extraterritorial Human Rights Breaches: Direct Attribution of Wrongfulness, Due Diligence, and Concurrent Responsibility' (2015) 36 *Michigan J Intl L* 129

Ulfstein G and Christiansen H, 'The Legality of the NATO Bombing in Libya' (2013) 62 *ICLQ* 159

Ushakov N, *Основания международной ответственности государств [Bases of International Responsibility of States]* (Moscow, International Relations, 1983)

Vagts D, 'The Traditional Law of Neutrality in a Changing Environment' (1998) 14 *American University Intl LR* 83

Valticos N, 'Pluralité des ordres juridiques internationaux et unité du droit international' in J Makarczyk (ed), *Theory of International Law at the Threshold of the 21st Century: Essays in Honour of Krzysztof Skubiszewski* (The Hague, Kluwer, 1996)

van der Wilt H, 'Corporate Criminal Responsibility for International Crimes: Exploring the Possibilities' (2013) 12 *Chinese J Intl L* 43

van Rossem J, 'Interaction between EU Law and International Law in the Light of Intertanko and Kadi: The Dilemma of Norms Binding the Member States but Not the Community'' (2009) 40 *Netherlands YBIL* 183

van Sliedregt E, 'Joint Criminal Enterprise as a Pathway to Convicting Individuals for Genocide' (2007) 5 *JICJ* 184

——, 'Complicity to Commit Genocide' in P Gaeta (ed), *The UN Genocide Convention: A Commentary* (Oxford, OUP, 2009)

——, *Individual Criminal Responsibility in International Law* (Oxford, OUP, 2010)

Verdirame G, *The UN and Human Rights: Who Guards the Guardians?* (Cambridge, CUP, 2011)
Verheyen R, *Climate Change Damage and International Law* (Leiden, Martinus Nijhoff, 2005)
Verhoeven J, 'La reconnaissance internationale: déclin ou renouveau?' (1993) 39 *AFDI* 7
——, 'Les "étirements" de la légitime défense' (2002) 48 *AFDI* 49
Verzijl J, 'La validité et la nullité des actes juridiques internationaux' (1935) 9 *Revue de droit international* 184
Vierucci L, 'Private Military and Security Companies in Non-International Armed Conflicts' [2009] EUI Working Paper AEL 2009/14
Villalpando S, 'On the International Court of Justice and the Determination of Rules of Law' (2013) 26 *LJIL* 243
——, *L'émergence de la communauté internationale dans la responsabilité des États* (Paris, PUF, 2005)
Virally M, 'Réflexions sur le "jus cogens"' (1966) 12 *AFDI* 5
——, *Le droit international en devenir: Essais écrits au fil des ans* (Paris, PUF, 1990)
Vitta E, *La responsabilità internazionale dello Stato per atti legislativi* (Milano, Giuffrè, 1953)
von Heinegg W, '"Benevolent" Third States in International Armed Conflicts: The Myth of the Irrelevance of the Law of Neutrality' in MN Schmitt and J Pejic (eds), *International Law and Armed Conflict: Exploring the Faultlines: Essays in Honour of Yoram Dinstein* (Leiden, Martinus Nijhoff, 2007)
von Pufendorf S, *De Jure Naturae et Gentium [On the Law of Nature and Nations]* (WA Oldfather tr, Oxford, Clarendon Press, 1934)
——, *Elementorum Jurisprudentiae Universalis Libri Duo [Two Books of the Elements of Universal Jurisprudence]* (WA Oldfather tr, Oxford, Clarendon Press, 1931)
Vos G, 'Linking Chains of Causation: An Examination of New Approaches to Causation in Equity and the Common Law' (2001) 60 *Cambridge LJ* 337
Voulgaris N, 'Rethinking Indirect Responsibility' (2014) 11 *IOLR* 5
Watts A, 'The International Rule of Law' (1993) 36 *German YBIL* 15
Weckel P, 'Convergence du droit des traités et du droit de la responsabilité internationale' (1998) 102 *RGDIP* 647
——, 'Les instantanés du droit international' in SFDI (ed), *Le droit international et le temps* (Paris, Pedone, 2001)
Weiler J, 'The Geology of International Law—Governance, Democracy and Legitimacy' (2004) 64 *ZaöRV* 547
Weiler J, Cassese A and Spinedi M (eds), *International Crimes of State: A Critical Analysis of the ILC's Draft Article 19 on State Responsibility* (Berlin, Walter de Gruyter, 1989)
Weil P, 'Towards Relative Normativity in International Law' (1983) 77 *AJIL* 413
Weir T, 'Complex Liabilities' in A Tunc (ed), *International Encyclopedia of Comparative Law: Torts*, vol 11 (Tübingen, Martinus Nijhoff, 1983)
Wellens K, *Remedies against International Organizations* (Cambridge, CUP, 2004)
——, 'Solidarity as a Constitutional Principle: Its Expanding Role and Inherent Limitations' in RSJ MacDonald and DM Johnston (eds), *Towards World Constitutionalism: Issues in the Legal Ordering of the World Community* (Leiden, Martinus Nijhoff, 2005)

Wells C and Elias J, 'Catching the Conscience of the Kings: Corporate Player on the International Stage' in P Alston (ed), *Non-State Actors and Human Rights* (Oxford, OUP, 2005)

Wengler W, *Völkerrecht* (Berlin, Springer, 1964)

Werle G, 'Individual Criminal Responsibility in Article 25 ICC Statute' (2007) 5 *JICJ* 953

Werner W, 'Responding to the Undesired: State Responsibility, Risk Management and Precaution' (2007) 36 *Netherlands YBIL* 57

Whiteman M, *Digest of International Law*, vol 8 (Washington DC, Department of State Publication, 1967)

Wigneswaran N, 'Responsive Responsibility: Counter-Terrorism Obligations and Responsibilities of States under International Law' in MJ Glennon and S Sur (eds), *Terrorism and International Law* (Leiden, Martinus Nijhoff, 2007)

Wilde R, 'Enhancing Accountability at the International Level' (2006) 12 *ILSA J Intl & Comp L* 395

Wittich S, 'Domestic Courts and the Content and Implementation of State Responsibility' (2013) 26 *LJIL* 643

——, 'Joint Tortfeasors in Investment Law' in C Binder et al (eds), *International Investment Law for the 21st Century, Essays in Honour of Christoph Schreuer* (Oxford, OUP, 2009)

Wolfers A, *Discord and Collaboration: Essays on International Politics* (Baltimore MD, John Hopkins Press, 1962)

Wolfram J, 'The Time Factor in the Law of State Responsibility' in M Spinedi and B Simma (eds), *United Nations Codification of State Responsibility* (New York, Oceana, 1987)

Wolfrum R, 'State Responsibility for Private Actors: An Old Problem or Renewed Relevance' in M Ragazzi (ed), *International Responsibility Today: Essays in Memory of Oscar Schachter* (Leiden, Martinus Nijhoff, 2005)

Wyler E, 'Quelques réflexions sur la réalisation dans le temps du fait internationalement illicite' (1991) 95 *RGDIP* 881

——, 'From "State Crime" to Responsibility for Serious Breaches of Obligations under Peremptory Norms of General International Law' (2002) 13 *EJIL* 1147

Wyler E and Papaux A, 'The Different Forms of Reparation: Satisfaction' in J Crawford et al (eds), *The Law of International Responsibility* (Oxford, OUP, 2010)

Yee S, 'The Responsibility of States Members of an International Organization for Its Conduct as a Result of Membership or Their Normal Conduct Associated with Membership' in M Ragazzi (ed), *International Responsibility Today: Essays in Memory of Oscar Schachter* (Leiden, Martinus Nijhoff, 2005)

Zanardi P, 'Aggressione armata indiretta ed elemento soggettivo dell'illecito internazionale', *Le droit international à l'heure de sa codification: études en l'honneur de Roberto Ago*, vol 3 (Milano, Giuffrè, 1987)

Zegveld L, *Accountability of Armed Opposition Groups in International Law* (Cambridge, CUP, 2002)

Zemanek K, 'The Unilateral Enforcement of Obligations' (1987) 32 *ZaöRV* 37

——, 'Does the Prospect of Incurring Responsibility Improve the Observance of International Law?' in M Ragazzi (ed), *International Responsibility Today: Essays in Memory of Oscar Schachter* (Leiden, Martinus Nijhoff, 2005)

Zimmermann A and Teichmann M, 'State Responsibility for International Crimes' in A Nollkaemper and H van der Wilt (eds), *System Criminality in International Law* (Cambridge, CUP, 2009)

Zoller E, 'Quelques Réflexions Sur Les Contre-Mesures En Droit International', *Mélanges Claude-Albert Colliard* (Paris, Pedone, 1984)

Zorzi Giustiniani F, 'The Responsibility of Accomplices in the Case-Law of the Ad Hoc Tribunals' (2009) 20 *CLF* 417

Zourek J, 'Enfin une définition de l'agression' (1974) 20 *AFDI* 9

Index

www.ingramcontent.com/pod-product-compliance
Lightning Source LLC
LaVergne TN
LVHW052219200926
848481LV00001B/155
* 9 7 8 1 5 0 9 9 2 6 7 7 0 *